HUNGRY AND STARVING

HUNGRY AND STARVING

Voices
of the Great Soviet Famine,
1928–1934

JAMES R. GIBSON

McGill-Queen's University Press
Montreal & Kingston • London • Chicago

© McGill-Queen's University Press 2024

ISBN 978-0-2280-1999-2 (cloth)
ISBN 978-0-2280-2000-4 (ePDF)
ISBN 978-0-2280-2001-1 (ePUB)

Legal deposit first quarter 2024
Bibliothèque nationale du Québec

Printed in Canada on acid-free paper that is 100% ancient forest free (100% post-consumer recycled), processed chlorine free

This book has been published with the help of a grant from the Canadian Federation for the Humanities and Social Sciences, through the Awards to Scholarly Publications Program, using funds provided by the Social Sciences and Humanities Research Council of Canada.

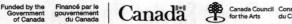

We acknowledge the support of the Canada Council for the Arts.
Nous remercions le Conseil des arts du Canada de son soutien.

McGill-Queen's University Press in Montreal is on land which long served as a site of meeting and exchange amongst Indigenous Peoples, including the Haudenosaunee and Anishinabeg nations. In Kingston it is situated on the territory of the Haudenosaunee and Anishinaabek. We acknowledge and thank the diverse Indigenous Peoples whose footsteps have marked these territories on which peoples of the world now gather.

Library and Archives Canada Cataloguing in Publication

Title: Hungry and starving : voices of the great Soviet famine, 1928-1934 / James R. Gibson.
Names: Gibson, James R., author.
Description: Includes bibliographical references and index.
Identifiers: Canadiana (print) 20230483240 | Canadiana (ebook) 20230483313 | ISBN 9780228019992 (cloth) | ISBN 9780228020004 (ePDF) | ISBN 9780228020011 (EPUB)
Subjects: LCSH: Collectivization of agriculture—Soviet Union—History. | LCSH: Famines—Soviet Union—History. | LCSH: Victims of famine—Soviet Union—History. | LCSH: Soviet Union—History—1925-1953.
Classification: LCC DK267 .G49 2024 | DDC 947.084/2—dc23

In memory of all in the Soviet Union who starved to death in 1928–34, especially the peasants and nomads and particularly their children.

As well as Vasily S. Grossman (1905–1964) and Lev Z. Kopelev (1912–1997) for their courageous compassion in memorializing the famine's victims.

And for Brian, my son.

Before the revolution Russia was able to feed itself. She even fed Europe. So what happened, then? Before collectivization there was an abundance of everything. We ate boiled, fried, and dried meat. In winter an average [peasant] household slaughtered 8–10 cattle. All kinds of fish. Pancakes with caviar. Butter was preserved in barrels. Where is all of this now?
— Yekaterina Trofimova, a Western Siberian peasant woman, 1930s, in Aleksei Martynenko, *Kollektivizatsiia i raskulachivanie*, 1.

And nothing remains of all that [peasant way of life]. Where can that life have gone? And that suffering, that terrible suffering? Can there really be nothing left? Is it really true that no one will be held to account for it all? That it will all just be forgotten without a trace?
— Vasily Grossman, *Everything Flows*, 148.

Who now remembers the hungry crowds in the cities and the peasants silently dying on their cold, crumbling stoves? In Russia people die in silence.
— Nadezhda Mandelstam, *Hope Abandoned*, 134.

I have always remembered … the great famine. And I have always told about it. But I did not begin to write it down until many years later. And while I wrote … forgotten persons stepped forward, voices long silent began to speak.
— Lev Kopelev, *The Education of a True Believer*, 248.

Let others sing of the hungry pain of love,
Let others sing of the hungry pain of life,
I will sing of the hungry pain of hunger.
— Moishe Nadir, "The Hungry Pain of Hunger," 18.

CONTENTS

Tables | ix

Acknowledgments | xi

A Note on Transliteration | xiii

Prologue: The 1928–34 Famine in Perspective | 3

1 A Special Famine | 16

2 A Hidden Famine | 85

3 A Natural Famine? | 124

4 An Unnatural Famine? | 134

5 A Manifold Famine | 202

6 The Relatively Worst Case: Kazakhstan | 240

7 The Absolutely Worst Case: The Ukraine – The North Caucasus | 258

Epilogue: The 1928–34 Famine in Retrospect | 282

Glossary | 295

Abbreviations | 297

Notes | 299

Bibliography | 437

Index | 471

TABLES

5.1 Official annual amount of grainland and average annual yield of grain and winter and spring wheat in the Soviet Union, 1928–34 | 203

5.2 Official total and per capita annual output of grain in the Soviet Union, 1921–34 | 205

5.3 Official production and procurement of grain in the Soviet Union, 1927–34 | 222

5.4 Exports of grain from the Soviet Union, 1928–35 | 232

ACKNOWLEDGMENTS

I am grateful to the resource-sharing department of the Scott Library of York University, Toronto, for the diligence of its staff, as well as to Philip Cercone of McGill-Queen's University Press for his support and patience. I am also indebted to Chaya Kapoor for her mapwork, several anonymous referees for their helpful comments on the manuscript, and Professor Brian Gibson of Université Sainte-Anne for his meticulous proofreading.

A NOTE ON TRANSLITERATION

References in the endnotes and the bibliography conform to the Library of Congress transliteration system, but in the main text and the text of the endnotes some Russian words are transliterated more phonetically for the sake of the general reader.

HUNGRY AND STARVING

PROLOGUE
THE 1928–34 FAMINE IN PERSPECTIVE

There is a master in the peasant commune; this master is merciless,
his name is famine.
– Nikolai A. Nekrasov, "Zheleznaia doroga," 1864.

In the village there is a deathly silence.
– [Izmailov], *Dnevnik*, 2 August 1934.

In his memoirs Nikita S. Khrushchev, the energetic and outspoken one-time leader of the USSR,[1] who famously launched the "de-Stalinization" (liberalization) of his country with his so-called "secret speech" ("about the cult of personality and its consequences") to a closed session of the Twentieth Congress of the Communist Party of the Soviet Union (hereafter CPSU) in 1956, recalled being a prominent participant in the most tumultuous and calamitous period of Soviet history – the quarter-century of Stalinist tyranny from 1928 until 1953. As such he had witnessed one of the period's searing events, the "provision difficulties" (Soviet officialdom's euphemism for "starvation") of 1928–34 that climaxed in 1932–33.[2] He recollected this famine: "After the 'all-out' collectivization of agriculture … a time of semi-starvation began for the Soviet Union, and in some areas there was fully-fledged famine. There was no food. We couldn't even ensure provisions for Moscow."[3] To his credit, Khrushchev not only acknowledged the famine but also lessened the likelihood of a recurrence with his opening of the "virgin and idle [disused] lands" to spring wheat in the Asiatic Russian steppe in the mid-1950s to complement the mainly winter wheat lands in the European Russian steppe.[4] Since Khrushchev's downfall in 1964 the famine climax of this food crisis has attracted a good deal of attention in both the popular and the academic literature, primarily because it has frequently been represented as having been both deliberate – "man-made," or "planned," or "organized"[5] – on the part of Joseph Stalin, the "great leader," and wilfully directed against Ukrainians especially (a *holodomor* [killing by starving], or "genocide"), who allegedly bore the brunt (if not the total force) of this "Ukrainian," not Soviet, famine.[6]

And the fact that it served to weaken peasant resistance to Stalin's Promethean project to hurriedly and ruthlessly transform the country from a backward agrarian empire into a modern industrial nation in the face of foreign hostility has also elicited interest. The attention has generated a voluminous literature,[7] some of it contentious and even polemical and nearly all of it specialized and impersonal, dealing with a specific locale (usually the Ukraine), a specific period (usually 1932–33), or a specific aspect (often the intent) of the famine. Nevertheless, the calamity remains little known outside academe, so this book offers a narrative of the famine in terms of its course, extent, duration, causes, and impact,[8] but, most important, as voiced by both the doctrinaire protagonists and the innocent antagonists – Russians and Ukrainians, Western Siberians and Central Asians, Volga Germans and Don Cossacks, Kazakhs and Kalmyks – in an attempt to put a human face on Stalin's assault on rural Russia. These dormant voices are derived from a panoply of insider and outsider evidence, comprising not only the words and deeds of the perpetrators (the policy-makers and their implementers, i.e., the Stalinist leadership, regional officials, and the secret police) but also those of Soviet witnesses (writers of prose and verse, journalists, and ordinary citizens) and the sufferers themselves (peasants and nomads, blue-collar and white-collar workers, and "former persons" [one-time tsarist officers, officials, titled and untitled nobles, priests, White Guards, etc.]). Additional evidence from a non-Soviet viewpoint comes from foreign observers – embassy and consul officials, journalists, Moscow correspondents, scientific and technical specialists, fellow travellers, emigrés, and tourists. Theirs are some of the voices of "the fate of peasant Russia" during the "times that were hard to bear."[9] It is time these voices were heard and to end what one writer has called the "silence of the West," a silence that has been a "blot on our civilization."[10]

Perspective

The great Soviet famine – what the Croatian witness Ante Ciliga called "Death's great harvest from 1929 to 1933"[11] and the Belgian witness Victor Kibalchich (aka Victor Serge) termed "the Great Wretchedness (1931–1934)"[12] – was another in a long line of disasters, natural and otherwise,[13] that had periodically afflicted Russia since its beginnings. From the eleventh to the middle of the twentieth century Russia endured more than 350 famines, including twenty-one severe, or *tsar* (king-sized), famines (so-called because of their omnipotence and pitilessness, i.e., their intensity, extent, and duration); four of these occurred in the 1800s and seven in the 1900s.[14] Famine, like drought, was so chronic that it was simply expected. President Mikhail Kalinin, the Soviet Union's nominal head of state (and of peasant stock), asserted in a speech at the end of 1921 to the Ninth All-Russian Congress of Soviets that an average famine struck every three years, a severe famine every five years, and an extreme famine every ten years.[15] Indeed, famine was so common (and so harmful) that it was central to the mentality of the peasantry, being an old and cruel enemy that threatened the livelihood of the peasants, who responded in accordance with their basic tenet – "the main thing is to survive."[16] The surrealist Soviet writer Andrei Platonov (Klimentov) depicts the traditional peasant strategy for surviving famine in his dystopian masterwork *Chevengur*, set in the steppe countryside in 1921 (and not published in its entirety in his homeland until 1988, on the eve of the Soviet era's collapse):

> Every fifth year half the village would go off to the mines and the towns, and the other half to the forests: the harvest had failed. From time immemorial it had been known that, even in dry years, herbs, greens, and cereals do well in forest clearings. The half of the village that had stayed would rush out to these clearings – to save their vegetables from being plundered instantly by hordes of greedy wanderers. But this time there was a drought the following year too. The village bolted up its huts and set out onto the highway in two columns. One column set off to Kiev to beg, the other to Lugansk in search of work; a few people turned off into the forest and the overgrown gullies, where they took to eating raw grass, clay and bark, and lived wild. The people who left were nearly all adults – the children had either managed to die in advance or had run off to live as beggars. As for the unweaned babies, their mothers had let them gradually die, not allowing them to suck their fill.

Platonov adds that infants were "cured" of hunger with an infusion of mushrooms and sweet herbs, whereupon "the children fell silent with dry foam on their lips" (a reference to the use of food substitutes from the wild as a last resort).[17]

Some post-revolutionary Russians could still recall the extreme famine of 1891–92, Russia's first national famine in terms of scale, affecting twenty-nine of the empire's ninety-seven oblasts, especially some 40 million inhabitants in the Central Black Earth and Volga Valley Regions. This calamity resulted from a decline in grain yields induced by a three-year sequence of winter cold and summer drought but was compounded by both a cholera epidemic (preceded in 1889 by an epidemic of "Russian flu," a virulent strain of influenza) and tsarist policy – Finance Minister Vyshnegradsky's policy of amassing gold and strenthening the ruble by means of higher taxes on the peasants and larger exports of peasant grain. The famine took 400,000 to 600,000 lives, despite the government's mounting of one of the largest relief campaigns in the country's history (more than 11 million subjects received state rations) and humanitarian contributions by prominent individuals such as the writers Leo Tolstoy and Anton Chekhov.[18]

Even more Bolshevik subjects could remember the so-called "Volga famine" of 1921–22 that, in fact, encompassed the Volga Valley,[19] the North Caucasus, the Ukraine,[20] the southern Urals, northern Kazakhstan, and Western Siberia with a population of some 70 million (about one-half of the country's total).[21] The final searing event of the "cursed years" of 1918–22,[22] it was generated by drought ("in the Volga Valley in the summer of 1921," recollected one memoirist, "the sun burned all of the grain");[23] by the requisition of agricultural production [*prodrazvyorstka*] – mostly grain but also livestock – from the peasants during the Civil War of 1918–22 by "food squads" on behalf of the infant and fragile Soviet state for the Red Army, the Cheka (secret police), Party officials, and factory workers;[24] and by plundering on the part of Red (Bolshevik), White (anti-Bolshevik), Green (peasant), royalist, and Ukrainian nationalist soldiers, as well as bandits and urban refugees (not to mention the "Red Terror" of demonic Felix Derzhinsky's secret police, whose 250,000 victims included aristocratic landlords).[25] In the words of a Moscow saying of 1918 recounted by the poet Marina Tsvetaeva, "When the Bolsheviks came to power, no more bread and no more flour."[26]

The Russian-cum-American sociologist Pitirim Sorokin, who witnessed the famine in the cities and the villages, noted that it illustrated the Russian proverb "A bad crop is from God, a famine is from the people," writing:

The 1928–34 Famine in Perspective

"There was a drought, it is true, but it did not cause the famine in all its horror. The Communistic policy of plundering the peasantry, thus leading them, in self-defense, to reduce the area of cultivation almost by half; the requisitions of corn [grain], even to seed corn, in the dry areas; this policy must be held responsible for the most catastrophic features of the famine."[27] Sorokin visited two of the starving rayons in 1921: Tambov for three weeks in the winter and Samara in the autumn. In the former he learned:

> In that rayon the requisitions and the beastly cruelties of the Communists [Bolsheviks] soon became unbearable. Not only did the agents take from the peasants all their corn and their poor belongings, often arresting or shooting them afterwards, but sometimes in the dead of winter they chased the peasants naked out of their houses, and threw water on them until they were living icicles. Once or twice a peasant turned on a Communist and murdered him. In retaliation the Communist agents mutilated peasants before shooting them, cutting off the ears, hands, legs, and pudendas of their victims, gouging out their eyes, or violating their wives and daughters in their sight. The peasants caught some of the agents unawares and mutilated them in similar fashion. Some they killed by binding their legs to the tops of two bent trees, [and] letting the trees slowly straighten. Others they tied to the tails of horses and dragged to death.[28]

In Samara Oblast the starvation was worse:

> "We entered the village of N. in the afternoon. This place was as though dead. Houses stood deserted and roofless, with gaps where windows and doors had been. The straw thatch of the houses had long since been torn away and eaten. There were no animals in the village, of course, no cattle, horses, sheep, goats, dogs, cats, or even crows. All had been eaten. Dead silence lay over the snow-covered roads until, with a little creak a sledge came in sight, a sledge drawn by two men and a woman and having a dead body on it. After drawing the sledge a short distance, they stopped and fell exhausted on the snow. Dully they looked at us as we approached, and with sick hearts we looked at them." I had seen starving faces in the cities, but such living skeletons as these three people

I had never seen. In rags, shaking with cold, they were not white of visage, but blue, dark blue with yellow spots.

Sorokin's party said "God help you" to them, and one of the starvelings replied: "God? We forgot God and He forgot us." The village constable then appeared and told the visitors that the makeshift morgue had to be locked and the local graveyard guarded in order to prevent cannibalization of the corpses.[29]

Some historians identify two distinct famines at this time: a northern urban famine in 1918–22,[30] caused mainly by the ravages of the civil war and the excesses of government procurement, and a southern rural famine in 1921–22, caused mainly by drought in a weakened countryside (which was to be struck by drought again in 1924 and weakened and alienated again by state underpricing of peasant grain in 1926–28). During the former an issue of the CPSU's newspaper *Pravda* (Truth) published – with unintentional irony – an editorial praising the creative energy of communism as illustrated by the government's decision to build the world's largest "crematory"![31] The 1921–22 famine also owed much to the fact that in the First World War the Russian army, composed primarily of able-bodied peasants, suffered huge losses that were not regenerated by the early 1920s (and not even by the late 1920s, when the next famine began). The cumulative effect of these factors climaxed in the first half of 1922, which the poet Boris Pasternak labelled the "black year." Another writer, the Nobel laureate (1970) Alexander Solzhenitsyn, was more explicit, declaring that peasants starved "to the point of cannibalism, to the point at which parents ate their own children ... and in the Volga Region they were eating grass, the soles of shoes, and gnawing at door jambs"; it was, he added, "such a famine as even Russia had never known, even in the Time of Troubles in the early seventeenth century," when at least "unthreshed ricks of grain survived intact beneath the snow and ice for several years."[32]

The situation was dire enough to menace the Bolshevik regime. The popular Ukrainian-born short story writer, journalist, and social activist Vladimir Korolenko, who had written a series of essays ("In the Famine Year") in 1892–93 about the great famine of that time, warned Bolshevik ideologue and commissar of education (and censor) Anatoly Lunacharsky in 1920 that, "captivated by unilateral destruction of the capitalist order, you [the Bolsheviks] have brought the country to an awful state" and "now the situation is much worse [than in 1891–92] and *all of Russia* has been struck by famine, beginning

The 1928–34 Famine in Perspective

with the capitals [Moscow and Petrograd (St Petersburg)], where there have been cases of people starving to death in the streets."[33] "Worst of all," he added, "you have destroyed the organic relation between the town and the village: the natural link of exchange." So, he wrote, "Each ploughman sees only that what he has produced is being taken away from him for remuneration that is obviously not the equivalent of his labour, and he concludes that he will hide his grain in pits. You find it, requisition it, and march through the villages of Russia and the Ukraine with a 'red-hot iron,' torching whole villages and rejoicing in the success of your food policy."

"If you add," continued Korolenko, "that many parts of Russia are already starving ... then the picture becomes even more startling than everything that befell me in the famine year [1891]."[34] Then he quotes a ditty that had been told to him by a former peasant:

> In olden days, dim Nicholas reigned
> And bread was hard to find.
> Clever communists we have since gained –
> No food now of any kind![35]

Korolenko was right to worry, for the next year (1921) drought struck as Bolshevik requisitions eased. Another Ukrainian, a young agronomist, described the drought in Kherson Oblast:

> And then out of spite, after the authorities had extorted all of the grain from the village [1920] and left only three puds [108 lbs] per person until the new crop of 1921,[36] nature herself rose up against the peasants: beginning in the summer of 1920 and during the winter [of 1920–21] and throughout 1921 not a drop of rain fell. The soil turned into ashes, into dust. Spring was the time to sow, but the land was dried-up ... The soil even lost its damp structure, the grain could not grow, and there was no rain. The ration left by order of the Bolsheviks until June 1921 was eaten. And they did not harvest a crop in 1921.[37]

The deadly result was described by a Muscovite in 1922:

> At this time we see, hear, and feel that there is a terrible famine in Russia. Images of it are displayed not only where the "elder of Russia,"

[Mikhail] Kalinin [the titular head of the Soviet state] travels (i.e., "in the starving rayons"), writing in his travel notes with the candour of "some sort of Korolenko" that "some die, others bury them, and others – luckier – try to use the remains of the dead, including the soft parts of the bodies, but even in Moscow itself along all of its streets."[38]

Mortality would have been higher but for relief efforts (begrudged by a suspicious Lenin), some domestic but mostly foreign, including Fridtjof Nansen's International Relief Organization, Save the Children, the Red Cross, the Society of Friends (Quakers), and future US president Herbert Hoover's American Relief Administration, which alone by the summer of 1922 was feeding 11 million people as well as fighting a typhus epidemic (altogether the ARA gave 75,000 tonnes of food to as many as half of the starving and saved at least 10 million lives).[39] Walter Duranty, who arrived in the Soviet Union in 1921 to become the Moscow bureau chief of the *New York Times*, guessed that the famine killed up to 7 million inhabitants (including Korolenko himself, the Symbolist poet Alexander Blok,[40] and Nikita Khrushchev's first wife); however, he cautioned that "few, save the children, died of actual hunger, but typhus (the so-called 'famine disease'), cholera, dysentery, typhoid, and scurvy, the diseases of malnutrition, took their plenteous toll."[41] Some desperate victims resorted to cannibalism, as the British consul in Leningrad was assured a decade later by the keeper of classical antiquities at the State Hermitage Museum (formerly the Winter Palace of the royal family), Oskar Waldhauer: "in the famine of 1922, on the Volga, if you heard of someone who had died, unless you got there at once there wouldn't be half a body to bury, the rest would have been eaten."[42] Indeed, it was this very famine that served as the basis for sociologist Sorokin's assertion that starvation could overcome society's strictest taboos, even reducing some members to committing the "supremely anitisocial act of cannibalism."[43] Estimates of the number of victims reach as high as 10 million, but the usual figure is 5 to 6 million souls, half of them children.[44] Additionally, many peasants panicked and migrated, mainly to Siberia and Soviet Central Asia (formerly Russian, or Western, Turkestan), and hundreds of thousands of orphaned and abandoned children appeared (in 1922 as many as 7 million of these urchins, primarily peasant children, may have been roaming the country).[45]

The famine had political as well as demographic repercussions. In Smolensk Oblast, at least, owing to the want of food, unrest grew among soldiers, workers, and peasants, seriously undermining popular support for the Bolsheviks. Communism in theory did not seem to match communism in practice; as a popular Moscow saying in 1917–19 put it, "Communism is wonderful, but communists are horrid!"[46] More soldiers deserted, factory strikes erupted, and peasant discontent flared. In one report of the spring of 1922 the Cheka noted:

> Among the peasants there are no limits to the grumbling against the Soviet Government and the Communists. In the conversation of every average peasant and poor peasant, not to speak even of the kulak [thriving peasant], the following is heard, "They aren't planning freedom for us, but serfdom. The time of [Tsar Boris] Godunov has already begun, when the peasants were attached to the landowners."[47]

The bumper harvest of 1922 ended the horror but not the widespread hunger and downright starvation. One specialist has argued persuasively that, from the beginning of 1919 until the middle of 1925, the Russian Republic (RSFSR), especially the Volga Valley (*Povolzhye*), endured a prolonged famine – with peaks in 1921–22 and 1924 – in the USSR as a direct result of the requisitioning of provisions by force from the peasants. These "seven years of starvation," he asserted, took the lives of at least 6 million peasants in the Volga Valley alone and ruined the entire republic's agrarian economy through, for example, the destruction of implements and livestock and the diminution of arable land; mass demonstrations during the collection of taxes and other payments and the recovery of seed loans; the simultaneous impoverishment of the peasants and enrichment of country officials in government, Communist Party, and cooperative bodies; the higher incidence of disease and the decrease in lifespan; the disappearance of traditional spiritual guidelines; the growth of moonshining/bootlegging, drunkenness, drug addition, and depravity; the surfacing of criminality, the lowering of standards of living, the strengthening of punitive bodies like the Cheka-cum-OGPU; and the proliferation of *besprizorniki* (the "neglected," i.e., waifs).[48]

And the 1928–34 famine was not to be the Stalin period's last. Harvest failures occurred in 1936 and 1939 and raised the spectre of famine, but it was kept at bay by 1937's bumper harvest. However, starvation reappeared in 1946–47 – just as the country was emerging bloodied but victorious from six years of savage warfare – and the extensive destruction and excessive requisitions of wartime and the extreme drought of 1946 put up to 100 million citizens (more than half of the USSR's population) at risk of starvation. As Khrushchev was to recall: "There was no rain; the economy had been ruined by the war; the collective farmers had no equipment, not even draft animals. The Germans had destroyed the machine and tractor stations (MTS's [agricultural machinery depots serving the collective farms]), and the war had done away with the horse herd."[49] The drought was extremely widespread but concentrated in the wooded steppe (parkland) and grassy steppe (prairie) of the south of the European quarter of the country; in scale and force it exceeded that of 1921–22 (in many areas no rain fell for up to seventy days in a row) and resembled that of 1891–92. At least 2 million inhabitants died of starvation and related epidemic diseases, and the famine's effects were felt as late as 1949.[50] And meanwhile, of course, throughout the Stalin period there was a covert famine in the network of Gulag camps, where hundreds of thousands of inmates were deliberately underfed and overworked to death,[51] as well as a famine in the early 1940s among the inhabitants of that part of European Russia occupied by German forces and even among those who were evacuated to the rear.[52] Thus, from 1928 until 1948 part or much of the population of the Soviet Union suffered from some degree of famine.

This food crisis was the country's last of the twentieth century, thanks mainly to the creation of another granary in the Asiatic Russian steppe to complement – not merely supplement – that in the European Russian steppe. According to Khrushchev, the Soviet Union's leaders, who had long worried about the want of grain reserves,[53] had also long been well aware of the existence of much virgin and disused (idle) land.[54] At the end of the 1920s the agronomist Nikolai Tulaikov headed a survey of usable land in the country's "eastern regions" (Asiatic Russia) and in 1930 reported 50 to 55 million hectares (1 hectare = 2.47 acres) suitable for grain-growing in Kazakhstan alone.[55] Stalin, however, was "categorically opposed" to the cultivation of new lands, again according to Khrushchev, who added, "It's possible that he wanted to concentrate attention on the cultural [agronomic] level of agriculture, to increase grain production through higher yields, through more intensive farming. This is the right road to take, but it is difficult and labor-intensive and requires a long time," as well as more investment.[56] Hence Stalin's trust in the neo-Lamarckian pseudo-genetics of Trofim Lysenko and his hollow promises to radically and quickly increase yields and livestock numbers.[57]

After his patron's death in 1953 Lysenko faded, and Khrushchev succeeded to the leadership and implemented his own program of agricultural betterment. It entailed the formation of a second granary of spring wheat on virgin and disused lands in the Asiatic Russian steppe (primarily by state farms) and, ipso facto, the replacement of some winter wheat acreage in the premier granary in the European Russian steppe with fodder crops, mainly corn ("sausage on a stalk"),[58] in order to put more and better meat on Soviet tables as well as more bread – plus much more investment in agriculture and the abolition of MTSS in 1958 (their equipment was sold to collective farms and they themselves were reorganized as RTSS [repair-technical stations]). Molotov – and Kaganovich and Malenkov – opposed what was later to be called (after Khrushchev's downfall) one of his "hare-brained schemes," deeming it an "unmanageable, absurd, and unnecessary" undertaking because of its excessive scale (40 to 45 million hectares) and high cost, and proposed, instead, the cheaper and faster expansion of cultivation in the non-black earth belt of central-northern European Russia, which, they contended, would double the yield per hectare.[59] But Khrushchev won the day, and in 1954 the ten-year Virgin and Idle Lands Program (VILP) was launched.

The program expanded the Soviet Union's sown area by almost one-quarter, and 25 million of the new 42 million hectares were in Kazakhstan (and 14 million of these 25 million hectares were opened iin the first year, 1954).[60] By the end of the program in the mid-1960s Kazakhstan accounted for up to one-third of the "new lands" (Western Siberia, the Urals, and the Middle and Lower Volga accounted for nearly all of the rest).[61] By then, too, more than 40 percent of Soviet grain output was derived from the new lands, compared with 25 percent from 1949 to 1953.[62] Thereafter Kazakhstan produced an average of 16 million tonnes of grain annually (one-half of the country's consumption in 1953), rendering it the Soviet Union's leading supplier (one-fifth) of wheat and relegating the Ukraine (one-sixth) to third place after the RSFSR.[63] Kazakhstan had also become, asserted Khrushchev, the country's cheapest producer of wheat.[64]

Inevitably with such a crash program decreed from above, as Khrushchev himself came to admit, mistakes were made in the early years in the new lands,[65] resulting in waste, soil erosion, and dust storms. These problems have commonly been underlined in the literature about the VILP, so much so that it has come to be seen as a failure, especially in view of the susceptibility of its interior location to drought, as in 1955. This view overlooks three compensating circumstances, however: first, the Soviets calculated that, even with severe drought two years of every five in the new lands, they would still produce 8 million tonnes annually on the average;[66] second, on the drier margins of the analogous spring wheat belt in the prairie oblasts, they eventually benefitted from the dryland-farming experience of Canadian growers;[67] and third – and most important – they took advantage, knowingly or unknowingly, of the so-called "pendulum principle" of drought occurrence in the USSR. This maxim refers to the fact that, owing to the circulatory characteristics of the atmosphere, in the vast land mass of the Soviet Union a region with below-normal moisture (drought-stricken) always borders a region with above-normal moisture, so that harvest failures in the former are offset by bumper harvests in the latter. For example, in the sixty-seven-year period of 1888 to 1955 drought struck the European Russian steppe (represented by Nikolayev Oblast) twenty-six times and the Asiatic Russian steppe (represented by Orenburg Oblast) twenty-nine times – but both regions simultaneously only three times (1888, 1889, 1923).[68] Thus, almost always drought would not strike Kazakhstan's granary and the Ukraine's granary at the same time, meaning that henceforth the Soviet Union would have both a larger and – most crucially – a more *reliable* grain supply, as well as fewer famines. Thus, the Russian droughts of 1957, 1959, 1963, and 1968 were partially mitigated by the VILP; Khrushchev's "hungry year" of 1963, caused by drought, would have been a famine year but for the 7.2 million tonnes of grain (one-half the procurement of the Stalin years) that were harvested in the "new lands."[69] On the rare occasions when drought did strike the two breadbaskets simultaneously, as in 1890, 1911, 1921, 1931, and 1972, a "catastrophic famine" resulted.[70]

At any rate, the point is that, as Zhores Medvedev, a Soviet biologist, historian, and dissident (and the twin brother of Roy, likewise a historian and dissident), wrote on the eve of the Soviet Union's collapse, "there have been several years in which only the good harvest in the virgin land areas has raised the total production of marketable grain above starvation level," and 1956 saw the largest grain harvest yet in the Soviet period, "when the weather was favorable in the eastern part of the Soviet Union and dry in the west (with Kazakhstan producing more wheat than the Ukraine)." He concluded that the VILP was Khrushchev's "boldest" and "most enduring" agricultural reform and a "lasting success."[71] That success struck Khrushchev's ally, Anastas Mikoyan, one day in 1955 when he found his government limousine blocked by a long, noisy line on a Moscow street, whereupon he asked his driver the cause of the hubbub and was told simply "Yevtushchenko." And when he asked who that was, he was again told simply "a poet," and only later did he understand: "I saw people queuing for poetry, not for food," and it was then that "I realized that a new era had begun" – an era of more attention to the basic needs of the people and no more famines. That fact of life had been made possible largely by VILP and was to be bolstered by an agricultural intensification program in 1965–75 (entailing the widespread application of mineral fertilizers) that would increase average grain yields by one-half, and by the purchase of grain abroad,[72] including wheat from Canada (giving rise to fictional Radio Armenia's anecdote about planting wheat in Kazakhstan but reaping it in Canada).

1
A SPECIAL FAMINE

> Earth and sky, sky and earth, such is the Russian land, and never in history has it reverberated so mightily with the voice of the peasant.
> – Maurice Hindus, *Red Bread: Collectivization in a Russian Village*, 355.

A Prolonged and Extensive Famine

Despite the historical familiarity of Russia's people with frequent famines, that of 1928–34 remains memorable. For one thing, it took place on a very wide scale (more or less the entire country) and over a very long time (seven years). Indeed, one demographic historian has gone so far as to say that "malnutrition was the norm for much of the [Soviet] Russian population during the 1920s and the 1930s."[1] Confidential reports from the secret police – the OGPU,[2] Stalin's "bared sword of the working class"[3] – indicate that the USSR suffered from "provision difficulties" from 1928 through 1934. And later in the 1930s some starvation reappeared. Another plausible time frame is from the end of 1928, when ration cards for food were introduced, until the beginning of 1935, when they were terminated.

Not surprisingly, the food crisis did not affect all of the country at the same time, varying from place to place and time to time. As John Vyvyan, third secretary of the British Embassy in Moscow, advised London in 1932, "in the case of the Soviet Union [owing to its vast size and physical and cultural diversity] it is more true than elsewhere that no section of the country is a microcosm of the whole," and "the condition of the agricultural population varies widely from place to place" – and not only from macro-region to macro-region but from micro-region to micro-region.[4]

The Moscow correspondent of the *Christian Science Monitor* (and briefly of the *Manchester Guardian*, too), William Chamberlin, found that "the high-water mark of plenty, cheapness and variety of food was 1926–27," and thereafter he and his Ukrainian-born and Russian-speaking wife, Sonya, had experienced a "great falling off";[5] he also said that "food was more plentiful and of better quality" during the mid-1920s, when he arrived, than when he left the country in 1934 during the last year of the famine.[6] In the experience of one of Chamberlin's American journalist colleagues, United Press International's Eugene Lyons (who had been born in Russia in 1898 as Yevgeny Natanovich Privin and who, just like Chamberlin, arrived in the Soviet Union in 1922 as a Communist sympathizer but left in the mid-1930s disillusioned by the famine and Stalin's purges), the food crisis grew "steadily worse" from 1928, the first year of the Bolsheviks' First Five-Year Plan (what Chamberlin called Russia's "Iron Age" because the plan stressed industry over farming and heavy industry over light industry).[7] Lyons vividly recalled the hunger/famine, although as a privileged foreigner (and fellow traveller) he did not suffer its pangs. Food, he wrote, became the "one absorbing subject, dominating all thought and conversation," and "the search for food, the struggle for sheer physical subsistence monopolized men's minds and drained their energies." Some, he continued, "changed their trades, their creeds, their friends in the hope of a little more sunflower seed oil or tea or bread," and "I saw men and women ... risk their careers or put themselves in danger of exile to a concentration camp for an extra ration." He also saw "the tremulous excitement that touched a Russian family when some member of it brought home a decaying herring or a verminous bit of meat." "Women offered their bodies in the hope of a real meal," and one woman "visiting the home of a General Electric engineer saw white bread, touched it incredulously, and burst into hysterical weeping." Lyons concluded that "it was not famine, but the shortage that causes men's bodies and minds and spirits to sag – the shortage that makes the stomach the core of existence, the center of every waking and dreaming thought – the shortage that makes all other human values, art, beauty, ideals, philosophies, an empty mockery." As a result, "a population meek by nature was made meeker by undernourishment, and therefore more amenable to manipulation by its rulers. People who spend every free moment looking for food have no time to mutiny or even to ask questions."[8]

The resultant widespread privation, which peaked in 1932–33, was expressed in two "anecdotes" (the black jokes that Soviet Russians liked to tell on themselves) heard by Mendel Osherowitch, a journalist for the New York newspaper *Jewish Daily Forward*, who returned to his Ukrainian birthplace in 1932 to visit his family and check the pulse of the "Republic of Workers and Peasants." One joke went as follows:

> This is a very popular story in Moscow. Once one of the soldiers standing watch by Lenin's dead body in the Mausoleum [in Red Square in front of the Kremlin] came running out, terrified. "Comrades," he said, "Lenin winked with one of his eyes ... I saw it myself."
>
> They thought this soldier's nerves had frayed because he had already stood watch by Lenin's body several times. They were certain he was out of his mind. But the soldier assured everyone that he remained fully in possession of his faculties and saw, not once, but several times, how the dead Lenin winked.
>
> So they sent a Red Army officer to stand watch by Lenin's dead body and closely observe the face of the deceased great leader Ilich. How surprised everyone in the Kremlin was when this Red commander also came running out, terrified, and told the same story as the soldier: "Comrades, Lenin winked with his eye ... I saw this myself."
>
> There was no reason to doubt the words of the officer, so a special conference was held in the Kremlin and it was decided that none other than Stalin himself should, at least for a few minutes, stand watch by Lenin's dead body. Perhaps the deceased Ilich was trying to communicate something which could not be entrusted to just anyone? As Stalin stood watch in the mausoleum, staring intensely in Lenin's direction, he, too, saw the same thing – Lenin was winking. Not losing control of himself, however, Stalin exclaimed loudly, in a full voice: "Comrade Ilich, what does this signify? Why are you winking? What do you want?" Out of Lenin's dead, sealed lips could be heard a voice, full of anguish: "I request, Comrade Stalin, to be turned with my head face down. I can no longer bear witness to the suffering of the Russian people." Such a story is told in Moscow.[9]

1928

The very first year of the Bolshevik blueprint did not bode well as the single-party (and by now) single-faction state under Stalin forcibly moved the several classes of peasants (the *bednyaks*, the worst-off, or poor, peasants; the *srednyaks*, the middling, or average, peasants; the *zazhitochniks*, the better-off, or prospering, peasants; and the *kulaks*, the well-off, or thriving, peasants) from their individual holdings or one of the two types of agricultural cooperatives that prevailed under Lenin's New Economic Policy of 1921–27 to the new state-owned and large-scale collective farms (*kolkhozes*) and state farms (*sovkhozes*).[10] Few went voluntarily – mostly the bednyaks – because, as one srednyak said, "they had nothing to lose but their chains" and everything to gain by pooling what little they had with the ampler means of the other peasants,[11] who had to be forced to move and share their hard-won gains.[12] As one Western Siberian peasant explained, "we entered the cooperative voluntarily but the kolkhoz by force ... In the cooperative we worked for ourselves. But in the kolkhoz for whom? In the cooperative the overseer was one of us, from the village. But in the kolkhoz he was always an outsider."[13] And there was a turnover of these managerial "outsiders" every couple of years. To the involuntary kolkhozniks collectivization amounted to plain theft, as one of them complained bitterly: "When collectivization commenced, real theft began. Outsiders arrived. Everything that they could take, they took. They seized the house, the livestock, clothing, the grain, the storehouses – everything up to the last handful of flour. They did not notice that the house was full of children who had to be fed something."[14] Another peasant added: "Among us it was said that the famine arose because of the kolkhozes. Everything was taken from people: livestock, inventory, seed. That is the famine that occurred."[15] Millions of peasants resisted; they protested in demonstrations, they left for the cities, and they destroyed their property before it could be seized, even torching kolkhozes. And as a visiting expatriate was told, "when the kolkhoz burns the peasants ... don't run to put out the fire, not unless they're driven to do so ... for the peasants hate the kolkhoz, even more than they once hated the nobleman's estate."[16]

Production declined, and already by the early spring of 1928 bread had become a "deficit product" and breadlines had become "longer, drearier, more sullen throughout the land."[17] Bread, especially so-called "black bread" (a dark brown sourdough bread made from dark rye flour), was a staple of the Russian diet, especially among commoners and particularly peasants.[18] In late spring a Muscovite writer noted in his diary: "in places there is already famine, 'as in 1891,' the 'socialists [communists]' say so as not to say 'as in 1920.'" He added: "Everywhere the news is startling: in Odessa they do [unpaid] civic duty [*dezhurstvo*] for bread; in the Caucasus they post notices in the restaurants [stressing] dinner with bread, as in 1922. There is no bread in Poltava. The Pre-Urals – Saratov, Chelyabinsk, Tyumen – are without bread." Even showcase Moscow experienced days with no meat and little bread, and weeks without tea and butter.[19] By the summer various forms of bread rationing as well as breadlines, which were especially long for cheaper black bread, had appeared throughout the country.[20] In July *Pravda* reported that in places there were night-long lines for bread, with parents sending their children to stand in line, where they were crushed by the adults and taken half-dead to the hospital every day; at one bakery there was a line round the clock. The report added that in some parts of the oblasts there was "disorder" on the part of disgruntled peasants equal to that of 1919–20 (which saw peasant rebellion against Bolshevik seizures of grain during the civil war), with "large and fearsome hunger strikes, and neither bread nor millet, and no oats at all at any price." And a Red Army soldier's letter to the newspaper lamented "the artificial famine ... [whereas] in [19]21 in our Union [of Soviet Socialist Republics] the famine was natural and not dependent on us ... [but] at the present time we are experiencing a famine that depends almost [solely] on ourselves" – that is, Bolshevik policy.[21] In early July a confidential report of the Norwegian chargé d'affaires said: "from more and more rayons one hears of actual want" and "over considerable areas there is neither flour nor meat to be bought." Two weeks later he stated, "if one is to believe all one hears from non-Bolshevik (but not, therefore, necessarily *bourgeois*) quarters, great areas of the country are on the verge of starvation and revolt," adding, "a social revolutionary [a member of a non-Bolshevik Marxist Party], who has travelled about a good deal in the country lately, told me a short time ago that in the southern corn [wheat] rayons the feeling is so bitter that a match would set the whole place in a blaze."[22] In the autumn the Norwegian Legation informed Oslo that "reliable reports from the country rayons confirm[ed] that several rayons [were] threatened with real famine, and, in any case, that there [was] a great lack of corn [wheat] in many places." Indeed, four Ukrainian rayons (Odessa, Kherson, Moldau, and Nikolayev) needed "immediate help," meaning that they were suffering from starvation.[23] The shortage of food was explained officially in terms of "kulak resistance," just as the shortage of manufactures was explained in terms of "industrial espionage."[24] By December the scarcity of food was being felt "even in Moscow, the most favored of Russian cities."[25] Food jokes began to be told in the capital, and Lyons quoted a couple of them: "You asked someone, 'How are you getting on?' and he replied, 'Lootche tchem zahvtra – better than tomorrow.' Or he said, 'Oh, like Lenin in his mausoleum.' 'How do you mean that?' you inquired, knowing that a joke was coming. 'Because they neither feed us nor bury us,' was the answer."[26] Food queues ("tails") had become "longer and more restive," Lyons noted,[27] and in all Soviet cities there were long lines for bread and fights in the lines, with an OGPU report saying that "it takes a fistfight to get some bread."[28] The OGPU also reported the "politically unhealthy mood" of the country's urbanites because of poor supply in general.[29] One citizen complained: "They send all the bread out of the country, and we ourselves sit here with no bread while our party leaders holler about achievements. We work eight hours at the factory, then stand four or five hours in a breadline. And there you have a thirteen-hour workday."[30] Another malcontent was more prophetic: "The government aims to turn us into living skeletons."[31]

1929

The hunger/famine worsened in 1929. Food rationing – in the form of "bread cards" – was finally implemented in the middle of the unusually cold winter of 1928–29. There were three categories of cardholders: blue-collar (manual) workers, children, and white-collar workers. Each category had a card of a different colour and was entitled to a different amount and kind of food. Cards were not issued to either *lishentsy* (literally the "deprived ones," i.e., the disenfranchised, also dubbed "one-time persons," namely, "enemies of the people" like former nobles, priests, private traders [Nepmen], and tsarist officials, who had to buy or barter on the expensive private market) or to peasants, who were expected to live off the land.[32] Moreover, not even cardholders were equally treated: Party and government cadres, industrial workers, and military and security personnel received more and better rations than others, as did foreign workers.[33] The rationing spawned a number of anecdotes, often in the form of riddles, for example: "Why is ours the most cultured country in the world?" "Because nearly everybody has at least one book and treasures it – the food book"; and "Papa," a boy asks his father, "Why don't Jews eat ham?" "And we Russians," replies the father angrily, "why don't *we* eat ham?"[34]

The two privileged metropolises – the new, inward-looking Soviet capital of Moscow and the old, outward-looking Tsarist capital of St Petersburg (1713)/Petrograd (1914)/Leningrad (1924) – were not spared the hardship. Ration cards were introduced in Moscow in the middle of March.[35] A resident of Leningrad stated that they were required from the very beginning of the year to obtain bread as "it was reckoned that this [measure] would obviate [the usual] lines, but today [3 January] the bread lines are worse." Much later – the end of May – she wrote: "the vexed question of bread lines, and other lines, remains in all its glory," adding that "there is still enough bread, [but] meat has disappeared."[36] A Norwegian citizen told a member of the British consulate in Latvia's capital of Riga at the beginning of the year that "the shortage of food-stuffs in Leningrad and Moscow ha[d] reached an appalling stage" and added, "probably the most amazing fact is the shortage of potatoes in Leningrad, a phenomenon in Russia which could be equaled only by England experiencing a shortage of coal, or Norway a shortage of herrings."[37] Yet the "Venice of the North" was relatively fortunate for, as the *Berliner Tageblatt*'s Paul Scheffer reported, "Leningrad is surrounded by a great belt of famine that begins not more than fifteen miles beyond the city limits."[38] Other cities and towns (particularly non-industrial centres) and especially villages fared worse. Between 1 January and 15 March 1929 the newspaper *Krestyanskaya gazeta* (Peasant gazette) received two hundred and seventy-six letters complaining of the scarcity and expense of grain and of starvation in the countryside. For example: "[peasants] are abandoning their farmsteads and migrating, just to avoid starvation" (Novgorod Rayon); "this year we have had a terrible famine" (Pskov Rayon); "we have neither bread nor fodder" (Leningrad Rayon); "the village is starving" (Rostov Rayon); "many of us do not have bread now" (Tambov Rayon); "we have a bread famine" (Vitebsk Rayon); and "we have no bread" (Galich).[39] Upon returning to the USSR in late winter after a trip home to the United States for a couple of months, the mining engineer John "Jack" Littlepage found that "the place

A Special Famine

had changed so much while I was gone that I could hardly recognize it." Prices had soared, and, particularly, "food was poor in quality and hard to get, and was outrageously high-priced."⁴⁰ In early spring the Norwegian consul at Arkhangelsk on the White Sea told British officials that in North Russia the bread ration for workers was six hundred grams daily, whereas "the Russian liked to eat the best part of 2 kilos," "there was no tea and very little sugar," and meat was "hardly to be had."⁴¹

The situation was not improved by the summer harvest. The populace grew more and more restive, resulting in hunger strikes and protest demonstrations. The authorities blamed "saboteurs" and "class enemies"; in the fall, forty-eight scapegoats (specialists in Narkomtorg, the state organ of trade and supply) were shot. As the head of the Czech mission in Moscow explained in a report to Prague:

> The Soviets are resorting to terror every time their situation becomes critical. They see terror as the only escape. The crisis in supply is increasing dreadfully in the USSR, and broad sections [of the population] do not hide their dissatisfaction with the authorities. The workers, one of the principal bulwarks of the present regime, are grumbling loudly, and they are demanding improvement. The bombardment with various slogans about the construction of socialism has ceased to help. The authorities have come to a dead end ... So it was necessary to find someone who could be held responsible for the general want and thereby deflect the anger away from the real culprits.⁴²

This "cleansing" (purge) did not lessen the hunger. In the middle of August an old peasant told Paul Scheffer, the German reporter: "life is no longer worth living."⁴³ Discontent grew, with the Norwegian Legation reporting that "unrest and revolt increase, both in the oblasts and the towns," the chief reason being the worsening availability of food.⁴⁴

Moscow was again not spared. An entry in a resident's diary in early fall read: "*Provisionment is deteriorating.* There are no eggs, no butter, and meat is scarce." Actually, milk and eggs were available but only to children – a fact that inevitably gave rise to another anecdote: "A foreigner, upon hearing in a store that eggs were available to children only, exclaimed that 'everywhere one must have eggs in order to have children but [here] you must have children in order to get eggs!'"[45] Later that season the capital was visited by a veteran correspondent of London's *Daily Telegraph*, Ellis Ashmead-Bartlett, famed for having publicized the Gallipoli campaign of the First World War as a "ghastly and costly fiasco." Like most visitors of that time, he found Moscow quiet and dreary, and Muscovites gloomy and sullen. He also found many beggars and long breadlines (but, "as usual, excellent" soups),[46] and he added, "the scarcity in milk, butter and cheese is so great that but few attempt any longer to obtain them," and that "the queues for all articles grow bigger and bigger as the winter progresses." "The search for food is a profession in Russia," he concluded.

Yet on the subject of famine the journalist cautioned his readers: "there is no subject on which it was more difficult to arrive at the truth"; although "your first impression ... on entering Moscow is that a horrible famine is already sweeping through the land," he added, "you must be careful to remember that everything is relative, and that these scenes of misery, however heartbreaking to the foreign observer, do not constitute a state of famine in Russia, either in the eyes of the people or of the government," for "a famine to the Russian means absolute starvation, when roots are devoured, thousands perish, and whole rayons are abandoned." He did admit that "last winter there were local famines involving many deaths in some parts, but no general famine devastating whole rayons," owing to an inferior harvest in the European Russian steppe being offset by a superior harvest in the Asiatic Russian steppe (in spite of inadequate railway capacity between east and west). Besides, he noted, "the needs of the population are very simple: a half kilo of bread per day, some vegetables and, whenever available, a lump of meat or ham to put in the soup."[47]

1930

Nevertheless, 1930 saw more of the same, including the disparity between large urban and small rural settlements. At the beginning of the year people returning to the town of Kashin from Moscow some one hundred miles (160 kilometres) to the south reported that "in recent months" in the capital "living conditions had changed for the worse": "A shortage of foodstuffs is noticeable – meat, milk, sugar, and such. In most of the dining places meat dishes are

A Special Famine

prepared not daily but every 3 or 4 days with a permit. Sausages and ham are hard to find. There is no cheese."[48] In the middle of January Scheffer found that "in Moscow there [was] an unparalleled shortage of food."[49] A month later the first British ambassador to the Soviet Union, Esmond Ovey, who upon his arrival was struck by the capital's "general aspect of dinginess," cabled that "difficulties regarding food and housing seem to occupy the attention of people ... to the exclusion of almost every other question."[50]

Leningrad seems to have been in worse straits. Its plight was recorded by Lyubov Shaporina, a representative of the Tsarist intelligentsia who, after having immigrated to France in 1925, returned five years later to found the first Soviet puppet theatre. In the middle of February 1930 she wondered:

> What will there be to eat? There is no butter, no eggs, no meat. We are issued 100 gr. per person once in 10 days, and we are members of the second category [of the four categories of ration recipients], not workers [who were members of the first category]. In the newspapers yesterday, after the cries for speedy and large-scale construction, it was noted in small type that in February children will be issued 200 gr. of butter and adults 200 gr. of *frityur* (i.e., margarine). How to live, what to feed my sick children, whom the doctors say need a variety and an abundance of nourishment. In 1918 we had rags and the peasants had produce. Now each of us is completely empty-handed.[51]

Kashin residents returning from Leningrad in the spring corroborated Shaporina's portrayal:

> Provisionment there is very bad: meat is rarely issued, there is scant fish and it is mostly salted, small loaves [of bread] are dispensed in slices, and fabrics, shoes, clothing, and hardware are not available. Long lines are often encountered at night and in early morning, for the issued articles do not suffice for everyone, and those who line up late risk being left with nothing. The food in the cafeterias is deteriorating. Under such conditions the white- and blue-collar workers are having a very hard time ... The mood is one of depression.[52]

At the beginning of summer Shaporina added, "I was at the morgue. It was terrible. But then I went along the Okhta [River] to the cemetery, and the people riding in the tram were more terrible than the corpses. Yellow faces, skin and bones, downcast eyes, people emaciated from prolonged malnutrition and doomed to death."[53]

Another summer witness was Fred Beal, a sympathetic American communist whose visit to the Soviet Union would prompt his political about-face.[54] When he arrived in Leningrad at the beginning of July his ship was met at the dock by a crowd of men, women, and children in ragged clothes begging for money, and he ate at a nearby workers' cafeteria where "hundreds" waited in line to eat thin cabbage soup, black bread, and weak tea plus boiled fish thrice weekly (and where his "scrawny and wasted" waiter devoured his leavings "because the Party decided to export food and other products to capitalist countries for machinery"). Beal found that food, clothing, and other articles were not allotted equally, with high Party and secret police officials, technicians, and workers who performed hazardous or strenuous labour receiving preferential treatment while "the Russian worker was just then having a hard time trying to keep alive."[55]

It was much the same in outlying smaller cities, such as the capital of the cotton republic of Uzbekistan, Tashkent, whose suffering was depicted in communications that had been intercepted by the OGPU: "Life in Tashkent is very hard. Everything is terribly expensive. You stand in line for bread, kerosene, etc." (4 August). "Typhus and tuberculosis have spread greatly. The mortality of children is 22 pers. out of 100 officially but I think that unofficially it is no less than 50%" (6 August). "Life has become impossible here. The expense is dreadful ... Can you imagine – I stood in line for two nights in order to get 4 kilos of potatoes for a ruble, and half of them had to be thrown away" (9 August). "Life here has become merciless, nightmarish, wretched" (10 August). "Flour is 100 rub. per pud [36 lbs.], rice is 150 rub. per pud. Butter is 8 rub. per pud, etc. ... Now everyone is coming to Tashkent, but they will starve to death here. There is nowhere to live. There are no apartments. They lie here and there right on the ground, in the streets" (27 August).[56] Beal himself visited Uzbekistan about this time and noted that "the workers were starving [in order] to build Socialism."[57]

The "provision difficulties" (officialese for "starvation") were worse in the villages. Secret OGPU reports documented hunger and starvation throughout the countryside at various times in 1930, and especially in the spring, entailing "swelling" (dropsy, or edema), "spotted fever" (typhus) from the unhygienic conditions, and "bloody flux" (diarrhea) from eating food "surrogates" (officialese for "substitutes") like carrion, the wholesale slaughtering of livestock for food, demonstrating en masse (mainly on the part of women), "dawdling" (working to rule), striking, destroying seed grain, raiding and smashing granaries, selling collective farm property and buying grain at very high prices on the private market, quitting the collective farms to seek food and work elsewhere, complaining bitterly ("It's better to bury grain in a pit and let it rot than to sell it to the state and then starve again"), responding angrily to official demands ("There is no grain now, come back when you begin to swell" and "We are hungry and we will not go to the steppe to work ... you have promised us everything but given us nothing"), and fomenting discontent and threatening rebellion ("You have taken the grain from us, now give it to us ... in the fall during grain procurement we will talk to you quite differently").[58]

But the peasants were largely defenceless, and procurement was unsparing and relentless, particularly to holdouts, as a peasant diarist in Western Siberia's Altai Kray recorded bitterly: "In the village the procurement campaign is intensifying. From the prosperous [peasants] grain is taken by force (for a certain payment), and from resisters it is confiscated to the last kernel and they are tried and put in prison. Compulsory loans are extended to every head of a peasant household unconditionally: take it or get nothing! The zazhitochniks are hostile to Soviet power, poverty, and distrust."[59] Nikita Khrushchev, at this time a middle-aged and fast-rising apparatchik (Party or government official), visited a kolkhoz named after Stalin near Samara (later Kuibyshev, the Second World War temporary capital in lieu of besieged Moscow) and discovered for himself "the real situation in the countryside ... a situation of literal starvation. People were moving around slowly, like flies in the autumn, because of malnourishment ... and all of them with one voice were begging us to give them bread."[60]

Near the end of 1930 an anonymous citizen wrote in desperation and exasperation to the famous writer Maxim Gorky (the pseudonym of Aleksei Peshkov)[61] – then living in Italy – in order to open his eyes to his motherland's plight (and probably in the hope of moving him to exert his influence for the people's welfare). He wrote:

You know, we are literally starving ... Take Belorussia, where the terror has reached the uppermost level and where there is nobody who believes in a bright future, for living conditions are worsening with each day. There is nothing to eat, the cafeteria has slops, salaries are withheld for months ... Where is the promised paradise? And alongside this [privation] the powers that be live otherwise. Everything is possible for them ... There is no firewood, we have not seen meat since the spring ... How can one exist on an empty stomach?

He ended: "Famine moves over the land, and we have nothing in the cafeterias except slops, but our leaders and bosses have everything, and on the skeletons of our famine they are constructing their personal well-being and 'socialism.'"[62] Gorky – now in thrall to the Bolsheviks as their literary darling as the author of the poem "The Song of the Stormy Petrel," the so-called "battle anthem of the revolution," and as one of the founders of "socialist realism" – may have been moved personally by the letter but there is no evidence that he reacted publicly.[63]

The suffering was creating malcontents even among the normally supportive and relatively privileged proletariat. The OGPU documented expressions of this discontent, including: "Long live the five-year plan of empty stomachs!"; on the wall of Astrakhan's Karl Marx Factory, "Any fool can rule, since all it takes to run the Soviet government is to know how to starve the people"; and on a locomotive in Siberia, "The USSR is a kind country – it sends all its bread [grain] across its borders, while it stays hungry."[64] Even Stalin himself was losing popularity. In the autumn a visitor quoted an anecdote about a seaplane pilot who, after rescuing a drowning man who proved to be Stalin, was granted any wish by the grateful dictator, so he opted to ask Stalin to promise to never tell a soul that he had saved his life, otherwise his own would not be worth living.[65]

1931

The year 1931 was marked by what another communist sympathizer, the English political activist and freelance researcher Freda Utley, called a "daily struggle for food" in the Soviet Union.[66] Ukrainian peasants nicknamed it the "hunger year."[67] In Leningrad the British consul Reader Bullard encountered beggars everywhere, and they pleaded for bread, not money: "In addition to the homeless children, one met many women with their children begging together for bread. These mournful groups – the living remains of what once were families – were a common sight throughout the USSR, and were particularly numerous around the larger railway stations. The stations themselves were emblems of Russia's suffering."[68] Soon Bullard was unable to stomach the scenes of starvation:

> After an initial exposure, I tended to avoid extended travels in the agricultural regions. It was [simply] too heartbreaking to see the endless hordes of people starving to death. When we did travel in the countryside we had to take care not to picnic too close to a village. On one occasion we failed to follow this precept, and when we threw away some orange peel a group of peasants approached us and asked if they could pick it up.[69]

Even Stalin's subtropical homeland of Georgia was facing famine. In the summer he ciphered Lazar Kaganovich (who with Stalin and Vyacheslav Molotov formed the de facto government executive) that "a number of rayons in western Georgia" had been reduced "to the point of *famine*" and that unless more grain were shipped there right away, "we may *face bread riots*."[70]

Siberia was suffering even more. An OGPU report cited "intolerable conditions" in Eastern Siberia,[71] and the authorities in Western Siberia reported famine "in the [steppe] rayons bordering the Kazakh ASSR [Autonomous Soviet Socialist Republic]," adding that in some rayons more than half of the kolkhozes were completely lacking in food grain, and in thirteen rayons there had been instances of famine-induced diseases and some suicide attempts because of starvation.[72] There had also been at least one uprising of starving peasants against Stalin's state. At the end of August some exiled peasants in the Chainsk Rayon of Tomsk Oblast revolted, demanding better living conditions; their slogan was "Down with communism and long live private trade, free labour, the right to land." They were brutally suppressed; only a few rebels were killed fighting, and the rest were summarily shot in front of their families (200 to 250 souls) and their bodies strung up along the roads and in the woods.[73]

Again Moscow, as well as other cities, was not immune to the privation. Like other visitors, Bullard found that the famine lent a dullness to the country's showcase capital: "My first impression of Moscow [May 1931] was of uninterrupted greyness: except for the green of the trees and shrubs, the only colours were grey and greyer. Men wore old suits, and women old dresses, usually grey. One sensed a mood of gloomy seriousness everywhere, and, indeed, there was good reason to be serious, since there were shortages of everything. Urban life was hard indeed and one felt it at once."[74]

When Fred Beal returned to Moscow in September he noted that the want of food "had taken a decided turn for the worse."[75] At the end of the year Beal also visited Kharkov (Kharkiv), very much a Russian city and the Ukraine's capital until 1934, when in the wake of the purge of Ukrainian nationalists it was supplanted by Kiev (Kyiv), primarily a Ukrainian city. There he discovered that even the large colony of privileged foreign workers at the Kharkov Tractor Factory "subsisted on a starvation diet": for lunch a bowl of cabbage soup with one or two herring bones in it, one slice of bread, and a few ounces of barley gruel, and for the rest of the day a voucher entitling one to a pound and a half of black bread costing twenty-five kopecks, and no meat except on special occasions and rarely any butter, cheese, eggs, or milk. So the colony's women, mostly German, staged a hunger march to the factory's headquarters and demanded "something to eat" because "they were starving." Also, "the foreigners were in despair at having to work alongside starving, stupefied and dazed Russian workers."[76]

Not just food but most goods had become scarce and costly – "deficit" goods in Soviet parlance. From the first day of his tour of the USSR – mostly to Soviet Central Asia – in 1932 the journalist Arthur Koestler, then a committed communist who was to gain fame as the author of the influential anti-totalitarian novel *Darkness at Noon* (1940), was struck by the lack of consumer goods, with the state stores boasting mostly empty shelves; in Kharkov, for example, the only goods that were easily obtainable were flypaper, contraceptives, and postage stamps.[77] In Moscow the wife of one of the capital's foreign correspondents complained that "all the things which seem so indispensable in our normal life were either unobtainable or of miserable quality," namely, stockings, cotton batting, needles and thread, bandages, hairpins, safety pins, soap, yarn, kitchen knives, nails, locks, clothes and hairbrushes, wicks for kerosene burners, light bulbs, electrical wire, wrapping, writing, toilet paper, buttons, fingernail files, eyeglasses, lipstick, hair dye, aspirin, diapers, typewriters, dust cloths, stethoscopes, gloves, scissors, can openers, shoes, galoshes, all clothing, hats, blankets, bed sheets, and

A Special Famine

"many more" items.[78] In Leningrad the cost of an apartment doubled between 1925 and 1930, and by late 1931 lemons, an "expensive fruit" at the best of times, "cost more singly than they used to cost by the dozen," while bricks soaked in kerosene for two days served in place of firewood (and reportedly gave more heat, although dirty bricks caked with lime also produced carbon monoxide).[79] Consequently, as William Chamberlin noted, "money lost most of its value because there was so little to be bought." Hence, he added, the anecdote that "the Russians are the richest people in the world – because they don't know what to do with their money." And it was suggested that Anastas Mikoyan, commissar of supply, should be put in charge of the struggle against prostitution for "he had already so effectively abolished meat, butter, shoes, and textiles."[80]

The suffering of Moscow and Leningrad was relative – they were still privileged cities. In 1930 they received about one-third of the country's urban supply of consumer goods, and in 1932 they were allotted more than one-third of the meat, fish, flour, groats, butter, and wine intended for urban consumption, although the two metropolises represented less than 4 percent of the Soviet population.[81] Consequently, as a survival strategy Soviet citizens who lived in villages and towns within striking distance of either metropolis took to travelling there to get whatever was available and returning with as much as possible. This phenomenon, which was to continue until the demise of the USSR, gave rise to an anecdote recited by a train passenger riding in third class and sitting on a bench laden with bags and pails brimming with foodstuffs: "Do you know why it's so easy to supply this huge country with food? Because they only have to supply Moscow and Leningrad. The rest of the country hops on the train, grabs what's left, and delivers it home."[82]

The same passenger cited another stratagem: "Look for a line ... The longer the better. If there's a line, there's something at the other end of it."[83] So whenever people went anywhere they always carried a net bag (*setka*) in the event of a scarce article suddenly appearing in a store, kiosk, or bazaar, for when it did it would sell out so quickly that one did not have time to fetch a bag and return to join the line. To these opportunists a net bag was an *avos'ka* – from *avos'*, meaning literally "perhaps" but figuratively "just in case," as Victor Herman, a Jewish American who arrived in Moscow as a sixteen-year-old at the end of 1931, discovered:

The civilians were all armed with string bags – sometimes three or four string bags – because who knew when and where a queue would set up for some food or something else that was suddenly being sold? So the people always carried them – "nets" they called them, and we learned to carry them too. It was all a question of luck – because you might happen on a queue anywhere, anytime. There was never any telling when there'd be a rush in some direction, and you learned to run with the crowd and not to bother to ask what it was they were selling until you had a place in line. It could be potatoes or cabbage or, once in a blue moon, soap. You got in line and you got whatever it was, no matter how long it took to get it, because who knew if you would ever get another chance?[84]

Koestler was equally struck by the custom of joining a line upon sight:

If it became known that any kind of goods had turned up in a store, the news spread immediately and everybody rushed to buy – whether the goods in question were toothbrushes, acid drops, soap, cigarettes, oil wicks, or frying pans. Wherever the people in the street saw a queue, they hurried to join it. Often, when the queue formed an angle round a street corner, the people in the rear had no idea "what they were selling," and amused themselves by passing on rumours and guesses. I soon became addicted to this sport.[85]

This propensity became so entrenched that the government produced a comic film that depicted a lone man pausing to contemplate suicide – and immediately a line formed behind him.[86] Soon, however, the habit of standing in line "for many hours under rain, snow, or scorching sun" became futile because the stores were empty; similarly, ration cards, which "were introduced for almost everything," became of little use because little could be bought with them.[87] The tactic appeared in the countryside, too, where everyone carried a basket in case they came upon a scrap of food. At the height of the famine in the spring of 1933 the Italian vice-cónsul in Novorossiisk in the North Caucasus observed: "the inseparable basket has now become quite a hallmark of the 'Soviet man.'"[88]

The setkas and lines were to prevail until after the collapse of the USSR in the early 1990s. I can still vividly recall one very cold winter day in 1964–65 when, upon leaving Moscow's Lenin Library (now the Russian State Library) and nearing the subway entrance, I spotted a long line for oranges being sold by a mittenless babushka (elderly woman). I immediately joined the queue, shuffled an interminable hour to reach the end and find with relief that the oranges had not yet sold out, bought my precious limit of one or two kilos, impatiently rode the crowded subway home to the university dormitory, rushed into our "block" (a two-room unit fronted by a vestibule with a toilet and a sink), and proudly displayed my antiscorbutic purchase to my wife – only to be told that she had been able to buy the same limit of the same oranges in the university that morning at its better-supplied and lineless *gastronom* (grocery)! My profound feeling of anti-climax, however, was tempered by our double ration, and we were quickly sobered by an awareness of our fortunate situation as privileged foreigners who could both access and afford such rarities.

In the early 1930s yet another strategy of survival, especially in the cities and particularly for those with the means, was resorting to Torgsin (the acronym for the All-Union Association for Trade with Foreigners on the Territory of the USSR), a chain of "special stores" (1930–36) where personal valuables could be bartered for scarce goods, including foodstuffs.[89] It was formed to mitigate the country's critical shortage of *valyuta* (foreign exchange, or hard currency, unlike the "soft" ruble) with which to fund industrialization. By 1923, when the new Soviet state had finally stabilized itself, little more than 100 million rubles remained to the Bolsheviks of the former Imperial Treasury's billions, owing to the expenditures, losses, and plundering of the First World War and the civil war, reparations under the separate peace treaty with Germany and the newly independent Baltic republics, assistance to Turkey and the Comintern (the Communist International, i.e., the international association of Communist parties), and famine relief.[90] Russia was a gold-rich country, but gold mining by individual prospectors and foreign concessionaires progressed slowly during the NEP, with production increasing from merely 7,400 tonnes in 1922 to only 28,100 tonnes of pure gold in 1930 – less than one-half of Tsarist Russia's annual output (66,400 tonnes in 1914).[91] At the end of 1928, the first year of the pivotal First Five-Year Plan, the USSR's hard currency reserve amounted to 130 million rubles, a "scant sum" for the requirements of industrialization.[92] Then in 1929 the economic depression in the capitalist West thwarted the Soviet government's plan of underwriting industrialization with hard currency from exports of raw materials, including grain. In 1929–30 the export prices of grain fell by more than one-third relative to the previous year, so the Soviet Union tried to offset the lower prices by raising the volume of grain exports at the expense of domestic needs.[93] However, right up to 1933 the outlay of hard currency on industrial imports substantially exceeded the income from exports, the peak of "absurd imports" being reached in 1931, when import expenses exceeded export revenues by half a billion rubles.[94] At the same time, in 1928–31 the state's annual output of gold did not, on average, exceed 30 tonnes of pure gold annually, that is, less than 40 million gold rubles' worth (at 1 ruble, 29 kopecks per tonne of pure gold), whereas in 1931 the outlay on foreign technical assistance alone cost more than 30 million gold rubles.[95] Hence Torgsin, founded on 8 July 1930 by decree of the Commissariat of Trade. Its development peaked in 1933, the worst famine year, when the number of stores skyrocketed from just over four hundred at the beginning of the year to 1,526 at the end.[96]

At first its "closed stores" sold antiquities (especially from the suppressed churches and monasteries but also from galleries, museums, and libraries, including Leningrad's Hermitage Museum and Moscow's Tretyakov Gallery) to foreign tourists and wealthy foreign collectors in Leningrad and Moscow and supplied foreign seamen in Russian ports. At the end of 1930, however, Torgsin expanded its clientele to foreigners working in the USSR and in the middle of 1931 to Soviet citizens themselves, who could buy hard-to-find and better-quality commodities, including foodstuffs, with Tsarist gold currency initially and eventually with domestic gold and later silver, silver plate, and precious stones – but not foreign currency. In 1931 Torgsin opened a store in Leningrad opposite the main hotel, and the British consul wryly observed: "The shop has been made so prominent that Russians have been straying into it in the belief that they could now buy something. The explanation that goods must be paid for in foreign currency was not well received by people who knew that, if they had been suspected of having any foreign currency, they would have been seated on chairs without backs and kept awake until they revealed its hiding-place."[97]

During the famine starving Russians, particularly one-time aristocrats and merchants, traded their valuables for provisions at the Torgsin stores simply in order to survive. In 1933 more than 80 percent of Torgsin's sales comprised foodstuffs, mostly bread.[98] But gold remained its prime target, and in the four years from 1932 to 1935 it procured almost one hundred tonnes of pure gold, including nearly twenty-one tonnes in 1932, which equalled more than one-half of the amount that was mined that year.[99] By value gold constituted almost one-half (44 percent) of Torgsin's income.[100] No wonder a skilled foreign worker called the Torgsin stores "golden pumps."[101] Their operation was observed by Lucy Lang: "A Torgsin store on Soviet Street [in Minsk, the Belorussian capital that she called one of 'the world's lowest depths'] sold food supplies for American dollars, and another Torgsin store, on Lenin Street, maintained an exchange. Anyone who could lay his hands on gold and silver took it to the exchange and got an order for provisions from the other store. Occasionally someone brought in old gold pieces or a wedding ring, but more frequently the desperate customer offered gold teeth or a denture with gold in it. False teeth leered at the passer-by from the window." "After all," Lang noted wryly, "one can eat without teeth. But of what use are teeth if there is nothing to eat?"[102]

For elderly Leningrader Olga Tolstaya-Voyeikova, a "former person" (in her case, a dispossessed noblewoman from the Volga port of Simbirsk [renamed Ulyanovsk in 1924 upon the death of its hallowed namesake, Ulyanov, alias Lenin]), Torgsin was "a means of sometimes getting a scarce commodity, although not cheaply." She dreamed of buying a paraffin stove there for five rubles instead of having to pay forty to fifty rubles on the free market. Undoubtedly, like many of her compatriots, she found the institution reprehensible, writing: "It is shameful to give so many things, unattainable in other places, to foreign buyers, or those who have foreign relations, and a crowd looking on with envious eyes. The whole thing is a disgrace, but when in Rome, do as the Romans do. We can't change anything."[103] Cynics came to read Torgsin as an acronym for *Tovarishchi, Osteregaites'* [or *Opomnites'*], *Rossiia Gibnet, Stalin Istrebliaet* [or *Iznuriaet*] *Narod* (Comrades, beware [or come to your senses], Russia is perishing, Stalin is destroying [or exterminating] the people).[104] The Torgsin stores were the prototype of the RSFSR's post-Stalin network of *Beriozka* (Little birch) stores, where anyone with hard currency could buy both popular foreign and scarce Soviet goods.

The scarcities were breeding more and more political discontent, some of it outspoken and menacing. At the end of the harvest season four kolkhozniks – all one-time Bolshevik supporters during the civil war of 1918–22 – on the

"Karl Marx" kolkhoz in the Volga German autonomous republic sent an "imprecation" directly to Stalin, complaining that:

> You have tormented and ruined us, you have enslaved us with your bureaucratic measures and plans, and you have taken away our freedom and conquered us bloodily, and now we are worse off than our enserfed grandfathers. We have neither clothes nor grain, we work like oxen, hungry, shoeless, and ragged, and we ask you if this will end? ... We are Red partisans who did not enthrone you so that you would squeeze the last drop of blood from our veins, and we will not forgive you our blood but take revenge ... Our overseers have learned nothing except big words; they are opportunists, and they have collectivized, taken away, confiscated, kulakized, and removed, but now they are the gendarmerie. They walk about like somebodies and taunt us like dogs.[105]

Such threats were idle, of course, in the face of the OGPU and the Red Army, but worrisome nevertheless.

1932

The hunger/famine peaked in 1932 and 1933. Andrew Cairns was a Canadian wheat expert and the director of the grain department of the UK's Empire Marketing Board who was sent to the Soviet Union in 1932 to determine the likelihood of Soviet dumping of "cheap wheat" on the world market. Between the end of April and the beginning of August he made four trips (with a diplomatic visa) to the Urals (twice), Kazakhstan, Western Siberia, the Ukraine, the Crimea, the North Caucasus, and the Central Black Earth Region – all of the country's granary, except the Volga Valley. The British Embassy reported that "Mr Cairns's practice was to approach local agricultural authorities for facilities for visits to State and collective farms in their rayons, and though in many cases he met with reluctance to show him any but the most successful concerns, his tours were sufficiently extended for the more typical aspects of Soviet agricultural conditions to be fully revealed to him." The embassy added, "His reports are eye-witnesses' accounts of semi-starvation, of people collecting grass for food, of men and women found dying of hunger in provincial towns, of crowds of migrant peasants living during the summer on a little black bread and melons, and of bitter and reckless complaints from members of all classes of the population in the oblasts, young and old, Communists and non-Communists, of low wages and steadily reduced rations."[106] Cairns himself cabled London that "there was acute widespread hunger and [a] not inappreciable amount of actual starvation."[107]

The starving were reduced to eating what OGPU reports rather euphemistically termed "surrogates," that is, substitutes: not only dogs, cats, and *susliks* (ground squirrels) but also frogs, slugs, chaff, weeds, and even each other (fresh and putrid). The starvation was severest where peasant "recalcitrance" to produce and provide grain – and thus official coercion – was greatest, that is, in the Ukraine and the North Caucasus,[108] the heart of the Soviet wheat belt, but also in the Lower and Middle Volga, Kazakhstan, and parts of Central Asia.[109] Temporally, winter and spring – after the harvested grain had been consumed by privileged persons and places and stored in "iron" (secure) reserves, and grain exports had been completed – were the leanest months, whereas late summer and early autumn afforded some leavings and pickings from fields and gardens for starving gleaners.

Like many others, Fred Beal toured the European Russian breadbasket, which was easier and faster to access than that east of the Volga by curious Western travellers and reporters. He saw thousands of starving and begging outcasts – runaway peasants and dismissed workers – a "condition [that] existed all over the southern part of the USSR."[110] The refrain heard by Cairns in the Ukraine was *Kushat nyet: nichevo nyet* (There is nothing to eat: nothing at all). The peasants were now so enfeebled by hunger, disease, and despair that they were unable to work or even walk. Arriving at a large village, a Ukrainian official (who would a dozen years later become one of the earliest and most famous Soviet defectors to the West) found an "unearthly silence," and a peasant explained that "all the dogs have been eaten, that's why it's so quiet," adding that "people don't do much walking, they haven't the strength." One of the few remaining villagers, a young mother, told him:

> I will not tell you about the dead. I'm sure you know. The half-dead, the nearly-dead are even worse. There are hundreds of people in Petrovo bloated with hunger. I don't know how many die every day. Many are so weak that they no longer come out of their houses. A wagon goes around now and then to pick up the corpses. We've eaten

everything we could lay our hands on – cats, dogs, field mice, birds. When it's light tomorrow you will see the trees have been stripped of their bark, for that too has been eaten. And the horse manure [containing kernels of undigested grain] has been eaten.[111]

One of Svetlana Alexievich's frontline female witnesses to the Second World War recalled a Ukrainian friend who had lost her family during the *holodomor* but "saved herself by stealing horse dung at the kokhoz stable by night and eating it. Nobody could eat it, but she did: 'When it's warm it's disgusting, but you can eat it cold. Frozen is the best, it smells of hay.'"[112]

Some "rather energetic and mobile" – and entrepreneurial – Ukrainian peasants, anticipating starvation, made timely trips to other parts of the country as far away as the Transcaucasus and the North to buy grain or potatoes, which they brought back for feeding their families and for selling at local bazaars at "fabulous prices," making enough money to be able to leave again and fetch more, as well as to pay taxes, which still had to be paid during the famine.[113] Others felt doomed, such as the peasant family interviewed in the Donets Valley in the late summer by Rhea Clyman, a Russian-speaking reporter for the Toronto *Evening Telegram* who toured southern European Russia by car for a month at the end of the summer: "It is autumn now. We have the vegetables from the garden, squash and pumpkins, and a few potatoes – from that we make flour ... Made of dried pumpkins and potatoes. When this is gone we'll have nothing else. The grain the village Soviet takes away. Our vegetables we grow in the garden will not last the winter. What shall we do in the spring?"[114]

As one would expect, given the priority of industry over farming, white-collar and blue-collar workers in the cities fared better than the peasants. Clyman spent two days in Kharkov, the Ukraine's second largest (and primarily Russian) city (1926) as well as its chief industrial centre. Nevertheless, she found that "this great Ukrainian capital was in the grip of hunger. Beggars swarmed round the streets, the stores were empty, the workers' bread rations had just been cut from two pounds a day per person to one pound and a quarter."[115] Clyman visited the "great tractor plant" – "piles of brick with lumps of mortar still clinging to the edges" like "a series of badly assorted chimneys flung up on a rubbish dump" – and was told by the manager of the timekeeper's office that the plant had a buffet for the workers but that it did not open until noon and was "very bad," offering "bread, nothing more." He also told her that the average wage for a skilled mechanic at the plant was 180 rubles a month, adding, "But what can he do with this money when meat sells at 12 rubles [6 dollars] a pound on the open market?" Finally, the time-keeper said, "You say you want to know what the Russian worker eats. I'll tell you" – the little man looked round furtively then leaned over the counter and whispered – "bread and potatoes. When he doesn't have potatoes he eats bread, and when he doesn't have bread he eats potatoes."[116] And any of the common black bread that was available was not infrequently adulterated by chaff, dust, straw, dead bugs, and even – as an American visitor in 1932 attested – "a regular museum collection of miscellaneous articles, including a broken button, several pieces of old matches, a small nail, and a healthy piece of chewed string" – and this in a normally better-supplied Intourist hotel dining room catering to guided tourists. He added, "Eating black bread in Russia is much like eating shad in America. You are continually removing debris from your mouth and placing it beside your plate."[117]

Another result of the famine in the Ukraine pertained to (but was not necessarily limited to) the Jewish populace. The American Jewish expatriate Mendel Osherowitch sojourned in 1932 in his family's Ukrainian rayon and found that there the Jews, once known for their temperance, had become drunkards. He was told the reason by a one-time "fine gentleman, a respectable Jew": "My fine fellow, it's simple. A loaf of bread costs 12 to 15 rubles. A litre of vodka costs only 2 rubles. So if you buy a litre of vodka, get drunk and pass out for a day, sometimes two, you forget you're hungry."[118]

In the Asiatic Russian breadbasket the peasant's situation was much the same, if not worse. Indeed, Western Siberia had undergone four years in a row (1929–32) of harvest failures.[119] Cairns's travelling companion, Otto Schiller,[120] the agricultural attaché of the German Embassy, told his Canadian colleague that "he had been in Russia for eight years and he knew that the agricultural situation was very serious, but he could not have imagined that conditions anywhere could be so terrible as in Western Siberia."[121] The peasants told Cairns: "'*rabotat, rabotat, rabotat, khleb nyet*' – we work, work, and work, but do not get bread."[122] As he trained through the southern Urals and across Western Siberia in the middle of spring he found that "the amount of begging (obviously not professional begging, but genuine cases of hunger) by children, women and men was simply amazing." "I expect," he added, "when I return to Canada I shall soon forget what little Russian I know, but never will I forget the Russian equivalent of 'please give me some bread,' or the expression on the faces of the tens to scores of people who made the request at practically every station at which I got out." At a small buffet in the town of Tatarsk Cairns and Schiller were having breakfast when some workers arrived with food chits and ate, and "as each worker finished his meal there was a scramble of children and one or two women and men for their soup plates to lick, and their fish bones to eat." The next day in Slavgorod in the Altai Kray they visited a bazaar, where "hundreds surged close around us to tell us all the people were hungry, that they (town workers, collective farm members, and individual peasants [farmsteaders] alike) worked and worked but got little bread, that people were eating all the dead horses and gophers [ground squirrels], many were dying every day of hunger, etc. etc."[123] The same kray's horrors were chronicled by the peasant diarist Konstantin Izmailov:

> 29 January. Hunger has begun in the rayon, and in places starvation. They [the authorities] are taking grain by force. They are seizing milk cows. They are also seizing pigs, sheep, and even chickens. There is no respect for, or belief in, the authorities. They [the peasants] sit and judge the members of the rural soviet who have taken the grain, cows, and pigs ... To feed and host human beings has gone out of fashion. Here, there, and everywhere one hears only "there is nothing," "there is no bread," "how will we live?" And no talk of meat.
>
> Nearby people are dining. These are communists and executive officials. GPU employees, the militia, etc. But these people require good conditions, [as] they are responsible for socialist construction. And in the economic organizations sit bureaucrats, and they are also dining. They are [all] dining, and the peasants are hiding their grain in pits and butchering their own cattle for meat. The poor peasants are starving ...
>
> 3 February. The poor peasants are living through a difficult time in the kolkhozes now: malnutrition and shortages of bread and shoes and clothes. It forces the poor peasants to work off the collective farm for the sake of a piece of bread. Here, there, and everywhere I hear daily only the words "there's no bread," "there's nothing to eat," "how will we live?"

2 March. Many white-collar and blue-collar workers will go without a piece of bread in March ... we are beginning to get used to starvation.

3 March. Gridnev, a [starving] teacher at the secondary school, shot his wife, Serafima Pavlovna, with a rifle at 7 o'clock this morning. Then, a little later, he shot himself.

8 April. We are suffering from hunger ... many are starving and without bread ... starvation among the white-collar and blue-collar workers and kolkhozniks and others in our village ... with the exception of executives, communists, and [foreign] specialists.

18 May. The starvation is reaching more and more terrible levels. More and more poor peasants are dying. They plead for a piece of bread or something to eat so as not to starve to death.

9 July. The starving beg insistently, obsessively, tiresomely to the extreme: "If only a piece, a crumb of black bread ... !" They [the villagers] shun them and hide from them, they have them at their mercy. They shut their windows and doors and answer through them: "there's no bread!, "there's nothing to give," "go away!" The starving implore relentlessly: "even a crumb, even a spoonful of milk, even a scallion ... at least give us a little water to drink!" The reply: "Go away, do you hear, go away!" Go to the devil, do you hear!" "You are plaguing us like dogs ... hundreds, even thousands of you come every day ... we ourselves are starving and live on rations." Dragging themselves from window to window, the emaciated starving receive one and the same answer.[124]

In Western Siberia's cities people were also starving, if relatively less so. At a bazaar in Novosibirsk, the rapidly growing industrial centre (nicknamed the "Chicago of Siberia") that had now surpassed Omsk as the kray's largest city and become its capital, Cairns asked a peasant vendor "if she was a collective farm member and she said she had been, but had left because now she goes hungry only 3 to 4 days a week whereas she was hungry 7 days a week when in the collective farm." "On our way home," he continued, "we saw a crowd on the street and went to have a look. A woman was sitting in the dust with a small baby at her breasts, and two young children were sitting crying for food. A woman went by and turned to us and said, 'you can see such sights all over the Soviet Union,' and a number of others spoke up and said, 'yes, she is right.'"[125] The city's workers fared better. Rudolf Volters, a young German architect who had signed a one-year contract with the Soviets in 1932 to design railway stations, told his fellow workers in Novosibirsk that even dogs in Germany would not eat what they had for breakfast, which was "very bad," but none believed him. "The Russian engineers," he explained, "are undemanding and are quite content if for breakfast at 12 o'clock [?] they have only a glass of hot water, a slice of black bread, and a fruit drop or even a lump of sugar." "For all of them," Volters asserted, "there existed but one problem: food."[126]

The populace was also starving at Omsk, which was visited in August by the American educator and historian Will Durant, who wrote: "Yes, Omsk itself was dying. Its population was falling day by day" as a result of what one official told him was "organized starvation."[127] But the city's soldiers, officials, police, and specialists, as Cairns noted, were better fed (and paid) than other residents.

Neighbouring Kazakhstan, where pastoral nomadism – not sedentary cultivation – predominated, was in worse shape than Western Siberia, thanks to the twin blows of collectivization and sedentarization of the Kazakh nomads.[128] A way of life based upon the seasonal movement of livestock and their herders was shattered. Schiller told Cairns that in 1925 he had taken a long camel trip through Kazakhstan and had found the plains "thickly dotted everywhere with cattle," but earlier this spring on a trip by car from Semipalatinsk he had not seen "one single head of livestock." Schiller added, "many, many thousands of the Kirgizians [Kazakhs] had died of hunger and, in his opinion, one million must die as they were all nomads and without their cattle (the bulk of which had been collected by the Government for meat), they could not live. Many thousands of Kirgizians were travelling into West China [Sinkiang] and North to [Western] Siberia in search of food."[129] Cairns himself at every train station "saw hundreds of them – all thin, cold, rag-clad, hungry and many begging for bread." "In two days motoring in one direction from Slavgorod," he continued, "I saw many small groups of Kirgizians camping on the prairie – every group beside a horse which had died and all eating the meat for food, and drying the skin in the sun to make boots etc."[130] On the Omsk-Moscow train at the end of May a woman from Karaganda, Kazakhstan's "city of coal," told Cairns that "the poor Kirgizians were dying in the streets, the bazaars, and stations faster than the army could bury them, people were eating mice and gophers [ground squirrels]."¹³¹ The sight of unburied famine victims was increasingly unexceptional. An American engineer, John (Jack) Calder, dubbed "Russia's miracle man" for his success as a troubleshooter in solving faltering Soviet projects in 1929–33, returned from a long tour of Kazakhstan to report its "roads lined with stiff corpses like so many logs."¹³² He was being driven across an arid plain in a snowstorm in the late winter of 1931–32 and for several hours had noticed what appeared to be logs lining both sides of the road; puzzled by their presence in a treeless desert, he queried his driver, who replied that they were not logs but the frozen corpses of starving peasants who had been trying to leave the country on foot in search of food.¹³³ At Balkhash on the lake of the same name in southeastern Kazakhstan a copper project was reportedly aborted partly because of the "secret diversion of food supplies from the job to the starving population surrounding that area."¹³⁴

"Hunger was stalking Moscow," too, recalled Khrushchev.¹³⁵ Homer Smith, an African American journalist seeking the vaunted equality of the classless Marxist society, upon his arrival in the capital found Muscovites "underpaid and underfed." "In my walks about the city," he wrote, "I found long lines of hungry men and women standing at grocery and butcher shops in the hope of getting something to eat. They began queuing up at daybreak, which was three o'clock in the morning during the summer. Most of them left, often several hours later, with only hunks of black bread and a few ounces of potatoes and sausage."¹³⁶ And the hunger, he added, was driving women into what he termed "sub-rosa prostitution," with foreigners especially.

Exploring Moscow upon his arrival in the USSR at the beginning of the spring, the Danish poultry-farming specialist Arne Strøm and his wife were struck by the sight of emaciated, hungry Russian commoners – "the most terrible living scarecrows one could think of."¹³⁷ About this time another privileged foreign specialist, the American engineer Zara Witkin, wrote to his mother that even for him, in the capital, "food is limited and poor; housing indescribably crowded; sanitary facilities so unsatisfactory that one wonders how certain human functions are performed." By September, he continued, the supply of food in the city – which was still favoured but the scarcity already "severe" and the variety "poor" – took a "sharp change for the worse." It was felt, of course, most keenly by the Russians, but even the entitled foreign experts had their rations reduced, with milk and eggs disappearing from their special stores.[138] "Food was the main topic of conversation everywhere," he noted. By the end of October Moscow's food crisis was "extreme," with meat being obtainable only at Torgsin in exchange for gold or foreign currency. Witkin correctly forecast that "there [would] be terrible suffering this winter," and he added the vain hope that "none [would] starve."[139]

An American teacher, Margaret Wettlin, who took a year's leave of absence to study abroad only to fall in love with a theatre director in Moscow and stay until her return to the United States in 1980, recollected that food was so scarce in the capital when she arrived at the beginning of the autumn that she "often wondered what Russians ate." She frequently roamed the city and checked the food stores, which repelled her with "those blue gobs of meat wrapped in bloodstained newspapers, or those eggs whose stench came through the shells, or those candies glued into a solid chunk by the jam fillings oozing out of them." She consoled herself with the belief that "food and clothes were scarce, but they were scarce for everybody,"[140] although in fact they were ample for the political and military elite but lacking for millions of peasants.

When Alexander Barmine, a Soviet diplomat (and "old Bolshevik," i.e., a pre-1917 Party member) who would defect during the purge trials years later from his post in Greece, returned to the capital on leave in 1932, he found that "a mere subsistence standard of living had become for everyone a matter of constant scheming and striving."[141] And in Leningrad the lack of food was such that by the summer workers were foraging in the countryside.[142] In the city itself, notably, infants suffered a "very high" mortality, owing to the malnutrition of mothers and babies alike.[143]

Even pampered foreign tourists, a prized source of *valuta* (hard currency), felt some pangs of hunger. An American travel writer who, with his wife, went hungry on a customized trip through the European Russian south wrote: "For anyone who is genuinely anxious to reduce, I recommend a month's unconducted tour of Soviet Russia. You can confidently count on losing weight at about one pound per day for as long as you can stand it. This is no figure of speech, because I am willing to state on oath that I myself lost twenty-six pounds and my wife sixteen pounds during the few [four] weeks we spent in Russia."[144] And, like other visitors to the Soviet Union, the couple found that theft – a natural result of going hungry – was rampant.

Not even Torgsin, another crucial source of foreign currency, was immune to the famine. The British consul in Leningrad reported that it had "a price-list like Harrod's and a stock that would disgrace an English country town," being reduced to importing flour, milk, butter, and eggs from neighbouring Finland.[145] Not even precious industry was unaffected. A six-month period in 1932 saw 339 industrial strikes in the country over "provision difficulties."[146]

1933

In an impromptu speech to the First All-Union Congress of Collective Farm Shock Brigaders in Moscow early in 1933, Stalin stressed that "the path of collective farming is the only correct path" and that "our immediate task is to make all collective farmers well-to-do," but he made no mention of the famine stalking the country – and his speech was greeted by "long persistent applause turning into an ovation" and cries of "long live the leading collective farmer" and "long live our leader, Comrade Stalin."[147] Meanwhile, the starvation was hellishly climaxing over a wide area, as attested by a variety of witnesses, visitors and residents alike, as well as demographic indicators. The annus horribilis was encapsulated by a Ukrainian poet, Mykola Rudenko: "It was the year of deaths, of hellish woes, it was the year of thirty-three."[148] An American psychophysiologist, Dr W. Horsley Gantt, the one-time chief of the Medical Division of the American Relief Administration in 1922–23 and a former student of Ivan Pavlov (the pioneer of the conditioned reflex) in 1925–29, returned to the Soviet Union in 1933 and, according to Consul Bullard, was "horrified at what he consider[ed] the change for the worse" and said, "no one is interested in anything but getting enough food."[149] The specifics were indeed horrific. In Ryazan, a couple of hundred miles (320 kilometres) southeast of Moscow, in early February an elderly teacher and archivist exclaimed, "My God! What is happening in Ryazan! People are dying like flies. There are no coffins, and lines at the undertaker's," and by the spring "whole villages" were dying around the city.[150] At the beginning of the year the parvenu (he had recently married into the British establishment) and financially struggling Malcolm Muggeridge, who succeeded William Chamberlin as the Moscow correspondent of the *Manchester Guardian* in 1932–33, was told by Dr Joseph Rosen, who was engaged in the agricultural settlement of destitute Soviet urban Jews, that the "peasants [were] wandering about in

[the] thousands with their bodies swollen by [a] lack of food." Several days later Muggeridge himself added, "in the Ukraine, in the North Caucasus, in Western Siberia, starvation."[151]

In late February an Italian engineer who was travelling from Moscow to Stalinabad (Dushanbe) in Turkmenistan and back reported: "the famine is great and widespread in the whole of the traversed Soviet territory."[152] About the same time the British ambassador, Sir Esmond Ovey, told the Foreign Office that the Ukraine and the North Caucasus were "the regions where the food situation [was] worst,"[153] but a month later Muggeridge, recently returned from a tour of the south, asserted in an unsigned article in the *Manchester Guardian* (which he had been allowed to dispatch in his embassy's diplomatic bag) that the famine in the Upper, Middle, and Lower Volga was "as bad as in the North Caucasus and the Ukraine" and "little, if at all, better" in Western Siberia.[154] At the very same time Gareth Jones, a young, bright, and eager Welsh student fluent in Russian, German, and French, had also just returned from a southern tour (some of it on foot through the countryside), and he reported in the New York *Evening Post* that the cry, "There is no bread – we are dying," was coming "from every part of Russia, from the Volga, Siberia, White Russia [Belorussia], the North Caucasus, Central Asia."[155] Two days later in another newspaper he wrote: "today the famine is everywhere, in the formerly rich Ukraine, in Russia, in Central Asia, in North Caucasia – everywhere."[156] And a week later in yet another newspaper Jones emphasized that, whereas the famine of 1920–21 had not been especially widespread, that of 1933 had "attacked the Ukraine, the North Caucasus, the Volga rayon, Central Asia, Siberia – indeed, every part of Russia" – and this after having "spoken to peasants or to eye-witnesses from every one of those rayons."[157] At Danzig on his way home in late March Jones, in a letter to his parents, said simply: "The Russian situation is absolutely terrible, famine almost everywhere and millions are dying of starvation."[158] Nevertheless, the rural was more dismal than the urban scene. A Czech engineer who had been arrested in 1929 and sentenced to ten years recalled: "During my travels in the country I noticed that barely ⅓ of the fields were cultivated. All of the rest remained an untouched expanse on which weeds grew profusely. The 'herds' that I saw numbered only 5–6 [head], each of them like a cow's skeleton. Almost nobody was visible in the fields, and those whom I did see were pulling ploughs and harrows and resembled phantoms."¹⁵⁹ The peasants called 1933, the famine's zenith, the "black year," meaning an evil or vile time.

The very long and very lean winter of 1932–33 between the previous summer harvest and the next produced the peak of the famine in the spring, when, as architect Volters found in Tashkent, "with the Uzbek, as with everyone else, there was only one topic [of conversation]: grain, there is no grain in the country, people are starving."¹⁶⁰ A much more personal account of the horror that spring – in this case in the North Caucasus – was given by an anonymous peasant woman of German origin who wrote a desperate plea for help to her uncle as she, her deaf-mute husband, and remaining three children waited to starve to death (her youngest son had already succumbed):

> The suffering of all of the inhabitants of the [North] Caucasus is indescribable. Nevertheless, I want to help you visualize what we are undergoing. We have been eating grass for the past two weeks. I even walked to a small hill where a dead horse lay and ate some of it. My husband is sick, his body is swollen, and my children are swollen. The doctor asserts that people will be dropping like flies because of the hot weather. Already forty people have been buried daily in a neighbouring Russian village. One German village lays claim to fifteen dead per day. Whole families lie unburied on the steppe trails for weeks. Nobody cares. Cats and dogs are being eaten.
>
> An underground trade organization has been established in the nearby town of Armavir, where people are slaughtered and made into sausages and cutlets to be sold as food. In our village some of our neighbours have desecrated graves by digging up bodies and pulling out gold teeth with pliers to sell in Torgsin for goods.¹⁶¹

The situation was no better in the Ukraine. In early February Poland's general consul in Kharkov had reported: "The famine in the Ukraine has become even more horrible and more severe. In this respect the situation is clearly worsening day by day, with more and more cases of theft, robbery, and murder – mainly at the markets – with the aim of getting food."¹⁶² Workers, as usual, fared better, but only relatively. In the late spring common workers in the republic were getting some bread at fixed prices, but for weeks they had been eating only bread and drinking tea with it; their staple was potato soup, which they usually made with hot water but seldom with much, if any, potato – as they put it, "one potato was trying to find another" (*kartoshka dogonyaet kartoshku*).[163]

The starvation continued into the summer. Otto Schiller, who made a tour in his own car in August, found "famine conditions ... probably on a worse scale in the Urals than elsewhere," and he was so "genuinely distressed" that he "set his face against further tours."[164] In Kazakhstan the famine was still raging, but in Central Asia it seems to have been less acute, owing partly to the prevalence of irrigation but mainly to the preoccupation with a so-called "technical," or "industrial" – that is, non-food – crop: cotton. After spending nearly three months in the USSR in the summer and autumn of 1933, mostly in Central Asia and partly with the renowned plant geneticist Nikolai Vavilov,[165] a cotton specialist from Trinidad informed the British Embassy: "In Central Asia everything, including food [crops], is being sacrificed to cotton. Unless people will consent to grow cotton they are not allowed water to irrigate their land." "In the same way," he continued, "peasants have been driven into collectives by the certainty that if they are recalcitrant their irrigation water will be cut off." But the Trinidadian found "no evidence that the mass of the people were on the verge of starvation, as in the grain rayons of European Russia," and undernourishment was more evident in the towns than in the villages, where the health of the cotton growers had to be maintained.[166]

Throughout the country starving peasants, as well as nomads, were on the move to cities and villages in a desperate search for food (just the reverse of the situation in 1918–19, incidentally, when the peasants still had plenty of grain and the trains were packed with "bag people," starving urbanites travelling to the countryside to seek food). This movement was described by diarist Izmailov in the Altai Kray at the village of Smolenskoe (with up to eight thousand souls), first in the middle of winter and then in the middle of spring:

> 18 February. Lately in February in Smolenskoe many Kirghizes [Kazakhs] have appeared. Singly and in large groups they walk through the village from house to house, pleading for bread in broken Russian; they pronounce Russian words badly and unintelligibly. At whichever house the Kirghiz or Kirghiza calls they start to beg for bread until nobody an-

A Special Famine

swers and nothing is given. Usually they [the villagers] lock their doors lest the Kirghizes not leave. And they can hardly afford them a piece of bread; such instances are very few, as they have nothing more to give.

16 May. More and more outsiders are arriving in Smolenskoe. They arrive every day. They come in the dozens and even hundreds. They stop everywhere to overnight: on the streets, on Bazaar Square, in clearings, and especially along the river. Here, there, and everywhere one can see them wandering, passing, crossing. They all walk through the village from door to door, begging for "just a small piece of bread." Some look for work here, some walk and ride farther. And this is repeated every day.[167]

Moscow and Leningrad (and republic capitals) were spared the worst, the Italian ambassador explaining, "as they are centres vital to Soviet power, as well as the seat of the Soviet government, they [the Bolshevik leaders] obviously look for every means of assuring their provisionment."[168] Nevertheless, the two national capitals, former and current, did not totally escape the food lacks, price rises, pay cuts, and job losses, as well as the housing shortage. In Leningrad the déclassé Olga Tolstaya-Voyeikova, reduced in means as well as status (although better supplied than many other residents), wrote to a relative early in the year: "Somehow our letters are distracted by this sore point of food, and conversations are inevitably reduced to the same subject; if you overhear conversations on the street, they vary between two topics: the question of housing and the question of food." In the spring she reiterated: "How we keep harping on about that subject of food difficulties. They absorb so much time and scheming." And in the summer she was besieged by beggars: "The [door]bell rings often in the morning, but only for some hungry beggar, a child or a woman, to whom we cannot refuse a bit of bread. A coin is not thankfully received."[169] The rampant begging in the city was remarked by a local worker and student who later became a prominent historian, Arkady Man'kov:

Whether you go along the Obvodny [Bypass Canal Embankment] or along October 25th [Nevsky] Prospect – on all sides, from all crannies, under portals, on the sidewalks – everywhere you hear the monotonously tiresome, pleading, or indifferently brief "give me a little kopeck." Everywhere you see withered, lined faces and wrinkled, extended hands. It is immense, all-powerful begging, the young and the old walking among us winter and summer, night and day ... And there is no end to it, no limit, it continually expands and grows. And together with it expands and grows the shame and the damnation of man by man.[170]

He added:

I ride the train to and from the city. Every day dozens of beggars pass through the cars! Most of them perform a different sort of musical number and only after that put out their hand. But many among them are cripples who, following each other through the cars, show off their deformity. Here comes a wizened, emaciated fellow on crutches. Blind. Begging pathetically, in almost a girl's voice he says: "I am half a man, but I want to drink and eat."[171]

Evidently Moscow was better supplied than Leningrad. Gareth Jones, the observant Welshman, found in the middle of spring that the capital did not appear "so stricken" as the villages, and that "no one staying in Moscow would have an inkling of what is going on in the countryside, unless he could talk to the peasants who have come hundreds and hundreds of miles to the capital to look for bread." "The people in Moscow," he continued, "[are] warmly clad, and many of the skilled workers, who have their warm meal at the factory every day, are well fed," although "the vast majority of the unskilled workers are feeling the pinch."[172] By the summer, however, the situation had evidently worsened, as reported by the Moscow correspondent of *Le Petit Parisien* at the end of July:

Even in Moscow, a more privileged centre and the seat of the government, hundreds of thousands of people are without ration cards and have to get what they need in the so-called "commercial" stores that belong to the state. There the state sells black bread for 3 rub[les] per kilo and white for 4 rub[les]. There is also the "private market," where speculation flourishes and a kilo of bread costs at least 7–8 rub[les] ... Already for a long time now there has been no butter, as well as mar-

A Special Famine

garine. On the private market a kilo of butter costs 50 rub[les]. Meanwhile, the average [monthly] salary is 100–150 rub[les]. We see [then] that in the "commercial" stores or at the private markets prices are too high for [blue-collar] workers and most white-collar workers. And if we still try to see what in the end the majority of Muscovites eat, then the answer is simple: bread and potatoes, when there are any, as well as meat twice a month, if they are lucky."[173]

Not only food but also housing was lacking in both metropolises, which had doubled to tripled their populations in the 1920s as a result of natural growth and the steady influx of peasants seeking industrial employment and more food. A British diplomat exclaimed: "Moscow must now [1931] be the most overcrowded capital in the world, and Leningrad is rapidly following its example."[174]

Disgruntled Muscovites especially had become politically disenchanted with the extreme and abiding shortages. In the summer a teenaged resident wrote in her diary: "Sixty kopeks for a kilo of white bread! Fifty kopeks for a liter of kerosene! Moscow's grumbling. The angry, hungry, tired people in the lines abuse the authorities and curse life. Nowhere can you hear a single word in defense of the detested Bolsheviks."[175] Gareth Jones found that some Muscovites were saying that the country's abbreviation of SSSR, which denoted Soyuz Sovetskikh Sotsialisticheskikh Respublik (Union of Soviet Socialist Republics), really signified *Smert Stalina Spacyot Rossiyu* (The Death of Stalin will Save Russia).[176]

More troubling to the Kremlin was the famine's impact on industry in terms of both production and employment. In early February the Polish general consul in Kharkov reported that workers in heavy industry in the Ukraine who had been receiving a ration of 1 kilogram of bread per day were now getting 600 grams, which would soon be reduced to 500 grams, while workers in light industry who had been receiving 700 grams of bread per day were now getting 300 grams, which would soon be reduced to 200 grams (indicating, incidentally, the difference in importance to the Soviet economy between heavy and light industry). Recently bread rations were being dispensed at certain places only, and if a worker failed to collect his ration at a given place on that day, then he forfeited it – which "frequently happen[ed]." The shortage of rations, added the consul general, as well as an insufficiency of raw materials and *khozraschyot* (literally, self-financing, but figuratively, unsubsidized), forced the Hammer and Sickle Factory in Kharkov to halve its workforce from fifteen thousand to seven thousand. Recently, too, a number of Ukrainian factories had been forced "to curtail production considerably and release thousands of workers."[177]

In late winter the OGPU reported that discontent among workers was widespread (the Ukraine, the North Caucasus, the Middle Volga, the Urals) as a result of food shortages, which had raised foodstuff prices sharply and caused starvation, demonstrations, and strikes (in March there were fifteen industrial strikes with 529 participants in various parts of the country "on the basis of provision difficulties"). The mood of the workers was expressed in such comments as "nothing is expected of the kolkhozes, and if they do sow anything, they won't harvest the crop, and the workers will have to starve, as in [19]18" and "under current conditions the workers will hardly have the strength to fulfill the second five-year plan [of 1933–37]." Moreover, "anti-Soviet elements" were inciting the workers with such cries as "help him who has been dismissed for no reason, help him who is starving and not working."[178]

The unrest spread during the spring and into the summer. An OGPU report of 1 April noted "acute provision difficulties" (code for severe famine) in parts of the Amur region in the Soviet Far East, where starvation and arrears in wages among the miners in the Kindinsk coalfield had created "anti-Soviet elements" whose agitation had put the workers in a "rebellious mood"; in the last ten days they had staged twenty-nine anti-Soviet demonstrations and issued a leaflet demanding "the overthrow of Soviet power and a struggle for the restoration of the monarchy." One worker was heard to shout, "Why have we struggled, in order to starve? Why have we been forced to work? This is what we have been reduced to. How long will this last?" The extraction of coal had been "sharply reduced" from 1,000 to 470 tonnes per day. Local officials were in "utter dismay," exclaiming, "What will we say if there is no bread, no money – don't agitate?" There had been a "growth of discontent" among the kolkhozniks, too, with one peasant sarcastically telling a meeting: "Soviet power has given women relief, there is no flour, [so] there is no need to bake bread – this is some kind of relief. How long will this continue?"[179]

The same source reported the same discontent at industrial enterprises in the West Region in June and in the Central Black Earth in July; the distribution of bread had "completely ceased" at small-scale enterprises in the former and at mostly small-scale and medium-scale enterprises in the latter. Some workers, including Party members, in the Central Black Earth were "agitating," with one of them declaring, "In the USSR they talk about fascist terror elsewhere, but our own workers are dropping from starvation at their machines and are eating leavings. Everyone [in Germany] freely agreed to have Hitler in power, and they [the Germans] do not starve like [we] do now." Another worker exclaimed, "We have fought for freedom and gained a better life for ourselves, but now they feed us slops. How long will we tolerate it? Nothing remains for us but to fight as we fought in the years of the civil war."[180]

In Western Siberia, too, industrial enterprises endured "grave difficulties" in provisionment. Only the workers in the Kuzbass were "satisfactorily supplied with bread," but even their nourishment had "worsened" and generated a "negative mood" as well as "activity by anti-Soviet elements" and two strikes.[181]

More alarmingly, the shortages of food and goods elicited "much discontent and many complaints" from officers in the Red Army. In some cases the dissatisfaction amounted to "anti-Soviet attacks," with one political instructor complaining, "Even in the capitalist countries there is not the beastliness that we have. In what capitalist army is a commander to be seen who is full but the family at his side (wife, children) are starving to death like dogs?" And a cavalry officer declared, "This is not service but a mockery; they drive us like dogs but feed us little. A fool is he who will go to war. Let those who get a lot do the fighting. If they declare war, I will desert right away."[182]

The regime did not really have much to fear militarily or even politically from such disaffection, but economically it did, for industry and agriculture were interdependent, with the latter affording the former not only foodstuffs but also raw materials and even labour, and an underfed and underpaid worker or soldier was an unproductive as well as a discontented one. Sooner or later the problem had to be resolved if the "new order" were to survive and prosper.

In the meantime the authorities tried to hide and even deny the famine through press and radio censorship and travel restrictions – but to little avail, as illustrated by an anecdote: Two friends happened to meet and one of them began to complain about his lot and to curse the authorities, saying, "There's nothing to eat," and he was overheard by a policeman on duty nearby who said, "Citizen, you are agitating here – come with me!," whereupon his friend intervened on his behalf and said, "Comrade policeman, he isn't normal, you know." "How the devil can he not be normal when he speaks the truth?" snapped the policeman and took the hapless complainer away.[183]

1934–?

The year 1934 represented the denouement – but not the termination – of the famine. An official dispatch from the British Embassy in the spring reported: "There appears to be some improvement in general agricultural conditions, as compared with last year, especially in the Ukraine. Considerable want still exists, however, and the hunger rayons are said to have now shifted north to Western Siberia, the Gorki and Lower Volga rayons, and even to the Moscow rayon, where conditions are said to be much worse than last year."[184] In the late summer the embassy updated the situation: "As regards the food situation in the countryside, I believe that there has been much less complete starvation than last summer," and "Western Siberia is said to have been one of the worst sufferers."[185]

Such was the case in the Altai region, which, noted a "former person," "before the revolution ... was famous for its fertility, its rich meadows, its herds of cattle, and, above all, its hard-working people" and had even become known as the "granary of Russia."[186] Here in the Altai steppe Konstantin Izmailov recorded the suffering in the spring and summer of 1934 on the part of the helpless peasants – but not the heartless authorities. In the village of Smolenskoe in the middle of May both a "closed" cafeteria and a "closed" bazaar, where only officials, foreign specialists, Chekists, the militia, and the military could eat as much "excellent" food as they liked, were "opened."[187] Meanwhile, Izmailov noted, "Children are dying, adults are dying. They die soon after falling ill [from typhus and typhoid], in 4 or 5 days. Diarrhea and stomach ache – such is the sickness, with a general weakess from starvation. Out of hunger they eat greens and die soon after. Not a day passes without a dozen deaths in the village."[188] Despite the danger of discovery of his frank diary (which would have condemned him as an "enemy of the people"), Izmailov could not resist recording his contempt for the state's hypocrisy: "They write [in the newspapers] that overseas in Japan, Korea, America, and other countries the peasants and workers are starving. But they do not write a word [about the fact that] here, in a grain country, its own peasants, individual farmsteaders, workers, and tradesmen are starving," adding that their leaders were seen by some as "Soviet bloodsuckers." And he was not afraid to repeat his sarcasm: "Earlier, before Soviet power, under the authority of tsars and priests, one had to fast 7 weeks [at Lent] per year (not eat forbidden foods [meat and milk dishes]), but now under Soviet power in the land of socialist construction, it is required to fast all year."[189]

A literate Belorussian peasant, Dionisy Gorbatsevich, who had immigrated to the United States in 1913 at the age of eighteen and returned in 1934 to spend the month of August in his native rayon, found the peasants far from fit, even though it was *strada* (suffering) – the harvest period of hard work: "Daily I met hundreds of peasant men and women, and they all looked tired, skinny, emaciated, anemic, sullen, sluggish, and lifeless, like corpses." "Why and from what," he asked, "were they all sullen, joyless, and sad?" But he already knew the answer – they had been reduced to "slaves of the land" by involuntary collectivization.[190]

Although the May Day slogan for 1934 of "abundance" was premature, the suffering was mitigated appreciably in the last half of the year by an abundant harvest and subsequent measures, thanks to favourable weather, as witnessed by Izmailov in the Altai Kray: "The summer of 1934 favoured good yields of everything. Unusually good grain and garden vegetables and a lot of thick grass in the fields. An abundance of various berries everywhere ... A good yield not only in the Smolensk Rayon but also throughout Biysk Okrug. Summer was warm and rain was timely."[191] In an August communiqué Otto Schiller reported: "at this time last year, the victims of hunger were counted by the millions; this year they are counted by the thousands."[192] Freda Utley recalled that for three years – 1934, 1935, and 1936 – there was "less actual starvation," although "ordinary people could not afford to buy" the food in the shops.[193] Bread rationing was ended on 1 January 1935, and the rationing of meat and fish products, cooking oils and fats, sugar, and potatoes was abolished on 1 October 1935 (and manufactures on 1 January 1936),[194] but prices increased and shortages persisted. As late as 1937 in Moscow, according to a resident American engineer, "there were still long lines sometimes extending for blocks before the food shops."[195]

By 1935, however, the worst was over, with hunger persisting but famine disappearing. That year a touring Australian stockman and politician, Charles Hawker, observed: "partly by unflinching coercion, and partly by a very skilful modification of the collective system so as to provide inducements and rewards for efficient work, they [the Bolshevik leaders] are actually getting the land worked according to their modified system." "Recovery," he continued, "is actually being achieved, and there is reasonable expectation of continued progress."[196] With this recovery, concurred Chamberlin, "a great step will have been made – the step from starvation to hunger." Thus, when Stalin told the First All-Union Conference of Stakhanovites, "Life has improved, comrades ... Life has become more joyous,"[197] he was right in terms of both urban and rural food supply, which had indeed improved relatively, as well as in terms of living and working conditions (more and better housing and goods and services – again relatively speaking) and even life expectancy (just before the bloody purges), although his words are often cited to demonstrate his hypocrisy.[198]

A Deadly Famine

The hunger/famine of 1928–34 exacted a heavy (if indeterminate) toll, reflected in a popular peasant saying of the time, *serp i molot – smert' i golod* (sickle [peasants] and hammer [workers] – death and famine). The mortality figures of observers are informed estimates at the best and outright guesses at the worst. The trustworthiness of official Soviet statistics varied between published and unpublished versions. Generally, in the opinion of one of the leading Western specialists on Stalinist statistics of population and agriculture, those "of the 1920s to the 1930s were, in spite of the extremely complex political situation, distinguished by the highest level of integrity and professionalism."[199] However, 1928 to 1932 was an aberrant period "of distortions associated with the psychology of constructivist planning," that is, the planning and creation of optimistic prognoses of population growth to please the authorities.[200] The year 1932 saw attempts to restore the reliability of official figures, but the statisticians were still unable "to provide a realistic evaluation of demographic and agricultural problems connected with the famine that would be politically acceptable, and subsequently they clashed with attempts by the authorities to portray their results in a favourable light."[201] The political pressure, plus the disruption and destruction of infrastructure in the countryside particularly, undermined the collection, registration, and even survival of reliable statistics on everything.

A Special Famine

Consequently, demographic historians have had to resort to estimates by means of adjustments and recalculations.[202] They indicate that the USSR's annual population growth after the 1926 census did not begin to decrease until the end of 1928 (the first year of the famine) and stopped decreasing at the end of 1934 (the last year of the famine).[203] Sergei Maksudov, a geologist-cum-historian who has spent his career studying the demographic catastrophes of Soviet, especially Stalinist, Russia, has calculated that the population's direct losses and indirect losses (direct losses plus lost births as a result of both the death of potential parents and the lower fertility of survivors) of the 1926–36 census period reached up to 10 million, one-half of which were direct losses – and in both cases primarily owing to the famine.[204]

Meanwhile, Russian and foreign specialists have calculated that the famine's climax in 1932–33 took more than 7 million lives,[205] so presumably the famine's other five years took the remaining 1 million of the shortfall of 8 million – if not more, as it seems highly unlikely that only two-sevenths of the reign of "king famine" would account for seven-eighths of its casualties. So it would not be unreasonable – if indeterminate – to conjecture a total of up to 10 million famine victims at the very least (approximately the population of Canada in 1930). By comparison, Maoist China's "Great Leap Forward" famine of 1959–62, which bears striking similarities to Stalinist Russia's of 1928–34, probably exacted at least 45 million lives.[206] Such was the result of the violence that, Stalin assured the English writer H.G. Wells in a famous interview on 23 July 1934, was unavoidable during a revolution because "Communists regard the substitution of one social system [socialism] for another [capitalism], not simply as a spontaneous and peaceful process, but as a complicated, long, and violent process" since the old system will always vigorously defend itself against the new.[207]

The few estimates by informed observers vary above and below this figure: psychophysiologist Gantt recalled that the estimates of famine deaths ranged from 2 to 15 million.[208] The diplomatic community may have been better informed, for the American acting chargé d'affaires in Riga told the US State Department that he had been told by a member of the Latvian legation in Moscow that, in the "general opinion" of diplomats in Moscow, the famine toll was 7 to 8 million.[209]

Most of the estimates of famine deaths by observers, however, are confined to the peak years of 1932–33, and they claim that in just those two years at least 3.3 million and at most 10 million starved to death (some 7 million is most often posited).[210] And Eugene Lyons, the United Press correspondent who arrived in Moscow in early 1928 and stayed six years, reported estimates by both foreigners and Russians of 3 million to at least 7 million.[211] Most of these victims came from the country's Eurasian steppe wheat belt, stretching from the Carpathian Mountains in the west to the Altai Mountains in the east.

The famine's climax at the end of the winter of 1932–33 was revealed to Western readers by several of the foreign correspondents in Moscow. Rumours of "wholesale starvation" in the countryside, especially in southern and southeastern European Russia and in Central Asia, had begun to reach their ears in the late winter, and the Soviet authorities, anxious to conceal bleak realities from the outside world, took the "unprecedented action" of forbidding the correspondents to leave the capital and travel to rural areas without the permission of the Commissariat of Foreign Affairs and the submission of a specific itinerary; however, no such permissions were granted until September, and by then the corpses had been removed and the harvest gathered.[212] In that month the *Manchester Guardian*'s William Chamberlin, whom the counsellor of the British Embassy rated "a cautious and conscientious investigator" whose "opinion may be accepted with confidence," made a ten-day trip with his wife to the Ukraine and the North Caucasus. On the basis of talks with peasants (who said that from a third to a half of their number had died) and of figures provided not by peasants ("who were often prone to exaggeration") but by local officials ("whose interest was rather to minimize what had taken place"), he estimated that, in the past year, the approximately 60 million inhabitants of the famine-struck regions had suffered a mortality rate of 10 percent for a total of 6 million deaths, including less than 2 million in the Ukraine, greater than 2 million in Kazakhstan, and 500,000 in the North Caucasus, and comprising "far more" men than women and "far more" individual farmsteaders than collective farmers (kolkhozniks).[213] Subsequently, based upon mortality figures given to him by locals, Chamberlin estimated nearly 4 million famine deaths in 1932–33 in the Ukraine and the North Caucasus.[214] So he was very near the "actual" mark, and he would have been right on it if he had added 1 million for the rest of the country.

A Special Famine

The peak of the famine exacted a high urban as well as rural toll. Indeed, in a number of large cities, against a background of low fertility (to be expected in an urban population), mortality rates were even higher than in the villages. For one thing, demographic enumeration was more accurate; for another thing, the large cities, especially, attracted numerous runaway peasants from the starving villages as well as from small cities – many, if not most, of them in a weakened condition. Also, those already living in the large cities, particularly children and pregnant women, were likewise in a feeble state because the food supply of their cities was irregular, and even the food norm gained through ration cards was inadequate. And finally, in spite of this meagre ration, the cardholders still had to undertake a full workload (and it was practically impossible to obtain more food than the norm).[215] Clearly, then, the cities were not islands of plenty in an ocean of hunger and famine.

Like Chamberlin, Schiller found that, at the height of the famine in the North Caucasus, starving men died sooner than starving women, and starving women with children sooner than those without children.[216] Similarly, a Polish diplomatic report stated that in the Ukraine the "women [were] more resistant than [the] men," resulting in a shortage of men "everywhere."[217] Also, one-half of all famine deaths in 1932–33 were males from nineteen to forty-nine years of age – both their most productive and most reproductive years.[218] This fact obviously weakened the capacity of the peasants to recover both their population and their agriculture, thereby prolonging their plight. In the peasant household it was the father who bore the brunt of the care of his family during the famine: he was primarily responsible for feeding his family, he went first of all to work in the fields of the kolkhoz with what little was left of his strength for a paltry ration, and usually he took the smallest portion of any food, while his wife commonly stayed at home "at the stove" and was less exhausted by lighter work indoors.[219] As Andrei Platonov expressed it (with a play on hallowed Marxist terminology), "the peasant woman [*baba*] is the foundation of the household, and the peasant man the superstructure."[220]

In the Lower and Middle Volga in 1933 males constituted 58 percent and 54 percent, respectively, of famine victims. The first victims included the aged as well as children, and sometimes the elderly decided of their own accord to eat less or to stop eating altogether and die so that the younger family members could survive. The least likely to starve were the families of kolkhoz managers, rural soviets (councils), and local Party activists because, as one survivor attested, they had "their own distributor" of provisions – themselves; they also enjoyed higher wages and larger rations. An official report (marked "strictly confidential, extremely urgent") on mortality in the Volga German Republic village of Staraya Popovka illustrates the crescendo of the famine: 76 deaths altogether in 1932 but 369 in 1933 – 4 in January, 4 in February, 34 in March, and 327 in April (before the 26th), equally divided between kolkhozniks and individual farmsteaders, mostly children (10 years of age and younger) and elders (60 years of age and older), and mostly from famine and related diseases. In 1933 in the Lower Volga village of Zyablovka so many peasants were starving to death so fast that there were not enough coffins in which to bury them, so they were simply dumped into pits, thirty to forty at a time.[221]

A Horrific Famine

In order to stay alive the starving peasants and nomads (and workers, too) resorted to a variety of expedients that had served them well in the past. Some of these recourses, however, were no longer available, including: the peasant commune's support of any of its needy members; the legal obligation of the landed gentry to help their peasants whenever the harvest failed; the Christian charity of the Russian Orthodox Church; the traditional role of the much maligned kulaks[222] (what one foreign diplomat called "the cream of the peasantry"[223] and one kulak's daughter called "Russia's best people"[224]) as not only moneylenders but also safeguarders of the indigent peasants during famines (as in 1921–22 and 1924–25), when they could always turn to them for help to sustain them until the next crop; and the peasant's personal property – his vegetable garden, livestock (cattle, horses, sheep, goats, pigs), poultry, and fruit trees, plus the gifts of nature in the woods (herbs, mushrooms, berries, nuts, honey).[225] All of these lifelines, however, had been broken by the doctrinaire and unflinching Bolsheviks, who abolished the commune, dispossessed the gentry, the church, and the kulaks (deporting or executing many of the latter, as well as nobles and priests ["popes"]), and collectivized most of the peasants and their property, which no longer belonged to them individually and personally. Those peasants who managed not to collectivize

A Special Famine

– the individual farmsteaders – did have the option during the famine of selling their livestock and implements and spending the money on grain, or of selling or eating their draught animals (horses and oxen), an expedient that had the additional advantage of eliminating the necessity of using grain for feed. The cow, however, was kept as long as possible for, as a peasant who survived the famine was to recall, "whoever had a cow, stayed alive."[226]

Nevertheless, for the collectivized as well as the independent peasants several survival strategies remained. At first, when they were merely hungry, many undoubtedly played what one post-Stalin memoirist has called the "crumb game," whereby mothers would divide a piece of bread into a "whole mountain of crumbs" so as to induce a semblance of abundance in their hungry children.[227] But at the height of the famine many, if not most, mothers could not resort to this artifice simply because they lacked a piece of bread to crumble. To get the grain for bread they tried to glean a few kernels by re-threshing grain straw, and to get a few spuds they dug up potato fields a second time. The Polish vice-consul in Kiev stated in the fall of 1934 that he had seen peasants doing so "on a number of occasions."[228] Two years earlier an OGPU spy had reported that the peasants of the Odessa Rayon had even dug out the stores of grain stashed by field mice and ground squirrels.[229] No sources remained untouched. Stalin's second lieutenant (after Molotov), "iron Lazar" Kaganovich,[230] in a speech of early 1933 to agricultural "shock workers" (overachievers), complained that peasants were stealing from storehouses, from seed drills during sowing, from reapers during harvesting, from threshers during threshing, and even from unripe standing grain.[231] The last stratagem, dubbed "scissoring," was, Solzhenitsyn wrote, "a totally new type of agricultural activity, a new type of harvesting" – "the nighttime snipping of individual ears of grain in the field" by "many tens of thousands of peasants ... because they had no hope of receiving anything from the collective farm for their daytime labor."[232] When seed grain was distributed by the government in the Ukraine in 1931 "the peasants," a visitor was told, "were so hungry that often they only sowed one half and ate the other, so that weeds had taken the place of grain."[233] Reaped grain was stolen not only in fields but at mills as well. At the end of the winter of 1932–33 the OGPU undertook a "special check" of fifty-one grist mills and affiliated hulling mills in the Ukraine, the North Caucasus, Western Siberia, Moscow Oblast, Tataria, the Central Black Earth, the Lower Volga, the Middle Volga, and Ivanovo Industrial Oblast and reported that, during the six months from September 1932 until March 1933, 1,902 tonnes of flour, 185 tonnes of grain, 568 tonnes of bran, 536 tonnes of fooder siftings, and 1 tonne of millet had been "misappropriated and squandered."[234]

The starving peasants stole from each other, too. At the beginning of 1933 a Polish student who was visiting the Ukraine wrote: "Horrible thefts. Peasants steal from peasants[,] workers rob workers. When a peasant owns a chicken or a pig, he has to sleep next to it throughout the night so that others who do not have 'so much luck' do not steal it at night and even before the dawn eat it with their hungry family."[235] By the spring, theft – normally unusual in the Ukraine – had become a "mass phenomenon" in the republic. "Not a cow, a sheep, or a pig is kept even one night in the barn," said an eyewitness. "So whoever still has any livestock, including cows, keeps them in the izba [peasant house]. Thus it was from Kiev to Chirigin and from Uman to the Dnepr. And it was the very same throughout the Ukraine and the North Caucasus."[236] Pilferage became so common that it was not regarded as a crime by the peasants, who felt that under collectivization "everybody's property is nobody's property."[237] The state, however, disagreed, and those who stole socialist property were condemned to death by shooting or, under mitigating circumstances, to ten years of imprisonment and the confiscation of all of the culprit's personal property under the law of 7 August 1932 (in Gulag argot "the law of seven-eighths" because on forms the date was written as 7/8/32; also dubbed "the law of three ears" because the theft of only three ears of grain was enough to warrant arrest). And a thief who stole personal property, even if starving, risked the death penalty. Journalist Clyman was asked by a *muzhik* (peasant) in the third-class carriage of a train in the North Caucasus whether people in Canada who stole a cow or a sack of grain were shot, for his brother-in-law had been shot by the OGPU for having "stole[n] a cow and slaughtered it for meat." He continued, "It was his own cow, [which] the collective farm took, and he stole it back, and now there are four children left orphans all because of a cow." "It's the new law," he explained. "The Communists want to protect state property, but does it help to shoot a man because he takes his own cow? There are so many shootings now."[238]

A safer option for the hungry and starving was to find "surrogates" – false foods, although not all were wholesome and some were even toxic. The peasants' use of food supplements and replacements to make "famine bread" was a long-time tradition. In the late nineteenth century they included straw, birch and elm bark, buckwheat husks, pigweed,[239] malt grains, bran, potatoes, lime leaves, various herbs such as goutwort and cow parsley (Queen Anne's lace), potato plant leaves, and lentils, and in some regions the inhabitants always had to eat pretend breads at least part of the year.[240] This list was lengthened by desperation in the spring of 1933, when Gareth Jones left his train in the northern Ukraine and, in order to avoid becoming lost in the snow-covered countryside, walked along the railway track from village to village, talking to the peasants, whose recurrent cries were *khleb[a] netu* (there's no bread) and *vse pukhly* (everybody is bloated).[241] Now the peak of the famine was impelling starving peasants everywhere to resort to an extensive and imaginative (and sometimes bizarre) array of substitutes. The most common – after dogs, cats, rats, and mice – were oilcakes made from the seeds of sunflowers, flax, and hemp; camelina (false flax); ground hemp; pumpkin roots; acorns (which were soaked for four days to make "acorn flour"); poppy seeds; cornstock pulp; goosefoot (*lebed*) ("goosefoot herbs" and "goosefoot flour");[242] "flour" made from vetch; potato peelings; "bits" (potato "purée," the residue from the making of potato starch); "rejects" (*otboi*), that is, discarded foodstuffs; water chestnuts (*chilim*); dried nuts, peanuts ("ground nuts"), and beechnuts (shelled and unshelled); *chekan* ("prunings," i.e., "flour" made from the rhizomes of bulrushes); "dwarf" flour made from seeds; cabbage leaves; the leaves and twigs of lime (linden) trees; horse (red) sorrel (*konevnik*); nettles; "stinkers" (*dushina*), that is, beet and potato greens; wild onion, wild garlic, wild horseradish, and wild mustard; "flour" made from dogrose berries; straw; chaff; silage; sawdust; rotten wood; tree bark, especially the inner bark of birch trees; infusions of the branches of fruit trees, especially apricot trees; moss; clay;[243] dried strips of horsehide that children could gnaw and suck endlessly; the blood and the bones of dead animals; and "aspic" made from the raw hides of dead animals.[244] Other substitutes used in the baking of bread included buckwheat flour, oats, bran, millet chaff, clover heads, cotton cake, beans, stewed onions, peelings, dried and ground wild pears, vetch, and dried birch bark.[245] As soon as the rivers thawed, the starving caught freshwater mussels (crayfish?) to boil, and once the snow cover had melted they hunted ground squirrels (susliks) en masse for meat. In the North Caucasus an official reported in 1933 that "numerous kolkhozniks go into the fields and flush out ground squirrels and do not even cut off their tails for submission to the rural soviet [for a bounty] but immediately singe and fry them to eat."[246] In the Volga German Republic, as elsewhere in the wooded and grassy steppes, however, although ground squirrels "served as a major prop for the starving ... it became difficult to catch them after meltwater from the snow had disappeared."[247] And they were nearly unpalatable, as a refugee child found in the Kazakh steppe during the Second World War: "Our mother was an excellent ... cook. Only she could prepare a gopher [ground squirrel] so that it became good to eat, though gopher meat isn't considered edible. A gopher on the table ... It stinks for a mile around, an unspeakably disgusting smell. But there's no other meat, and we have nothing else. So we eat these gophers."[248] Jones found that starving peasants in the northern Ukraine were even driven to killing and eating their horses, although they were normally as averse to consuming horsemeat as Orthodox Jews were to consuming pork and had scorned the (Muslim Crimean) Tatars for profaning themselves by consuming horse flesh.[249] Some were not above devouring horse carrion, and an eyewitness recorded this gruesome indulgence not far from Kiev in the grim spring of 1933:

> We overtook a crowd of twenty kolkhozniks armed with shovels and axes. Some of them carried sacks of horsemeat on their shoulders and others simply armfuls of the same that emitted an unbearable stench. But we had [already] experienced this smell, and the kolkhozniks, moving their feet with difficulty, hurried home in anticipation of a filling supper of this carrion. Hope shone in their eyes, and slobber flowed from the mouths of some. Others could not bear it and gnawed the rotten meat without pondering the dreadful act.
>
> They vied with each other in complaining to us that nine days ago in the rain several horses had dropped dead in a single day in the field and had immediately been buried. The kolkhozniks working there had returned on foot at night, unearthed the flesh, carried it home, and eaten it, and they had not told anyone else where the horses were buried. But now these had discovered the secret, and they would eat some here. It ended in a fight over the carrion, and they killed two who wanted to take the large chunks for themselves, leaving them to lie with the bones of the dead horses.

When they were asked how they could possibly eat carrion, one of them replied: "It is obvious, comrade, that you have never starved." The shocked comrade added that, besides carrion, mice and frogs were "delicacies for millions of unfortunates," whose staples were plant roots, tree bark, tree buds, and even algae. "Everything," he concluded, "absolutely everything, went for food, including man himself."[250]

The desperate scrounging for substitutes was epitomized by scenes in the Lower Volga. An observer there wrote: "The people are grazing, the cattle are grazing. They eat mussels to the utmost. Along the riverbanks you meet entire families engaged in the preparation of this tasty dish – cracked oysters."[251] Another observer in a letter to a friend said of the region: "This is the current state of the Lower Volga in a number of villages and rayons: most of the population ekes out a wretched, starving existence. They live on anything that happens to come to hand: they eat sorrel, *konyovik* [either willow herb or swamp loosestrife], and other plants, and flour from the bulbs of swamp plants (so-called *kuchakamysh*); they mix *barda* [lees], the sediment left by distillation, with flour from marsh plants and bake 'flatcakes.' After flatcakes, God only knows." He added, "almost nobody is left in the villages."[252] And finally, a resident of the Lower Volga saw for herself what the starving peasants were reduced to consuming: "After nothing was left in the house to eat, they ate mussels from the Khopyor [River], they ate grass, they barked trees, they ate rotten potatoes, ground squirrels, mice, cats, and dogs, and horse and cattle carrion that had been doused with carbolic acid they soaked in the Khopyor and ate."[253] The faux fare also included retted and boiled hides, roots dug out of marshes, and rotting turnips that were gathered in the fields, mixed with flour dust, and baked into "buns."

Starvation in the Central Black Earth was recalled by a Russian historian who became a prominent specialist on collectivization, Nikolai Ivnitskii. He experienced the famine as a boy in the region after his father was arrested and deported, his mother lost her job, and the family went to live with one of her sisters. He described how his family struggled to survive:

At first the relatives helped us, but by the winter of [1932–33] their provisions had run out. Famine began. In order not to die, people began to kill anything living, they caught pigeons and [other] birds, and when snow came they began to gather last year's rotten potatoes from the kolkhoz fields. They flooded out ground squirrels and caught them to use as food. They dug out their burrows so as to collect the leftover grain that they had readied for the winter. From the starch of the rotten potatoes mama cooked a dark brown *kissel* [a kind of blancmange], and from this starch, goosefoot, and pounded bark she baked dark green flatcakes, similar to cowdung patties. We ate them, filling our stomachs with the surrogates, but the hunger did not pass. In the spring our entire family – mama, my brother, and I – swelled up. The whole body filled with some sort of liquid, the face swelled, and the stomach swelled. They put mama in the rayon hospital. I was already 10 years old, my brother 8. By the summer, when the ears [of grain] ripened, we walked to the fields, snipped spikes of the "milky-waxen ripeness," and ate [them]. Many had already died by this time. How we survived, I do not know.[254]

The faux fare generated an epidemic of gastric disorders, and many peasants, particularly children, died agonizing deaths from constipation or "bloody flux" (diarrhea).[255] Such was generally not the case in the cities, however, where the residents had less need – and less choice – of substitutes, principally dogs (whose cooked flesh was nutritious as well as tasty). Some mothers became so distraught over not being able to feed their children that they committed suicide.[256] Others went insane. A prominent member of Moscow's privileged scientific community learned from his former janitor of "frequent instances of madness among the peasants."[257] And cannibalism and even necrophagy appeared, with not a few starving peasants eyeing other peasants (alive and dead, and kin and non-kin) as food. Cannibalism became common enough to warrant a poster that was seen by Lucy Lang in the office of a Moscow official that depicted "a mother in distress, with a swollen child at her feet, and over the picture was the inscription, 'The eating of dead children is barbarism.'" When Lang questioned the functionary about the poster, he said, "It is one of our methods of educating the people … We have distributed hundreds of these posters, especially in the villages of the Ukraine."[258]

How peasants could become so depraved is illustrated by the plight of a starving kolkhoz family in Western Siberia as described rather clinically by a physician:

> Filipp Borodin has earned 650 workdays [on the kolkhoz] and has a wife and five children from 1½ to 9 years of age. His wife lies sick on the stove;[259] three of the children are sitting on the stove, pale as wax, with swollen faces; the one-and-a-half-year-old sits on the window sill, pale and bloated; the ten-year-old boy lies sick on the dirt floor, covered in rags; and Filipp Borodin himself sits on a bench and constantly smokes hand-rolled cigarettes of disgustingly pungent tobacco [*makhorka*?], cries like a baby, and begs for death for his children. With tears he begs [kolkhoz manager] comrade Sukhanov: "Give me even a kilogram of potatoes, even a litre of milk, you know that I worked all summer and am now working tirelessly" (at present he looks after the bulls, but in summer he tends the cows). According to comrade Sukhanov and the brigade leader of the kolkhoz "Red Partisan," Borodin was a meek worker.
>
> Borodin does not even have [any] surrogate food. Two days ago he and his family ate two dead piglets discarded by the kolkhoz. In Borodin's izba there is unbearable filth, dampness, and stench mixed with tobacco smoke. Borodin curses his children: "You devils, you're not dying, would that I didn't have to look at you!"
>
> Studying Borodin's condition objectively, I can say that he is beginning to fall into a psychosis because of starvation and is drawn strongly to the idea that he will eat his own children.

Then the doctor proceeded to describe the village context:

> The izbas are dirty. Around them there is filth from human faeces as a result of diarrhea from [eating] surrogates. The people move like phantoms, silently, dully. The izbas are deserted, their windows sealed (about 500 householders have abandoned their homes in the village of Karpovo and gone who knows where). Very rarely are animals encountered in the streets (apparently the last have been eaten). In the entire village

(1,000 households) I met only two hens and one rooster. From time to time a scrawny dog is seen.

He added, "The straw roofs of the izbas and barns have been stripped for livestock fodder."[260]

"Absolutely confidential" OGPU reports documented a number of instances of cannibalism at the end of the winter and in the spring of 1933 throughout the country.[261] For example, a secret report of 31 March 1933 cited "a number of cases of cannibalism, the sale of human flesh at markets, and murder for this purpose" in several regions, including the North, the Lower Volga, the North Caucasus, and Kazakhstan.[262] In an Uzbek cemetery at a town in Kazakhstan a Kazakh man was found with the body of a child that had been cooked and cut up, and in the snow near the cemetery the body of a twenty-two-year-old Kazakh woman was found cut into pieces and minus the flesh of her arms and thighs.[263] The same report described a similar instance in the Urals:

> During the night of 23 March in Chelyabinsk on the property of the Ferrosplavov Factory one T. killed an unknown woman in his *zemlyanka* [makeshift shelter]. In a trunk in the zemlyanka were discovered about 30 chunks of boneless human flesh weighing 16 kg. and in a bowl some soup made from this flesh.
>
> A sack with parts of the woman's body was found in a pile of snow 50 m. from the zemlyanka.
>
> T. was arrested and under interrogation indicated that on 19 March last he had killed the unknown 20-year-old woman, who had come to spend the night. After murdering her, T. butchered and salted the soft parts of the body and buried the bones and the rest in a sack in the snow. From this flesh they [T. and his wife] cooked soup, which all of the family ate.

The report added that T.'s wife was planning to butcher and eat one of the children.[264]

Russian witnesses told the British consul in Leningrad that by the summer cannibalism was "a matter of course" in the Ukraine and "common" in the North Caucasus.[265] A Polish official in the Ukraine had reported in late spring: "instances of cannibalism continue as before; nowadays in Kiev the militia [police] bring pieces of legs and arms, as well as female breasts, as evidence of the guilt of the criminals who have been caught."[266] Touring the republic in the summer, an American journalist observed: "in the Ukraine just now cannibalism has become a commonplace."[267] Usually it was a case of unburied corpses being harvested or buried bodies being unearthed for, as an official in Kiev Rayon said, "What does it cost to pick up a fresh corpse or to dig up a dead body at night and use it for food? Who will know of this, when corpses cover the roads and fill the ditches, and they themselves and the rest are dying?"[268] Occasionally it was a case of premeditated murder, as in the instance of a stout lady who visited her sister and brother-in-law, both of whom decided to butcher her, so during the night the wife stunned her sister while she slept, slit her throat, cut her up, and salted the chunks, and the next day, instead of going to work on the kolkhoz, they arranged a banquet, which was attended by half a dozen others, who drank vodka and ate only meat in various guises without bread, with the host shouting, "Thank you, comrade Stalin, for a happy and joyful life! Hurrah! Long live Stalin!"[269] In a signed and witnessed statement in August by a Ukrainian farm official who had fled to Poland to escape the horror, it was asserted that starving peasants often ate their dead children and that the authorities did not allow the corpses of famine victims to be buried until they had decomposed for fear that they would be dug up and eaten by the starving. He added that cannibalism was being punished by summary execution but with little effect because death had lost its sting.[270] Cases were even reported of the killing of starving peasants to make soap – a scarce product – from human tallow.[271] But it was more common to kill and eat one another, including one's own children. The OGPU reported one such case in a *khutor* (Cossack hamlet) in the Tsimlyansk Rayon on the lower Don, where the husband, an individual farmsteader, of Kristina Yermakova had died in 1933, leaving her with four children, two of whom then died, so she moved to a kolkhoz with her two remaining children but was unable to work because of illness and lived on charity. In late April she and an old woman living with her killed her eight-year-old son and ate part of him, the mother later explaining:

> While enduring the great famine, I decided to kill my 8-year-old son, Ivan, and to that end I asked the advice of the old woman, Anna

Predkova, telling her, "We will perish anyway, so let's kill Ivan and eat him." Predkova did not object to this, saying to me, "Strangle him, that's all." The older son did not agree to this and objected. I told him that we will perish anyway, so you and the old woman together kill him. Whereupon my son Nikolai wound a strap around Ivan's neck and began to choke him. At this juncture I asked the old woman for help, saying, "Grannie, quickly, lend a hand." Whereupon she approached and hit him on the head with a stick and killed him. Right after this the three of us cut the flesh into pieces and cooked them.[272]

Cannibalism was no less prevalent in the North Caucasus. On 1 August 1933 a French newspaper, *Le Journal des Débats Politiques et Littéraires*, ran an article on the famine that quoted a recent foreign traveller to the North Caucasus as saying that he had encountered instances of cannibalism "everywhere" there, adding that reports of cannibalism had been "completely confirmed by reliable sources in Krasnodar and Sevastopol, with descriptive details and personal names."[273] In March the OGPU had reported that, in the Yeisk Rayon along the coast of the Sea of Azov, it had caught one gang of three persons who had knifed and eaten four children and another gang of four (ranging in age from sixteen to sixty-five) who had "systematically engaged in cannibalism" and knifed and eaten three children, including the eleven-year-old son of the sixty-five-year-old female leader of the gang.[274] Worse still, in May the OGPU uncovered what it termed a "kulak terrorist organization" at four villages near Armavir, headed by the Koshelev brothers, who had murdered some 150 adults and children and used their flesh partly to feed themselves and partly to sell at markets in Armavir. They were motivated by class revenge, hunger, and money, one of them saying, "We urge these communists to come to our place with their children, knife them, and eat their flesh but mostly sell it at Armavir as dried, cooked, and jellied meat, sausage, and cutlets. In general it is tasty and wholesome."[275] An anonymous letter writer summarized the horror of the North Caucasus in the summer:

> The famine is such that people are dying on the roads, ten at a time. Many people have turned purple from hunger, are swollen and covered with sores. Some desperate mothers abandon their children in the street, attaching a piece of paper to them where their name is written.

> Others, in desperation, kill their children or kill themselves. Everywhere you can see people lying around starving, in post offices, public gardens and in the markets. The state is not helping and is indifferent to all those who do not qualify under the category of worker, because they are no longer able to work. The endless queues of beggars that resemble walking corpses look for anything to eat in the rubbish. They dig up the tombs of the dead in the cemeteries, exhuming the corpses as soon as they are buried [in order] to eat them. Deaths from the contagion of eating human flesh are common. The sale of human flesh, especially that of children, has become almost a routine thing. Mothers are afraid to leave their children on the street, because they can be stolen and then will be killed and eaten. Just in Stavropol, during a single month, 80 cases of missing children were confirmed. Cannibals who not only eat human flesh but also sell it in the markets are often sentenced to death.

The writer concluded: "a formerly thriving country [region] has been turned into a cemetery, reduced by ruthless barbarians to the appearance of a desert."[276]

As if to absolve themselves, some peasants contemplating cannibalism either requested permission from the authorities to do so or asked the opinion of friends or neighbours. The same issue of *Le Journal des Débats* reported receiving an April letter from a North Caucasus village telling of a widow (whose husband had just starved to death) asking a visiting neighbour whether she and her children should bury him or eat him; the newspaper also received a March letter from a German resident of the Lower Volga telling of parents asking the village soviet whether they could eat their dead children.[277] Not surprisingly, parents or relatives who ate children had usually lost their minds.[278]

Even the 1932–33 peak of the hunger/famine of 1928–34 took more lives than the famines of 1921–22 or 1924–25, partly because the peak was both longer and more extensive. All of his peasant informants told Gareth Jones in 1933 that the current famine was graver than that of 1921–22, when it was more localized, mainly along the Volga, whereas "today the famine is everywhere."[279] And this ubiquitous famine lasted longer (and cost more lives) partly because, unlike the 1921–22 famine, which was officially recognized as such – if belatedly – by the state and was mitigated by both foreign relief and some state relief (e.g., the creation in the villages of "grain reserves" in case of harvest failures, the deferment of taxes, collections by state organs and social agencies like the Red Cross), it was not acknowledged by the state and was not moderated by foreign relief[280] – and it was blamed on the peasants and the nomads themselves.[281]

But some surviving peasants in the Lower Volga and southern Urals regarded Stalin himself as directly and personally responsible for the famine, which, they believed, he expressly engineered in order to extract gold for industrialization and food for the cities and the Red Army. *Kogda Lenin zhil*, they said, *nas kormili. Kogda Stalin postupil, nas golodom morili* (When Lenin lived, we were fed. When Stalin came, we were starved dead).[282] Gareth Jones was quoted as saying that Stalin was "the most hated man in Russia."[283] And when the peasant diarist Izmailov finally left the Altai Kray at the end of the thirties for the Leningrad front, he also left a message for the "father of the people": "So I want to say no thanks to you, comrade Stalin, for your 'joyful and happy life' that you have given to working people! It is but a fairy tale of a happy life. Terrible and agonizing starvation has become our permanent guest. Every day we have to starve."[284]

The Kremlin could have allayed the famine or even averted it altogether by reducing or halting the export of foodstuffs, buying provisions abroad, or soliciting foreign relief,[285] but, as the head of the Ukraine's Poltava Soviet told correspondent William Chamberlin: "To have imported grain would have been injurious to our prestige. To have let the peasants keep their grain would have encouraged them to go on producing little."[286] The same Latvian informant in Moscow who told the American diplomat in Riga about the famine's high toll also told him that the Soviet government would not accept outside charity because one of the famine's causes – collectivization – was, in his words, "too closely associated with the name of Stalin for an open admission of its failure to be made without grave injury to his prestige as the leader of the Communist Party." For the same reason, the informant added, the policy of collectivization would not be abandoned. Besides, he noted, unlike 1921–22, in the aftermath of the First World War, a civil war, and foreign intervention, by 1933 the Soviet regime was much surer of its power to suppress any attempt at popular rebellion, and it was determined "to deal with peasants who [were] reluctant to work under the collective farm system by means of severe punitive measures," including confiscation, eviction, deportation, imprisonment, and execution.²⁸⁷

At first, when the famine was less severe and the peasants were still able to survive by farming, they did so and in the winter sent some family members to work in the cities, whence these "winterers" sent money home to the village to defray various taxes in money and kind and to purchase supplies before themselves returning in the spring. But as the state's exactions increased and the famine worsened, and without any foreign and with little domestic relief, the desperate peasants – both the individual farmsteaders beset by relentless strictures and the kolkhozniks beset by the kolkhozes' failings – migrated to find some.²⁸⁸ Migration – either permanently as a family to a less stricken region or seasonally by the muzhik to another region for agricultural work or to a city for industrial work – was another age-old survival measure. The migrants might not only find work but could live "grazing" (*na podnozhom kormu*) in the forest, collecting wild plants and hunting animals; moreover, they could rely upon the locals, whose material condition was better than that of their former starving neighbours and therefore responded more mercifully to their pleas for work and some bread. In order to survive they – particularly the women, children, and elderly – had to beg, and charity was a venerable Russian tradition with deep Christian roots; besides, help for the weak and the poor was the primary obligation of members of the peasant commune.²⁸⁹

And so it was in 1928–34. Solzhenitsyn termed the period 1929–33 the "exhausting years," when, starving and – if they had been dispossessed – landless and unemployed, the peasants roamed the country in the hundreds of thousands in search of food and work. Their quest was more fruitless than fruitful, however. As an official of Intourist, the state travel agency, aboard a tour boat on the Volga River confided to Andrew Cairns, the peripatetic Canadian agronomist, "everybody in Russia was crazy because they were all travelling to look for better conditions, but there were no such conditions as they were terrible everywhere."²⁹⁰

From 1930 some disaffected peasants, chiefly those with relatives in neighbouring Poland or Romania, even fled their country across the "cordon," a one-hundred-kilometre-wide border zone, especially to Poland.²⁹¹ And many of those Russians who were able to travel abroad made sure to return with as much food as possible. When Arthur Koestler entered the USSR in the summer of 1932, the Soviet customs officials at the railway junction of Shepetovka in the western Ukraine – as was their wont – completely unpacked and unwrapped the contents of every piece of baggage and then repacked everything, taking half a day to do so. "Most of the travellers in the train were Russians," he wrote, "and most of the contents of their baggage was food. Hundreds of pounds of sugar, tea, butter, sausages, lard, biscuits, and conserves of every variety were piled on the counters and grimy floor of the Customs shed." He added that he was startled by the look of greed and resignation on the faces of the famished customs officials as they inspected the food, as well as the deference of their touch and the gleam in their eyes.[292]

Not a few blue-collar and white-collar workers were also on the move in the hopes of improving their lot. A former White Army officer who visited the Ukraine at the outset of 1933 estimated that from one-fifth to one-quarter of the republic's factory and office workers had been dismissed from their jobs for want of provisions for the workplace, resulting in unemployment and malnutrition (and one-third of the "angry and hungry" workers turned to thievery and robbery for a living). The officer claimed that thirty thousand workers, for example, had left the Dneprostroi dam project, the showcase of Lenin's electrification program that had been started in 1927 and had begun generating power in 1932.[293] These hungry urbanites resorted to intensive gardening (*dacha*,[294] allotment, courtyard, roof-top, and even window-box), bartering (odd jobs for payment in kind), black marketeering (pricey and risky), Torgsin, soliciting a higher food-ration category (improbable), and foraging in the countryside for mushrooms, roots, nuts, berries, honey, fish, and game.

However, the majority of the wanderers – as Cairns himself discovered – were peasants who had simply quit their collective and individual farms, leaving the fields uncultivated and infested with weeds and the livestock untended, being, in the words of an ex-pat American repairman in Kiev, "too hungry and angry to work" them.[295] The most grievous sufferers were the individual farmsteaders, who received neither sympathy from the state nor succour from the kolkhoz, and the children of large families. The plight of the former was recollected by a family member of an individual farmstead (*khutor*) in Rostov Oblast of the North Caucasus. The family's means were appropriated by the authorities, and:

Left without grain ... we starved. We began to go to the field to flush ground squirrels out of their burrows and eat them; we gathered ears of grain (to glean ears was not permitted, and more than once patrols seized our ears and sacks); and we took chaff and baked flatcakes ("flaps") from it. Without potatoes, we made broth from bits of beet and cabbage. I remember that we often made chickpea porridge ... We were emaciated, like skeletons, and some even had swollen legs ... All of our thoughts centred on eating.[296]

Children begged everywhere, and they even gathered at the grain depots, grist mills, and grain elevators (where the workers furtively ate the grain) and picked seeds to eat out of their excrement.[297] In some cases in large families the parents fed only some of them in order to save the rest, the doomed being locked in storerooms, cellars, and barns to starve to death.[298]

At first, those starving peasants who lived in villages within striking distance of towns and cities began to resort to "bagging" (*meshochnichestvo*) – that is, walking or riding to them with bags in search of bread. This practice had arisen during the period of War Communism (1918–21), when starving workers, not peasants, had taken sacks of scarce goods to the countryside and exchanged them for plentiful provisions, which they then took home and ate or sold; however, during the great famine the process was reversed, except for the fact that the sacks of the starving peasants were empty when they left their villages and not full when they returned. As the most privileged cities, Moscow and Leningrad were the favourite destinations; in March 1933 a peasant woman hawking milk on a street in Moscow told Gareth Jones: "I live 50 versts [53 kilometres] from Moscow, & there we have no bread. They took the bread away and the potatoes away. We come to Moscow & bring bread back. Moscow is feeding us. If it were not for Moscow, we should die."[299] However, bagging drained the capital of vital food for its own residents. An OGPU check at the beginning of spring 1932 revealed that every day baggers were leaving Moscow's railway stations with an average of more than seventeen thousand puds of grain, and every day one to four thousand baggers were waiting to board trains at the stations of the North Caucasus and travel north.[300] As the larger cities ran out of bread the peasants began to travel as far as possible in whatever direction to find food, swarming the railway stations and jamming and even jumping the trains.[301] At the end of the summer a Polish agent reported: "almost the whole of Ukraine is traveling in search of bread, the trains are filled to the highest possible degree, and one has to wait for days in line to get on a train."[302] It was at this time that Arthur Koestler found that millions of peasants had been "nomadized" by the famine, which "had turned a considerable percentage of the population into railway-nomads who were travelling thousands of miles, attracted by vague rumours of better conditions in some other region." It was a period, he added, of upheaval officially labelled "nomadism in agriculture and industry," when whole villages were abandoned and entire rayons were depopulated by the exodus.[303] Koestler's train made frequent stops as it moved slowly across the Ukrainian steppe. "At every station," he wrote, "there was a crowd of peasants in rags, offering ikons and linen in exchange against a loaf of bread," and "the women were lifting up their infants to the compartment windows – infants pitiful and terrifying with limbs like sticks, puffed bellies, big cadaverous heads lolling on thin necks."[304] "They choked the railway stations, crammed the freight trains, squatted in the markets and public squares, and died in the streets," he recalled, adding, "I have never seen so many and such hurried funerals as during the winter [of 1933] in Kharkov."[305] At the end of summer later that year Harry and Lucy Lang trained through the Belorussian and Ukrainian countryside and witnessed the peasant-jammed stations: "At every station we saw scores of peasants, men and women, huddling together on the wet ground, their mud-stained bundles scattered about them. Mud-encrusted rags covered their feet, and filthy pieces of sacking clothed their bodies. A drizzling rain fell, and the peasants were blue with cold. They did not even turn their eyes to look at the train."[306] The charnel-house stations would have been noticed by Soviet citizens, too, although very few would have dared to talk or write about it. One who did was Rina Zelënaia (1901–1991), the actress, singer, and comedian (born Ekaterina Zelënaia), who was already horrified by them in the autumn of 1928. In her diary she wrote:

> Really, can one quite forget the train stations – terrible, cold, and dark, and full of hungry people – filthy and lousy and lying asleep side by side [torn-out page] … where the personnel stand on the track line, and one cannot imagine them moving. Nobody comes and nobody goes – for months people have been collapsing in the stations. Really,

can one forget the piles of corpses that are packed into carts and dumped in the cemeteries like firewood. And the horses dying on the roads and looking at us with such eyes that it is impossible to turn or run away?[307]

The most vivid description of this human anthill of transient peasants was written by Frederick Griffin, who toured European Russia for the *Toronto Star* in the spring and summer of 1932:

Peasants pouring in and out of the river boats. Peasants piling off and on the trains in a kind of changeless phantasmagoria, the places of those getting off being immediately taken by those getting on, without end. Perpetual peasant motion. Peasants swarming along the banks of the Volga like human ants. Peasants crowding the railroad stations of the Northern Caucasus and the Ukraine, squatting and sprawling about the platforms, spread with their bundles all over the waiting rooms so that it is almost impossible to walk along without trampling on men, women and children.

Peasants breaking in waves over the fringe of cities, clustering the waterfronts, infiltrating through the streets, as if the horde of them threatened to overrun and swamp the urban people.

Peasants everywhere, thick as the Russian flies, restless as if stirred by some vague wanderlust, seeking barter, bread, change, work; placid, patient, stolid, long suffering, slow as yoked oxen; mute myriads, dull, dark, squalid, tragic, seemingly pitiable masses who yet can sing and dance, laugh and love when the fancy takes them.

Who are they? What are they? Where are they all going thus endlessly? What are they all seeking? On what quest are these thousands of seemingly aimless wanderers embarked with their sacks, their bundles, their suitcases and their baskets?[308]

Some of the most distraught of the fleeing peasants, however, chose to end their struggle. Homer Smith, the well-established "black man in Red Russia," witnessed this horror on his return to Moscow by train from the Ukraine in 1932:

I saw a tragic scene which illustrated the desperation to which these peasants were being driven. As my train was gathering speed out of the station at Bakhmatch [Bakmut, now Artemovsk], it jerked to a sudden halt. Looking out the window, I saw pedestrians rushing toward the locomotive. I got down from my coach and rushed after them to see what had happened. Peering through the crowds that had gathered, I saw with horror that a peasant, holding his wife and two children in his embrace, had thrown himself under the wheels of our fast moving train.

My porter was unmoved. "It happens on almost every trip," he remarked with resignation in his voice. "They even throw themselves under the train between stations and we know nothing about it until our next trip."[309]

Most of the fleeing peasants, as George Burrell noted in 1930, "flocked to the cities to work in the factories."[310] On the outskirts of those overcrowded and underhoused magnets they fashioned *zemlyanka*s, makeshift shelters sunk into the ground.[311] Their principal destinations were Moscow (especially) and Leningrad, which, they knew, enjoyed preferential provisionment and offered more employment possibilities than small cities. The Italian ambassador, Count Bernardo Attolico, reported to Rome in late March of 1932 that "hundreds and thousands of peasants ... driven from the countryside for different reasons, now overrun the streets of Moscow."[312] There, recalled Mary Leder, the teenaged daughter of one of the many American left-wing sympathizers who immigrated to the USSR during the Great Depression and eventually became disenchanted,[313] "old men, women, and children sat on the curbstone or stood in front of bakeries, pleading for the *doveski* (the small pieces of bread placed on the scales to make the exact weight) and begged from door to door and in suburban trains."[314] Leder's compatriot, the travel writer Carveth Wells, saw throngs of starving peasants scrounging for food during the night in the streets of the capital, particularly near the railway stations: "men, women and children, some of them so weak that their friends were helping them along while they groped in the gutters and among piles of garbage for food." "Moscow," he added, "was said to have at least twenty thousand" of these beggars.[315] Thus, unlike the famine of 1921–22, during which urbanites travelled to the villages in search of food, that of 1928–34 saw the opposite movement. This switch prompted the inevitable anecdote: One peasant asks another, "What is the difference between Bolshevism and Communism?" "Bolshevism," the other replies, "is when there is no food in the cities, and Communism is when there is no food in the country."[316]

As grain became scarcer and scarcer in the villages, more and more peasants fled. Until 1933 they were able to quit the famine regions and to seek help anywhere. The rub was the fact that the famine was more or less ubiquitous. Moreover, only a few large administrative or industrial cities (and a few privileged groups: the Party elite, the OGPU, the Red Army, intellectual and scientific luminaries) were sufficiently provisioned; so many of the starving just went to beg wherever vegetable gardens and fruit trees were common.[317] Nevertheless, in only the first half of 1932, 2,654,500 people migrated from the villages to the cities, and it was partly for this very reason – urban succour – that fewer people starved to death in 1932 than in 1933.[318] In just two months – December 1932 and January 1933 – 85,217 peasants (9,213 families), nearly a half of them individual farmsteaders and a third of them kolkhozniks, left the villages of the 215 rayons of the Ukraine alone.[319]

From 1933, in an attempt to control the demographic displacement and general disorder stemming from the rural-to-urban exodus, the state tried to prevent both fleeing and begging by taking several measures: issuing internal passports to most citizens but not the peasants (among others), who were thus unable to reside in the cities; deporting "hardened beggars" from cities and regions; prohibiting urban workers, members of the military, and the inhabitants of neighbouring regions from sharing their rations with kolkhoz beggars; and by decrees of 22 January and 16 February forbidding peasants from leaving the Ukraine, the North Caucasus, and the Lower Volga.[320] Thus, as Solzhenitsyn wrote, "the long lines of those dying of famine trudged toward the railroad stations in the hope of getting to the cities, which was where the bread grains were evidently ripening, but were refused tickets and were unable to leave – and lay dying beneath the station fences in a submissive heap of homespun coats and bark shoes."[321] A member of the troupe of Moscow's Vakhtangov Theatre that toured the industrial centres of the Urals in the spring of 1933 recalled in his memoirs: "at the station of each town through which we passed we saw hundreds and thousands of starving peasants who with their last ounce of strength had come from their villages in search of a scrap of stale bread." "They sat," he continued, "against the station walls in long drab rows, sleeping and dying there and then, and every morning the station guard would take away the corpses in carts covered with tarpaulins."[322] An aspiring "proletarian" writer (i.e., a working-class writer who wrote about the "realities" of socialism) was travelling westward by train from the Urals to Moscow in the summer as a guest of the OGPU, and he described with empathy the begging, dying peasants lining the railway:

> I eat, I drink, and I recall bitterly the Magnitogorsk-Moscow train. One after the other we glimpsed the platforms, stations, stops, and waiting places. And everywhere along the line stood ragged, barefoot, emaciated children and old men. Skin and bones, walking skeletons. And all of them stretched out their hands to the passing cars. On the lips of all of them there was one easily guessed word: bread, bread, bread. They begged for alms. For centuries they have fed and watered the townspeople, but now ... And this [penury] despite relatively good harvests in the years before last. What's happening? Why have the peasants been reduced to beggary? Because the state grain procurers rampage in the villages. They seize the last particle of grain. Even for seed and feed.

He added, sardonically, that "from the minute we became the guests of the Chekists absolute communism began for us" because "they ate very well and paid nothing."[323]

The famine bolstered a pitiable element that had blighted the Soviet Union since its beginnings: the waifs, "those sparrows of Russia," in the words of one observer[324] – homeless, or street, children who had deserted their starving peasant or worker parents or had been abandoned or orphaned by them and who then flocked to the cities to scrounge, surviving by begging, peddling, pickpocketing,[325] robbing, and even prostituting themselves.[326] Their numbers swelled during the turmoil of the so-called revolutions of February and October 1917, the civil war of 1918–22 and the concomitant foreign intervention, and the famines of 1921–22 and 1924–25. By 1922 they numbered at least 7 million.[327] Predictably, the beginning of the great famine in 1928 produced another generation, and by 1932 Moscow alone hosted at least 1 million waifs, according to an unpublished letter to the government newspaper *Izvestiya* at the beginning of the year[328] – one-quarter of the official estimate (underestimate, more likely) of the country's total of 4 million in April of that year.[329]

As the famine intensified, their number increased, peaking in 1933. Between 1 January and 31 July of that year the number of ragamuffins in orphanages alone – a fraction of the overall number – rose from 6,000 to 7,000 in the North, from 14,650 to 43,000 in the North Caucasus, from 16,300 to 21,500 in the Urals, from 6,000 to 12,000 in the Lower Volga, from 9,600 to 13,500 in the Middle Volga, from 8,209 to 11,269 in Western Siberia, and from an unknown number to 61,000 to 70,000 in Kazakhstan.[330] Walter Krivitsky, a security official who defected in 1937, recalled his shock at seeing these starving orphans while indulging in the luxuries of the Marino Sanatorium (a pre-1917 palace) for Soviet elites near Kursk in February of 1934:

> That evening seated in the brilliantly lighted dining hall of Marino, everyone was chatting gaily after an excellent supper. Outside, it was bitterly cold, but within, a roaring fireplace gave us cozy warmth. By some chance I turned suddenly and looked toward the window. I saw the feverish eyes of hungry peasant children – the *bezprizornii* – their little faces glued like pictures to the cold panes. Soon others followed my glance, and gave orders to a servant that the intruders be driven off. Almost every night a few of these children would succeed in eluding the sentry and sneak up to the palace in search of something to eat. I sometimes slipped out of the dining hall with bread for them, but I did this secretly because the practice was frowned upon among us. Soviet officials have developed a stereoetyped defense against human suffering: "We are on the hard road to socialism. Many must fall by the wayside. We must be well fed and must recuperate from our labors, enjoying, for a few weeks each year, comforts still denied to others, because we are the builders of a Joyous Life in the future. We are the builders of socialism. We must keep in shape to continue on the hard road. Any unfortunates who cross our path will be taken care of in due time, in the meanwhile, out of our way! If we stop to drop you a crumb, the goal itself may never be reached."[331]

The data on 1,656 waifs who were removed from trains in the Urals Region in the last nine months of 1931 are indicative of the composition of their population in terms of gender, age, class, and ethnicity: 96 percent were boys and only 4 percent were girls, two-thirds were aged eleven to fourteen years, more than one-half were from worker families and fewer than two-fifths were from peasant families, and more than four-fifths were Russians and fewer than one-tenth were Ukrainians. Also, two-thirds said that they had no parents at all, and two-thirds were runaways from children's homes.[332]

During the summer these wretched children rode the rails in order to reach Moscow and other cities and to wander the country, and – as Carveth Wells observed – begging and stealing from passengers and hawkers aboard the train and at the stations, jumping off the train just before it entered a station, hiding in nearby woods, and jumping on the train as it left, with the locals trying to knock them off.[333] On the Trans-Siberian Railway they seem to have been better treated, perhaps because so many of the passengers were foreigners and perhaps because of the traditional kind treatment of "unfortunates" (exiles) by Siberians. One passenger, the German architect Volters, en route from Moscow to Novosibirsk, remarked, "A small pack of ragged 5–10-year-old orphans accompanied us all the way [at 60 kph] on the footboards and in the boxes for tools under the cars. Some of them enjoyed the journey on the roofs of the cars." "At the stations," he added, "they bade farewell to the passengers, who, I saw, treated them well."[334] Another German, a diplomat, compassionately recollected these urchins, a "pitiable group of young boys and girls ... as resilient as they were colourful":

> Only the toughest among them could survive. Individually and in bands, they roamed the country in railway cars. At goods yards and other stops, they would build bonfires and sit around them in large groups, warming their hands before setting out in search of food. Many *besprizorniki* in Moscow would pass the night in one of the numerous large barrels that had been used to carry asphalt and which were everywhere in evidence in those years. In the late evening, one might even encounter such children sleeping in Red Square.[335]

The diplomat was often warned, however, especially by Russians, to be wary of the waifs lest they rob or even murder him. Nevertheless, he developed "a great respect for these homeless urchins, so full of life and with a remarkable capacity for endurance." He noted that many of them had lost an arm or a leg by falling from moving trains, so they lent "a sad hue to public places."

A Special Famine

Thanks to "re-education camps," he concluded, they gradually disappeared from city streets.[336]

The waifs "disappeared" because they were periodically apprehended by the militia (police) and the OGPU and placed in various shelters: orphanages, "children's homes," "feeding stations," and "medical stations," which were understaffed, underequipped, undersupplied, and "overflowing," so both death and escape rates were high. By June of 1933 there were up to 100,000 waifs in the Ukraine, for example, and they lived in "exceptionally difficult" conditions, accommodated in wooden barracks, three to four per bunk, and subject to a "very high" death rate.[337]

All of the foregoing signified the end of a way of life. The peasants – and it bears noting that at least four-fifths of the country's population was rural in the late 1920s[338] – were not only decimated but "decultured" as well. At first the muzhik could move to kinder places or seek work on construction projects and in industrial enterprises, but soon malnutrition and his lack of an internal passport made him, in the words of the Duchess of Atholl, a British relief lobbyist for famine victims, "practically a prisoner in his village, as he ha[d] no horse to travel by, and [was] not strong enough for long distance walking" and "thus he ha[d] no other way but to remain in his village and await the gradual approach of the end." Such was especially the case by the summer of 1933 in the North Caucasus:

> The fact that, in spite of the immense mortality from famine no attack of any importance is made upon the State apparatus is proof on the one hand of the strength of that apparatus, and on the other of the complete helplessness of the population. One can traverse the famine-stricken oblasts [of the North Caucasus] almost without risk, in spite of the growth of banditry, and of the countless homeless tramps [–] adults and children [–] who wander far and wide. Resigned despair and complete apathy characterize the people rather than wrath and bitterness.[339]

Rural Russia had been traumatized as well as transformed; the Russian peasantry – to many Russians, especially romantics, the "salt of the Russian earth" – had been cruelly crushed into the very soil that they had worked for centuries, and their old way of life was gone.³⁴⁰ This result has been lamented as the "depeasantization" of Russia, when "collectivization broke the backbone of the Russian people, depriving them of a caretaker of the land."³⁴¹ The transformation from "peasant" (a semi-independent and mostly subsistent cultivator) to "farmer" (an independent and mostly commercial cultivator) was incomplete, however, the peasant having simply exchanged one landlord (the gentry) for another (the state).

2
A HIDDEN FAMINE

Under the stultifying throttle of censorship they [Moscow's foreign correspondents] are obliged to limit their investigation and their expression.
– Zara Witkin, *An American Engineer in Stalin's Russia: The Memoirs of Zara Witkin, 1932–1934*, 24–5.

It was not possible to talk about the famine. It was forbidden to say that it existed.
– a Western Siberian peasant, in N.L. Lopatin and L.N. Lopatina, *Kollektivizatsiia i raskulachivanie (ochevidtsi i dokumenty svidetel'stuiut)*, doc. 134:404.

Despite its extent and severity, the great famine of 1928–34 was for quite some time little known – or not known at all – outside the USSR, and it did not attract even scholarly attention until the 1960s, a decade after Stalin's demise.[1] The silence was due to denial and deceit on the part of the Soviet authorities (including and especially the leadership), the non-admission of both Soviet and foreign scholars to the pertinent archives until the 1990s, the hoodwinking of flattered personages and artless tourists,[2] the self-delusion of fellow travellers, and the complicity of many (but not all) reporters, Soviet citizens (of various stripes) themselves, and the economically depressed Western powers. The Duchess of Atholl advised the first British ambassador to Moscow, Sir Esmond Ovey (who, a colleague noted, was "at first rather disgustingly pro-Soviet"[3]): "[a] distinctive feature of this famine is that the authorities have not acknowledged and do not acknowledge that famine exists," adding that "they even officially deny it"[4] – either because as hidebound ideologues they could not bring themselves to believe that a collective enterprise was failing or because as practical careerists they were afraid to report failure to their superiors, particularly the unforgiving trio of Stalin, Molotov, and Kaganovich.

Certainly an overarching conditioner was a scornful attitude towards the peasant on the part of the Soviet "new man," an attitude expressed by the idealistic revolutionary and writer and journalist Boris Pilnyak (the pseudonym of Boris Vogau), who is reported to have said, "Peasants always complain. They keep on whining, from the time they're born till the day they die. It has always been thus in Russia."[5] Peasants were commonly regarded as "black" or "dark," that is, benighted. The innovative filmmaker Sergei Eisenstein, the cinematic favourite of the Bolsheviks, illustrated this demonization in his 1927 film *The General Line* (re-edited and re-issued in 1929 as *Old and New*) that condemned the "100 million illiterate, dark, backward peasants" (and extolled collectivization as their salvation). The American correspondent Walter Duranty once met a "comrade" (Bolshevik loyalist) who referred to "these dumb dark peasants."[6] Duranty himself, however, and his compatriot reporters in Moscow were not immune to the same prejudice. Excited and blinded by the Bolsheviks' overdue, essential, and dazzling project to speedily transform the country, they disparaged the "Russian national character" generally and the peasantry particularly, regarding the peasant – in the words of one Bolshevik – as "little more than an animal," docile, apathetic, fatalistic, conservative, and a dispensable impediment to progress.[7] An American engineer added his voice to the chorus, declaring that peasants were "illiterate, densely ignorant, poverty stricken, and superstitious" and "pursued primitive methods of living and working."[8]

Indeed, as avowed Marxists the Bolsheviks had at best an ambivalent and at worst an antagonistic attitude towards the peasantry. Marxist theory was developed in Western Europe on the basis of industrial capitalism, not agrarian serfdom, resulting in what David Mitrany has called the "Marxist creed of proletarian supremacy," whereby the peasantry is subordinate to, and at the mercy of, the proletariat. Marxists, Mitrany wrote, "paid attention to the peasants only because they looked upon them with a dislike in which the townsman's contempt for all things rural and the economist's disapproval of small-scale production mingled with the bitterness of the revolutionary collectivist against the stubbornly individualistic tiller of the soil." "Marxism," he added, "has always justified its scorn of the peasants on the grounds, among other things, that they were brutish and could not be organized," and "Marxists have been taught to count the peasants as probably enemies rather than as possible allies."[9] Indeed, in 1928 the Bolshevik leaders were only half a dozen years removed from the violent response of many peasants to the agricultural depredations of the Red (and White) armies during the "war communism" period of 1918–21.[10] Particularly threatening had been the "Caftan War" of 1918–19 in Samara and Ufa Oblasts; the "Pitchfork Movement" of 1920–21 in Kazan, Samara, and Ufa Oblasts in the Volga Valley; the "Tambov Brotherhood" under Alexander Antonov in 1920–22 in Tambov Oblast (the country's most rural oblast [92 percent of its population]); the united uprisings of Cossacks and peasants in 1920–21 in the Altai Kray; and the Western Siberia peasant revolt of 1921, with its call for "councils without communists."[11] In this respect the famine can be viewed as part of the process of the "grinding right down" (*domolyvanie*) of all of those who offered a political alternative to the Bolsheviks – not just Ukrainian, Tambov, Volga, and Siberian peasants but Cossacks, ex-Whites, the clergy, and the aristocracy, too.[12]

So the individual farmsteader (*edinolichnik*), the least communal peasant, was especially demonized. Workers deployed to the villages during collectivization in order to guide him saw him as "an enemy of Soviet power, so one can do anything with him."[13] This prejudice was echoed by a Party inspector, who reported from the Lower Volga that "'the individual farmsteader is the enemy of Soviet power, so that one can do anything to him' – such is the view of the rural workers, although among these individual farmsteaders there are unquestionably hard-working peasants" but "they treat them all as one."[14] One such worker was the writer (and, much later, dissident) Lev Kopelev, an idealistic communist and Bolshevik activist who ashamedly acknowledged this disdain at length in his memoirs:

> In reviewing my youth ... I was proud of having been part of the events of the 1930s, which I saw as heroic high tragedy. Instead of Fate, the action was moved by [Marxist] "historical necessity," in which I believed more ardently than, as a child, I had believed in God. That is why I was proud that I had helped take bread away from peasants; that I, a twenty-year-old city know-nothing, had instructed people who had grown old farming as to how they should live, how they should work, what was good for them and what was bad. And no wonder: I had looked down on them from the pinnacle of the one, true, all-redeeming social science [Marxism]. Of course, I had never regarded them as condescendingly and inimically as did my more militant comrades, who saw these "country hicks" – especially those who did not join the kolkhoz as "cheats," "turkeys" and "Hindus" – as a pernicious kulak element or, at best, as ignorant boors lacking in class consciousness.

Kopelev added, "private property [to Marxists the fundament of capitalism] was seen by us as a wretched and despicable sin, the basis of a 'petit bourgeois outlook.' So I was convinced of my ideological superiority to the peasants and was ashamed of feeling pity while we robbed them."[15] Given this outlook, it is no wonder that the Bolsheviks had little, if any, empathy or sympathy for the peasants and their plight.

Kopelev's wife, Raisa Orlova, who accompanied him to exile in Germany in the early 1980s (his sin was having spoken and written about indiscriminate killing, raping, and looting by Red Army soldiers as they advanced victoriously westward in 1944–45), believed that the Bolshevik abuse of the peasantry stemmed from a "conception of different moralities" that had been cultivated from the beginning of the October 1917 coup d'état, a notion embodied in Lenin's declaration at the Third Congress of the Komsomol (Young Communist League) in 1920 that "whatever is useful to the proletariat is moral," a principle that he adopted from the nineteenth-century radical anarchist Sergei Nechayev[16] – just as the Bolshevik faithful would come to hold that the individual could be mistaken but not the collective. It was because of this abuse, she felt, that the sensational publication in the USSR in 1962 of Solzhenitsyn's *One Day in the Life of Ivan Denisovich*, which recounts the course of one eventful day in a Gulag *lager* (penal camp) for the peasant Ivan from a wretched kolkhoz, "aroused not only feelings of guilt over those who were imprisoned, but something more profound as well: a feeling of historical guilt over the peasant."[17]

The antipathy of the Bolsheviks towards the peasantry began with Vladimir Lenin,[18] the founder of the Soviet Union, which, ironically, proudly proclaimed itself the workers' and peasants' state.[19] The muckraking American journalist Lincoln Steffens made a three-week visit to St Petersburg in 1919 and interviewed Lenin, who, he reported, "foresaw trouble with the fixed minds of the peasants, their hard conservatism."[20] And Boris Pilnyak told another American visitor that Lenin, while talking about the peasant during a conversation with some Soviet writers, put his hand to his throat and said: "Either we choke him or he chokes us!"[21] He undoubtedly had in mind the kulak, whom he loathed as the countryside's most proficient and prosperous capitalist, the "implacable enemy."[22] In a speech in the summer of 1918 to a meeting of workers, Lenin referred to "the avaricious, bloated and bestial ku-

A Hidden Famine

laks" as "the most brutal, callous and savage exploiters," and he demanded a "ruthless war on the kulaks!" and "death to them!"[23]

Lenin's successor (although not his heir apparent), Joseph Stalin,[24] disdained both agriculture and its practitioners. Stalin's eventual confessor, Nikita Khrushchev, who called his former chief a "barbarian," stated that he "taught us to think of agriculture as a third-rate branch of our economy." He added, "For Stalin, peasants were scum. He had no respect for them or their work. He thought the only way to get farmers to produce was to put pressure on them." Furthermore, said Khrushchev (whose own parents were peasants), "Stalin considered peasants on collective farms to be like sheep whose wool has to be shorn as soon as it reaches a certain length."[25] And Stalin's second lieutenant, Lazar Kaganovich, citing Marx, asserted that the Bolsheviks had gained power "in order to deliver the peasants from 'the imbecility of village life.'"[26]

Perhaps it was this aversion to the peasants by their masters – despite their receiving hundreds, if not thousands, of damning reports from local, rayon, and regional Party and state officials and the OGPU,[27] as well as numerous pleading letters from the suffering peasants themselves, about the ravages of the famine throughout the country – that made them deny the existence of the famine. Or perhaps they were blinded by the Marxist belief that their path was historically inevitable and absolutely infallible, so that errors simply could not and would not occur. Or perhaps they believed that if errors did occur somehow, then they were justified for the sake of the advance from capitalism to communism ("Revolution is not a dinner party," went Mao Zedong's version of the Russian excuse "You can't make an omelette without breaking eggs").[28] Or perhaps as a sensitive socialist model for the rest of the world – and the world's *first* socialist state – they wanted to save face. For whatever reasons, they went to great lengths to deny and to hide the disaster.

Stalin himself actually did acknowledge the famine at its height a couple of times, albeit not directly and not fully. On one occasion he told the January 1933 Party plenum that the country's peasants had "forgotten the destruction and starvation" of the famine and "had made themselves prosperous."[29] Another occasion was a private conversation on 13 May 1933 between Stalin and Colonel Raymond Robins, an American Christian socialist and Progressive

Party member, who made bold to question the general secretary about the famine. Stalin promptly replied by blaming the starving peasants themselves for not having joined the kolkhozes in time to earn their own bread: "These peasants did join the kolkhozes," he explained, "but under our rules and our laws bread is given only for work. He who does not work does not get bread. These peasants joined the kolkhozes in winter but had not worked in the busy season [of seeding and reaping], so they did not receive any grain. For this reason some of the peasants are now starving. That is our way: whoever works can live well." He continued by denouncing the starving peasants as dependants (i.e., parasites): "They believed that if they joined the kolkhozes the state ought to provide for them ... the [other] kolkhozniks still curse them: 'One should not help loafers, let them perish ...' These are the reasons why the harvest in some places, especially the Ukraine, has not been satisfactory." Stalin added, "You will be in the south and you will see individual farmsteaders who did not join the kolkhozes ... Those peasants are starving terribly and even dying. Why has this occurred? For a year now they have refused to cultivate. They had hoped to steal grain and live on the stolen grain. But to us it is very bad to steal. They have got used to living this way because they do not respect public property."[30] Stalin acknowledged the famine privately again on 9 September 1940, when at a meeting of the Party's Central Committee during a discussion of Avdeenko's film of Jack London's *The Law of Life* he said that, during collectivization, "25–30 million of us [excluding himself and other worthies, of course], for example, starved, there was not enough grain, but now we have come to live well."[31] His comments were not published, however, and another half-century would pass before the famine could be mentioned in print.[32]

At the time of the famine, then, Stalin was well aware of its existence as he had received many reports about its occurrence from various officials and quarters; for example, a long letter (marked "secret") about its ravages in Kazakhstan from a top official there[33] and even an oral account from his wife, Nadezhda Alliluyeva, of instances of cannibalism and trafficking in human flesh that had been related to her by students at the Institute of the National Economy.[34] Stalin simply either disregarded or dismissed the reports. On one occasion he resorted to mockery. At a meeting in Moscow at the end of 1932, for instance, the secretary of the Central Committee of the Ukrainian Communist Party, Roman Terekhov, mentioned to Stalin the desperate situation of the starving villages in the Kharkov Rayon and requested the dispatch of grain to them but was interrupted and sarcastically humiliated by his boss: "We've been told, Comrade Terekhov, that you are a good speaker but it seems you are a good storyteller, too – you have concocted this tale of famine and thought to intimidate us, but it won't work! Wouldn't it be better for you to leave the post of secretary of the oblast committee and of the central committee of the Party and go to work at the Writer's Union? Then you can write your fairy tales and fools will read them."[35] Two weeks later Terekhov, one of the few "old Bolsheviks" from the peasantry, was removed from his position.

Ordinarily Stalin and his inner circle[36] blamed any shortcomings on "class enemies" ("counter-revolutionaries" or "anti-Soviet elements"), "wreckers" ("saboteurs"), or "idlers" ("slackers") in the countryside – officials or peasants – who did not deserve to eat or to live.[37] In his speech of 19 February 1933 to the First All-Union Congress of Collective Farm Shock Brigaders he reminded his audience of the words of Lenin, "our great teacher" (who in turn was quoting St Paul): "He who does not work, neither shall he eat," words aimed at "exploiters" and "loafers" (in the countryside the kulaks, "who do not work themselves, but compel others to work for them, and get rich at the expense of others," and in the towns the Nepmen, the private traders who proliferated during the NEP period) and idlers, "who loaf and want to live at the expense of others [in the countryside the protesting peasantry]."[38] Again, in several letters to Stalin from 1931 to 1933 the Don Cossack novelist Mikhail Sholokhov complained of the want of grain on the lower Don for food, feed, and seed. In one letter of 4 April 1933 he wrote: "In this rayon, as in others [of the North Caucasus], collective farmers and individual farmsteaders are now dying of hunger; adults and children are swelling and are feeding on everything that a person ought not to live on, starting with carrion and ending with oak bark and all sorts of marsh roots." In his reply a month later Stalin thanked Sholokhov for bringing such "shocking things" to his attention but stressed that the novelist had seen only one side of the matter and that it was necessary for him to see the other: "And the other side consists of the fact that the esteemed peasant cultivators of your rayon (and not only your rayon) have conducted an 'Italian' (sabotage!) and have been quite willing to leave the workers and the Red Army without grain. The fact that the sabotage was quiet and outwardly inoffensive (bloodless) does not change the fact that the esteemed peasant cultivators essentially conducted a 'quiet' war against Soviet power."[39]

Vyacheslav Molotov (pseudonym of Skryabin), Stalin's right-hand man, shared the viewpoint of his boss, Koba, as he was known to his inner circle. Late in life Molotov told an interviewer that the allegations of famine were "absurd" for he had travelled to the Ukraine (twice), the Urals, and parts of Siberia at the time and "saw nothing of the kind," adding that starvation "couldn't have just escaped [him]." He did admit that "deaths had been reported of course in some places" but asserted that the famine death figures were "an exaggeration" and "ha[d] not been substantiated," while only "enemies of communism" had contended that the famine was deliberate."[40] Lazar Kaganovich (pseudonym of Kogan), Stalin's other right-hand man, also did not acknowledge the famine. In speaking to the same interviewer as had Molotov, he did not once mention the famine, nor did he do so in his own memoirs.[41]

On the other hand, Nikolai Bukharin, the editor of first *Pravda* and then *Izvestiya* who, after Leon Trotsky's exile in 1929, was Stalin's chief rival for power (and who advocated a much more lenient policy towards the peasants), was quite aware of the famine, according to his wife, Anna Larina: "At the time of the collectivization in 1930, when he was traveling through the Ukraine, he saw packs of children begging for alms at the little local stations, their stomachs swollen from hunger. Nikolai Ivanovich gave them all his money. When he got back to Moscow, he stopped by to see my father, told him about the trip, cried out, 'If more than ten years after the revolution one can see such things as this, what was the point of doing it?,' collapsed on the couch, and sobbed hysterically."[42] Bukharin did not, however, see fit to confront Stalin about the famine or even resign from the Party, such was his faith in the rightness of the almighty revolution.

Regional officials – provincial (*oblast*), territorial (*krai*), rayon (*raion*), and local (city [*gorod*] and village [*derevnya*]) – denied the famine, too, likely mainly out of fear: fear of losing face, or fear of losing their positions of privilege (better rations, higher salaries, and greater prestige), or worse (prison, exile, or even execution) if they were to admit to making mistakes or failing to produce. In the spring of 1933 a physician in Kiev Oblast reported that the year before "it was impossible to even talk about famine, 'timidity' reigned

A Hidden Famine

supreme. Given such 'timidity,' of course, very little was done." "This year, too," he added, "[up to the beginning of March] to talk about famine is considered almost counter-revolutionary."[43] Otto Schiller told a colleague several times about his visits to villages in the company of local Soviet administrators who were complicit in the conspiracy of silence, forbidding any public discussion of the famine. If the peasants asked the officials for bread, they would simply not answer; if the peasants asked about the scale of the famine, the same officials would reply: "You must fulfill the plan and do what the Party has ordered and everything will then be all right." Such officials, said Schiller, "simply refused to acknowledge that the famine existed."[44] Some of them even tried to disprove its existence by misleading their superiors with deceitful information. Peter Kulagin, an OGPU chief in Leningrad, confided to the British ambassador in the summer of 1932 that many lower officials submitted favourable reports about agricultural production that they knew to be untrue "because they have not the courage to report the fact, so that the Kremlin never really knows what the situation is."[45] Consequently, as unlikely as it may seem, it is possible that the Bolshevik leadership was not *fully* aware of the severity of the peasant's situation.[46]

Apparently some lesser Party members in the countryside, appalled by what they witnessed, were fully aware and said as much. One such was an N. Zhivanov, who wrote bluntly to Ukrainian Party secretary Stanislav Kosior (or Kossior) at the end of 1932:

> Open your eyes to the reality of what you – tacit slaves of Moscow – have created with your policy. For two years now you have ruined the Ukraine and agriculture ... We have finally ruined Ukrainian agriculture, not to mention the collective farms. The collective farmers say bluntly that it is Polish landlordism. But Polish landlordism never reduced the village to such a state as we have these past two years. The peasant has been turned into a starving pauper, and on the collective farm they give soup only to those who work, and the elderly and the children are condemned to death from starvation, provided they have managed not to die this winter; we have completely undermined the defensive capability of our country. The Red Army is our strength, but a child or a father of every Red Army soldier has died of starvation. Ukrainian communists are ignorant of the work of the masses and are

gendarmes in the village. They have provided all of the conditions for Polish landlordism and kulakism. The basis for counter-revolution has increased 95% and for the Party 5%.

He added, "In 1930 our collective farmers struggled miraculously and heroically for grain. But in the last two years the Party has completely opposed itself to the village. We have incurred heartless management and silent mockery, with no concern for the collective farmer."[47] Zhivanov's fate is unknown (but not that of Kosior, who was to be shot in 1939).

For most officials, however, it was easier and safer to blame the peasants themselves. Indeed, on the rare occasions when officials did acknowledge the famine, their usual explanation was that the starving peasants refused to work, and "he who does not work does not eat" was a Bolshevik mantra. A physician at a Kiev hospital, Doctor P. Blonsky, found that "very widespread among managers and ordinary workers is the politically harmful 'theory' that the starving themselves are to blame for the famine, that they [the starving] said that they did not want to work, and, that being the case, they [the managers and the workers] say that even if they die they do not feel pity [for them]."[48] Some officials, too, felt that the lofty and noble goals of the plan were worth any sacrifice, including millions of starving citizens. In November 1933 at a meeting of the workers of the Elektrozavod factory in Moscow the Party secretary told an American specialist in reply to his charge that peasants in the Volga Valley were starving: "Don't worry that you saw people dying of hunger. If twenty millions die of hunger, we will still have plenty of people to continue our work. And what does it matter if millions of people die, as long as we are building Socialism?"[49] The Bolsheviks under Stalin, in other words, were simply blinded to reality and morality by ideology. When, wrote Lev Kopelev, "he [Stalin] said: 'The struggle for grain is the struggle for socialism' ... we believed him unconditionally."[50] This obduracy was expressed by the poet and novelist Marietta Shaginyan, who described herself as an "eternal optimist," but even she had lost faith in the system by the spring of 1932:

> Explain to me, she asks [the Chekist Yakov] Serebryansky and [the artist Vasily] Yermilov (we are all sitting together), why sixteen years after the revolution we have been brought to this state ... I was just in Leningrad. Do you know that famine typhus has erupted there, as in 1920? ... I

was always able to see ... in everything new the movement towards socialism. Now I have lost it. We are overstuffed with ideology. Once we became used to varnishing and rationalizing everything, we lost the feel of the real facts of life.[51]

Cultural as well as political leaders were culpable. Admittedly, all writers and artists were subject to censorship, which was rationalized by the commissar of education (and literary critic and dramatist) Anatoly Lunacharsky in a 1927 article entitled "On the Place of the Writer in the State": "Of course, when we [as the world's first socialist state] are surrounded by enemies, it is not possible to exist without censorship."[52] The intelligentsia cooperated and even collaborated with the authorities either because they could not bring themselves to believe that their political overlords were really capable of such evil-doing or because they were simply determined to save themselves and keep their privileges (special rations, access to writers' clubs, clinics, and spas, leave to travel abroad, etc.) or because they believed that they were still serving art, literature, or science and Mother Russia, not Stalin and the Party. Few were immune to these sentiments. The popular Don Cossack writer Mikhail Sholokhov, smarting from criticism by Bolshevik leaders over his even-handed treatment of Reds and Whites during the civil war in his epic *Quiet Flows the Don*, responded with *Virgin Soil Upturned*, a propagandistic treatment of collectivization.[53] One of the foremost of the Soviet Union's literati, Kornei Chukovsky, a literary critic and a popular writer of literature for children, especially poetry, did not once mention the famine in the 1928–34 entries of his rather fragmented and spare diary (admittedly, it would have been risky to do so had he wished). He did mention the kolkhoz, which in 1929 he deemed "the sole savior of Russia, the sole *solution* to the country's peasant question!," adding, "within ten years a millennium of Russian peasant culture will be radically different, will be re-born magically, and life therein will have become happier than the [nineteenth-century] Populists could ever have imagined – and all thanks to kolkhozes." He ended by predicting that "by 1950 the productivity of the kolkhoz village will increase fourfold."[54] One wonders whether Chukovsky ever visited a kolkhoz in his lifetime. Finally, in the autumn of 1930, while being shaved in Leningrad, his barber told him that he had fled the Ukraine, leaving his wife and daughter there, and then he suddenly exclaimed "hysterically" that "there we see the destruction of humanity," adding, "I know, I think, that you serve in the GPU, but I don't care – the destruction of humanity is occurring there."[55] Chukovsky, apparently, did not ask the barber what he meant.

Perhaps the most flagrant literary example of culpability, however, is that of Maxim Gorky, a politically opportunistic writer who spent much of his life abroad. Famously sympathetic to the underclass, he nevertheless despised the peasantry. In his 1922 booklet *On the Russian Peasantry* Gorky described "the half-savage, stupid, ponderous people of the Russian villages and hamlets" as conservative, ignorant, cruel, cunning, uncreative, untruthful, suspicious, and fatalistic – brutish obstacles to progress who had to be removed or reshaped.[56] According to Andrey Platonov, who nowadays is considered one of the most original and creative Soviet writers of the Stalin period but was unsung at the time, Gorky once said, "You'll pardon my saying so, but the peasant is not yet human … He's our enemy, our enemy."[57] And, Gorky wrote, "if an enemy does not surrender, he must be exterminated."[58] So he was indifferent to the plight of this "enemy of the people." Although he had sought relief for the starving in the famine of 1921–22, Gorky stood aloof from that of 1928–34, despite being made aware of the tragedy by letters from its victims.[59] And when one of his son's friends, appalled by the famine's impact in the Ukraine, begged the famous father to bring it to the attention of the country's leaders – to whom he had access – Gorky became very angry, accused her of lying, and told her to stop spreading enemy propaganda.[60]

On the other hand, some literary notables did acknowledge the famine in their work – and suffered accordingly. The "peasant" poet Nikolai Klyuev (1887–1937) was a native of the Olonets area in the Russian North, one of the centres of the Russian epic tradition and of the Old Believer faith. He was arrested in 1933 for "idealizing" the kulak class and deported to Siberia, where he was executed. One of the reasons for his prosecution was his writing and reading at secret gatherings (which sooner or later included informers) of his masterpiece, "Burnt Ruins" (never published in the Soviet Union), an epic poem depicting the rape of his beloved Russian village by new "Saracens" (Stalinists) and a "dragon" (Stalin). He wrote:

October, a lean wolf bitch,
Gnaws at the forest icon shelf
While ovens long for loaves
And dismay gropes through threshing barns

For a pinch of mother-flour.
Eel pouts have left the lake;
Yoke leather and harness loops. Fur boots and bark have been devoured,
Yet bellies still ache with hunger

...

Sigovets was captured by a dragon,
And blue-eyed Vasyatka was salted in a vat by his own parents.

...

The day chirped with sparrows
When they called the boy into the yard –
As if for mushroom hunting.
For the smack of beef and kidney
My neighbor dressed out his son,
Sprinkling gray salt
Along his bird-like ribs and sinews.
The old woman scrubbed the blood
From the log beneath the beam.
And later – like a fox in a trap –
She wailed in the closet.
Terrible were the old woman's wails –
Shifting from lullabies
To the clicking calls of magpies.[61]

The Acmeist poet Osip (Mandelshtam in Russian) Mandelstam (1891–1938),[62] one of the galaxy of poets of Russian literature's own Silver Age (1890s–early 1920s), met the same fate. His epiphany was triggered by a visit in May 1933 to "starving Old Crimea," where he saw "the starving peasants," "fearsome shadows cast from the Kuban and Ukraine," in the words of his poem "Stary Krim" (Old Crimea).[63] The peninsula was "overrun with fugitives – 'terrible wraiths from the Ukraine, Kuban.'" In Koktebel Mandelstam bought milk to give to the begging young children of a Ukrainian refugee. "This particular family," his wife recalled, "were not even victims of the campaign against the kulaks. They had simply joined in the headlong flight with everybody else. In the Ukraine and the Kuban the famine had raged unchecked and whole villages had died. Many of those who fled fared no better and simply perished by the roadside."[64] Upon his return to Moscow Mandelstam could not bear to remain silent any longer, and in November he sealed his fate by penning a sixteen-line poem attacking Stalin (the "murderer and peasant slayer" and "Kremlin highlander" [i.e., man of the Caucasus Mountains] for whom "every killing is a treat") and reciting it to some friends, one of whom betrayed him to the OGPU, which then arrested and deported him to a penal camp in the Soviet Far East (he died en route).[65]

Two other luminaries of literature, the poet and novelist Boris Pasternak (1890–1960) and the Russian Jewish journalist, short-story writer, and translator Isaac Babel (1894–1940), were also aware of the famine but did not protest publicly. Pasternak, who would decline the 1958 Nobel Prize in Literature for fear of falling further into official disfavour, was sickened by what he saw in the countryside:

> In the early 1930s it became fashionable among writers to travel to the collective farms and gather material about the new Soviet village. I wanted to be like everyone else, and so I set out on such a trip with the idea of writing a book. What I saw there cannot be conveyed in words, any words. There was such inhuman, unimaginable misery, it was such a terrible disaster, that it began to seem almost abstract, beyond the bounds that the conscious mind could admit. I felt ill. For an entire year I could not write.[66]

So traumatized was Pasternak by collectivization that at a conference in Paris in the summer of 1935 he told some correspondents that "only God can save Russia."[67] In print he did at least manage to have a character in his epic novel *Doctor Zhivago* say that collectivization was a mistake and a failure,[68] although the book was first published abroad in 1957 and not in the Soviet Union until the late 1980s.

The awakening of Babel, probably the country's most celebrated writer, apparently did not occur until late 1933. In the fall of that year he was sent to the Ukraine and the North Caucasus on a writing assignment. After leaving the Ukraine and reaching Nalchik in the North Caucasus, he said to his wife: "The bounty of the past is gone – it is due to the famine in [the] Ukraine and the destruction of the village across our land."[69] Babel once confided to a friend that what he saw in the Ukrainian countryside was "more horrifying than anything he had encountered during the civil war," whose brutality and violence he had vividly described in his acclaimed cycle of stories, *Red Cavalry*, and he retained from his visits to Ukrainian villages "the sharpest memory of all [his] life."⁷⁰ He began to write *The Great Krinitsa*, a collection of stories about a village (where "no dogs dare to bark") in the Kiev Rayon in the throes of collectivization, but it was left unfinished when he was arrested as a "Trotskyist" and "foreign spy" and executed in 1940 in Moscow's infamous Butyrka Prison.⁷¹

One Soviet writer of the 1920s–1930s did write a lot about collectivization, although allegorically, but little of it – unsurprisingly – was published at the time. Andrei Klimentov (1899–1951), who came from a poor peasant family, adopted the pseudonym "Platonov" in honour of both his father and the Hellenic philosopher. As a youth he was a passionate supporter of the October Revolution and a staunch believer in the new world of communism to be constructed rationally. The famine of 1921–22 shocked him, and afterwards he devoted himself to land reclamation work before resuming his writing in 1928 and experiencing collectivization first-hand between 1929 and 1932, when he was sent on several tours of inspection of kolkhozes in central and southern European Russia by the Commissariat of Agriculture.⁷² He penned a number of scathing satirical works, including four about the absurdities and tragedies of collectivization: the 1930 novel *The Foundation Pit*, a surreal satire about a team of workers who dig a foundation for a huge home for the working class, but the more they work, the more things go wrong, and the pit becomes a grave for both workers and peasants;⁷³ the 1930 play *The Hurdy-Gurdy* (or *The Organ Grinder*), a black comedy about collectivization; *Benefit: A Poor Man's Chronicle*, which was published in 1931 with the censored passages mistakenly not deleted but printed in boldface, thereby earning Stalin's condemnation as a "kulak's chronicle" and its author as "scum"; and the 1932 play *Fourteen Little Red Huts*, which savagely lampoons the horrors of collectivization at a village in Central Asia. In that dystopian portrayal the kolkhoz manager is named Futilla (futility?) and two writers Latrinov (latrine?) and Glutonov (glutton?); an elderly kolkhoznik says, "Our salted beef, and the grain that belongs to us poor peasants, in the patched-up sacks – that's all gone out to sea in our ship too, towards the far shore of Imperialism [i.e., exported to capitalist Western countries]"; a very old touring foreign savant named Bos (probably representing George Bernard Shaw, who derided the notion of famine in the USSR when he visited it on the occasion of his seventy-fifth birthday), tells the manager, "Thank you for your hospitality. I've had a nice meal of desert grass"; the elderly kolkhoznik Topov (from *topit'*, "to wreck"?) tells Bos, "They're [i.e., the kolkhozniks] gnawing at one another – it's worse than tears. Hunger never makes the people weep, they sink their teeth into one another and die of rage." Whereupon Bos asks him, "What about you? Don't you want to eat?," and Topov replies, "No, what keeps me alive is [class] consciousness. You can't stay alive here from food, can you?" And then a peasant woman tells the manager, "Futilla, there's no food – the men are all collapsing. Anton's throwing up – he's eaten some poisonous herb," and the manager replies, "They should have protected our grain and our sheep from kulaks. Let them suffer now – it'll teach them a scientific [i.e., Marxist] lesson."[74] Nearly all of Platonov's score of works remained unpublished in his country in his lifetime. He somehow survived his literary effrontery, predeceasing Stalin by two years, likely dying of tuberculosis contracted from his son, who, as a teenager, had been sentenced to the Gulag for anti-Soviet agitation and had caught the disease there before being released in 1941. Since the publication of his works after the collapse of the USSR, Platonov has been acclaimed as one of the most gifted writers of the Soviet period.[75]

Surprisingly, some of the foreign reporters in Moscow seem to have been as unaware of the famine as were many Soviet citizens, who were kept in the dark by their own press and radio, which not so much denied the disaster as left it unwritten and unspoken. Foreign citizens were also kept in the dark because foreign correspondents in the USSR were tightly controlled by the Soviet authorities, so much so that in recalling his dozen years of reportage from Moscow William Chamberlin said that he was "impressed by the number of important events which either were never reported abroad or were described in such evasive fashion as to convey no real idea of what was happening." As an example he cited the famine peak of 1932–33 that "was so deliberately concealed from foreign journalistic observers that many Soviet apologists denied its authenticity."[76] As a French correspondent, Pierre Berlan of *Le Temps*, France's leading daily paper, explained to his readers at that time:

> A catastrophe that even the blind could have foreseen and that we forecast here already more than a year ago (*TAN*, 31 May 1932) has befallen the country. The silence of the press about this [event] is one of the

more curious phenomena of contemporary Russia. A kind of conspiracy of silence surrounds the food situation, whose catastrophic character, however, appears to be an open secret. Naïve people in Paris or elsewhere, even if they studied the Soviet press thoroughly, could not dare to say that they learned anything from it. The official censor is the head of the telegraph, who relentlessly distorts the telegrams of foreign correspondents and permits only euphemistic expressions, such as "serious food difficulties," which are telltale enough for those who know Soviet Russia but appear as dissimulations of the first order by comparison with the actual situation.[77]

All of the foreign correspondents had to labour under the vigilant scrutiny of the Soviet censor, Konstantin Umansky, a brilliant linguist and a long-time correspondent of TASS, the Soviet news agency, who in 1931 had joined the Press Department of the Commissariat of Foreign Affairs of the USSR, which, like all revolutionary governments, was extremely sensitive to publicity, especially of the unfavourable sort. Umansky, who was later to become Soviet ambassador to Washington, had the power to revoke an uncooperative correspondent's accreditation and even to expel him or her. Before foreign press dispatches were submitted to, and accepted by, the one window in the sole telegraph office in Moscow that was authorized to transmit them, they required the signature and the seal of the Press Department, their "precise wording having been bargained over, passages deleted, and compromise formulas found for telling the news while blurring its meaning."[78] So, concluded Eugene Lyons, owing to inertia, procrastination, and a desire to keep their jobs, the capital's foreign reporters shamefacedly colluded with the government's concealment of the famine by simply not writing about it or referring to it obliquely and vaguely in circumlocutions.[79] They also laboured under their own prejudices, most of them having leftist sympathies (initially, at least) and being loath to criticize the noble Bolshevik project of a utopian society.[80]

If, however, the correspondents were to cover the famine, then it behooved them to go to the famine-struck regions (preferably by automobile, which afforded more mobility than the train) and see it for themselves – or else remain in relatively comfortable Moscow and depend upon Soviet press propaganda. The former, journalistically responsible alternative, however, was rendered unattractive (and unacceptable to some) by a number of weighty obstacles, including dissuasion on the part of the Soviet authorities (and even their own embassies), the necessity of a working knowledge of the Russian language (or, failing that, the hiring of an expensive and watchful translator), the lack of road maps, the crude state of the roads or even their absence, the shortage of gasoline, the scarcity of food en route, the want of hotels off the main roads, and bedbug-infested quarters (hotels and izbas). Journalist Rhea Clyman overcame these challenges in the summer of 1932, even though the British ambassador had recently attempted a short excursion by car and had been forced to return for want of fuel, and the night before her departure the British Embassy (responsible for Canadian citizens) had called to dissuade her from the "foolhardy venture." Walter Duranty of the *New York Times* also warned her against going (and he added that he had already written her obituary but assured her that it was a flattering memorial). Comrade Umansky's Press Department told her: "You'll be back in Moscow within a week. There are no roads. You won't get any gasoline, and there are no hotels on the route that you are following. You can't live without your hot bath and three meals a day. You'll come running back to Moscow when you feel the first bedbug bite!"[81] But Clyman persisted and endured the "swarming" bedbugs in her peasant quarters and the "untold tortures" of black bread made from corn chaff and straw, completing an eventful and revealing month-long journey from the capital to Tbilisi that she described the next year in a series of fifteen articles in a Toronto daily. She also advised anyone wanting to tour the Soviet "famineland" to choose the least comfortable but most informative mode of travel:

> If you want to hear the true voice of Russia, go for a trip on a train: not in the deluxe first-class carriage, where commissars and foreigners ride, nor in the second-class (soft) compartments where "responsible workers" take up so much room, but in the third and fourth-class wagons; that is where the real truth is told.
>
> The people pile in as thick as ticks on a sheep's wool, with their household furniture and goods stuffed in a sack on their back, a tea kettle and slab of black bread tied in a handkerchief, and once the wheels start moving, tongues are loosened and the barriers of restraint and fear are let down.[82]

Not only were intimidating officials, police, or political activists absent from the "hard" cars but the higher volume of train noise shielded conversations.

The conditions for journalists were so adverse that it was not until the midpoint of the climax of the famine that Moscow's foreign press corps became aware of its existence and undertook to report it.[83] In the summer of 1932, Eugene Lyons filed a dispatch (by telephone to UPI's London office from Berlin) about the eviction and deportation of some forty thousand inhabitants of three Cossack *stanitsas* (large villages) in the Kuban Valley. Early the next year Lyons's Russian secretary spotted a mention in a Rostov-on-Don newspaper of a lack of food there; however, since he was bound to his Moscow office by UPI policy, Lyons told two colleagues, whose employers encouraged them to travel: Ralph Barnes of the New York *Herald Tribune* and William Stoneman of the Chicago *Daily News*. With their interpreter they went by train to Rostov-on-Don and witnessed the famine horror in the city's southern hinterland for nearly two weeks before being intercepted by the OGPU, but they had scored their scoop, which they dispatched via two German furriers returning to Berlin (Barnes's account began with the words "hunger and terror stalking southern Russia").[84] Their indiscretion prompted a crackdown by the Soviet authorities. In the middle of February of 1933, Stalin complained to Kaganovich and Molotov about snooping in the Kuban by American reporters and decreed: "it is necessary to put an end to this and to forbid these gentlemen from travelling around the USSR," adding that "there are so many spies in the USSR."[85] On 23 February foreign reporters were forbidden to leave Moscow without submitting a detailed itinerary and securing official approval. Then, in the middle of March, attention was temporarily diverted from the famine by the sensational show trial of six English and eleven Russian engineers at Metropolitan Vickers, a British electrical engineering company, on charges of espionage, "wrecking" (sabotage), and bribery.[86]

Meanwhile, another foreign reporter, Malcolm Muggeridge, had made his way to the south in early February by having the Russian wife of a colleague (the wittily cynical Alfred Cholerton, who loathed the Soviet regime) buy him a train ticket to Rostov-on-Don. Then he sent his dispatch via the British Embassy's diplomatic pouch in order to avoid the censor, and in three "heavily sub-edited" articles at the end of March in the *Manchester Guardian* he recounted his "nightmare memory" of "abandoned villages, the absence of livestock, neglected fields; everywhere famished, frightened people and intimations of coercion, soldiers about the place, and hard-faced men in long overcoats."[87]

These reports afforded only glimpses of the famine, however. More detailed and more reliable exposés came first from Gareth Jones, a Welsh student of both Nazi German and Soviet Russian affairs and a freelance cub reporter who had already visited the USSR twice (in 1930 and 1931).[88] He arrived on his third visit in early March of 1933, talked to Muggeridge (who apprised him of the starvation in the steppeland of "South Russia"), and resolved to ignore the travel ban and visit the Central Black Earth and the Ukraine to see for himself. Unlike many other Russia-bound journalists, Jones possessed both a diplomatic passport and a command of Russian, so he was able to tour unescorted; also, not being one of the accredited resident correspondents in Moscow, he was not subject to their restrictions. But even after journalists were banned by the authorities from travelling to the countryside, he would simply "take a train, not knowing my destination, drop out at some small station and walk for miles until I was in the Real Russia," for "if I had asked for a railway ticket to a village it would have been politely refused me," so "the only thing to do was to take a ticket to a big city and drop out of the train in a small station without any one noticing me." Once in the countryside, Jones continued, "I wandered alone on foot through a number of Russian villages, sleeping on [the] hard floors of peasants' huts, and speaking to the rank and file of the real folk, to the 'forgotten men,' in their own language, Russian." "And then," he added, "I learned from the mouths of the peasants themselves why there is not enough soup."[89] Taking his own food (bought in US dollars at the capital's *valyutny gastronom* [foreign currency grocery], which still existed in the mid-1960s), Jones visited a score of villages on foot in the vicinity of Moscow, the Central Black Earth, and the Ukraine ("parts of which are far from being the most badly hit in Russia"). Two recurrent cries of the peasants formed the leitmotif of his journey: *khleba netu* (there's no bread) and *vse pukhly* (everyone's swollen). He also collected evidence from "peasants [arriving in the cities in search of bread] and foreign observers and residents" – including up to thirty foreign consuls and diplomatic representatives – about the Ukraine, the Crimea, the North Caucasus, the Nizhny-Novgorod rayon, Western Siberia, Kazakhstan, the Tashkent rayon, and the areas of the Ukrainian and Volga Germans. Jones concluded

A Hidden Famine

that the famine had been caused primarily by collectivization and "the peasants' hatred of it." After leaving the Soviet Union in late March, he summarized his findings in an uncensored letter from Danzig: "The Russian situation is absolutely terrible, famine almost everywhere, and millions are dying of starvation."[90]

Meanwhile, Jones's startling revelations were being corroborated by another reporter, correspondent William Chamberlin,[91] whose wife and travelling companion, like Jones, enjoyed the advantage of fluency in Russian, although, unlike Jones, they did not travel rough. Nevertheless, as Chamberlin himself asserted:

> I saw much more of the Russian village than the average correspondent. The *Monitor* was more receptive than most newspapers would have been to mail [i.e., posted] articles describing the everyday life of the people and the new social and economic conditions in the countryside,[92] and I scarcely let any year pass without at least one long trip into the vast Russian rural hinterland. Thanks to Sonya's native knowledge of Russian, I was able from the beginning to get on without [the] benefit of interpreters living in the shadow of the Gay-Pay-Oo. At the time of our first trip ... I knew extremely little Russian ... [but] later I was able to take a more active part in talking with the peasants myself, and I have always considered these trips as one of my most valuable sources of Russian information. They were without any element of official stage management or junketing. We simply picked out a promising region, obtained some conventional credentials from the Commissariat for Foreign Affairs and went off by ourselves.[93]

Right after the ban on unauthorized travel to the countryside was revoked in September 1933, the Chamberlins took a three-week tour of the Ukraine and the North Caucasus. In the Ukraine's Poltava and Cherkass Rayons they went "cross-country walking" in order to shake their guides and talk alone to the peasants, and by staying at the German agricultural concession of "Drusag" in the North Caucasus they again evaded the official guides and found the huge farm to be "an oasis of order and plenty in a desert of surrounding unkempt neglected fields."[94] Chamberlin found the area's gardens and fields choked with weeds and the Cossack villages "ghostly quiet," the formerly numerous and "fierce, snapping dogs, trained to guard sheep and cattle," having starved to death or been eaten.[95] Probably because peasant resistance to collectivization was stiffer here than elsewhere – for many of the peasants were Cossacks, who had enjoyed a higher standard of living than other peasants before 1917 and who had mostly fought with the reviled Whites during the civil war – *kraikom* (territorial Party committee) secretary Boris Sheboldayev, who had "a reputation for cruelty in 'liquidating' kulaks in the lower Volga rayon," was put in charge, and under him entire villages were deported en masse to the far north in the dead of winter, while other villages were "blockaded" in order to prevent urban supplies from reaching them. His methods, Chamberlin found, "turned what would otherwise perhaps have been a hunger into a famine, and they left a diseased and weakened population (there was a tremendous epidemic of malignant malaria in the Kuban Valley in 1933) and a ravaged and devastated countryside which will require years of reconstruction before it can hope to regain its former prosperity."[96] Chamberlin concluded that, as far as he could "observe and learn from reliable information," the famine regions included the Ukraine, the North Caucasus, parts of the Middle and Lower Volga, and much of Kazakhstan, while northern and central European Russia and Siberia "suffered a good deal of hardship and undernourishment, but not actual famine."[97]

Gareth Jones's exposés were confirmed, too, by another Russian-speaking reporter, the Russian-born socialist Harry Lang of New York's *Jewish Daily Forward*. During a year's world tour of nineteen countries, he and his Ukrainian-born wife in the late fall of 1933 visited Leningrad, Moscow, Kharkov, Kiev, and Minsk, and they "traveled extensively off the beaten track" in the Ukraine and Belorussia, where they witnessed "the harvest of famine, the crop of death." A high Soviet official in the Ukraine told him confidentially that 6 million of that republic's inhabitants had starved to death in 1932–33. It was in Belorussia, however, where he found that "the pall of hunger and terror was heaviest"; his wife felt that in its capital of Minsk she "was in the world's lowest depths." Even in privileged Leningrad "there was hunger for milk as well as for bread; for kerosene as well as butter; for paper as well as for meat; and even for cloth to make shrouds for the dead."[98]

The famine exposés were downplayed, doubted, or even denied by a few reporters, most infamously by the canny Walter Duranty of the *New York Times*.[99] His euphemistic description in an oft-cited dispatch to his news-

A Hidden Famine

paper of 30 March 1933 – "There is no actual starvation but there is widespread mortality from diseases due to malnutrition" – became among Moscow's foreign press corps the classic example of journalistic understatement (more correctly, euphemistic dissembling), and to Eugene Lyons it epitomized the "shabby episode" of the failure of the capital's foreign newshounds to report the famine honestly instead of withholding, minimizing, and even rejecting its existence.[100] William Chamberlin regarded Duranty as "a consistent apologist for every case of *Schrecklichkeit* [terrorization], on the argument, rather trite through overuse, that one couldn't make an omelet without breaking eggs."[101] In the fall of 1932 he reported that "the food shortage must be regarded as a result of peasant resistance to rural socialization, or, perhaps, more accurately, as a result of measures taken to overcome that resistance."[102] It was not until the travel restrictions on foreign reporters were rescinded in September of 1933 – after the worst of the famine was over in the wake of a bumper harvest, thanks to extremely favourable spring and summer weather and the deployment of Red Army guards in the fields – that Duranty made his epiphanous trip to the Ukrainian steppe and then belatedly acknowledged the starvation, at least privately, but publicly he would state only that "the cost has been heavy in lives and human suffering."[103] By then, however, the *New York Times* had scooped its own correspondent by reprinting a Paris *Le Matin* account by a Russian-born American couple who had visited their native villages in the Ukraine in the summer of 1933 and were "horror-stricken" to find "everybody ... suffering from swollen legs ... the result of malnutrition in a country where the harvests had been good," and "all dying of starvation."[104]

Expatriates, heads of state, celebrities, tourists, and fellow travellers were equally gullible and equally capable of rationalizing their myopia and excusing Soviet "excesses."[105] This behaviour was particularly unpardonable on the part of expats, who were usually fluent in Russian and familiar with the country and its people. Perhaps the most famous – or infamous – was Maurice Hindus, who had been born and raised in the last decade of the nineteenth century in Belorussia in what he called "a village where time stopped," one of eleven children whose kulak father's death in 1905 had impoverished the family and prompted it to immigrate to the United States. There he worked as a farmhand to finance his education and became a freelance writer and lecturer. *Century Magazine* sent him to the Soviet Union to study the socialist experiment, especially farm life, and he returned to his native village to see for himself the transformation of the countryside by collectivization (the sympathetic grassroots result was *Red Bread* [1931], one of his twenty books about Soviet Russia). Muggeridge met Hindus and described him as "an American of Russian-Jewish extraction with black curly hair and a winning smile."[106] To Lyons he was one of "the most industrious apologists for Stalin."[107] Hindus believed that the Russian peasant was so resistant to change ("they would take no chances with a new way lest it prove a failure and they lose their grain") that, "clearly, coaxing and persuasion would need to be supplemented by no small amount of compulsion."[108] Even with the benefit of a decade of hindsight he was still able to condone the social and economic costs of compulsory collectivization. In 1938, while admitting that in parts of the country, especially the North Caucasus and the Ukraine, "the reckless generalship of the early years of collectivization had led to endless misfortunes that finally culminated in the famine of 1932–33" and that "the stupidity, incompetence, the sheer villainy of the bureaucracy ha[d] been a prolific cause of mishap and often enough of horror," he nevertheless concluded that, "in spite of its enormous cost in substance and in human and animal life, collectivization in my judgment constitutes the most triumphant achievement of the Revolution" and that "the collectives are the Magna Charta [*sic*] and the Bill of Rights of the new order in the Russian village" and "are so firmly intrenched [*sic*] that they have become an organic part not only of the new and still enormously crude civilization of the country but of its physical integration and of its fortification against alien attack," the reasons being that they entailed "the superiority of large-scale mechanized farming over the former strip system of primitive tillage" and offered "the most formidable guarantee Russia has as yet evolved against the recurrence of the periodic famines that for over a thousand years have been devastating the peasantry in many regions."[109] So the ends justified the means. However, perhaps because his own father had been a kulak (although not a successful one), Hindus did concede that "many of the koolaks died prematurely in exile" and that "the ordeal to which they were subjected in the early days of their liquidation was one of the momentous tragedies of all time."[110] Reading Hindus, a patriotic agrarian son of Belorussia, one senses that he was so desirous of his motherland becoming a progressive and prosperous nation that he was only too willing to minimize or even overlook Bolshevik atrocities.

Another deluded expatriate, a contemporary of Hindus but of princely rather than peasant origin, was the literary and political historian Dmitry S. Mirsky, the pen name of Prince Dmitry Petrovich Svyatopolk-Mirsky (1890–1939). The son of the tsar's minister of the interior, Mirsky served with the White forces during the civil war before immigrating to Great Britain in 1921, securing a lectureship at London University, and publishing *A History of Russian Literature* (1926), a long-time standard. Meanwhile, he gravitated to Marxism, and in 1931 he unwisely asked Maxim Gorky to secure a pardon for him from the Soviet authorities, who allowed him to return in 1932. Muggeridge took a liking to him but couldn't resist unkindly repeating the jibe of a correspondent for a Paris daily that Mirsky had accomplished the remarkable feat of surviving as a parasite under three different regimes: a prince under tsarism, a professor under capitalism, and a *homme de lettres* under communism. Kornei Chukovsky came to know him and admired "the vast erudition, the sincerity, the literary talent" but noted that he ate too much fine food and drank too much vodka.[111] Although he must have known better, Mirsky wrote to an English friend in the fall of 1933: "Things are changing here very rapidly. The harvest as I suppose you know was first class and the peasants have sprung into unprecedented wealth."[112] At the height of the Great Terror in 1937 he was arrested as a British spy and perished en route to the Kolyma Gulag in 1939.

Western leftist radicals likewise stayed silent, but at least they had a better excuse than the expats, usually knowing neither Russia nor Russian. American and British leftists were just as attracted by the Marxist promise of egalitarian prosperity and international brotherhood as they were repelled by the exploitation, inequality, and bloodiness of capitalism – so much so that some of them even characterized Stalin's cruelty as "necessary."[113] The socialist activist and bohemian journalist John Reed led the American homage in 1917, he and his feminist wife, Louise Bryant, occupying the barricades with the Reds and he publishing the triumphalist *Ten Days That Shook the World* (1919) before dying, somewhat disillusioned, the next year of typhus in Moscow, where he was buried at the Kremlin wall. Reed was followed by one of his mentors, muckraker Lincoln Steffens, who made three trips to Lenin's Russia (1917, 1919, 1923). Returning from his second, when he had interviewed the Soviet leader, he was asked by Bernard Baruch, the wealthy stock-market speculator, "So you've been over into Russia?," and Steffens replied, "I have been over into the future, and it works."[114] He was to repeat and even rehearse this pronouncement, refining it into his famous mantra: "I have seen the future, and it works." He became a staunch defender of the Bolshevik cause, even justifying, like Lenin himself, its high human cost. He died in the summer of 1936 at the outset of the Great Terror, which he would have undoubtedly rationalized.

The radical labour activist and journalist Anna Louise Strong (1885–1970) was also seduced by – in terms of Bolshevik parlance – the "Big Idea." Moulded by an evangelical Christian conscience and the sorry plight of needy children and striking workers in the United States, she was understandably attracted to the ideals of the Soviet state. Upon the advice of her friend Lincoln Steffens she visited the USSR for the first time in 1921 as a correspondent for the American Friends Service Committee that was aiding the famine victims, and then she was appointed the Moscow correspondent for the International News Service. She lived in the Soviet Union but travelled regularly and extensively outside as well as inside the country, lecturing frequently and publishing prolifically. Described meanly by Muggeridge (himself initially a sympathizer) in 1933 as "an enormous woman with a very red face, a lot of white hair, and an expression of stupidity so overwhelming that it amounted to a kind of strange beauty,"[115] she toured the villages and kolkhozes of southern European Russia in late 1929 and "was left with the impression that, whatever might be the faults of the new system, it could not fail to be an improvement on the old one," to the "medieval" methods of which "she ascribed a greater part of the famines in Russia, and she thought that with modern methods ... the danger of widespread famines in the future so greatly reduced as to be already almost eliminated."[116] Would that she had revisited these places in 1932–33. Strong promoted and defended the Soviet system in many books and articles and lectures, although the purge trials of the Great Terror apparently distressed her. Partly because of her strong support of the communist revolution in China, she was arrested in 1949 in Moscow for espionage but released and deported, and she spent nearly all of the rest of her life in Beijing, where she may or may not have witnessed an even deadlier famine as a result of the Great Leap Forward (1958–61) than that which she had forgiven in the Soviet Union three decades earlier.

The peripatetic, radical, and proud black American writer Langston Hughes, an innovator of "jazz poetry" and a shaper of the "Harlem Renaissance" of the 1920s, was just as unobservant as Strong in the Soviet Union, whose vaunted boast of non-racism he wanted desperately to confirm. He spent nearly a year there in 1932–33 and also seems to have missed the famine's climax, despite having travelled fairly widely. In Moscow he wrote the poem "Letter to the Academy," which was published in *International Literature*, edited by a member of the radical American colony in the capital. In it he said:

> Speak about the Revolution – where the flesh triumphs
> (as well as the spirit) and the hungry belly
> eats, and there are no best people, and the poor
> are mighty and no longer poor, and the young by
> the hundreds of thousands are free from hunger
> to grow and study and love and propagate, bodies
> and souls unchained ...[117]

At the same time he wrote to a friend and business associate in the United States: "I would like to see Harlem once more before everybody starves to death"[118] – not that life was good there, but it had yet to reach the level of the Soviet famine.

The interest of British leftists in the Soviet experiment began later and peaked in 1932,[119] when one of them noted: "the entire British intelligentsia has been to Russia this summer."[120] That included the retired Sidney and Beatrice Webb, respected (and affluent) socialists, Fabians, Labourites, and founders of both the London School of Economics (1895) and the political weekly *New Statesman* (1915). They "fell in love" with what they found in the Soviet Mecca, and upon their return they published, in 1935, a panegyrical philosophical rigmarole of their experience entitled *Soviet Communism: A New Civilization?* (later editions even omitted the title's question mark). In it, they stated how they "saw" the famine that was then raging widely. They did this by posing the question: "Was there or was there not a famine in the USSR in the years 1931 and 1932?" They answered by saying that in both years "there was a partial failure of crops in various parts of the huge area of the USSR"; that "the partial failure of crops certainly extended to only a fraction of the USSR"; that "this partial failure was not in itself sufficiently serious to cause actual starvation, except possibly, in the worst rayons, relatively small in extent"; and, finally, that even there (the Ukraine and the North Caucasus) the "sullen farmers" had nobody to blame but themselves because of their "widespread refusal to sow, neglect to weed, and failure to weed [*sic*: reap?]."[121] So essentially the peasants had deservedly reaped what they had sown.

The Webbs' close friend and a fervent socialist, the witty Irish writer George Bernard Shaw (who after the death of the Webbs successfully petitioned to have their remains moved to Westminster Abbey), displayed some of the humour but none of the insight of his plays during his own Soviet tour the previous year, when he bypassed the rural crisis in spite of – or perhaps on account of – having Maurice Hindus as his guide. His visit could have been the stuff of one of his comedies. In mid-September, while eating a meaty soup in Leningrad's best hotel, Shaw concluded that Russians boasted "the best diet in the world – black bread and cabbage soup." This observation prompted the British consul to say that "Mr Shaw enjoyed his black bread because it was made from good flour and well cooked, and because he had not had to stand in a queue to get it; and as to cabbage soup, the Leningrad housewife would be justified in repeating the gibe that if she had some meat she could make some cabbage soup, if she had the cabbage."[122] Earlier in Moscow the playwright had duelled verbally over lunch with Sonya Chamberlin, the wife of the *Manchester Guardian*'s correspondent. The previous evening Shaw had celebrated his seventy-fifth birthday by giving a speech replete with "enthusiastic encomiums for the Soviet regime," saying, among other things, that as he had neared the Russian frontier he had become so certain that there would be no want of food in the Soviet Union that he had thrown out of the train window all of the hampers of victuals that anxious friends had given him. This cocksureness was too much for Mrs Chamberlin, whose husband in his 1924–34 diary recalled the ensuing exchange:

"I think, Mr Shaw, many Russians would have appreciated it if you had thrown away that food in Russia and not Poland," Sonya began. "Where is there any food shortage here?" retorted Shaw, pointing to the well-appointed dining room of the Metropole Hotel, largely patronized by foreigners with comfortable bank accounts, with a gesture that suggested Marie Antoinette's "Let them eat cake." Sonya is literal-minded and persistent, and she returned to the charge. "I have a four-year old daughter. As a foreigner I can buy all the milk she needs. But if she had depended on the Soviet milk ration she would have had milk only once or twice during this last winter." "Why don't you nurse her yourself?" inquired Shaw, with a trace of irritation. "I think she is a little too old for that," replied Sonya with a smile. "Oh, nonsense,' said Shaw, with Dr. Johnson's determination to win the argument at any cost. "The Eskimos nurse their children until they are twenty years old." "Well, Mr Shaw, I'm not an Eskimo," was Sonya's final shot.

Her husband added, "It is a little amusing and surprising that Shaw, who has such a genius for stagecraft, seems to be quite oblivious of the really superb histrionic efforts which are being made for his benefit during his ten-day sojourn here."[123] Evidently none of those ten days was spent unescorted in peasant villages for on his return to Britain he wrote a new play, *On the Rocks: A Political Comedy*, in the preface to which he says that, in the Soviet Union, "I saw no underfed people" and "the children were remarkably plump."

Eugene Lyons of UPI may have detected the cause of the 1925 Nobel laureate's naïveté, observing that he was "more interested in being seen than in seeing, in being heard than in hearing," so he saw and heard nothing and learned nothing, such was his conviction of the rightness of socialism and the wrongness of capitalism. But Lyons also believed that Shaw was not deceived by his hosts and that he simply used the USSR as a platform from which to taunt the capitalist world and to make light of Soviet hardships.[124] The more intemperate Muggeridge simply rated Shaw "a preposterous old fool."[125]

Shaw had foolish company. Hugh Dalton, who was to become chancellor of the exchequer of Britain's Labour government in 1945, was one of a party of forty-five Fabians (including the Webbs) who took a guided tour of the Soviet Union in July 1932. He returned "immensely stimulated," having "caught a quick but vivid glimpse of a quite new world" that "remained with [him] as an abiding influence." He concluded euphemistically that "they [the Soviets] had an agricultural problem ... but so had we in the capitalist West," adding, "most of the Russians I saw looked better fed than my unemployed Durham miners and their families."[126] He did not say whether he had mingled, unguided, with any Donbass miners or Kuban peasants. But he did admit that "there was no political freedom," just as "there never had been under the Russian Tsars," adding, "perhaps, some of us thought, we had overvalued this in the West, relatively [*sic*] to other freedoms."[127]

Arthur Koestler, an "innocent abroad" who sojourned longer and travelled more widely than most others in the Soviet Union, did acknowledge the famine but was not disillusioned. "I remained a convinced Communist," he recollected, because "I had learned that facts had to be appreciated not on their face value, but in a dynamic way." Thus, living standards were low but they had been even lower under the tsars, and those of the working class in the capitalist countries were steadily falling while those of the working class in the USSR were steadily rising, so: "I not only accepted the famine as inevitable, but also the necessity of the ban on foreign travel, foreign newspapers and books, and the dissemination of a grotesquely distorted picture of life in the capitalist world."[128] Eventually, however, even the faithful Koestler recanted, disabused by the Great Terror. He wrote: "I went to Communism as one goes to a spring of fresh water" – quoting Pablo Picasso – "and I left Communism as one clambers out of a poisoned river strewn with the wreckage of flooded cities and the corpses of the drowned."[129] His epiphany was expressed in his novel *Darkness at Noon* (1938), the story of an "old Bolshevik" who is purged by the very regime that he helped to create – an example of the revolution devouring its elders rather than its young.

The sarcastic Muggeridge had little patience with the "innocents," or so-called "useful idiots" (on account of their PR value to the Soviet leaders). They provided Moscow's foreign press corps, he wrote, "with our best – almost our only – comic relief."[130] The correspondents held a contest among themselves to determine which one of them could produce the most striking example of credulity on the part of the "flower of our western intelligentsia," and "Cholerton, rightly, received the Grand Prix when, overhearing an eminent British jurist ask Oumansky whether Habeas Corpus operated in the USSR, he broke in to tell him, to his complete satisfaction, that, whatever might be the case with Habeas Corpus, the authorities strictly adhered to Habeas Cadaver." Muggeridge never ceased to marvel at these gullible visitors and never forgot them, regarding them as "one of the wonders of the age." He swore: "I shall treasure till I die as a blessed memory the spectacle of them travelling with radiant optimism through a famished countryside, wandering in happy bands about squalid, over-crowded towns, listening with unshakeable faith to the fatuous patter of carefully trained and indoctrinated guides, repeating like school-children a multiplication table, the bogus statistics and mindless slogans endlessly intoned to them ... – all, all chanting the praises of Stalin and his Dictatorship of the Proletariat. It was as though a vegetarian society had come out with a passionate plea for cannibalism, or Hitler had been nominated posthumously for the Nobel Peace Prize."[131]

However, the confident Muggeridge was too quick to forget what British socialist Margaret Cole did not, namely, that "the continuing high hopes of the Revolution, the knowledge of what its makers had set out to achieve and were in part achieving, compared with the dead hopelessness of breadlines and the dole, were more than enough to outweigh or even dispel any beginnings of doubt for the excited [fellow] travellers" who, "like so many more of us, saw in Soviet Russia the negation of the immoralities of industrial capitalism and the system of private profit."[132] Or, as Michael Foot, the future leader of the British Labour Party (1980–83), put it: "How deeply the Left craved to give the benefit of all the doubts to Moscow! No one who did not live through that decade [1930s] can quite appreciate how overwhelming that craving was."[133] The Duchess of Atholl concurred, recalling that "for many perfectly honest members of the Labour Party it [the 1917 Bolshevik takeover] represented a genuine and inspiring attempt to raise the conditions of the world's workers" and "any evidence which tended to prove the contrary could only be a forgery."[134] Then, too, the Soviet Union was seen by Western leftists as not only the saviour of the working class from rapacious capitalists but also as an ally against fascist regimes in Germany, Spain, and Italy. As a result of these perceptions, as well as the efficacy of Soviet censorship and propaganda, foreign public opinion was loath to criticize the USSR.[135]

Another group of Westerners who went to the "socialist paradise" not only to tour but also to work were skilled workers and technicians, especially engineers – many of them out of work and leftist and all of them needed by Soviet central planners to realize their project of several large-scale bases of modern heavy industry in both European and Asiatic Russia.[136] The teenaged Victor Herman's father, Sam, an auto worker in Detroit, went in 1931 to Gorky (Nizhny Novgorod) to help Henry Ford build a factory and make the Model A car for the Soviets ("it didn't matter what the politics were; it only mattered where the marketplace was") because, as the son said, "He saw that he was doing something for the good of the world. Making Russia strong meant making Socialism work, and that was for the good of everyone everywhere – because didn't that mean there would be more fairness for everyone and the good life for all?"[137] Another foreign worker was the engineer Zara Witkin, who envisioned the "vast panorama of Soviet engineering possibilities" and believed that "the Soviet Union planned to reconstruct human society ... on a vast new technological foundation." For this noble task, he added, "Engineers were vitally needed. Their creative powers, perverted by the crass exploitation of capitalism, were to be used for the benefit of society. This great call to the socially minded technical brotherhood of the world rang in my soul, a challenge to the best energies of mind and imagination."[138] Witkin, however, was eventually defeated by the "subterfuge, duplicity, laziness, venality, jealousy, and stupidity" of Soviet bureaucrats and technicians.[139] Unfortunately, these foreign workers did not incline or aspire to literary efforts, so they left few accounts of their experiences. And even these pass over the famine, for their authors lived and worked in the hungry cities, not in the starving villages, and they received special treatment.[140]

Even heads of state were fooled. The most infamous case was that of French prime minister Édouard Herriot, who paid an official visit to the USSR in the late summer of 1933 and toured the Ukraine and the North Caucasus for several days. He asked to see a collective farm, and near Kiev he was shown a "Potemkin village," that is, one that had been specially prepared in order to impress visitors.[141] Afterwards in Moscow Herriot was assured by President Kalinin – "a peasant by birth and conviction" – that "the stories of people dying of starvation are absurd myths ... though there may possibly have been shortages."[142] Near the end of his published travelogue the prime minister mentions "the fable of the famine in the Ukraine,"[143] and he told the newspaper *Le Nouvelliste* after his return that he had crossed the Ukraine and had seen "such a garden in full flower"[144] – thereby virtually admitting that he had truly been led down the garden path. An American journalist's wife, Lucy Lang, let the Soviet cat out of the Ukrainian bag, writing that she and her husband, upon returning to their Kiev hotel late the night before Herriot's visit,

> were amazed to discover that the streets were being washed by an army of men and women. My OGPU cousin provided the explanation: Édouard Herriot, the French statesman, was to arrive in the Ukraine the next day, and orders had been given to eliminate every trace of the famine. The hotel, too, was being refurbished, for the distinguished visitor was to make it his headquarters for a few hours. Worn carpets were taken up, and plush rugs were put in their place. New furniture ap-

peared from somewhere, and members of the staff were clad in shining uniforms.

When Herriot arrived, she added, "the city was spotless, and the streets were filled with cheering throngs. Even the Red Army horses were all dressed up."¹⁴⁵

Many, if not most, of the country's hoi polloi were also complicit in Stalin's charade, and, unlike many, if not most, Western visitors, they must have been aware of the famine's horrors, either directly from personal involvement or indirectly from rumours, letters, reports from friends or relatives, and the sight of starving runaways¹⁴⁶ – although not from Soviet radio broadcasts or newspaper reportage.¹⁴⁷ In late 1929 Galina Zatmilova, a twenty-three-year-old Komsomol member in Sverdlovsk in the Urals, "saw kulakization and collectivization with [her] own eyes": "Those crowds of people driven out of their homes, the wild howling of the women, and the wailing of the children, were so awful that I did not recover for a long time after. I applied to leave the Komsomol."¹⁴⁸ The plight of the kulaks was also witnessed by a theatre director:

> In the spring of 1933 our theatre [Moscow's Vakhtangov] went on a tour of the Urals to the large iron and steel factories. During this trip my friends and I had the dismal opportunity to see with our own eyes the role it [collectivization] played in our country. I will never forget the endless freight cars with their doors sealed crosswise and their single little window barred. People in rags with pale, emaciated faces were visible through the bars. The cars were escorted by numerous guards with rifles in the persons of OGPU soldiers. They were conducting "kulaks" to the concentration camps.¹⁴⁹

A young teenager in Moscow wrote in her diary in the summer of 1933: "People arriving from the oblasts tell all sorts of stories. They say they can't clear all the dead bodies off the streets fast enough, that the provincial towns are full of starving peasants dressed in tattered rags. That the thieving and banditry everywhere is [*sic*] appalling." She added that the Ukraine was reportedly "unrecognizable now. Nothing but the lifeless, silent steppe ... overgrown with high weeds."¹⁵⁰ A Bolshevik official, Victor Kravchenko (who later famously defected to the United States), even contended that "the famine that raged throughout southern Russia and Central Asia was a matter of common knowledge" but that Party members, himself included, were constrained to denounce as "anti-Soviet rumors" the obvious fact that "the first dividends of collectivization were death."[151]

Presumably, then, Russians generally were aware of, and horrified by, the rural trauma, but they either said nothing or wrote discreetly, like Olga Tolstaya-Voyeikova, who wrote of "the present time, when every morsel counts."[152] As a doctor in Kiev Rayon said, in a letter to the Ukrainian Commissariat of Health in the spring of 1933, "this year (right up to the beginning of March) it was considered virtually counter-revolutionary to speak of a famine."[153] Towards the end of the Khrushchevian "thaw" in the post-Stalin period, Nadezhda Mandelstam wrote compellingly about the fact that people knew about the famine but kept quiet:

> For [the] half a century [since 1917] the most unspeakable things have been perpetrated without the slightest attempt at self-justification, and the people who witnessed them are still silent. It is a wonder we have not lost the use of our tongues through silence! But actually there has been no sign of such a thing happening even to those who, far from being silent, have gone out of their way to praise all the crimes that have been committed. We have the prospect of living through another half-century of shameless panegyrics, since to speak out is not only dangerous but futile: "Ten steps away no one hears our speeches" [quoting her husband's "Stalin Epigram"]. By the time a hundred years of this have gone by, our tongues no doubt really will have withered away. We have learned to be silent, so we can learn to do without our tongues.

She added, "We all held our tongues because of our cravenness and the terror that gripped us. The only slight consolation I have is that not only we but 'they' [the authorities] too were cowards and also sweated with dread."[154]

Some who stayed silent confined their knowledge to diaries (which, if found by the OGPU, could have cost them their lives).[155] The fifty-year-old artist and translator Lyubov Shaporina told her diary on 3 February 1930: "It seems to me that Russia is being governed by the monstrous ravings of a madman. Suddenly within half a year a [peasant] population of a hundred million has been transformed into slaves, and its best part, the most industrious and enterprising [the kulaks], are being shot or utterly ruined." On 16 March she added: "And all of Russia is sliding headlong into some sort of abyss." Later the same month she concluded: "When I close my eyes and think of Russia it seems to be a living being whose skin is flaying and its blood spouting. Russia has never suffered such destruction and such punishment, of course, not even under the Tatars [Mongols]."[156] And Mikhail Prishvin (1873–1954), an agronomist by training who became a popular writer on naturalist and folkloric themes (thereby avoiding the pitfalls of socialist realism), likewise confided his anguish to his personal journal. Stalin, he wrote, was a "man of real steel" who had caused "all of the horror of this winter [1929–30], the rivers of blood and tears." "Here," he added, "is a man in whom there is not even a mustard grain of the influence of literature and humaneness: without clothes, a savage man of the Caucasus."[157]

Some Russians who were aware of the famine dealt with that fact by playing what a woman raised in the post-Stalinist USSR recollected as the *"vran'yo* [deception] game," the "pretending" or "suspension of disbelief." She elaborated: "The rules are simple: they [the authorities] lie to us, we know they're lying, they know we know they're lying but they keep lying anyway, and we keep pretending to believe them" (as in "they pretend to pay us, and we pretend to work").[158] So it was possible to pretend that the famine was caused by sabotage by enemies of the people or even that there was no famine at all. It was a way of avoiding unpleasant (and unmentionable) realities. Similarly, a defence lawyer who practised in the Soviet Union for thirty-seven years (until she and her husband were deported in 1977, he for writing anti-Soviet literature and she for meeting with foreign agents masquerading as journalists – but actually for doing her job conscientiously and principledly) admitted that in the 1930s she and her friends, "surrounded by the most appalling human suffering," were afflicted with a "dreadful myopia." This absence of insight, she believed, could not be "explained entirely by our youth, our ignorance of life, the circumstances of our upbringing" but, rather, by "something far more difficult: how a combination of two kinds of hypnosis – the hypnosis of revolutionary idealism and the hypnosis of cynical, barefaced lies – was capable of dulling the senses of an entire nation, depriving it of the desire to see and comprehend what was happening."[159]

The Party faithful deceived themselves by refusing to believe what was occurring in their homeland. In 1938 in a Kazan prison Nadezhda Grankina, who was serving a ten-year sentence as the wife of an "enemy of the people" (a former Red Army commander), had several cellmates – one-time Party activists – who continued to believe in the righteousness of the Party and the correctness of the Party line: "I was extremely surprised that my present comrades, former Party members, did not know what was going on in the country. When I used to tell them about the famine in Orenburg during my exile there in 1932–33, they would say that it was a lie, that I was exaggerating so that I could slander our Soviet way of life. When I talked about the 'excesses' that had been allowed during the campaign to collectivize peasant farming, they used to say that I was a Trotskyite – although Stalin himself had already condemned these excesses." She added, "They thought I got what I deserved because I was critical of the excesses. Yet when the same thing happened to them, they thought it was a mistake that would be fixed – because they had never had any doubts whatsoever." Grankina called this phenomenon "some kind of universal psychosis."[160] This "psychosis" was abetted by the conviction of the faithful that the rosy, near future necessitated current privations, including starvation. This belief was expressed indignantly by an Intourist guide to an American travel writer in the summer of 1933 when he unintentionally mocked her spare attire (hundreds of foreign tourists must have heard this very same rationale from their Intourist guides): "I am proud to be in rags! I am proud to eat poor food! I am only one of millions of Russians who are living like this for the sake of our country! We love luxuries as much as you Americans do, and when the Five-Year Plan [of 1928–32] is over we shall have better things than you have. We too shall have our silk stockings and fine clothes and fruit to eat, but now we are sacrificing ourselves so that we can save money and buy your American machinery [for industrialization]!"[161]

She was convinced because she believed the Party line to this effect (and there were no other political parties to question that line). As Walter Duranty reported in a special cable in the *New York Times* of 9 July 1932, "the Kremlin believes with fanatic fervor that the hardships [including starvation and attendant diseases] are worth while [*sic*]."[162]

The doctrinaire Bolsheviks came to look upon starving peasants heartlessly as people who could not cope with the "new order" and were therefore disposable. In his infamous famine-denial article in the *New York Times* at the height of the starvation Duranty stressed that "the Bolshevist leaders are just as indifferent to the casualties that may be involved in their drive toward socialization as any General during the [First] World War who ordered a costly attack in order to show his superiors that he and his division possessed the proper soldierly spirit." "In fact," he added, "the Bolsheviki are more indifferent because they are animated by fanatical conviction"[163] – a conviction expressed by the Futurist poet Vladimir Mayakovsky when, on the eve of the coup d'état of his beloved Bolsheviks in 1917, he declared: "Today the thousand years of the Past are over, today we revise the world's foundations. Today we recut life to fit our cloth, right down to the very last button."[164] Stepan Podlubny, a worker of peasant origin who was desperate to remake himself as an accepted proletarian (and who became an OGPU informant in 1932), had this reaction in his diary when his mother returned from a visit in the summer of 1933 to their native village in the Ukraine with news of the famine there:

> About the news that Mama reported: an incredible famine is going on over there. Half of the people have died of hunger. Now they are eating cooked [sugar] beet tops. There are plenty of cases of cannibalism ... All in all it's a terrifying thing. I don't know why, but I don't have any pity for this. It has to be this way, because then it will be easier to remake the peasants' smallholder psychology into the proletarian psychology that we need. And those who die of hunger, let them die. If they can't defend themselves against death from starvation, it means that they are weak-willed, and what can they give to society?[165]

It became easier for Podlubny to condemn the peasants thusly once he held them in contempt. He expressed that contempt early the same year against what he called the "Rodin village" of a neighbouring apartment in his Moscow block of flats, an apartment overflowing with the Rodin family's friends, as well as relatives who had recently arrived in search of work: "These young people are all from the village – girls and fellows from a backward, extremely low milieu ... their relation toward each other, their thoughts and manners are just animal-like ... there you see a thief, a bandit and what have you, someone who it is very difficult, if not impossible, to put on their feet, and lead to the path of truth, the path of a cultured person."[166] He even held his father, who had been kulakized and deported for three years, in contempt for remaining "old," "backward," and "useless" instead of trying to transform himself into a "new Soviet man" (and he displayed his disrespect by not referring to him by his first name and patronymic).[167] So, being contemptible and unreformable, peasants who starved to death were not to be lamented as they were incapable and unworthy of redemption as *homo sovieticus*. In effect, the muzhik was an embarrassment to the modernizing proletarian state.

Thus, the new proletariat adopted the Party's attitude towards the old peasantry. Correspondent Rhea Clyman witnessed a minor episode in this "class war" in a third-class train carriage in the North Caucasus in the summer of 1932, when "a fierce fight broke out – [a] symptom of the class-struggle being waged throughout Russia – the fight between the workers and the peasants." A group of shock workers huddled in the aisle was furious at the peasant women for occupying so much space on the benches with their bulky bundles and complained loudly, whereupon one peasant woman shouted, "We've as much right to be on these trains as you. We're workers, too; and we work harder than you," whereupon one of the shock workers hurled the epithet "kulak," and the woman retorted, "I've lost everything that I have to lose." "Workers," she exclaimed more harshly, "they think they're important now. The government deceives them with promises, but we peasants aren't such fools. You wanted our land, you took it, you've got our horses and our cows, but look at your kolkhozes," she taunted, "have you got any bread?"[168] This animosity predated collectivization, as the Croatian communist Ante Ciliga discovered during a train trip southward to the Crimea in the winter of 1926–27 while talking to a group of Ukrainian peasants, who complained that "all … was for the factory workers" and "nothing for the peasants," adding, "today, as before, the peasants were counted second-class citizens."[169] The urban workers tended to regard the rural peasants as ideologically uninformed, backward, stupid, and lazy, while the peasants saw the workers as the hoodwinked supporters of the state that had seized their property and impoverished them, as well as doctrinaire and arrogant class snobs. The starving rural producers of grain disdained the urban consumers of grain, supplied by the state, as freeloaders (*darmoyedy*). As a correspondent for *Le Temps* reported in the summer of 1933, "in the eyes of the peasant the city dweller has become a parasite living at his expense, a 'sponger'" because the large cities had grain, "the product of his labour that the state took from him in order to feed the privileged classes of the country, namely, the army, the OGPU, specialists, and skilled workers."[170]

3
A NATURAL FAMINE?

Famine is not your friend.
– Russian peasant proverb, in Ivan Khripunov, *Dnevniki 1937–1941 godov*, 374.

For our country as a whole, drought is no joke.
– Nikita Khrushchev, in Sergei Khrushchev, *Memoirs of Nikita Khrushchev*, 2:325.

The normally jocular Premier Khrushchev, who knew whereof he spoke, was not joking. The amount of grain that was planted, grown, and reaped on Russian farmland – Tsarist or Soviet – varied, of course, from year to year and from region to region, but not only because of human actions. Policy may have been the major cause of the great famine of 1928–34, but it was certainly abetted by nature. Such has always been the case in Russian history; indeed, not infrequently nature was more to blame than people. If the Russian peasant's worst human enemy was the landlord, then his worst natural enemy was the weather, chiefly drought; in Tsarist Russia the village priest commonly prayed expressly for rain to end the drought, and the peasants beseeched God with prayers, incantations, and even sacrifices to avert drought and grant a bountiful harvest.[1] Drought plus frost limited the peasant's working season to 125 to 130 days of the year (late April to late October) and exacted enormous effort for an uncertain result; so even in a crop year most peasants were barely able to make ends meet.[2]

Surprisingly, in the spring of 1933 at the peak of the famine the redoubtable Gareth Jones told the readers of one of his ordinarily trustworthy newspaper articles that "climatic conditions have[,] in the past few years, blessed the Soviet Government."[3] He was wrong, however, if he meant to include the year 1931; in the last month of summer of that year he did indeed visit the Soviet Union with John ("Jack") Heinz II, heir to the American food company for-

A Natural Famine?

tune, but Jones's bloodhound reporting did not extend to the Asiatic Russian steppes of Kazakhstan,[4] Western Siberia, or the southern Urals, or even to the European Russian steppes of the southern Transvolga, the Lower and Middle Volga, and the North Caucasus, so he was unable to witness one of the infrequent "catastrophic" droughts of the century.[5] Memorialist Alexander Solzhenitsyn erred, too, when in his magnum opus on the Gulag he described the height of the famine as "a strange three-year famine – a famine that came about without drought and without war"; in fact, he was wrong on both counts for the famine was also caused in part by a war – a class war. Victor Kondrashin, one of the most productive and most authoritative Russian scholars of collectivization, was closer to reality when he wrote that "throughout the years of collectivization the problem of drought was pressing in the Soviet village."[6]

Drought was just one – albeit the worst – of several natural hazards that commonly conditioned the Russian peasant's existence. An analysis of twenty years (1918–39) of OGPU reports on the rural situation showed that the most frequently mentioned problem – 48 percent of all reports – was drought, followed by downpours (mostly in the early fall) at 21 percent, hail at 10 percent, floods at 8 percent, insects at 8 percent, fire at 3 percent, and frost at 2 percent.[7] These hazards loomed larger in this country than in most others, especially those of Western Europe, and even the rest of Eastern Europe, as well as the Americas, because its geography is less conducive to productive agriculture.[8] Nature has been called more of a stepmother than a mother to the USSR; its vastness (it occupied one-half of the world's largest land mass) meant extremes of temperature; its northerly location (close to Arctic cold) meant early and late frosts and a short growing season; and its interior position (distant from sources of moisture, except westernmost European Russia) meant dryness.[9] Nature shortchanged the Soviet Union with respect to both temperature and precipitation. Some four-fifths of its cropland was found within the least productive thermal zone of two hundred degree-months or less,[10] compared with only one-third of North American (and one-fifth of US) cropland; in addition, three-fifths of the Soviet sown area was found within the two least favourable moisture zones, compared with two-fifths of North America's (and only one-third of the United States') sown area.[11] More dauntingly, less than 2 percent of Soviet grainland was found in zones of the optimum combination of temperature and precipitation, compared with 56 percent of American grainland.¹² Relative to other grains, wheat is more vulnerable to low temperatures and acidic soils, which restricted its growing primarily to the wooded steppe and grassy steppe. The Asiatic Russian steppe, with its late but hot summers, dry autumns, and often light snow cover, excluded winter wheat, whose yield is double that of spring wheat;[13] on the other hand, the Soviet Union's climate favoured not soft but hard wheats, which have a higher protein content and are more suitable for bread – the Russian preference – than pastry. Unknown to Khrushchev, apparently, the climate did not favour corn, which requires a long growing season and ample moisture – and corn was the most important feed grain.

Droughts were frequent and intensive in Russia,[14] Tsarist and Soviet, thanks to its huge size (the world's largest country in the world's largest land mass) and resultant continental climate (which was exacerbated by either sheer distance from, or mountain barriers to, maritime influences on the west, east, and south or by pack ice on the north). Twenty-four of the seventy years from 1885 through 1955 were drought years[15] – one drought about every three years, and six "catastrophic" droughts (one involving both the European steppe and the Asiatic Russian steppe) from 1890 to 1972. During this period drought struck Uralsk 78 percent of the time, Volgograd 70 percent, Saratov 55 percent, Orenburg 46 percent, Nikolayev 46 percent, Rostov-on-Don 34 percent, Voronezh 24 percent, Kharkov 23 percent, Kazan 22 percent, Nizhny Novgorod 13 percent, and Kiev 6 percent.[16] The droughts occurred most often – three years of every five on the average – in the steppe and semi-desert lands bordering the Caspian,[17] that is, the lower reaches of both the Volga and Ural Rivers. There, then, drought was normal and expected, not abnormal and unexpected. Nikita Sergeyevich recognized the risk of undependable precipitation: "It's true that inadequate precipitation sometimes caused great damage. We were all completely dependent on the rainfall. If you were to be judged by the harvests in the southern part of our country, you could be touted as a genius one year and be dismissed the next as a complete idiot. If the rainfall was good, the wheat harvest could be as high as 30 centners per hectare[18] ... If the winter wheat was affected by drought in the autumn or in April, the harvest would be only 5–10 centners per hectare. That's how dependent on the weather we were."[19]

At least Khrushchev appreciated the drought problem and approached it rationally with his Virgin and Idle Lands project. Stalin, by contrast, did what

A Natural Famine?

many of his victims were accused of doing, namely, he "sabotaged" agriculture by having agricultural officials, technicians, and scientists arrested, imprisoned, and executed. One such specialist, the founder (in 1929) and director of the country's Hydrometeorological Service, Alexei Wangenheim, was arrested at the beginning of 1934 and accused of conspiring to sabotage socialist agriculture by fabricating weather forecasts and destroying the network of weather stations that he himself had created, especially those designed to forecast drought. As one of the many scapegoats for agricultural shortcomings, he was imprisoned and interrogated in the OGPU's headquarters, Moscow's infamous Lubyanka, the one-time headquarters of the All-Russia Insurance Company, now devoted to ensuring that the country was safe from "enemies of the people" and "counter-revolutionary elements," including Wagenheim, who was sentenced to ten years of hard labour on the White Sea's Solovetsky Islands, where his faith in Stalin and the Party remained unshaken; he was executed in the fall of 1937.[20]

Russian droughts are almost always accompanied (and intensified) by *sukhovei*[21] – what Andrew Cairns called the "dreaded hot winds" of the Volga Valley that blew northwestward out of Central Asia in the summer.[22] All of the Middle and Lower Volga is subject to at least twenty-five sukhovei days annually (as well as drought days 50 percent of the time).[23] "It can be said that sukhovei are as characteristic of droughts as droughts are of a continental climate," stated a prominent Soviet climatologist.[24] The droughts are worsened, too, by *mgla* – dust storms, which occur from the spring (mainly) until the autumn in the south and the southeast of the Great Russian Plain. These "black storms" are created by high winds in the steppe and desert zones that pick up dirt and sand – sometimes together with seeds or young plants – and blow them away, burying crops and even buildings elsewhere, as well as covering roads and railway tracks, filling irrigation channels, creating drifts, and reducing visibility. The areas with the most sukhovei days are also the areas with the most *mgla* days.[25]

During the famine period, then, it was normal, or expected, that drought would not only occur but also vary in terms of time (season or month) and place (all or part of the same area); in other words, in some years some grain areas would be droughty in whole or in part and for all or part of the season – and some not. For example, for two winters in a row (1927–28 and 1928–29) the Ukraine suffered "a calamitous loss of [winter] wheat," owing to severe cold with little snow cover (winter drought),[26] but in 1930 it (and the North Caucasus) enjoyed what Andrew Cairns rated "a year of ideal climatic conditions,"[27] and the 1930 grain crop was deemed by Maurice Hindus to be the best since 1917.[28] However, 1931 was a year not of normal but of "catastrophic" drought,[29] only the fourth to strike the European and the Asiatic section of the Russian steppe at the same time since that of 1890 (1911 and 1921 were the other two).[30] The Central Black Earth, the southern and eastern Ukraine, the northern and eastern North Caucasus, the Lower and Middle Volga, southwestern Bashkiria, the southern Urals, Western Siberia, and Kazakhstan – all of the chief grain areas – were drought-stricken, and the drought lasted from April until August.[31] The "principal reason" for the resultant harvest failure, especially of wheat, stated Andrew Cairns, was the "serious drought in many important regions, including all the chief spring wheat areas"; other causes, he added, were the "unfavourable harvesting weather," late seeding, and poor ploughing.[32] Precipitation during the country's vegetative period of eighty days was below the average amount by as much as 56 percent.[33] The drought was intensified by sukhovei in the central and eastern sections of the steppe zone, including the Middle Volga, whose "petition" to Moscow for assistance explained the region's plight. It had been one of the country's first regions to finish spring sowing, owing to "favourable climatic conditions": plenty of moisture in the soil, thanks to abundant rainfall in May (130 percent more than normal), and "very favourable" temperatures, which had facilitated the "rapid sprouting" and the "luxuriant growth" of all crops. But then sukhovei began in the middle of June and lasted until the end of July, raising temperatures to as much as 42°C in the shade and 55° to 60°C on the surface of the ground, without any precipitation in the second half of July, so that wheat yields on the left bank in centners per hectare fell from 7.7 on 1 and 15 June to 5.7 on 1 July, 4.8 on 15 July, 4.2 on 1 August, 3.9 on 15 August, and 2.7 on 1 September. About one-quarter of all grainland was lost, and the grain that was reaped was "very low" in quality.[34] The story was the same in the Lower Volga, with the Stalingrad Party secretary, Vladimir Ptukha (shot in 1938), telling the October plenum of the Central Committee in Moscow that just ten days of "extraordinary heat" and sukhovei had reduced grain yields twofold to threefold compared with 1930, with the yield varying from 0.5 centners per hectare on the border with Kazakhstan (windward) to 9 on the border with the Central Black Earth (leeward), so that the harvest was reduced by 20 percent.³⁵ This "catastrophic" occurrence prompted the convening of a conference on drought in October in Moscow, where Molotov stated that several million hectares of grainland had been struck by the drought, resulting in the loss of several hundred million puds of grain. Delegates recommended several practical remedies, including the prohibition of treefelling in the Middle Volga (in order to retain soil moisture) over an area of half a million hectares and the undertaking of irrigation (in order to regulate water supply) of an equal area with water from the Volga-Don Canal and the Volga itself.³⁶

The next two years reverted to the usual pattern (temporal and spatial) of mostly bounty with some want. Margaret Cole, the wife of economist and fellow Fabian socialist G.D.H. Cole, visited the Soviet Union in the summer of 1932 and neatly summarized the aftermath of 1931:

> Nature has a nasty way of turning sulky at the wrong moment. But new Russia was thinking mechanistically, even of her farming. Drought ruined the 1931 grain harvest of five important sections of the Union, viz. the Lower and Middle Volga, Southern Urals, Western Siberia and Kazakhstan. The Government, therefore, had to provide, in addition to the normal domestic and the abnormal export requirements, another 1,800,000 ton[ne]s of grain to these regions for seeds and food. This was extracted from the Ukraine at a cost of considerable disaffection, and the Ukrainians responded by, in their turn, eating into a good part of their seed grain intended for the 1932 sowing. All the graingrowing areas planted thinly, the Ukraine seriously diminishing its acreage. Then the unusual happened for Russia. Last winter [1931–32] opened with heavy frosts instead of a customary protective covering of snow. The thin sowings were even more thinned by the destructive frosts. The following summer's growth was slow; thin crops mean heavy weeds, and the stalks, or "straw," proved too short in many areas for the modern combine to do its work properly even when it was available. To cap it all, about half-way through the gathering of the 1932 harvest the weather broke across Southern Russia, still further spoiling an indifferent crop and further dispiriting the harvesters.³⁷

Andrew Cairns concurred with Cole's assessment that 1932's poor grain crop was attributable to both climatic and non-climatic factors but that the latter were more detrimental. They included: (1) late and insufficient tillage (owing to the "catastrophic" losses of draught power), resulting in an infestation of annual and perennial weeds; (2) the late seeding of both winter and spring grains, resulting in losses from winter cold, drought, and sukhovei; (3) the miserable living and working conditions, resulting in widespread discontent and passive resistance (on the part of both individual and collective farmers) as well as a very low productivity of labour; (4) the want of seed (most of it untreated for disease); and (5) the inefficient harvesting with inadequate horsepower and equipment. The climatic factors included: (1) alternate freezing and thawing during the winter of 1931–32, causing very heavy losses of fall-sown crops (winter grains), especially wheat and particularly in the Ukraine and the North Caucasus; (2) the lack of precipitation, the high temperatures, and the sukhovei during the critical period of plant growth in the European Russian steppe, especially the left bank of the Middle Volga; and (3) the hot and humid weather (conducive to the development and multiplication of rust spores) that exacerbated the losses from stem rust, particularly in most of the North Caucasus and much of the Ukraine.[38] In the Ukraine a lot of money and time had been spent during the winter on a "snow preserving" campaign that entailed the making of small ridges in the fields in order to retain the snow, but high winds "cut [the] enormous drifts of firmly caked snow to pieces." From 20 to 40 percent of fall-sown grain was winter-killed.[39]

Drought struck the North Caucasus and the Lower Volga as well as the Ukraine in 1932.[40] Leonard Elmhirst's companion, identified only as "X," told him that "the grain was parched by the hot wind ... all down the Volga."[41] Andrew Cairns reported that in late June and early July drought and sukhovei "practically ruined" the wheat crop of the "upper Volga" and the left bank of the "lower Volga"; then, on both sides of the "lower Volga," "incessant rains" during the harvest period caused a "heavy loss in both quantity and quality," and "to make matters worse ... they had an extremely heavy infection of stem rust, and a good deal of wheat was not worth harvesting."[42] Consequently, the year's average yield of kolkhoz grain in centners per hectare was 5.1 in the Ukraine, 3.9 in the North Caucasus, and 3.7 in the Lower Volga, compared with 7 to 10 in northwestern European Russia (the West, the Central Industrial Rayon, and the Central Black Earth).[43] Walter Duranty reported that even the sacred "iron grain fund" (Red Army reserve fund) had to be tapped for food and seed.[44]

By contrast, in 1933, recalled Freda Utley, "the weather helped to produce the best harvest in years."[45] The dry spring had been negated by favourable summer weather in most of the country, yielding an "unprecedented" crop, reported the German ambassador.[46] Weather conditions in the Ukraine, waxed the Italian consul in Kharkov, were "exceptionally favourable" and "exceptionally superb, wondrously superb."[47] At summer's end the procurement authorities told Stalin that the grain harvest was the largest since 1917, even though along the drier southern edge of the steppe belt stretching from the Middle and Lower Volga to the southern Urals and northern Kazakhstan it was "very small," owing "not to poor tillage but solely to climatic conditions," that is, to drought and sukhovei.[48] And in northwestern European Russia the opposite extreme occurred: "soakings," or "downpours" (*vymochki*), brought by strong low-pressure systems coming from the North Atlantic via the Baltic Sea corridor, ruined sowings in the West Region and elsewhere.[49]

Nevertheless, the crop remained – as described by locals to Whiting Williams – the "biggest for fifty years," but, he stressed, much of it (up to one-third) was not harvested. He saw "field after field covered with ungarnered grain that had been allowed to rot where it had been grown and ripened and been cut." Many peasants had starved to death or had been deported, and those still alive were too malnourished or too disaffected to work well or at all; some of the harvest was salvaged by the deployment of the industrial proletariat (and Red Army soldiers) to the fields as emergency harvesters, but they were unaccustomed to hard physical farmwork and were themselves weak from malnourishment (Williams cited one case of only seventy of the one hundred workers who had been sent to one kolkhoz returning alive); fewer and weaker horses remained to transport the sheaves of grain, and their motorized replacements were insufficient (so the authorities tried moving the scarce tractors, trucks, and combines around the country from areas of earlier to areas of later reaping); and much of the reaped grain was pilfered by the starving.[50] So even when the Soviet Union produced a bountiful harvest, it was not necessarily bountiful everywhere or even completely harvested; and, conversely, whenever it produced a meagre harvest, it was not necessarily meagre everywhere.

The latter was the case in 1934, the last year of the famine (and – true to form – bumper harvests in 1935 and 1937 were to alternate with harvest failures in 1936 and 1938 and even 1939).[51] The cause was a spring-summer drought from April through July;[52] precipitation during the country's eighty-day vegetative period (the period of growth between germination and flowering, generally starting at 10°C) was up to 41 percent below average in 1934 (compared with 56 percent in 1931).[53] A Soviet agricultural specialist, I.V. Yakushkin, spoke of a "disastrous drought" that affected nearly all of the Soviet Union, particularly the Ukraine (except the western Ukraine), the North Caucasus, and the Middle and Lower Volga, and especially winter wheat.[54] Autumn sowings of winter wheat and early sowings of spring wheat "suffered severely" from light snow and heavy cold during the winter and sukhovei-induced drought in March and April; 90 percent of the winter wheat was "ruined" and most of it was replaced by spring sowings of corn and millet, but by the middle of May half of these had been lost.[55] The drought was "absolute" in the Ukraine, the North Caucasus, and the Volga Valley, where no rain fell for more than two and a half months and the "hot steppe wind" blew steadily for two months and "desiccated the land even more" (but, despite the drought, weeds flourished in the fields).[56] In most grain areas the crop was salvaged by early summer rainfall, but in the eastern Ukraine the rain fell in "torrents" in July, when, the peasants told Louis Fischer, "we didn't want rain," and the crop was only half that of the "bumper year" of 1933.[57] In the middle of the harvest failure Otto Schiller reported that the crop was so poor throughout the Ukraine and in some parts of the RSFSR that, after state procurement, the peasants, particularly those of the individual farmsteads and the weakest kolkhozes, would not have enough left to sustain themselves.[58]

The weather during the famine years of 1928–34, then, was rather more severe than normal. The harvest failures of the "catastrophic" drought of 1931 and the "disastrous" drought of 1934 meant that much less grain was available for procurement than usual, and under pre-1928 agronomic conditions the peasants would simply have marketed less in order to subsist and survive until the next and likely better harvest. Under collectivization, however, the resolute Bolsheviks ruthlessly persisted in forcibly exacting as much grain as possible, regardless of the harvest outcome, thereby dooming millions of peasants and nomads to starvation. In the words of an individual farmsteader, "there was a famine not because there was a harvest failure but because all of the grain earned [by the peasants] was seized."[59] So policy was the primary cause of the famine, but it was not the only factor for it was unquestionably exacerbated by the extreme droughts of 1931 (especially) and 1934. The weather was a secondary factor – but a factor nonetheless.

4
AN UNNATURAL FAMINE?

A bad crop is from God, a famine is from the people. – Russian proverb.
– quoted by Pitirim A. Sorokin, *Leaves from a Russian Diary* and *Thirty Years After*.[1]

As Tacitus' Romans "made a solitude, and called it peace," so the Soviet Govt. have "made a famine, and called it communism."
– Laurence Collier to the Foreign Office, in Carynnyk, Luciuk, and Kordan, *Foreign Office and the Famine*, doc. 5:78.[2]

The Context

From the available evidence there seems to be little, if any, doubt that the primary cause of the great famine of 1928–34 was state policy, namely, collectivization generally and its modus operandi particularly[3] – in other words, Father Stalin, not Mother Nature, and coercion, not volition. As a member of the Latvian legation told the chargé d'affaires of the US legation in Riga, "the famine is directly attributed in diplomatic circles to the disorganization of agriculture brought about by Stalin's policy of collectivization."[4] Malcolm Muggeridge was characteristically less diplomatic and more immoderate and categorical: "This particular famine was planned and deliberate; not due to any natural catastrophe like failure of rain, or cyclone, or flooding. An administrative famine brought about by the forced collectization of agriculture; an assault on the countryside by party *apparatchiks* ... supported by strong-arm squads from the military and the police."[5] More specifically, then, it was the way that collectivization was implemented – coercively, hurriedly, blindly, and ruthlessly – that caused so much havoc, not the concept itself. As a "former person" noted, the Bolsheviks had been inspired and inflamed by such epithets as Lenin's "Who is not with us is against us" and that of the proletariat's literary favourite, Maxim Gorky, "If the enemy does not surrender, liquidate him!"[6]

This outcome may have come as a shock to many, but it should not have come as a surprise. The Bolsheviks were, after all, doctrinaire Marxists and as such committed to the abolition of private property (nationalization of the means of production), the "dictatorship of the proletariat" (one-party – the workers' party – governance),[7] and central planning of the economy. Moreover, the Bolsheviks had already shown themselves to be quite capable of ruthlessness – witness the "Red Terror" against their opponents (declared and suspected) following their seizure of power in October 1917. Furthermore, the Bolsheviks were bound to make economic mistakes, thanks mainly to the vagueness of the Marxist doctrine (as outlined in Karl Marx and Frederick Engels's *The Communist Manifesto* (1848) and elaborated in Marx's *Capital: A Critique of Political Economy* (1867), which was a destructive critique of industrial (but not agrarian) capitalism but not a constructive and detailed blueprint of communist construction (apart from such general prerequisites as the abolition of private property and the adoption of central planning). So the builders of the "new order" had to work largely by inference and by trial and error. Mistakes were going to be made, especially in agriculture, which, being more dependent upon natural factors (particularly temperature and precipitation), was less amenable to planning than industry. As Otto Schiller said in 1931, "it had to be realized that in agriculture it is not the machine alone which decides, but that it is necessary to pay attention to natural conditions also."[8] This truism was blithely ignored by the faithful adherents to the "General Idea" (the dogma of Bolshevism). The *Guardian*'s correspondent Malcolm Muggeridge, for instance, happened to dine with some officials in the North Caucasus who were "so friendly and sincere." "About this peasant business!" I asked. "They smiled, having an answer all ready. As the factories were in 1920 so now the farms. We've built up heavy industry; the next task is agriculture." Muggeridge wanted to say, "are you quite sure ... that the parallel is correct – factories and land! Isn't agriculture somehow more sensitive, lending itself less to statistical treatment! Will people [peasants] torn up by the roots make things grow, even if you drive them into the fields at the end of a rifle!" However, he ended, it is "as impossible to argue against a General Idea as against an algebraic formula."[9] Nikita Khrushchev, nicknamed the *kukuruznik* (corn man) after one of his "hare-brained schemes" (the planting of corn in the insufficiently humid Ukrainian steppe), reminds us that farming is the "most capricious" branch of the economy because it is highly dependent upon the vagaries of weather and entails coping with animate objects ("living organisms") rather than inanimate machines, or, as he also said, "agriculture depends too much, as the peasants used to say, on the Lord God."[10] He elaborated: "Agricultural production is a capricious sector of the economy. Nature introduces its corrections every year, now allowing you to accumulate, ever so slightly, some reserves of grain, now creating such difficulties that bread rationing is necessary."[11] This truism was acknowledged – if not heeded – by Kaganovich of the Bolsheviks' governing triumvirate: "To raise industry to a higher level, to build new factories, is much easier than to rebuild agriculture. This is especially true of the type of agriculture we had in his country with its millions of tiny farms."[12]

To make matters worse, few of the Bolshevik leaders had any practical agricultural experience; one of the few (and most notable) exceptions was President Mikhail Kalinin, but he seems to have wielded little power in his figurehead position (as evidenced by the fact that he was one of the few old Bolsheviks to survive the purges shortly before and shortly after the Second World War).

Finally, agriculture was bound to be subordinated to industry, owing to the hostility of the rest of the world to the communist experiment. The Bolsheviks made no secret of their detestation of the inequality and instability of the capitalist system and of their determination to not only shun it but also to undo it, so the capitalist world tried to isolate (through non-recognition) and even overthrow (through military intervention) the Bolshevik regime. Thus, the brash Soviet state was forced to go it alone – which it probably preferred to do anyway in order to avoid dependence upon, and contamination by, capitalist economies. Sectorally, this estrangement entailed a favouring of industry (capital goods), notably heavy industry for militarization, over light industry (consumer goods) and agriculture. It also meant more self-sufficiency (import substitution).[13]

The "Peasant Problem"

Sooner or later, then, the Bolsheviks could be expected to put the "new order" in place. Indeed, very soon after their coup d'état of October 1917 (essentially a peasant, not a worker, rebellion) they tried to do so during the period of so-called "war communism" (1917–21), when, following a brief flirtation with

An Unnatural Famine?

private ownership in agriculture, small-scale industry, and retail trade, in 1918 they nationalized land, all industry, and all trade (and even introduced central planning in the form of 1920's State Commission for the Electrification of Russia [GOELRO]). The result was economic collapse, with production plummeting and prices skyrocketing; by 1920 agricultural production was less than two-thirds, and industrial production only one-fifth, that of 1913. The population was subjected to hyperinflation à la Weimar Germany (in 1920 the ruble had 1 percent of its 1917 purchasing power), food rationing, and the industrial conscription of labour.

The principal roadblock was the peasantry. Lenin had come to power with the popular slogan of "peace, land, and bread." The war-weary soldiers (primarily peasants) got peace when the Bolshevik government ended Russia's cannon-fodder participation in the "Great War" in 1918 by suing for peace under the harsh terms of the Treaty of Brest-Litovsk; the land-hungry peasants (and urban refugees) got the seized estates of the royal family, the nobility, and the church. Bread, however, proved elusive. Often the peasants simply seized the land for they had always believed that the soil that they had worked for centuries was theirs. As they were wont to say, "I may belong to the *barin* [gentry master], but the land belongs to me."[14] And now they refused to sell grain from their "own" land to the Bolshevik state for the latter's fixed prices, so in June 1918 the Bolsheviks created "committees of the poor," or *kombedy* – purportedly representing the poor peasants but in fact controlled by Bolshevik cadres, and ostensibly in order to redistribute the land but actually to requisition its output, seizing enough to feed the Red Army during the civil war (1917–20) and essential government and industrial personnel while coercing the peasants into new socialist farms called "communes." The peasants were quick to react (sometimes violently)[15] by consuming and hoarding more of their output and by reducing their sown area, resulting in shortages of provisions in the cities and the flight of urbanites to the countryside in search of food – all aggravated by the disruption of transport between the grain-producing and the grain-consuming regions.

The privation and confusion generated widespread discontent. Industrial strikes multiplied and peasant unrest increased; many peasants were rebelling violently by 1921, when famine struck. The disaffection even reached the armed forces, culminating in an uprising in March 1921 at the Gulf of Finland's naval base of Kronshtadt, whose sailors had fired the battleship

Aurora's guns four years earlier to signal the Red assault on the Winter Palace. Leon Trotsky (Leo Bronstein), the fiery orator who had so successfully organized the Red Army, later wrote that "the collapse of the productive forces surpassed anything of the kind history had ever seen. The country, and the government with it, were at the very edge of the abyss."[16] Clearly Lenin had to take drastic action in order to retain popular support and lasting control of the world's first socialist state.

His answer was the New Economic Policy (NEP) of 1921, which was intended to stimulate production (the economic goal) by permitting some private ownership and to restore the linkage, or solidarity (*smychka*), between peasants and workers (the political goal) by giving the former the freer use of land and its output so as to provide more grain for the latter. A peasant was allotted the amount of land that was considered necessary to provision his household's number of "eaters" (mouths to feed).[17] The compulsory requisition of a fixed amount of grain was replaced by a percentage requisition (about 50 percent) of net output (the surplus remaining after subsistence requirements were met), and the peasants were free to sell the rest on the open market. They were also allowed to rent land and to hire hands. In addition, private domestic trade was permitted in order to improve distribution (this gave rise to private traders called "Nepmen," later vilified as carpetbaggers), and small-scale industry was denationalized (even foreigners were allowed to operate concessions). The state, meanwhile, retained control of the "commanding heights" (crucial sectors) of the economy: large-scale industry, banking, foreign trade, transportation, and communications. At the same time, more spoken and written criticism and dissent were tolerated, and there was an experimental flowering of the arts in painting, design, literature, stagecraft, and architecture.

The outcome was a mixed economy of socialism and capitalism – what Lenin called "state capitalism" – wherein state monopolies and private enterprises combined to revive the economy. And swiftly revive it they did, with agriculture regaining its 1913 level by 1926 (despite a drought in 1924–25) and industry by 1927. The French journalist Pierre Dominique was told repeatedly by peasants during his extensive tour of the USSR in 1932 that "in 1926, 1927 and 1928 we had so much wheat, so much bread, that we did not know what to do with them."[18] After a decade's hiatus, the country was able to resume grain exports already in 1923–24, and they contributed one-half of the country's export earnings from 1923–24 through 1925–26 and two-thirds in 1926–27.[19]

However, by restoring agricultural production the peasants again became an obstacle to Bolshevik progress. Instead of safeguarding peasant-worker solidarity, the NEP threatened it, for the state desired more grain in order to expand urban industry, especially heavy industry (iron and steel), for the purposes of both industrial modernization and military expansion (the latter in light of the persistent aloofness and sometimes outright antagonism of other capitalist powers), but in order to do so the state would have to offer more for peasant grain or charge less for state goods; the former would favour the most efficient and most prosperous peasants (the hated kulaks) and thereby widen disparities in the countryside (ideologically unpalatable),[20] and either the former or the latter would lower the state's accumulation of capital for the expansion of heavy industry (strategically unacceptable). The state refused to follow this course, so the price of manufactures (scarce) rose and the price of grain (ample) fell after 1922, with the peasants consuming more and marketing less of their grain crops (by 1926 grain output was as much as in 1913 but grain sales were only one-third to three-quarters as much). The peasants simply refused to market grain if the prices of state procurements were low or if the prices of state manufactures were high (while, not infrequently, drought-induced harvest failures, as in 1920–21 and 1924–25, further reduced the grain supply). In the early winter of 1927–28 in Ulyanovsk Oblast in the Central Volga the official price of grain (what the state paid) was 1 ruble, 20 kopecks per pud for wheat and 70 kopecks per pud for rye, whereas the market price was 2 rubles, 20 kopecks per pud of wheat and 1 ruble per pud of rye.[21] According to Stalin, the state needed 500 million puds (8,190,000 tonnes) of grain annually in order to meet the demands of the country's cities, industrial centres, regions of non-food (so-called technical, or industrial) crops, and the Red Army,[22] but it procured only 430 million puds (7,043,000 tonnes) from the 1926 crop and 300 million puds (4,914,000 tonnes) from the 1927 crop,[23] prompting Stalin to denounce what he called this "peasant revolt." Will Rogers, the American homespun humorist, visited the Soviet Union at this time and summed up the situation – what he called "the real and the serious trouble" – in his inimitable fashion:

The Government tells the farmer what he shall get for his products — based, of course, on the market value at that time. Well, he is not kicking so much on that as he is on this: When he sells his grain, he can't take the money and go buy what he needs. He can't buy his plows and his wagons and his harness and many other things that ha[ve] to be made by a factory. They cost him more than his grain brought him; and if he did happen to have enough, then the things are not to be found to buy. They have to import most of them and the cost to the farmer is tremendous. So what does the old Farmer do? He won't sell them the stuff.

Rogers added, again keenly: "The Russian Peasant may be Illiterate, but he is not what you call Dumb ... He knows what's the use raising anything if you can't trade it or sell it for what you want. So he is just raising it for his own use," and if he does raise more and the government demands it, then "he illiterally replies, 'No, I eat that. My family very big bread eaters, eat lots of wheat. I have none for sale.' ... The old farmer just grinds his extra up into Vodka, lays in a lot of wood and hibernates for the winter."[24] The peasants simply stored their surplus grain and waited for prices to rise, logically reasoning: "It doesn't hurt for grain to lay in one place for long" and "Why sell grain for one ruble now, since if we wait until spring we can get four or five rubles for it?"[25] In the North Caucasus in 1930 market prices for grain were from eight to ten times higher than state prices.[26]

Certainly the fledgling socialist country was confronted by an agricultural predicament in the second half of the 1920s. It was rightly called a "sales-crisis" by Paul Scheffer, the astute Moscow correspondent of the *Berliner Tageblatt* from 1921 until 1928 (when he was not allowed to return "because of articles that had been increasingly unfriendly over the past three years").[27] "The wheat is there," he reported, "but the peasant is not bringing it to market in sufficient quantities," adding punningly, "That is the kernel of the ... problem."[28] There had been three good harvests in a row by 1928, when grain output was virtually the same as that before the First World War on virtually the same acreage of cropland, but grain sales were 25 to 50 percent lower. This disparity arose because, before the Bolshevik seizure of power (and land) in 1917, the gentry estates and the holdings of the prosperous peasants dominated commercial production (four-fifths), while the much smaller holdings of the srednyaks and bednyaks dominated subsistence production (although each of the two groups accounted for one-half of gross output).²⁹ By 1928, however, the gentry (and church) estates were long gone, leaving commercial production primarily to the kulaks (especially) and srednyaks, and they were unwilling to sell their surplus grain to the state so long as the state offered them low prices for their grain and charged them high prices for its insufficient and inferior manufactures, especially textiles. As Ciliga noted at the time: "There was corn [wheat] in the villages, but the peasants were not interested in giving them up to the State at ridiculously low prices, for this same State sold them its mediocre industrial products in insufficient quantities. Peasant life was returning to [a] natural economy. The town no longer received corn, the countryside no longer received manufactured goods." "The State," he explained, "had neither the means of buying cereals at a higher price, nor of developing its industry on a large scale."³⁰ In withholding their grain the peasants were in effect staging what Ciliga called a "corn strike," especially in 1928 and particularly by the kulaks.³¹ So to extract more grain the state took "extraordinary measures," which were not infrequently "perverted" (abused) by regional and local officials, including arbitrary confiscations and even "road ambushes," but which averted the "danger of famine in the towns" and harmed mainly kulak speculators.³² From 1925 more and more taxes were imposed on the hapless kulaks, whose plight was voiced in a ditty:

> For each rick that was stacked in the field,
> For each horn that the cattle did yield,
> For each cart that was taken to the vale,
> For all of the cats' and dogs' tails,
> For the light and even its lack,
> And everything – just like that!³³

"Chips fly when wood is chopped," noted Scheffer, who added that "this [peasantry] is certainly the thickest of all trees to which the political axe has ever been applied."³⁴

The peasants were not completely blameless for the situation (or at least their age-old agrarian system of choice was not) as part of the problem did lie in the commercially insufficient scale and technologically backward state of peasant farming. At the beginning of 1928 (and the termination of the NEP) only a quarter of the country's 24 million peasants holdings were "surplus farms" – farms with ample land (owned or rented) and some machinery and therefore with output in excess of their needs for subsistence (food, feed, seed) and these 4 million farms were the chief basis of the Soviet Union's export trade and of its grain supply for urban white-collar and blue-collar workers, soldiers, and Chekists. On the average a peasant holding comprised four to five hectares of sown land, one to two cows, one horse, and five to six mouths to feed (including two to three who worked the fields). Peasant labour was primarily manual, with only 15 percent of the holdings having any agricultural machinery (seeders, binders, threshers), wooden ploughs, sickles, and scythes being commonplace.[35] Cereal yields were seven to eight centners per acre, and one peasant could produce enough to feed two persons.[36] Peasant farming was improving but not quickly enough to provide food, labour, and capital for accelerated industrialization. Certainly the Bolsheviks did not believe that the peasants could rapidly increase commercial grain production for larger grain exports in the name of the needs of industrial expansion,[37] even though from the late 1800s to the early 1900s they had managed to make Russia the world's principal producer and exporter of grain – and at a time when the country was undergoing a considerable "industrial revolution" (albeit mainly at the cost of high domestic taxes and large foreign debts).

Meanwhile, the restoration of the economy to pre-war levels by the mid-1920s had raised the question of what path to take next, for the NEP, unlike "war communism," had been intended from the beginning to be a temporary expedient, not a permanent condition – Lenin's famous "one step backward" before taking "two steps forward." Accordingly, from 1925 private business was subjected to increasing restrictions, such as higher taxes and lower priorities. The question of direction triggered the "great industrialization debate" of the last half of the 1920s among the Bolshevik leaders. All of them agreed that much more industrialization – what Bolshevik believers referred to as the "song of steel and iron"[38] – was necessary in order to modernize and strengthen the country not only for its own sake but also for the sake of defence against foreign enemies; they differed, however, on the kind, the means, and the pace of industrialization. The "Leftist" faction under Trotsky, military commissar, favoured the unbalanced development of the economy in the form of hyperindustrialization, financed by the "primitive socialist accumulation of capital," that is, the bleeding of the peasants by means of high prices for manufactures; the Trotskyists also favoured antagonism towards the capitalist countries and the promotion of world revolution – Trotsky's notion of "permanent revolution" – in order to counter foreign hostility (on the assumption that other socialist countries would be friendly). The "Rightist" faction under Nikolai Bukharin, editor of *Pravda*, advocated a more balanced development of industry and agriculture (more or less a continuation of the NEP) by encouraging the peasants, including the kulaks, to prosper and to invest their savings in industry (Russia, he allegedly said, was "to ride into socialism on a peasant nag"); the Bukharinists also urged the normalization of relations with the capitalist world and the abandonment of the notion of world revolution in order to stimulate foreign trade and to lessen the need for heavy industry (defence). The "Centrists" under Stalin first co-opted the Rightists in order to marginalize the Leftists (who were denounced by Stalin as "superindustrializers") and then promptly adopted the latter's policy (with Stalin attacking what he called the "right deviationists" and accusing them of advocating "calico industrialization," i.e., light industry for consumer goods like textiles, and achieving socialism "at a snail's pace"); the Stalinists also argued that instead of fomenting world revolution the regime should first develop a viable model of socialism at home – Stalin's notion of "building socialism in one country" – in order to preserve the world's first example of a socialist state by rendering it impregnable to both foreign (capitalist) enemies and domestic (Nepmen and kulaks) opponents.[39] Stalin emerged victorious, isolating his adversaries at the Fifteenth Party Congress at the end of 1927 and eventually suppressing them (Trotsky was deported in 1929 and assassinated in 1940, Bukharin was demoted in 1928 and a decade later arrested and executed). The cry of the Bolshevik hardliners was "we must become independent of the peasants!"[40] – a question, incidentally, of the fate of 130 million of the 160 million Soviet citizens. But Stalin was not about to be held to ransom by the muzhik, particularly the kulak. He took drastic action, just as Lenin had done in 1921 after the failure of "war communism." This time, however, there would be no appeasement of the peasants; that course had been tried under the NEP and had led to the current stalemate. In effect, Ciliga wrote, Stalin said, "To hell with the NEP!,"[41] and launched collectivization to control agricultural production and its distribution.

Stalin's decision to follow the Leftist path was sparked by the "grain procurement crisis" of 1927, which saw another shortfall in the amount of grain acquired by the state. The deficit was caused partly by hoarding in response to a war scare (Great Britain severed diplomatic relations in 1927, when the Anglo-Russian Trading Cooperative Society [ARCOS], the Soviet trading agency in London, was accused of espionage) and partly by weather-induced mediocre harvests in the southern Ukraine, the Lower and Middle Volga, Western Siberia, and Kazakhstan,[42] but the chief cause was the refusal of the peasants to sell more grain to the state until it offered higher prices and supplied more goods.[43] Instead, as Commissar of Trade Mikoyan, echoing Will Rogers, told his commissariat comrades, given "the fact that the muzhiks are not fools, that they aren't stupid," they hoarded until the war scare faded and prices rose, meanwhile diverting their surplus grain to more profitable beef and milk cattle, as well as *samogon* (homebrew).[44] Stalin said that his nemesis – the kulak – was demanding three times the price offered by the state, which objected and consequently acquired one-third less grain from the 1927 than from the 1926 crop.[45] The shortfall threatened the country's defence capacity, social stability, and heavy industry, and Stalin blamed the profiteering of the private traders (Nepmen) and kulaks, as well as the ineptness and leniency of local officials, so he shifted from economic measures against them to repressive measures ("administrative methods" in officialese), even though the majority of the peasantry now comprised srednyaks, not kulaks or bednyaks.[46]

The militant campaign began on the very first day of 1928, when Stalin sent Molotov first to the Ukraine (and then to the Urals) "to extort grain ... from everyone who had grain," Molotov recalled much later in retirement, adding proudly, "We took away the grain. We paid them in cash, but of course at miserably low prices. They gained nothing. I told them that for the present the peasants had to give us grain on loan" because "industry had to be restored and the army maintained." Molotov travelled through the Ukraine in a "special railroad car ... protected by a security detail" and was careful not to overnight in the villages. Upon his return to Moscow he told Stalin how he had used "all kinds of rather harsh methods of persuasion," and his "boss" was so delighted that he exclaimed, "I would [could] cover you in kisses in gratitude for your actions down there!"[47]

According to Molotov, Stalin "too wanted that experience, and soon afterward set off for Siberia."[48] For three weeks he travelled in a secret government train as far as Irkutsk, stopping along the way at the large cities of Omsk,

Tomsk, and Novosibirsk "to exert desperate pressure" on local officials and "to arrest speculators, kulaks, and other disrupters."[49] At the same time, "brutal pressure" was also to be put on local officials in the European Russian south, in both cases in order to obtain grain from "hoarders" in the two and a half to three months left in the east and the one and a half to two months left in the south before the disruption of transport by spring break-up (*rasputitsa*). Stalin also ordered that as many manufactures as possible (up to 80 percent) be taken from the cities and the non-grain-growing areas and sent to the grain-growing areas.[50] "The situation," he declared, "hinges ... on grain procurements," which "we must capture at any cost." That "cost" included the alienation of the population. Josif Girsa, the Czech consul in Moscow, declared that the "shock" campaign of state grain procurement in 1928 "was in fact nothing more than the forcible robbery of the peasants and the seizure of grain at absurdly low prices, and it did not differ at all from the requisitioning of grain during War Communism." The peasants were "offended and embittered"; at a meeting of Bolshevik leaders on 10 April 1928 it was admitted that 85 percent of the peasantry was "politically disloyal."[51] Two months later, in a letter to the Politburo (the Political Bureau of the Central Committee of the Communist Party of the Soviet Union),[52] the deputy commissar of finance warned: "we must not close our eyes to the fact that the countryside, with the exception of a small segment of poor peasants, is against us, [and] that these attitudes are already beginning to spill over into workers' and urban centres."[53] Stalin, however, argued that the USSR could only develop industry on the basis of "internal accumulation," that is, its own resources in the form of the labour of the working class and the output of the peasant class (including the peasants' tax payments and their purchases of costly goods), because it lacked reparations (unlike Germany at the end of the Franco-Prussian War), exploitable colonies (unlike Great Britain), and European loans (unlike the United States), so that the procurement of grain from the peasants at low prices was "something like a tribute, something like a surtax, which we are forced to take temporarily" – although it was "unpleasant" – until industry had been fully developed.[54] He added, "We can't live like Gypsies, without grain reserves, without certain reserves in case a crop failure occurs, without reserves for maneuvering in the market, without reserves in case war breaks out, and, finally, without some reserves for export."[55]

The "war against the peasants" was underway.

The Course of Collectivization

In December 1927 the Fifteenth Party Congress authorized collectivization,[56] Stalin's solution to the impasse between the peasantry and the government over the marketing of agricultural production, and in the spring of 1928 a Party conference formally approved Stalin's ascendancy and his policy swerve to the left.[57] The First Five-Year Plan (1928–32) of GOSPLAN (the State Planning Commission) was launched, stressing three measures: complete nationalization (only personal effects remained private), heavy industrialization (capital goods, at the expense of consumer goods [light industry]), and agricultural collectivization (at the expense of individual peasant holdings). These measures, which represented the so-called "second communist revolution," meaning the economic revolution, as opposed to the political revolution of 1917, were not widely popular, so Stalin needed absolute control of Soviet society in order to implement them. Accordingly, he commandeered and strengthened the OGPU and the Red Army (and even formed his own palace guard, a cavalry regiment in the Kremlin of some eight hundred Caucasus loyalists),[58] eliminated all economic opponents as well as political rivals, and suppressed all sources of dissent, spoken and written, including within the Party, producing what the Czech consul in Moscow termed "Soviet Bonapartism" with Stalin as the "Bonapartist dictator."[59] Together with Molotov and Kaganovich, he was left to rule with an iron hand.

Collectivization entailed the amalgamation of the individual farmsteads of the peasants into much larger, and many fewer, collective farms (kolkhozes) and state farms (sovkhozes).[60] The former were commonly centred in the peasant villages and the latter primarily on the former gentry estates and,[61] later, often on unused or disused marginal land in frontier regions for experimental undertakings. Kolkhozes, which were formed mainly in the older, settled parts of the country (especially where peasant resistance was strong), overwhelmingly predominated, for they bore a closer resemblance to the age-old peasant commune than did sovkhozes, which were fewer in number and larger in size and were staffed by salaried employees – sovkhozniks, the "rural proletariat," whose entire output went to the state (hence the sovkhozes were sometimes called "factories in the fields" or "grain factories" or "meat factories," etc.). The collective farmers – kolkhozniks – were also required to deliver their output to the state but in fixed amounts and at fixed (and generally low) prices, and the remainder (if any) then went to the collective farm itself (for feed and seed, for example) and lastly to the kolkhozniks themselves (on the basis of their labour input, calculated in "workdays") for food or even sale. Thus, the collective farmers were residual sharers in the output of the kolkhozes and thereby bore the brunt of harvest failures, so that sometimes their own "acre and a cow" (a small plot of land, a couple of head of livestock, and a few fowls) kept them alive. Eugene Lyons declared that the kolkhozniks were simply sharecroppers for the state, with the peasants themselves bluntly putting their status thus: "In the old days we worked for the landlords, now we work for the government. What's the difference?"[62]

On the one hand – at worst – collectivization was a ruthless measure undertaken by Stalin in order to nationalize agriculture by imposing state control over farmland and over the production and marketing of foodstuffs. On the other hand – at best – it was an audacious attempt by the Bolshevik leadership to abruptly transform rural Russia into a more productive and more egalitarian landscape through the communalization and secularization of the peasants and through the consolidation and mechanization of their holdings, hopefully through persuasion (but from 1929 through pressure and brute force).

The Bolsheviks, as Maurice Hindus noted, were determined to modernize the virtually medieval condition of Russian agriculture, with the malignant squalor and numbing hardships of village life,[63] the age-old superstitions[64] and pragmatic conservatism[65] of the muzhik, the wasteful "fences" separating the peasants' scattered strips of ploughland under the venerable three-field system,[66] and the isolating *bezdorozhye* (roadlessness) during rasputitsa – the "impassableness" of spring thaws and fall rains.[67]

Most peasants, however, were unwilling to join the kolkhozes voluntarily as it meant surrendering their personal property and individual freedom for the unproven merits of collective enterprise. Victor Serge, the anti-Stalin Marxist who witnessed the process, estimated that only about 15 percent of the peasants were in favour of the kolkhozes.[68] As Eugene Lyons noted, under the NEP "for the first time almost in Russian history, the vast majority [of the peasantry] acquired land that it could call its own and had not the slightest inclination to relinquish it."[69] As one elderly peasant told Hindus: "Without anything of our own we'd feel as though we didn't belong anywhere at all, and yet they [the Bolsheviks] say that possessions are no good. They are all the time telling us that. Lecturer after lecturer is coming and telling us that we ought to forget possessions and have everything in common. Why then is the desire for it in our blood? Why?"[70] Similarly, another oldtimer told Hindus that, "happy with his family on his own land, he saw no reason for scrapping his individualistic household, joining a kolkhoz and losing his independence."[71] A daughter who had been born (1923) into a peasant household that had migrated to Siberia in the 1920s recollected the unwanted transition from individual farmstead to kolkhoz:

> Before the kolkhoz we had our own ploughland and we planted grain [wheat], millet, and buckwheat. We lived well then. We had a large granary, and it was always full. We were middling, not rich. But collectivization ruined both us and the rich [the kulaks]. Before the kolkhoz my father usually worked for himself in the summer and stocked everything on his own, and in winter he drank and had a good time. Around us he was hardworking, and he made good little tubs. I remember him selling the tubs at the market and coming home and putting three litres of homebrew on the table. He would drink half and fall asleep. And then – to work. At that time everyone made homebrew. The men liked to drink but also to work. When collectivization began, our good life ended. Our granary was emptied. Father sold everything and joined the kolkhoz in 1931. He said that everything would be seized anyway and we would even be deported to the north. They [the authorities] gradually dispossessed those [peasants] who did not want to join the kolkhoz and exiled them. Whether rich or poor, it didn't matter. The main thing was not joining the kolkhoz. Thus were my sister and her husband deported. After serving their terms, many did not return.

She added, "The kulaks did not want to join the kolkhoz. They lived prosperously, you see, and people worked for them. It is true that the kulaks varied – some paid well for work and some did not. It was [also] said that they poisoned the kolkhoz fields and committed arson."[72]

The peasants simply did not want to abandon their age-old life for the uncertain prospects of the vaunted kolkhoz, especially when the initial kolkhozes faltered.[73] The situation was described by William Chamberlin:

The average peasant's desire for a sense of personal ownership, which to him meant freedom and independence, his deep distrust even of his own neighbors, to say nothing of alien city Communists who came to tell him how farming ought to be carried on, could have been overcome only if the collective had meant a swift and marked rise in the peasants' standard of living. But just the reverse occurred. Determined to achieve the maximum amount of industrialization within the shortest possible time, the Soviet leaders found themselves obliged to place heavier and heavier burdens on the peasants. The state needed more grain, more meat, more milk, more cotton, flax, wool, and sugar beets, both for the needs of the city population and for purposes of export. Concentrating on the heavy industries, it did not possess sufficient stocks of manufactured goods to offer the peasants a fair equivalent for their produce.

The result, continued Chamberlin, was the virtual seizure of the output of the peasants at fixed prices in paper rubles. "During the last few years no words have been so hated in the Soviet countryside as *khlebozagotovki* (grain collections) and *kontraktatsiia* (contracting), the former meaning 'the ruthless squeezing out of the last bushel of the peasants' surplus grain' and the latter an arrangement 'under which they were obliged to deliver up all of the surplus of their more important crops for paper rubles and a doubtful chance of buying manufactured goods.'" During his frequent and extensive trips into the countryside during collectivization, Chamberlin found that "the peasants had one keenly defined sense of grievance: that more was being extracted from them, in the form of products and labor, than they were getting in the form of clothes and boots, tea and sugar and soap."[74] One of the most popular black jokes of the time held that the Russian initials of the All-Union Communist Party of the Bolsheviks, VKP (b) (*Vsesoiuznaia Kommunisticheskaia Partiia* [*b*]), really stood for the *vtoroe krepostnoe pravo bolshevikov*, "the second serfdom of the Bolsheviks."[75] Indeed, the Rightist leader Nikolai Bukharin asserted (and later recanted) that collectivization was equatable with "the military feudal exploitation of the peasantry," and the Trotskyist economist Yevgeny Preobrazhensky (whose surname figuratively, and aptly, meant "the transformer")"[76] theorized (and later recanted) that the peasantry represented a colony that the socialist state must exploit.[77] Molotov held the same view. Late in life he recollected that "all of us [Stalin's circle] agreed on ... the building of socialism ... at the expense of the peasant ... because the workers were already giving everything they had" and "we had already taken everything from the bourgeoisie," so "only the peasantry remained from whom we could take something so as to move forward."[78]

Besides, the Bolsheviks did not trust the peasantry, as Andrew Cairns's official guide explained to him in June 1932 in Kiev: "The communists, she said, realized very well that the French revolution had been broken by the peasants,[79] and they were very much afraid the Russian peasants would break the Russian revolution if they were left alone as they were in [the] NEP (when things were very good, and there was an abundance of food and she could take a holiday and spend money and not worry about tomorrow). The Party was, therefore, determined to change the psychology of the peasants and eventually to make good communists of them."[80]

To do so would not be easy, for the village was distinctly stratified. As an example, in the spring of 1929 the village of Novaya-Mikhailovka in the Minusinsk Rayon of Western Siberia consisted of 371 households: 224 households of srednyaks, 80 of bednyaks, 67 of zazhitochniks and kulaks (or "rich," peasants, as the Bolsheviks preferred to label them because some had very large holdings of arable land, agricultural machinery [mowers, threshers], mills, churns, and hired workers), and 0 of batraks (hired hands).[81] The bednyaks and batraks, although fearful and distrustful, were the most willing to collectivize, but they brought little or nothing with them, and, besides, they were illiterate and unskilled. As a bednyak in a village in Arkhangelsk Oblast admitted, "The srednyak is already able to live on his own, but necessity drives us [bednyaks] into the collective."[82] Their entry meant, however, as Consul Girsa correctly predicted in the spring of 1928, that "primarily the worst layer of the rural population will enter the kolkhozes, willingly entering enterprises subsidized by the state because they have nothing to lose," adding that "these villagers are professionally and morally the least qualified, so it will soon become clear that this new and expensive experiment of Soviet power will end in great confusion."[83] A witness to Girsa's forecast recalled the experience of one kolkhoz: "The bednyaks hankered to enrich themselves at the expense of the kulakized srednyaks. These bednyaks were Grisha (Ol'kin), Peter, and Dmitry Krutov; Dmitry became a foreman in the kolkhoz, appointing himself. But the bednyaks lived up to their name. They led a wild life, and they did not put manure on their fields, so their crop was poor and thus there was nothing for their livestock to eat, and they kept fewer cattle." He added that "two years after collectivization everything was broken, nothing was left – neither cart nor sledge," and "they all regarded the kolkhoz not as they had at first but as something alien."[84]

Although the kolkhoz offered several benefits, notably lower taxes and more goods, the srednyaks and especially the kulaks were loath to join it, having to relinquish their property (land, livestock, implements) and autonomy to the collective. As peasants in the northern Ukraine told Gareth Jones in the spring of 1933: "They [the Bolsheviks] took away our land. Why should we work if we have not our own land? They took away our cows. Why should we work if we have not our own cows and if we have to share what is our own with all the drunkards and lazy fellows in the village? They took away our wheat. Why should we work, if we know that our wheat will be taken from us?"[85] And the novelist Mikhail Sholokhov, who witnessed the process, portrayed the same reaction on the part of a Don Cossack peasant: "I've built up my farm, and got a hump on my back and callouses on my hands into the bargain, and now have I got to give everything into the common stock: my cattle, and grain, and fowls, and my home too? That way it works out that you give your wife up to others, and you go yourself to the whores, that's all … I'll be giving the collective farm a yoke of oxen … a mare with foal, all my implements and grain. And another will be giving only his lousy pants."[86]

Siberian peasants, who had a reputation for independence,[87] reiterated this feeling of a lack of vested interest in the kolkhoz to the French journalist, Pierre Dominique: "the peasant no longer has the feeling that he is working for himself, and he works only half as hard," for in the kolkhoz he knew that as long as he did the minimum amount of work – "above all, no more than his neighbour" – his livelihood was assured.[88] Moreover, as a local Party official in the Lower Volga stressed, the middle-peasant member of the kolkhoz "*does not consider the kolkhoz his*" because he was subjected to marginalization (*ottiranie*, literally "pushing aside") and thus weakly represented in its management, as well as in the membership of the rural soviet. The official added, "to the peasant who in past years knew beforehand from memory what had to be done in the spring, it is really terrible and ridiculous to wait until planting without knowing concretely [from the manager] how it will be organized."[89]

Furthermore, the earliest kolkhozes in particular were so badly conceived and so badly organized as to be unattractive alternatives to the individual farmsteads. A report of a rayon Party committee in the West Region of 1 February 1931 did not paint a pretty picture of the recently organized kolkhozes there, complaining of shortages of seed and fertilizer, the lack of labour discipline, drunkenness, theft, and simulation – so much so that some long-time members were leaving in disgust and even bednyaks were loath to join, saying, "We shall not enter the kolkhoz until we slaughter our last cow. How stupid it was to call oneself a poor peasant [in order to gain preferential admission] – now we are expected [by the Bolsheviks] to be the first to enter the kolkhoz ... the kolkhozniks do nothing. Food is rotting. We will all starve to death in the kolkhoz."[90] Little wonder that labour productivity would prove so low on the collective farms.

The kulaks were the strongest resisters to collectivization because, being the most successful of the peasants, they had the most to lose.[91] To the Bolsheviks they were the prime class enemy in the countryside – the most individualistic, the most exploitive, and the most prosperous of the peasants, or at least of those with capitalist instincts. In one of Andrei Platonov's stories his protagonist expresses the Bolshevik view of kulaks: "Beneath the hunter crawled diligent ants, burdened like respectable little people with heavy loads for their households. They are vile creatures, he thought, with the character of kulaks. They spend all their lives dragging goods into their kingdom; they exploit every solitary animal, big and small, that they can dominate; they know nothing of the universal common interest and live only for their own greedy, concentrated well-being."[92] As such the kulaks under Stalinist socialism were as doomed as were the captains of industry.[93]

Contrary to Bolshevik taxonomy, however, kulaks – literally, "fists" (or a "strike force" in military parlance) – were not all "rich." They were defined fairly by Eugene Lyons as "the more industrious, more unscrupulous, and more prosperous peasants."[94] Whiting Williams concurred, observing: "they weren't really very rich, these kulaks, but they were the best farmers in the villages – and usually the hardest workers," so "when they were dispossessed and driven into exile, the standard of farming, never particularly high, fell alarmingly."[95] Sometimes the kulaks rented extra land and hired extra labour, and in Tsarist Russia they were commonly regarded as the villages' tightfisted entrepreneurs and moneylenders (Chamberlin's "Shylock"). In

Russian literature and folklore the kulak was depicted as a bloodsucker and cutthroat.[96] Hindus, who knew whereof he spoke (his father was a kulak in the Belorussian village of Bolshoye Bikovo, where he was raised in one of four Jewish families),[97] wrote that "the chief social sin of the koolak was lending money and even more often grain, hay or straw to his poorer neighbor, who would be charged an exorbitant interest in cash, in kind and most commonly in labor to be performed in the future during the busy seasons in the field."[98] By virtue of this very role, however, the kulaks, as well as the srednyaks, "served as a guarantee against hunger for poor peasants and those with small landholdings" by lending them food, feed, and seed until the next harvest, and during the 1928–34 famine starving peasants were heard to say, "return the kulaks, they will feed us."[99] Fyodor Mochulsky, a Gulag boss during the Second World War, recalled that "a great number" of his prisoners were "simple farmers," kulaks, "whose only fault was that they loved the land and were able to produce food on it." He added, "[they] were the hardest-working people we had in our countryside. They loved the land, and they learned how to work it well," and "the earth, in turn, rewarded these workers, and they prospered."[100]

Initially the regime tried to coax the kulaks – and all individual farmsteaders generally – to join the kolkhoz, but when they balked it coerced them from the outset under the slogan "whoever does not enter the kokhoz is an enemy of Soviet power" with so-called "extraordinary" (repressive) measures, including higher grain quotas, higher grain taxes, lower prices for grain but higher prices for goods, lower priority for equipment and materials, and "voluntary" insurance premiums and bond purchases – and eventually confiscation, eviction, deportation, and even execution. One peasant couple wrote despairingly to their Red Army son in early 1928: "The payments, Seryozha, are impossible. They've added further voluntary insurance for 500 rubles. Nobody gets insurance voluntarily, they divvied it up by force and collected it. Now they've sent in a lottery bond for 1,100 rubles, also voluntary, but they're making people take it by force. So, Seryozha, it's payment after payment. Nobody is happy with Soviet power, not one citizen, and how can you be happy, Seryozha? The Bolsheviks turn out not to be rulers but robbers, not a proletarian government but an SR [Socialist Revolutionary, i.e., bourgeois] one."[101] By demonizing the kulaks, the Bolshevik leadership did release a long repressed popular desire for vengeance against them,[102] so that there was undoubtedly less popular sympathy for their plight than that of other peasants.

Private traders ("profiteers"), both rural and urban, were also targeted. In January 1928 alone the OGPU arrested (on charges of speculation) some three thousand private grain traders throughout the country; the largest stockpiles of grain hidden by private traders were discovered in the Ukraine.[103] The impact on urban supply could be sudden and drastic, as Shaporina discovered when she went shopping in early 1930:

> Yesterday, 16 February, I went to the market to look for butter. All of the private traders had been closed. It is remarkable that they had not been closed by violence, no, but by the imposition of a tax of 20 thousand [rubles]. The other day I. told me that her parents traded on Sennaya [Haymarket Square, St Petersburg's oldest market]. Completely unexpectedly they [the vendors] were suddenly notified that they had to pay an additional 8,000 [rubles] for 1927, 1928, and 1929. Today they were notified that tomorrow morning they [the authorities] would come and inventory all of their property, and they left one bed and one dress. And then they still threatened to deport them. Where, why? I am horrified.[104]

Despite the draconian measures, the harvest of wheat and rye in 1928 was 500 to 600 million puds (8,190,000 to 9,828,000 tonnes) less than in 1927, owing partly to harvest failures (from frost and drought) in the Ukraine, the North Caucasus, and the Central Black Earth; by 1 April eight times less grain was procured than by the same date in 1927 from the Ukraine and the North Caucasus, which together normally contributed from one-half to two-thirds of the country's output.[105] So the regime tried to squeeze more and more grain from more and more peasants, such that in 1929 the kulak became any peasant who resisted collectivization – that is, procurement.[106]

Stalin called 1929 "the year of the great break [*velikii perelom*]" (the Russian precursor of Mao's "Great Leap Forward"), meaning the gaining of the upper hand in the rural class struggle against the bourgeoisie by the proletariat (and the resultant "furious upheaval" [*la tourmente déchaînée*], as Leningrader Olga Tolstaya-Voyeikova put it). Solzhenitsyn was more brutal in deconstructing "the Great Turning Point, or as the phrase had it, the Great Break," for we were "never told what it was that broke." "It was the backbone of Russia," the "backbone and mainstay of the Russian people" – the peasantry.[107] Economically, the rupture was marked by the termination of private trade, the acceleration of collectivization, and the intensification of oppression, particularly against the individual farmsteaders, notably the kulaks. In the spring the regime introduced the so-called "Ural-Siberian method" of grain procurement – more accurately, the "gouge-the-kulak method" – whereby special village commissions consisting of bednyaks and srednyaks assigned grain requisition quotas to the peasant households on a "class" basis. So the kulaks were ordered to surrender their surplus grain and thereby meet most of the village's quota, and those who failed to do so faced fines, imprisonment, expropriation, or deportation.[108] By the end of the year enough grain had been obtained not only to fulfill the plan but also for the first time to create a "reserve grain fund" of 100 million puds (1,638,000 tonnes) for the needs of industrialization.[109]

As well as extorting the labour and the output of the peasants, the regime attacked their traditional institutions, such as the household (*dvor*), the peasant assembly (*skhod*), the village mill (a meeting place for informal politics), the village market (*rynok*), and the church – the bases of peasant society. By the end of the First Five-Year Plan in 1932 that way of life, which had prevailed for a millennium, would no longer exist.[110] Thereafter the relationship of the peasants to the land was radically different, as one of them attested:

> Before the kolkhoz the peasant was always drawn to the land. He had a conscientious attitude to work, he had a lot of energy, and he knew why he worked and what he would get for his work. After collectivization he understood that none of it was his, that he would get nothing and so he worked only in order to pass the day quickly. He was not interested in his work whatsoever. He strove to pay a lot of attention to his personal plot [in accordance with the kolkhoz charter of 1935, the plot measured from about 100 feet by 100 feet up to about 200 feet by 200 feet (about 35 metres by 35 metres up to about 70 metres by 70 metres) beside his house], for he knew that if he abandoned his personal plot, he would perish.[111]

Politically, 1929 was marked by the demise of the Rightists. They made their last stand at the Central Committee's plenums in April and November, when they advocated the importation of grain to meet the deficiency of procurement until the problem of grain supply was overcome by encouraging the efforts of the more prosperous peasants.[112] But Stalin's Centrists believed that outlays for grain imports would lessen investment in heavy industry as well as outlays for imports of industrial equipment and raw materials for light industry, and, moreover, give free rein to their "implacable" class enemy in the village, the kulaks.[113] In a speech to the April plenum Stalin explained the role of the kulaks in the grain problem, namely, the fact that in the previous two years (1927–28) the state had needed to procure 500 million puds (8,190,000 tonnes) of grain each year for the cities, industrial centres, the Red Army, and regions of technical, or industrial (non-food), crops but had been able to get only 350 million (5,733,000 tonnes) by means of voluntary marketing (*samotyok*) and had had to get the other 150 million puds (2,457,000 tonnes) "on the basis of managed pressure [i.e., coercion and force] on the kulaks and the prosperous strata in the village." He concluded:

> Grain is not an ordinary commodity. Grain is not cotton, which cannot be eaten and cannot be sold to just anyone. By contrast with cotton, grain under current conditions is a commodity that everyone gets and without which it is not possible to live. This fact the kulak takes into account, and he holds grain back, thereby infecting grain holders in general. The kulak knows that grain is the money of hard currency. The kulak knows that a surplus of grain is not only the means of his own enrichment but also the means of enslavement of the poor. Under current conditions grain surpluses in the hands of the kulaks are the means of the economic and political empowerment of kulak elements. So in taking these surpluses from the kulaks we not only facilitate the supply of the cities and the Red Army with grain but also undermine the means of the economic and political empowerment of the kulaks.[114]

As for the Rightist contention that some capitalist countries would be willing to give the USSR grain on credit, Stalin dismissed it as "nonsense," declaring, "wouldn't it be laughable to think that the capitalists of the West have suddenly begun to pity us and want to give us several dozen million puds of grain virtually gratis or on long-term credit?," and adding, "the fact is that for half a year now various capitalist groups have wanted to probe us, our financial potential, our creditworthiness, and our stability."[115] Neither foreign nor domestic capitalists were to be trusted.

At the end of the year, at a conference of agricultural functionaries, Stalin raised the slogan of "the liquidation of the kulaks as a class." A week later, on 5 January 1930, "all-out collectivization" was decreed by the Politburo; the legislation stipulated the elimination of the kulaks and the total collectivization of agriculture within the shortest possible time (the most important grain-growing regions – the Ukraine, the North Caucasus, the Middle and Lower Volga – were to be completely collectivized in 1930 and the others in 1931). Stalin was in a hurry, and he was not one to suffer opposition. Now the peasants were enrolled in kolkhozes primarily by "administrative repressive-punitive methods," whereby the political authorities employed "mainly force, with the help of threats, arrests, dispossession of the kulaks, and deportation 'to Solovki' [a Gulag archipelago]."[116] As many as 338,000 kulak families were subjected to one of three forms of kulakization in 1930: destitution, deportation, or destruction. Those considered "non-threatening" were simply dispossessed; those regarded as "dangerous" were exiled to remote and unarable regions; and those deemed "hostile" were imprisoned or executed. Most of them belonged to the first category, which entailed expropriation of their property and relocation to the worst land in their rayon.[117] Those kulaks who were deported rather than relocated were allowed to take twenty puds (720 pounds) of baggage (per family) with them into exile, and their remaining moveable and immoveable property was expropriated for the use of kolkhozes and kolkhozniks.[118] The watchword was "Bolshevik tempo," which was explained to Muggeridge by his Russian-language teacher anecdotally:

> A peasant visiting Moscow started asking what was meant by "tempo." His guide took him to a large building and said, "Before the Revolution that building would have taken twelve years to build, but now we finish it in one year." Back in his village, the peasant wanted to explain what he had learned to his father, but in the village there were no buildings large enough for him to illustrate his point, only miserable huts. At last he thought of an idea. He took his father to the cemetery and said: "You want to know what 'tempo' is – well, before the Revolution it

would have taken us twelve years to fill the cemetery, but now we fill it in one year."[119]

The inevitable "excesses" (*peregiby*), some of them barbaric, on the part of overenthusiastic and unsympathetic officials at the local level prompted Stalin's "Giddy with Success" speech of 2 March 1930, which demanded moderation in order to pre-empt outright rebellion following what Lyons called "a conquest of the peasantry."[120] Moscow's pressure to quicken the tempo of collectivization had prompted local Party workers to use even more threats and more force on the peasants to join the kolkhozes. One zealous official in a Komi Republic village told his underlings: "If they do not enrol voluntarily, then enrol them by force of arms."[121] It was said that some enrollers told the peasants to form two lines and choose either the one on the left for going into the kolkhozes or the one on the right for going into exile. Kolkhozes formed in this way were represented as having been established voluntarily as local officials did not want to disappoint their superiors for fear of being "purged" (demoted, dismissed, or "liquidated") from their politically and economically safe jobs. Similarly, a high Party official who was sent in 1931 to a rayon in the Central Black Earth to check peasant complaints that had been mailed to President Kalinin reported:

> The mistakes [of 1930–31] even exceed those of 1929–30 in their nature and depth ... All-out collectivization has, as a rule, been put into practice regardless of the result of peasant voting. In the village of Zelyony during the vote almost all of the individual farmsteaders abstained, with none voting either for or against collectivization. Nevertheless, the chairman of the meeting declared: "Since nobody voted against, all-out collectivization is approved." If the individual farmsteaders persisted, "all kinds of repression" were undertaken – under various pretexts their horses, cows, fodder, and even their household plots were taken from them.[122]

The mood of the disaffected peasantry in the face of this mounting pressure and arrogant trickery was captured by the Party secretary of the Middle Volga Kray in a letter in spring to Stalin:

Under the conditions of a harvest failure we [nevertheless] took all of the payments from the villages for 6 months (autumn 1929–winter 1930) – more than 60 mil[lion] rub[les], including 13 mil[lion] rubles as advances on tractors. For many peasants their conception of collectivization is inescapably connected with all of these difficulties and the increasing financial pressure on the villages ... If we add to this [plight] such facts as not giving the kolkhozniks a single kopeck for his work ... not letting the peasant women have a horse to ride to the hospital, the inclusion of dozens of villages and towns in the formation of every "giant" [kolkhoz] without their consent, and the scandalously careless and wasteful attitude of the majority of kolkhoz managers to the issuing of orders for every sort of work (and all of these facts have occurred), *then one is surprised only by the sufferance of the peasants, who have endured these outrages in silence until the beginning of March*.[123]

Peasant outrage culminated in uprisings, some of them involving hundreds of rebels and armed violence that required suppression by not just the militia (police) but even OGPU and Red Army soldiers. The revolts peaked in the spring and came close to civil war; March saw some 1,650 peasant revolts throughout the country – excluding the Ukraine – involving 750,000 to 800,000 peasants.[124] Some kulaks, the most abused, resorted to terrorism; in Western Siberia in nine months of 1930 they committed one thousand "terrorist acts," almost two-thirds of which involved killings and most of which took place in the late winter and early spring.[125] These were to be the last in a long list of peasant revolts on Russian soil.

Following Stalin's call for moderation there was an exodus of peasants from the kolkhozes, a "former person" observing that "people streamed out of the collective farms. In some cases only the chairman remained, in other cases the whole collective disappeared. Some remained in existence thanks to the 'zealous class-consciousness' of a few members, usually layabouts, rogues and drunkards, who had nowhere else to go."[126] Collectivization and particularly kulakization continued nonetheless, albeit in a less frenetic and more orderly fashion. And the relentlessly increasing procurements, which left the peasants little or even no grain for seed the next spring or for food over the winter, forced them to butcher their livestock, including family cows and work horses – which in turn meant less plowing and carting in the future.[127] One kolkhoznik's son described his father's hard toil for zero gain in the Altai Kray: "His year-round fanatical work on the kolkhoz provided absolutely nothing: neither grain nor money. Serf labour for corveé. He was a shock worker on the kolkhoz, and he earned more workdays in the year than most of the kolkhozniks – but what came of it! There would be no workdays, no shoes sewn from them. Work was depreciated 100% then! Everything went to the state."[128] Sometimes the struggling kolkhozes were unable to pay their members for their work in cash or kind, and instead their unrequited workdays were recorded as notches on a stick – prompting them to lament: "how many years we worked for sticks [i.e., peanuts]."[129]

Rather than face starvation, many peasants simply abandoned their farmsteads, quit the kolkhozes, and migrated to the cities for work and food, especially from the Ukraine, the North Caucasus, and the Middle and Lower Volga, leaving free land, livestock, and implements for the kolkhozes and – in the case of exiled kulaks – supplying free labour for remote mines, logging camps, and construction projects.[130] As Gareth Jones noted in 1931, "Bread is not the only produce of the collective farm," for "the collective farm has the duty of supplying the factories not only with grain but with men," explaining that "the use of machinery and the better organization of work upon the farms will, it is argued, liberate for the factories many millions of workers who will not be needed in an agriculture so mechanized as to cut down the number of hands required." These "leavers" (*otkhodniki*) were to be recruited for industrial centres. The resultant impression, incidentally, was "the most striking of all" – the absence of unemployment, with even beggars disappearing from the streets.[131] Altogether the First Five-Year Plan saw 10 million peasants leave the villages to join the ranks of urban workers;[132] in 1929–30 alone Soviet cities increased their total population by 3 million persons,[133] primarily through migration (and in the process incurred a long-standing urban housing shortage). In the face of this increasing rural-to-urban migration, as well as decreasing grain output (owing not only to the declining number of growers but also to the declining sowings on the part of the remaining growers), from 1930 Soviet cities experienced food shortages. In early 1931 the provision allotment for urban citizens in the second and third rationing categories was reduced by 21.4 million puds (350,519 tonnes) nationwide.[134]

An Unnatural Famine?

After a slow start in 1928, the number of kolkhozes increased sharply (and, conversely, the number of individual farmsteaders decreased sharply) with the intensification of collectivization. There were 33,000 kolkhozes (comprising 416,000, or less than 2 percent, of all peasant households) on 1 July 1928 but 106,000 (comprising nearly 15 million, or 58 percent of all peasant households) by 10 March 1930 (right after Stalin's "Giddy with Success" admonition) – all of which were not formed "without grave errors, excesses, and passions," in Kaganovich's euphemistic understatement.[135] Whereas less than 2 percent of peasant households had joined kolkhozes – primarily voluntarily – by the end of 1928, by the beginning of 1934, 65 percent had joined, primarily involuntarily, and the remaining 35 percent accounted for less than one-sixth of Soviet grainland (meaning that they were quite small-scale).[136] Meanwhile, the sown area under kolkhozes increased from 63 million hectares in 1929 to 92 million in 1932, and of this increase of 29 million hectares 12 million were lands seized from kulaks and 8 million were lands gained from individual farmsteaders, while 9 million were disused lands.[137]

The growing yearly squeeze from early 1927 until the end of 1933 on the individual peasant farmsteaders and their resultant privation are illustrated in letters sent by some of them – in this case ethnic Germans – from the Ukraine (mostly), the Middle Volga, and Western Siberia to relatives and friends in North and South Dakota describing their worsening predicament and desperately soliciting help:[138]

> 24 February 1927: "Our harvest was good and much grew. Only money is lacking. And why? Everything we grow is sold so cheaply. Since [the] fall, wheat is only one ruble per pud [36 lb.] ... That is under the regime's control. Corn is 40 kopecks per pud. Whatever a person must buy is terribly expensive. So that is why we have no money."[139]
>
> 6 June 1928: "Overall, compared to the year 1926, our lives are now at least 75% worse."
>
> 30 July 1929: "There are no more large[-scale] farmers who seed 100 or more dessiatines [*desyatinas*] of land. Instead, each soul is allotted 2½ dessiatines. Figured in with that amount is the yard, livestock pasture, and garden, and so not much remains for seeding [grain]."
>
> ? December 1930: "Everyone has to become a member of the collec-

tive" and "It has been strictly prohibited that any of us say 'my' any longer, but instead we have to say 'ours.'"

? January 1931: "They [the authorities] take all the grain away, paying 80 kopecks per pud, and then the farmer himself must buy it back again, at the rate of 10–12 rubles per pud [a fifteenfold difference]."

? January 1931: "If you do not enter [the kolkhoz] of your own accord, they will take away all your belongings, fining you so heavily it can't be paid."

7 August 1931: "The whole year through it goes this way: grain procurement, meat procurement, vegetable procurement, whatever it is to be found is then procured, or, as it is said in good German speech, extorted or robbed. Everything goes for [to] the regime, and if you don't have what they demand, then go to the market and buy it there from the swindlers, for a scandalously high price" and "The business [commercial] booths stand empty: there is no sugar, no soap, no kerosene, no tobacco, no dry goods, no writing paper, or cigarette paper – nothing, completely empty."

Summer 1931: "There were such heavy taxes levied against us that we couldn't pay them. Then they took everything away from us and chased us from our house. Our belongings and also our sister's were sold at auction. We have nothing but what we carry on our bodies."

24 August 1931: "We have come to a time when people are glad there is not a harvest. If much grows, the produce must be given up; if little grows, a person has to give that up too. With a good harvest, there is no bread and with a poor harvest there is no bread either. People here prefer a weak harvest over a good harvest, for with a weak harvest there is not as much work, not as much torn clothing, for they have need of clothing, but no need for a harvest that does not belong to them anyway."

27 March 1932: "Everything is wasted and empty here with us, so there isn't even a handful of straw that can be found in the threshing area. Dozens of horses are so malnourished that they can't pull anything any more, and the same with cows, which must be lifted up so they can stand. People don't know anything about milk anymore, and have forgotten they once drank it, and we don't remember either how bread tastes. We don't see sugar, and are short of everything, so that we are poor, miserable, and naked in our distress."

Spring 1932: "Bread has climbed to 3 rubles a pound, a price at which nobody can buy any.[140] People await the growth of sorrel and stinging nettles – there is nothing else for which to hope. There were stores of potatoes buried in the ground during [last] autumn as provisions for [this] spring, as well as seed potatoes, but people were commanded in February to uncover them, and ... [t]hat cost many people their lives, for when the great cold came ... the greatest part of the potatoes froze, and people remained without provisions, so that a full[-fledged] famine raged ... There was an epidemic of spotted typhus this past summer, and this winter smallpox was severe ... After the potatoes were taken away ... at least half the people in the villages who took part in an uprising fled. The farmers had destroyed grain storage bins and buildings that held provisions, and where there weren't any, the farmers divided up the collective's livestock, not as property ... but to rescue themselves from the hunger-death. No more Red Army units are sent to places of unrest. Now, they send only communists who get their rations from the [O]GPU secret police. One Red Army division, sent out of Samara at the beginning of March, came through a peaceful village and found such a situation there that they divided up their provisions to [with] the people, refusing to go further."

? March 1933: "Thousands have starved, and thousands more will starve. People walk around, searching for bread, but there is none. The robbers [authorities] have taken the last of everything away from us."

23 December 1933: "In 1900 we went to Siberia with our four children ... a distance of 4,000 kilometers from the old homeland. It is a somewhat cold, but also a rich and fertile region. Land was good and plentiful, and also cheap. Because of a land shortage we left our old home ... We came here poor, and we started to build up our property and belongings ... By our 12th year here, we had all of the necessary machinery, even a threshing machine ... We had twenty work horses, a yoke of oxen, cows, sheep, pigs – and enough of everything ... When the communists began to come here in 1919, they began to levy taxes, and so little by little we began to lose what we had built up. In 1929 came the command that anyone owning a threshing machine, or having hired men and maids, would lose their rights, and all of their property was annulled, that is, everything was taken from us and sold at auction. People were taken

far away from here, into a strange, cold region, to a primitive forest, where those poor people had to work and were fed so badly that thousands of them died of hunger. That is the lot of those who worked so diligently, to get something for themselves."[141]

Peasant Reaction

Many – and probably most – peasants resisted collectivization, either passively or actively, and sometimes violently, especially at the beginning, when the Bolshevik presence in the countryside was weaker.[142] John Scott, Magnitogorsk's American booster, asserted that Soviet citizens grumbled but did not revolt because they were willing to help build what they believed would be a better society, so they accepted what they assumed would be short-term privation in return for long-term prosperity. Besides, he continued, Russians were famously accustomed to hardships, while the starving were too weak to rebel. The same view was expressed by one of Scott's fellow welders, a Russian: "Just wait five or ten years and we won't need one single thing from the capitalist world," he said, adding that "then we won't have to export food. We'll eat it all ourselves."[143]

In fact, however, while Russians may have been willing to suffer until better times, most peasants were unwilling to tolerate force and theft – and their unwillingness increased as collectivization intensified. Their resistance included the writing of letters and telegrams of protest to the heads of Soviet organs, the editors of newspapers, and higher officials, notably President Kalinin (the one-time peasant) but even First Secretary Stalin,[144] pamphleteering (the distribution of anti-Soviet leaflets and posters), the voicing of complaints and demands at official meetings and public demonstrations, the deliberate destruction of their livestock to prevent their expropriation,[145] "terrorist acts," and open revolts. Many others simply did what a peasant family known to Leningrader Shaporina did: "they have sold their cow and horse and abandoned their farmstead, and everywhere they [the peasants] are slaughtering livestock, fleeing to the forest and the city – total ruin."[146]

For those peasants who stayed, demonstrations quickly became frequent and massive. In 1926 and 1927 together there were only 63 mass demonstrations, 22 of them in Siberia (where the peasants were generally more prosperous and more independent-minded),[147] but there were 709 in 1928 and

1,307 (with 350,000 demonstrators) in 1929.[148] It was much worse in 1930, when the OGPU recorded some 1,500 demonstrations with 350,000 participants in January and February together and more than 6,500 demonstrations with 1,600,000 participants in March alone.[149] Women, incidentally, dominated the protests in the villages and the cities alike because the care of their families traditionally fell to them, not the men; also, in light industry, where women were paid less and fed less than workers in heavy industry, where men predominated.[150] In the villages, observed a small-town disenfranchised person, "almost everywhere the women opposed the formation of collective farms,"[151] owing to both rumours that collectivization would affect their traditional social and religious roles in the household and to actual policies (particularly the collectivization of livestock and poultry) that would undercut their basic economic role in the household. Their opposition may also have arisen from the fact that the authorities tended to deal less harshly with women than with men.[152]

Peasant resistance was more effectual when it took one form or other of the only tactic at their disposal – their refusal to feed the urban population, the industrial workforce, the army, and the police by planting less grain ("sowing for oneself") and breeding fewer livestock, or by consuming more grain and meat and marketing less, or by hoarding and even destroying output, or by working to rule or not at all (the so-called Italyanka)[153] – what might be called the tactics of peasant guerilla warfare.[154] Some peasants sabotaged spring sowing by not doing what Kaganovich exhorted them to do, namely, to prepare the seeds by collecting, winnowing, cleaning, testing, treating, and drying them, and to plough early and plough deep ("as soon as the soil begins to warm," he said, "immediately begin plowing and plow properly, deep" because "every day counts," and he cited the sayings "sow a day earlier and you will reap a week sooner" and "the deeper you plow the more bread you will chew"). The Polish trade advisor in Moscow reported in 1932 that during sowing Ukrainian peasants resorted to "cheating," which was done by mixing sand with seed to show that they had met the predetermined amount of sown grain by weight, or by sowing fewer seeds than normal on the predetermined acreage, or even by sowing something – whatever they liked – other than grain in the soil.[155] At the height of the famine in the spring of 1933, claimed an old Kazakh, the authorities did not even entrust sowing to the peasants because they simply ate the seed, so it was sown by airplane, and wherever it fell outside the fields the starving flocked there like chickens to scavenge it.[156]

Similarly, the peasants subverted harvesting by ignoring another Kaganovich behest, namely: "When you have a good crop, it is important not to lose a single day. It is said that one day feeds a year. If you are late in harvesting, the grain shells and is wasted."[157] So, spitefully, not only was the harvest delayed but only some of it was reaped while some of it was looted. At the end of 1932 the Politburo vilified the Lower Volga rayon of Nizhne-Chirsk for

> the massive loss and spoilage of the harvest ... through the extremely inferior sowing of winter and spring ploughland in 1931–32, the leaving of 26,000 hectares of standing grain in the fields and 7,000 hectares of mown grain in windrows under the snow, the spoilage of stacked grain, and the criminal delay of grain threshing (on 15 December [only] 95 thous. of 142 thous. hectares of mown grain had been threshed) – which has resulted in colossal losses of the 1932 crop in the rayon, the delay of grain threshing, the transfer of very inferior grain to the state, and the fulfillment of a criminally small amount of the plan for grain procurement.[158]

The theft of grain – both seed and crop – increased, of course, as the famine worsened. In late 1932 Stalin and his inner circle blamed procurement shortfalls on "looting" and "pilfering" of grain by the peasants in order to insure themselves against a repeat of their starvation in the spring of 1932.[159] Kaganovich noted one common way of skimming seed grain: "Seeds are thrown into the drill, the lever is put at eight poods [puds] and screwed up, then the sower unscrews this lever, puts it at five poods instead of the eight required per hectare, sows five poods and keeps the remaining three poods for himself" – which deprives the kolkhoz and the state of twenty to thirty puds at harvest time, and "the same thing happens with hand sowing."[160] Kolkhoz officials themselves sometimes colluded with the kolkhozniks in the theft of grain, as the Polish consul in Kiev reported in the summer of 1933:

> Some kolkhozes specifically designate oldsters 60–70 years of age as guards [of the grain stores and fields] so as to make it easier to steal

and hide dozens of centners. These so-called 'barbers' [i.e., snippers] cut whole sacks of spikes [ears].¹⁶¹ Everywhere the fields are guarded fairly closely, for which a disproportionately large number of people are recruited. In some rayons the guards on foot and horseback number in the thousands. Despite this [precaution], they steal at night, and in one rayon 127 of the 947 guards [themselves] were caught stealing. For guarding the fields all hunting rifles are confiscated, and in Kiev at the present time it is impossible to find gunpowder and small shot.

He added that the thieving peasants were severely punished, but often the fate of those who were not caught was no better, the Polish military attaché writing that "numerous instances of the death of whole groups (several dozen persons) as a result of the eating of unripe ears of grain have been observed."¹⁶² The survivors tried, often in vain, to hide the stolen grain, "generally ... everywhere: in the ground [in pits], in stoves, under floors, and even behind icons," said a government inspector's report.¹⁶³ Such "theft" of their own grain was immortalized in the apocryphal legend of Pavlik Morozov, who was said to have dutifully reported the hiding of some sacks of grain by his father, who was then shot for this crime against the state, whereupon Pavlik was killed by his own vengeful family and became a martyr to the Soviet cause.

The widespread loss of grain to theft – from whole sheaves to several kernels in secret pockets (especially in the country's breadbasket heartland of the Ukraine, the North Caucasus, and the Lower Volga) – was instrumental in the promulgation on 7 August 1932 of the notorious "Law on the Preservation of Socialist [Public] Property," or, as the peasants dubbed it, the "law of five spikelets," because it was used to prosecute them for gleaning as little as a handful of grain from harvested fields. This law stipulated the "supreme penalty" (shooting) for offenders or, under "extenuating circumstances," imprisonment for ten years. It gave rise to a saying in the village: *Von on, von on zaderzhalsya. Von on, von on pobezhal. Desyat let emu dadite, koloski on sobral* (There he is, he's dawdled. There he is, he's skedaddled. Give him ten years, he's picked some ears).¹⁶⁴ Kaganovich called the measure the "great law" and declared that, under it, "we have shown that the state will get the grain it envisions in the plan."¹⁶⁵ By the end of the year, in the RSFSR alone 54,645 persons had been convicted under this law, and 2,100 of them had been shot.¹⁶⁶

Outright warfare on the part of the peasants began early, indeed even before the commencement of collectivization. The OGPU reported 901 "terrorist acts" against grain procurers and Party activists in 1927, 1,153 in 1928, and 9,137 in 1929, most of them committed in the grain belt in response to procurement and dekulakization.[167] The secret police recounted one such protest in Western Siberia's steppe, where "the kulak Pshenichnikov [derived, ironically, from the word for 'wheat,' *pshenitsa*] assembled a crowd of 150 [peasant] women and 50 [peasant] men, armed with stakes and axes, who prevented the sale of his [confiscated] property. There were shouts from the crowd that the Soviet authorities want to kill all peasants by starvation and that it was necessary to drag off and break up the authorized rayon executive committee."[168] At the end of 1928 a diplomatic eyewitness reported: "The village, which half a year ago was on the whole adhering to passive resistance, has recently begun to defend itself actively ... including using force. The agents and supporters of the authorities among the muzhiks in favour of collectivized management are being subjected to assault and not infrequently murder. The peasants are setting fire to collective enterprises. The matter has become large in scale."[169]

The diplomat, the Czech Josif Girsa, saw even worse in 1929, which he called the year of "ruthless persecution":

In the village there was, properly speaking, a small civil war, with catacombs of the dead and wounded, an uninterrupted stream of death sentences, and frequently desperate attempts at bloody revenge. The corpus of individual terrorism of the Socialist Revolutionaries under tsarism (Savinkov-Azef) pales by comparison with today's sudden struggle of the village's oppressed class and the enormous organized vengeance of the government authorities. Even in the worst years of the civil war there was not such a flow of blood as last year's.[170]

An OGPU report on the "forms and dynamics of the class struggle in the village" revealed 709 "mass demonstrations"; 1,027 "terrorist acts" (torchings and killings); and 845 instances of "pamphleteering" nationwide in 1928; 1,307, 9,093, and 2,391, respectively, in 1929; and 13,453, 13,794, and 5,156, respectively, in 1930.[171] In 1930 acts of terrorism against Party and village activists were "widespread" and many protests involved "thousands," lasted "months," and required artillery and even aircraft to be suppressed.[172] Armed uprisings were

An Unnatural Famine?

deemed "terrorist" actions and did not persist in the face of state might; the OGPU recorded 68 armed peasant uprisings involving 83,846 participants in 1930, 26 involving 28,077 participants in 1931, 2 involving 2,150 participants in 1932, and 1 involving 600 participants in 1933.[173] The deployment of the Red Army against the rebellious peasants was problematic, however, as most of its recruits came from the villages – 85 percent at the commencement of collectivization.[174] Not surprisingly, as a former White Army officer noted, they "often" disobeyed orders to shoot fellow peasants in revolt.[175] So the Kremlin resorted to the more dependable and less fastidious OGPU police and soldiery to suppress peasant revolts and redeployed Red Army soldiers as political activists in the villages.[176] Thus, Gareth Jones found in the early spring of 1933 that, when some Red Army soldiers refused to shoot rebellious peasants in a village in the south of European Russia, members of the Komsomol willingly and happily complied, such was their ideological fanaticism. "We must be strong and crush the accursed enemies of the working class," they told him, "Let them suffer now. We have no place for them in our society."[177] Many more peasants were arrested and deported, however, than were killed, either in combat or by execution. In the 1930s most of the *zeks* (prisoners, or convicts) in the Gulag were peasants,[178] thanks to collectivization. During the NEP years of 1923–27 peasants constituted an average of less than one-third of all OGPU arrests (429,587) for anti-Soviet activity, but from 1928 through 1934 they formed an average of more than two-fifths of all arrests (2,444,273).[179]

Ultimately, of course, peasant resistance was futile in the face of the Red Army, the OGPU, and doctrinaire Bolshevik supporters in both the cities (bureaucrats, intellectuals, workers) and the villages (Party activists). And Stalin was adamant; he might temporize or even moderate, but he would not change course. As he told Molotov in the late summer of 1930, "the collective farm movement ... is the major and decisive factor in our current agricultural policy."[180] And the 1932–33 climax of the famine, for which this "movement" was responsible, administered a terrible coup de grâce to peasant resistance. After a ten-day trip to the south in September 1933 Chamberlin reported that he had still encountered passive resistance in the villages but that "the active resistance of the peasants had been broken both by terror and by mass deportations."[181] The Polish vice-consul in Kiev concurred, declaring that the secret of the Bolsheviks' success lay "primarily in their total disregard for the means and victims through which a goal is attained," applying "systematic terror" in the process.[182]

Dekulakization and Kulakization[183]

The terror had been directed especially against the kulaks as the chief enemy – political and economic – of the Bolsheviks in the village. They bore the brunt of expropriation and banishment under "dekulakization," the euphemistic "liquidation of the kulaks as a class" that the government announced at the end of 1929. The methods were "fairly varied" and included taxation pressure (higher and higher rates) to the point of insolvency, the outright confiscation of property (with implements, livestock, and fodder being transferred immediately to a kolkhoz and the house given to a poor peasant or a communal organization), the expropriation of land and its replacement by a very small amount of poorer land, and deportation.[184] The taxation of kulak holdings, for instance, more than doubled between 1929–30 and 1930–31 on the national average.[185] Kulaks were even subjected to summary execution. Igor Torgov, a future academician and prominent organic chemist, recalled that, when he was a seventeen-year-old boy in Kazan in the second half of 1929, collectivization and dekulakization were at their height in the villages, and the newspaper *Red Tataria* had begun to publish the names of those kulaks who were being shot for opposing collectivization. "I saw with horror," he wrote years later, "how the dozens of them increased to the hundreds, and I dimly guessed what a bloodbath [*krovavaia bania*] was occurring in the countryside," and he added that "Kazan was full of rumours [so] that the air itself seemed saturated with [the smell of] violence and death."[186] Little wonder the kulaks regarded mandatory collectivization as the implementation of a "new serfdom."[187] The term "kulak," recalled a one-time security official, had come to mean not much more than "victim."[188]

The dekulakization process was so marred by "excesses" – mistakes caused by the over-enthusiastic, subjective, and haphazard application of the term "kulak" – that even Stalin was moved to order a slowdown at the beginning of March 1930 with his "Dizzy with Success" edict (i.e., "enough is enough!"). The chief excess was to simply classify *all* peasant resisters to collectivization (not just actual kulaks but also zazhitochniks and srednyaks) as kulaks and then dekulakize them, resulting in two processes – dekulakization and kulakization-cum-dekulakization. Thus, in one village in the Central Black Earth in the summer of 1931 the srednyaks and even the bednyaks were first kulakized and then dekulakized, whereupon their confiscated property was squandered by the drunken workers of the rural soviet, leaving the kolkhoz in disarray and the population cowed.[189] Indeed, it was mostly not the "rich" kulaks or the "poor" bednyaks (those who could say "we've made nothing except three children") who were dekulakized but the majority of the peasants – the prospering zazhitochniks (those who "had enough, and the whole family worked from dawn to dusk") and the middling srednyaks.[190] As a one-time village woman told the Belorussian Nobel laureate Svetlana Alexievich: "In our village, all of the best families were subjected to kulakization; if they had two cows and two horses, that was already enough to make them kulaks. They'd ship them off to Siberia and abandon them in the barren taiga forest … Women smothered their children to spare them the suffering."[191] Solzhenitsyn called their journey into the unknown the "peasant's *Via Crucis*,"[192] his or her own Way of the Cross to some remote Russian Golgotha. Their transport by train was nightmarish, as another informant of Alexievich's, an old communist, recalled: "The town of Orsk, near Orenburg. Freight trains full of kulak families rolling through night and day. On their way to Siberia. We were guarding the station. One time, I opened the doors of one of the train cars: a half-naked man was hanging from a belt in the corner. The mother was cradling the little one in her arms, while her older boy sat on the floor next to her eating his own shit with his hands like it was kasha [porridge]. 'Shut that door!' the Commissar shouted at me. 'That's the kulak bastard! There's no room for them in our new life!'"[193]

Some kulaks tried to avoid the fearful process altogether through "self-kulakization," whereby they changed their status to srednyaks by reducing their sown acreage and selling or killing many of their livestock, or simply by selling their property and migrating voluntarily to faraway Siberia – a long-time peasant sanctuary – or even the Far East rather than risking deportation with an axe and saw to a "bear's corner" (hellhole).[194]

Most "kulak" exiles, like other euphemistically denominated "special settlers" ("enemies of the people" sentenced to "internal exile"), were dispatched to the European Russian north (the North Kray, Karelia, and the Kola Peninsula), the Urals, the Western Siberian north, Kazakhstan, and the Soviet Far East, and some were resettled in the more arid and less fertile parts of the

North Caucasus and the southern Ukraine and even in the mountainous parts of Central Asia.[195] For example, at the beginning of 1931 the OGPU asked its regional branch in the North whether it could accept up to 100,000 kulak families (some 500,000 persons) from the "southern regions" by the coming spring. The North branch replied that it could accommodate fifty to seventy thousand families but recommended that only the able-bodied men be sent before the opening of the navigation season (end of May) so that, by summer, they could prepare the sites allotted for permanent settlement; otherwise, in order to transport everyone nearly all of the kray's logging horses and logging trucks would have to be mobilized and delivered over thousands of kilometres, thereby disrupting the valuable procurement of timber for export. The kulak families would be settled in groups in unpopulated or sparsely populated areas and used as a workforce in a number of rayons, so they should bring a "minimal inventory" of axes, saws, and the like, as well as – if possible – one horse per five to ten households as they would have to haul timber for building their settlements. Finally, at first the kulaks would have to be issued "starvation rations" (*golodnie normy snabzheniia*) because there were no people or markets where they were to be settled.[196] So many kulaks were exiled to the North that when Chamberlin visited Petrozavodsk in the heart of the Karelian lake area his elderly drayman told him, "This isn't Karelia any more, it's Katorga [Russian for 'exile to hard labour']."[197]

After the demise of the Soviet Union, the recollections of some of the kulak exiles came to light.[198] The daughter (and only child) of one peasant family in Krasnoyarsk Kray, for example, recalled the fate of her illiterate parents – who had entered a kolkhoz in 1929 with their izba, cow, sheep, pigs, two horses, two sacks of flour, some canvas, and a sewing machine – and worked "conscientiously." In 1931 the family was dispossessed and "sentenced to exile as kulaks." With "thousands" of others from the kray they were taken in boxcars to Tomsk and barged up the Ob River to the Vasyugan tributary, which "drained" Vasuganye, or the Great Vasyugan Mire, the northern hemisphere's largest wetland, beset by very long and very cold winters and very short and hot summers, plus myriad *gnusy* (biting insects). There they lived at first in birch shacks amidst "marsh and mud" below the line of high water, and a monthly ration of six kilograms of mouldy and lumpy flour was "given only to those who could work, and the feeble were doomed" to an early death. The children lugged clay for their parents to make stoves but were too weak to haul more than two or three shovelfuls in a pail. Soon the exiles "began to swell and die" and "were buried without coffins in common graves, which were dug every day." "God knows how many people perished" trying to escape, the daughter recollected. Their settlement was called Mogilny (meaning "grave") but later renamed New Vasyugan; however, "by then barely one-half of the exiles remained – New Vasyugan stands on bones." Then, she ends poignantly, "in 1937 my father was taken away as an enemy of the people [and likely shot]. He was a tireless toiler, and he knew only his family and work. He had been orphaned as a child, and all his life he did not hurt a fly. What kind of enemy was he? To whom?"[199] In the very same region two years later two thousand of six thousand exiles died of cold, hunger, and disease on an island in the middle course of the Ob that was then dubbed Cannibal, or Death, Island.[200]

The kulak exiles were used to open industrial and agricultural enterprises in sparsely peopled and remote parts of the country, mainly in heavy work (mining and construction but notably timber-felling and timber-hauling, for timber was a prime export and therefore a source of hard currency).[201] Their labour was cheap but inefficient and wasteful.[202] The head of the convict complex at Norilsk near the mouth of the Yenisei River acknowledged: "who else could have done it [resource-opening on a large-scale in remote and harsh places]?" Because: "If we had sent civilians, we would first have had to build houses for them to live in. And how could civilians live there? With prisoners it is easy – all you need is a barracks, an oven with a chimney and they survive. And then maybe later somewhere to eat ... So they had to bring, first of all, specialists who could build. And in the second place, people who could be used."[203]

Their living and working conditions were so punitive that the head of the Gulag, Matvei Berman, considered it pointless to send his charges to these "special settlements" after their release because conditions there were "in the majority of cases worse than in the camps."[204] The death rate exceeded the birth rate by fivefold in 1932 and by ninefold in 1933.[205] Many resorted to suicide but even more to flight; from the spring of 1930 through the summer of 1931, 101,650 of the 1,365,858 inhabitants of the "special settlements" in the North, the Urals, Western and Eastern Siberia, the Soviet Far East, and Kazakhstan – that is, one-eighth of them – fled, and only one-quarter of these runaways were caught (sometimes they were harboured by the locals, who provided them with food, clothes, transport, and even forged documents). Most of the runaways were kulaks who had been exiled in 1931. Their reasons for fleeing included the primitive living arrangements, the lack of food, the separation of heads of households from their families, the want of proper security, the belief that they had been sent to the settlements to die, and the arbitrariness of the administrators of the settlements.[206]

Some of the kulaks, at least, met their fate with vaunted Russian stoicism.[207] A dozen years after the commencement of kulakization, the German observer Wolfgang Leonhard met some kulak exiles in late 1941 near Kazakhstan's Karaganda, one of the new strategically positioned crucibles of heavy industry (coal) founded by the Soviets, and one of the exiles recalled their deportation "indifferently and unconcernedly" as follows: "There was nothing at all here in those days. There were just some pegs stuck in the ground with little notices on them saying: Settlement No. 5, No. 6, and so on. The peasants were brought here and told that now they had to look after themselves. So then they dug themselves holes in the ground. A great many died of cold and hunger in the early years. Well, after that they gradually built themselves [adobe] huts, and then things were better."[208]

Many Soviet citizens were unsympathetic, maintaining that the kulaks had only themselves to blame for their plight, which they richly deserved. An Intourist guide for an American travel writer responded heatedly when he asked about them: "I will tell you about these Kulaks!" she almost screamed. "They have rebelled against the Government ever since nineteen-twenty-three when they were asked to pay a tax on grain. Many of our tax collectors were sent into the Ukraine, but the Kulaks murdered them, disemboweled them, filled their bodies with grain and sent them on freight trains to Moscow with notes pinned to them saying, 'Here is your grain!'" She added callously, "Collectivization is what the peasants need, but until all the Kulaks are dead, we cannot make collectivization succeed."[209] Similarly, in 1933 the prolific Belgian novelist and peripatetic journalist George Simenon (the creator of Inspector Maigret) visited Odessa, where, according to his tour ship's captain, every night the corpses of fifty famine victims were collected from the streets, and his guide – whom he called his "guardian angel" – assured him at their luxury hotel that the starving people on the street outside whose faces Simenon was simply unable to describe and who "would fight to the death for a bowl of soup" were "not wretched" and "not starving" but rather just kulaks, "peasants who ha[d] not adapted themselves to the regime." He added, "You are a foreigner. You cannot understand. For you several thousand deaths count. For us we can let millions die. Besides, we are importing machines instead."[210]

This rationalization of revolutionary violence was likewise expressed, if less callously, in 1935 by Olga Adamova-Sliozberg, a thirty-three-year-old Moscow white-collar worker, who had hired a kulakized peasant, Marusya, as a nanny. Marusya's husband had been sentenced to forced labour on the Belomor Canal and her children had lived in a hole in the ground with their grandmother until they died of scarlet fever. After hearing this tragic story, a shocked Olga related it to her husband, Judel Zakheim, a university lecturer in biology (soon to be arrested and executed), whose response was all too typical:

> You know, you can't make a revolution wearing white gloves. The destruction of the kulaks has been a hard and bloody process, but it had to be done. Marusya's tragedy may look straightforward to you, but things aren't as simple as they seem. Why did her husband get sent to the camps? It's hard to believe he was totally innocent. People don't get sent to [a] camp for nothing. I wonder if we shouldn't get rid of Marusya; there's always been something fishy about her ... maybe she's a perfectly decent woman, maybe there was some mistake in this particular case. But if you chop down trees, you know, the chips are bound to fly.[211]

Altogether, from 1930 until 1935, 9 to 10 million peasants were dispossessed and deported, including 5 to 6 million kulaks.[212] The OGPU reported that from the beginning of 1930 until the end of September 1931 – the heyday of kulakization – a total of 2,437,062 kulaks (517,665 families) were deported, about one-quarter of them elsewhere within their native oblast or kray (mainly Western Siberia) and about three-quarters of them beyond (mainly the Urals), excluding the thousands who died in transit or who fled after their arrival.[213] And from 1928 "urban kulaks" ("speculators" – private traders, or Nepmen) were likewise "liquidated." The victims were observed closely by John Littlepage (1894–1948), the American mining engineer who worked for the Soviet Gold Trust from 1928 until 1937 (even becoming its deputy commissar) and lived with his family in the USSR and motored widely in the oblasts: "Traveling through Siberia after the summer of 1930, we encountered thousands of men, women, and children, packed with their bags and bundles into mixed passenger and freight ['Maxim Gorky'] cars,[214] often wedged in so tight they could hardly sit down, being shifted around by guards armed with rifles. There seemed to be no end to them; they filled up almost every station for a time, and all the available rolling-stock seemed to be used for them." He added, "The newcomers all seemed to be completely bewildered by what had happened to them, and very few of them ventured to make complaints of any kind ... They had lost their homes, had been forcibly removed from lands occupied by their families for generations, and put at unfamiliar work in unfamiliar surroundings."[215] Littlepage seems to have been unaware, however, that many of the deportees did not live to reach their destination or that many of those who did arrive did not live long.[216] Perhaps one-quarter to one-third of all deported peasants perished.[217] The outside world generally remained oblivious to the tragedy for, as Eugene Lyons wrote, owing to Soviet censorship, the silence or evasion of foreign correspondents (and foreign governments), and Soviet propaganda, it was much more concerned with Soviet "dumping" of cheaper products on world markets. To him kulakization was "the most drastic enterprise in the whole course of the revolution" as well as the event that induced a basic shift in his thinking and feeling about the USSR.[218] He claimed that even the blinkered Anna Louise Strong was moved to call the campaign "the most spectacular act of ruthlessness which occurred in those years."[219] Solzhenitsyn, the memorialist of the Gulag camps, called the deportation of the kulaks a "tidal wave" of "forced resettlement of a whole people, an ethnic catastrophe," resulting in the destruction of "the essence of the village, its energy, its keenness of wit, its love of hard work, its resistance, and its conscience."[220]

Peasant Resignation

As Otto Schiller noted, by 1932–33 sloganeering and exhortation by the authorities had been replaced by "brutal coercion,"[221] which rendered peasant resistance futile and often fatal and the peasants themselves apathetic, without any interest in producing surpluses, especially on land that was not their own to use as they saw fit. As a peasant woman told Rhea Clyman: "We don't have the harvest we used to get when the fields were our own. Who cares what grows now?" And a muzhik said, "On this land we were born and bred, but now the fields are not ours, and the bread [grain] we are now cutting will go into other mouths, not our own."²²² In his moving novel *Everything Flows* Vasily Grossman has a one-time kolkhoz manager and brigade leader put it this way: "The collective farms often failed to fulfil the plan. Too little land had been sown; or there would be a severe drought; or the land had been squeezed dry and it no longer yielded anything; or everyone except the old women and children had managed to escape to the city ... And if a collective farm failed to deliver its quota of produce, then its members would receive only six or seven kopeks per labour-day [workday], plus a hundred grams of grain. And there were years when they did not receive even a single gram. And people don't like working for nothing."²²³

By 1932, four years of coercion had drained the peasants of resistance, and it was replaced by what Lyons described as "a supine despair manifest in indifference, laziness, and neglect." They raised enough for themselves and left crops to rot.²²⁴ When the Ukrainian peasant's situation became hopeless by 1932, he simply "lost his faith in his age-old benefactor – the land," according to a Polish diplomatic bulletin.²²⁵ He refused to plant or to reap, reasoning, in the words of the *Nation*'s Louis Fischer: "What is the use of plowing, planting and harvesting when the authorities seize a large part of my crop? The peasants accordingly sabotaged – and had nothing to eat."²²⁶ Fischer spent a month at the end of the 1932 harvest campaign travelling throughout the Ukraine, and "all over the countryside [he] saw grain which the peasants had left on the fields [to rot]."²²⁷ Duranty reported that only two-thirds of the summer's grain crop had actually been reaped in the Ukraine, the North Caucasus, and the Lower Volga, and the autumn sowing (of winter wheat) was lagging because, in the parlance of the local officials, "the peasants are lying on their stoves."²²⁸ Not only did the peasants lose any interest in working, they also lost the strength to do so, as the Polish consul general in Kharkov found. In early 1933 he reported "a dangerous psychological phenomenon: people exhausted by hunger and the cold, thinking only about how to get bread for themselves and their families, and quivering constantly from the fear of arrest and the seizure by the OGPU of the remains of their property, and not only do not want to work but are unable to work."²²⁹ At this very time Kaganovich, in a long speech to the First All-Union Congress of Collective Farm Shock Brigaders, complained of laziness and idleness on the part of the peasants. He accused them of working listlessly, ignoring crop rotations, manuring and fertilizing insufficiently, harrowing badly, and weeding inefficiently, thereby depleting and reducing yields. There were "numerous instances," he added, of the peasant's actual working day amounting to four and a half hours and his yearly labour to fifty days on kolkhozes as well as cases of half of the kolkhozniks doing no work at all,[230] such was the loss of incentive. Kaganovich did not seem to realize – or want to admit – that many of the peasants simply did not care any more. Otto Schiller found in the North Caucasus that, "even with the immense mortality from famine, no attack of any importance is made upon the State apparatus" – which he saw as "a proof, on the one hand, of the strength of that apparatus, and, on the other, of the complete helplessness of the population." The starving peasants displayed "resigned despair and complete apathy" rather than "wrath and bitterness"; now, he added, they were "callous and [in]different to the fate of those near to them."[231] Schiller's assessment was supported by a Polish vice-consul in the Ukraine in the autumn of 1933; he wrote that there the peasants had been reduced to a state of "utter despair and hopelessness" and were silently awaiting their fate. He added, "I talked to many families who did not have even a kilogram of supplies for the [coming] winter. When I asked how they intended to pass the winter, they answered that they did not have even a hope of lasting until the spring, certain that they would die of hunger, but in spite of this [prospect] there was no sign in their voice of even the slightest protest or a shadow of any indignation. They had accepted it as God's will."[232]

The Italian ambassador in Moscow even identified peasant apathy as the chief cause of the famine, asserting that "it is necessary to seek ... the primary cause of the actual famine in the absence of interest felt by the peasant in working land that no longer belonged to him and in his reluctance to give the state the fruit of his own labour."[233]

Many peasants were disheartened enough to abandon farming completely. As Eugene Lyons put it, "peasants deserted the collectives as rapidly and more joyously than they had entered them."[234] Altogether in 1931–32, when 650,000 peasant families were dispossessed, including more than 250,000 who were deported, another 250,000 families dispossessed themselves by selling or abandoning their holdings and leaving their villages.[235] In just the two months of December 1932 and January 1933, 85,219 peasants (9,213 families), including 40,888 individual farmsteaders and 28,196 kolkhozniks, quit their villages in the Ukraine alone.[236] This alienation reduced the number of peasant households in the Soviet Union by one-fifth (5.2 million) between the end of 1928 and the end of 1935.[237] The exodus from the countryside was seen as a national calamity by Osip Mandelstam's wife (and amanuensis), Nadezhda: "I cannot believe that Tamerlane [1382] and the Tartar invasions [1237–40] had an aftermath anything like that of collectivization. Fleeing from the Tartars, people at least kept together for mutual protection or the settling of new lands, but collectivization really scattered its victims in a literal sense – everybody made off on his own, or at most with his wife and children. The old were just left to die."[238]

Alarmed by this exodus, which plugged the roads, jammed the trains, and choked the cities, the Kremlin tried to control it. On 22 January 1933, the Party's Central Committee decreed the arrest and forcible return to their previous domiciles of those peasants who had left their oblasts or territories.[239] Within exactly three months 258,401 fugitive peasants had been apprehended (including 52,334 in the Central Black Earth, 47,217 in the North Caucasus, and 37,924 in the Ukraine), and of these 230,633 – 89 percent – were returned.[240] Some of the runaway peasants managed to avoid capture, however, and found refuge in the cities and work in the factories, where they stayed. To fill the void left by the fleeing peasants, as well as those who had starved to death, other peasants were relocated both within and outside their region, particularly in the Ukraine and Kazakhstan, where entire rayons had been depopulated. In 1933 the Ukraine saw 16,000 of its kolkhozes with some 90,000 kolkhozniks shifted within the republic, and 21,856 kolkhozes with 117,149 kolkhozniks (and 425,482 head of livestock) were moved to the republic from elsewhere in the USSR – an operation that required 329 special trains.[241]

As if they had not suffered enough, starving peasants were subjected to an additional affliction – epidemic diseases. Malnourishment lessened their resistance to dysentery, typhoid fever, scorbutus (scurvy), smallpox, malaria, bubonic plague, influenza, cholera, and chiefly "famine fever," namely, typhus, or spotted fever. None was uncommon during the famine, and they peaked in 1933.[242] W. Horsley Gantt, the American physician who spent half a dozen years in the Soviet Union in the 1920s studying first the impact of war and famine on Russian health and later Pavlovian behaviouralism (meanwhile becoming fluent in Russian), stated that in 1931–33 the principal epidemic diseases were typhus and scorbutus, the latter resulting from the collapse of vegetable and fruit production and the former from the growing poverty, which entailed undernourishment, overcrowding, and a lack of soap and hot water. He added that the 1932–33 epidemic of typhus, whose peak in the spring of 1933 coincided with that of the famine, "probably" equalled that of 1920–21, which caused "several million" deaths.[243] In June 1933, four hundred new cases daily were admitted to the hospitals of Moscow alone (and half as many to those of Leningrad); in May one of the large Moscow hospitals reported fifteen deaths daily from typhus.[244] Rudolf Volters, the German architect who spent 1932 plying his trade in the Soviet Union, found that "there was a lot of malaria, cholera, and here and there individual cases of the plague," plus typhoid fever in the summer, "but worst of all was spotted fever"[245] – that is, typhus (*sypnoi tif*). Epidemic typhus is caused by a parasitic bacterium (*Rickettsia prowazeki*) and is transmitted by lice, which thrive in unhygienic and crowded conditions. Its symptoms include a rash, a fever, joint and muscle pain, and headache; if left untreated, it kills up to 60 percent of its victims. The number of cases in the country rose and fell in tandem with the famine: from about 40,000 in 1930 to nearly 100,000 in 1931, 200,000 in 1932, and more than 800,000 in 1933, then 400,000 in 1934 and just over 100,000 in 1935.[246] Typhus raged in the Ukraine, which saw 8,384 cases in 1931 and 15,458 in the first eleven months of 1932; the Italian consul in Kharkov deemed the disease endemic by the autumn of 1933, when the city had about 300 new cases daily (up from 50 to 60 the previous summer), with a death rate of up to 40 percent (up from 20 percent in 1932).[247] The struggle against the malady was hampered by not enough hospital beds, bed linen, blankets, and soap; in Kharkov "fines upon fines" were imposed for inadequate sanitation, and the Italian consul reported that "the practice of raising chickens and rabbits in people's rooms has been abolished, as this had been widespread," adding that now "this particular practice is permitted only in the houses' bathrooms."[248] Also, as a Polish bulletin reported, the afflicted "are not treated because even in the capital of Kharkov they are lacking the most basic means of disinfection and medicines (for example, quinine, aspirin, etc.)."[249] Other Soviet cities were not spared. One Dr Bell, a Russian-born British subject and a lecturer at Leningrad State University, told the British Consulate that a "serious epidemic" of typhus was "raging" in the city in the last half of November 1932, with "some hundreds of fresh cases a day"; the

An Unnatural Famine?

disease, he added, was "brought to Leningrad mainly by peasants who come here to buy *bread*," 40 percent of the stricken dying because their resistance had been lowered by starvation.[250] Bell also noted that there was "much typhus in Siberia also."[251] Indeed, the French chargé d'affaires in Moscow reported that typhus was especially prevalent in Siberia, particularly in Novosibirsk and Chita.[252] William Wood was to recall that in the spring and summer of 1933 "thousands upon thousands of people" succumbed to the dreaded disease in Western Siberia.[253] Rudolph Volters, who called typhus "the perpetual companion of Russian winter," provided details of its impact on Novosibirsk. It erupted in February, and soon the number of victims admitted daily to the city's hospitals rose to three hundred and stayed at that level for two months; Volters was told by the city's chief physician that 40 percent of admissions died. The disease was, as usual, spread by body lice, and two weeks after infection a victim had a high temperature, and a few days later a red rash. Thereafter, said the physician, "everything depends upon care," but Novosibirsk's "overly small hospitals and inadequately trained personnel" could not cope, so that "many of those admitted to the hospitals died simply from inadequate care." The hospitals were able to feed only 20 percent of the victims. So many died that the locals said that "the epidemic has won out, the populace has died out." The plight of the waifs was notably pitiful. Volters wrote: "The homeless children, the 'orphans,' who on cold winter nights infiltrated entryways, stairways, and corridors so as to save themselves from the frost, were thrown pitilessly onto the street. Lice ridden, they carried the disease with them."[254]

Frequently the morbidity was worsened by the simultaneous occurrence of several epidemic diseases. Besides malnutrition, the most common causes of death among both adults and children over the age of one during the climax of the famine in 1932–33 were typhus, typhoid, dysentery, and tuberculosis[255] – which could strike simultaneously, particularly in 1933. In the late winter of 1932–33 a Polish diplomat reported that typhus, typhoid, and "a particularly severe type of dysentery" were "widespread" in the Ukraine (he added that the stricken peasants were refusing anti-typhus injections and "very often" begging for poison instead), and the OGPU reported 1,636 cases of disease outbreaks in Kazakhstan, including 1,349 of typhus, 194 of typhoid, and 93 of smallpox, in addition to scurvy and intestinal ailments (it added that 42 to 45 of the 4,300 waifs in the special children's homes were dying daily). At the beginning of spring 1933 there were 8,327 cases of typhus, 1,327 of typhoid, 588 of smallpox, and 317 of scurvy in the Urals from January through March, according to the OGPU; and the autumn saw epidemics of typhus, typhoid, and smallpox in various parts of the country, mainly among workers, owing to malnutrition and unsanitary conditions (shortages of soap and medicines, infrequent bathing, dirty bedding, head lice, and even sabotage by caregivers).[256] To combat the epidemics temporary hospitals were established, mass vaccination and inoculation were undertaken, special medical teams were deployed, sanitation measures were undertaken on passenger trains, and disinfection wards were established[257] – all to only some avail.

Typhus (or spotted fever) was much more rampant than typhoid fever. The number of cases of typhoid (and paratyphoid) fever in the Soviet Union increased from 115,000 in 1928 to 175,000 in 1929, almost 200,000 in 1930, 260,000 in 1931, 300,000 in 1932, 210,000 in 1933, 200,000 in 1934, and 140,000 in 1935.[258] In both 1930 and 1931 typhoid fever was "raging" in Leningrad as a result of contaminated drinking water.[259]

Both malaria and tuberculosis had been suppressed during the 1920s, but both rebounded strongly during the famine, the former because of migration from non-malarial to malarial regions in both European and Asiatic Russia.[260] The number of cases in the country rose from 2.7 million in 1930 to 3.2 million in 1931, almost 4.5 million in 1932, 6.5 million in 1933, 9,477,000 in 1934, and 9,024,000 in 1935.[261] The humid and exceptionally rainy summer of 1933 in the Ukraine prompted an outbreak of malaria there; in September William Chamberlin reported "a great deal" of malaria in the Kuban, where one-third of the members of some kolkhozes were stricken.[262]

Malaria afflicted many more Soviets than smallpox, the number of cases of which rose from 10,000 in 1930 to 30,000 in 1931, 60,000 in 1932, 38,000 in 1933, 18,000 in 1934, and 4,000 in 1935,[263] the figures reflecting – as in the instances of typhoid fever and malaria – better treatment and better nutrition by the mid-1930s.[264]

The onslaught of epidemics included bubonic plague in parts of the USSR, especially Siberia. In the late spring and early summer of 1933 pneumonic and septicemic plague "of swift attack and high mortality" struck the Urals and Western Siberia. It was spread by marmot fleas, one conduit being the excavation of marmot burrows by starving peasants in search of the rodent's store of grain.[265] An American engineer living and working in Siberia told

Horsley Gantt that "all the inhabitants of badly afflicted villages were shot and the houses set fire to."[266]

The unhealthful environment prompted the following advice, given to Arne Strøm by a German engineer on the train to the former's job at Povorino in the eastern Central Black Earth in the spring of 1932:

> The best thing I could do [the engineer said] was to send my wife and my child back to a civilized country as soon as possible, as typhoid, cholera, venereal disease and starvation reigned everywhere, except in the propaganda centres like Moscow, Leningrad and the other big towns ... We were to remember *never* to touch unboiled water, *never* to drink out of glasses used by Russians, but *always* to carry our own glasses about with us. We must be very careful in our choice of friends as nearly everybody was infested with lice, and lice were terrible carriers of infection. Towards beggars we had to be brutally firm otherwise we would be overwhelmed by them. As soon as we had arrived at our destination we were to be vaccinated against typhoid and smallpox. It was true that the vaccine they used here was generally no good, but still it left one free from responsibility if one did fall ill. We must be sure to insist on having our own lavatory, and we must immediately put it under lock and key, and we must do our best to live in rooms that are as isolated as possible, preferably in a house to ourselves.[267]

Strøm thought that the engineer must be "mad," but he soon discovered from his own experience that he was not. The situation was indeed alarming for foreigners, but for residents, especially the peasants, it was terrifying.

Agricultural Repercussions

The peasants faced an array of obstacles to higher yields, bumper harvests, and larger procurements for domestic consumption and foreign exportation. Production was handicapped not only by the haste ("Bolshevik tempo") and uncoordinated implementation of collectivization, the excessive requisitions, and the forcible measures but also by the insufficiency and the defectiveness of the agricultural machinery that was supposed to lighten labour and supplant redundant peasants, the incompetence of machinery operators and of kolkhoz managers (the latter were politically dependable but agriculturally ignorant, often being born and bred in the cities), the unwieldy size of the kolkhozes and especially the sovkhozes (thanks to the obsession of Bolshevik economists with the notion of "increasing returns to scale," or what was popularly referred to as "gigantomania"), the shortage of fodder, the paucity of seed, and the inadequate transport, plus the invariably unreliable weather.

There was an unrealistic drive for total mechanization – what the Soviets called "Americanization" – in the face of a rural labour supply that was abundant, cheap, and unskilled.[268] Initially, however, not enough agricultural machinery was produced as industrialization's priority was heavy industry, not light industry, and heavy industry's priority was the military, not the peasantry. The persistent manufacture of defective products – *brak*[269] – was a general problem. The few trucks, tractors, combines, mowers, and the like that were made were "often not of the best quality"[270] – surprising in view of the buying and copying of standard foreign models (Fordson, John Deere, and the like) and the hiring of foreign experts and skilled workers, but not surprising in view of the "qualifications" of domestic factory workers. In the summer of 1932 Andrew Cairns was told by three disillusioned French tourists who had just visited Stalingrad (Tsaritsyn until 1925 and Volgograd from 1961) that an Italian engineer there had told them that "if a man could put in one screw nail he was a skilled worker in Russia and if he could put in three he was an engineer."[271] The users of the machinery were as unskilled as its makers, and the inferior machines were easily damaged by peasants unable either to operate or to repair them. As the one-time minister of state for commerce of Australia observed diplomatically during his tour of inspection of the Soviet countryside, "if the almost servile conditions of the peasants made the imposition of a collective system less difficult, the ignorance and inexperience inseparable from such backward conditions rendered technical progress exceedingly difficult."[272] So it should not have come as a surprise to a visitor to the depot of agricultural implements at State Farm No. 2, "Verblyud," a model grain sovkhoz of 375,000 acres (151,757 hectares) in the North Caucasus just east of Rostov-on-Don in 1932, when he found that "acres of ground were occupied with broken-down or discarded machinery, much of it of the most expensive imported variety." The engineer there told him that "the wastage of grain with some of our [machinery] workers rises as high as 30 and 40%." The machinery difficulties were such that the peasants

An Unnatural Famine?

were again hitching cattle to ploughs.[273] Rhea Clyman also visited "Verblyud," arriving in the spring of 1933 just after it and the nearby "Gigant" (Giant) sovkhoz – the two showcases of state farms – had been removed from Intourist's itinerary and closed to foreign tourists in the wake of rumours about the failure of their crops and the arrest and even shooting of their managers. She came across a "large field ... filled with old broken-down machines: tractors, combines and threshers ... tools and spare parts lay forgotten and rusty in the tall grasses. Some of the machines looked quite new; a few were imported and others were Soviet make, but they were all rusty and dismantled." A workman told her, "Here's all our wealth: machines thrown out on the scrap heap after a few months' use. But why should we treat a machine better than the government treats us?"[274] The situation was the same in the Ukraine, where Party secretary Stanislav Kosior, in a report in the autumn of 1933 to Stalin, noted the resultant "extremely low labour productivity at grist mills, in field brigades, and with tractors" and stated:

> It is necessary to add the enormous [degree] of idleness of tractors. At the present time [only] 60–70 percent of the pool of 40 thousand tractors is working; some of the rest need major repairs and some are not used because of minor breakages, the lack of certain parts and babbitt, and so on. In my telegram I have already reported that more than one and a half thousand tractors have been standing idle for want of babbitt. Now this number has increased. Since neither we [the republic authorities] nor the oblasts have any babbitt at all, the number of such tractors will increase daily and inevitably hamper all remaining work – milling, haying, the digging of sugar beets, and the harvesting of inter-row crops.[275]

At the beginning of December, according to the Polish vice-consul in Kiev, some thirty-five thousand tractors and fifteen thousand trucks in the Ukraine were in need of repair.[276] Draught animals were obvious alternatives to unusable machinery, but they were in no condition to be of much help since the peasants' livestock (at least those that the starving had not already eaten) were also starving to death. Officially, between 1928 and 1933 the country's livestock population decreased by more than one-half (from 277 million to 117 million head): horses by one-half, cattle by almost one-half, sheep and goats by nearly two-thirds, and pigs by one-half.[277] The 1928 total would not be regained until thirty years later, in 1958. In the RSFSR alone, which comprised three-quarters of the country's territory, in just one year (spring 1928 to spring 1929) the number of pigs fell by one-half, sheep by one-third, cattle by one-quarter, and work horses by one-eighth[278] – cattle and horses the least because of the latter's primacy as a draught animal and the former's primacy as a family feeder as well as a draught animal. In his story "The Cow" Andrei Platonov has a peasant boy (perhaps himself) describe the importance of the family cow, which had just been killed by a train:

> We had a cow. While she lived, my mother, my father and I all ate milk from her. Then she had her son – a calf – and he ate milk from her too, there were three of us and he made four, and there was enough milk for us all. The cow also ploughed and carried loads. Then her son was sold for meat, he was killed and eaten. The cow was very unhappy, but she soon died, run over by a train. And she was eaten too, because she was beef. Now there is nothing. The cow gave us everything, that is[,] her milk, her son, her meat, her skin, her innards, and her bones – she was kind.[279]

The peasant diarist Izmailov was more cryptic when his work pony starved to death: "3 May [1930]. This morning old Voronchik ['little raven'] died. He starved to death. Since February 15 there has not been a wisp of hay or grass."[280]

Otto Schiller attributed the high losses to the "mass slaughter" by the starving peasants, the higher incidence of diseases resulting from the indiscriminate amalgamation of herds during collectivization, and the insufficient protection of – and attention to – livestock during the agrarian upheaval.[281] The "mass slaughter" was intensified by the Party decree of 30 July 1930 On the Development of Socialist Stockbreeding, which was intended to occasion a "great advance" in livestock production but in fact facilitated the confiscation of peasant livestock by the kolkhozes, with the Commissariat of Agriculture subsequently reporting "the mass slaughter of milk cows and the squandering of work horses" as the peasants – rather than see them seized by the kolkhozes – killed, sold, or simply abandoned them "like so many unwanted kittens or puppies," in the words of one observer.[282] A retired peasant recalled his family's experience at this time, when he was yet a boy: "All of my parents' livestock were seized by the kolkhoz, leaving the family only one cow; they took nearly all of the agricultural implements without payment, of course. At first the horses ran home from the kolkhoz stable; as soon as they were let out, they galloped home. They put their heads on the window sill and neighed. The childrens' and adults' hearts bled so."[283]

Nevertheless, rather than have their precious livestock seized by the kolkhoz, peasants often simply slaughtered and consumed them. Novelist Sholokhov imagined the killing and gorging in the Don Cossack village of Gremyachy Log:

> Livestock began to be slaughtered every night in Gremyachy. Hardly had darkness fallen when the brief and stifled bleatings of a sheep, the mortal scream of a pig or the bellowing of a calf would be heard piercing the silence. Not only those who had joined the collective farm, but individual farmers also slaughtered. They killed oxen, sheep, pigs, even cows; they slaughtered animals kept for breeding. In two nights the horned cattle of Gremyachy were reduced to half their number. The dogs began to drag entrails and guts about the village, the cellars and granaries were filled with meat ... "Kill, it's not ours now!" "Kill, they'll take it for the meat collection tax if you don't" "Kill, for you won't taste meat in the collective farm" ... And they killed. They ate until they were unable to move. Everybody, from the youngest to the oldest, suffered with stomach-ache. At dinner-time the tables groaned under the weight of boiled and roasted meat. At dinner-time everybody had a greasy mouth, everybody belched as though they had been at a funeral repast in memory of the dead. And all were owlish with their intoxication of eating.[284]

The village bazaars and city markets overflowed with meat; there were even instances of "leaving horses at hostelries as payment for stays," and not infrequently dobbins and bullocks were left on the road or in a field with a note: "It's nobody's, whoever needs it – take it."[285] In 1932 an American observer "saw stray horses rambling over the snowy Ukrainian steppes"; they were called *besprizorny* horses, having been "orphaned" by their one-time masters, who were either unable to feed them or could not bear to kill them.²⁸⁶ Some peasants got rid of livestock in order to avoid being damned with the label of kulak and paying the attendant price. In the Middle Volga, reported a Party official in late 1929, the kulaks and the better-off srednyaks "earnestly and quickly adapt[ed] themselves to the new situation, restructuring their farmsteads, downsizing, and liquidating some of their livestock" in order to avoid expropriation and deportation as kulaks. He explained: "Coming to the kolkhoz, this or that better-off srednyak, having three head of cattle, sells two, and with the third joins the kolkhoz because he does not want to invest more in its indivisible capital fund than his neighbour, who has one head." "For all of these reasons," he added, "we have a colossal increase in the dumping of draught livestock on the market. We have a situation such that a work horse that usually costs 100 rub[les] goes for 20–25 rub[les] in the harvest-failure rayons."²⁸⁷

Livestock numbers plummeted, too, as a result of malnourishment (a paucity of fodder),²⁸⁸ overwork (fewer draught animals working harder), and improper care (inadequate grooming and shelter) – all of which promoted animal diseases. The years 1931 to 1933, for instance, saw a "substantial spread" of epizootic diseases in the Urals Region: scabies (mange), meningitis, Siberian "sores" (anthrax?), glanders, and piroplasmosis (babesiasis), one of several parasitic infections like tick, or Texas, fever.²⁸⁹ In the Central Black Earth from July through September 1933, up to 15 percent of its horse stock contracted meningitis, which killed up to two-thirds of the stricken animals – and these statistics were incomplete; some kolkhozes lost more than three-quarters of their work horses.²⁹⁰ In the Ukraine a Polish diplomat reported that the oblast's horses had suffered "much loss" from eating dry chaff, which caused stomatitis (inflammation of the mouth).²⁹¹

The decimation of livestock resulted in a loss not only of animal products (meat, milk, butter, cheese, wool, leather) but also of draught and manure, which in turn resulted in lower yields. Andrew Cairns found that this was the case especially in 1930–32, when the relative loss of livestock was double that of 1928–30, the period of all-out collectivization. He also found in 1932 that the output of milk per cow in the the Soviet Union was less than half that of most other countries, and that because of underfeeding it was "very doubtful" whether two Russian horses were equal in draught power to one horse elsewhere.²⁹² In the spring of 1932 Stanislaw Kosior, Party chief in the Ukraine, told Stalin that draught power was the "main problem everywhere

An Unnatural Famine?

now" in his republic; in the rayons visited by him about a quarter of the horses had died, and the rest had been reduced to "skin and bone."²⁹³ A Polish consular official toured the Lugansk Rayon by car in May 1932 and found that the ditches lining the rural roads abounded in horse carcasses and skeletons, while those horses that were still alive staggered on their legs and were "so emaciated that all that remained was literally skin on bones." Those that were driven to pasture to graze something were too weak to stand up and had to be propped up with boards.²⁹⁴ Throughout the First Five-Year Plan the Middle Volga saw an "extreme overstraining of draught power" from an average of 6.2 hectares per draught animal in 1928 to 10.4 in 1932 (and even 12 on the river's left bank).²⁹⁵ The OGPU reported that one of the main reasons for the slow pace of fall sowing (of winter grain) in the region in 1933 was the depletion of work horses (especially on the left bank, where up to 40 percent had been lost) owing to various diseases (especially meningitis), unqualified veterinarians, and insufficient medicines as well as, the agency added – perhaps falsely – "sabotage," that is, deliberate infection with epizootic diseases by "anti-Soviet elements."²⁹⁶ In the same year a British Embassy report noted the "deplorable condition of draught animals almost throughout the Soviet Union, which is mainly due to lack of fodder," and added that milk cows were being used in place of work horses, many of which had been killed for food or had starved to death.²⁹⁷ In the wake of the want of both horses and tractors the peasants composed a sardonic doggerel: "Cats, not tractors, will work the plough, / In the collective farms that we have now."²⁹⁸

Meanwhile, however, at the outset of 1933 Kaganovich had proudly announced that "the sickle has been replaced by the combine, the flail by the threshing machine, the wooden plow by the tractor."²⁹⁹ The output of agricultural machinery had indeed increased; for example, 148,480 tractors were made in 1933, compared with 34,943 in 1929 (almost a 400 percent increase in terms of the relative numbers favoured by Soviet boosters).³⁰⁰ And tractors were indeed more efficient than horse-drawn ploughs, especially on large-scale farms such as the kolkhozes and sovkhozes. Ukrainian Party chief Kosior told Stalin that in the Ukrainian steppe a team of four to five horses could plough 0.5 to 2.5 hectares per day but a tractor from the Kharkov or Stalingrad factory could plough 5 to 6 and sometimes 8 to 10 hectares daily (which he still considered "unsatisfactory").³⁰¹ Gareth Jones estimated that in terms of draught power one Ukrainian tractor equalled sixteen horses.³⁰²

The problem, however, was – as often with Soviet statistics – the unsaid quality of the product as well as the unsaid ability of the handler. At first, at least – as might be expected – production was problematic. Rhea Clyman "heard" in Moscow in the spring of 1933 that the Kharkov Tractor Factory, the "great Soviet showpiece" of agricultural mechanization that cost 10 million rubles to build, had a labour turnover of 30 to 40 percent and that the First Five-Year Plan had stipulated that it produce 140 tractors daily but it had never made more than 101 daily and averaged only 44, so that Russians had taken to calling it a *traktorzloi* (tractor villain) instead of a *traktorstroi* (tractor builder).[303] Moreover, the machinery that was produced was often defective, and after its delivery to the kolkhozes and sovkhozes it was just as often mishandled by untrained operators, as the British consul in Leningrad reported: "The Putilov tractor takes twice as long to produce as it ought, then waits its turn to be tinkered up so that it will go [work] after a fashion, and finally (according to the press) is left out in the open at the port for weeks waiting to be shipped south. When it reaches its destination it falls into the hands of mechanics who, according to competent foreign observers, are so ignorant and careless that the life of foreign agricultural machinery, which ought to last for five years, is reduced to about one year, and that of Soviet machinery is shorter still."[304]

One Ukrainian peasant recalled that, in his village in 1930, new tractors ("Farsons," i.e., Fergusons modelled upon the American line of Massey Ferguson machines) were used for spring sowing on a new kolkhoz: "They brought these tractors with wheels ... But they weren't very powerful, that was how they were built. Nobody was trained, nobody knew anything. They started off – over went the tractor. There wasn't any place there that was level, it was all up and down. It tipped over and the [winding] drum filled up with oil. And that was it. The sowing was finished – they didn't sow anything."[305]

The director of the Ukraine's thirty and the Crimea's four grain sovkhozes told an inspection commission in the summer of 1932 that their combine operators were "extremely badly trained" and that less than 15 percent of them were "familiar with the work of combines" for they had taken training courses lasting only two to three weeks instead of the requisite four "on account of the shortage of food." He added that their tractors were used "exceptionally badly."[306] The peasants, of course, were simply not used to machines, preferring horses to tractors; indeed, a recorder of the local lore of the one-time kray of Mologa (whose deliberate flooding created the Rybinsk Reservoir, or Sea of Rybinsk, completed in 1941) asserted that "the production of grain by the former peasantry was unthinkable without horses" (and he noted that the term "horsepower" even became the measure of the strength of most machines).[307] As an elderly Ukrainian peasant told Gareth Jones: "A horse is better than a tractor. A tractor goes and stops, but a horse goes all the time. A tractor only works in certain times of the year, but a horse you can use all the time. A tractor cannot give manure but a horse can."[308] Even Kaganovich acknowledged that "a man who has been accustomed to pulling the tail of an ox, to handling a whip, to following a wooden plow, finds it difficult, at first, to get used to a tractor." So some peasants, he continued, failed to drain tractor radiators and they froze or they tapped the lubricating oil (for their own use) and the parts became overheated. "To pour water into a tractor is not as simple a thing as to water a horse," he added, with the result that some peasants poured muddy water from puddles into tractor radiators, clogging and overheating the parts.[309] Indeed, it seems that the foremost problem was not so much the shortage of tractors and their mishandling as their lack of spare parts.[310] The OGPU reported that, in the Middle Volga in the fall of 1932, the shortage of draught power was "catastrophic" because the number of horses had been halved since 1929 and the tractor pool was in a "sorry state: of 10 thous[and] tractors ... only 3.5 thous[and] tractors altogether are operational, and even then [only] intermittently on account of their bad condition, lack of spare parts, etc."[311] A peasant himself offered another reason for the breakdown of machinery:

> After the introduction of collectivization the peasant came to have a negative attitude to horses because he knew that they were not his and that there was no advantage in taking care of them. He had the same attitude to agricultural machinery. It was usually thus: he worked a little, abandoned the machine without even lubricating it, and then quit just in order to get through his workday. The fact is that the presence of machinery in the kolkhoz deprived the kolkhoznik of part of his income, for it was necessary to pay for the machinery. So when the MTS was organized, the peasant was not pleased.[312]

Famine and disease weakened peasant labour as well as draught power. Dr Fritz Dittloff (1894–1954), the German First World War veteran who managed the Krupp-funded German agricultural concession of "Drusag," which employed forty German agricultural specialists and encompassed seven thousand hectares of farmland along the Kuban River near Kropotkin from 1922 until 1933, observed that between 1928–30 and 1930–32 the efficacy of labour decreased by 50 percent; in order to accommodate the enfeebled labourers the weight of grain sacks was halved (from 100 to 50 kilograms each), and the number of operators for a steam-powered threshing machine was doubled (from 25 to 50), while horses and oxen were reduced to doing barely one-half of their usual work.[313] Consequently, timely spring and autumn sowing were thrown off-course. The consequences were described by Andrew Cairns:

> In order to avoid very low yields it is imperative that spring crops be sown in time to utilize for root development the soil moisture accumulated during the autumn, winter and early spring. Late seeding frequently results in the young plants being killed, or irreparably injured, before the seasonal [spring] rains fall. Late seeding also often results in the plants being too weak to withstand the dreaded late June and early July hot winds [sukhovei] from the southeastern desert regions.

The low grain yields of 1931 and 1932, added Cairns, stemmed partly from late seeding. The "early sowing of autumn crops," he continued, "while not so vital as in the case of spring grains, is essential if the young plants are to attain a vigorous growth before the dry late autumn and/or severe winter weather [hard frost] sets in."[314]

Yields of grain (and of other major crops in the south of European Russia, like sugar beets and potatoes) were also reduced by weeds. Kaganovich asserted that this "scourge" of weeds arose from careless winnowing and poor cultivation: "they [the peasants] did not winnow the seeds properly, they did not hoe the fields, they did not plow, sow, harvest in time – they were late."[315] Fields were so weedy that they needed to be ploughed two or three times before seeding.[316] But the peasants had lost many, if not most, of their draught animals (horses and oxen), which, moreover, had yet to be replaced by sufficient functional machinery. As Dittloff said, "to be successful a campaign against weeds ... can only be waged by extensive ploughing and by the timely use of the harrow to stir up the surface of the soil," but "it was no uncommon sight in the Ukraine and the North Caucasus to see women dragging a harrow over the land ... a party of eight women would be employed to drag a harrow a couple of yards in width."³¹⁷ Furthermore, by now the peasants had lost their will to work. At the beginning of 1933, in a letter to the Polish Consul in Kiev, a student wrote: "The peasants (80% of the entire population [of the Ukraine]) have no motivation to work in the fields, since everything will be taken away anyhow (according to the planned purchases). As a result, a large portion of the fields remains uncultivated or is sown carelessly (only [in order] to fulfill the set quota). Only weeds grow in the chernozem [black earth] fields of [the] Ukraine. The crops are at minimum levels: 15–20 poods per 1 hectare."³¹⁸

And, of course, peasants were simply too weakened by starvation to be able to work. Arne Strøm met an Austrian sugar beet specialist at Voronezh in the fall of 1932 who told him that the growing of sugar beets was going "badly," and he explained that "the peasants were so underfed that they could hardly keep on their feet in the fields, let alone use a hoe. Often they lay down and died amongst the beets, which were in turn strangled by weeds."³¹⁹

In the Ukraine and the North Caucasus weeds became a serious problem in the autumn of 1931 during the planting of winter wheat; heavy rain, said a sovkhoz official, prevented the ploughing of fallow and promoted the growth of weeds, "which began to choke the sowings," so that the weedy crop had to be harvested in the summer of 1932 with mostly simple reapers rather than faster combines, which, he lamented, "can harvest only clean, weed-free fields," the weeds choking the machines.³²⁰ In the meantime, Cairns observed: "all spring crops late and very weedy, much land recently in cultivation now idle, much good grass but no livestock, practically no hay made, virtually no summer fallow, and everywhere a magnificent crop of weeds."³²¹ The British Embassy reported that the "deplorable neglect of fallow land" with its resultant infestation by weeds was "a feature of the Soviet countryside that immediately strikes a foreign observer."³²² Two such observers, Carveth Wells and Leonard Elmhirst, noted in the summer of 1932 in the south of European Russia that "hour after hour the train passed through country that ... was covered with weeds as far as the eye could see," and in "most of South Russia [the Ukraine and the North Caucasus] ... weeds were seeding everywhere" after rain fell during harvesting and turned fallow into fields "three to five feet high of solid weeds."[323] A year later Walter Duranty wrote: "I saw for myself when I visited the North Caucasus in August how the high road from Rostov to the Kuban ran at times for miles through a wilderness of lofty weeds which had been golden wheat fields only three years before."[324] More damning were the observations of Commissar of Defence Kliment ("Klim") Voroshilov (1881–1969), another of the few "old [pre-1917] Bolsheviks" to survive Stalin's purges. He travelled through South Russia at the same time as Duranty by train, by car, and "by touch" (on foot) but reported his impressions to Stalin, not the press. In the North Caucasus he saw a "painful picture of the shocking weed infestation of grain," and he concluded that "in general the North Caucasus is experiencing an utter disaster," such that he could assert: "this year in only the N. C. weeds have consumed no fewer than 120–150 million puds [1,966,000–2,457,000 tonnes] – if not all of 200 [million, or ca. 3,276,000 tonnes] – of our grain." And this despite the weather in the spring and the summer having been "exceptionally favourable" to a bumper crop; instead, "at best it has been average or worse." In the Ukraine, too, Voroshilov saw a "shocking weed infestation of grain," although "somewhat less" than in the North Caucasus; harvesting had already begun but it "had been going sluggishly, not well, and was quite uncharacteristic of a busy harvest time."[325] In Western Siberia weeds likewise flourished on ploughland. There Andrew Cairns "was astonished at the tens of thousands of hectares of good land in unbroken stretches which was lying idle growing weeds" because of abandonment by the peasants.[326] When Leningrad's Party secretary Sergei Kirov undertook an inspection tour of grain-growing and stock-rearing in June 1934 (just six months before his sensational assassination), he found the fields infested with "flower gardens of wild mustard."[327]

In spite of a vaunted "war on weeds," they continued to be pervasive.[328] In 1934 an Italian diplomat reported that, despite a heat wave, there was an "exuberant" infestation of weeds in the European Russian steppe, possibly, he thought, because of their "exceptional" growth the year before.[329] And in 1935 Charles Hawker, the Australian specialist, found that weeds were still "bad or very bad" in the fields of half of the villages in the main grain belt and "more plentiful than they should be" in many fields of the other – and better – half. He guessed that 85 percent of the crops in southern European Russia had not been weeded enough. The problem, he continued, was the cropping

An Unnatural Famine?

of all of the fields every year, with no allowance for fallow that could be easily cleaned of weeds by ploughing them under. This problem, in turn, was aggravated by the re-seeding in spring of autumn-sown but winter-killed wheat. Technical crops, he added, such as sugar beets, potatoes, sunflowers, and corn, were more easily weeded because they were sown in more widely spaced rows that could be easily worked by single-horse scarifiers.[330]

Weeds were not the only problem. Grain crops were harmed, too, by smut and especially rust, both of them fungal diseases (*Ustilago tritici* and *Puccinia triticina*, respectively). Smut – rather, loose smut – infects wheat during flowering and turns parts of the ears into blackish powder. Three types of rust – stem, leaf, and stripe – may affect wheat during its life cycle. Stem rust causes perhaps the most damage, the wind-borne spores consuming the moisture and the nutrients needed by the plant in order to develop kernels, which shrivel to as much as one-half or two-thirds of their normal size; leaf rust, the most prevalent of the three, simply reduces the size and the number of kernels instead of shrivelling them.[331] The development of leaf rust is facilitated by warm, damp – that is, sultry – weather, which in the USSR was confined essentially to the southeastern Ukraine-northwestern North Caucasus area, where the pathogen can survive the milder winters and infect winter wheat. Aeolian dispersal of the fungal spores could result in large-scale epidemics, as in 1932, when Andrew Cairns was told by a correspondent of the Polish Telegraph Agency in June that much of the wheat crop in eastern Poland and in Romania had been ruined by rust blown from the Soviet Union.[332] A Soviet study reported that rusts caused "huge losses annually in the USSR" of grain, notably wheat, the losses amounting to millions of centners; indeed, their harmfulness was "axiomatic," owing to their widespread and frequent (almost annual) occurrence and intensive infection. In the rayons of Kursk and Voronezh (the southern half of the Central Black Earth), rusts reduced the crop of wheat by 15 percent in 1932 and 20 to 27 percent in 1933, of oats by 6 percent in 1932 and 26 percent in 1933, and of rye by 10 percent in 1932 and 3 percent in 1933.[333] Especially the Ukraine's crops suffered from pests in 1932, with Andrew Cairns reporting "extremely heavy" losses of both winter and spring wheat from a "heavy infection of stem rust" and "very large areas [of] oats not worth harvesting due to smut" as well as "sugar beets very poor smothered with weeds and much caterpillar damage."[334] Furthermore, "very large bugs (Anisphia Austrica or something like that) ... were doing considerable damage by eating holes in the [wheat] kernels."[335] Cairns added that rust and smut were rampant partly because herbicides like copper sulphate were "deficit articles."[336]

Reflecting the Marxian concept of increasing returns to scale, the size of the farms was certainly not wanting; indeed, the size of the kolkhozes and sovkhozes, particularly the latter, was simply too large, too unwieldy, for effective management. In the North Caucasus the sovkhoz "Gigant" was established in the summer of 1928, and two summers later it covered 445,000 acres (695 square miles), 210,000 of which were virgin soil, employed 2,500 permanent and 2,000 part-time workers, and reaped mostly wheat and rye; it was planned to increase its size to 618,000 acres (965 square miles).[337] Another gigantic North Caucasus sovkhoz was the Agricultural Training Farm and Experimental Station of "Verblyud," which, a visitor learned in 1932, covered at least one-quarter of a million acres, employed 3,300 workers, served additionally as a training ground for 1,200 students, and housed a population of 10,000. The visitor also reported that, "in general, the State farms have proved to be white elephants: they have been unmanageably large and many of them have had to be split up."[338] A year later the reporter Rhea Clyman found that "Verblyud" was in the process of being subdivided into twelve smaller sections.[339]

Management remained problematic, however. As the First Five-Year Plan progressed, more and more *vydvizhentsy* – "advanced ones," parvenus who were promoted hurriedly to positions of authority more on the basis of their class origin than their professional capabilities – were appointed to managerial positions, and with predictable results.[340] Fritz Dittloff, the head of "Drusag" (shorthand for the German-Russian Seed Company), which tested its seeds and tillage methods on seven thousand hectares (17,290 acres) of land in the Kuban until 1933, confided in an interview that the management of the kolkhozes was "hopelessly bad," with each farm usually run by a Party official – "a Red Director, with only a few political and agricultural catchwords in his vocabulary and no knowledge of agriculture, stock-farming, or the theory of farm management."[341] Andrew Cairns found most agricultural officials to be confident and enthusiastic but also untrained and unrealistic, certain that communism would overcome everything. Even foreign "experts" who wanted to help build socialism had first to qualify on political grounds. In June 1932 in Kiev, Cairns's guide admitted: "they [the Bolsheviks] had made many mistakes in Russia and people who had been barbers or waiters in foreign countries had been brought here as industrial and agricultural specialists, but even they were better than many of their [our] own people."[342] Sergio Gradenigo, the Italian consul general in Kiev, gave voice to the peasants' opinion of these outside "experts": "The peasants [of the Middle Volga and the Dnepropetrovsk-Belgorod belt] all say: 'When we were independent, each had a sufficient supply [of seed] to plant right at the time judged to be the most opportune. Now it is necessary to await the approval of the government's agronomists, who ignore the peculiarities of the soils, giving permission to begin new ploughings and plantings when precious days – if not weeks – have been lost, and they prescribe seeds that are not always suited to all of the region and then ... the seeds arrive when they are no longer of any use and so we must eat some in order not to starve.'"[343]

To make matters worse, the managers were transferred with excessive frequency. An American visitor in 1932 noted: "competent agricultural managers seem to be very scarce in Russia at present and much harm is done by the constant moving of men from one post to another, before they have had a chance to prove themselves if they are any good and just long enough to do plenty of harm if they have no capacity."[344] It was the failure of managers to meet ever higher targets that resulted in their removal and replacement by more ruthless overseers. The very high turnover was exemplified by the Lower Volga's Serdobsk Rayon, where in 1931 alone twenty-four kolkhoz and sovkhoz managers and fifteen rural soviet chairmen were replaced.[345]

Initially, too, crop rotation was ignored, in spite of the old Russian adage "sow grain over grain and you will neither thresh nor winnow."[346] So yields stagnated or declined. The Middle Volga reported in the summer of 1932 that there had been a "total lack" of regular crop rotation in the kray, with the sowing of wheat year after year on the same land for five to seven and more years.[347] The resultant depletion of nutrients in the soil was compounded by a neglect of manuring in favour of fertilization. Kaganovich himself stressed that the new chemical fertilizers were not meant to replace manure, especially since the former was for use primarily on technical crops. He cited the saying, "Use plenty of manure and your barn will be full."[348] The decimation of the livestock population, however, inevitably resulted in much less manure. Sooner or later, though, what Otto Schiller called the "old agronomical rules," including crop rotation and manuring, were rediscovered and reintroduced when, he added, "after only three years practice it appeared that wheat growing alone upset the composition of the soil, rapidly reduced its fertility, favoured the spreading of weeds, and resulted in such an increase of the typical wheat pests as to make further wheat growing to some extent problematical."[349] All in all, much of the grain that was reaped was lost. In 1933 alone some 800 million puds (13,104,000 tonnes) of grain, including as much as 40 percent of the crop in parts of the Ukraine and the Lower Volga and an average of 22 percent of Kazakhstan's grain crop and sunflower crop, were lost, mainly because it was overripe, stolen, fed to livestock, left as kernels in straw and chaff, or poorly milled.[350]

Whatever was finally produced had to be delivered, of course, and delivered expeditiously: to the domestic market for essential personnel but especially to the foreign market in exchange for the requirements of heavy industrialization (expertise and machines). Transport, however, was not up to the task. In 1931 Stalin regarded "*transport* – above all, *railroad* transport – to be the most important issue in the coming months" and the "principal threat to the national economy."[351] The UK's Empire Marketing Board, which was concerned about Soviet competition for sales of Canadian and Australian grain, was advised by Andrew Cairns on 22 August 1932: "one of the most difficult problems in Russia to-day [is] the lack of transport; the very heavy loss of horses and the great shortage of machinery mean[s] that much of the grain crop must lie for weeks in the fields and be spoiled by rain."[352] Roads were primitive – they were rarely paved or even gravelled and usually dirt; indeed, "roadlessness" (*bezdorozha*) was commonplace during spring thaws and autumn rains. Returning in the middle of May 1932 from a ten-day trip to southern European Russia, the British ambassador reported: "except for a considerable distance from Moscow there appear to be few roads worthy of the name unless in the immediate vicinity of the towns."[353] Appeals to Moscow on these grounds, however, could be dangerous as well as unsuccessful. In the early spring of 1931 the Party first secretary of the Middle Volga, Mendel Khatayevich (shot in 1937), applied to Moscow for leave – now that the winter sled roads had melted – to give the peasants one to one and a half puds of feed oats for each of their carts in order to enable them to haul up to 4 million puds (ca. 65,518 tonnes) of grain from five rayons that were "especially distant from railroads," thereby ensuring that their grain would reach the railheads and not spoil. Stalin and Molotov, who were wont to blame oblast and rayon subordinates for shortcomings and to reject their excuses and to deny their pleas, refused, calling the request extortionate and unnecessary and declaring that the kray's leadership had misled Moscow and that Khatayevich himself would bear full responsibility for failing to deliver the grain unspoiled.[354] The *Economist*'s correspondent wisecracked in 1932 that "Russian transport arrangements appear, indeed, to be based on the Chinese proverb that it is better to travel than to arrive," and he noted that the usual form of road transport was "still the wagon drawn by horses little larger than Shetland ponies and carrying an incredibly small load at a snail's pace." Rail transport, he continued, was not much better. Most of the rolling stock was old, much of it was in disrepair, it ran on beds ballasted with sand or dirt rather than metal (gravel or cinders), and the rails were usually light and spiked in sleepers (ties) rather than affixed to baseplates, so that the trains could neither travel fast nor carry much freight or many passengers.[355] In 1930–32 so much grain (wheat, barley, corn) was being procured and exported that the railway boxcars and the riverboats that hauled it to the ports of the Black Sea were unable to keep pace with the demand.[356] Bottlenecks developed and multiplied, and the delays spoiled precious foodstuffs. In the autumn of 1932 a "huge mass of grain" in the Ukraine and in the Kuban in the North Caucasus was stockpiled at railway stations in heaps several metres high, and the grain became warm and mouldy; when rail fell some of the piles were soaked and they rotted, "for it was difficult to save a mountain of wheat with the help of tarpaulins."[357] Furthermore, "in view of the shortage of tarps," everywhere the stockpiles of grain were covered with sacks, so that "many" of the piles "completely rotted and during the winter froze into a solid mass, which [workers] broke into pieces with the aid of picks and crowbars and took partly to distilleries, simply burying the rest"[358] (at the same time, at all of the railway stations in the North Caucasus, a "colossal number" of stockpiled watermelons and cantaloupes were rotting while peasants were being prosecuted for making their melons into marmalade).[359] In 1933 in the Altai, Izmailov recorded: "It is astonishing where the grain goes; in our kray we have thousands of centners of it. If you look at any depot in our village [Smolenskoe] or in the neighbouring town of Biysk, the mountains of piled grain are awesome! We do not have enough housing for the grain! Threshed grain is heaped right on the ground for want of barns and sacks. We are wallowing in grain, surrounded by grain … yet we are starving."[360]

The upshot of all of these problems was what Otto Schiller in late 1933 called a "crisis of collectivization," a crisis that was "cumulative, since each year owing to inadequate cultivation the land becomes more overgrown with weeds, while each deficient harvest lessens the resources of fodder for the cattle [livestock], which still provide the main draught power for cultivation, and at the same time has an adverse effect on the health and efficiency of the peasants."[361] This crisis was epitomized by the situation in the Middle and Lower Volga. The former was the subject of a report of 12 August 1932 from the kray's Party secretary, Khatayevich, to the Party's Central Committee and the Sovnarkom (the Council of Peoples' Commissars, the executive body of the Soviet government) in Moscow "about the low yield level in the kray and measures for their elimination."[362] For the four-year period from 1929 to 1932 yields in the principal wheatlands on the left bank of the kray had been "sharply reduced" to an average of three centners per hectare, owing mainly to the "droughty climate" but also to a "complete absence" of "proper crop rotation," with wheat being sown for five to seven and more years in a row, thereby "greatly weedifying and exhausting the soil" – a crucial absence because the authorities were trying to change the system of land use from the old fallow system (of three fields) to a more intensive system (of seven to eight fields) without fallow that could only succeed with adequate crop rotation. More and more virgin and disused – that is, marginal – land was being worked. Also, there had been an "extraordinary overstraining of draught power throughout the kray – an average of 10.4 hectares per draught animal (compared with 6.3 hectares in 1928), and about 12 hectares on the left bank (up to 13–14 hectares in some rayons) – which does not ensure the proper quality of cultivation and prolongs the haying period intolerably." The fields were "choked with weeds" because of shallow ploughing (only two and a half to four inches), which had been prescribed in order to bring more land under cultivation. It was advisable to begin sowing as soon as the snow melted, especially in arid areas, in order to take full advantage of the soil moisture accumulated during the winter and early spring for crop growth instead of waiting for the soil to dry out – but to do so required caterpillar tractors, which could work the muddy fields ten days earlier than wheeled tractors, and draught animals; however, on the left bank there were enough caterpillar tractors to do only 23 percent of kolkhoz field work in 1932, and the number of horses had fallen from 1,140,000 in 1928 to 740,000 in 1932, and in 1931–32 at least 200,000 head of oxen had been lost, and even cows had to be used in some rayons for both light and heavy field work, but they ploughed so "very badly" that 25 percent of the sowings failed. On the kray's right bank, up to 40 percent of the sown area of the kolkhozes was harvested by sickles and threshed by flails – "antediluvian implements." The kray's MTSs had 20 to 25 tractors each for a total sown area of 40,000 to 45,000 hectares but needed 60 to 70 each in order to reduce the sown area to a manageable 25,000 hectares (and they also needed 1,000 trucks). Secretary Khatayevich concluded by understating that, without more agricultural machinery, "there is no way we will be able to manage."[363]

5
A MANIFOLD FAMINE

> When you cut timber, chips fly.
> – Bolshevik apologists

The Production of Grain

While collectivization diminished the Soviet Union's livestock numbers enormously, its impact on grain-growing during the period of the famine was much more mixed: grainland expanded (although spring wheat yields declined) and production increased (although exportation faltered) – at least according to foreign estimates and official statistics, with the latter not always being more accurate than the former.[1] In the face of falling yields – resulting undoubtedly from the application of less manure as livestock decreased, infestation by more weeds as peasant labour declined, and the cultivation of more marginal (less fertile or more arid) land – the area sown to grain had to be enlarged in order to produce (and export) more, especially wheat (table 5.1).

The yield of winter wheat averaged one-third more per hectare than that of spring wheat – less than the common disparity of two to one. During this period wheat constituted one-third of all grainland; rye was a close second, followed by oats.[2] During the famine period, then, grain and wheat yields fluctuated but remained modest or worse[3] – despite the supposed superiority of collectivized agriculture. Andrew Cairns found that official Soviet figures attempted to illustrate the progress of agriculture by underlining the increasing area of grain while downplaying the decreasing yield of grain; also, some

Table 5.1
Official annual amount of grainland and average annual yield of grain and winter and spring wheat in the Soviet Union, 1928–34

Year	Grainland (hectares)	Grain yield (centners per hectare)	Winter wheat yield (centners per hectare)	Spring wheat yield (centners per hectare)
1928	92,200,000	7.9	7.8	8.?
1929	96,000,000	7.5	7.9	5.9
1930	101,800,000	8.5	10.6	7.3
1931	104,400,000	6.7	9.1	4.0
1932	99,700,000	7.0	7.4	5.1
1933	101,600,000	8.8	10.8	7.1
1934	104,000,000	8.5 [7.3?]	?	?

Sources: Narkomzem SSSR, *Sel'skoe khoziaistvo SSSR*, 266, table 103, 268, table 105; and Tsentral'noe upravlenie, *Narodnoe khoziaistvo SSSR ... 1932*, 121, table 1. See also Stalin, *Works*, 13:325. However, according to Nikolai Briukhanov (shot in 1938), deputy chief of the Central Commission on the Determination of Yields within Sovnarkom (Council of the National Economy), the 1934 grain yield was only 7.3 centners per hectare (Danilov, Manning, and Viola, *Tragediia sovetskoi derevni*, 4:18, 19).

of the expanded grainland involved marginal land (in terms of temperature, precipitation, or soil) that was incapable of high yields, while not a little of the best land lay fallow.[4] The causes of the lower yields were detailed by the Party's first secretary of the Ukrainian rayon of Dnepropetrovsk in a report in the autumn of 1933 to Stalin. The secretary said that the average grain yield of the rayon's 3,600 kolkhozes that year was 10 centners per hectare (instead of the prescribed 13), and in some rayons only 5 to 8 centners, owing to poor seed, sparse seeding, thick weeds, and poor reaping; in the autumn of 1932 in "very many cases" kolkhozes had sown only 2 to 4 puds of winter wheat per hectare instead of the requisite 7 to 9 and had reaped very little or nothing at all the following summer. Then he described the consequences:

> The severe neglect and the weediness of the fields – besides the fact that the weeds choke the grain – lead further to the heavy infestation of the

fields by all kinds of harmful non-flora: Hessian flies, wheat moths [*oz-imnie sovki*], [saw-toothed] grain beetles [*zhuki kuz'ka*], cicadas, and the like. Now all of our fields, especially in those rayons having the worst battles against weeds, are literally swarming and teeming with such pests. The Hessian fly in the autumn and spring and the grain beetle during harvesting eat a very large part of our crop. During the harvest I saw for myself the brilliant external appearance of the winter and spring wheat, but when I looked more closely I found the ears in those fields empty [of kernels], and the surviving remnant of grain proved very inferior, having been sucked dry by the grain beetles.

On the whole our struggle against harvest losses has been conducted insufficiently throughout the rayon ... at present it is still possible to find a small number of ears in our fields. And half of a pud [18 lb.] of seed is left in the bucket chains of the machines that sow the fields thickly. This inadequate struggle against losses and the low quality of the harvest are also attributable in no small degree to the acute shortage of hands and the extreme strain on draught power.

Consequently, concluded the secretary, the rayon's kolkhozes would be providing about 220 million puds (3,603,000 tonnes) of grain to the state instead of the 250 million puds (4,095,000 tonnes) that had been estimated in August.[5]

Little wonder that, at the beginning of 1934, the Party's Central Committee resolved that the main agricultural task of that year was "the raising of the yields of everything and especially of technical crops" through the improvement of cultivation and the use of machinery and implements, as well as the strengthening of labour discipline on the part of kolkhozniks.[6]

The annual output of grain increased gradually but irregularly, both in total and per capita terms (table 5.2). The average annual grain harvest was 73.6 million tonnes during the First Five-Year Plan (1928–32) and 72.9 million tonnes during the Second Five-Year Plan (1933–37);[7] by comparison, Tsarist Russia's average annual output of grain in 1909–12 (within the country's 1933 boundaries) was 78.5 million tonnes in total and 585 kilograms per capita.[8] The trend of Soviet wheat output was similar to that of grain: 21,362,397 tonnes in 1925; 24,909,362 in 1926; 21,171,662 in 1927; 21,961,852 in 1928;

Table 5.2
Official total and per capita annual output of grain in the Soviet Union, 1921–34

Year	Total (tonnes)	Per capita (kilograms)
1921	42,300,000	317
1922	56,300,000	415
1923	57,400,000	415
1924	51,400,000	364
1925	74,700,000	518
1926	78,300,000	532
1927	72,800,000	483
1928	63–73,000,000	409–55
1929	62–69,000,000	395–440
1930	73–77,000,000*	456–81
1931	57–65,000,000**	320–65
1932	55–60,000,000***	288–314
1933	70–77,000,000****	430–72
1934	77,000,000	[?]

Sources: Cairns, "Agricultural Production," citing GOSPLAN for the 1921–30 figures and himself for the 1931–32 figures; Danilov, Manning, and Viola, Tragediia sovetskoi derevni, 3:854, table 6, 4:18; Davies and Wheatcroft, Years of Hunger, 446, 448–9, table 1; Kondrashin, Golod v SSSR, vol. 1, bk. 1, doc. 327:489; Narkomzem SSSR, Sel'skoe khoziaistvo SSSR, 208, table 29; Tsentral'noe upravlenie, Narodnoe khoziaistvo SSSR ... 1932, 121, table 1. See also Stalin, Works, 13:326.

* William Chamberlin estimated fewer than 80 million tonnes for 1930 (United Kingdom, FO 371/17253, no. 7753). And the Politburo boasted that the 1930 crop "exceeds the harvest of any since the revolution" (Kondrashin, Golod 1932–1933, 2nd ed., 122).
** Andrew Cairns estimated 63.4 million tonnes for 1931 (United Kingdom, FO 371/17253, no. 7753).
*** For 1932 William Chamberlin estimated about 60 million tonnes and Andrew Cairns 60.4 million tonnes (United Kingdom, FO 371/17253, no. 7753).
**** William Chamberlin estimated about 75 million tonnes for 1933 (United Kingdom, FO 371/17253, no. 7753).

18,855,585 in 1929; 26,893,732 in 1930; 17,574,931 in 1931; and 19,100,817 in 1932 for an annual average of 21,478,792 tonnes, compared with an annual average of 22,125,340 tonnes in 1909–13.[9]

Much of the crop was lost between field and table. Otto Schiller contended that as much as 30 percent of the 1933 harvest was not forthcoming.[10] It has been estimated that in 1930–33 the discrepancy between the harvested and the marketed crop averaged some 12 percent (one-eighth), owing to wastage, spoilage, and pilferage between reaping and storing.[11] One official asserted that some 800 million puds (13,104,000 tonnes) were lost as a result of letting ripe grain stand too long, leaving ears of grain that had been dropped in the reaped fields, storing grain too long in stooks and piles, leaving milled grain in the chaff, feeding reaped grain to livestock during harvesting, and stealing.[12] In the middle of August the editorial board of Pravda informed Stalin that, a week earlier, a group of "shock workers" from the press had undertaken a surprise inspection "to check the struggle against losses of grain at elevators, grain collection stations, processing enterprises (mills and the like), and places for loading and unloading grain" and had found that the safeguarding of grain at all of these facilities was "completely unsatisfactory" and their personnel "careless" and "unprofessional." They also found that grain was often delivered in a weedy, dirty, or damp state and was stored in antiquated and dilapidated facilities with inadequate fire protection.[13]

Thus, again collectivized agriculture proved wanting, producing no more (and often less) in total or per capita than the peasants had during the last half of the NEP (after recovering from the severe droughts of 1921–22 and 1924–25) and even less than they had during the five-year period prior to the First World War.

The Procurement of Grain

Despite the disappointing performance, the procurement of grain by the state was not lessened or even suspended but actually increased, for Stalin was resolute. Apart from needing to procure more grain for the burgeoning urban population (which grew by 12.4 million souls between 1928 and 1931 alone),[14] more vitally – in the view of the country's leaders – it was strategically necessary to procure more grain for exportation in order to finance industrialization and militarization as well as agricultural mechanization. Stalin and company were certain that it was just a matter of time before the Western capitalist powers declared war on their brave new world: a militaristic Japan was behaving aggressively in the Far East (invading Manchuria in 1931), Adolf Hitler's Nazis were on the rise in Germany, Great Britain had just severed relations, and the United States had yet to recognize the legitimacy of the USSR (and, only a decade earlier, several Western powers had intervened militarily in the civil war on the side of the reviled Whites). The supervisor of the nickel mines and prison camps at Norilsk near the mouth of the Yenisei River recalled the country's siege mentality at the time: "Our country was preparing for war ... but it is important to realize that this was not necessarily a war against the Germans. From the beginning we knew perfectly well that the outside world would never leave our Soviet revolution alone. Not only Stalin realized it – everyone, every ordinary communist, every ordinary person realized that we had not only to build, but to build in the full knowledge that soon we would be at war. It was inevitable – the Soviet Union would never be left in peace."[15]

Victor Herman, who went to the Soviet Union as the American son of one of the Ford Motor Company workers at Gorky and spent eighteen years in Siberia's Gulag, "found out pretty fast [in 1932] that [target] shooting was a very big thing over there – most everybody did it, practiced all the time with whatever sort of firearm they let you use," for "everybody was given to understand that this was an important thing, a way to protect the USSR from all the capitalist nations they figured were getting ready to invade it."[16]

The Soviet Union had inherited from Tsarist Russia two modest bases of heavy industry, the Donbass and the Urals, but they needed to be modernized and expanded, and capital was scarce. The means would be the sale of raw materials abroad for hard currency with which to buy machinery and technology for industrial development – primarily heavy industry for the making of capital goods (goods that make other goods) like iron and steel for armaments, not light industry for making consumer goods like clothing and appliances. "Everything possible," wrote a Russian chronicler, "was used to buy equipment abroad and to hire foreign specialists for the new factories: manganese ore from Chiatura, petroleum, timber, gold, copper and tin from church bells, antiques, handicrafts, grain, butter, eggs."[17]

Grain was included from the outset. In a directive at the beginning of 1928 Stalin stressed the cruciality (and warlike nature) of grain procurement, urging the need for "brutal pressure" to be exerted on Party bodies everywhere, for "grain procurement represents a fortress that we must take by any means" – and which "we certainly will, provided we do our work in a Bolshevik manner with Bolshevik pressure."[18] In the summer of 1929, halfway through the second year of the First Five-Year Plan and the first of its four procurement campaigns, Stalin declared in a letter to Molotov: "grain procurement this year will provide the basis for everything we're doing – if we foul up here, everything will be wiped out."[19] A week later Stalin told Molotov that "the grain procurements ha[d] gone well," adding, "if we can beat this grain thing, then we'll prevail in everything, both in domestic and foreign policies"[20] – meaning that, internally, the peasants will have been subjugated and, externally, the capitalists will have been countered. A year later Stalin exhorted Molotov: "Force the export of grain to the maximum. If we can export grain, the credits [for foreign purchases] will come."[21] And, finally, a couple of weeks after this urgent behest Stalin reminded Molotov: "*we must force through grain exports with all our might*, otherwise our hard currency could become really desperate," and "we must *push* grain exports *furiously* ... otherwise we risk being left without our new iron and steel and machine-building factories," and he urged that daily grain exports be raised from 1 million to 1.5 million puds (16,380 to 24,570 tonnes) to 3 million to 4 million puds (49,140 to 65,520 tonnes) "at a minimum."[22] This strict policy of meeting foreign trade obligations through the exportation of foodstuffs became, in the opinion of Eugene Lyons, "perhaps the deepest of the silent grievances of the Soviet people." The cost of militarization disgusted a Leningrad worker, Arkady Mankov, who complained: "it is no secret that fully ⅔ of the state budget is spent on the army, the military, that fully ⅔ of all loans and returns are cast into the jaws of the bloody monster – war." He added, "At the same time that in the southern oblasts (the most grain-rich!) people are swelling from famine and fleeing in panic to the cities, and at the same time that in the cities they throw 80–120 rub[les] a month at the overwhelming majority of people, dooming them to poverty and starvation, they are giving military rations to the army, i.e., in other words, payment in kind."[23]

The methods of grain procurement became more and more draconian as the Kremlin demanded more and more grain for export, the military, the cities, and various central reserve stocks. Procurement was executed initially under the "contract system," whereby the peasants had to surrender from one-quarter to one-third of their harvest, with, however, considerable variation from region to region and from holding to holding. In 1930 the norm was set at one-quarter to one-third of the crop for the chief grain-producing regions and one-eighth in the others, but in fact more was taken, thanks to the imposition in 1931 of so-called "counter plans" of procurement, that is, exactions over and above the planned targets. So in accordance with the norms of 1930 and 1931, respectively, 30 percent and 41 percent of the harvest was taken from the Ukraine, 33 percent and 42 percent from the Crimea, 34 percent and 38 percent from the North Caucasus, 41 percent and 40 percent from the Lower Volga, 39 percent and 32 percent from the Middle Volga, 27 percent and 29 percent from Western Siberia (the lowest percentage, presumably in view of its lengthy drought), and 33 percent and 40 percent from Kazakhstan. The average norms for these chief grain-producing regions were 32 percent in 1930 and 37 percent in 1931. Norms were even fixed for all of the chief grain-consuming regions, for example, in 1930 and 1931, respectively, 15 percent and 20 percent for the Moscow Region, 9 percent and 10 percent for the Leningrad Region, 11 percent and 15 percent for Nizhny Novgorod Kray, and 8 percent and 10 percent for the West Region.[24] The 1930 norm for an individual farmstead was 19 percent of output, for a kolkhoz 32 percent, and for a sovkhoz 60 percent; in the Ukraine kolkhozes had to render twice as much grain as individual farmsteads.[25]

The Kremlin was still not satisfied, however, so the contract system was replaced by the "conveyor" or "assembly line" system in order to extract as much grain as possible for the state in fulfillment of Stalin's "first commandment of the kolkhoz" – "first render grain to the state and then use the remaining surplus for your own needs." The conveyor method was intended to "save" harvested grain from plunderers, and for this purpose it was not stooked but instead threshed immediately and – bypassing the kolkhoz granaries – taken right to the storage depots. In practice, however, the conveyor was always "spinning its wheels," and the grain strewn in the fields spoiled and rotted while waiting to be threshed. The resultant loss of grain in 1930 amounted to one-fifth to one-quarter of the harvest.[26] As a kolkhoz official told the Party plenum of June 1931, "last year we embraced the famous newspaper cry of 'conveyor' without reason or thought until the grain was lost."[27]

At the suggestion of Anastas Mikoyan, the 1932 norm for the grain-producing regions was raised to 30 to 40 percent for kolkhozes and 40 to 45 percent for those served by MTSS, so that, compared with 1930, in 1932 the Ukraine's kolkhozes rendered 37 percent more, the North Caucasus's 56 percent more, the Middle Volga's 46 percent more, and the Central Black Earth's 29 percent more; the new norms were calculated – based upon local conditions – in centners per hectare, but kulaks had to render 150 percent more than kolkhozniks, and kolkhozniks with personal plots had to render 5 percent more than kolkhozniks without them.[28] Moreover, a Politburo decree at the beginning of 1932 authorized regional officials to procure grain "above the plan"; 60 percent of these additional requisitions were to be sent to the central reserve funds and the rest kept for local needs.[29] Overall, from 1928 through 1934, the state exacted an annual average of 28 percent of total grain output; by contrast, during the NEP the peasants did not sell more than 22 percent of their grain output, keeping 12 percent for seed, 25 to 30 percent for feed for livestock, and up to 30 percent for food for themselves.[30]

Meanwhile, the aggregate of monetary payments to the state by the peasants increased two-and-a-half-fold between 1930 and 1932; some 40 percent was mandatory (rural taxes, insurance charges, cultural contributions) and the rest was "voluntary" (loan, ration, and stock charges). The peasantry became the Soviet Union's foremost taxpayer, its exactions representing 55 percent of all monetary payments to the state in 1930, 68 percent in 1931, and 75 percent in 1932.[31]

To overcome peasant resistance to these extortionate demands, the state took a variety of measures, ranging from coercion to violence. In 1929 the Kremlin introduced "measures of social influence," that is, shaming, in order to extract more grain from peasant "hoarders." Two such measures were prohibitions and boycotts. For example: a ban on lighting entailed a blackout – the covering of the windows of the offender's izba in order to keep the interior dark; a boycott against greeting forbade the salutation of an ostracized peasant by other peasants; and an outcast peasant's gates and windows could be smeared with tar and a sign put on his gates: "Do not come here – I am an enemy of Soviet power" (if the sign was removed, the outcast was fined).[32]

Still not enough grain was procured, so harsher measures were applied, and social tension mounted in the villages, with the peasants hating the workers as the favourites of the Soviet leaders, and the srednyaks hating the bednyaks as recipients of state supplies, and both the srednyaks and the bednyaks hating the kulaks as beneficiaries of their misfortune by buying their livestock cheaply and lending them grain dearly (so that they had little sympathy for the kulaks when they were subsequently dispossessed and deported).[33]

The harsher measures climaxed in 1931–33. In 1931 the summer-autumn procurement campaign was assisted by special activists, the so-called "Twenty-Five Thousanders" (actually, 27,500): industrial workers from the cities, who were chosen from some seventy thousand volunteers on the basis of their organizational and political experience (70 percent were Party members) and who were given a crash course on the rural economy and dispersed throughout the countryside to defend collectivization against the misgivings and "petty property instincts" of the peasantry.[34] The exhortations of one of these activists were fictionalized colourfully by Sholokhov:

> "I am a worker from the Red Putilov works [in Leningrad], comrades," he opened his speech. "I have been sent to you by our Communist Party and the working class, in order to help you organise a collective farm and to destroy the kulaks, our common bloodsuckers. I shall not say much. You must all join together in a collective farm, socialise the land, and all your implements and cattle. Why must you join a collective farm? Because it is impossible to go on living as we are! The difficulties we're having with the grain have arisen because the kulak lets it rot in the ground. We have got to get the grain from him by force! But you would be glad to give your grain, only you haven't got much. You can't feed the Soviet Union on the grain of the poor and middling peasants. We've got to sow more. But how are you going to sow more with only a wooden or a single-share plow? Only the tractor can get us out of that difficulty."
>
> "The Party proposes complete collectivisation," he added, "so as to hitch you on to the tractor and lift you out of your want. What did comrade Lenin say just before his death? 'Only in the collective farm can the peasant find salvation from his poverty. Otherwise he is doomed. The vampire kulak will suck him flat as a board.' And you must walk quite firmly along the road he pointed out. In alliance with the workers the collective farmers will sweep away all the kulaks and enemies."[35]

Mostly young men with the outlook of the years of the civil war and bent on a career in the Soviet administration, the Twenty-Five Thousanders (dubbed the "light cavalry" by one observer)[36] served as Stalin's trusted and staunch allies in the field, with little knowledge of, and even less sympathy for, the peasants by virtue of their upbringing and experience. They did not spare the reserve, feed, or even seed funds of the kolkhozes from the extra exactions. One village oldtimer in Volgograd Rayon recalled that "there were Twenty-Five Thousanders [here], and they didn't understand anything."[37] Nevertheless, the state procured 1,240,800,000 puds of grain (20,324,000 tonnes) – 297 million puds (4,865,000 tonnes) more than in 1929 – from a "record" harvest (thanks to very favourable weather) of 835,400,000 tonnes (1,841,723,00 puds) officially (but 772 million tonnes [1,701,951 puds] actually).[38]

Sometimes, on the local level, activists undertook punitive measures on their own initiative. During the 1931 spring sowing campaign, some fanatical Party officials in the countryside formed the Union for the Struggle for Discipline, which even resorted to the whipping of peasants (reminiscent of Tsarist serfdom). With the connivance and impunity of rayon Party leaders, Union members whipped peasants for being late to work, leaving unplanted or unploughed places in the fields, "having taken someone else's wife," coming to work in *valenki* (traditional peasant felt boots), or even "having strolled on the street." The whipping was described as follows: "The condemned was forced to lie on the ground, and they beat him with the palms of their hands or a spoon but most often with reins, a belt, switches ... they beat the men and the women." Some activists also bullied the peasants by various means, for example, in a village in the Turkovsk Rayon of the Lower Volga a kolkhoz woman was forced to kiss a simpleton whom "they had forced to kiss a horse" beforehand.[39] These instances reflect the hostile and even contemptuous attitude of some Party activists towards the peasants. And this attitude enabled the activists to justify their cruelties.

Often, however, the local countryside authorities were not severe enough and had to be pressed by Moscow. Victor Kravchenko was mobilized in 1931 for a brigade to be sent to some villages in the Ukraine's Dnepropetrovsk Rayon to extract more grain, and his brigade was told by a Central Committee member: "Your job is to get the grain at any price. Pump it out of them [the villagers], wherever it's hidden," and "don't be afraid of taking extreme measures" because "it's a war – it's them or us!" They were also ordered to steel the local village officials, who "need an injection of Bolshevik iron."[40]

The peasants, of course, bore the brunt of this "war" waged by "iron" officials. A team of reporters from *Pravda* spent ten days in Moldavia at the beginning of 1932, investigating peasant complaints about grain procurement, and recounted them in a private letter to their editorial colleagues. They checked "ultra-leftist" excesses and found "clear and in most cases open counter-revolutionary acts on the part of the local workers vis-à-vis the village." The worst "excess" was the search for grain, usually conducted at nighttime and very thoroughly and destructively: the searchers wrecked stoves looking for hidden kernels of grain and thatched eaves looking for cobs of corn; if they found any, they imposed a fine in money and kind in an amount that they knew the peasants could not pay, and so, that night or no later than the next day they sold all of their belongings (and in some cases just destroyed them), literally "undressing" the peasants by taking their boots and skirts. Rarely was much grain found; the search usually ended with the seizure of "very meagre amounts," although the peasants may well have hidden much more "rather cunningly" (the authorities told the reporters that "the peasants hide grain in bottles, match boxes, and one-pound bags that they hang under tables"). Another "excess" was the bashing of peasants in a number of villages and rayons; fingers were broken, arms were wrenched, hair was pulled out, heads were beaten with iron bars, and in one village a peasant woman was lowered upside down in a well and asked whether she had any grain to surrender.[41]

This exposé did not become public, and the excesses continued, as local Party careerists, hoping to gain the favour of higher rayon, region, and national Party bosses, engaged in "excessomania" – the imposition of completely impossible targets. Indeed, procurements became so unreasonable that they often exceeded output levels and left the kolkhozes, sovkhozes, and individual farmsteads without enough grain for seed, feed, and even food, let alone workday payments in kind for the kolkhozniks. As one kolkhoz manager told Andrew Cairns in 1932, the procurement plan necessitated a yield of 132 puds of buckwheat and 480 puds of vetch per hectare from his kolkhoz, whereas its average yields were only 26 and 175 puds, respectively; moreover, the plan's demand for potatoes exceeded the kolkhoz's average harvest by 11,140 puds (182 tonnes). And, as another kolkhoz manager near Kiev explained to Cairns, "when a [collective] farm did not sow as much as the plan called for, or if there was crop damage due to winter frosts, hail or drought, the Government still collected the full amount of the plan, and the peasants went hungry."[42]

The Ukraine's Party chief, Stanislav Kosior, epitomized the purblind attitude of the authorities, central and regional, towards disappointing procurement, blaming it not on flawed policy but on the enforcers and sufferers of that policy. In a speech at a joint meeting of the Moscow and Kharkov central committees, he boasted that the Ukraine had enabled the country to increase grain procurement one and a half to two times during the First Five-Year Plan, that is, from 500 million to 600 million puds (8,190,000 to 9,828,000 tonnes) from non-collectivized agriculture in 1928 to 1.2 billion to 1.4 billion puds (19,656,000 to 22,931,000 tonnes) from collectivized agriculture in 1932, "but," he said, "despite the larger amount of grain, it is still difficult for us to obtain it for a number of reasons ... in a number of rayons and regions we have overlooked the penetration of the kolkhozes by harmful elements, the fouling [*zasorennost'*] of Party organizations, and the enhancement [*aktivizatsiia*] of nationalistic counter-revolutionary elements," and "we will mount the severest attack on these elements in order to uncover and unmask them so as to destroy and neutralize them." He added, "Although we have more grain [now], unfortunately the kolkhoz grain is being devoured by spongers and loafers who are still present in the kolkhozes, as well as by a large number of parasites who live in the village and do not plant or reap and live on stolen kolkhoz grain." True to Party form, Kosior especially faulted the non-collectivized sector, saying that "particularly the large villages that have 1,000–1,500 households are bound to have 100–150 households of so-called individual farmsteads that do not engage in agriculture ... parasitic elements ... living on stolen kolkhoz grain ... with the result that a huge amount of kolkhoz and sovkhoz grain is plundered, reducing our resources."[43]

The Kremlin's impatience came to a head at the end of 1932 after the loss of one-half of the harvest that year – two and a half times as much as that of 1931.[44] The target of grain procurement had been set at 1,173,000 puds (19,210 tonnes), which was 439,000 puds (7,190 tonnes) less than 1931's, but there was still a shortfall of 80,400 puds (1,317 tonnes), most of which was attributable to the Ukraine (notably), the North Caucasus, and the Central Black Earth.[45] On 22 October the Party secretary of Dnepropetrovsk Rayon,

A Manifold Famine

Mendel Khatayevich, reported to Stalin that by 15 October the first (and most decisive) three and a half months of the grain procurement period in the Ukraine had achieved only three-eighths (140 million puds [2,293,000 tonnes]) of the planned target of 375 million puds (6,142,000 tonnes), leaving the next two and a half months (the least decisive) of the period to procure the remaining five-eighths; furthermore, he estimated that only 70 million puds (1,146,000 tonnes) of the remaining 235 million puds (3,850,000 tonnes) would be procured. Never since the formation of the Soviet Ukraine in 1922 had so little grain been forthcoming in the first three and a half months of its harvest.[46] On the very same day the Politburo decided to form "extraordinary commissions" to go to the southern steppes of European Russia – responsible for most of the country's procurement deficiency – in order to enforce state grain procurements by purging spineless local officials and exiling listless peasants. Their attitude was illustrated by one participant who declared: "Grain has to be got at any price! We will do so until blood flows! Follies will be committed but grain will be gotten!"[47]

One commission under Kaganovich (with Mikoyan and the OGPU's deputy but actual chief Genrikh Yagoda) was sent to the North Caucasus, another under Molotov was sent to the Ukraine, where he was eventually joined by Kaganovich, and still another under the "old Bolshevik" Pavel Postyshev (shot in 1939) was sent to the Lower Volga. The situation in the North Caucasus had been reported to Stalin in August by the kray's Party secretary Boris Sheboldayev (shot in 1937), another "old Bolshevik," who had written that the harvest of grain, especially of winter and spring wheat, was lower than in 1931 and therefore the procurement would be "substantially lower," too. He explained:

> It is difficult to establish the importance of the individual reasons for the outcome in July of a dramatic reduction in harvest prospects. There is no doubt that the ripening of the grain was affected by the mismanagement of the kolkhozes and sovkhozes (the late sowings, the lack of crop rotation, the poor cultivation of the fields) and the prolonged weediness and thinness of the grain, but there were also special natural conditions (withering [*zapal*], lodging [*stek*], and haze [*tuman*], etc.), as these phenomena are called by agronomists and peasants alike, which sharply reduced the number of ears [spikes] and in some rayons

nullified them ... Finally, the harvesting conditions (rain for a month and a half) also led to some losses (germination).[48]

In the Lower Volga Postyshev's commission found that the shortfalls in seeding and reaping had been due not to "kulak sabotage" but to "agrotechnical" factors such as faulty planning, mismanagement, and crop choice.[49]

As was his habit, however, Stalin blamed "distortions" of the Party line on its cadres, not policy, let alone the elements. So in the North Caucasus Kaganovich was "to work out and carry out measures for smashing the sabotage of grain sowing and procurement organized by counter-revolutionary kulak elements in the Kuban" by the end of the year. He was tasked with "making an immediate breakthrough" in the pace of wheat, sunflower, and corn procurements.[50] At the beginning of November in Rostov-on-Don at a series of meetings with local officials Kaganovich's commission was told that the kray's stock of grain was so low that it was impossible to fulfill the procurement plan, but the commission paid no heed and told them that they were simply blind to "obviously emerging sabotage" and were serving as "envoys of peasants infected with a kulak spirit." Particularly individual farmsteaders of the Cossack stanitsas, where the situation was most problematic, were "repressed," that is, dispossessed and deported, if not jailed or shot, and Party officials, too. Kaganovich declared: "It is necessary that all of the Kuban Cossacks learn how in [19]21 the Terek Cossacks who opposed Soviet power were relocated. And we can do so now, too, in order that they do not foul rather than seed the golden Kuban lands and do not spit on them, and in order to settle accounts with them we will relocate them."[51] Between the beginning of November 1932 and the middle of January 1933 thirteen Kuban Cossack and two Don Cossack stanitsas were "blacklisted" – designated for "repression" – and more than 61,600 *stanichniks* were deported to northern rayons, including 45,600 of the 47,500 of the three stanitsas of Poltavskaya, Medvedovskaya, and Urupskaya.[52] The purged stanitsas were resettled with kolkhozniks from the North and demobilized Red Army soldiers, and Poltavskaya, Urupskaya, and Umanskaya were renamed Krasnoarmeiskaya, Sovetskaya, and Léningradskaya, respectively.[53] Also, by the spring of 1933 nearly half (45 percent) of rural Party bosses in the North Caucasus had been purged.[54]

A Manifold Famine

From the North Caucasus Kaganovich went to help Molotov in the Ukraine, which had reported the greatest shortfall (both absolutely and relatively) in the country's European breadbasket. The Party bosses in the Ukraine, Kosior and Vlas Chubar (both "old Bolsheviks" and both shot in 1939), protested the republic's procurement target, which they deemed too high. At the beginning of July Stalin proposed to Molotov and Kaganovich that both be fired, or "Chubar's corruptness and opportunistic essence and Kosior's rotten diplomacy ... and criminally frivolous attitude toward his job will eventually ruin the Ukraine." Stalin added, "these comrades are not up to the challenge of leading the Ukraine today," and he had in mind to replace them with Kaganovich.[55] They were "persuaded," not replaced, however, and Molotov's commission even agreed to reduce procurement by 70 million puds (1,147,000 tonnes), for Stalin was concerned about the Ukrainian rayons bordering unfriendly Poland, fearing their loss in the event of the worsening of the republic's grain crisis. In a cipher to both Molotov and Kaganovich Stalin said, "it is necessary to make an exception for the specially suffering rayons of the Ukraine, not only from the point of view of justice, but also in view of the special position of the Ukraine, its common frontier with Poland, etc." (and he thought that a similar exception might have to be made for the Transcaucasus).[56] Someone had to take the blame, however, so lesser officials and peasants took the fall. Between 1 November and 5 December 1932 the OGPU arrested 1,230 rural managers, plus 140 brigaders, 265 foremen, and 195 other kolkhoz workers in the Ukraine, and 206 groups of "kulaks" and "anti-Soviet elements" were found and tried; in addition, the Ukrainian Central Committee blacklisted 6 large villages and up to 400 kolkhozes. Communists themselves were likewise persecuted: in October–November 327 Party members were tried, nine of whom were shot for helping or hiding "kulak saboteurs."[57] Half a century later it was still possible to hear it said in the Ukraine and the North Caucasus that "Kaganovich passed through just like Mamai [the brutal Mongol warlord invader of the 1300s] had passed through."[58]

The repression was inflicted elsewhere, too, if not as bloodily. In a "strictly secret encoded message" of 7 December Stalin and Molotov told Party bosses in the Urals that they would not "evade responsibility for unfulfillment of the plan by sovkhozes" and that "in the event of non-fulfillment of the plan they would be arrested as fraudsters, saboteurs, and enemies of the Soviet state, just as a number of managers of sovkhozes in Western Siberia, the Ukraine, and the North Caucasus have been arrested." Moreover, they were "to explain to the managers that a Party card would not save them from arrest and that an enemy with a Party card would merit even greater punishment than an enemy without one."[59] And in another such telegram a week later Stalin authorized the Party boss of Gorky Kray to repress two rayons for not meeting their grain, flax, potato, meat, and timber targets by means of the following measures: "the cessation of the delivery of goods to, and the shipment of goods from, the rayons, the absolute prohibition of kolkhoz trade, the prompt exaction of credit and other payments from the kolkhozniks and individual farmsteaders, the purging of state, cooperative, and kolkhoz personnel of alien and harmful elements, the removal of counter-revolutionary elements from organs of the OGPU, and the prompt purging of Party organizations."[60]

In order to improve labour discipline in the kolkhoz-sovkhoz system and thereby safeguard procurements, "politotdels" (political departments) – what Victor Kravchenko called an "army of more than a hundred thousand stalwarts [including himself], selected by the Central Committee"[61] – were established at the beginning of 1933 and deployed at sovkhozes and MTSs, where they liaised closely with the OGPU to exert more direct control over agriculture by Moscow, to which they were directly subordinate (rather than local bodies). Their "primary task" was "to guarantee the unconditional and opportune fulfillment by the kolkhozes and kolkhozniks of their obligations to the state and in particular to resolutely combat the misappropriation of kolkhoz property and the occurrences of sabotage of Party and government measures in the matter of kolkhoz grain and meat procurements."[62]

The "politotdelniks," as newly minted communists, were often doctrinaire and enthusiastic and not infrequently committed serious "excesses" with regard to the cadres of the kolkhozes, sovkhozes, and MTSs, arresting and expelling honest workers as "enemies" and often classifying production shortfalls, personnel inexperience, machinery breakdowns, and the like as "sabotage." In 1933 the politotdels, in conjunction with the OGPU, had 271,048 peasants (206,494 of them individual farmsteaders) arrested, which was 83,057 more than in 1932, and the OGPU independently arrested 64,554 kolkhozniks, compared with 30,249 in 1932.[63] Also in 1933, nearly one-third of kolkhoz and sovkhoz agronomists, one-half of their bursars, more than one-third of their storehousemen, and one-quarter of their bookkeepers, stocktakers, grooms, and the like were dismissed; and nearly one-third of the managers of kolkhozes in Kazakhstan, the Lower Volga, and the North Caucasus were declared "enemies" of the kolkhoz system.[64] At least one manager made it easy for these "eyes and ears" of Moscow by purging himself. He oversaw the grain sovkhoz "Red Perekop" in the Ukraine, and on his third attempt at suicide he shot himself to death because of depression over his poor performance and left a note: "To not fulfill the orders of the party of Lenin means not to live. Apologize to my family. Bury me wherever you want, but in a field."[65]

Most rural officials and especially activists, such as the politotdel members, heeded the slogan "the struggle for grain is the struggle for socialism!" To them the ends justified the means, and some even felt that "it is better to exceed than not to achieve [the sowing and the procurement targets]."[66] There were exceptions, however. In the face of unattainable targets some lower-level cadres beseeched Moscow to reduce them (although their pleas were usually rejected, and the plaintiffs themselves were threatened with "harsh measures" – including arrest as liars, wreckers, and traitors – if they failed to deliver). In 1931 the manager of one kolkhoz in the Volga German ASSR even "actively opposed the taking of grain" and declared: "the plan given to the village is unrealistic, and no more grain will be surrendered, otherwise the villagers will starve to death." Elsewhere in the Volga Valley in the same year, a rayon Party secretary ordered the publication in the rayon newspaper of a telegram from Stalin and Molotov about grain procurement in order to explain to kolkhoz managers and activists why the rayon's authorities were being forced "to actually extract all of the village's grain," for he did not want the kolkhozniks to reckon him an "enemy" to blame for the seizure of their grain "to the bottom of the barrel." For his pains the secretary was removed from his position and expelled from the Party.[67] Still in the same year in the Ukraine, according to official Polish reports, the procurement target was so impracticable that even the lowest-ranking officials expressed "repeated warnings and protests" to their superiors that were flatly rejected as punishable evidence of "kulak ideology."[68] Maurice Hindus found that grain procurement had been undertaken with "especial vigor," owing to "the fatal falsification of figures on acreage and yield, on the part of officials in the Ukraine, which caused the authorities in Moscow to impose heavier collections of grain than the crop warranted." The peasants implored the procurement authorities to relent, he continued, but "they knew that peasants always wailed, and they were ever conscious of party discipline – of the fact that they must not fail in the achievement of the mission on which they were sent." He added, "At times, of their own volition, they gathered more grain than their instructions called for. They were brave and faithful and they wished to demonstrate their devotion to their superiors by proving that in spite of difficulties they could more than fulfill their program." Subsequently, "hundreds of these officials all over the Ukraine were dismissed, disciplined, tried, jailed, or expelled from the party."[69]

Some higher officials also objected to the targets. At the end of the 1932 harvest season the commissar of agriculture himself, Yakov Yakovlev (Jacob Epstein) (another "old Bolshevik," shot in 1938), told Stalin that the "crucial flaw" in the system of grain procurement was the fact that the amount of the target for each kolkhoz was determined "at the whim of the rayon authorities" without "any fixed criteria, set by law, to ascertain the amount of grain that can [realistically] be procured." He added that this flaw, which made procurement look more like requisition, was worsened by the fact that rayon officials really did not know the resources of each of the seventy to eighty kolkhozes that were found in many rayons.[70] But it was the starving peasants who paid the price of unreasonable procurement. In the autumn of 1930 a kolkhoznik in the Middle Volga wrote in a letter to "Comrade Stalin":

> In our kolkhoz there are about 400 members with families, and a total of some 90 thousand puds of grain have been milled. The procurement task was 85 thousand puds. The kolkhoz administration informed the executive committee, which ordered the unconditional fulfillment of the plan. When 50% of the plan was reached, the chairman of the kolkhoz, after seeing the grain left for its own use, declared that it could not furnish any more grain. He was removed by the executive committee. The second chairman furnished additional grain to the point where only seed grain remained and then refused to provide more. A third chairman was appointed who took all of the grain ... The kolkhozniks

were given 400 grams per day and nothing more. And now there are kolkhoz families who sit at home without a piece of bread.

The kolkhoznik added, naively, "dear comrade Stalin, you must thrash those who undermine the authority of, and trust in, the Party and Soviet power."[71]

Stalin's team remained unmoved, however. As early as 1929 Reader Bullard had observed: "the Government are determined to get large supplies of grain at all costs, and with the OGPU their chief instrument, having powers of life and death, anything can happen."[72] And in the autumn of 1933 the Italian consul in Kharkov, Sergio Gradenigo, reported "the pitiless requisition of anything that can still be found among the peasants." "The harvested grain," he added, "has all been taken and carried off to Moscow, Leningrad, to military warehouses, and to ports of export overseas."[73] The country was building its industry and military by starving its peasants. As a disillusioned Will Durant sardonically put it, "the peasants must be compelled to grow more grain, the grain must be exported, machinery must be imported, Russia must starve itself into security."[74] Or, as the conflicted Louis Fischer told two American visitors, "this country is starving itself great."[75]

The repressive measures did succeed in procuring an irregularly increasing amount of grain for the state in both absolute and relative terms, although procurements were reduced during the famine's climax (table 5.3).

The state procured most of its grain from the Ukraine, the North Caucasus, the Central Black Earth, and the Lower and Middle Volga in 1931 (two-thirds), 1932 (two-thirds), and 1933 (three-fifths), with the Ukraine alone providing one-third in 1931, one-third in 1932, and one-quarter in 1933.[76]

Thus, between the start and end of the First Five-Year Plan the state increased its procurement of grain more or less twofold,[77] and two and a half-fold by the end of the great famine. By the end of the grain harvest in 1935, when the state took up to two-fifths of the crop (compared with about one-sixth during the NEP), Kaganovich wrote triumphantly to his fellow Politburo member, Grigory ("Sergo") Orzhonikidze (1886–1937 [suicide]): "what is happening ... with this year's grain procurement is an absolutely fantastic, stunning victory of Stalinism."[78] The "war against the peasant" had been won.

The war's losers, both the peasantry and agriculture, paid a heavy price. The deterioration of agriculture is illustrated by a statistical accounting in

Table 5.3
Official production and procurement of grain in the Soviet Union, 1927–34

Year	Production (tonnes)	Absolute procurement (tonnes)	Relative procurement (percent of harvest)*
1927	72,800,000	10,808,435	15
1928	63–70,000,000 [73,100,000]**	10,790,000	15 [14.7]*
1929	62–69,000,000 [71,700,000]**	15,348,449 [11,200,000]**	17 [22.4]*
1930	73–77,000,000 [83,525,000]**	22,357,542*** [21,405,000]**	27 [26.5]*
1931	57–65,000,000 [55–56,000,000]**	24,247,232 [22,460,000]**	37 [32.9]*
1932	55–60,000,000 [54–55,000,000]**	18,277,759 [18,275,000]**	31–34 [26.9]*
1933	70–77,000,000	23,100,000	30–32 [25.9]*
1934	77,000,000	26,200,000	? [29.2]*

Sources: Davies and Wheatcroft, *Years of Hunger*, 446, 448–9, table 1; Davies et al., *Stalin-Kaganovich Correspondence*, doc. 10:73, 238; Tsentralnoe upravlenie, *Narodnoe khoziaistvo SSSR ... 1932*, 121, table 1. See also Ivnitskii, *Golod 1932–1933*, 25, 44, 104, 110; Kondrashin, *Golod v SSSR*, vol. 1, bk. 1, doc. 119:252; Kondrashin, *Khlebozagotovitel'naia politika*, 147, table 10; Kondrashin and Tiurina, "'Govorit' o golode," 94, 95; and Danilov, Manning, and Viola, *Tragediia sovetskoi derevni*, 4:18 – all of whom give more or less the same figures for various of these years.
* Narkomzem SSSR, *Sel'skoe khoziaistvo SSSR*, 267, table 103.
** Kondrashin, *Golod 1932–1933*, 2nd ed., 117, 122, 145, 178–9, 188, table 9; 246, table 10.
*** According to Kaganovich, 20.2 million tonnes (Davies et al., *Stalin-Kaganovich Correspondence*, doc. 10:73).

one Lower Volga rayon. On 12 March 1933 an official reported that the Yelansk Rayon, which he considered a microcosm of the Lower Volga Kray, had experienced "in the last 3 years a steady decline in yield, output, and especially grain procurement by the state," with the wheat area increasing from 97,000 hectares in 1930 to 128,000 in 1931 and 116,000 in 1932, the wheat crop decreasing from 791,000 centners (79,086,000 tonnes) in 1930 to 745,000 (74,486,000 tonnes) in 1931 and 491,000 (49,091,000 tonnes) in 1932, state wheat procurements decreasing from 420,000 centners (41,992,000 tonnes) in 1930 to 253,000 (25,295,000 tonnes) in 1931 and 208,000 (20,796,000 tonnes) in 1932, and the number of horses decreasing from 16,500 in 1930 to 15,000 in 1931 and 7,000 in 1932 (and 4,000 by 1 March 1933). So procurements as a proportion of production fluctuated – but generally decreased – from just over one-half (53 percent) in 1930 to one-third (34 percent) in 1931 to just over two-fifths (42 percent) in 1932. The official added, "if the quality (poor) of soil cultivation is added to the huge losses during harvesting and the colossal theft of standing grain and from sheaves, threshing floors, barns, etc., then it will be understandable why in 1932 the rayon met less than 70 percent of the initial grain procurement target ... for which the rayon was put by the territorial administration on its blacklist [of underachievers]." The chief causes, he asserted, were the disarray in management and planning in the rayon and the lack of incentives for the kolkhozniks.[79] Both factors – and others – were about to be addressed by the regime.

The "New NEP"

Eventually – in the face of increasing and irrefutable evidence – the Stalinist leadership seems to have become not only fully aware of, but also alarmed by, the disastrous situation in the countryside. Presumably even Stalin's inner circle must have realized that, if the situation were to continue, then there would soon not be enough peasants alive to produce ample grain and other foods for the country, let alone export; besides, by the end of the First Five-Year Plan in 1932 the highly touted heavy industrial base had been more or less built, if rather crudely, so grain exports were much less crucial than in 1928. Or perhaps the Kremlin's "belligerent attitude" disappeared simply because it was no longer necessary, for it had won the "war against the peasants," or, as Otto Schiller put it, "a victory has been gained by the government, the peasant brought to his knees."[80] Alexander Barmine, the "old Bolshevik" Soviet diplomat who wisely defected before the 1936–38 purges, contended that Stalin knew that the famine threatened his leadership – "another poor harvest and disaster might descend on him" – so that every effort was exerted during the spring 1933 sowing to ensure a good crop, which was indeed obtained. Consequently, he continued, "many who had doubted began to think that, despite Stalin's authoritarian methods – or perhaps because of them – the country would, after all, overcome its difficulties."[81]

The more pragmatic view holds that the leadership finally realized that it had an agrarian calamity on its hands, so it decreed a number of measures to try to alleviate the situation,[82] measures that were encapsulated under the rubric "neo-NEP" (although the term was disavowed by the leadership) and were intended to produce a "reconciliation" (*umirotvorenie*) between the regime and the peasants. Stalin saw the measures as "a combination of the general [i.e., common] interests of the kolkhoz with the particular [i.e., private or personal] interests of the kolkhozniki."[83] The earliest measure was the distribution from 1931 of millions of puds of grain for seed, feed, and food to kolkhozes, sovkhozes, and individual farmsteads as loans, commonly repayable from the next crop at the rate of tenpuds for every loan of one hundred puds.[84] The first such relief (interest-free and repayable in the autumn from the next crop) seems to have been made in early February 1931 to kolkhozes and sovkhozes throughout the country but especially in the drought-stricken Lower and Middle Volga, Bashkiria and Tataria, the Urals, Western Siberia, and Kazakhstan.[85] Belorussia, which found itself in a "strained situation" from 1 July 1931, owing largely to the flooding of a number of rayons and the loss of 50,400 hectares of winter grain that were re-sown to non-grain crops, was loaned 38,444 tonnes of grain in the third quarter and 41,974 tonnes in the fourth quarter of 1931 and 36,286 tonnes in the first quarter of 1932, although its plight was "complicated" by a "substantial and systematic" failure to deliver all of the relief.[86] In the first half of 1932, 75.9 million puds (1,220,000 tonnes) of grain – primarily (80 percent) for seed and most of the rest for food – were loaned nationwide, with the Urals being the foremost recipient of seed grain and Kazakhstan, Western Siberia, and the Middle Volga the chief recipients of food grain; in the first half of 1933, 82.5 million puds (1,351,000 tonnes) of grain (primarily food grain) were distributed nationally, some 90 percent of it going equally to the Ukraine and the North Caucasus; and, in the autumn of 1933 and the winter of 1933–34, 145 million puds (2,375,000 tonnes) of grain (mostly food grain) were fairly evenly distributed throughout the country.[87] Frequently loans were subsequently supplemented, and sometimes more than once. Food relief was also sent to industrial centres and army bases. In May 1932 the Politburo even ordered the recall of 15,000 tonnes of corn and 2,000 tonnes of wheat from the country's ports and the purchase of 3.5 million puds (57,328 tonnes) of grain in the Far East and 3 million puds (49,138 tonnes) of wheat in Persia, as well as the delivery of 4 million puds (65,518 tonnes) of grain from the Central Black Earth to the Ukraine and the cessation of the export of grain from the Ukraine to the North Caucasus.[88]

Inevitably, shortcomings materialized. Sometimes the relief did not reach its intended recipients; from October 1932 through June 1933, for instance, 22 percent of the 391,366 puds (6,410 tonnes) of food destined for 205,000 persons in 104 rayons of Kazakhstan was "misappropriated."[89] Sometimes, too, as in the Ukraine in the late winter of 1932–33, the delivery of relief was delayed by "bureaucratic sluggishness" on the part of rayon officials to the point of ineffectiveness.[90] Kiev's Doctor Blonsky attributed the "untimely receipt" of "food help" to the attitude among the workers that the starving peasants did not deserve relief because they themselves were to blame for their plight by refusing to work. "Given such a mood among those who should combat the famine," he wrote, "their actions in the fight against the famine cannot, of course, produce any tangible results." He added, "There is a sort of commercial and purely exploitive approach to the starving. They are regarded not as unfortunate people but as a workforce that needs to be used for labour. Hence it is not a struggle against famine as a national disaster but merely a job of restoring the workforce, with a horse being more esteemed than a person."[91] The principal shortcoming, however, was the ulterior motive behind relief: discrimination against individual farmsteaders, the hated class enemy of the Bolsheviks in the countryside, especially if they also happened to be kulaks. Grain loans to the Ukraine were distributed by Party and OGPU officials, who dispensed assistance first of all to kolkhozniks "having a large number of workdays," brigade leaders, tractor drivers, and the Red Army families of kolkhozniks and individual farmsteaders. However, with regard to other individual farmsteaders (who constituted up to two-fifths of the rural population of some Ukrainian oblasts), relief was given only to those who voiced a desire to join a kolkhoz or to make a contractual agreement with a sovkhoz; it was withheld from those who did not want to work in a kolkhoz, and they were categorized as "non-working or parasitical elements" and subjected to "deportation to the north." In fact, most of the relief went to the sugar beet areas of the Ukraine and their sovkhoz workers.[92]

Elsewhere, the policy of the authorities that late winter and early spring was to provide food relief on the same terms in order to preserve and enhance the kolkhoz economy at the expense of individual farmsteads, with grain being given to kolkhozniks only and leaving the rest to starve to death. As one peasant told the authorities during spring sowing: "Many of the individual farmsteaders and those kolkhozniks having a small number of workdays are dying, of course. The slogan 'he who does not work does not eat' is interpreted unamended by the rural bodies – let them die." If any kolkhozniks, such as the very old, the very young, or the sick, refused to go to work or did not fulfill their cultivation norm, they were denied food relief. Individual farmsteaders received food help only if they fulfilled the seed-preparing and seed-planting plan that had been established for them (and for this task the implements and draught animals that had been taken from them for various arrears were returned), whereupon they were given food "on a par with the kolkhozniks," especially if they then joined a kolkhoz and went to work in its fields.[93] But some who were entitled to relief were deliberately humiliated by the dispensers – for example, in the spring of 1933 in the German Autonomous Republic an elderly kolkhoznik asked the kolkhoz chairman "to issue grain to him," and the chairman forced him "to beg on his knees for it in the presence of all of the kolkhozniks," some of whom wept.[94]

Nevertheless, in 1933 grain loans for seed, feed, and food to kolkhozes, sovkhozes, and individual farmsteads were more timely and larger than in 1931–32, when they were not made until the autumn and early winter instead of early in the year for late winter and early spring sustenance. From the autumn of 1933 until the spring of 1934, 145 million puds (2,375,000 tonnes) of grain were loaned – mostly to the Ukraine (nearly one-half) and the North Caucasus (nearly one-quarter) – compared with only 75.9 million puds (1,243,000 tonnes) in the first half of 1932 and 78.8 million puds (1,291,000 tonnes) in the first half of 1933 – mostly to the Urals, Kazakhstan, the Ukraine, Western Siberia, and the Middle Volga, in that order.[95] However, as Victor Kondrashin has cautioned, these loans can hardly be termed "help" because: "They were not disinterested and, in contrast to the situation at the time of the 1921–1922 famine, were aimed not at the saving of the starving peasants but at their 'enserfment' in the kolkhozes. To force them to submit to their fate and to work uncomplainingly in the kolkhoz – that is what Stalin wanted. In this sense he successfully achieved his aim."[96] Also, the loans were normally repayable in kind after the next harvest at an interest rate of 10 percent. Furthermore, the loans were not distributed equally, more being given to the

A Manifold Famine

kolkhozniks than to the individual farmsteaders, always the rural pariahs, leading William Chamberlin to conclude, following his September 1933 tour of the south, that "the food shortage had been used as a weapon against the individual peasants."[97]

Food relief came in the form of livestock as well as grain. Two Politburo resolutions of August and November 1933 ordered the acquisition of 1,665,000 calves from kolkhozes and individual farmsteads (in return for a reduction of their milk and meat procurements by 20 to 25 percent) and their sale "on preferential [credit] terms" to "cowless kolkhozes" and sovkhozes throughout the country for "propagation and fattening." Many peasants, however, could not afford to buy them or had no feed for them, so that in the winter of 1933–34 and the spring of 1934 they either ate their fresh stock or sold them.[98] Horses were forthcoming, too; at the end of 1933 the Politburo decreed the purchase of sixteen thousand work horses in the West Region and Belorussia for the Ukraine.[99]

Long-term relief was afforded in the winter-spring of 1932 by a number of decrees by various state bodies with the intention of stimulating an alienated peasantry to better efforts.[100] Probably the most salutary feature of what Trotsky derided as "Stalin's Neo-NEP" was the promotion of the "artel" model over the "commune" model of the kolkhoz. Under the latter the peasants did not have a garden or livestock of their own, prompting the complaint that "everything is ours but nothing is our own," and often lived in a dormitory, and all kolkhoz members were paid equally in cash and kind (and many of them were recruited from the poorest peasants, peasants who had departed but later returned, and political refugees). Under the artel model, however, the peasants had their "personal subsidiary economy" (i.e., "subsidiary" to the kolkhoz's economy) – their own small house and small garden, or "personal plot" (which they used, but did not own, privately), as well as perhaps a cow, a pig, and some poultry, whose output supplemented (and in bad years even replaced) their share of the kolkhoz's output in accordance with the amount and nature of their input (measured in "workdays"). The artel, then, afforded the peasants more personal economic freedom and less risk of hunger, namely, a lifeline.[101] Further relief came in 1935 with the adoption of a new kolkhoz charter; the old charter of 1930 had sanctioned their personal plots but had not specified their size or exempted them from state interference, but under the new charter the plots were legally guaranteed and their size limited to one hectare (plus three cows), and the peasant members were allowed to sell any surplus output privately.[102] However, they remained residual sharers in kolkhoz output (last, actually), with managers, combine drivers, and the like earning the most workdays, but thereafter (until 1958) the kolkhozes' first obligation of the delivery of output to the state was made in fixed amounts at fixed prices.

Other measures included: allowing the peasants (both kolkhozniks and individual farmsteaders) to sell their personal output on the "peasant" (private) market upon fulfillment of their state procurements; more severe penalties for the theft of grain during harvesting, hauling, storing, and milling (the misappropriation of grain in 1932 had been large-scale, and in 1933 it still amounted to 1,280,000 tonnes); the establishment of fixed rates of grain procurement that were not liable to increases during procurement campaigns (this measure represented a restoration of the tax in kind of the NEP period);[103] the authorization in early 1934 of free trade in grain in the large cities (although, as some peasants and workers said, "they've acted after they fleeced the peasants" and "the workers have no money and the peasants have no grain for trade");[104] the payment of MTSs in kind (grain), not money, for their work on kolkhozes, thereby stimulating production by both; the deployment of Red Army soldiers (most of them from the countryside and therefore experienced in harvesting) to the villages to help with the harvest instead of, as in 1932, blue-collar and white-collar workers (who disrupted their familiar urban work and deranged the unfamiliar rural work, like harvesting); a decision to switch from horizontal to vertical expansion of agriculture – to "abandon the policy of indiscriminate expansion of cropland" on the part of both kolkhozes and especially sovkhozes in favour of improving cultivation, increasing crop yields through crop rotation and fertilization, "developing and improving cadres," and more efficient management; the supply of more consumer goods to the villages in order to stimulate agricultural production (the countryside was to receive at least 55 percent of total output, and Stalin declared that "the fate of the *smychka* [solidarity between workers and peasants] depend[ed] on the development of consumer goods"); the authorization at the end of 1933 of the establishment in 1934 of urban allotment gardens of one-eighth to one-quarter of a hectare per worker's family for 1.5 million Soviet workers (one-third of them in the Ukraine) in the country's large industrial cities, to be worked "by their own labour and in their free time" (although in some places the local authorities simply ignored the authorization);[105] and the curtailment of grain exports: 118,153 fewer tonnes in 1933–34 than in 1932–33 (albeit partly owing to a fall in the world price of grain as traditional exporters such as Argentina, Canada, and the United States emerged from the Great Depression).[106]

All of these measures directly or indirectly improved the lot of the hungry and the starving – peasant and worker – to a greater or lesser degree. As one peasant recollected, "in 1934 [life] became a little better, they [the authorities] began to provide more bread and to publish kolkhoz laws."[107] Another factor, in the view of the British Embassy, was "the famine itself, which [had] convinced the peasants that, unless they made a desperate effort [themselves], they would starve again [the] next winter." "A great step forward will have been made," it added, "– the step from starvation to hunger."[108] As Otto Schiller said, "at this time last year, the victims of hunger were counted by the millions; this year they are counted by the thousands."[109]

The reform measures of the "new NEP," however, were too little and too late to undo the despoliation of the countryside. Its agriculture had been exploited too much and too long – mainly for urban mouths – in order to attain the holy grail of heavy industry. And, Ciliga believed, although the amelioration of the plight of the peasants curtailed their passive "sabotage," they continued to regard kolkhoz labour as a form of serfdom, and their ideal remained a return to individual farmsteading: "even if they despaired of ever achieving a return to the past," he wrote, "it still remained their dream."[110]

The Export of Grain

All of the Bolsheviks, of course, were determined to preserve the Soviet Union as the world's first socialist country, but their methods differed radically. Bukharin favoured the development of a mixed domestic economy through amicable political and economic relations with the outside world; Trotsky advocated the development of a socialist economy both internally and externally through the promotion of worldwide revolution in the capitalist countries; and Stalin, who argued that the rest of the world was not ready for socialist revolutions and that the capitalist West was ideologically untrustworthy, favoured the development of "socialism in one country," namely, the USSR, through autarky (import substitution), apart from essential exchanges for the purpose of developing heavy industry for defence against surrounding and antagonistic neighbours. This "fortress mentality" was to persist until the collapse of the Soviet Union sixty years later.

At the outset of Stalin's xenophobic disposition, both of the Soviet Union's heavy industrial bases (the Donbass and the Urals) and both of its light industrial bases (the Central Industrial Region around Moscow and the Leningrad Region) were antiquated and inefficient, and its industrial workforce was underskilled. Grain exports promised "quick money," that is, faster and easier returns than other sources, for modernization and expansion of the country's industry.[111] As the Soviet diplomat to an international conference on grain in 1931 said, "We export [grain] in order to discharge our import obligations. Our country's imports exceed half a million American dollars per year and tend to increase from year to year. A number of countries that import our grain, for example, Italy, England, and Germany, are interested in the normalization of conditions for our exports, since the Soviet Union does not have any other sources for payment of its imports, such as, for instance, revenue from foreign loans, investments abroad, or invisible exports."[112]

And in order to control and increase the output of grain the largely subsistent peasant holdings were collectivized and commercialized, and in order to secure their output the state resorted to larger and larger and harsher and harsher requisitions – all of which helped to create famine. As the *Guardian*'s Malcolm Muggeridge reported at the beginning of the spring of 1933, "to feed the cities and to provide even very much reduced food exports it was necessary for the Government's agents to go over the country and take everything, or nearly everything, that was edible." In the North Caucasus he talked to a peasant out of earshot of both their minders, asking, "How are things with you!" "He looked round anxiously to see that no soldiers were about. 'We have nothing, absolutely nothing. They have taken everything away,' he said, and hurried on. This was what I heard again and again and again."[113]

The voluminous exportation of grain would also allow the Bolsheviks to realize their desire to regain Russia's pre-war position as the leading supplier of grain to Western Europe, a position that had been usurped by the United States, Canada, and Argentina.[114] A plan to do so was announced at the November 1929 Party plenum by Commissar of Trade Anastas Mikoyan, who said that in 1930 a limited amount of barley, oats, and perhaps corn but no food grain would be exported; however, he added, "from the summer of 1930 a real problem of grain exports will arise to face us," and in 1931 a "substantial amount" of food grain would be shipped abroad and "in order to undertake substantial exportation it [would be] necessary to begin the construction of large-scale mechanized elevators at the most important ports on the coast of the Black Sea, particularly at Ukrainian ports, for the Ukraine and the North Caucasus will be the chief exporting regions"[115] – because together they constituted the country's chief source of surplus wheat and the closest source (via sea lanes) to the markets of Western Europe. From 1930 Soviet diplomats sought favourable terms for their country's grain exports in order to regain its pre-1914 "natural markets" in Europe and provide "no less than 50 percent of the world's export of grain," that is, at least the 5 million tonnes that Tsarist Russia exported annually.[116] Stalin was impatient to do so as he was in a hurry to develop industry; indeed, the Politburo admitted that the object of grain procurement was "export grain" in exchange for industrial equipment.[117] In the summer of 1930 Stalin told Molotov: "Mikoian reports that grain procurements are growing, and each day we are shipping 1 to 1.5 million poods [16,379 to 24,569 tonnes] of grain. I think that's not enough. The quota for daily shipments should be raised to 3–4 million poods [49,138 to 65,518 tonnes] at a minimum. Otherwise we risk being left without our new iron and steel and machine-building factories (Avtozavod [at Nizhny Novgorod on the upper Volga River], Cheliabzavod [at Chelyabinsk in the Urals], etc.)." He warned Molotov that some comrades would advise deferring exports until the world market price peaked, but he declared: "In order to hold off, we must have hard currency reserves. But we don't have them. In order to hold off, we would have to have a secure position on the international grain exchange. And we haven't had any position *at all* for a long time there – we'll only obtain it now if we can exploit conditions that have arisen at the present moment and are particularly favorable to us."[118]

Stalin, however, was wrong about the conditions, which were not generally favourable. The worldwide economic recession following the stock market crash of 1929 and the collapse of the gold standard resulted in depressed commodity export prices and fewer import credits. Prices on agricultural products, the chief Soviet exports, fell, and prices on industrial products, the chief Soviet imports, rose,[119] so that even more grain had to be exported.[120] Mikoyan told the October 1931 Central Committee plenum that the global

Table 5.4
Exports of grain from the Soviet Union, 1928–35

Year*	Target (tonnes)	Amount (tonnes)	Percentage of production	Percentage of procurement
1928–29	?	80,000	0.11–0.13	0.7
1929–30	?	1,330,000 [260,088]	1.92–2.4	8.7
1930–31	5,146,000	5,840,000** [4,841,293]***	7.6–7.7	26.1
1931–32	4,500,000	4,790,000 [5,177,882]***	7.4–8.4	19.8
1932–33	2,457,000	1,610,000 [1,808,132]***	2.7–2.9	8.8
1933–34	3,520,000	1,210,000–2,319,000	1.6–3.3	5.2–10
1934–35	4,749,000	768,668	1.0	2.9

Sources: Danilov, Manning, and Viola, *Tragediia sovetskoi derevni*, 3, supp. 1, 858–9: tables 9a and 9b; Davies and Wheatcroft, *Years of Hunger*, 470–1: table 15; Kondrashin, *Golod v SSSR*, 1, bk. 1, doc. 183:341, 2, doc. 299:410, 3, doc. 494:581; Kondrashin, *Khlebozagotovitel'naia politika*, 97; Narkomzem SSSR, *Sel'skoe khoziaistvo SSSR*, 263.
* The double year refers to the year of the harvest (first year), some of which was not exported until early the next (second) year.
** In the spring of 1931 Mikoyan told Stalin that 5.6 million tonnes had been exported (Kondrashin, *Khlebozagotovitel'naia politika*, 97).
*** These amounts are given by Kondrashin, *Golod 1932–1933*, 2nd ed., 158: table 6.

economic crisis had led "to a sharp drop in prices on agric[ultural] products, including our exports," so that the USSR "had to augment its original plan for grain exports by virtue of the need for hard currency for industrial equipment."[121] Table 5.4 sharply reflects these "augmentations" before the famine's peak.

The first year of the export drive was frustrated by insufficient state procurement; 1,805,000 fewer tonnes of grain were exported in 1928 than in 1927, and the USSR even had to *import* 246,200 tonnes of grain by the middle of the year[122] (although much of it was higher-quality seed grain).[123] Thereafter the exportation of grain increased sharply to highs in 1930 and 1931 (even exceeding export targets, thanks to increasingly ruthless procurements), decreased markedly in 1932 and 1933 as the famine climaxed, and plummeted in 1934 upon completion of the rudimentary foundation for modern heavy industry. Throughout the period exports constituted a very low proportion of both production (especially) and procurement as most grain output – and more and more of it – had to be kept to satisfy growing domestic demand (cities, industrial centres, defence and security forces, and reserve stocks), with fewer and fewer producers supplying more and more consumers under urbanization, industrialization, and militarization.

Most of the grain exported by the Soviet Union came from the southern wooded steppe and grassy steppe belts of southern European Russia – the Ukraine, the North Caucasus, the Lower and Middle Volga, and the Central Black Earth (more or less in that order) – because, with its large and adept peasant population, fertile soil, and better supply of moisture (than the Asiatic Russian steppe), the European Russian south was the country's principal producer of grain and was located closer to major ports so that exportation was faster and cheaper. In 1930–31 the Ukraine and the North Caucasus together provided 70 percent of grain exports; in 1931–32 it was planned that 55 percent of grain exports would come from the Ukraine and the North Caucasus, but actually the Middle Volga and the Lower Volga provided most; and in 1933–34 grain exports came mostly from the Ukraine, the North Caucasus, and the Lower Volga.[124] Their export grain did not have far to go. The Council on Labour and Defence ordered in the summer of 1931: "the reservation [of grain for export] is to be derived first and foremost in regions that gravitate toward ports"[125] – the Ukraine, the North Caucasus, and the Lower and Middle Volga, with their river and rail links to ports on the Black Sea. Indeed, so much grain was delivered to these ports that they could not always cope. The OGPU reported at the beginning of August 1933 that more than 100,000 tonnes of export grain had accumulated at the Crimea's ports – twice as much as their storage space – and fifteen to twenty thousand tonnes were arriving daily. So, the secret police understated, "the grain lay under the open sky in bales under threat of spoilage and plunder, since its preservation in this manner is difficult."[126]

The road abroad for Soviet grain was rocky, too. In the wake of the depression in the international capitalist economy, prices slumped, controls tightened, and trade declined (between 1929 and 1932 the volume of world trade fell by 25 percent).[127] The prices of primary products, including grain, fell much faster than those of industrial goods, so the terms of trade disadvantaged the Soviet Union. And, generally, the only Soviet commodities that were saleable in the West were raw materials: grain, furs, oil, timber, minerals, fibres (as late as 1938 grain, timber, furs, and fibres constituted more than two-thirds of Soviet exports).[128]

Moreover, increasing global grain output after the First World War but almost static international demand produced an excess of supply. By the middle of 1929, just as the USSR began to export more grain, about one year's export of grain was in storage throughout the world.[129] The oversupply and resultant falling price undermined the Soviet strategy of increasing grain exports in order to maintain large-scale imports for its industrial offensive. In 1930–31 it exported nearly two and a third times as much grain as in 1926–27 but obtained only about one-sixth more in proceeds.[130]

Nevertheless, the grain exports were "large enough ... to alarm the international markets," noted Eugene Lyons.[131] In the United Kingdom, the United States, Canada, and Australia, said wheat expert Andrew Cairns, there was considerable apprehension about the "terrible competitive menace of Bolshevik agriculture."[132] Indeed, the USSR's efforts to increase exports faced foreign charges of "dumping," "slave labour," "godlessness," non-payment of Tsarist debts, the seizure of private property, the confiscation of concessions, and the like, as well as political animus, so that Soviet trade with Western countries (the United States, the United Kingdom, France, Germany, Canada, and others) was sporadically interrupted by embargoes, reduced or cancelled credits, tariff barriers, and so on, although these deterrents were seldom coordinated.[133] Besides, Soviet wheat was not welcomed everywhere, especially by the United States and Canada, which were anxious to protect their depression-ravaged and drought-stricken farmers. In 1930 five countries (including France and Canada) imposed anti-dumping restrictions on the Soviet Union, but Soviet trade with these countries was slight anyway, and France in 1931 and Canada in 1935 lifted theirs.[134]

In order to offset the falling price of grain on the global market, the Soviets exported more and more of it, Mikoyan telling a Party plenum in 1931 that, because of the drop in price, "we had to increase the original target for export grain because of the need for hard currency for industrial equipment."[135] However, this strategy lowered grain prices even more, and the massive exports to Western (and even Eastern) Europe provoked protests from competitors, which feared being ousted from their traditional markets for agricultural products. Among the objectors were Europe's agrarian countries, including Poland and Romania, as well as overseas suppliers (Argentina, Australia, Canada, the United States); they created an "agrarian bloc" and formed a united front against "Soviet dumping." Their stance, however, was not backed by the principal European importers of Soviet grain, who sided with the USSR. At international conferences on agricultural exportation in 1931 in Rome, Geneva, and London, especially Italy, France, and the United Kingdom supported Soviet participation in Europe's grain trade, with France, for example, arguing that the USSR had every right to occupy Tsarist Russia's place in Europe's grain market.[136] The Soviet delegation declared: "Any proposal directed towards the exclusion from the economic community of nations of the country occupying ⅙ of the earth's surface is doomed to failure beforehand."[137]

By the summer of 1931, as Stalin informed Kaganovich, Germany, Italy, and the United Kingdom had given the USSR preferential terms of trade (and France – whose chief source of oil was the Soviet Union – was intending to do so), whereas the United States demanded "*draconian credit terms*" and penalties for the cancellation of orders.[138] In 1931 the Soviets were even willing to reduce the volume of their grain exports to Western Europe, provided it receive in return hard currency credits from its customers. A directive from the Politburo of 15 March 1932 to the Soviet delegation at the First International Wheat Conference in Rome stated: "The USSR could come to an agreement on the reduction of the tempo of growth of grain exports from the USSR or on the establishment of the principle of uniformity by the month or the quarter of grain exports from the USSR on the condition that it be guaranteed the necessary terms, especially compensation in the matter of credits and loans."[139] Alexander Barmine, then a Soviet trade official in Paris, countered charges of deliberate dumping by his country by asserting that "foreign importers knew how desperately the Soviet Union needed gold [earnings], and offered prices for our exports so low that they were often less than the cost of production," causing a loss that "was not considered decisive by Moscow, and we accepted such offers in many cases."[140] And Walter Duranty assured the American embassy in Berlin at this time that Moscow did not want to dump Soviet wheat on the world market "at any price" in order to undermine capitalism; rather, he said, its sole purpose was to sell its products, and it was "actually dependent upon the maintenance of capitalism and high prices" (for its exports) until it could stand on its own two feet.[141]

Not surprisingly, the Soviet Union allotted its industrial orders to those countries that created the most favourable conditions for its exports, including grain; for example, in a Politburo directive of 25 August 1931 to Soviet diplomats in Italy it was advised: "In discussions with [Prime Minister Benito] Mussolini ... hint at the possibility of additional expansion of our purchases in Italy with the establishment of a favourable attitude to our exports."[142] The USSR collaborated with only those Western European countries that played an "honest game," that is, operated under mutually beneficial terms. For example, in examining the question of Soviet grain sales in Belgium the Politburo resolved, on 30 July 1931, "to suggest to Narkomvneshtorg [Commissariat of Foreign Trade] that it answer the Belgian firm [handling the sales] that a high rate of interest is unacceptable to us."[143]

Under these favourable conditions Europe became virtually the sole market for Soviet grain, for almost every country of Western Europe – with the exception of France (thanks to winter wheat in the Paris Basin and both winter and spring wheat in Algeria) – either did not produce enough grain to meet its own needs or lacked colonies that did. From 1929 through 1932 the Soviet Union shipped 12,087,395 tonnes of grain – evidently all of its export grain – to Europe; from one-third to one-half was wheat, except in 1929, when most of the paltry 260,088 tonnes was barley.[144] The primary European market was the United Kingdom, which took 53 percent of export grain in the 1930–34 period, followed distantly by Germany at 13 percent and Italy, the Netherlands, Belgium, Norway, and Estonia the rest. The Soviets estimated that in 1933 alone Europe would import 4.8 million to 5.8 million tonnes of wheat, of which the United Kingdom would take half, or 2.4 million to 2.9 million tonnes.[145] The UK lost first place only in 1934 to Germany, which took one-third that year.[146]

On the other hand, the foreign products (principally industrial equipment) obtained in return for grain and other exports came from a greater variety of countries – and not just European – but mainly from Germany (notably), the United Kingdom, Poland, and the United States: 2,855,900 tonnes in 1930 (more than one-half from Germany, Poland, the United Kingdom, and the United States), 3,563,500 tonnes in 1931 (two-thirds from Germany, Poland, the United Kingdom, and the United States), 2,322,100 tonnes in 1932 (two-thirds from Germany [mainly] and the United Kingdom), 1,236,100 tonnes in 1933 (one-half from Germany [mainly] and Poland), and 1,025,200 in 1934 (nearly one-half from the United Kingdom, Belgium, Poland, Germany, the United States, and France).[147]

The hard currency earned by the Soviet Union from the sale of its grain (and other raw materials) in Western Europe was spent on the construction of new factories and the installation of industrial equipment as well as the acquisition of superior varieties of crop seeds and livestock breeds. In 1931, for instance, the Politburo allocated 5.5 million rubles' worth of hard currency for the construction of two combine factories in Rostov-on-Don and Saratov, 19 million rubles' worth for the purchase of tractors in the United States, 8 million rubles' worth for the purchase of bloodstock in Germany, the United Kingdom, and South America, and 550,000 rubles' worth for the purchase of drought-resistant seeds in the United States, southern Europe, and North Africa.[148] Soviet exports, however, were subject to the fluctuations of the capitalist market. Thus, during the First Five-Year Plan (1928–32) the USSR's foreign trade fetched only three-fifths (3,282,600 rubles) of the planned total earnings abroad of 5,426,400 rubles, and the shortfall for industrial development was 1,873,000 rubles[149] – meaning that the industrial blitzkrieg was slowing, so more grain had to be exported in order to compensate, which meant that more had to be procured, meaning that it had to be procured more forcefully, which in turn meant that starvation worsened and more Soviets died, for industrial development was paramount.

The exchange of Soviet grain for Western industrial (mainly) and agricultural technology raises the rather obvious – but neglected – question of Western complicity in the great famine of 1928–34.[150] The USSR's forced industrialization and collectivization – and hence the resultant famine – is explainable in not only internal but also external terms. Stalin's economic program was made possible not only by Bolshevik tyranny but also by the collusion of the industrialized countries of Western Europe (notably the United Kingdom, France, Germany, Italy, and Belgium) and the United States, from which the Soviet Union acquired the necessary machinery and foreign hard currency in exchange mainly for cheap grain (as well as timber, furs, and minerals). Western Europe imported more than 12 million tonnes of Soviet grain during the famine period[151] – well-nigh all of the Soviet Union's export grain. Respectable Western European firms themselves, realizing the obvious commercial advantages and ignoring their ideological differences, offered their services to the USSR for the purchase and sale of Soviet grain, and Soviet trade delegations guaranteed its uninterrupted delivery.[152] The United Kingdom, known for its postwar anti-Bolshevik position, became amnesiac when it was a question of cheap grain for British workers. As a memorandum of February 1931 by the Commissariat of Foreign Affairs said: "In spite of all its hatred towards the USSR, leaders of the Liberal government have had to declare that the industrial population of Great Britain must have the opportunity to enjoy cheap items of nourishment."[153] The Soviet grain was traded while famine raged in the Soviet Union, a fact that became known – although limitedly and belatedly – in the purchasing countries, thanks to reporters, travellers, diplomats, and specialists. As a German diplomat recalled, despite being aware of the famine, Western countries like his own continued to export industrial goods to the USSR on the grounds that the shipments would alleviate domestic unemployment; besides, they argued, even if the shipments were to cease, it would not stop the Soviet government from continuing to terrorize its peasants.[154] Little wonder that the trade was decried by some as "export on bones," that is, the skeletons of Russian peasants and Kazakh nomads.[155] Nevertheless, the formula of "grain in exchange for hard currency and machinery" was accepted by the leading Western European countries, and their support of the economy of the Soviet Union during the First Five-Year Plan guaranteed the success of Stalinist industrialization during its most decisive stage.[156]

The USSR's trade with the West was mutually beneficial, of course. With its orders the Soviet Union helped Western Europe and the United States to better endure and begin to recover from the economic crisis of the Great Depression, and the hard currency that they spent on Soviet exports came back in the form of payments for industrial equipment and technical specialists. So, just as the West was complicit in the making of the great Soviet famine, so was the Soviet Union complicit in the recovery of Western capitalism from the Great Depression, thereby aiding and abetting its ideological adversary. Thus, although the horrors of the famine were known in the West, mutual commercial interest trumped morality, humanitarianism, and ideology.[157]

The industrialization (and hence militarization) of the USSR was made possible by the commercial cooperation of the capitalist West, especially the United Kingdom and Germany. This cooperation muted the West's response to the famine, at least on the official level.[158]

Finally, the mutual complicity that had enabled the Soviet Union to burgeon industrially, militarily, and politically was favoured, too, by the changing global geopolitical situation. The rise of a re-armed and fascist Germany in 1933 and of a militarized and expansionist Japan (which occupied Manchuria in 1931) broke the balance of power that had taken shape in the wake of the First World War and created a new threat to Soviet security on the west and the east, and, with its newfound military power, the USSR was seen as a check to both Nazi Germany and Imperial Japan.[159] In 1933 it was officially recognized by the United States, and in 1934 it was accepted into the League of Nations (one year after both Germany and Japan had withdrawn). Ironically, the Soviet Union achieved its greatest diplomatic successes since Lenin's death at the very time that the famine peaked.

6
THE RELATIVELY WORST CASE: KAZAKHSTAN

> The entire population of Kazakhstan is dying of starvation.
> – an anonymous Kazakh to President Kalinin, 10 February 1932 (Nusinbaiev and Zhienfaliev, *Golod v Kazakhskoi stepi*, 2:120).

The collectivization of agriculture was especially destructive in Kazakhstan (which was to become the USSR's second largest republic after the RSFSR) and to the eponymous Kazakhs, reducing them to a minority within their own republic.[1] To their cost, the nomadic (primarily) and semi-nomadic Kazakh pastoralists in their *auls* – the migratory encampments of yurts (felt tents) of Kazakh clans – had little tradition of sedentary cultivation and little in common with the kolkhoz-like village commune (*mir*) of the Eastern Slavic peasants. The dual blow of mandatory sedentarization and mandatory collectivization would make them – proportionately – the primary victims of the great Soviet famine.

The Bolshevik campaign was the latest manifestation of colonialist oppression of what were then called the "Kirgizhes." From the eighteenth century, imperialist expansion had been gradually rendering them subjects of the Tsarist empire, and especially since the 1890s their lands had been usurped by Cossack, Russian, and Ukrainian peasant settlers in the steppe to the north and the foothills to the southeast.[2] Kazakh resentment over pastureland alienation, aggravated by Russification, onerous exactions, and wartime exigencies, exploded in rebellion in the summer of 1916, sparked by a decree on the mobilization of Muslims. The uprising formed part of a national liberation movement – the Basmachi Revolt of Turkestan's Muslims against Tsarist and

Soviet rule.³ The rebellion was not suppressed until the early 1920s (although Basmachi guerillas were active in Soviet Central Asia into the 1930s), with atrocities being committed by both sides. In the meantime, famine struck, chiefly in southern Kazakhstan, taking about 1 million lives.⁴

During the NEP some accommodations with the Kazakhs were conceded by Moscow, but the Bolsheviks did not fully trust them. The Kazakhs had reacted with indifference to both the overthrow of the monarchy and the establishment of Soviet power, so long as they were left in peace to their nomadic and semi-nomadic ways. This indifference, however, made them appear suspect at best and disloyal at worst to the Bolsheviks and unreliable to their own authorities. So in 1926–27 Moscow began to impose firm Soviet political and economic control over Kazakhstan under the banner of "little October" and the despotism of Party secretary Filipp Isayevich (Shaya Itskovich) Goloshchyokin (1876–1941), another "old Bolshevik." He had dropped dentistry for politics in 1903, and in 1918 he had participated in the killing of the Romanov royal family in Yekaterinburg in the Urals. With Nikolai Yezhov (shot in 1940), the future head (1936–38) of the NKVD (the OGPU's successor), Goloshchyokin was posted to Kazakhstan, arriving at the end of 1925, whereupon he began to purge the local leaders and to settle the nomads. As a Party man he proved arrogant, demagogic, and cynical; generally speaking, he barely regarded the Kazakhs as human beings, and not once during his seven years in the kray did he leave the capital (1925–29) of Kyzyl-Orda (now Kyzylorda) to see what he had wrought in the countryside.⁵ The purges began in 1926, and the first arrests were made in early 1928.

Goloshchyokin had been given the task of creating "barracks socialism" in Kazakhstan in the form of kolkhozes and communes.⁶ They were totally alien to the nomadic and even the semi-nomadic Kazakhs, who in 1928 numbered some 4 million in the USSR, 3.8 million of whom lived in Kazakhstan (and most of the rest in neighbouring Siberia), where 85 percent of them were nomadic or semi-nomadic (although some cultivation had already taken root, with the Kazakhs eating considerable grain, notably millet).⁷ Most were poor and illiterate as well as exempt from taxation and conscription. Most of them relied upon stock rearing for their well-being; in 1927 it was the "mainstay" of the kray's economy, engaging 75 percent of the population (and 90 percent of Kazakhs) and affording 50 percent of the value of gross output.[8] The republic's livestock population increased from 16 million in 1920 to 32 million in 1928, for Kazakhstan was very well suited to nomadic and semi-nomadic pastoralism, 53 percent of its area being fit for grazing and 2 percent for haying but only 17 percent for cultivation.[9] Nevertheless, the doctrinaire Bolsheviks believed otherwise. John Littlepage correctly identified the motive behind denomadization as the Party's view that "nomads [were] backward and [could not] be raised up to the Communist notions of a higher civilization until they [were] taken away from the steppes and their roving life and changed into proletarians, or wage-earners, either in industries or on state-controlled farms."[10] A November 1927 Kazakhstan Party conference asserted: "The typical feature of stock rearing in Kazakhstan is its extreme backwardness (archaic, crude forms of management, the uncontrolled development of herds, nomadism over long distances, inferior breeds of livestock, year-round grazing, periodic livestock plagues because of *dzhut* [ice-covered pasture],[11] epizootic diseases, etc.); this backwardness (in the forms of management) is the cause of the smallness of the settlements (5–7 *kibitkas* [nomad tents] per *aul* [nomadic community]), the backwardness of social relations (a mixture of clan, feudal, and commercial relations), and the economic dominance and political influence of the clan head – the *bai*." The conference resolution added: "only a radical change in the form of management of stock rearing, as well as a change in the form of settlements and a real rise in the economic well-being of most stockbreeders (after having broken the economic dominance of the bais and changed the aul to srednyak status) will change the social relations and create the conditions for a shift to a socialist framework."[12] Thus, sedentarization facilitated political and economic control while "civilizing" the nomads.

In 1928 Goloshchyokin, ever Stalin's enthusiastic instrument, launched his ruthless campaign of denomadization (the sedentarization of more than 100,000 nomadic and semi-nomadic families – 480,000 persons – into kolkhozes, removing them from their auls) and kulakization, or "bayization" (the dispossession and deportation of the *bais*, the better-off pastoralists, i.e., Kazakh kulaks), plus the conscription of the Kazakhs and the re-opening of the republic to Slavic colonists.[13] It was planned to complete the sedentarization of the Kazakhs by the end of 1933 by moving them to large villages of five hundred farms each in northern and southern Kazakhstan to grow field crops, meanwhile abandoning central Kazakhstan (to the detriment of stock rearing), three-quarters of which was in pasture and unsuited to productive cultivation because it received fewer than 255 millimetres of precipitation annually and had little water for expensive irrigation.[14] Goloshchyokin exhorted local Party bosses not to be "afraid of excesses."[15] And they were not. The upper ranks of the republic's bureaucracy were mostly Russians and Ukrainians who brutally enforced Goloshchyokin's sedentarization and collectivization drive, and, moreover, they were assisted by lower-level Kazakh cadres bent upon settling old scores, gaining personal benefits, and proving their ideological credibility.[16]

The campaign, much as in the case of the country's peasants, was hastily planned and arbitrarily implemented, with, predictably, even more disastrous results because it targeted a primarily nomadic or semi-nomadic rather than a sedentary population. Twenty-Five Thousanders were dispatched to the republic to assist its own activists, many of whom were indigent and ignorant, resorting to beating, whipping, and even shooting to have their way. Their conduct reminded one famine survivor of a Kazakh proverb: "If you give someone your hair to cut, then they will cut off your head instead."[17] And after being forced into the kolkhoz, one official stated, the newcomers were "only left the right to work steadily and starve."[18] Kazakhs who refused to join kolkhozes were encouraged to reconsider by being subjected to mock shootings by firing squads, being paraded naked through villages in sub-zero weather, and being dunked in holes in frozen ponds.[19] And campaigns were mounted to find the livestock that they had supposedly "hidden" or "driven away into the mountains and deserts."[20] The steppe nomads, like the steppe peasants, resisted. The OGPU reported a "wave" of 372 mass demostrations and violent uprisings involving eighty thousand participants in 1929–31, describing them as "acts of terror, arson, and banditry."[21] The revolt was suppressed by Stalin's loyal ally, General Semyon Budyonny, the founder of the Red Cavalry. Some 25,000 "enemies of the people" were executed and more than 100,000 imprisoned.[22] By the beginning of 1935, six years after its commencement, the process of sedentarization of the nomadic way of life of the Kazakhs had been completed, with their auls replaced by kolkhozes. Already, by the middle of 1932, 90 percent – 200,000 – of nomadic and semi-nomadic Kazakh households had been sedentarized, in the process raising their share of the republic's sown area from just less than one-third to one-half.²³ Being neither accustomed, nor committed, to collectivized agriculture, the settled Kazakhs suffered more than the Russian settlers; the latter also had more arable and more fertile land and better implements and, unlike the Kazakhs, their own plots.²⁴ Moreover, as a member of the Economic Council of the Council of National Commissars, Turar Ryskulov (shot in 1938), admitted in a letter to Stalin, Kaganovich, and Molotov in 1933, anti-Kazakh feeling – "out-and-out chauvinism" and "Great-Power chauvinism" (likely tinged with racism) – prevailed on the part of "non-Kazakhs," that is, Russians and Ukrainians, especially on the livestock kolkhozes.²⁵ Little wonder, then, that although between 1928 and 1940 Kazakhstan's grainland increased one-and-a-half-fold, its output decreased by the same proportion, and its yield decreased by one-half (from 9.2 to 4.3 centners per hectare).²⁶ And drought struck in 1929 and in 1931. So grain procurement targets were underfulfilled, incurring Moscow's wrath. In 1928 the target of 164,000 tonnes was met, but the 1929 target of 655,000 tonnes had to be lowered to 647,000 tonnes in light of the drought (and only 619,000 tonnes were secured), and in 1930 only 758,000 to 794,000 tonnes of the target of 1,015,000 tonnes were obtained, despite Stalin's behest to Molotov in August 1929: "Maintain a firm policy [on grain procurement] with respect to Siberia, Kazakhstan, and Bashkiria. No concessions."²⁷

The Kazakhs were perhaps even more traumatized by the confiscation of their precious livestock than by their denomadization. In 1928, 75 percent of their income was derived from stockbreeding, for, as Turar Ryskulov attested, "Kazakhs virtually do not cultivate gardens or breed poultry, [although] many grow grain with low yields."²⁸ A nomad victim, Mukhamet Shayakhmetov, who wrote one of the few accounts by a survivor, has asserted that "the Kazakh nomads could not imagine an existence without their livestock: they knew of no other kind, and believed that to be left without their animals would mean certain death." He added that their animals were treated virtually as kin, the death of one being seen as a death in the family.²⁹ So they were devastated when their animals and pastures were seized and redistributed and their barter economy was replaced by a money economy. In addition, although to a lesser degree, those Kazakhs who were devout Muslims were staggered by the desecration of mosques, much as those Russian and Ukrainian peasants who were devout Christians were staggered by the desecration of Orthodox churches.

The confiscation of their property and livestock (sheep and goats, horses, cattle, camels) and its distribution to kolkhozes, poor peasants, and hired hands began in the summer of 1928 with "Bolshevik tempo." Already on 18 November *Pravda* reported from Kyzyl-Orda that the "confiscation and eviction" of the "bais and semi-feudalists" of Syr-Darya Okrug, for instance, had been completed and that 24,656 head of livestock had been seized, of which 15,820 had been given to 3,119 poor peasants and agricultural labourers, 3,254 to 62 kolkhozes, and the rest to sovkhozes.[30] A "rapacious slaughter" of livestock followed.[31] Thousands of head were slaughtered for meat for export to other Soviet republics. Stalin ordered that Moscow and Leningrad be supplied first with the meat and then the large cities and the Red Army. At every large railway station a killing ground was established for slaughtering and butchering livestock, and the meat was loaded in boxcars and taken to the country's large cities.[32] Millions of livestock died from mistreatment, exposure, malnutrition (in 1933 they had little fodder or shelter, with kolkhozes feeding them oat, millet, and wheat straw),[33] overcrowding, epidemic diseases (brucellosis and tuberculosis), abandonment or slaughtering by the Kazakhs themselves (to preclude seizure), and even depredation by Russian peasants (an official admitted: "in a number of places an old tradition has been revived: if Russian villages lose any livestock, they are unfailingly regained [taken] from Kazakhs").[34]

The pace of collectivization was so frenzied that the republic's livestock population plunged within five years. Whereas it had doubled from 16 million in 1920 to 32 million (Russian sources) in 1928 (or increased one-and-a-half-fold to 40 million [Kazakh sources]), it fell from 40,294,000 head in 1929 to 3,699,000 in 1933 – a decrease of 91 percent in four years.[35] Particularly sheep decreased: between 1928 and 1932 they declined by 75 percent, followed by camels (60 percent), cattle (15 percent), and horses (9 percent),[36] presumably indicating that meateaters preferred mutton to beef and horsemeat, that sheep and camels were particularly vulnerable to mistreatment, and that camels as beasts of burden were being replaced by trucks. Also, between 1929 and 1932, at least two-thirds of the livestock losses occurred on individual farmsteads and kolkhozes and one-third on sovkhozes – and overall mostly in Russian, not Kazakh, parts of the republic,[37] indicating that Russians were mainly responsible for the losses. And the Kazakhs were the chief losers. On 1 May 1932 less than one-third of the republic's 5,542,000 livestock (28 percent, or 1,555,900 head) belonged to Kazakhs, compared with four-fifths in 1928 (and, in 1932, 80 percent of their 1,555,900 head were found on kolkhozes); moreover, in 1932 a Kazakh household averaged two to three head of livestock, compared with thirty-five thousand in 1929, and this "circumstance had already created much difficulty for draught and transport in the vast steppe."[38] In his report to Stalin in August 1932, the chairman of Kazakhstan's Council of Peoples' Commissars, Uraz Isayev (shot in 1938), tried to put the best face on the situation by stating that, although his republic reflected "the victory of socialism in [his] country ... the most important branch of the national economy of Kazakhstan, stock rearing, despite fundamental changes in its development (sovkhozes, kolkhozes), [was] in a quantitative sense really in a catastrophic state."[39] State procurements of meat, wool, and hide from Kazakhstan were merely one-sixth of those of 1929–30, when the republic was the Soviet Union's "primary livestock base," accounting for 11 percent of its livestock, 15 percent of its commercial meat output, and 34 percent of its commercial wool output.[40] No longer were Kazakh herders able to greet each other with the traditional salutation of "How are the livestock faring?"[41]

The social cost was horrific: famine and flight, plus attendant diseases – all of which came to be known as "Goloshchyokin's genocide." From the beginning of 1932 – officially, at least – the depletion of livestock, plus a shortfall in the expansion of the sown area (1 million hectares in 1932 instead of the planned 14 million) and three successive harvest failures wrought by summer drought in 1931, 1932, and 1933, resulted in starvation and epidemics.[42] Turar Ryskulov, a communist nationalist official, in his long report to Stalin ascribed the Kazakh famine to the drastic decline of livestock by 1932, "excesses and deception" during sedentarization and collectivization, and the small share of Kazakhs (less than one-third) in the republic's sown area by 1932.[43] Two post-communist Kazakh historians attribute the starvation primarily to livestock depletion as well as to harvest failures in the sown area, the unaccustomedness of the Kazakhs to vegetarian foodstuffs, and their inexperience in such alternative livelihoods as fishing, hunting, and gathering.[44] They add that, without immunity, it was easy for Kazakhs to become "virgin victims" of typhus and other epidemic diseases,[45] just as without sheep or goats

The Relatively Worst Case: Kazakhstan

it was easy for them to starve and without horses or camels it was not easy for them to flee. Both Kazakhs and non-Kazakhs were victimized, one of the former writing to President Kalinin in early February of 1932: "some of the population has left for Siberia, and the rest have been overtaken by starvation and are dying off."[46]

The famine, which began no later than 1929, climaxed in 1932–33.[47] Described by nomadic survivor Mukhamet Shayakhbetov, it mirrored the desperation of the peasantry elsewhere in the country. He recalled that at first the starving continued to roam but in order to beg, not herd, and they were greeted with alarm but charity in the auls, which, however, soon tired of their growing number. Once the snow had melted and the fields had dried in late winter, they gleaned ears of grain left in the fields and cooked the kernels. After none was left and the fields had been ploughed, they shook the straw chaff from old sacks to find grain; some died in the process, however, because the kernels became toxic after lying under the snow all winter and had to be washed and cooked thoroughly. By the summer of 1933 these meagre sources were gone, and "famine now swept through the entire region." "Everywhere you look," he continued, "you could see starving people with swollen faces wandering about or, worse still, living skeletons, all skin and bones, in tattered clothing. There were corpses lying in the streets, the steppe and the roads." He added that most of the bodies on the streets and roads lay face down because "when a person has starved for so long that he has no strength left, he falls forward as he is walking along, as though tripping, and never gets up again."[48] The corpse-lined routes afforded a grotesque experience to a Kazakh boy, who recollected it much later in life:

> When I was around ten, we were out in a cart gathering fuel. Brushwood, rushes, dry grass – they would all go into the stove. We had hardly left the town when the wooden wheels began to creak, as they lurched over something. The ground seemed even, just sand, but we were making heavy weather of it. The creaking sound was strange and sinister; it made you feel uneasy. I jumped down from the cart. In the sand all round me there were bones. Who had scattered them there? As we gathered grass and dry branches, we saw bones, bones everywhere. They were lying on the surface or slightly covered over with sand. Then skulls began to appear, human ones ... The grown-ups explained that

starving people had been trying to reach the town, but had perished on the way. There was nobody to bury them and that was why dead bodies were strewn about.[49]

Another witness, Uraz Isayev, admitted in his report to Stalin in the summer of 1932: "Starving Kazakhs and their abandoned children gather around industrial enterprises and sovkhozes in the Semipalatinsk and Aktybinsk Rayons and at railroad stations and engage in theft and besiege kolkhoz fields and snip off ears [of grain]. The starvation and crowding and filth are the grounds for the spread of epidemics (smallpox, typhus, dysentery, and other diseases)."[50] The following winter saw the famine's peak, which was acknowledged in a report of the politotdel of an MTS: "The winter of 1932–1933 was particularly severe. Mass denomadization, [high] mortality (especially among the population's Kazakhs), the slaughtering and squandering of cattle, the lack of grain for nourishment and for fodder for draught animals, the unavailability of seed ... The kolkhozniks have fled to the mountains and deserts or collect the roots and seeds of wild plants. The remaining kolkhozniks could not work because of extreme exhaustion and disease."[51]

Towards the end of the winter Turar Ryskulov reported similarly: "[The starving Kazakhs] eat refuse as well as the small roots of wild plants and small rodents. All of the dogs and cats have been eaten by them, and the piles of garbage around their huts are full of the boiled bones of dogs, cats, and small rodents. They talk of cases of cannibalism."[52]

An elderly survivor recalled his winter journey in 1932 to his place of exile. On the way his party came upon a "dead town" of white yurts and white-felted wagons whose occupants, deported Kazakhs, had starved to death, and when they entered one wagon a "high, piercing sound rang out" and "made everyone's blood run cold": "From a tiny hole in the little 'hut' a small living creature leapt out and threw herself at the group of men. It was covered in blood. Its long hair was frozen in bloody icicles sticking out to each side; its legs were thin and black like those of a raven. It had wild eyes and a face caked with dried blood, smeared with drops of fresh blood. It bared its teeth, and red foam came out of its mouth." The four men recoiled from this fiend and fled in terror, whereafter one of them explained: "It was human. It was a child. A little Kazakh girl of seven or eight."[53] There were many rumours – and some actual instances – of hunger driving some to "murder cannibalism" (killing people for their flesh) and, worse, to "survivor cannibalism" (eating the flesh of corpses, i.e., necrophagy); others, again like the steppe's peasants, resorted to substitutes, especially *masaq*, the rotting remants of the harvest, the thorns of *dzhigim*, a local plant, and even bedding, according to an official in Chu Rayon.⁵⁴

In 1932–33 the Soviet government undertook famine relief, which, although belated and limited, did save some lives.⁵⁵ Turar Ryskulov said that it was difficult to provide famine relief because of a lack of detailed and reliable information about the victims, owing to its suppression by the Goloshchyokin regime, under which "it was forbidden everywhere (even in Alma Ata, where they removed the bodies of Kazakhs from the streets) to say officially that a famine existed and famine deaths had occurred."⁵⁶ Another problem was graft. An "absolutely secret" report of the OGPU of 7 July 1933 revealed that there were 206,000 persons in Kazakhstan's 104 rayons in need of food aid (*prodpomoshch*) and that between October 1932 and July 1933 391,366 puds of grain had been given to them; however, "checking of the course of distribution" had found "numerous instances of abuse and theft on the part of rayon and aul pseudo-activists" amounting to more than 20 percent, or more than eighty-six thousand puds, since December 1932, including twenty-seven thousand puds in the last two and a half months.⁵⁷ The embezzlement was described by a Kazakh woman in a letter of early February 1932 to President Kalinin:

> If they [local officials] just see some citizen with a bit of bread, a pound of flour, or a piece of meat, then they take it for their consumption as if it had been surrendered to the state, whereas in fact they themselves devour it, and in addition they seize money, good clothes, and various other things, and they conduct searches and take bribes of what they want from whomever they want, and if anyone does not want to pay a bribe, despite the fact that he is a bednyak or srednyak, they silence him and confiscate [anything], and [so] now he is a kulak.⁵⁸

Another letter from an anonymous Kazakhstani confirmed this abuse of power by local officials, complaining: "if some Party or rural soviet member or simply any activist does not like some srednyak or even bednyak, then quick as a wink they make him a kulak and drive him out of the village, and the rayon executive says that they hold the power in the countryside and once the rural soviet makes him a kulak, it means that he must be a kulak."[59]

Many of the starving tried to survive by migrating elsewhere within Kazakhstan, elsewhere within the Soviet Union (about 1 million), or even elsewhere within Asia (up to 200,000 to China, as well as unknown numbers to Mongolia, Afghanistan, Iran, and Turkey).[60] During the famine period a total of 1,130,000 persons – primarily Kazakhs – quit Kazakhstan; 454,000 of them eventually returned (voluntarily or otherwise), and 676,000 did not,[61] remaining members of the Kazakh diaspora. According to the nomadic survivor and eyewitness Makhmet Shayakhmetov, the traditional response of the Kazakh nomads to persecution (and even family quarrels) was to move far away, either within the vastness of the "great steppe" or across the border into Chinese, or Eastern, Turkestan (Sinkiang), where they had kinfolk; from 1928 until 1933 perhaps up to 200,000 Kazakhstanis, primarily Kazakhs, relocated to Sinkiang.[62] Such exoduses had occurred before, as in 1881–82 with the demarcation of the boundary between Russia and China and in 1916 with the promulgation of the decree conscripting young Kazakhs for the front. Goloshchyokin's ruthless campaign of denomadization and collectivization prompted another, starting in 1928 and peaking in 1931.[63] In his crucial report of 9 March 1933 to Stalin (it was instrumental in Goloshchyokin's subsequent removal), Turar Ryskulov acknowledged that – officially, at least – 100,000 had fled to Kirgizia, 50,000 to Western Siberia, 40,000 to the Middle Volga, 30,000 to Central Asia, 20,000 to Karakalpakia, and others to Kalmykia, Tadzhikistan, and even the North, as well as China.[64] "This," he admitted, "is not simply nomadism (which usually occurs in summer for a short distance and with livestock) but to a considerable extent the flight of starving people in search of sustenance."[65] Many died on the way. For every one who fled, two (children, women, the elderly) died, and all eyewitnesses asserted that the main roads were lined with the bodies and bones of the dead.[66] Most of the fleeing Kazakhs, unable to feed their children and unwilling to watch helplessly as they starved to death, abandoned them at railway stations or in towns and cities,[67] where they might at least scrounge some morsel by begging or stealing and perhaps even find shelter. As Ryskulov reported, "many of the migrants leave their children to their own fate"; "masses of orphaned children have gathered in the cities and at the r[ail]r[oad] stations

The Relatively Worst Case: Kazakhstan

in Kazakhstan," he added, and often "the Kazakhs bring their children to institutions and to residences and dump them there."[68] These waifs numbered (officially) 50,000 to 57,000 by the end of 1932, 61,000 by the spring of 1933, and 70,000 by the summer of 1933,[69] but actually they were probably much more numerous.

Because the Kazakh steppe lay in the north of the republic and all of its north bordered Western Siberia (mostly), the Urals, and the Volga Valley, many, if not most, of the weak and sick fleeing nomads went to nearby Western Siberia and the Middle Volga, especially to cities just over the border. In early February 1932 the Party secretary of Western Siberia, Robert Eikhe (another "old Bolshevik," shot in 1940), in a letter of complaint to his Kazakhstan counterpart, described the influx of Kazakh migrants, mostly kolkhozniks (they said), who had begun to arrive in the autumn of 1931 and whose numbers had recently assumed "massive dimensions":

> The Kazakh arrivals settle in [local] Kazakh auls, whose population has as a result nearly doubled, as well as in abandoned houses and in apartments already occupied by Kazakhs, and those without shelter spend their nights on the street. With no work and no belongings, most of them literally starve, and begging is growing among them and infectious illnesses are appearing. Numerous instances of the consumption by the Kazakhs of surrogates as food and of meat from livestock carcasses have been observed.
>
> In the streets the militia [police] annually [*sic*: daily] pick up Kazakhs who are sick from starvation. There are also cases of Kazakhs starving to death, with the mortality from starvation, exhaustion, and freezing increasing, especially recently with the onset of cold snaps and raging snowstorms ...
>
> Owing to the famine, horse rustling has developed among the Kazakhs ... and there are many cases of stealing, robbing, and the theft of bread from citizens not only in the streets but in apartments, which the Kazakhs invade in gangs of 5–8 persons and demand to be given bread. The cafeterias of Slavgorod are overflowing with emaciated Kazakhs, who glean bread crumbs there, lick the plates clean, and sometimes grab food from the diners.

In Slavgorod the Kazakhs come almost daily to the rayon organizations with their children and abandon them there. Recently 4–5 abandoned Kazakh children have been picked up daily in the streets. The children's homes and the hospitals are overflowing, and we cannot provide children's homes for all of the youngsters collected in the streets.[70]

Why the migrants had to resort to crime in order to survive was explained by one of them, Umurgali Aukeyev, who wrote to the authorities in July 1932 that the Kazakhs had sought refuge in Western Siberia because the livestock requisitions of 1931 had left them without any animals and caused the famine and the exodus. He explained that it was difficult for the migrants to find work in Western Siberia's cities, for factory managers were loathe to hire them because they were weak and sick, burdened with families, and unused to industrial tasks. They were also, he added, subject to "anti-Kazakh feelings [prejudice]" on the part of local Siberians, who often assaulted them simply "because they [were] Kazakhs."[71] A pitiless doggerel was in circulation at the time:

When I at one time was Kirghiz
I ate my meat and drank koumiss.
But now that I've become Kazakh
The front of my belly meets my back.[72]

As a consequence of these circumstances, the Kazakh migrants found little or no relief outside their republic. One eyewitness in Omsk, a teacher's fifteen-year-old son, recalled that "at that time the city was inundated by hungry bands of Kazakh nomads" who "would stretch out their tin cups to passersby hoping for a handout and imploring, 'Oh, pap-man, the belly's empty!'"[73] Some "Siberians" – in this case a group of sympathetic political deportees – were sufficiently appalled to write to the "central organs" in Moscow to declare that they "no longer had the right to remain silent and unconcerned eyewitnesses to the famine befalling the population of the Pavlodar Rayon":

For about one and a half months swollen people dressed in rags, primarily Kazakhs, have been thronging from the famine regions into Pavlodar. The city is flooded with them. Unbelievable beggary is grow-

The Relatively Worst Case: Kazakhstan

ing. During the day dozens of people call at every house. The starving are of all ages: the young, the old, children. The dumps are strewn with starving people picking and eating garbage.

The medical establishments are inundated with those starving to death. The famine has generated epidemics (a special three-man commission has even been formed to fight typhus). The corpses of those who have frozen to death, the homeless, and those who have starved to death are constantly being found near the city's out-patient departments within view of those arriving for admission. We know of houses where the starving, coming to beg for bread, have dropped dead. Not infrequently one can meet families of Kazakhs dragging themselves somewhere and pulling a sled after themselves with their belongings, atop which lies the body of an infant who has died en route.

The starving, half-frozen children are thrown into institutions. The children's homes are overcrowded and do not accept them. Daily one meets throughout the city dozens of children of all ages, abandoned, half-frozen, and swollen from starvation. Their usual cry is: "father died, mother died, no home, no bread" ... Individual citizens accost the children and direct them, of course, to the police, but the latter do not accept them, simply driving them back into the street.[74]

It was the same scene in the Middle Volga, which contained 100,000 Kazakh migrants in the summer of 1930.[75] By the spring of 1932 there were more than fifty thousand (30 percent of them children) in just eleven rayons of the Middle Volga, many of them in the city and rayon of Orenburg, where a few worked in kolkhozes, sovkhozes, and timber mills, but most were unemployed and wandered from rayon to rayon. Some of the Kazakh children lived in rickety zemlyankas, which were unheated, dark, damp, and crowded (ten square metres for up to seventeen youngsters). They were only partly clothed, and some were naked, barefoot, and covered in tattered rags. All of them were emaciated, some were swollen from malnutrition, and they suffered from mange, herpes, boils, and lice, rarely – if ever – taking baths or seeing doctors. Mortality was high – in Orenburg, from three to four children daily.[76] Victor Serge, the unrepentant Left Oppositionist who for his internationalist pains spent three years in exile in Orenburg, found upon his arrival in June 1933 that "a hideous famine was raging" and that the city abounded in "Kirkhiz [Kazakh] families lying heaped together, dying of hunger." "The Kirkhiz folk," he added, "lay on waste lots in the sun; one could not be sure if some of them were alive or dead."[77]

The famine lasted until the removal of the uncompromising Goloshchyokin in 1933 and a bumper harvest in the autumn of 1934,[78] but by then it had exacted what Rysulkov blandly termed a "heavy toll," of children especially.[79] At least 1.7 million to 2.2 million Kazakhs and possibly 3 million perished during the famine.[80] As one Kazakhstani historian has concluded, "Goloshchyokin did to Kazakhstan what Pol Pot did to Kampuchea."[81] What happened in the Kazakh "killing fields" has been variously labelled – besides "Goloshchyokin's genocide" (eradication of a people) – an "ethnocide" (eradication of an ethnic group), a "steppe golodomor" (a killing by starving), a "Kazakhicide" because the Kazakhs suffered disproportionately and were maltreated more grievously and more pitilessly than non-Kazakh victims, and a "great disaster" (*velikii dzhut*).[82] This unequal mortality has been noted by Kazakh historians, who have asserted that from 1930 through 1933, for example, 49 percent of the republic's Kazakhs perished, compared with 25 percent of its Kirghizes; 13 percent of its Uigurs; 12 percent of its Mordvinians; 11 percent of its Ukrainians and Germans; 10 percent of its Tatars, Belorussians, and Dungans; 8 percent of its Uzbeks; 6 percent of its Russians; and 10 percent of its remaining nationalities. And in the same period (1 June 1930–1 June 1933), when 94 percent of its Kazakhs were rural, Kazakhstan's rural population decreased by more than one-half (from 5,873,000 to 2,493,500).[83] The longer intercensal period (1926–39) reveals the same disproportion. The republic's Kazakhs numbered 3,628,000 in the 1926 (17 December) census and 2,307,000 in the 1939 (15 January) census for a decrease of 1,321,000, or 36 percent. In the same period Kazakhstan's Uzbeks decreased by 124,600 (55 percent), its Uigurs by 25,700 (41 percent), and its Ukrainians by 201,300 (23 percent), for a total decrease of the four nationalities of 1,672,000 by 1939 (or 1.7 million in the "executed" [suppressed] 1937 [5–6 January] census).[84] However, the 1926 census undercounted the Kazakhs in Kazakhstan by 12.3 percent, so that in the early 1930s, before their population began to plummet, they probably numbered 4,120,000 to 4,317,000, meaning that by 1937 they decreased by 50 percent and by 1939 by 2,137,500, or 49 percent, while at the same time 616,000 Kazakhs fled their republic (411,000 to other Soviet regions and 205,000 to other countries). Consequently, from famine and flight the

The Relatively Worst Case: Kazakhstan

Kazakhs decreased by 2,754,000, or 64 to 67 percent, between 1930 and 1937–39, with the decrease varying from 70 percent in northern Kazakhstan to 50 percent in southern Kazakhstan to 65 percent in western Kazakhstan, and reaching 80 to 90 percent in some rayons.[85] This relative decrease was larger than that of any other major ethnic group in the Soviet Union.

The first famine of 1919–22, which chiefly affected southern Kazakhstan, cost about 1 million or more lives, and the second famine of 1930–33 took 1.5 million to 2 million or more lives, so in a span of fifteen years the republic lost 40 percent of its population.[86] The Kazakhs themselves did not regain their 1930 population until 1962, thanks to a postwar population explosion, but the influx of Russians and Ukrainians during the Virgin and Idle Lands Program of the last half of the 1950s slowed them from becoming a majority in their titular republic until the repatriation of Kazakhs and the departure of Russians and Ukrainians in the wake of the collapse of the USSR at the beginning of the 1990s. And it was not until 2012 that a monument to the famine's victims, the "Wall of Sorrow," was erected in Kazakhstan's new capital of Astana.

In 1933 a nineteen-year-old Russian girl, Tatyana Nevadovskaya, the daughter of a "special settler," in this case a professor deported to work at an experimental agricultural station, where she assisted, became "deeply troubled" by the Kazakh carnage and penned a poem in the hope that later generations of Kazakhstanis would "not forget the people who died from hunger, the children and old people, the *kishlaks* [villages] and *auls* [encampments] now empty and deserted, the people who froze to death in the steppe and those who suffered from disease." The heartfelt and poignant lines written by this relatively privileged observer, entitled simply "Kazakhstan Tragedy," could serve as a requiem for the victims:

> Heady March is here with notes of spring,
> So full of memories – so sad and bleak.
> The young grass has a bitter sting
> After snows once strewn with bodies weak.
> The poverty and dirt I do not see,
> Nor the rags and lice of which we read.
> What makes me suffer bitterly
> Is the fate of all the hapless dead.

Hunger scythed them down, while I could eat.
My feet were shod, while theirs were bare.
I recall a begging granny in the street
And I still hear a mother in despair.
From under her rags she drew a breast
To show us no drop of milk was left.
Her baby's body could not come to rest,
Clutched by his mother of hope bereft.
I do not shudder at this ghastly sight,
Yet gaze on it calmly no one could.
As people fall who have no strength to fight,
Gleaning grains where once ripe corn had stood.
Stacks of straw are still large, intact,
Despite pouring rain, strong wind and snow.
Inside rotten ears of corn are packed,
Covered in mould – poisonous you know ...
A helpless infant's little hand
Might still find a rotten ear.
Although he now can hardly stand,
His thin cracked voice you will hear.
Where is their guilt? Why all this pain?
Here in this huge homeland of ours?
Why such thin fingers must rummage for grain?
Why such sick children go begging for hours?
Through their skin poke shoulder blades
And ribs so painfully protrude.
Stomachs swell as the last hope fades.
Why this tragic lack of food?
Winter crops sprout in the warm blue haze.
Larks in the sky are soaring aloft,
As children's hunger blurs their gaze,
A Kazakh's corpse lies on soil so soft.
Who gave the orders? I want to understand.
Who made us sink to poverty and die?
Since ancient times, throughout this land
The nomads have led forth their herds – so why

The Relatively Worst Case: Kazakhstan

Make camels and donkeys suffer so long?
Why strip from farmers their very last shirt
And force a whole people once supple and strong
To miserably starve in the cold and the dirt?
Who needed all this – Allah or Our Lord?
To take all they had and give nought in return?
Which despot would brandish so high his sword?
Which lunatic heartlessly take all they earn?
Last wagons, last felts and also last sheep
Are seized without protest or any cries.
Shepherds cannot plough with furrow deep:
With no *yurt* in winter, death is no surprise.
Without a herd or sheep, hunger is their lot:
Neither nature nor the weather is to blame.
We cannot say it is too cold or hot,
Or that harvests did not bring the land great fame.
It should have brought the people meat, bread and tea.
But no! They took away the first-class wheat,
Leaving giant straw stacks in every field and lea;
Round them cluster peasants with not enough to eat.
Neither Jesus nor Allah would invent such a fate,
To leave a Kazakh without wool, without felt,
With no skins for his shoes till far too late,
No warm cap, no warm coat and no belt.
He would not know that all around Moscow
The peasants they plant, sow and reap.
It is hard to watch such sorrow
And at night I can no longer sleep.
The lark trills up in the sky so bright,
While down below all is so grim.
Evil and beauty, darkness and light,
Blend into one troubling hymn.[87]

7
THE ABSOLUTELY WORST CASE: THE UKRAINE – THE NORTH CAUCASUS

The famine is especially grave in the Ukraine and the North Caucasus. There the cases of death from emaciation are countless.
– the Moscow correspondent of *Le Petit Parisien*, 31 July 1933.

The Primacy of the Granary of the Steppelands of European Russia

While it is certain that Kazakhstan (or, more properly speaking, the Asiatic Russian steppe and the Kazakhs) suffered the most in relative terms from the famine, losing up to one-half of its Kazakhs (2.5 million out of 5 million), it is equally certain that the Ukraine and the North Caucasus (or, again more properly speaking, the European Russian steppe and the Ukrainians) suffered the most in absolute terms, losing 9 million or even 12 million Ukrainians, or from one-third to two-fifths of the Ukrainian population of both the Ukraine (24 million) and the North Caucasus (2 million) in 1926[1] – but even in the latter case still proportionately fewer than Kazakhstan's loss. Also, like the Kazakhs, many of these Ukrainians were lost to rural-urban migration and rural-rural deportation rather than to starvation. Still, those Ukrainians who lived outside the Ukraine – up to 8 million – were mostly peasants who had migrated to accustomed steppelands in the adjoining Central Black Earth (23 percent of its population) as well as the North Caucasus (62 percent of the Kuban's and 44 percent of the Don's population), plus Kazakhstan (13 percent of its population, primarily in the north),[2] which were likewise prime grainlands, so they, too, were among the famine victims. Thus, many Ukrainians starved to death because they were the dominant Soviet ethnic group ("nationality" in Soviet parlance) in the dominant Soviet grainland – the fertile chernozyom ("black earth") belt of the "great steppe," which stretched from southern European Russia (the Pontic, or Ukrainian, Steppe) eastward into Asiatic Russia as far as the Ob River (the Kazakh Steppe), where, however, it was less densely settled and more subject to cold and aridity. So the Ukrainian grainland was more productive (even if its chernozyom was more "degraded," or less "virginal") and its skilful peasants more productive, so they stood to lose more under prescriptive collectivization and were bound to dominate the casualties in the "war against the peasants" and bear the brunt of the ensuing famine.[3] As one-time premier Nikita Khrushchev, who had considerable Ukrainian experience, asserted in his memoirs, the "Ukraine held a special place as the 'breadbasket' of our country, the major source of grain and [beet] sugar." "Its relative importance," he added, "in providing food for our country was very great." This dominance was explained, continued Khrushchev, by two factors: the Ukraine's "good black earth and a good climate," and the "cultural level of agriculture," which was higher than elsewhere in the country, for "the people had already accumulated knowledge and experience."[4] As Svetlana Alexievich was told by one of her informants, "the soil there is so fertile you can stick a stake in it and it'll grow into a tree."[5] It was owing to this superior fertility of the steppe that the "kulak capitalism" of individual farmsteading, as Ciliga termed it, was most developed in the Ukraine, the North Caucasus, and Western Siberia and "as a result the resistance to the bureaucratic collectivization was particularly bitter."[6]

So the Stalinist leadership placed its highest hopes for the success of collectivized agriculture on the southern European, primarily Ukrainian, steppelands, and when these expectations were frustrated the peasants there were vengefully punished more severely than peasants in less promising farmlands. Consequently, as British ambassador Esmond Ovey told the Foreign Office in early 1933, the Ukraine and the North Caucasus were "the regions where the food situation [was] worst and where the most violent measures ha[d] been taken to secure the execution of the grain-collection plan."[7] In the three years 1930, 1931, and 1932 the Ukraine and the North Caucasus together supplied an average of just over two-fifths (41 percent) of the country's total grain procurement, with the Ukraine alone providing an average of almost one-third (31 percent), followed by the North Caucasus in second place at almost one-eighth (11 percent) and the Central Black Earth in third place at one-tenth (10 percent)[8] – all of them wholly or partly sharing the highly fertile and densely farmed European Russian steppe. Similarly, the Ukraine and the North Caucasus together were the chief source of exported as well as procured grain, supplying 70 percent in 1930 and 65 percent in 1931, for example.[9] Thus, the more that a Soviet region specialized in the growing of grain, the more that it was collectivized, the more grain was procured from it, the more grain was exported from it, and the more that it starved.[10] Little wonder that when an anonymous American worker left the Soviet Union in June 1933 he said, "the famine rages everywhere in Russia, but especially in the Ukraine."[11]

Outside the steppe zone of either European or Asiatic Russia agriculture was more marginal, less fruitful, and less commercial, so collectivization was less intrusive and the population more compliant. This correlation was noted by the Polish ambassador to Moscow, Waclaw Grzybowski, when in 1939 he reflected at length about the special severity of the famine's impact on the Ukraine and the North Caucasus and on Ukrainians:

> The negative attitude of the majority of the peasants [of the Soviet Union] to the kolkhoz was not expressed everywhere with the same force. It can be said that it was manifested in direct proportion to the fertility of the soil and the benefit derived from it by the local population. In most of the black-earth zone, where the working of the land had always been the principal livelihood, the peasantry felt the worsening of life as a result of the transition to the collective farm system much more keenly than in other zones and their potential displeasure with the institution of the kolkhoz was greater. This [circumstance] applies particularly to the Ukraine, the Don, and the North Caucasus, where heretofore the process of eviction of untrustworthy elements had not completely ended. In Central Russia, where agricultural work only partly satisfied the necessities of life of the inhabitants, the chief source of earnings was industry (factory and cottage), and it was much easier to be in accord with the current agrarian regime.

Additionally, the ambassador asserted, "Psychological differences and local mores also exerted great influence in this matter. For the Great Russian, passive by nature and long used to the land commune, the collective [farm] was not the contrast that it was for the Little Russian [Ukrainian] or Cossack, whose life and psyche were formed in somewhat different [frontier] conditions." "It is these very factors," he concluded, "that explain the fact that the resistance of the population during the introduction of collectivization in the south of Russia was much greater than in the central regions. So in the first place Soviet power relied upon the Great Russian element as a more loyal element."[12] Thus, as Otto Schiller found, by 1932 the chief grain region of the Ukraine-North Caucasus was "almost completely collectivized," while the so-called "supplementary" (secondary) grain regions were collectivized "to a smaller extent."[13]

Grzybowski also insinuated that Ukrainians were less loyal to Party policy than Great Russians (who formed only one-tenth of the Ukraine's population) because they were more partial to private than to common property and hence produced more kulaks, who, of course, were anathema to the Stalinist leadership.[14] Vasily Grossman noted this phenomenon: "In the Ukraine, we [Party activists] were told, they had an instinct for private property that was stronger than in the [Great] Russian Republic [RSFSR]. And truly, truly, the whole business [of kulakization] was much worse in the Ukraine than it was with us [Great Russians]." "It was clear," he continued, "that Moscow was basing its hopes on the Ukraine [as the primary granary]. And the upshot of it was that most of the subsequent anger was directed against the Ukraine. What they said was simple: you have failed to fulfill the plan, and that means that you yourself are an unliquidated kulak." "The conclusion reached on top," ended Grossman, "was that the grain had all been concealed, hidden away. By kulaks who had not yet been liquidated, by loafers! The 'kulaks' had been removed, but the 'kulak' spirit remained. Private property was master over the mind of the Ukrainian peasant."[15] Perhaps the Ukraine (and even the North Caucasus) really was more kulak-prone, but, if so, then it likely stemmed from its superior chernozyom and its superior cultivation, which generated a more productive, more prosperous, and less compliant rural population than elsewhere (with the possible exception of Western Siberia, likewise a frontier region).

President Kalinin agreed with the Polish ambassador's sentiment, but he added another possible factor when he told France's prime minister Herriot that the Bolshevik attempt to win the hearts and the minds of the peasants had been hardest to prosecute in the Ukraine and the North Caucasus, "the land of the kulaks … where the White Army had been raised."[16] Indeed, the gravest military threat to Bolshevik victory during the civil war had come from the Whites in the south, who had even besieged Moscow before being routed. This conflict, as vicious as all civil wars, had raged only a decade before the introduction of collectivization, so the memory of it still festered on both sides.[17] Politically, then, the Bolsheviks undoubtedly felt less secure in the Ukraine and the North Caucasus, although at least in the latter Great Russians were in the majority, if only barely, and in the former appreciable in the eastern portion only. At any rate, given this animus, Moscow may well have been less responsive to pleas from Kharkov or Kiev for sympathy and assistance during the famine and thereby failed to moderate its impact.

The Ukraine featured another distinctive circumstance. True to its name (meaning "on the periphery"), it was a frontier on the international boundary of the Soviet Union. This feature was not unique for, as one of the country's fifteen union republics, or SSRs, it had by definition to border on another country, but the Ukraine's western boundary adjoined Romania and – much more significantly – Poland, whose relations with Russia, Tsarist and Soviet, had long been unfriendly (indeed, Russia had been instrumental in removing Poland from the map of Europe via three partitions in the eighteenth and nineteenth centuries, and as recently as 1920 they had fought each other).[18] Moreover, the Ukraine's western borderland was the heartland of Ukrainian nationalism, with its secessionist propensity (and, constitutionally, the USSR was a voluntary union of SSRs and therefore each had the theoretical right to secede). Stalin himself called the Ukraine "a large and distinctive republic,"[19] presumably because Ukrainians were second only to Great Russians as the Soviet Union's most populous ethnic group; they were concentrated overwhelmingly in the Ukraine;[20] their language, religion, and culture were similar to, but distinct from, those of Great Russians; and they shared the country's primary granary and its primary iron and steel base (the Donbass) with the RSFSR as well as a border with capitalist Poland[21] – all of which generated more nationalist and secessionist sentiment, primarily on the part of intellectuals and white-collar workers. Norwegian captain Vidkund Quisling, whose surname would become synonymous with treason after he collaborated with the German invaders and occupiers of his country during the Second World War, represented British interests at the Norwegian Legation in Moscow in 1927–29, and he reported at the end of 1928 that "there had been a very great change in the last few years in the Ukraine, and all official correspondence was now carried on in the Ukrainian and not in the Russian language." He added that "here, too [as in Georgia], a Communist was Ukrainian first and a Communist second."[22]

Stalin acknowledged these tensions and Moscow's need to counter them, declaring in a cipher to Kaganovich in the summer of 1932 that "*the most important issue* right now is the Ukraine," where "things are bad with regard to the *party* … the soviets … the [o]GPU" because of their vacillating leadership and their overlooking of Ukrainian separatism and Polish influences ("Petlyura adherents" and "direct agents of Pilsudski"),[23] as well as their resistance to the grain procurement plan, so that "unless we begin to straighten out the situation in the Ukraine, we may lose the Ukraine."[24] Stalin added that the Central Committee must implement measures for "the economic and political strengthening of the Ukraine" – "above all its *border* rayons" – with "the goal of transforming the Ukraine as quickly as possible into a real *fortress* of the USSR, into a genuinely exemplary republic," and "we should be unstinting in providing money" – otherwise, "I repeat, we may lose the Ukraine."[25] Moscow reacted by purging the Party leadership in the Ukraine in 1933, replacing Stanislav Kosior and Vlas Chubar with Pavel Postyshev (all of whom would eventually be executed) and undertaking Russification. Postyshev attacked deviations from the Party line in the Ukraine, including "bourgeois nationalist activities."[26] The Italian consul in Kharkov asserted that the purge was "most assuredly designed to paralyze any attempted manifestations of Ukrainian separatism," and he believed that Moscow was motivated by "the necessity or expediency, more or less openly acknowledged, of denationalizing those regions in which Ukrainian or German consciousness ha[d] reawakened, threatening possible political difficulties in the future, and where, for the sake of the unity of the empire, it [was] better that a preponderantly Russian population reside."[27]

Moscow, in the consul's words, was indeed watchful of "Ukrainian separatist nationalism" and "Ukrainian particularism" and responded with Russification, but it did so, too, in the case of nationalistic manifestations by other non-Great Russian minorities elsewhere. Moscow's response was more forceful in the Ukraine because it was the USSR's second-ranking republic. For the same reason resistance was stronger in the Ukraine. The Italian consul reported in early 1933 that Moscow's "unrelenting requisition" of the republic's resources, especially provisions, was reawakening "Ukrainian consciousness," and he added that the Ukraine was "the region that ha[d] by far most openly sabotaged its collectivization and even industrialization."[28] The stronger resistance on the part of Ukrainians undoubtedly cost them more dearly in lives.

The Ukrainian Calamity

Certainly the peasants of both the Ukraine and the North Causcasus suffered grievously as well as inordinately. In July of 1932, as the famine began to peak, Carveth Wells trained across the Ukrainian countryside and saw empty villages and starving peasants: "Farm houses were in ruins everywhere, roofs gone, fences broken down, wagons without wheels, farming implements lying about in every stage of kapootness while wretched-looking peasants with rags tied around their feet were to be seen wandering about aimlessly and watching the train go by without a smile on their faces."[29] Likewise, a month later Rhea Clyman, after leaving Kharkov and driving down the Donets Valley, passed kilometre after kilometre of "forlorn and deserted villages" where "the houses were empty, the doors were flung wide open, the roofs were caving in." She found the starving children especially pathetic. One peasant woman told her: "Our children were eating grass in the spring ... they were down on all fours like animals, eating grass. There was nothing else for them." Then "she undressed them one by one, prodded their huge sagging bellies, pointed to their spindly little legs, ran her hand up and down their tortured, mis-shapen, twisted little bodies to make me understand that this was real famine. I shut my eyes. I could not bear to look at all this horror."[30]

The horror was even worse by the spring and summer of 1933, when the famine climaxed. Now there was little, if any, difference in the level of starvation between urban and rural dwellers. Dmitry Goichenko, a thirty-year-old Party activist of peasant background, toured the city and rayon of Kiev in the spring with a friend who held a "major post" in the city. They walked through it: "At every step we met the starving, who formed an enormous proportion of all of the passersby. Millions of these unfortunates roamed the city in search of [the means of] saving themselves. They were visible in the courtyards as they rummaged in garbage containers and, finding something edible, hurriedly shoved it into their mouths together with filth." By that spring, they estimated, about 500,000 had died in Kiev and its rayon,[31] and the same number had fled, "many of whom were dying without reaching the promised land [cultivated countryside] of grain and potatoes." Goichenko continued:

> Already on the outskirts of Kiev I saw many of the starving lying on the streets and squares, dead and still alive. Outside the city along the road that we travelled we saw the same scene. There were many pedestrians, but just as many had collapsed on the road and in the ditches. All of them were either emaciated or swollen. Instead of eyes there were slits, and the faces, bloated with water, were even shiny. Their arms and legs were swollen, too. All of these people were filthy and most of them were ragged. We often encountered corpses lying across the road, and we rode around all of them.
>
> It was the very same in the villages through which we drove. Here there was a terrible emptiness and devastation. There was not a single fence anywhere; all of them had gone for fuel, for the kolkhozniks did not have any straw, which with the stooks of grain had rotted in the fields. Firewood was also nowhere to be had, and even to go to gather twigs in the forest was forbidden under the law of seven-eighths. Nearly all of the barns had also been dismantled for fuel or kolkhoz construction. Every large shed [*stodol*], an invariable building in all peasant farmsteads, had long since been torn down and taken away for the construction of kolkhozes. Here and there the *khata* [house] roofs were almost totally gone. The thatch from them had also been used for fuel or feed for cows, if they had any, since a kolkhoznik did not even get rotten straw for cattle fodder. He lived and worked solely for the state.

Goichenko added that "invariably in every village there were corpses upon corpses in the streets, in the yards, and in the ditches," and "it was already warm, and the country air, instead of smelling sweet with the coming spring, was saturated with the putrid stench of corpses, for in places the bodies had not been removed for a week."[32]

Official Polish reports attested to the deserted villages, the littered corpses, and the zombified peasants. One Polish agent wrote: "Dozens of uncollected bodies lie on the roads, in the fields, and in the woods. In the villages, even in those near cities, there are often boarded-up and abandoned houses. Neither dogs nor cats are to be seen almost anywhere – all have been eaten.

In the woods there are many half-wild people, who eat mushrooms, moss, and roots. On the roads one often meets families of peasants fleeing the villages in carts in an uncertain direction."³³ The reason for their flight – repeated in the Polish reports – was the fear of widespread cannibalism. One report stated:

> An absolutely reliable informant from Berdichev says that in the evenings around that city there is an actual hunt for children. After night falls no mother allows her child on the street. In spite of this [precaution], there are instances of the stealing of children from their homes. They [the starving] eat the remains of horse carcasses, and there are cases of families eating their deceased members after waiting for several days for coffins and permission for burial. The famine manifests itself most terribly in the villages. In a number of rayons, such as Tsvetkovo, Zvenigorod, Uman, Busk, Tarashcha, and Berdichev (partly), cannibalism has become a kind of habit.³⁴

Perhaps the most gruesome description was left by an anonymous eyewitness:

> I went into one of the small houses and froze on the threshold. Next to the wall on a wooden bench lay the almost dried out body of a child aged five or six. Its mother was leaning over it, holding a knife and was trying with difficulty to cut off the child's head. The knife and her hands were covered in blood and the child's legs shook convulsively. For a moment I caught her eye and she looked at me. She was unlikely to have taken anything in, her eyes were dry, the light had gone out of them; they were like the eyes of a corpse that had not been closed. An hour later we went back into the same house to record this – yet another case of cannibalism – but this time we saw that same woman lying on the earthen floor, her face turned upwards with the staring eyes of the dead. She was holding the severed head of her child to her breast.³⁵

The suffering of the children was horrific, as a seventeen-year-old Ukrainian girl, Hava Volovich, saw for herself. The famine "was like a cholera epidemic – people dropped like flies," she said. A friend's sixteen-year-old sister whose father had starved to death left her baby with her mother and "went off to find something better"; her mother, whenever she got any food, gave it to her own children, but "she gave Vera, her granddaughter, nothing: that way she'd die quicker." Hava continued:

Verochka turned into a living skeleton, with a coat of whitish fluff covering her yellow shrunken skin. Day after day she lay in her cot, eyes wide open like shining glass buttons on her corpse's face. But still she would not die. Her mouth, which hadn't yet learned to form the word "mama," whispered "issi" – she wanted something to eat …

I saved Verochka a small share of my food [a thin gruel of flour flavoured with goosefoot and sorrel] if we had anything to eat at home. She would fasten her skinny hands (they were like chicken feet) on the bowl and swallow the contents in seconds. Then she would point at the window. My friend would carry her out and put her down on the grass in the sun. Verochka would roll over on[to] her belly in an instant. With her yellow old woman's hands, she'd start snatching at the grass and stuffing it in her mouth.

That child was made of iron!

A grass diet finished off many, many other children and adults. But Verochka survived.

Hava ends her account unsparingly:

Once I saw a little boy about six years old by the cemetery fence. His greenish puffy face was covered in cracks, out of which some kind of liquid was oozing; his bloated, cracked legs were running in it too. Something green and wet was trickling out from under his homespun trousers. It must have been the grass he'd just eaten. His stomach had atrophied, and he could no longer digest anything at all.

The boy stood immobile. From his half-open mouth came a thin cry: "ee-ee-ee!" It wasn't a call for help; he didn't expect that from anyone. He'd seen adults – who were supposed to take care of children, not exterminate them – come and snatch his family's last crust of bread, condemning them to death by starvation. People were enemies; he was afraid of them. And so he'd come away from the busy streets, where there was nothing for him, to the cemetery fence, perhaps hoping to find something to eat. But it was death that found him.[36]

Like Gareth Jones and Rhea Clyman, Whiting Williams found the starving children, particularly the orphaned or abandoned ones, the most pitiable of all the victims. The waifs had been brought to the towns and cities by their starving parents in search of work and food but were soon ejected by the authorities, and the parents, believing they were returning to certain starvation, left their children behind to have a better chance of surviving by begging or stealing. Williams found that "there [were] hordes of those wild children in all the towns" and that "they live[d] and die[d] like animals." By the summer of 1933, he guessed, eighteen thousand children had been abandoned in this fashion in Kharkov alone. Eventually, he added, these waifs were rounded up but instead of being placed in orphanages were put on trains and unloaded in the countryside at a distance from which it was too far for them to walk back to town.[37] In 1933 alone the OGPU apprehended 228,065 ragamuffins on streets and at railway stations in the Ukraine, of which 188,872 were released to kolhozes and sovkhozes.[38]

The shortage of staples gave rise, as elsewhere, to embezzlement and speculation, especially as the famine peaked. At the beginning of 1933 the OGPU reported that it had uncovered "mass" fraud at baking plants and bakeries in the Ukraine that involved the changing of baking norms for the moistness, acidity, and admixtures in bread, resulting in "savings" of tens of thousands of puds of flour and bread that were mostly stolen and used as bribes.[39] In late spring speculators, who officially qualified as criminals, stood several hours in long lines to buy half a loaf of bread for three rubles and then sold it for eight rubles without having to stand in line. A speculator's daily income was reckoned to be twenty to thirty rubles, while a skilled worker earned only five to seven rubles per day.[40]

A multitude of livestock also perished. Between 1929 and 1933 the Ukraine lost at least one-half of its livestock population.[41] The depletion of milk cows and work horses had the most drastic effects, for obvious reasons. The number of work horses fell by one-third – from 3,400,400 to 2,268,400 – between 1 January 1932 and 1 July 1933, mostly on kolkhozes and individual farmsteads. The OGPU did not blame policy for the "die-off" (*padyozh*), which occurred in all parts of the Ukraine; rather, it faulted "exhaustion in connection with the lack of coarse and particularly concentrated feed," the "extreme increase in work load during spring sowing," the "continuing depersonalization of horse care and the criminally negligent and slipshod attitude to the horse stock in sovkhozes and kolkhozes," and the "wrecking activities of c[ounter] r[evolutionary] kulak elements in the kolkhozes and sovkhozes." Epizootic diseases (especially meningitis) were also blamed, but – as was its wont – the OGPU focused on the "enemies of the people":

> During spring sowing and harvesting OGPU organs uncovered and liquidated a whole series of c[ounter] r[evolutionary] kulak groups whose activities were directed at the destruction of the horse stock in the kolkhozes. The kulaks who had wormed their way into the kolkhozes disabled the horses in the following way: they did not feed or water them for several days, or the feed that they did provide was clearly inferior, sometimes they put glass, nails, and the like in the feed, they overloaded the horses or simply worked them to death, they did not isolate the sick from the healthy horses, they did not clean them, they left them at pasture without supervision, etc. and so on. We uncovered a whole series of cases where the management of kolkhozes – littered with kulaks, Petlyurists, and other a[nti]-s[oviet] elements – deliberately wrecked the resolutions of the Party and the government on the organization of round-the-clock pasturing of exhausted horses. In Pyatikhatki Rayon, where during the last 2 months 300 horses have died of glanders, a c[ounter] r[evolutionary] group of 5 veterinarians was uncovered. At several kolkhozes the members vaccinated completely healthy horses with glanders, and they died as a result.[42]

The OGPU's obsession with subversives aside, it is possible, of course, that starving peasants did vent their resentment through sabotage of the kolkhoz, particularly when they had little or no personal stake in it.

In late 1933 the Ukrainian situation moderated, partly because of the weakening, if not cessation, of peasant resistance, thanks to what a report from the German consul general in Kharkov, Karl Walther, called the "most cruel repression and hunger," that is, defeat and death. Stricter enforcement of Party decrees tightened governance in the countryside, reducing disorder, inaction, and sabotage; as Stalin was quoted by Walther, "the reasons behind the difficulties with grain procurement are not to be found with the peasants, but among us because we have the power."[43] In the ten months from February to November 1933 1,340 Party members were appointed to managerial positions in the rural Ukraine and an additional 12,500 Party members were posted to the villages, while 640 incumbent Party secretaries and rayon Party chairmen were recalled; furthermore, 643 kolkhoz and 203 sovkhoz political positions were filled with 3,000 Party members.[44] Also, the complement of agricultural machinery was improved by the dispatch of industrial repairmen and the delivery of 15,000 new tractors, 2,400 new combine harvesters, and 3,000 new trucks to the republic.[45] The newer machines were better than the older models, and the operators were more skilful than before. Even the weather improved. Walther quoted Pavel Postyshev, the secretary of the Ukrainian Party's Central Committee, in this respect: "the crops have been outstanding due to favorable weather everywhere this year [1933]; winter crops, compared with the previous years, did not suffer with mild snowfall and quite low temperatures, the spring brought abundant rainfall, and the summer sufficient heat."[46] The crop would have been even better if more seed had been available for planting (even though the Ukraine had received 555,000 tonnes of seed from Moscow), a larger portion of each field had been sown, and the sown area had been better worked. The crop would have been even better, too, if "much" of it – up to 25 percent – had not been wasted. As the German consul in Odessa reported: "In some cases, not all the grain was reaped and much of the mowed grain was left in the fields. The grain which was mowed too early or badly reaped was lost, while much was also stolen."[47] Nevertheless, for the first time the Ukraine's grain procurement target was reached by the deadline of 1 November – about 6 million tonnes (about one-half of the total crop), compared with about 4 million tonnes in 1932.[48]

The North Caucasian Calamity

The North Caucasus duplicated and possibly exceeded the Ukraine's devastation, although the "mountaineers" (the several smaller ethnic groups of the Caucasus Mountains, such as the Chechens and Ingushes) were largely spared. At the famine's apogee in the spring of 1933 the impressions of a German agronomist (probably Otto Schiller) were cited by an Italian diplomat:

The Absolutely Worst Case: The Ukraine – The North Caucasus

The agronomist was able to state that the villages are almost completely abandoned and the houses in ruins. When he questioned the few survivors, they replied that their neighbours were all dead from starvation and they themselves were awaiting the same fate with resignation: "In a few days we will end like the others," they said. Along the country roads one often sees people starving to death and unburied corpses. People pass without noticing them. The first to perish are the men, who generally offer less resistance than the women; the mothers have to nurse their own dying infants in front of those who are no more. In the villages, then, one sees only women and children: these have scrawny limbs and heads, unlike their bodies, which appear bloated. Food consists of grasses and roots; bread has become an unknown item; one finds at the very most a little corn flour. They speak of ... cannibalism ... A Russian of German background, a trustworthy person, asserted having seen ... corpses from which pieces of flesh had been torn.[49]

The resort of the starving to grazing had been noticed by Carveth Wells the previous summer, when, he wrote, "from the train windows, children could be seen eating grass," "their stomachs enormously distended."[50]

The treatment of the peasants by the local authorities could be barbaric. An "absolutely confidential" official report in April 1933 described how one rayon's authorities, led by a factory director, "terrorized" the kolkhozniks with "medieval inquisitorial methods":

They removed the roofs of their houses, dislodged the frames, broke the stoves, drove the peasants barefoot into the freezing cold, put them in frigid granaries (in their underwear in 20°–25° [F.] of frost) for hours. They put a revolver in their mouth and forced them to drink kerosene and salty water, to goosestep, to stand on tiptoe sticking out their tongues, and to stand with upraised arms and squeeze their hands with pencils between their fingers, and they sat their buttocks on a hot cooker and gave them cold water to drink. For any word of criticism they were put in a cellar – all of this [cruelty] with the leave of the former rayon leadership and some territorial representatives.

The report blandly added that "these outrages greatly sapped the energy of the [peasant] population" and made them secretive, distrustful, and passive.[51]

Such "outrages" occurred because the authorities were convinced that there was plenty of grain to be had but that the peasants were hiding it. And the peasants were indeed hiding as much as they could because procurements were not leaving them enough for food, seed, and feed. The OGPU reported at the end of 1932 that during the 1 November to 10 December period of that year it had discovered 4,764 pits and 238 "black [illicit] granaries" in the kray, from which 93,108 centners of grain were seized, and had arrested 16,864 "counter-revolutionary kulaks and anti-Soviet elements," comprising 3,680 kulaks, 271 prosperous individual farmsteaders, 6,473 srednyaks, 482 bednyaks, 3,130 kolkhozniks, 1,896 soviet and kolkhoz employees, and 932 former traders and others.[52] In one rayon the individual farmsteaders employed the "most refined methods" of concealment, with grain "hidden under dinner tables and in double-bottomed tubs half full of water, daubed under stoves, buried in graves, hung in toilets, etc."[53] The peasants continued to resist and to conceal grain, however, and their masters continued to procure insistently and repress ruthlessly. The North Caucasus Party secretary, Andrei Andreyev (one of the few of his rank not to be shot but to die in his bed), told Stalin at the end of 1929 that, in order to enforce grain procurement in the North Caucasus that autumn, more than 5,000 Party workers had been sent to the peasant villages and Cossack stanitsas and 30,000 to 35,000 peasant holdings had been fined or sold, 20,000 peasants had been tried, and some 600 shot.[54] The Polish general consul in Kharkov, Jan Karszy-Siedlewskie, reported that "nowhere [in the USSR other] than in the North Caucasus was grain procurement conducted with such brutality, and, properly speaking, it really represented the confiscation of nearly all agricultural output."[55]

As in the Ukraine, the situation in the North Caucasus was aggravated by a distinctive circumstance – the animosity of the Bolsheviks to the Cossacks of the Don and the Kuban, the commingled remnants of the former several Cossack groups of the northern seaboard of the Black Sea. The Bolsheviks' enmity stemmed from the Cossacks' loyalty to the imperial family (they were prominent members of the palace guard), their military prowess as guardians of the empire's southern frontiers, the participation of many of them – especially the Kuban Cossacks – in the White Army,[56] and perhaps even their quasi-democratic governance (with a popular assembly elected by adult males that in turn elected an *ataman* [chieftain]). Thus, when the Don and especially the Kuban Cossack peasants resisted collectivization, they were more severely repressed than non-Cossack peasants.

The victorious Bolsheviks disbanded the Cossack "hosts" (armies), and many of their members emigrated, but thousands remained in their stanitsas (villages or garrisons) and farmed the steppe astride the Ukraine-North Caucasus border. William Chamberlin, who toured the North Caucasus and the Ukraine at the famine's height, opined that in the former peasant resistance "was doubtless stiffer than in other sections of the country, because a considerable part of the population consisted of Cossacks, who had enjoyed a higher standard of living than the mass of the peasants before the October Revolution and who had mostly fought on the side of the Whites during the civil war."[57] Dr Fritz Dittloff, the former manager of the German agricultural concession "Drusag" in the Kuban, testified in 1934 in England that the persecution of the Kuban Cossacks began in 1929 because, "from their position of economic advantage, they had obtained a controlling influence in the villages" and were "men skilled in the use of arms." Their stanitsas, he continued, were embedded with anti-Cossack Russians, and the Cossacks themselves were forbidden to carry sabres or daggers and were deprived of their horses. "I have often heard Communists remark," he said, "that the Cossack must be made to plough and travel with the aid of oxen, so as to deny him permanently all practice in horsemanship."[58] The Cossacks suffered much more, too, thanks to the exceptional ruthlessness of the *kraykom* (Party kray committee) secretary, Boris Sheboldayev, who had already gained notoriety for his ferocity in the same rank in the Lower Volga before being appointed to the North Caucasus in 1931 (and who was to be shot for his pains in 1937).[59] The Cossacks resisted his repression passively and in some places actively but were suppressed "by the most rigorous measures."[60]

Whole stanitsas were emptied by deportation and others were starved to death by "blacklists" that prevented them from receiving outside supplies.[61] According to Otto Schiller, the Cossack stanitsas were thinned and emptied primarily by deportation, which began on a mass scale in the autumn of 1932,[62] and the Russian villages primarily by starvation, with the individual farmsteads being treated more harshly than the kolkhozes. The Cossacks, he continued, who, "by tradition and mentality, were the most resolute antagonists of agricultural collectivization," bore the brunt of deportation; most were exiled to the Urals and the rest were "thinned through famine," so that the Kuban host was "practically annihilated" and the Cossack danger "eradicated." During the winter of 1932–33, Schiller estimated, the populations of the Cossack stanitsas of Timishbek and Ust-Labinskaya plummeted from 15,000 to 1,000 and from 24,000 to 10,000, respectively, while the Russian villages of Dmitriyevka and Tlinskaya, respectively, shrank from 6,000 to 2,000 and from 3,000 to 1,500 inhabitants (by the spring of 1933 twenty to thirty peasants were dying daily in the Russian villages, and with the advent of warm weather most of the rest would "doubtless die from malaria," which had "prevailed to an unprecedented extent since last autumn"). During the winter, too, Stavropol's population fell from 140,000 to 90,000 and Krasnodar's from 230,000 to 190,000.[63]

The North Caucasus landscape was devastated, transformed from a breadbasket into a battlefield. At the beginning of 1933 an English visitor found that the Kuban resembled "an armed camp in a desert – no work no grain no cattle no draught horses, only idle peasants or soldiers."[64] In February Malcolm Muggeridge toured the Ukraine and the Kuban and described the latter as being in the process of "becoming a desert, inhabited by starving peasants and occupied by well-fed troops."[65] By late spring the ruination had peaked, the Italian ambassador to Moscow telling Rome:

> The situation in the North Caucasus and the Kuban is without any doubt the worst in all of Russia, and this is the result of the violent repressions taken against the Cossacks, who have been offering the fiercest resistance to measures of agricultural collectivization. Those who have not been eliminated on the spot have been deported to the North, the Urals, and Siberia. Many have died during the journey, made in closed cattle cars.[66]

Finally, when William Chamberlin made his ten-day trip to the Ukraine and the North Caucasus in September he found that the latter "ha[d] been the arena of a terrible class struggle, and [bore] every sign of the ordeal through which it ha[d] passed." "Formerly a rich and prosperous region," he added, "it is now a scene of terrible poverty." He elaborated the situation in the Kuban:

The first thing that struck me when I began to walk about in the Cossack villages in the neighborhood of Kropotkin was the extraordinary deterioration in the physical condition of what had once been an extremely fertile region. Enormous weeds, of striking height and toughness, filled up many of the gardens and could be seen waving in the fields of wheat, corn, and sunflower seeds. Gone were the wheaten loaves, the succulent slices of lamb that had been offered for sale everywhere when I visited the Kuban Valley in 1924. At that time every Cossack settlement had its large number of fierce, snapping dogs, trained to guard sheep and cattle; now there was an almost ghostly quiet; the bark of a dog was never heard. "The dogs all died or were eaten up during the famine," was the general explanation of their disappearance.

He found, too, "a physical change in the population of the North Caucasus, where the Cossack element ha[d] been largely eliminated, whether from death [by starvation] or deportation, and a poorer but more docile class of peasant ha[d] taken its place."[67]

The Blockade of Peasant Migrants in 1933

By 1933 so many peasants had starved to death or taken flight that the Stalinist leaders took drastic action in order to keep as much of the grainland as possible in production (for the rest of the country as well as export) and to ease the clogging of roads and railways, as well as the flooding of large cities, by starving and begging peasant refugees. This problem was most acute, of course, where peasant production was greatest and peasant resistance was strongest, namely, the European Russian steppe of the Ukraine, the North Caucasus, and the Lower Volga. In December 1932 and January 1933 alone 85,217 peasants (9,213 families) left the Ukraine, nearly one-half of them individual farmsteaders and one-third kolkhozniks (and more than one-half of all of them from the oblasts of Kiev and Kharkov).[68]

In January 1933 the Party's Central Committee instructed the security agencies to implement measures for "the prevention of the exodus of starving peasants" (without special permits) from and between the chief grain areas, primarily the Ukraine and the North Caucasus, as well as (a month later) the

Lower Volga – the "mass exit of peasants 'for bread' to the Central Black Earth, the Volga, the Moscow Region, the West Region, and Belorussia" that was "undoubtedly ... organized by the enemies of Soviet power, SRs [Socialist Revolutionaries, quasi-Marxists who saw the peasants, not the workers, as the revolutionary class], and agents of Poland with the aim of agitating 'through the peasants' in the northern rayons against kolkhozes and generally against Soviet power."[69] The desire to prevent or lessen the spread of "anti-Soviet" and "anti-kolkhoz" sentiment was secondary, however; the primary reason was the need to exert more control over the mobility of the peasants of the chief grain areas in order to safeguard the agricultural workforce and hence production, as well as to curtail the spread of criminality and morbidity in the form of a multitude of desperate and often diseased (chiefly typhus- and dysentery-stricken), starving peasants.[70] Regardless, the measure – roadblocks/checkpoints (*kordony na dorogakh*) – doomed innumerable peasants to starvation.

The political and security authorities of the North Caucasus were ordered to "not allow the mass exit of peasants from the North Caucasus to other territories and their entry to the kray [of the North Caucasus] from the Ukraine," the same authorities of the Ukraine were ordered to "not allow the mass exit of peasants from the Ukraine to other territories and their entry to the Ukraine from the North Caucasus," and the same authorities of the Central Black Earth, the Moscow Region, the West Region, Belorussia, and the Lower and Middle Volga were ordered to "arrest those 'peasants' of the Ukraine and the North Caucasus stealing northward and, after the counter-revolutionary elements have been removed, ensconce the rest in their [original] places of residence."[71] Genrikh Yagoda (Enokh Iyeguda) – the de facto head of the OGPU at the time and yet another "old Bolshevik," shot in 1938 – was keen to oblige because, like his Kremlin masters, he saw the exodus as a "counter-revolutionary sally," the "best way of spreading counter-revolutionary and provocative rumours against kolkhozes and Soviet power" – that is, a political, not an agrarian, problem. Yagoda ordered his agents in the Moscow Region, the Central Black Earth Region, the West Region, the Lower Volga, the Middle Volga, and the Transcaucasus "to arrest forthwith all those stealing from the Ukraine and the North Caucasus, subjecting them to thorough screening," and "to confine all malicious counter-revolutionary elements in concentration camps and to return the rest to their [original] places of residence, sending those who refuse repatriation to the special settlements of kulaks in Kazakhstan." He also ordered his operatives "to erect pickets on all roads leading from the Ukraine and the North Caucasus" and the OGPU generally "to create cordons, especially around railway junctions, and to organize a systematic check of peasants travelling on the railways, immediately arresting all those arriving from the Ukraine and the North Caucasus."[72] Within three months of the initial decree 258,401 peasant fugitives (including 52,334 in the Central Black Earth, 47,217 in the North Caucasus, and 37,924 in the Ukraine) had been apprehended, of whom 230,633 (89 percent) were repatriated.[73] The blockade was abetted, incidentally, by another control measure – "passportization," which entailed the issuance of identity cards to Soviet citizens for travel and residence purposes but excluded the peasants, thereby immobilizing them and purging the large cities and industrial centres of transient peasants.

These draconian restrictions, however, were too late to sufficiently revitalize the peasantry of the Ukraine-North Caucasus-Lower Volga granary; too many peasants had already departed either that area or that life. So in 1933 and early 1934 kolkhozniks and demobilized Red Army soldiers resettled there – some on their own accord but most under state auspices. Three hundred families of kolkhozniks were shifted from the Moscow Region to a rayon in the Lower Volga, and an "absolutely secret" OGPU memorandum at the end of 1933 listed 105 echelons, totalling 38,504 former soldiers with 57 horses, 2,551 cattle, 2,800 "small stock" (including 440 rabbits), and 7,466 fowls, which had been relocated to places in the North Caucasus that had been forcibly emptied of those Kuban Cossacks and peasants who had "sabotaged" grain procurement.[74] This latter movement experienced a "number of shortcomings," however, including not enough uniforms, bedding, and money; long waits at loading points without sufficient provisions; transportation in unequipped and unsanitary boxcars; and decrepit housing (without doors, stoves, window glass) at their destinations – all of which prompted the migrants to return by flight (1,084 fled from the nineteen rayons of the Kuban).[75]

Most of the resettlers, however, went to the Ukraine, as the region having lost the largest number of peasants. And most of this resettlement was "organized," that is, sponsored by the state. The relocation plan for the "resettlement of kolkhozniks in the steppe rayons of the Ukraine" stipulated 41,300 families (7,500 from the Central Black Earth Region, 6,800 from the West

Region, 4,500 from Belorussia, 3,500 from Ivanovo Rayon, and 2,000 from Gorky Kray), plus 17,000 families of "unorganized" internal migrants (7,000 from Chernigov Rayon to Donetsk and Dnepropetrovsk Rayons, 5,000 from Kiev Rayon to Odessa, Dnepropetrovsk, and Kharkov Rayons, and 3,000 from Vinnitsa Rayon to Odessa Rayon).[76]

For many of both the voluntary and involuntary migrants the Ukraine did not prove to be a "promised land," despite their substantial privileges, for example, money for repairing khatas, the voiding of arrears on rural taxes, insurance payments, and obligatory deliveries of milk and meat to the state, and the halving of grain procurements.[77] A security service report at the end of the summer detailed their "desire to return" (*obratnichestvo*), which by then was called "massive."[78] Only about three-quarters of the migrants (43,100 families numbering 219,110 kolkhozniks, with 27,625 horses, 36,670 cows, and 60,000 "small stock") arrived in Donetsk, Dnepropetrovsk, Kharkov, and Odessa Rayons. Already in March the first returnees appeared at their former abodes in Belorussia and the RSFSR, and in June–July the trickle became a stream (by the middle of July, for instance, 15 percent of those who had migrated from the West Region – one thousand families – had returned). Most of the defaulters returned without their belongings and livestock. Their motivations for returning included underfunding and underfeeding; placement in unrepaired and unsuitable housing in the Ukraine; the unsympathetic and sometimes hostile attitude of the local Ukrainian authorities; the "grossest distortions" on the part of local Ukrainian rural workers, including illegal evictions of migrants from dwellings, the groundless penalizing and searching of migrants, their exclusion from kolkhozes and employment, the withholding of grain from migrants, and the taunting and assaulting of migrants; and, "in a number of rayons," the wounding and killing of migrants and the torching of their property, especially by "runaway kulaks or those returning from interrogation or deportation" to find their khatas occupied by migrants, many of whom then starved to death in 1934.

To supplant the migrants who did not remain, and to augment those who did, the authorities resorted to, literally, the rustication of urbanites. A Polish consular advisor wrote in July 1933: "For work in the fields all of the remaining able-bodied rural population (at most one-half of it remains, and at least 20 percent has died from starvation and disease), the army, and Party and Komsomol organs have been mobilized; and a mass of the urban population has been sent under duress to the villages – employees of governmental and communal organizations and students in higher and middle educational institutions; summer holidays have been temporarily cancelled."[79]

Employees were usually released for two weeks, during which they received all of their salary, plus two rubles a day and "meagre food," and those sent to the harvest lived in the fields.[80] Some fifty thousand were mobilized in Kiev and even more in Kharkov, according to a Polish military attaché.[81] The mobilization was so massive that it paralyzed life in the cities, as the Polish consulates in Kiev and Kharkov stated in a joint report in August:

> Establishments in Kiev are almost totally deserted, as most of their employees have been deployed to [agricultural] work; in establishments where 5 employees worked, only one remains. All factories and mills are closed. The civilian population is being registered in the streets, at the markets, etc. Long columns with bands and banners stretch along the streets to the railway station, and behind them stretch wagons with baggage. One gets the impression that these people will not be returning to Kiev soon. This [deployment] helps the Soviet authorities to further purge the cities [of undesirable elements] and makes it possible to permanently reinforce the depopulated villages with these elements. Some of those leaving the station in Kiev weep; they are alone, clutching a small bundle and taking the train to the fields, leaving their apartments to the mercy of fate. It should be added that theft is flourishing to an extraordinary degree in Kiev. The figures of completely weakened people are visible in the lines of those leaving [the city], and not much benefit will be derived from them during the harvest. Fifty such persons are needed to replace one sound rural toiler in the fields.[82] The labour of these echelons cannot last very long, since after several days they will have collapsed, and their transfer to other rayons for more work – given the awful state of railway transport – will not produce the desired results.[83]

Indeed, added the report, railway transport was "not fulfilling its task at all," and river transport was "in the same state," resulting in logjams of both labour and grain.[84]

The same report, entitled "The Situation in the Ukraine," faulted not only mobilization and transport but also shortcomings in what it termed the "organization of work," namely: (1) the recruits spent too much time walking to work (often ten kilometres) in the fields and back, so they were ordered to overnight in the fields, but on account of the misallocation of tasks they roamed the fields uselessly and did not fulfill their norms, and they could not cope with the work, which lasted from sunrise until late evening, because they were not used to it (e.g., their weakly bound sheaves came undone), so that generally more work was assigned to the resident peasants; (2) there was a "very great" shortage of tractors, mowers, binders, and threshers, which were in a "sorry state" of disrepair for want of spare parts, so that many of them "stood idle"; (3) the grain was delivered to receiving points "very slowly" because the kolkhozniks took their time, the roads were in a "sorry state," and the horses were too few and too weak, and the crop was subject to "an enormous amount of theft of kernels and spikes," despite the watching of the fields "rather closely" by many guards (who themselves sometimes stole grain);[85] and (4) upon leaving the cities for the villages the echelons of blue-collar and white-collar workers received a travel ration (usually three loaves of bread and one pud of flour each), all or part of which many of them left with their families in the hope that they would be fed upon reaching their destinations, where, however, they were obliged for the first few days to live on their ration, so some of them were already starving at the outset; moreover, their food norm was reduced for all who did not fulfill their fixed work norm – all of which enfeebled the workforce and reduced the harvest.[86]

Finally, at the end of July, Moscow ordered an "unconditional" halt to the "incorrect" mass mobilization of urban workers for harvesting in "all rayons of the Ukraine and some rayons of the North Caucasus and the Urals" because they had proven "completely unsuited to agric[ultural] work," and their absence from the cities was "wrecking the work of the factories." They were to be replaced with kolkhozniks and sovkhozniks as well as army recruits.[87] On the surface, however, little improvement was observable. In August, Polish consul Stanislaw Sosnicki toured the Ukraine by car and reported: "the impassable roads to the poor villages present a very sad picture of whole kilometres of uncultivated land and sown fields full of weeds, and the number of hands for reaping even these small crops is minimal."[88]

The Absolutely Worst Case: The Ukraine – The North Caucasus

Nevertheless, by the end of summer, according to a Polish diplomatic bulletin, the Soviet authorities had gained control of the "situation" in the Ukraine, owing to two factors: the "decisive and consistent policy of the Communist Party," enabling it "to break the passive resistance of the village [i.e., even more ruthless procurement] and to destroy the decentralizing nationalistic attitude of the Ukrainian intelligentsia [i.e., more Russification], and the unexpectedly successful results of this year's harvest [i.e., clement weather]."[89] The bulletin did not mention that at the same time, fortunately, Moscow's malignant agricultural policy was being moderated to enable the recovery, if only slowly and partly, of the bounty and the beauty of the great Eurasian steppe and the lives of its peasant cultivators and nomadic pastoralists.

EPILOGUE
THE 1928–34 FAMINE IN RETROSPECT

> In the people's memory collectivization remains as an unjust, cruel, and unwarranted punishment of the well-off peasantry that doomed millions of peasants to starvation.[1]
> – Angelina Kazmina-Borkbakka, *Russkoe schast'e: Semeinaia khronika stalinskikh vremen*, 17.

> The one thing I haven't gotten sick of is watching the wheat turn yellow. I've gone hungry so many times that the thing I love best is ripening grain, seeing the sheaves swaying in the wind. For me, it's as beautiful as the paintings in a museum are for you.
> – a babushka (elderly peasant woman), in Svetlana Alexievich, *Second-Hand Time*, 128–9.

> Hunger ... has the power to destroy the body, to cripple the soul, to annihilate millions of lives.
> – Vasily Grossman, *Love and Fate*, 540.

"It was one of the most terrible epochs in the history of Russia," flatly stated the Soviet theatre musician (and 1930s survivor) Yury Yelagin of the 1928–34 period of the great famine.[2] George Burrell went even further, declaring that "it will rank with the great infamous chapters of the world's history of man's inhumanity to man."[3] Certainly it was one of the grossest calamities of the three-quarters of a century of Russia's Soviet period, comparable to the battlefield slaughters and civilian casualties of the First World War (1914–18) and the Second World War (1939–45), Lenin's "Red Terror" of 1918–21, and Stalin's "Great Terror" of 1936–38. Three of these calamities occurred during the quarter-century (1928–53) of Stalinist tyranny – hence the recollection by one of the confidants of the poet Anna Akhmatova: "Stalin, Anna Andreyevna would say, is the greatest executioner that history has ever known. Compared to him, Genghis Khan and Hitler are just boys."[4] Or, as the full extent of Stalin's responsibility for the deaths of as many as 40 million people became more widely known in the 1990s, a black joke said that a future encyclopaedia would carry the following entry under the letter "H": "Hitler, a petty tyrant of the Stalin period."[5] To Solzhenitsyn, Stalin was simply the "Great Butcher."[6] And more generally Józef Czapski, a writer and painter who spent 1941–42 in the USSR in the Polish army of General Anders, wrote that the "extreme wastefulness and disregard for human life" that he observed there was "the normal Soviet attitude toward human beings" (at the same time that he remarked the generosity of ordinary Russians) – the necessary and somehow acceptable price of constructing and safeguarding Stalin's utopia.[7]

Of the human carnage wrought by Stalin and his minions (particularly Kaganovich and Molotov but others, too), at least 10 million victims – more than those of either the *Stalinshchina*, or Great Terror, of 1936–38 or the Nazis' Holocaust (Shoah) of 1941–45 – are attributable to the great famine,[8] which was not even officially acknowledged by the Stalinist leaders, who recognized only "provision difficulties." As an individual farmsteader asserted, "the famine took place on a huge scale," and "it squeezed hundreds of thousands of people with its foul hand, squeezed them to the last drop."[9] This disaster was neatly (and not accidentally) coincidental with both the collectivization of agriculture and the rationing of food[10] – respectively the solution to, and the result of, what the British Embassy rightly identified in 1932 as the Stalinist leadership's "most vital problem, that of feeding the people under socialism."[11] The consolidation of scattered peasant holdings under communal oversight into much larger and many fewer kolkhozes (chiefly) and sovkhozes under state control was implemented in order to secure returns that could be used to develop heavy industry through the purchase of foreign machines and expertise from capitalist countries in order, in turn, to enable the Soviet state to survive in a hostile capitalist world. Indeed, during the First Five-Year Plan (1928–32) and afterwards industry did develop very rapidly quantitatively (if less so qualitatively) and helped the country to survive the onslaughts of Nazi Germany and Imperial Japan a decade later. Molotov even went so far as to say: "I believe our success in collectivization was more significant than victory in World War II" because, "if we had not carried it through, we would not have won the war."[12]

This "success," however, as the perceptive and sympathetic Gareth Jones observed, was achieved "at the expense of profound suffering."[13] The equally observant William Chamberlin concurred:

> The Soviet Union during the last five years [1929–33] has undergone ... fundamental and sweeping changes ... The decisions of the Soviet leaders to drive forward the industrialization of the country at a feverish pace, to take away from the peasants the individual method of farming the land, to banish the last remains of private ownership and initiative from the economic life of the country, to institute a gigantic all-embracing system of centralized state economic planning ... all these changes were brought about with ... uncompromising and ruthless disregard of the human cost involved.[14]

This cost was paid – paradoxically, as others have noted[15] – chiefly by the peasants and the nomads, the very producers of food (grain and meat, respectively),[16] thanks to excessive output targets that they were unwilling or unable to meet and to ruthless procurement methods that they were ultimately powerless to resist. As the novelist Vasily Grossman has one of his characters recollect, "the peasants said that however hard they worked, they'd still have their grain taken away from them."[17] They were among the principal ingredients of Joseph Stalin's often-cited "meat grinder."[18] Not that the urban population had an easy time of it; at the height of the famine in 1932–33 in the large and the industrial cities – one and the same in many cases – the housing crisis (overcrowding in small and shared apartments; dilapidation from inferior construction and heavy use; infestation by vermin like rats, cockroaches, and lice; and inadequate heating from insufficient firewood) was worse, money was scarcer (from reduced salaries and wages, while most valuables had already been cashed at Torgsin), and consumer goods were few in number and low in quality (thanks to industry's preoccupation with producer goods). Urbanites were also going hungry and not infrequently succumbing to starvation; however, they were not starving to death in the millions like their compatriots in the countryside. The result of Stalin's "construction of socialism" was the destruction of peasant and nomadic society. As the son of a prominent Russian and Soviet historian declared, "industrialization ... was very necessary but not at any price."[19] That price was the derangement of agriculture, the impoverishment of the population, and widespread suffering, notably of the peasantry. As an avowed Social Democrat (Menshevik opponent of the Bolsheviks) told a visiting American expatriate in 1932, "one of the greatest crimes the Bolshevik government is committing is in the attitude it has taken toward the peasants. If anyone is suffering in Russia, more than all others, that is none other than the peasant."[20]

In the "war against the peasantry" the primary victims were usually the individual farmsteaders, that is, those peasants and nomads who, despite coercion, refused to submit to collectivization by joining the kolkhozes.[21] This bias demonstrates that the war was a class, or ideological, war, for to the doctrinaire Bolsheviks the peasants generally and the individual farmsteaders particularly (and above all the kulaks, of course) represented "capitalism in the countryside" (indeed, it could easily be deemed an occupational war as the Bolsheviks had little respect for either nomads and their primitive lifestyle or peasants, the "black people" – uneducated, coarse, and hidebound, emblematic of Russia's supposed "backwardness").[22] As Muggeridge concluded in the fall of 1932, "Soviet society is based on the lust of class hatred," and he noted in his diary: "the chief thing I have learnt from coming to Russia is the reality and the strength of class hate."[23] This class war primarily affected peasants and nomads, not mainly or solely Ukrainian peasants or Kazakh nomads, although they suffered the most in absolute and relative terms, respectively. The famine was a nationwide, not a regional, catastrophe – a Soviet, not just a Ukrainian or a Kazakh famine (indeed, it may well be that more Great Russian peasants than Ukrainian peasants or Kazakh nomads perished from starvation). The famine did not select its victims by ethnicity; peasants starved to death in all parts of the Soviet Union and nomads in several parts of Russian Turkestan. As the one-time Soviet diplomat Alexander Barmine recollected, the famine "raged in the Ukraine and in central asia [Kazakhstan]" but "was felt in very corner of the country."[24] Muggeridge agreed, reporting that "all the available evidence goes to show that conditions in the Upper, Middle, and Lower Volga regions are as bad as in the North Caucasus and the Ukraine; in Western Siberia they are little, if at all, better."[25] He was echoed by Victor Serge while witnessing the "nightmare": "famine comes to the Ukraine, the Black Lands [areas of *chernozyom*], Siberia, to all the Russian granaries."[26] The Russian and Georgian language and history specialist, Donald Rayfield, has written that by approaching the 1928–34 famine as more than simply a Ukrainian, or Kazakh, or even Soviet famine but as overwhelmingly a peasant and nomad famine, one can better comprehend the food crisis, especially through the voices of the victims – which in turn affords an antidote to the indifference, then and now, of the rest of the world to Stalin's "eradication of the Russian peasant."[27]

Nevertheless, not a few nationalistic Ukrainian Canadian, Ukrainian American, and Ukrainian historians insist that the rapacious requisition of grain under collectivization was deliberately and specifically aimed at the Ukraine as punishment for its nationalist/separatist tendencies. As evidence, they cite such testimonies as the following from Polish consul Jan Karszo-Siedlewski (intelligence codename "Mikado") in Kharkov in 1933:

> It is typical that this situation [the famine] applies not to the south of Russia as such but just to the Ukraine, for, if one crosses the northern boundary of the U[krainian] SSR, the picture changes radically. In the Central Black Earth Region, which from a climatic and economic standpoint differs little from the Ukraine, the situation of the peasantry is incomparably better. This [difference] is attested by the fact that the economic policy of the central government with respect to the Ukraine has been much more ruthless and predatory than in regard to the neighbouring regions of the R[ussian] SFSR, with the sole exception of the North Caucasus.[28]

However, compared with the Ukraine and the North Caucasus the Central Black Earth's chernozyom was much less extensive and its climate less droughty and more favourable to the growing of potatoes as a substitute foodstuff. Also, the region was closer to Moscow and its privileged food supply. And why include the North Caucasus, where more Great Russians (the plurality and perhaps even the majority of the kray's population in 1926)[29] than Ukrainians would suffer? Moreover, any deliberate starvation of the peasants would fuel, not foil, nationalism, which was the province of the intelligentsia, not the peasantry. Besides, according to the German consul in Odessa, Paul Rot, the number of supporters of Ukrainian nationalism was "still not significant."[30] The compilers of a collection of official Russian documents about nationalism/separatism show that Soviet policies of antinationalism and anti-separatism were inclusive and not directed solely against Ukrainians as such, although they did loom large in such policies simply because of their relative number (the country's second largest ethnic group) and their economic and political weight.[31]

Much of the misunderstanding surrounding this issue is attributable to the referencing of administrative (political) instead of environmental (natural) subdivisions, that is, the treatment of the southern European breadbasket as a complex of separate political units (the Ukraine, the North Caucasus, the Lower Volga) rather than as a single agricultural zone – the European Russian wooded and grassy steppe, whose portion west of the Volga was the country's chief granary and for this very reason was the chief target of collectivization, not because much of it happened to be occupied by Ukrainians.[32] Another source of misunderstanding was the tendency of Western, especially English-language journalists and travellers, to confine their excursions to, and observations of, the countryside during the great famine to the Ukraine and the North Caucasus and to neglect the rest of peasant and particularly nomad Soviet Russia (Andrew Cairns and Otto Schiller were exceptional in this respect, but they were scientists whose reports were not publicized). They did so mainly because the former were closer and easier to access, with more and better links by road and rail to their base in Moscow; also, their readership included numerous expatriate Ukrainians in Canada and the United States but few, if any, Great Russians from the Volga Valley or Western Siberia, let alone Kazakhs (and a few of the journalists, such as Harry Lang, William Chamberlin, and Maurice Hindus even had familial connections with the European Russian south). By so doing most reporters provided their readers (including politicians and academics) with a skewed picture of the famine, a picture that portrayed Ukrainians especially as deliberate and exclusive victims of the famine (although the best reporters, like Gareth Jones and William Chamberlin, were aware of the famine's national scope – and said so).[33] Stalin's policies – political, economic, social, cultural – were aimed at *all* opponents, regardless of ethnicity, religion, language, or occupation. They did not target solely or even mostly Ukrainians; to posit otherwise is special pleading for particular victimhood – at best chauvinistic myopia, at worst a callous affront to the memory of non-Ukrainian famine victims. Chauvinistic Ukrainians have nationalized the famine, appropriating it as theirs only, and – even worse, as Viktor Kondrashin, probably the most knowledgeable and authoritative Russian specialist on the famine, has asserted – they have exploited it as an ideological instrument in a campaign of Russophobia.[34] And there were not simply "several" or "multiple" famines in the USSR in 1928–34; there was not just a "Ukrainian *holodomor*" or a Kazakh "catastrophe" but a "Soviet *golodomor*,"[35] with the same basic cause – agricultural policy, principally collectivization and especially its implementation. It was Solzhenitsyn's "slaughterous collectivization" or "peasant plague."[36] Only the famine's intensity varied from place to place. The entire Soviet Union, not just the Ukraine or Kazakhstan, suffered a "harvest of sorrow"; the Apocalypse's Third Horseman rode his black horse throughout the USSR, grassland and woodland, lowland and highland. Or, as a victimized independent homesteader expressed it, "I do not consider famine years to be those when starvation rages only in individual regions rather than throughout the USSR."[37] The 1928–34 Soviet famine, then, serves as a salutary example of the dangers of seeing a subject of passionate interest out of its spatial context, in this case the USSR as a whole (and even that national disaster ought to be viewed in the global context of hunger and starvation in the world's urban slums and rural wastes stemming from economic depression and severe drought in the "hungry thirties").

Nor was the famine deliberate, or at least there is no available evidence to prove that the regime implemented collectivization with the intention of generating starvation. It would simply have been self-defeating to wilfully deplete the very producers of grain, which was required as a vaunted export and a domestic staple. As historian Stephen Kotkin has stated flatly, "the famine was not intentional."[38] Nevertheless, the regime did not hesitate to punish the peasants lethally for their resistance to excessive requisitions. As Germany's consul in Kiev, Karl Walther, informed his Moscow embassy: "There is a conviction among the countryside population that although the Soviet authorities have not initiated the hunger on purpose, it [they] nevertheless used it as a means to carry out its [their] own plans to break the resistance towards the system and the aversion towards collective work."[39] And towards the end of the famine in the summer of 1934, Otto Schiller, probably the most knowledgeable foreign investigator of Soviet agriculture, wrote: "If it should not be assumed that the government incited the famine intentionally, in any case it can be claimed that consciously, or by disregarding the consequences, it did not undertake all the steps that it could to prevent the mass deaths."[40]

The famine was long-lasting as well as nationwide. Many people – both Ukrainian peasants and Kazakh nomads – were starving to death as early as 1928 and as late as 1934, not just in 1932–33, which was simply the apogee of starvation. The length of the famine raises the question: Why did the Bolsheviks maintain such a clearly deadly policy for so long? The answer seems to be found in their absolute certainty that they were pursuing the correct line for the sake of the survival of the world's first socialist state (Stalin's "socialism in one country" rather than Trotsky's "world revolution") in the face of predatory capitalist neighbours[41] – in other words, their doctrinal dogmatism.[42] As cocksure ideologues the Marxists knew they were right, and they would brook no dissent, especially since they felt alone and under siege from the rest of the world. As the Constructivist poet Eduard Bagritsky (Dzyubin) (1895–1934) wrote:

We look around and all we see
Are enemies – no friend.
Yet if the times demand we lie, then lying it shall be –
And if they do demand we kill, killing will know no end.[43]

Even more to the point was the profuse mea culpa of one of the keen Twenty-Five Thousander enforcers, Lev Kopelev, who acknowledged late in life that, like the rest of his generation, "I firmly believed that the end justified the means. Our great goal was the universal triumph of Communism, and for the sake of that goal everything was permissible – to lie, to steal, to destroy hundreds of thousands and even millions of people, all those who were hindering our work or could hinder it, everyone who stood in the way." He elaborated:

That was how I had reasoned, and everyone like me, even when I did have my doubts ... when I saw what "total collectivization" meant – how they "kulakized" and "dekulakized," how mercilessly they stripped the peasants in the winter of 1932–33. I took part in this myself, scouring the countryside, searching for hidden grain, testing the earth with an iron rod for loose spots that might lead to buried grain. With the others, I emptied out the old folks' storage chests, stopping my ears to the children's crying and the women's wails. For I was convinced that I was accomplishing the great and necessary transformation of the countryside; that in the days to come the people who lived there would be better off for it; that their distress and suffering were a result of their own ignorance or the machinations of the class enemy; that those who sent me – and I myself – knew better than the peasants how they should live, what they should sow and when they should plow.

Despite what he did and what he saw – "women and children with distended bellies, turning blue, still breathing but with vacant, lifeless eyes ... corpses in ragged sheepskin coats and cheap felt boots" – Kopelev did not lose his mind or commit suicide, he did not curse those who had sent him, and he did not lose faith in the cause. As he added, "I believed because I wanted to believe," and "when we saw the base and cruel acts that were committed in the name of our exalted notions of good, and when we ourselves took part in those actions, what we feared most was to lose our heads, fall into doubt or heresy and forfeit our unbounded faith."[44] Kopelev was echoed by an elderly and unrepentant communist, who expostulated to Svetlana Alexievich: "We [*sovoks*, those who adhered to Soviet values and attitudes] wanted to build a new world where everyone would be happy. We thought that it was possible. I sincerely believed in it! ... The future we died and killed for."[45]

The infallible and inflexible Bolsheviks grievously miscalculated, however, with collectivization, failing to foresee the acute dissent of the peasants and the strength of their resistance. The Stalinist leadership figured that, in order to compel the peasants to accept the kolkhoz, it was necessary only to crush their most successful members – the kulaks – but it was the majority of the peasants, not just the kulaks, who became the chief danger to the regime. Coerced into the kolkhozes, the stubborn peasants chose "weak weapons" as their form of resistance: a negligent attitude to kolkhoz labour and the use of livestock in their own interest (hence the selling and killing of horses, oxen, and cows on a huge scale – which in turn drastically lowered the quality of field work) as well as mass migration from the villages to the cities and

"Italyankas" (work-to-rule actions) by those who stayed.[46] Such reactions stemmed, too, from the unfair system of payment for the peasants' kolkhoz labour; in 1930, despite its bumper harvest, they worked "for peanuts" (*za palochki*, literally "for sticks") and again in 1931, while for their workdays they received crumbs, which did not suffice until the next crop.[47] And the responsibility for what Robert Conquest called this "terror-famine" lay directly with Stalin and his inner circle of Molotov, Kaganovich, and Mikoyan – all of whom were to die in their beds without any reckoning, as part of the country's refusal to come fully to grips with the atrocities of the Stalin years, including not only the great famine but also the Great Terror (when, a Soviet defector said, "the Soviet government became a gigantic madhouse")[48] and the carnage of the Second World War.[49]

Finally, the great famine was a tragedy because it was unnecessary, or at the very least the very high toll was unnecessary. The country's goal of rapid industrialization could have been moderated with lower grain exports; the Russian historian of collectivization, Victor Danilov, has calculated that the amount of grain exported in 1932 alone would have fed 7 million people under a normal harvest (as many as starved to death in 1932–33) and kept 14 million alive under a harvest failure (more or less the range of possibly all famine deaths in the 1928–34 period).[50] Indeed, during the famine grain was not even the chief export. At its height in 1932–33, in terms of ruble value, the leading Soviet exports were timber, petroleum products, textiles, furs, and grain – in that order (and the leading importers were – by far – Great Britain and Germany, each with from one-sixth to one-fifth of the total ruble value).[51] Exports of timber, petroleum products, textiles, and furs could have been increased and grain decreased, as was indeed the case between 1932 and 1933, when the regime relented and curtailed the amount of exported grain by one-half and augmented the amount of exported textiles by two-fifths.[52] Or, even more radically, wrote Eugene Lyons, the Bolsheviks could have used industrial capital, gold reserves, or foreign credit to import foodstuffs, appealed to the charity of the outside world, or backpedalled to private farming, but instead they went to great lengths to downplay the starvation and thereby save face for the "almighty plan."[53] Another – and more doctrinally palatable – alternative to the export of grain for hard currency was Torgsin (although it entailed a substantial loss of cultural heritage). The state's profit on

Torgsin's trading was 6 million rubles in 1931, 49 million rubles in 1932, and 106 million rubles in 1933.[54] In the first half of the 1930s the worth of the valuables received by Torgsin was sufficient to cover 20 percent of the cost of the Soviet Union's imports of industrial equipment, technology, and raw materials; in 1933 alone – at the famine's zenith – the worth of valuables received sufficed to pay one-third of the cost of industrial imports, and the agency's income exceeded the amount of foreign currency obtained from the country's export of grain, timber, and oil.[55] The fact that the Stalinist leaders chose not to relent on grain exports – except in 1933, for fear of rendering the peasants and nomads dysfunctional – attests to their doctrinaire willingness to sacrifice millions of their citizens for "the cause."

Regardless of the Soviet leadership's alternatives, the West remained complicit in the tragedy. It preferred commercial collaboration to principled opposition. If foreign markets had taken less Soviet grain, or none at all, Soviet peasants would have been left with enough food, feed, and seed grain for survival. The demand in the sputtering Western capitalist economies for profitable employment, production, and consumption, however, was irresistible, given the privation of the Great Depression, which trumped sympathy and humanity. Western political and business leaders were aware of the famine and their own role in it, and their embarrassment or even their shame possibly tempered the famine's coverage in American, British, French, and German media.

Even after the famine ended in 1934 the hardships of the peasants and nomads did not cease. Drought wreaked a harvest failure in 1936, creating the "grain crisis" of 1936–37 that encompassed "a whole series of regions" of the country and that could have been worse than that of 1932–33, for in 1936 the harvest was smaller than that of 1931 and of 1932, procurements were higher, and the stock of grain in the villages was lower. However, only "several thousand," not millions, of peasants starved to death, for several reasons: the harvest failure was preceded by a normal harvest in 1935 and followed by a record harvest in 1937; the peasants had already recovered somewhat from the trauma of forcible collectivization with the help of their personal plots and local markets; food loans were granted on a "much larger scale" than in 1932–33; the great famine had taught the regime a lesson that mass starvation damaged not only the peasantry but the economy; and by 1936 the kolkhoz was securely established, and most of its opponents had yielded or fled or been deported or executed, leaving mostly loyal proponents who this time were not blamed by the authorities for the starvation.[56] Nevertheless, the kolkhozniks – residual sharers in kolkhoz output – remained pessimistic and cynical, saying after the bumper harvest of 1937: "even if this year every ear [of grain] yields a pud, we will still get nothing."[57]

Meanwhile, Stalin had launched a bloody purge of the Party that also engulfed the peasants. Indeed, Gareth Jones believed that "it was among the hungry masses" that he found the "real reason" for the outbreak of Stalin's reign of terror in 1935 – "throughout the country a feeling of revolt and of hatred of the Communists that Stalin can only crush by terror."[58] From 1 October 1936 to 1 July 1938, 700,000 to 800,000 peasants were arrested by the OGPU's successor, the NKVD, and about half of them were shot.[59] What one of Stalin's bodyguards called the "black years" (1936–38) of the Great Terror (and he lived to recall them to his grandson)[60] were followed by the horrific ravages of the Second World War, which in turn were immediately followed by the drastic drought of 1946–47 – all of which unduly affected the peasantry. They had to await Stalin's death in 1953 and his succession by Khrushchev for some relief. By then a quarter-century had passed since the onset of what novelist Vasily Grossman called the "savagery of general collectivization."[61]

The great famine left a lasting legacy – the centrality of food in Soviet life (much as the "hungry thirties" taught a generation of Americans and Canadians to not waste food) – and no wonder, given the fact that during twenty of the twenty-five years of Stalin's regime (from 1928 until 1948) there was continual starvation in all or much of the country and among all or many of its citizens. In her book about the Soviet culinary experience the author Anya von Bremzen and her mother, resident witnesses to the challenges of everyday existence under Stalin, Khrushchev, Brezhnev, and Gorbachev, noted that the want of food helped to undermine the Tsarist regime of Nicholas II in 1917 and the Soviet regimes of Khrushchev in 1964 (following a meagre grain harvest in 1963 and his misguided campaign for growing corn) and Gorbachev (the prohibitionary "mineral [water] secretary," who, incidentally, lost two uncles and an aunt to the famine) in 1991.[62] But, they added, "even in calmer times … the daily drama of putting a meal on the table trumped most other concerns" and "food anchored the domestic realities of our totalitarian state, supplying a shimmer of desire to a life that was mostly drab, sometimes absurdly comical, on occasion unbearably tragic, but just as often naively optimistic and joyous."⁶³ More than a little of the "unbearably tragic" was attributable to the great famine of 1928–34.

The Chilean filmmaker Patricio Guzmán, in *Nostalgia for the Light* (2010) and *The Pearl Button* (2015), the first and second parts of his epic trilogy contrasting the natural beauty and human horrors of his native Chile, has wondered if water has a memory, with the corpse-laden South Pacific waters of the long coast of his country remembering the innocent indigenous and political victims of oppression on the part of ruthless colonizers and presidents, particularly General Pinochet. If he is right, then perhaps soil has a memory, too, and the bone-studded and blood-stained "black earth" of Russia's Eurasian steppelands remembers the equally innocent peasant and nomad victims of Generalissimo Stalin's tyranny. If so, long may it remember them – and we as well.

GLOSSARY

apparatchik: a Communist Party or government official
ataman or *hetman*: a Cossack chieftain
aul: a Kazakh migratory encampment
babushka: an elderly woman or grandmother
bai: a better-off head of a Kazakh nomadic clan
batrak: a hired hand
bednyak: a worst-off, or poor, peasant
bezdorozhye: "roadlessness"
bezprizornik: a waif
Cheka: shorthand for the All-Russian Extraordinary Commission (Bolshevik secret police until 1922)
chernozyom: "black earth" soil
Comintern: the Communist International
derevnya: a village
desyatina: a land measure of 2.7 acres or 1.09 hectares
dzhut: ice-covered pasture
"eastern regions": Asiatic Russia
edinolichnik: an individual farmsteader
gorod: a city or town
Gulag: shorthand for the Main Administration of Corrective Labour Camps and its regional network of camps
hectare: a metric measure of area equal to 2.47 acres
holodomor: a killing by starving
izba: a peasant house
khata: a Ukrainian house
khutor: an individual farmstead or Cossack hamlet
kibitka: a Kazakh nomad's tent
kishlak: a Central Asian village
kolkhoz: a collective farm

Komsomol: shorthand for the Young Communist League
kray: a territory
kraykom: a Party kray committee
kulak: literally, a "fist"; figuratively, a well-off, or thriving, peasant
lager: a penal camp
lishenets: a disenfranchised person or "non-person"
mgla: dust storms
mir: a pre-1917 village commune of peasants
muzhik: a peasant
Narkomtorg: shorthand for the People's Commissariat of Trade
Nepmen: private traders under the New Economic Policy
oblast: a province
Politburo: shorthand for the Political Bureau of the Central Committee of the Communist Party of the Soviet Union
politotdel: a political department
Povolzhye: the Volga Valley
pud: a measure of weight equal to 36 pounds or 16⅓ kilograms
rayon: a district
rasputitsa: the "impassableness" of spring break-up or autumn rains
Region: a political-economic region
samogon: homebrew
smychka: the solidarity between the workers and the peasants
sovkhoz: a state farm
Sovnarkom: acronym of the Council of People's Commissars
srednyak: a middling, or average, peasant
stanitsa: a large Cossack village or garrison
sukhovei: a hot, dry wind
suslik: a ground squirrel
Torgsin: shorthand for the All-Union Association for Trade with Foreigners on the Territory of the USSR
Transcaucasus: the three SSRs of Georgia, Armenia, and Azerbaijan on the south side of the Caucasus Mountains
veliky dzhut: a "great disaster"
yurt: a Kazakh felt tent
zazhitochnik: a better-off, or prospering, peasant
zemlyanka: a makeshift shelter

ABBREVIATIONS

ARA: American Relief Administration
ASSR: Autonomous Soviet Socialist Republic
CPSU: Communist Party of the Soviet Union
GOELRO: State Commission for the Electrification of Russia
GOSPLAN: State Planning Commission
MTS: machine-tractor station
NEP: New Economic Policy of 1921–28
NKVD: People's Commissariat of Internal Affairs (successor to the OGPU in 1934)
OGPU: United State Political Directorate (Bolshevik secret police from 1922)
RSFSR: Russian Soviet Federated Socialist Republic
RTS: repair-technical station
SR: Socialist Revolutionary
USSR: Union of Soviet Socialist Republics

NOTES

Prologue

1 The Union of Soviet Socialist Republics, or USSR, also known more informally as the Soviet Union, was not proclaimed until 1922 (and lasted until 1991), but in this book the two terms are used to denote the country after the Bolshevik coup d'état of October 1917.
2 "Famine" is an admittedly problematic term. It connotes an extreme scarcity of food that results in an excess mortality from starvation or hunger and related diseases. But how "extreme" must the scarcity be – in terms of mortality, extent, or duration – in order to qualify as a "famine"? During the Soviet food want of 1928–34 people were starving to death every year, and more people were hungry and starving in more places in 1932 and 1933 than in 1928–31 or 1934. The anti-Marxist diarist Ivan Shitts recorded in mid-1928 that "news from the provinces [spoke] bluntly of starvation" (Shitts, *"I strakh, strakh bezumnyi,"* 49), and the pro-Marxist witness Victor Serge observed that, "beginning with 1929–1930, the famine [spread] over the immense country like leprosy," and that "in 1932–1933 the famine [was] general in the countryside of Russia" (Serge, *Russia Twenty Years After*, 170, 178).
3 Khrushchev, *Memoirs*, 2:303. Khrushchev added that the chronic problem of hunger was illustrated by the satirical anecdote about a camel being unable to walk from Moscow to Vladivostok on the Pacific because it would get no farther than Sverdlovsk (Yekaterinburg) in the Urals before being eaten (356). Moreover, as an American woman noted during a visit to Moscow, Belorussia, and the Ukraine in September of 1933, it was more than a famine of food generally or bread especially: "There was hunger for milk as well as for bread, for kerosene as well as for butter, for paper as well as for meat, and even for cloth to make shrouds for the dead" (Lang, "Soviet Nightmare," 257–8). Incidentally, the title of Lang's chapter refers to the "nightmare" of the "strangled mass of the Soviet people" (259).

4 The percentage of state grain purchases derived from such "new lands" rose from about one-third in 1953 to about one-half thereafter, and the RSFSR (primarily southern Siberia) accounted for one-half to two-thirds of the increase and Kazakhstan (primarily northern Kazakhstan) the rest (Zelenin, *Agrarnaia politika*, 103). This augmentation of wheat output, incidentally, allowed planners to replace a good deal of the wheat acreage in the European Russian steppe with fodder crops such as corn and sugar beets to boost the lagging livestock sector and put more meat, milk, and eggs on Russian tables (and, in the process, Khrushchev's beloved Ukraine lost its role as Russia's traditional breadbasket).

5 Although these three adjectives are used interchangeably in the literature, an important distinction should be kept in mind. The outcome of any human action can be construed as "man-made" (i.e., not a "natural" action or an "act of God" such as a tornado), deliberate or otherwise, but "organized" implies a purposeful (i.e., "planned") outcome.

6 These have been the predominant interpretations (especially before the collapse of the USSR at the beginning of the 1990s), based upon selective documents and selective eyewitnesses. This special pleading has resulted in a veritable holodomor industry. For example, see: Applebaum, *Red Famine*; Carynnyk, Luciuk, and Kordan, *Foreign Office*, xvii–lxi; Commission on the Ukraine Famine, *Oral History Project*; Commission on the Ukraine Famine, *Report to Congress*; Conquest, *Harvest of Sorrow*; Dolot, *Execution by Hunger*; Graziosi, "Uses of Hunger"; Graziosi, Hajda, and Hryn, *After the Holodomor*; Hryn, *Hunger by Design*; Hunczak and Serbyn, *Famine in Ukraine*; Isajiw, *Famine-Genocide in Ukraine*; Klid and Motyl, *Holodomor Reader*; Kulchytsky, *Famine of 1932–1933 in Ukraine*; Kurlyiw, *Holodomor in Ukraine*; Luciuk and Grekul, *Reflections*; Madden, *Holodomor*; Marples, *Holodomor*; Rudnytskyi, Levchuk, Wolowyna, and Shevchuk, "Famine Losses"; Serbyn and Krawchenko, *Famine in Ukraine*; and even a periodical, *Holodomor Studies* (plus several films [e.g., *Famine-33*, a 1991 drama by Oles Yanchuk, and *Bitter Harvest*, a 2017 romance by George Mendeluk], a couple of plays, and an opera). With care these works – notably their primary sources – can be of value, but, as Ben Jonson has a character say in *Catinline's Conspiracy* (act 3, scene 2), "the dignity of truth is lost with much protesting."

Opponents of these interpretations have been labelled "deniers" (à la Holocaust deniers), for example, Tottle (a long-time labour union organizer and journalist), in *Fraud, Famine and Fascism*, who does not, in fact, deny the occurrence of the famine (which he ascribes to a variety of causes, not just Stalinist excesses and mistakes) but does reject the notion of intentional starvation designed to exterminate the Ukrainian people (in his view a notion advocated by Ukrainian ultranationalists, particularly those who collaborated with the German invaders during the Second World War, and based upon fraudulent evidence that was nevertheless publicized by conservative newspapers controlled by the "yellow journalism" publisher William Randolph Hearst, who opposed the Soviet Union's entry into the League of Nations).

Russian historians, who did not publish on the Soviet Union's famines until after the collapse of the USSR, have responded with largely contrary views (and Mironin, in *'Golodomor' na Rusi*, 163, even asserts that Stalin was "not to blame" for the famine, which he attributes to the "chaos" of the mixed economy of state and private ownership under the New Economic Policy (hereafter NEP) of 1921–28 and the "urgent measures" required to resolve the country's "usual geopolitical impasse" of facing enemies on both its western and eastern borders). Their interpretations have benefitted from the easier access (for themselves and foreign scholars) from the early 1990s to the pertinent archives (including those of the Communist Party of the Soviet Union [hereafter CPSU], the People's Commissariats [federal ministries], and security services such as the OGPU [1922–34], the successor to Lenin's bloody Cheka) as well as from the publication from the mid-1990s of a number of voluminous documentary collections about Stalin's agrarian policies, notably: Resis, *Molotov Remembers*; Danilov and Berelowitch, "Les documents"; Lih, Naumov, and Khlevniuk, *Stalin's Letters to Molotov 1925–1936*; Danilov, Manning, and Viola, *Tragediia sovetskoi derevni*; Berelovich and Danilov, *Sovetskaia derevniia*; Danilov, Khlevniuk, and Vatlin, *Kak lomali NEP*; Davies et al., *Stalin-Kaganovich Correspondence*; Bratiushchenko, *Kogda arkhivy otkryvaiut sekrety*; Pokrovskii, *Politbiuro i krest'ianstvo*; Kotova, *Kollektivizatsiia*; and Kondrashin, *Golod v SSSR 1929–1934*.

A number of Russian (and a few Western) scholars have exploited these primary sources to very good effect in the form of authoritative and comprehensive works on collectivization generally and the food crisis particularly. See especially Ivnitskii, *Golod 1932–1933*; Klimin, *Rossiiskoe krest'ianstvo nakanune "velikogo pereloma"*; Klimin, *Rossiiskoe krest'ianstvo v pervyi period sploshnoi kollektivizatsii*; Klimin, *Rossiiskoe krest'ianstvo v zavershaiushchii period sploshnoi kollektivizatsii*; Kondrashin, *Khlebozagotovitel'naia politika*; and Kondrashin, *Golod 1932–1933 godov*. Recently, regional treatments grounded in the documents have begun to appear (e.g., Krasil'nikov, Salamatova, and Ushakova, *Korni ili shepki*, and Rakov, "*Derevniu opustoshaiut*").

Recently, Russian researchers have accused their Ukrainian counterparts of "politicizing" the famine by construing it as exclusively or primarily Ukrainian and deliberately genocidal (see Chichirin, *Fenomen ukrainiskogo "goloda"*; Chichirin, *Mif i pravda*; Kondrashin, *Sovremennaia rossiisko-ukrainskaia istoriografiia*; Prudnikova and Chichirin, *Mifologiia*; and Vaniukov, *Golodomor*). To counter this special pleading, in 2009 Russia's Federal Archival Service held a press conference, distributed a documentary collection (Antipova, *Golod v SSSR 1930–1934 gg.*), and subsequently placed on the internet a partially bilingual DVD collection of downloadable documents ([Federal Archival Agency], *Famine in the USSR 1929–1934 New Documentary Evidence*) and another assortment of downloadable documents ([Federalnoe arkhivnoe agentstvo], *Kollektsiia dokumentov GARF, RGAE, RGASPI, TSAFSB Rossii*).

Thus, it appears that most, if not all, of the most informative and trustworthy archival documents on the food crisis are now available in print for the use of researchers. Other underused primary sources include British, German, Italian, Polish, and Vatican diplomatic and intelligence reports and memoirs (e.g., Zlepko, *Der ukrainische Hunger-Holocaust*; Graziosi, "'Lettres de Kharkov'"; Shishkin, *Rossiia v gody "velikogo pereloma"*; [Bullard], *Inside Stalin's Russia*; Bruski, "Bol'shoi golod"; Bednarek et al., *Holodomor*; and McVay and Luciuk, *Holy See*); agronomic reports by Australian, Canadian, and German specialists (notably Cairns, *Soviet Famine, 1932–33*; and Schiller, "Agriculture in the Soviet Union in the Year 1931," as well as three articles by Schiller in the *Daily Telegraph*); recollections by Soviet blue-collar and white-collar eyewitnesses (particularly Shitts, *Dnevnik*; Mankov, "Iz dnevnika"; Hellbeck, *Tagebuch aus Moskau*; Hellbeck, "Fashioning the Stalinist Soul"; Hellbeck, *Revolution on My Mind*; Lugovskaya, *I Want to Live*; Prishvin, *Dnevniki*; Zima, "Golod 1932–1933 godov"; Gorokhova, *Mountain of Crumbs*; Vodopianova and Kondrashin, "... Nasha derevenia opustoshena do poslednego zernyshka"; Zhober [Jobert], *Russkaia sem'ia "Dans la tourmente déchaînée ..."*; Cherepnin, *Dnevnik lishentsa*; Gaidukov, *Aleksei Vasil'evich*

Oreshnikov, vol. 2; Shaporina, *Dnevnik*, vol. 1; Kazmina-Berkbakka, *Russkoe schast'e*; and Zhober [Jobert], *Kogda zhizn' tak deshego stoit* …); letters and memoirs of peasant and nomad victims (particularly Danilov and Ivnitskii, *Dokumenty svidetel'stvuiut*; Nusinbaev and Zhienfaliev, *Golod v Kazakhskoi stepi*; Kovalev, *Golosa krest'ian*; Litvinenko and Riordan, *Memories of the Dispossessed*; Leshuk, *Days of Famine, Nights of Terror*; Vossler, *We'll Meet Again*; Goichenko, *Skvoz raskulachivanie i golodomor*; Shaiakhmetov, *Silent Steppe*; Milova, *Izgnanniki s svoei strane*; Bondar and Matveev, *Istoricheskaia pamiat'*; Gritsensko, *Rossiiskaia oi Sovetskaia derevnia*; Lyssyvets, *Raconte la vie heureuse* …; Nurtazina, "Great Famine of 1931–1933 in Kazakhstan"; Storella and Sokolov, *Voice of the People*; [Izmailov], *Dnevnik*; Shvydkov, *Moi put'*; and Khripunov, *Dnevniki*); accounts by a variety of visitors and travellers, including writers, reporters, tourists, dignitaries, foreign technicians, left-wing sympathizers, physicians, and others (e.g., [Witkin], *American Engineer in Stalin's Russia*; Wettlin, *Fifty Russian Winters*; Gerstein, *Moscow Memoirs*; Leder, *My Life in Stalinist Russia*; Volters, *Spetsialist v Sibiri*; Gheith and Jolluck, *Gulag Voices*; Gamache, *Gareth Jones*; and Jones, "General Survey of Agricultural Conditions in the USSR"); and weather records (e.g., Borisov, *Climates of the USSR*; Lydolph, *Climates of the Soviet Union*). All of these primary sources – a veritable embarrassment of riches – enable more detailed, more balanced, and more reliable, as well as more dispassionate, interpretations of the Stalin regime's "war against the peasants." They are not flawless, of course; for example, reports from embassies and consulates could be kept confidential or moderated by superiors, and their authors often did not venture far afield, while "stories" by journalists could be censored by the authorities or tempered by the journalists themselves or their editors (as Muggeridge's were by the *Guardian*'s editor) for fear of expulsion. And, of course, not all observers had a sufficient knowledge of Russian or agriculture or travelled widely enough to be able to understand what was happening in the Soviet countryside.

7 I know of no up-to-date bibliography of the English-language literature, which is simply too prolific to list here. For recent bibliographies of Russian (mainly) and Ukrainian publications, see Kondrashin, *Golod 1932–1933*, 2nd ed., 21–78; Kondrashin, *Sovremennaia rossiisko-ukrainskaia istoriografiia*, 456–66; and Stepanov, *Otechestvennaia istoriografiia*, here and there throughout.

The famine has also been fictionalized, most famously by Vasily Grossman, the popular Second World War frontline reporter, in his *Everything Flows* (for another translation, see Grossman, *Forever Flowing*). See also Koval, *Krushilovka* – "a peasant son's tale of collectivization and the famine of 1930–1933" – and Stadnyuk, *People Are Not Angels*.

8 The only other general account of the famine is the late Robert Conquest's *Harvest of Sorrow: Soviet Collectivisation and the Terror-Famine* (1986), which was published just before the collapse of the USSR and thus before the publication of many volumes of official documents and a large body of secondary literature on the famine as well as more than a few memoirs. It is also preoccupied with the famine in the Ukraine. R.W. Davies and Stephen Wheatcroft's *The Years of Hunger: Soviet Agriculture, 1931–1933* (2004) is also a comprehensive account but intended for specialists, not laypeople; also, it examines much more than the famine per se and is largely limited to the years 1932–33, not the entire famine period.

9 Ozerov, *Portraits without Frames*, 51, 122.
10 Rayfield, *Stalin and His Hangmen*, 190.
11 Ciliga, *Russian Enigma*, 498.
12 Serge, *Russia Twenty Years After*, 178.
13 A famine may not be purely "natural," of course, because even if its root cause does lie in the physical environment (drought, flood, frost, etc.), it may also have been induced by human action and/or inaction, such as deforestation, mismanagement, and so on.

Also, some writers, notably Amartya Sen, an Indian economist, have adopted the anthropocentric view – not uncommon in the case of both economists and historians – that famines are caused not by "Mother Nature" but by humankind, who – at least in democratic societies with various rights – can always find food by buying, trading, sharing, or migrating (see Sen, *Poverty and Famines*), and if they fail to do so, then society, not nature, is at fault. In his words: "Starvation is the characteristic of some people not *having* enough to eat. It is not the characteristic of there not *being* enough to eat." And, as one-time communist supporter and *Christian Science Monitor* and *Manchester Guardian* correspondent William Chamberlin declared following his trip through the starving Ukraine and North Caucasus in September 1933:

> Is there any recorded case in history where famine – not poverty or hardship or destitution, but stark famine, with a toll of millions of lives – has occurred in a democratically governed country? Is it conceivable that the famine of 1932–1933 could have taken place if civil liberties had prevailed in the Soviet Union, if newspapers had been free to report the facts, if speakers could have appealed for relief, if the government in power had been obliged to submit its policy of letting vast numbers of the peasants starve to death to the verdict of a free election? The countless graves of the humble and obscure famine victims, the peasants of Ukrainia and the North Caucasus, of the Volga and Central Asia, are to me the grim, unanswerable refutation of the specious Communist contention that freedom of speech and the press and political agitation is only humbug by which the bourgeoisie tries to delude the masses. (Chamberlin, *Russia's Iron Age*, 377–8)

However, besides ignoring the fact that often in the past the trigger, or basic cause, of famine has been drought or flood or some other natural action, this thesis assumes that democratic societies are sufficiently endowed in natural and human resources to be able to store or buy or trade or share or move.

14 Kondrashin, *Golod 1932–1933*, 2nd ed., 97. See also Borisenko and Pasetskii, *Tysiacheletniaia letopis'*, especially 236–478; Dando, *Geography of Famine*, chap. 9; Dando, "Man-Made Famines"; Kahan, "Natural Calamities"; Milov, "Prirodno-klimaticheskii factor"; and Pashuto, "Golodnie gody v Drevnei Rusi."

15 Kalinin, *Izbrannie proizvedeniia*, 1:306. The country's worst famine took place in 1601–03; it cost the lives of as much as one-third of the Russian population and may have contributed to the overthrow of the tsar himself, Boris Godunov, and helped to create the hiatus of the "Time of Troubles" and the advent of the Romanov dynasty in 1613.

16 Kondrashin, "Golod v krest'ianskom mentalitete," in Danilov and Milov, *Mentalitet i agrarnoe razvitie Rossii*, 115, 117; Kondrashin, *Khlebozagotovitel'naia politika*, 188.

17 Chandler, *Portable Platonov*, 22. Perhaps it was for this reason (and others) that peasant mothers were inured to the frequency of child death – as

recounted to a foreign correspondent's Russian wife by a peasant neighbour in their apartment building, a woman who had had seven children, all but one of whom had died:

> When a child died in a village ... it was as natural as when day turns into night. One was not even supposed to cry when a baby died. Why was that? Was it because we were told that our lives were in God's hands and that we were not to question His deeds? Or because children didn't cost money like a horse or a cow, and one could get more of them? Or because children dying young had always been as much part of a peasant's life as a drought or a storm? ... My own mother said that it is forbidden to cry over a newborn baby when it dies. (Fischer, *My Lives*, 67–8)

18 See Kondrashin, *Golod 1932–1933*, 2nd ed., 100, 101; Robbins, Jr, *Famine in Russia 1891*; Sims, Jr, "Crop Failure of 1891"; and Wheatcroft, "1891–92 Famine." For eyewitness accounts, see Reeves, *Russia Then and Now*; Stadling and Reason, *In the Land of Tolstoi*; and Anonymous, "Starving on the Volga." For a map of the famine, see Anonymous, "Map of Russia."

19 Although the drought was quite widespread, it seems to have struck the Volga Valley the hardest. A teacher and archivist in the Volga German Republic astride the middle Volga, Peter Sinner, wrote in his autobiography that the villagers starved to death in 1921–22 like flies in the autumn, with the republic losing one-third of its population to starvation, disease, and emigration (Walters, *Wir Wallen Deutsche Bleiben*, 167, 189). For a documentary collection on the famine in Samara Oblast in the Middle Volga, see Galygina et al., *Golod v Srednevolzhskom krae*, vol. 1.

20 The toponym "Ukraine" (literally, "frontier") is used herein with the definite article, as was generally the case in both academic and popular discourse before the demise of the USSR. Thereafter a concerted and successful campaign was conducted – mainly by Ukrainian nationalists, particularly those of the diaspora – to have simply "Ukraine" written and spoken in English. The grounds are unclear, although they likely have something to do with the fact that, in the three Eastern Slavic languages (Russian, Ukrainian, and Belorussian), the definite and indefinite articles are implicit, not explicit (which they definitely are in English, the language of this book). Whatever the reasons, to

the ear of this native speaker "Ukraine" without the definite article does not ring true and sounds broken and awkward (as do "Yukon" or "Congo" or "Sudan" without it). To sound right in English without "the," it needs to become "Ukrainia," as in "Argentina" vis-à-vis "the Argentine" (conversely, but for the same reasons, "The Gambia" is objectionable). Similarly, Ukrainian nationalists insist upon using "Kiyiv" in place of the commonly recognized "Kiev" – which makes as much sense as Great Russians insisting upon using "Moskva" in place of "Moscow" or "Sankt-Peterburg" in place of "St Petersburg" (which they do not).

21 For a map of the famine, see Anonymous, "Map of the Famine Area."
22 See [Vladimirov], *Russia Accursed*, for a contemporary Russian painter's depictions (plus photographs) of the tribulations of this period.
23 Ivanova, *Vospominaniia Nikolaia i Mariny Chukovskikh*, 104. In 1921 in the Volga basin in May, June, and July (the heavy-growth period of spring grain), rainfall was less than 10 percent of normal (United States, *Russia Relief*, 4).
24 Both Reds and Whites (i.e, communists and monarchists) took part. As a Volga peasant told the touring Herbert Hoover, the US secretary of commerce, "The reds took all they could get, and then the whites came along and took what was left" (United States, *Russia Relief*, 32). The one-time noblewoman Edith Sollohub (Sologub) asked a Bolshevik convert in 1919, "how do you like Communism, and he replied: 'Well, Communism is not so bad as long as there are things to be taken. But when everything has been taken – we won't need Communism anymore'" (Sollohub, *Russian Countess*, 217).

The requisitioning was effective, with the state acquiring 108 million puds of grain in 1918–19, 213 million puds in 1919–20, and 284 million puds in 1920–21 [1 pud = ca. 36 pounds] (Veselovskii, *Problemy nashei zhizni* 1:141), but the policy decimated and alienated the peasants. The diehard communist politician and diplomat Vyacheslav Molotov, one of the principal architects of Stalinism, described and defended this policy in his rambling memoirs: "Balking at nothing, the state took from the peasants what it needed ... there was no other way out ... there was no food for the army, and we had to feed the workers ... the army was large and we couldn't exist without it." He added that the "peasants tolerated this for a while, but once the [civil] war was over [1921], the uprisings began," so the Bolsheviks had to "save the cause and carry out the reforms of the NEP, that is, make concessions to the peasantry," for "Lenin said we have reached the point with the peasants where if we do not make certain concessions to them, they will drive us from power" (Resis, *Molotov Remembers*, 151).

25 The peasants mounted several formidable uprisings, notably the "Antonovshchina," the Blue Army of peasants under Alexander Antonov in Tambov Oblast in 1918–21 (see Aleshkin and Vasil'ev, *Krest'ianskaia voina v Rossii v usloviakh povoennogo kommunizma*; Aleshkin and Vasil'ev, *Krest'ianskie vosstaniia v Rossii v 1918–1922 gg.*; and Sennikov, *Tambovskoe vosstanie, 1918–1921*). For a general treatment of peasant uprisings against the Bolsheviks during the civil war of 1918–22 (and its resultant shaping of Stalin's policy towards the peasants), see Kondrashin, *Krest'ianstvo v gody Grazhdanskoi voiny*.

26 Tsvetaeva, *Earthly Signs*, 28n.

27 Sorokin, *Leaves from a Russian Diary*, 282.

28 Ibid., 257–8.

29 Ibid., 285, 286–7.

30 Notably in Petrograd, where the famine's impact was observed by H.G. Wells, the versatile English writer who visited "starving Russia" in the fall of 1920. "Most" of the city's populace, he wrote, was "nearly starving," and since his first visit in 1914 its death rate had nearly quadrupled and its birth rate had almost halved (Wells, *Russia in the Shadows*, [3–5]). Mrs Sollohub found that "by summer 1918 the [city's] food problem had become really acute," such that by the next year "some people, if they saw a [starving] horse falling in the streets, would wait for it to die, and then run to cut meat from the carcass" (Sollohub, *Russian Countess*, 184, 224). The starvation soon produced a crop of urban waifs, what Hoover described as "dirty, half naked, lousy, half starved, mere skeletons with helpless, hopeless, hunted looks in their eyes" (United States, *Russia Relief*, 26).

Incidentally, Wells's opinion of the Russian peasant victims was unsympathetic: "The peasants," he scoffed, "are absolutely illiterate and collectively stupid, capable of resisting interference but incapable of comprehensive foresight and organisation" (Wells, *Russia in the Shadows*, [71]) – a view not unlike that of most Russians on both the political right and left.

31 Ibid., 232.

32 Solzhenitsyn, *Gulag Archipelago*, vol. 1, bk. 1:342–3, 344.

33 Unless otherwise stated, all emphasis that occurs within quotations is in the original.

34 Negretov, *V.G. Korolenko v gody revoliutsii i grazhdanskoi voiny*, 415–16.
35 Ibid., 16. On a like note Sorokin found in the spring of 1920 that "on all sides one hears such comments" on the Bolshevik regime as: "When there was a Czar we had plenty of *svin'ia* [pork], now there is Lenin and we haven't even *konina* [horsemeat]" (Sorokin, *Leaves from a Russian Diary*, 238).
36 One pud (40 funts), the old Russian unit of weight, equals 36.11 pounds (16.38 kilograms).
37 Gritsenko, *Rossiiskaia i sovetskaia derevnia*, 207–8.
38 Okunev, *V gody velikikh potriasenii*, 832–3.
39 Sorokin, *Leaves from a Russian Diary*, 288. To date scholarship in English on the famine of 1921–22 has been preoccupied with American relief (see Edmondson, "Politics of Hunger"; Engerman, *Modernization*, chap. 6:103–23; Fisher, *Famine in Soviet Russia*; Golder and Hutchinson, *On the Trail of the Russian Famine*; Long, "Volga Germans and the Famine of 1921"; Patenaude, *Big Show*; especially and even chauvinistically, Smith, *Russian Job*; Tsikhelashvili and Engerman, "Amerikanskaia pomosh'"; and Weissman, *Herbert Hoover*; also Sorokin, *Leaves*, 282, 288). A domestic relief agency, the All-Russian Committee for Aid to the Starving, was formed in the summer of 1921 but was terminated by Lenin after five weeks (see Topolianskii, *Vserossiiskii komitet*). For the confrontation between the atheistic Bolshevik state and the Russian Orthodox Church (and other faiths) over the famine, see Zima, *Golod 1921–1922 godov*.
40 The Russian Symbolist poets arose in the 1880s from the Symbolist movement in European art. They tried to evoke feelings rather than depict reality. Their movement flourished in the first decade of the twentieth century, and Alexander Blok and Andrei Bely became their leading members.
41 Duranty, *I Write*, 128, 130. For a study of typhus, or spotted fever, during the early years of Soviet power, see Mironova, *Velikaia epidemiia*. From 1918 to 1923 *sypniak* ("little rash"), as it was called colloquially, infected some 25 million citizens, thousands of whom (including Stalin's first wife, Ekaterina Svanidze) perished (ibid., 43). Typhoid (*briushnoi tif*), or typhoid fever, was a bacterial infection (*salmonella enterica*) fostered by unsanitary and unhygienic conditions, principally food or water contaminated by faeces. Lenin lost his sister, Olga, to the disease in 1891.
42 [Bullard], *Inside Stalin's Russia*, 85.
43 See Sorokin, *Man and Society*, 68.

44 Danilov, "Dinamika naseleniia SSSR za 1917–1929 gg.," 246; Kondrashin, *Golod 1932–1933 godov*, 1st ed., 319, 323, 2nd ed., 497; Klimin, *Rossiiskoe krest'ianstvo*, 1:19–20; Williams, "Confidential Circular"; and Williams, "My Journey." Duranty's estimate is corroborated by one demographic analysis that produces a toll of 6 to 7 million, with eleven epidemic diseases accounting for about half of the deaths (Adamets, "Famine in Nineteenth- and Twentieth-Century Russia," 163, 171).

45 Mikhailov, *Great Disaster*, 290.

46 Tsvetaeva, *Earthly Signs*, 71.

47 Fainsod, *Smolensk*, 41–3. The "time" refers to the aptly named "Time of Troubles," the interregnum between the death of the last tsar of the Rurik dynasty in 1598 and the ascension of the first tsar of the Romanov dynasty in 1613, a *hiatus horribilis* marked by foreign intervention, short-lived pretenders to the throne, rebellion, famine, and plague.

48 Poliakov, *Golod v Povolzh'e*, 10, 669–71 (see also his *Pervyi sovetskii golod*, 1:66, where, after dating the famine from 1919 to 1925, he ranks it as the first of the "three Soviet golodomors" of the first half of the 1920s, the first half of the 1930s, and the mid-1940s). In 1926 both a Soviet magistrate and a Soviet ambassador's wife told the mercurial Romanian writer Panait Istrati (1884–1935), Romain Rolland's "Maxim Gorky of the Balkans" (because of his years of vagabondage among the masses), that there were an estimated 400,000 to 600,000 ragamuffins in the Soviet Union (Istrati, *Russia Unveiled*, 24). These unfortunates were observed in Moscow in the mid-1920s by a "former person" (Sergei Golitsyn, a one-time nobleman who managed to survive in the Soviet Union until his natural death there in 1989): "By night the gangs of orphaned *bezprizorniki* (homeless children) kept themselves warm around burning pieces of asphalt in metal drums and huddled for shelter in the foundations of the unfinished buildings of Kazansky Station. Clad in rags, with wind-burned faces and shining eyes, they wandered about the streets in search of prey, slipped through the crowd in shops or on the trams, or stood in groups beating time on old spoons as they intoned songs and collected coins in their caps" (Golitsyn, *Memoirs*, 130 [subtitled *The Golitsyn Family in Stalin's Russia*, this memoir was written "for the drawer," i.e., in secret, during the last decade of the author's life and finished just a month before his death]).

49 Khrushchev, *Memoirs*, 2:310. He also recollected that he had reported the famine to Stalin, who refused to believe his account (ibid., 4–7).
50 See Dando, "Soviet Famine"; Ellman, "1947 Soviet Famine"; Ganson, *Soviet Famine of 1946–47*; [Khrushchev], *Khrushchev Remembers*, chap. 7; Kondrashin, *Golod 1932–1933 godov*, 1st ed., 324–5; Veselova et al., *Golod v Ukraïni 1946–1947*; Volkov, "Drought and Famine of 1946–47"; and Zima, *Golod v SSSR 1946–1947 godov*. For a map of the famine, see that from the *Russian Economic Bulletin* (no. 9) online at https://upload.wikimedia.org/wikipedia/commons/c/c6/Famine_en_URSS_1933.jpg.

For the context of state food supply during what Russians came to call the Second Great Patriotic War (the first being that of Napoleon's invasion of 1812), but excluding the famine of 1946–47, see Goldman and Filtzer, *Hunger and War*.
51 For a more detailed comparison of the three famines of 1921–22, 1932–33, and 1946–47, see Kondrashin, *Golod 1932–1933*, 2nd ed., 496–511.
52 For some voices of this little-known famine, see Alexievich, *The Unwomanly Face of War*; and Alexievich, *Last Witnesses*, here and there throughout, especially the former. A recent compilation of memories of wartime famine in the rear lines in the middle Volga Valley is Matlin, comp., *Golod 1941–1945 gg.*; and Matlin, *Ustnie rasskazy*.
53 In 1953, for example, just over 31 million tonnes of grain were procured but 32 million tonnes were consumed, so the state reserve had to be tapped (Brezhnev, *Virgin Lands*, 65). The metric, or long, tonne equals 2,204.6 pounds (1,000 kilograms), compared with the imperial, or short, ton of 2,000 pounds (907.2 kilograms).
54 Khrushchev, *Memoirs*, 2:311, 312.
55 Brezhnev, *Virgin Lands*, 62, 63.
56 Khrushchev, *Memoirs*, 2:312–13, 322–5. Years later Leonid Brezhnev, who succeeded Khrushchev after having made his name in the "new lands" project, would say that the extensive route to agricultural improvement via the new lands had been quicker and cheaper than the intensification route via higher yields and better breeds (Brezhnev, *Virgin Lands*, 69).
57 Another example was the grandiose "Great Plan for the Transformation of Nature" (1948), which, among other things, entailed the planting of a vast network of shelterbelts in order to protect crops from desiccating winds in

the steppe – where, because of insufficent precipitation, trees did not grow naturally.

In this regard Stalin's daughter Svetlana observed that her father's endless changes to his country retreat meant that "he was unable merely to contemplate nature; he had to transform it." He intended, it seems, to transform not only the population into the new ideal man of *homo sovieticus* but also the country itself into a new communist Garden of Eden.

58 Hence Khrushchev's nickname of *kukuruznik*, "corn man." For a general study of his corn plan, see Hale-Dorrell, *Corn Crusade*.
59 Resis, *Molotov Remembers*, 346, 347. However, the non-black earth was much less fertile than the black earth of the new lands; on the other hand, the corn program faltered because of insufficient summer humidity in southern European Russia as well as the disincentives of centrally planned and government-controlled agriculture.
60 Brezhnev, *Virgin Lands*, 20–1.
61 Tsentral'noe statisticheskoe upravlenie, *Sel'skoe khoziastvo SSSR*, 160.
62 Zelenin, *Agrarnaia politika*, 103.
63 Brezhnev, *Virgin Lands*, 138; Khrushchev, *Memoirs*, 2:345; Tsentral'noe statisticheskoe upravlenie, *Sel'skoe khoziastvo SSSR*, 162–3. Consequently, whereas before the launch of VILP (the Virgin and Idle Lands Program) often more winter than spring wheat was produced in the country, afterwards 50 to 100 percent more spring wheat was grown because the new lands were too dry and too cold to produce the snow cover that was necessary for fall-sown winter wheat. The latter is more dependable and more productive than spring wheat, yielding about twice as many centners per hectare, but varieties of spring wheat are generally harder and more suited to the making of bread (Tsentral'noe statisticheskoe upravlenie, *Sel'skoe khoziastvo SSSR*, 161).
64 Khrushchev, *Memoirs*, 2:345.
65 Ibid., 2:328–33.
66 Brezhnev, *Virgin Lands*, 134.
67 Khrushchev, *Memoirs*, 2:332.
68 Rudenko, *Zasukhi v SSSR*, 50.
69 Talbot, *Khrushchev Remembers*, 127, 129–30.
70 The pendulum principle was actually invoked in the summer of 1928, the first year of collectivization, by M.M. Volf, the head of the agricultural department of GOSPLAN, who stated that "a good harvest in Kazakhstan would

compensate for [a] crop failure in [the] Ukraine" (Tauger, "Grain Crisis or Famine?," 152, citing *Visty*, 24 July 1928, 5). At that time, however, little grain was grown in Kazakhstan, and action on this notion had to await the death of Stalin in 1953 and the "thaw" of his eventual successor, Khrushchev, in 1956, when it became safer to float fresh ideas, or, as the latter put it, "the locks had come off people's tongues" (Khrushchev, *Memoirs*, 2:337, see also 320). In the meantime Soviet climatologists had presumably been aware of the phenomenon (and probably pre-revolutionary climatologists, too), but it took Khrushchev to act on it, wittingly or not. In his memoirs he hints at his awareness of the principle, saying, "We too were dependent on the weather, that is, on favorable climatic conditions coming together in one year or another and in one region or another. Ours is a huge country, and inevitably in some places there will be a lot of rain and in other places dry spells" (ibid., 338, see also 325, 340).

71 Medvedev, *Soviet Agriculture*, 167, 173, 175. Another Russian historian, in his monograph on Khrushchev's agrarian policies, makes no mention at all of the pendulum effect (but he does castigate Lysenko for insisting that Kazakhstan's virgin lands be ploughed deeply, thereby causing disastrous dust storms [Zelenin, *Agrarnaia politika*, 92]). Leonid Brezhnev, in his rather vain and overstated account of his own role in VILP, also says nothing about the pendulum principle (see Brezhnev, *Virgin Lands*).

72 In the 1970s and 1980s the USSR was the world's foremost importer of grain (Dronin and Bellinger, *Climate Dependence and Food Problems*, [xv]). The imports were bought with the petrodollars earned from the export of oil and gas from the new petroleum fields in Western Siberia.

Chapter One

1 Adamets, "Famine in Nineteenth- and Twentieth-Century Russia," 177.
2 One of the "endless number" of "anecdotes" (black jokes) circulating in the summer of 1933 held that the acronym OGPU stood not for the Obyedinyonnoe Gosudarstvennoe Politicheskoe Upravelenie (United State Political Directorate) but for *O, gospodi! Pomogi ubezhdat'* (Oh, good Lord! Help me to flee) or for *Ubezhish – poimiut, golovu otrubiat* (Run – they will catch you and chop off your head) (Mankov, "Iz dnevnika," 151).
3 Stalin, *Works*, 13:160.

4 Carynnyk, Luciuk, and Kordan, *Foreign Office*, doc. 7:82–3.
5 [Bullard], *Inside Stalin's Russia*, 21. According to official figures, the food supply peaked in 1926 (Osokina, *Our Daily Bread*, 3).
6 Chamberlin, *Confessions*, 67, 111.
7 Lyons, who rated Chamberlin "the best-informed and least sensational of my American colleagues in Moscow," said that he could think of no more apt description. "Iron symbolizes industrial construction and mechanization. Iron symbolizes no less the ruthlessness of the process, the bayonets, prison bars, rigid discipline and unstinting force, the unyielding and unfeeling determination of those who directed the period. Russia was transformed into a crucible in which men and metals were melted down and reshaped in a cruel heat, with small regard for the human slag" (Lyons, *Assignment*, 147).
8 Ibid., 177–82.
9 Osherowitch, *How People Live in Soviet Russia*, 27–8. For the second anecdote, see ibid., 28–9.
10 Most of the peasants were placed in the kolkhozes, where they became residual sharers in output. On the so-called state farms (the "sov" prefix actually means "soviet," not "state") the peasants became salaried workers, paid in cash and kind – hence the sovkhozes were dubbed "factories in the fields" and "wheat factories." Sovkhozes were larger in scale and fewer in number than kolkhozes, and they were established especially on the margins of cropped or grazed districts where the climatic and pedologic conditions were less conducive to productive agriculture, and they were sometimes operated as experimental stations.
11 Shvydkov, *Moi put'*, 27. This remark, incidentally, may have been a pun on *tsep'* (chain) versus *tsep* (flail).
12 Lopatin and Lopatina, *Kollektivizatsiia i raskulachivanie*, doc. 103:319.
13 Ibid., doc. 3:27–8. In fact, there were even some cases of kolkhozes being headed by bednyaks, who were illiterate and unskilled (ibid., doc. 26:103–4).
14 Ibid., doc. 109:388.
15 Ibid., doc. 110:341.
16 Osherowitch, *How People Live in Soviet Russia*, 103.
17 Lyons, *Assignment*, 97, 99.
18 As a Russian ethnographer has noted, to the peasants "bread was almost sacred" (Berdinskikh, *Rus' krest'ianskaia*, 59), a sentiment that was echoed by one of them in his diary: "Without bread life is impossible" ([Izmailov], *Dnevnik*, 1:626). Bread's role as the staff and stuff of life was impressed upon

the author of this book when he was a *stazhor* (post-graduate student) at Moscow State University in 1964–65, eating at cafeterias, and usually choosing a bowl of soup but not always choosing bread, whereupon the server would invariably ask with a mixture of concern and puzzlement, "khleba ne nado?" (You don't need any bread?). Soviet workers boasted that they could breakfast on nothing more than a half to a whole kilogram of bread, and in 1935 – which saw a bumper harvest – a touring Australian official observed that Russians were "enormous bread eaters," consuming from two to three times as much as his compatriots (Osokina, *Our Daily Bread*, 3; Hawker, *An Australian*, 57). Especially rye ("black") bread was prized, so much so that in prerevolutionary times most of Russia's arable land was sown to rye, rendering the country a "kingdom of rye" (Goldstein, *Kingdom of Rye*, 9).

19 Shitts, *Dnevnik*, 31, 50; see also 30. Ivan Shitts (1874–1942), a "former person," was a versatile writer who sent his diary clandestinely to an old friend (a Slavicist) in France in the early 1930s.
20 Osokina, *Our Daily Bread*, 26.
21 Danilov, Manning, and Viola, *Tragediia sovetskoi derevni*, 3, doc. 116:317, 318, 318–19.
22 Watt, *British Documents*, 12, doc. 60:135, doc. 63:140.
23 Lievan, *British Documents*, 9, doc. 71:164, doc. 84:206.
24 Lyons, *Assignment*, 100.
25 Utley, *Lost Illusion*, 90.
26 Lyons, *Assignment*, 158. Such anecdotes would not, presumably, have been appreciated by the Party's devotees for, as Chamberlin experienced, the two essential qualities of revolutionaries were an "intolerance [of dissent] and [an] absence of any sense of humor" (Chamberlin, *Confessions*, 55).
27 Ibid., 148.
28 Osokina, *Our Daily Bread*, 30.
29 Ibid., 26.
30 Ibid., 30.
31 Ibid.
32 Jarman, *Soviet Union*, 3:633; Littlepage and Bess, *In Search of Soviet Gold*, 67. Bess, incidentally, succeeded Chamberlin as the *Christian Science Monitor*'s Moscow correspondent upon the latter's departure in 1934. Littlepage himself gained so much favour with Stalin that he was allowed – exceptionally – to leave the country at the height of the latter's Great Terror.
33 As hunger and starvation increased, so did the use of bogus food cards; in

just March alone in 1932 in Magnitogorsk, the new "steel town" in the Urals, the authorities seized more than eight thousand cards that had been issued, Gogol-like, to "dead souls" – that is, deceased persons (Sevost'ianov et al., "Sovershenno sekretno," vol. 10, pt. 1, doc. 31:116).

34 Lyons, *Assignment*, 181. Note the illogical inference that Russians cannot be Jews or vice versa.
35 Lievan, *British Documents*, 9, doc. 97:220.
36 Zhober, *Russkaia sem'ia "Dans la tourmente déchaînée ...,"* 311, 365, 366.
37 Lievan, *British Documents*, 9, doc. 86:207, 208.
38 Scheffer, *Seven Years*, 16.
39 Antipova et al., *Golod v SSSR*, doc. 42:86–92; Kondrashin, *Golod v SSSR*, 1, doc. 2:60–3. All of the letter writers were investigated and punished.
40 Littlepage and Bess, *In Search of Soviet Gold*, 61, 63. Littlepage (1894–1948) called the campaign of agricultural collectivization the "Second Communist Revolution," aimed at the peasants, nomads, and private traders – that is, the economic revolution as opposed to the political revolution of 1917.
41 Lievan, *British Documents*, 9, doc. 99:225.
42 Shishkin, *Rossiia v gody "velikogo pereloma,"* 166, 167.
43 Watt, *British Documents*, 9, doc. 139:299.
44 Lievan, *British Documents*, 9, doc. 139:298.
45 Shitts, *Dnevnik*, 144, 145.
46 Soups have long been one of the most nutritious and delicious mainstays of the diet of the Eastern Slavs, that is, the Russians, Ukrainians, and Belorussians (the one-time terminology of Great Russians, Little Russians, and White Russians, respectively – as in the tsar's official designation of "Emperor of All the Russias," Great, Little, and White – has fallen out of fashion because it was seen to rank Russians higher than Ukrainians, although it connoted population numbers and political and economic weight, not cultural ranking, and politically confused White Russians with the Whites who opposed the Reds during the 1918–21 civil war).
47 Ashmead-Bartlett, *Riddle of Russia*, 32, 33, 34, 125, 126–7, 127, 128, 129, 129–30.
48 Cherepnin, *Dnevnik lishentsa*, 36.
49 Lievan, *British Documents*, 9, doc. 139:298.
50 Jarman, *Soviet Union*, 3:633; Lievan, *British Documents*, 9, doc. 159:323.
51 Shaporina, *Dnevnik*, 1:88.
52 Cherepnin, *Dnevnik lishentsa*, 67.

53 Shaporina, *Dnevnik*, 1:94.
54 Beal (1885–1964) was a Massachusetts millworker and an organizer for the National Textile Workers, a communist labour union that called a famous (or infamous) strike at the Loray Mill in Gastonia, North Carolina, in 1929 over wretched working conditions. The strike, like most at the time in the United States, was violently suppressed by the authorities, and it ended in deaths (including vigilante killings) and a mistrial. The strikers were retried and sentenced to long jail terms but the indicted vigilantes were released; Beal and several others jumped bail and took refuge in the USSR. Following his disillusionment there, Beal returned to the United States (where he was befriended and supported, incidentally, by Eugene Lyons) and was imprisoned but was pardoned in 1942.
55 Beal, *Proletarian Journey*, 227, 231, 232, 239.
56 Kondrashin, *Golod v SSSR*, vol. 1, bk. 1, doc. 141:281–8.
57 Beal, *Proletarian Journey*, 254. His words echo the catchphrase "starving itself great," an oxymoron coined by Moscow's American correspondents.
58 Antipova et al., *Golod v SSSR*, doc. 1:30–1, doc. 2:33, doc. 3:34–7, doc. 4:38–41, doc. 5:42–5, doc. 6:46–7, doc. 7:48–50, doc. 9:57–8, doc. 10:51–6 , doc. 11:75–6, doc. 12:77; Berelovich and Danilov, *Sovetskaia derevnia*, vol. 3, bk. 1, docs. 116–19:354–72; Danilov, Manning, and Viola, *Tragediia sovetskoi derevni*, 2, doc. 174:473–8, doc. 191:530–6; [Federal Archival Agency], *Famine in the USSR*, docs. 2, 4, 8; Vaniukov, *Golodomor*, doc. 2:12–14, doc. 4:18–22, doc. 7:25–9, doc. 9:35–6, doc. 10:37–57.
59 [Izmailov], *Dnevnik*, 86.
60 Khrushchev, *Memoirs*, 1:35.
61 As we shall see, not a few of the Bolshevik leaders and their loyalists favoured aliases, dating from their conspiratorial days as an underground movement; the aliases, like the de rigueur tunics, also lent them an activist political cachet.
62 Kondrashin, *Golod v SSSR*, vol. 1, bk. 1, doc. 147:297–300.
63 Two years later, at Stalin's personal invitation, Gorky returned from his Italian exile and edited a grotesque literary whitewash of the building by some 125,000 exiled convicts – thousands of whom perished – of the Belomor (White Sea) Canal (officially the Stalin White Sea-Baltic Sea Canal), a 240-mile (386-kilometre) route intended to circumvent the longer seaway around North Cape (but doomed to failure by shallow draught) and to rehabilitate

"enemies of the people" (see Gorky et al., *Belomor*). One of the contributors to the anthology, the writer and literary theorist and critic Victor Shklovsky, later said that the project was "more horrific than the war [First World War]" (Gerstein, *Moscow Memoirs*, 39).

64 Osokina, *Our Daily Bread*, 54, 55.
65 Jones, "My Russian Diary."
66 Utley, *Lost Illusion*, 115. Winifred (Freda) Utley (1898–1978) emigrated from England to the USSR after marrying a Russian economist employed by Arcos, a Soviet trading firm in England. In 1936 she fled her adopted country with her son after her husband was arrested and sentenced to five years in a labour camp at Vorkuta, where he was executed by firing squad in 1938 for leading a hunger strike. Freda moved to the United States, where she became a politically controversial writer.
67 Bednarek et al., *Holodomor*, doc. 56:189.
68 [Bullard], *Inside Stalin's Russia*, 38.
69 Ibid., 39.
70 Davies et al., *Stalin-Kaganovich Correspondence*, doc. 2:54.
71 Antipova et al., *Golod v SSSR*, doc. 19:100–1.
72 Malysheva and Poznansky, "Golod na iuge Zapadnoi Sibiri," doc. 1:74, 75. The report of January 1932 stressed the situation's political repercussions:

> In recent months with respect to the kray's [Western Siberia's] harvest-failure districts there has been an acute shortage of not only food but also seed grain, as well as instances of excesses in the conduct of grain procurement, and the political mood of some strata of the peasantry in these districts – not only on the part of the individual farmsteaders but also the kolkhozniks – has worsened appreciably. At present this [mood] has not yet changed the generally positive political situation in the kray, but it is already being reflected in a general discontent, moods of panic, and mass flight from the rayons to the cities, and these feelings will undoubtedly intensify in proportion to the aggravation of provision difficulties. At the same time, there has been a revival of anti-Soviet activity on the part of counter-revolutionary cadres. (Ibid., 74–5)

73 [Izmailov], *Dnevnik*, 1:540n2.
74 [Bullard], *Inside Stalin's Russia*, 37.

75 Beal, *Proletarian Journey*, 275.
76 Ibid., 284, 291. Beal added that, so extreme was the despair over living and working conditions, "all over Russia the workers were engaged in a great spontaneous campaign of silent sabotage" (289). So when the authorities blamed production shortcomings on "wreckers" and "saboteurs," their accusations may not have been totally baseless.
77 Koestler, *Invisible Writing*, 68.
78 Fischer, *My Lives*, 35.
79 Zhober, *Russkaia sem'ia*, 441; Zhober, *Kogda zhizn' tak deshego stoit* ..., 40, 97.
80 Chamberlin, *Confessions*, 145. Stalin told Kaganovich that Mikoyan was "bumbling and disorganized" – hardly assets for a commissar of supply during a famine (Davies et al., *Stalin-Kaganovich Correspondence*, doc. 46:158).
81 Osokina, *Our Daily Bread*, 77.
82 Gorokhova, *Mountain of Crumbs*, 129.
83 Ibid., 128.
84 Herman, *Coming Out of the Ice*, 37. Herman (1915–1985), whose memoir was ghostwritten, went to the Soviet Union because his father was one of the three hundred Ford Motor Company workers from Detroit with communist sympathies who were sent to Gorky (formerly Nizhny Novgorod) on the upper Volga River on a three-year contract to help build a Ford factory. A gifted athlete, in 1934 he set the world record for the highest parachute jump from 24,000 feet (7,300 metres) and became known as the "Lindbergh of Russia," but he refused to renounce his American citizenship, and in 1938 he was arrested for "counter-revolutionary activities" and spent the next eighteen years in the Gulag. Upon his release he was not allowed to return to the United States until 1976, and two years later he filed a lawsuit for $10 million against the Ford Motor Company that remained unresolved at the time of his death. For an account of the general context of Herman's experience – "the never-before told story of Americans lured to Soviet Russia by the promise of jobs and better lives, only to meet tragic ends" – see Tzouliadis, *Forsaken*.
85 Koestler, *Invisible Writing*, 68. A Soviet boy later recollected that "people in these lines got to know one another and had worked out a system for keeping each other's place so that they could be in several lines at the same time" (Konstantin, *Red Boyhood*, 58). The political epiphany of the Hungarian-born, Austrian-educated, British-naturalized, Jewish Koestler (1905–1983)

started during his Soviet tour and climaxed with *Darkness at Noon* (1940), wherein an Old Bolshevik, Rubashov, is purged by the very apparatus that he helped to create under "Number One" (Stalin).

86 Burrell, *American Engineer*, 12.
87 Fischer, *My Lives*, 33.
88 Commission, *Report to Congress*, 421.
89 More than half of the items sold by Torgsin in 1933 were breadstuffs (Osokina, *Alkhimiia*, 79).
90 Ibid., 16–17.
91 Ibid., 17.
92 Ibid., 21.
93 Ibid., 22.
94 Ibid, 23.
95 Ibid., 24.
96 Ibid., 81.
97 Jarman, *Soviet Union*, 4:132. The consul self-righteously added, "However, 'Torgsin' is a valuable institution to foreigners in that it provides food and useful articles at prices in foreign currency which are reasonable, and it is not our fault if the Soviet Government treats us much better than its own citizens" (ibid.).
98 Osokina, *Our Daily Bread*, 123. This channel could be risky; at the height of the famine in June 1933 an American worker, while strolling in a park in Gomel in Belorussia, discovered in the bushes the body of a man who had been shot and his gold teeth extracted for bartering in Torgsin (Kondrashin, *Golod v SSSR*, 3, doc. 415:502).
99 Osokina, *Alkhimiia*, 95; Osokina, "Torgsin," 716.
100 Osokina, *Alkhimiia*, 133.
101 Volters, *Spetsialist v Sibiri*, 236.
102 Lang, "Soviet Nightmare," 264–5.
103 Zhober, *Kogda zhizn' tak deshego stoit*, 164–5, 165, 174.
104 Kondrashin, *Golod 1932-1933*, 2nd ed., 654; Mel'nichenko, *Sovetskii anekdot*, no. 770, 217.
105 Danilov, Manning, and Viola, *Tragediia sovetskoi derevni*, 3, doc. 69:188.
106 Jarman, *Soviet Union*, 4:577.
107 Carynnyk, Luciuk, and Kordan, *Foreign Office*, doc. 8:101. Andrew Cairns (1899–1958) visited the USSR in a professional capacity first in 1930 and again

in 1932, when he inspected Soviet agricultural conditions on behalf of the Empire Marketing Board, travelling to Western Siberia as far as Novosibirsk (10 May–5 June), the Central Black Earth, the Ukraine, the Crimea, and the North Caucasus (15 June–30 July), and the Volga Valley (Voronezh, Saratov, and Stalingrad [Volgograd]) (12–22 August). The British Foreign Office considered posting him to Moscow in 1933 as its embassy's agricultural attaché, and Cairns himself intended to write a book about his Soviet experiences, but neither came to pass (his wife believed that he did not return because the Soviet government refused to issue him a visa). Laurence Collier, a first secretary in the Northern Department of the Foreign Office, described Cairns in 1932 as a "wheat expert" who spoke Russian "fluently" (although Cairns himself stated that he knew only a "little Russian" and that he was often accompanied by an interpreter [i.e., a minder]) who was "clearly a careful and trustworthy observer" (Carynnyk, Luciuk, and Kordan, *Foreign Office*, doc. 2:9). His diligence in the field went so far as an examination of the human excrement in a village for its texture (coarseness indicating excessive fibre from offal) (Cairns, *Soviet Famine 1932–33*, 20). His reports are a rich fund of reliable data on Soviet agricultural conditions in the spring and summer of 1932. He died in a plane crash on a consulting assignment in India in 1958.

108 Lyons, *Assignment*, 490.
109 Ibid., 578; Chamberlin, *Russia's Iron Age*, vii, 4, 67, 76–7, 373.
110 Beal, *Proletarian Journey*, 296.
111 Kravchenko, *I Chose Freedom*, 112, 113. Kravchenko (1905–1966) was prompted by these "village horrors" to "break with the Party" and to defect to the United States in 1944. In 1948, in what was billed as the "trial of the century," he won a libel suit against the Paris Communist weekly *Les Lettres Françaises*, which had reported that he had not authored his book. A troubled soul, Kravchenko committed suicide in New York City in early 1966. See Kern, *Kravchenko Case*.
112 Alexievich, *Unwomanly Face of War*, 27.
113 Goichenko, *Skvoz raskulachivanie i golodomor*, 236.
114 Clyman, "Children Lived on Grass," 36.
115 Clyman, "Girl from New Toronto," 1, 3. Ethnically more Russian than Ukrainian, Kharkov had been made the capital of the Ukraine in 1765, and it became the capital of the Ukrainian SSR upon its formation in 1921 but was replaced by Kiev in 1934.

Rhea (Rachel) Clyman was an unmarried Canadian Jewish journalist. Born Rachel Kleiman in Poland in 1904, she and her family immigrated two years later to Toronto, where she lost part of a leg in a childhood streetcar accident and, a year later, her father. At the end of 1928 she went to Moscow, where she was hired by Walter Duranty as his secretary and assistant, and nine months later – after having rented a room with a Russian family, acquired a Russian boyfriend (who was to be exiled to Siberia for speculation), and learned Russian – she undertook her roughly 1,700-mile (2,700-kilometre) road trip intrepidly and resourcefully through the eastern Ukraine and the North Caucasus to Tiflis (Tbilisi) in Georgia as a guide and interpreter for two young, independent, and wealthy American women in their "flivver" nicknamed "Beckie," and in the spring of 1933 she sold a series of twenty articles to the conservative Toronto *Evening Telegram* and the London *Daily Express*. She spent four years as the "special correspondent" in Moscow for both of these (and other) newspapers. At the end of her southern journey to what she called the Soviet Union's "Famine Land," she was expelled from the country for defamation – an earlier exposé of conditions at a logging camp in Soviet Karelia – whereupon she went to Germany as a freelancer to cover the rise of National Socialism. After leaving Berlin three days after Kristallnacht (9 November 1938), she survived a crash landing at Amsterdam's Schipol Airport. Late in life she lived in obscurity and poverty in New York City. See the 2018 documentary film *Hunger for Truth: The Rhea Clyman Story* by Andrew Tkach; and Balan, "Rhea Clyman."

Unfortunately, Clyman's reportage has been overshadowed by eight articles with lurid titles in the *Chicago Tribune* (18–24 January 1933) by one of her duo of American employers, Alva Christensen (with Mary De Give), who, incidentally, deemed Clyman an "unwise choice" because she proved to be "quite unpleasant." After leaving Clyman in Tbilisi (where she was arrested by the OGPU and escorted back to Moscow), the two Atlanta adventurers continued eastward through the Transcaucasus and into Soviet Central Asia (where they encountered Langston Hughes), going as far as Tashkent before they were stopped by the Soviet authorities. Although more general, their impressions were much the same as those of Clyman. For example: "Here [at Kharkov] we were in the richest wheat producing section of the soviet realm, the Ukraine, and here were people all underfed and many of them on the verge of starvation. Every peasant we questioned had a tale of woe" (Christensen, "Girls Find Filth and Famine," 8).

Clyman, incidentally, met Beatrice and Sidney Webb, members of the Fabians (a society of respectable British socialists) and authors of the delusional *Soviet Communism: A New Civilisation?* (1935), on the eve of their carefully controlled visit to the Soviet Union in the spring of 1932. Beatrice Webb did not like Clyman because of her lower class ("a common little thing, with no intellectual background and no moral scruples"; "an unsavoury little mortal") and her gloomy outlook on their destination ("the people are virtually starving"), and Beatrice added – insinuatingly – that Clyman "says she reads and speaks Russian fluently" ([Webb], "diary," 4 January 1932–29 December 1934, 70–2).

116 Clyman, "Girl from New Toronto," 3.
117 Wells, *Kapoot*, 67. Shad is an anadromous herring of the Atlantic Coast of North America prized as a tasty commercial fish and a feisty sport fish, once known as "the poor man's salmon."
118 Osherowitch, *How People Live in Soviet Russia*, 82.
119 Poznanskii and Malysheva, "Golod na iuge Zapadnoi Sibiri," 128.
120 Dr Otto Schiller (1901–1970) was the German counterpart of Cairns (although Cairns spent much less time in the Soviet Union and, by his own admission, was "more critical of the Russians"). Schiller had worked on a model farm near Saratov in the Volga German Republic in 1924–27 and at the German agricultural concession of "Drusag" (an acronym for the "German-Russian Seed Joint-Stock Company") in the Kuban in 1927–30 before becoming the agricultural attaché at his country's embassy in Moscow in 1931–37. Schiller's diplomatic colleague at the German Embassy, Hans Heinrich Herwarth von Bittenfeld (a member of the aristocratic opposition to the Nazis who supplied the Allies with intelligence before and during the Second World War) appraised him thusly:

> His Russian was fluent, and he spent so much time roaming the countryside that we [at the German Embassy] called him "the *kolkhoznik*" – the collective farmer. Thanks to his practical training and to the excellent preparation that he had had earlier at university, Schiller was the finest observer of the agricultural scene in any of the embassies. His reports were treated as the Bible; his analyses were quoted and paraphrased by diplomats of many countries. (Von Herwarth, *Against Two Evils*, 77)

During the height of the famine in 1932–33 Soviet officials considered Schiller's agricultural intelligence "extremely serious" because it "became the point of departure of the entire international campaign against the USSR"; his behaviour in the country was "completely unparalleled," they said, for he "travel[led] around the kolkhozes and overnight[ed] with the kolkhozniks in the field at the very height of the intensification of the class struggle in [their] village [countryside]," which the officials deemed "insolent and unconcealed espionage that [they could not] forgive" (Kondrashin, *Golod v SSSR*, 3, doc. 403:493). Actually, Schiller's conduct was not really "completely unparalleled" for Andrew Cairns and Gareth Jones were doing likewise.

Schiller remained in the country until 1937, when he was removed not at the request of the Russians but as a result of Nazi Party intrigues. In 1937–45 he was employed as an agricultural specialist at IG Farben, a German chemical and pharmaceutical company (a subsidiary of which produced the lethal gas for the Jewish death camps). During the Second World War, as part of the *Generalplan Ost* (a blueprint for the German occupation and settlement of Central and Eastern Europe), "he developed detailed plans for converting Soviet Collective Farms into cooperatives, and they were successfully implemented in the North Caucasus, where they appeased the peasants and forestalled partisan activity and sabotage" (Von Herwarth, *Against Two Evils*, 77, 230–1).

121 Cairns, *Soviet Famine*, 10.
122 Ibid., 16.
123 Ibid., 4, 13, 14.
124 [Izmailov], *Dnevnik*, 1:392, 394, 399, 405, 412, 423.
125 Cairns, *Soviet Famine*, 12.
126 Volters, *Spetsialist v Sibiri*, 118. This memoir was published in Berlin in 1933 and 1937, the second time with sketches by the author's colleague, Heinrich Lauter.

Similarly, a joiner at a factory at Khabarovsk in the Soviet Far East wrote a letter (unpublished) to the government newspaper *Izvestia* deploring the living and working conditions: "We, the workers of the Sormovsk Factory, are suffering from shortages. From dusk to dawn we stand in lines for a piece of bread. They reduce our pay, the supply of the workers worsens, and the prices of all goods increase. There is nothing in the stores except powder, perfume, and vodka. We are starving and barefoot." He ended by saying that, out of disgust with their "hard living conditions," he and eighty-two other workers had left their jobs and set off to Moscow without tickets or documents (he himself had trashed his Party card because of the "lies"), but en route three of them had died and six had been murdered (Kondrashin, *Golod v SSSR*, vol. 1, bk. 2, doc. 473:62, 63).

127 Durant, *Tragedy of Russia*, 16, 20.
128 Yet a French visitor, the journalist Pierre Lucchini, wrote that in Siberia and Turkestan (Central Asia) he did not observe the "seething discontent" among the peasants that he saw in European Russia (Dominique, *Secrets of Siberia*, 237). Dominique was Lucchini's pen name; he was a polemicist whose political leanings were to shift from left to right, presumably as a result of his exposure to the realities of Stalinism.
129 Cairns, *Soviet Famine*, 10.
130 Ibid., 10–11.
131 Ibid., 31.
132 Lyons, *Assignment*, 574.
133 Abbe, *I Photograph Russia*, 282–3. Other travellers were less observant; Ella Maillart, a famous Swiss adventurer, explorer, and journalist, crossed Russian Turkestan from west to east and from east to west in 1932–33 and either completely overlooked the Kazakh famine or noticed it but decided not to report it (see Maillart, *Turkestan Solo*).
134 [Witkin], *American Engineer*, 115. Witkin was an idealistic and socialistic American engineering prodigy of Russian Jewish background who went to the Soviet Union because of his disillusionment with capitalism and his infatuation with a Russian film star.
135 Khrushchev, *Memoirs*, 1:55.
136 Smith, *Black Man in Red Russia*, 17.
137 Strøm, *Uncle Give Us Bread*, 28. Strøm spent a year at a poultry farm in Povorino near Voronezh.
138 These special stores were operated by Insnab, shorthand for the "Special Office for Supplying Foreign Specialists and Workers with Provisions and Manufactures."
139 [Witkin], *American Engineer*, 79–80, 97, 114.
140 Wettlin, *Fifty Russian Winters*, 8.
141 Barmine, *One Who Survived*, 201.
142 [Bullard], *Inside Stalin's Russia*, 119.

143 Jarman, *Soviet Union*, 4:382.
144 Wells, *Kapoot*, 113. Wells went to the Soviet Union to debunk negative reports about the country but soon became disenchanted with the woeful realities of the "Land of the Great Experiment."
145 Jarman, *Soviet Union*, 4:381.
146 Sevost'ianov et al., *"Sovershenno sekretno,"* vol. 10, pt. 2, doc. 294:388. Such strikes multiplied as the famine intensified. They constituted 20 percent of all strikes in the same period in 1930, 11 percent in 1931, and 38 percent in 1932 (ibid., 391).
147 Stalin, "Stalin's Speech," 1. See also Stalin, *Works*, 13:242–63. A "shock" worker (*udarnik*, from *udar*, "blow") was an especially enthusiastic and productive worker; a brigade was a work team on a kolkhoz.
148 Quoted by Kopelev, *Education*, 224. Rudenko (1920–2004) was also a Soviet dissident.
149 [Bullard], *Inside Stalin's Russia*, 220.
150 Iakhontov, *Vospominaniia*, 694, 697.
151 Bright-Holmes, *Like It Was*, 61, 63. Rosen, an American citizen of Russian birth, had returned to work for the American Relief Association during the famine of 1921–22 and subsequently participated in Jewish relief efforts. Muggeridge and his wife, Kitty, the favourite niece of Beatrice Webb, were soon disabused of their leftist leanings by, among other things, the famine horror.
152 Graziosi, "'Lettres de Kharkov,'" doc. 16:48. These diplomatic reports were subsequently published in book form in Italian (see Graziosi, *Lettere da Kharkov*).
153 Watt, *British Documents*, 11, doc. 49:62.
154 [Muggeridge], "The Soviet and the Peasantry," 3:9.
155 Anonymous, "Famine Grips Russia." Jones and Muggeridge were among the first, if not the very first, journalists to publicize the famine in the West, although Muggeridge tried to take credit for being *the* first and cribbed some of Jones's material (see Cherfas, "Reporting Stalin's Famine").
156 Jones, "Famine Rules Russia."
157 Jones, "Seizure of Land."
158 Jones, letter to his parents.
159 Kondrashin, *Golod v SSSR*, 3, doc. 415:501–02.
160 Volters, *Spetsialist v Sibiri*, 210.

161 Anonymous, A letter.
162 Bruski, "Bol'shoi golod," doc. 1:129.
163 Ibid., doc. 3:138, 138–9.
164 Watt, *British Documents*, 11, doc. 171:235.
165 Nikolai Ivanovich Vavilov (1887–1943) – botanist, geneticist, geographer – was one of the country's foremost scientists, with a worldwide reputation (and his brother, Sergei, was a leading physicist). His principal contribution to botany was the identification of the centres of origin of cultivated plants. He took part in numerous expeditions around the globe and amassed the world's largest collection of plant seeds in Leningrad (the seed bank, incidentally, was preserved during the city's nine-hundred-day German siege in 1941–43, and – ironically but heroically – nine of Vavilov's colleagues starved to death while tending the edible samples). He worked mightily to combat famine by improving the yield of crops. In the late 1930s he incurred Stalin's displeasure by opposing the Lamarckian quackery of Trofim Lysenko, who claimed, for example, that he could endow the seeds of spring wheat with those of winter wheat through the process of "vernalization." Motivated by professional jealousy and class enmity, Lysenko succeeded in having Vavilov purged; again ironically (and tragically), three years after his arrest in 1940 for "wrecking" Soviet agriculture, Vavilov was starved to death in a Saratov prison. Lysenko was denounced and dismissed in the post-Stalin years, but he died in his bed in 1976. See Pringle, *Murder of Nikolai Vavilov*.
166 Watt, *British Documents*, 11, doc. 209:301. He added that Central Asians were being provisioned mainly with wheat brought from Western Siberia on the new Turk-Sib Railway (the subject, incidentally, of a celebrated 1929 documentary film of the same name by Victor Turin).
167 [Izmailov], *Dnevnik*, 1:483, 510. On 9 May Izmailov had noted that "Kirghizes from Kazakhstan in particular" were arriving in the village (ibid., 507).
168 Graziosi, "'Lettres de Kharkov,'" doc. 21:62.
169 Zhober, *Kogda zhizn' tak deshego stoit*, 210, 238, 255. In the summer, when more food was obtainable, the "sorest point" was housing (ibid., 264).
170 Man'kov, "Iz dnevnika," 156.
171 Ibid.
172 Jones, "Famine Rules Russia."
173 Kondrashin, *Golod v SSSR*, 3, doc. 392:481. *Le Petit Parisien* (1876–1944), one of France's most popular newspapers before the First World War, had a leftist

and radical orientation. From 1940 until its closure in 1944 it collaborated with the Vichy regime.
174 Jarman, *Soviet Union*, 4:132.
175 Lugovskaya, *I Want to Live*, 56. Lugovskaya (1918–1993) has been – perhaps inaptly – called "Russia's Anne Frank." In 1932 she began to keep a candid diary, which was discovered by the NKVD, the OGPU's successor, in 1937 at the height of the mass arrests, show trials, and executions and deportations of the "Great Terror." She, her older twin sisters, and her mother were sentenced to five years of hard labour in Kolyma, the most distant and most brutal island of the Gulag archipelago. They survived, and upon her release Nina went to Vladimir to live with her artist husband, whom she had married in exile.
176 [Jones], "Tell Them We Are Starving," 150, 190.
177 Bruski, "Bol'shoi golod," doc. 1:133.
178 [Federalnoe arkhivnoe agentstvo], *Kollekstsiia dokumentov*, doc. 83:4, 6, doc. 113:2.
179 Ibid., doc. 100:1, 2, 2–3.
180 Ibid., docs. 152, 165, 172.
181 Ibid., doc. 168:1, 2.
182 Kondrashin, *Golod v SSSR*, 2, doc. 326:436, doc. 328:438.
183 Man'kov, "Iz dnevnika," 151.
184 Watt, *British Documents*, 12, doc. 65:75.
185 Ibid., doc. 164:189. Oddly, the author of this dispatch, Lord Chilston, the ambassador, qualified it by adding that "the Russian peasant is, however, able to subsist on little nourishment."

The rather vague and bland nature of this and other summations from the British Embassy have been addressed by Michael Hughes, who has argued that "the restrained tone of their dispatches sometimes failed to capture the full drama of the events on which they reported"; that "the collectivization of agriculture ... was always something of a second-hand experience for British officials" and, "since they were largely confined to two major cities [Moscow and Leningrad], neither of which was situated in an important agricultural region, they rarely had the opportunity to see the process in action for themselves" – which "perhaps accounts for the curiously bloodless texture of the reports sent to London"; that "the Embassy staff were initially inclined to treat collectivization as an essentially economic [rather than political] affair" so that "their early dispatches, in particular, were filled with dry reflections on ... arcane technical problems" with the result that they "sometimes found it difficult to comprehend the sheer brutality and violence of the whole process"; that "although a number of British officials ... were able to tour a few of the [collective] farms, they were invariably taken to showcase establishments"; that "in spite of all this evidence [from journalists and peasants themselves] British diplomats based in the comparative comfort of the Moscow Embassy still found it difficult to comprehend the sheer scale of the tragedy taking place in the countryside"; and – finally – that "they seldom witnessed the suffering with their own eyes, which perhaps tended to inculcate a degree of aloofness that could easily appear to outsiders as unfeeling indifference" (Hughes, *Inside the Enigma*, 240–5). A third secretary at the embassy, however, sounded a contrary note after returning from a "personally conducted" trip to the Crimea and the southern Ukraine in the summer of 1932 with Andrew Cairns:

> At Sinelnikovo ... we were accompanied by an official, who would not leave us ... Nevertheless, it is impossible so much as to have one's shoes blacked without being met with the same outcries: "We have no leather here like yours, no bread, no meat – nothing. There is nothing to live for!" This was said to me with a GPU officer within 2 yards. Except in the case of rare Communists, there seems to be no patriotic inclination to hide conditions from a foreigner. He is the natural receptacle for complaints against the "system," in whom I found on two occasions that even Communists were willing to confide. (United Kingdom, FO 4621/4621/38, no. 410)

186 Golitsyn, *Memoirs*, 446.
187 [Izmailov], *Dnevnik*, 1:484.
188 Ibid., 1:628.
189 Ibid., 1:600–1, 609.
190 Minskii Muzhik, *Chto ia videl*, 339.
191 [Izmailov], *Dnevnik*, 1:631.
192 Bednarek et al., *Holodomor*, doc. 202:543.
193 Utley, *Lost Illusion*, 220.
194 Osokina, *Our Daily Bread*, 135–44; Lih, Naumov, and Khlevniuk, *Stalin's Letters to Molotov*, letter 82:217n1.

195 Wood, *Our Ally*, 190. Wood and his wife lived in the USSR in 1931–34, 1937, and 1941. On the other hand, Markoosha Fischer called the period between 1933 and 1936 the "fat" years relative to the famine period, notably in terms of provisioning, even though "one had to stand in line several hours in an overcrowded, stuffy store," but "the wooden imitations of cheese and sausage which had filled the windows of food stores together with cobwebs and dead flies made way for real food products of excellent quality" in "rebuilt and freshly painted or brand-new food stores, well stocked with a great variety of foodstuffs" sold by "patient and polite" salesgirls (Fischer, *My Lives*, 100, 103). Perhaps she was referring to what might be termed the "special stores for special persons in special cities."

196 Hawker, *An Australian*, 7, see also 13.

197 Stalin, *Selected Writings*, 371. Stakhanovites were those workers who overachieved by exceeding their norms. The term honoured Alexei Stakhanov (1906–77), who allegedly mined sixteen times his quota of coal on 31 August 1935. The constant exhortations to become Stakhanovites generated a scatological ditty among youngsters (Konstantin, *Red Boyhood*, 77):

They've just announced a new plan:
To shit no less than a kilogram!
Those who seven can afford,
Will receive a nice reward.
Those who shit only a pound,
Will be beaten to the ground.

198 Even Stalin did not have the gall to authorize the publication of *the* Soviet cookbook, the *Book of Tasty and Healthy Food*, until 1939, when the recommended ingredients were still unavailable to most Soviet citizens.

199 Kondrashin, *Golod v SSSR*, 3:721.

200 Ibid., 720. Two other Western specialists have written that "in the USSR in the 1930s statistics on population as well as planning, [sic] reveal[ed] an increasing divergence between word and deed," that is, between published and unpublished figures, and that this disjunction "resulted in conflict between the political leaders and the statisticians" such that, between 1918 and 1941, the central statistical agency had eight different directors, five of whom were shot in 1937–39 and one of whom (the agency's founder) was fired in 1926 for

openly and actively opposing Stalin politically (Blium and Mespule, *Biurokraticheskaia anakhiia*, 9, 13). And two recent books demonstrate how Stalinist statistics were exploited to serve ideology rather than reality through distortion and deception, especially vis-à-vis Tsarist Russia and famine in particular (see Oreshkin, *Dzhugafilia i sovetskii statisticheskii epos* and Kuriaev, *Russkii khleb v zhernovakh ideologii*). Stalinist statistics should be taken with a pound, not a pinch, of salt.

And so should Stalinist maps. At the outset of General Secretary Gorbachev's "restructuring" and "openness" campaigns in 1988, the head of the USSR's mapping agency admitted in an interview published in *Izvestia* that, since the late 1930s, virtually all official maps had been falsified (streets and rivers misplaced, boundaries moved, features omitted) in order to foil enemy agents (Keller, "Soviet Aide," 2).

201 Kondrashin, *Golod v SSSR*, 3:720.
202 Ibid., 73, table 1. For estimates – not "corrections" – of population losses in the Ukraine, the heart of the famine, see Vallin et al., "New Estimate of Ukrainian Population Losses" and Rudnytskyi et al., "Demography of a Man-Made Human Catastrophe," whose authors calculate that the famine took the lives of 4.5 to 4.6 million Ukrainians (although it is unclear whether these were ethnic or census Ukrainians, as the Ukraine as a census unit contained not a few Great Russians, who were mostly urban).

The calculations also assume the soundness of the population registration figures in the archives; however, as an elderly and unrepentant communist – one of the dwindling number of witnesses remaining to talk about all those who lived in the Soviet period – told Svetlana Alexievich: "Who else will you find to tell you the truth? All that's left are the archives. Pieces of paper. And the truth is ... I worked at an archive myself, I can tell you first hand: paper lies even more than people do" (Alexievich, *Second-Hand Time*, 262). Regarding the compilers of the statistics, the observant British consul in Leningrad, Reader Bullard, asserted that there was a "belief held by many that Soviet statistics are compiled largely by persons whose conception of quantity is that of the cook who estimates the amount of salt she put in the soup as 'a good knob [dollop]'" (Jarman, *Soviet Union*, 4:384).

203 Kondrashin, *Golod v SSSR*, 3:731, table 2. The figures date from 1 January of each year.
204 Maksudov, *Pobeda nad derevnei*, 394–5. Maksudov is the pseudonym of

Alexander Babyonyshev, who was expelled from the USSR in 1981 as a dissident.

205 This is the figure that the State Duma of the Russian Federation accepted in 2008. Kondrashin agrees with Wheatcroft, however, that the famine toll of 1932–33 was 5.6 million (Kondrashin, *Golod 1932–1933*, 2nd ed., 422).

206 Dikötter, *Mao's Great Famine*, x, 298, 324–5, 333–4.

207 Stalin and Wells, *Marxism vs. Liberalism*, 16, 17.

208 Gantt, *Russian Medicine*, 154. The Gulag's memorialist, Alexander Solzhenitsyn, wrote that what he called the "Peasant Plague," the amalgam of rural evils of 1929–34, starved 15 million peasants to death (including 6 million in the "great Ukrainian famine" of 1932–33) (Solzhenitsyn, *Gulag Archipelago*, vol. 3, bk. 6:350, 353). And Robert Robinson, a black American toolmaker with the Ford Motor Company who lived and worked in the Soviet Union from 1930 until 1974, was told by "a number of Communist Party sources" that altogether 17 to 19 million Soviets perished (Robinson, *Black on Red*, 39n1).

209 United States, Felix Cole to the Secretary of State, 1.

210 Abbe, *I Photograph Russia*, 255; Carynnyk, Luciuk, and Kordan, *Foreign Office*, doc. 72:407; Danilov, Manning, and Viola, *Tragediia sovetskoi derevni*, 3, sup. 2:885; Graziosi, "'Lettres de Kharkov,'" doc. 21:66; United Kingdom, FO 371/17253, no. 7182; Hawker, *An Australian*, 17; Ivnitskii, *Golod 1932–1933*, 243; [Ivnitskii], "Real Story," 2; Kondrashin, *Golod v SSSR*, 3:653; Osokina, "Victims of the Famine," 13; Tawdul, "Famine in Russia," 2; Watt, *British Documents*, 11, doc. 168:232; 12, doc. 237:287; Zelenin, "O nekotorikh 'belykh piatnakh,'" 319. The Langs, man and wife, were told in September of 1933 by a "high official" of the Ukrainian government that "six million people have perished from hunger in our country this year" (Lang, "Soviet Nightmare," 259–60).

211 Lyons, *Assignment*, 579; Lyons, "My Six Years in Moscow," 271. A committed communist, Lyons (1898–1985) arrived in the USSR from the USA as a devoted partisan and left with a hatred of Bolshevism and Stalinism (but with a strong affection for Russia and Russians). By his own admission, "few foreigners outdid the United Press man [himself] in the glorification of the new socialist objectives" (Lyons, *Assignment*, 196). A compatriot, the photojournalist James Abbe, who deemed Lyons more of a writer than a reporter, said that Lyons felt matters "intensely," especially injustice, and that his ideals

"suffered shock after shock" during the First Five-Year Plan (Abbe, "Men of Cablese," 30). A close friend, the "brilliant and hard-headed young California engineer" Zara Witkin, dedicated his Soviet memoir to Lyons, "whose soul was fired by the heroic struggle of the Russian people for liberty – whose heart was racked by their suffering." Witkin added that Lyons's UPI office was "a sort of unofficial American embassy in Moscow to which crowds of Americans and Russians flocked" ([Witkin], *American Engineer*, [21], 80).

212 Chamberlin, *Russia's Iron Age*, 82–3.

213 Ibid., 83, 84, 87, 88, 88n5, 367–8. See also Carynnyk, Luciuk, and Kordan, *Foreign Office*, doc. 73:417; United Kingdom, FO 371/17253, no. 7753; Watt, *British Documents*, 11, doc. 203:292. Rhea Clyman met Chamberlin in 1932 and told Lady Beatrice Webb a year later that he "does not say what he really thinks of Soviet Russia" ([Webb], "diary," 4 January 1932–29 December 1934, 73).

In the same month a ten-day trip to the Ukraine and the North Caucasus was also made by Walter Duranty of the *New York Times* with Stanley Richardson of the Associated Press. Upon his return to Moscow Duranty told a member of the British Embassy that he thought "it quite possible that as many as 10 million people may have died directly or indirectly from lack of food in the Soviet Union during the last year," with the Ukraine's population decreasing by 4 to 5 million and that of the North Caucasus and Lower Volga by 3 million (United Kingdom, FO 371/17253, no. 7182; Watt, *British Documents*, 11, doc. 189:271). Duranty may have obtained his figures from Otto Schiller, who estimated 5 to 10 million deaths (Watt, *British Documents*, 11, doc. 168:232) and/or from Fritz Dittloff (1894–1954), the former manager of the German North Caucasus concession "Drusag," who estimated 10 million casualties (Carynnyk, Luciuk, and Kordan, *Foreign Office*, doc. 72:407), for Edward Coote described Duranty as "a totally unqualified agricultural observer," one who would "have no difficulty in obtaining sufficient quantitative experience in tour hours to enable him to say whatever he may wish to say on his return" (United Kingdom, FO 371/17253, no. 6878). In like vein Clyman told Lady Webb that Duranty was "vain and ignorant of what goes on" ([Webb], "diary," 4 January 1932–29 December 1934, 73). In this particular case, however, he was not ignorant. Not every villain is completely villainous.

214 Chamberlin, *Confessions*, 157. Whiting (Charles) Williams, a progressive American businessman, author, and lecturer who visited the USSR in 1928

and returned in 1932 to check the rumours of starvation in the Ukraine, reported 5 million famine deaths there but cautioned that "nobody can know" because officials, including doctors, dared not record deaths as famine-caused (Williams, "Confidential Circular," n.p.). (Williams [1878–1975] was a multilingual charity organizer and management consultant from Ohio who famously went underground in the late 1910s and early 1920s in various countries in the Americas and Europe to investigate working conditions.) Polish diplomats, who motored throughout the Ukraine periodically from their bases in Kharkov and Kiev, interviewed peasants, workers, and officials and conjectured a consensus of at least 5 million victims, too (Bruski, "Bol'shoi golod," 126, 126n83). On a fantastical note, the one-time president of the Ukraine (2005–10), Viktor Yushchenko, asserted on 21 November 2008 (a memorial day for Ukrainian victims of the famine) that "every day for two years [1932–33] 25 thous[and] people starved to death" – which, if true, would make a total of 18,250,000 victims, or 60 percent of the Ukraine's population of some 30 million at the time (Ovchinnikov, "Kiev otmechaet den' pamiati")!

215 Kondrashin, *Golod v SSSR*, 3:654.
216 Schiller, "Corn Growing in Fields." Women are able to store greater reserves of fat than men.
217 Bednarek et al., *Holodomor*, doc. 197:535. And one of Svetlana Alexievich's witnesses (as children) to the Second World War recalled that, during the siege of Leningrad, "everybody lost their papa, the papas died sooner, but the mamas stayed alive," adding, "I guess they couldn't die. Otherwise who would have been there for us?" (Alexievich, *Last Witnesses*, 236).
218 Kondrashin, *Golod v SSSR*, 3:657.
219 Kondrashin, *Khlebozagotovitelnaia politika*, 200.
220 Platonov, *Zapisnie knizhki*, 34. Also, this male "superstructure" tended to be undermined by excessive drinking and smoking.
221 Kovalev, *Golosa krest'ian*, 218.
222 As one peasant said, "Who were these kulaks? In the village there were no such kulaks. This ignominious, offensive name was endowed by the Soviet authorities" (Lopatin and Lopatina, *Kollektivizatsiia i raskulachivanie*, doc. 108:333).
223 Jarman, *Soviet Union*, 3:705.
224 Semenova, *Unichtozhennie kak klass*, 1:[1].

NOTES TO PAGES 60-3

225 Kondrashin, *Khlebozagotovitel'naia politika*, 189–90, 192–3.
226 Ibid., 191.
227 Gorokhova, *Mountain of Crumbs*, 3.
228 Bednarek et al., *Holodomor*, doc. 204:546.
229 Ibid., doc. 77:234.
230 Molotov himself called Kaganovich Stalin's "most devoted" right-hand man (Resis, *Molotov Remembers*, 190), and Beria asserted that Kaganovich was the most vigorous member of Stalin's inner circle (Kremlev, *Lavrentyi Beria*, 622). Clyman found that he was popularly known as the "tsarevich," that is, the heir to Stalin's throne (Clyman, "Wrecks Litter Railroad," 12).
231 Kaganovich, "Ukreplenie kolkhozov," 2.
232 Solzhenitsyn, *Gulag Archipelago*, vol. 1, bk. 2:57–8.
233 Elmhirst, *Trip to Russia*, 160.
234 Sevost'ianov et al., "*Sovershenno sekretno*," vol. 10, pt. 1, doc. 64:209.
235 Bednarek et al., *Holodomor*, doc. 94:280.
236 Goichenko, *Skvoz raskulachivanie i golodomor*, 235, 235–6.
237 Jones, "Seizure of Land," 7.
238 Clyman, "Russian Peasant Shot," 23.
239 Pigweed is an amaranth whose leaves, stems, and seeds are edible and highly nutritious, although its nitrate-laden leaves can be harmful to livestock.
240 Smith and Christian, *Bread and Salt*, 349.
241 Jones, "There Is No Bread."
241 Goosefoot, or orach[e], was likely *Atriplex hastata*, a variety of goosefoot (so-called because of its leaf shape). It is a herbaceous weed with a farinaceous veneer.
243 One of the surviving children of the siege of Leningrad later told Svetlana Alexievich: "People even ate dirt ... at the market, we could buy dirt from the destroyed and burned-down Badayev warehouses; dirt with sunflower oil spilled on it was particularly valuable, or dirt soaked in burned jam. Those two were expensive. Our mama could only afford the cheapest dirt, which barrels of herring had stood on. That dirt only smelt of salt, but didn't contain any salt. Only the smell of herring" (Alexievich, *Last Witnesses*, 238–9).
244 Kondrashin, *Khlebozagotovitel'naia politika*, 192. In his epic *Life and Fate* novelist Vasily Grossman has an old botanist from Moscow explain how he survived the famine in the Ukrainian countryside:

> You know why I stayed alive? Because I know plants. And I'm not talking about things like acorns, linden leaves, goosefoot, and nettles. They all went in no time. I know fifty-six plants a man can eat. That's how I stayed alive. It was barely spring, there wasn't a leaf on the trees – and there I was digging up roots. I know everything, brother – every root, every grass, every flower, every kind of bark. Cows, sheep, and horses can die of hunger – but not me. I'm more herbivorous than any of them. (Grossman, *Life and Fate*, 546)

245 Bednarek et al., *Holodomor*, doc. 113:320; Osokina, *Our Daily Bread*, 34.
246 Kondrashin, *Golod v SSSR*, 2, doc. 353:469.
247 Ibid., doc. 391:512.
248 Alexievich, *Last Witnesses*, 61.
249 Jones, "There Is No Bread."
250 Goichenko, *Skvoz raskulachivanie i golodomor*, 218–19. As a survivor of the siege of Leningrad told Svetlana Alexievich, "I know that a man can eat anything" (Alexievich, *Last Witnesses*, 238).
251 Kondrashin, *Khlebozagotovitel'naia politika*, 171, citing the Centre for the Documentation of Recent History (TSDNI), f. 98, op. 1, d. 17, fol. 47.
252 Kondrashin, *Golod v SSSR*, 2, doc. 413:535.
253 Kondrashin, *Khlebozagotovitel'naia politika*, 193.
254 Ivnitskii, *Golod 1932–1933*, 6.
255 Kondrashin, *Khlebozagotovitel'naia politika*, 169.
256 Ibid.
257 Gaidukov, *Aleksei Vasil'evich Oreshnikov*, 2:524.
258 Lang, "Soviet Nightmare," 259.
259 The traditional Russian stove, or oven (*pech'*), is a unique type of masonry stove dating from the fifteenth century. Usually located in the centre of the izba, it burns firewood and is used for cooking (mainly baking) and heating. It retains heat for a long time by channelling the smoke and hot air through a labyrinth of passages and thereby warming the constituent bricks. It is large enough and flat enough for people to sit, lie, or sleep on or even to hide in.
260 Malysheva and Poznanskii, "Golod na iuge Zapadnoi Sibiri," doc. 2:76.
261 See here and there throughout: Antipova et al., *Golod v SSSR*; [Federal Archival Agency], *Famine in the USSR*; and [Federal'noe arkhivnoe agentsvo], *Kollektsiia dokumentov*.

262 Kondrashin, *Golod v SSSR*, 2, doc. 317:424–5.
263 Ibid., 424. And a man who had fled Kazakhstan told his nephew that upon his return in 1933 "people told him the roads were lined with corpses and that wild animals, particularly wolves, were eating the corpses," and even "more shocking were the tales of gangs of cannibals roaming the countryside," and he himself narrowly escaped capture by one such gang (Pannier, "Kazakhstan").
264 Vaniukov, *Golodomor*, doc. 95:245–6.
265 [Bullard], *Inside Stalin's Russia*, 205, 206.
266 Bruski, "Bol'shoi golod," doc. 3:149.
267 Williams, "My Journey," n.p.
268 Goichenko, *Skvoz raskulachivanie i golodomor*, 222.
269 Ibid., 222–3.
270 United Kingdom, FO 371/17251, no. 6565.
271 Carynnyk, Luciuk, and Kordan, *Foreign Office*, doc. 72:408.
272 Danilov, Manning, and Viola, *Tragediia sovetskoi derevni*, 4, doc. 43:120.
273 Kondrashin, *Golod v SSSR*, 3, doc. 303:483.
274 [Federal'noe arkhivnoe agentstvo], *Kollektsiia dokumentov*, doc. 108:1.
275 Sevost'ianov et al., "Sovershenno sekretno," vol. 10, pt. 2, doc. 320:495.
276 McVay and Luciuk, *Holy See*, doc. 36:52.
277 Kondrashin, *Golod v SSSR*, 3, doc. 393:484.
278 Kondrashin, *Khlebozagotovitel'naia politika*, 198. On the other hand, sometimes parents sacrificed themselves in order to save their children (ibid.).
279 Jones, "Famine Rules Russia."
280 There were exceptions, including some food parcels dispatched from abroad by relatives and charities (but not always received) and state loans in kind of mostly food, seed, and feed grain in 1932–33 that were normally repayable from the future harvest at an interest rate of 10 percent (i.e., one pud for every ten puds loaned).
281 Kondrashin, *Khlebozagotovitel'naia politika*, 203. Also, the 1921–22 famine struck both villages and cities, whereas in 1932–33 the stockpiling of food in the major cities and the blockading of starving migrants by "passportization" (the issuing of internal identity cards at the end of 1932 to all citizens except peasants) lessened the urban impact in the view of the French chargé d'affaires in Moscow (McVay and Luciuk, *Holy See*, doc. 13:17). The "passports" were introduced "with the aim of ridding the large industrial cities, primarily

Moscow, Leningrad, and Kharkov, of unwanted elements" (Bruski, "Bol'shoi golod," doc. 1:134). Holders were not to leave their homes without them, and they were required for travel between republics; infringement risked incarceration. The authorities used them to reduce rural to urban migration by the starving peasants. They were not terminated until 1974, five years after having finally been issued to collective farmers and individual farmsteaders.

282 Kondrashin, *Khlebozagotovitel'naia politika*, 204.
283 Anonymous [Jones], "Famine Grips Russia."
284 [Izmailov], *Dnevnik*, 2:538.
285 In 1932–33 the temporary cessation of grain exports, the lowering of grain procurement targets, and the granting of food, seed, and feed loans to various regions afforded some relief but niggardly and belatedly, and it was certainly far too little and far too late to prevent the demographic catastrophe.
286 Chamberlin, *Russia's Iron Age*, 89n.
287 United States, Cole to Secretary of State, 1–2, 2.
288 The antipathy of those who quit the kolkhozes in despair generated the following anecdote:

> One day a kolkhoz chairman was walking home from work across the hayfields and there on his path sat some wolves, who did not get out of his way. He shouted at them, but they did not move. So he set fire to the hay, but still they didn't budge. "I'll enrol you in the kolkhoz right away," he yelled, whereupon the wolves put their tails between their legs and fled. (Kondrashin, *Golod 1932–1933*, 329)

289 Kondrashin, *Khlebozagotovitel'naia politika*, 2nd ed., 194.
290 Cairns, *Soviet Famine*, 114.
291 Bruski, "Bol'shoi golod," 105–6; Kondrashin, *Golod v SSSR*, 3, doc. 376:456–8.
292 Koestler, *Invisible Writing*, 63.
293 Bednarek et al., *Holodomor*, doc. 88:256. Subsequently, Dneprostroi was destroyed by the retreating and scorched-earthing Russians (1941) and again by the retreating Germans (1943) and was finally rebuilt permanently in the last half of the 1940s.
294 The dacha, a venerable Russian institution, is a "cottage" (ranging from a shack, hut, or cabin to a house or villa) in the countryside that serves as a retreat in the summer months or on winter weekends for urbanites.

295 Cairns, *Soviet Famine*, 53.
296 Khripunov, *Dnevniki*, 370. The author also provides a unique account of ground squirrel catching:

> A picture of the past comes to mind. An April morning. The sun is already high above the horizon. Katya, Raika, and I are walking to the pond, 4 or 5 kilometres from the khutor. It is hard to walk when you are weak. On the way we eat up a ground squirrel (they are round, like a cucumber, and are roasted in the stove). We carry water from the pond to a ground squirrel's burrow. One of us puts a hand over the burrow, and then another pours water into it. After 3 or 4 pails, the burrow is full, and the wet little beast climbs out. There is no time to lose. You have to quickly grab the squirrel by the throat, raise it high, and smash it on the ground to kill it. Sometimes it bites your finger with its sharp teeth. If you miss your chance, the squirrel will run off. And in the open it can't be caught. (Khripunov, *Dnevniki*, 370–1)

Incidentally, the author, who was only ten years old at the time (1933), asks: "Why do adults remember themselves well from the ages of 10–12 but not from the ages of 1–10? ... I remember my life only from the year 1933 onwards, but I know almost nothing before that" (ibid., 372).

297 Kondrashin, *Khlebozagotovitel'naia politika*, 197–8.
298 Ibid., 197.
299 [Jones], "Tell Them We Are Starving," 35, 111.
300 Sevost'ianov et al., "Sovershenno sekretno," vol. 10, pt. 1, doc. 15:101.
301 Bruski, "Bol'shoi golod," 109–10.
302 Bednarek et al., *Holodomor*, doc. 56:190.
303 Koestler, *Invisible Writing*, 73; Scammell, *Koestler*, 73.
304 Koestler, *Invisible Writing*, 63.
305 Ibid., 70.
306 Lang, "Soviet Nightmare," 257.
307 Zelënaia, *Dnevnik 1928–1938*, 57, 59. The missing page was very likely ripped out by the author herself *na vsiakii sluchai*, that is, "to be on the safe side."
308 Griffin, *Soviet Scene*, 216. Generally Griffin (1890–1946) was hopelessly handicapped by, in his own words, "ignorance of the Russian language and the

constant need of an interpreter [from Intourist]," who dutifully shepherded him everywhere, even on occasion sleeping with him (presumably platonically). His naive impressions were serialized in the *Star* and later published in book form (see above). He had been sent by the Toronto daily because by 1932 Canadian interest in the Soviet Union had reached "fever heat and possibly no other country viewed Red Russia with greater alarm and even hatred" than Canada because "the Communist state loomed in many Canadian minds as a monstrous threat, not only in social terms but as an economic enemy in terms of wheat, lumber, pulp, fish, and minerals" (Griffin, *Variety Show*, 314).

309 Smith, *Black Man in Red Russia*, 20.
310 Burrell, *American Engineer*, 11.
311 In late 1941 around Karaganda, Kazakhstan's coal-mining and steel-making centre, zemlyankas were described by a young German communist (who had just been deported to the republic) as "holes in the ground covered over with cardboard or wood and a layer of earth about two feet thick, with a few poles to support the roof" (Leonhard, *Child of the Revolution*, 140).
312 Graziosi, "'Lettres de Kharkov,'" doc. 3:23.
313 On this topic see Tzouliadis, *Forsaken*. More generally speaking, seventy to eighty thousand foreign workers, specialists, and exiles from around the world went to the Soviet Union to live and work between the overthrow of the Tsarist regime in March 1917 and the outbreak of the Second World War in September 1939, with many of them recording their impressions (Graziosi, "Foreign Workers," 38).
314 Leder, *My Life in Stalinist Russia*, 62.
315 Wells, *Kapoot*, 79, 80.
316 Gantt, *Russian Medicine*, 152. This anecdote originally referred to the situation at the end of the 1910s that helped to create the famine of 1921–22.
317 Kondrashin, *Khlebozagotovitel'naia politika*, 195.
318 Ibid.
319 Kondrashin and Tiurina, "Govorit' o golode," doc. 19:120.
320 Kondrashin, *Khlebozagotovitel'naia politika*, 195–6.
321 Solzhenitsyn, *Gulag Archipelago*, vol. 1, bk. 2:198.
322 Elagin, *Ukroshchenie iskusstv*, 46.
323 Avdeenko, "Otluchenie," 11. Avdeenko, a former "famine orphan," was en route to the Baltic Sea–White Sea (Belomor) Canal through Karelia to join

Gorky's Writers' Brigade of 120 officials and writers who were to travel the canal with a view to discovering and proclaiming the rehabilitative effects that its construction was having on the convict builders.

324 Dominique, *Secrets of Siberia*, 51.
325 Lucy Lang observed the heart-breaking abandonment (or infanticide) of a child during her tour of a collectivized Ukrainian village that was under investigation for suspected sabotage in September of 1933:

> While I was watching the Soviet investigators at work, a peasant woman, dressed in patched sacking, appeared from a side path. She was dragging a child of three or four years by the collar of a torn coat, as one might drag a heavy bag. When she reached the main street, she simply dropped the child in the mud and went away. Everyone saw what had happened, but no one made a move. The child's face was bloated and blue, and its hands and tiny body were swollen. Obviously it was near death, but it was still alive. The mother left the child in the road in the hope that someone might do something to save it. (Lang, "Soviet Nightmare," 260)

> The pilfering expertise of the waifs impressed Arthur Koestler, who wrote that the overcrowding of the country's towns and cities had "made Russia into a paradise of pickpockets who displayed a virtuosity as nowhere else"; in Kharkov he found that most of the pickpockets were "the notorious waifs and strays who had been roaming about the country like a plague of locusts ever since the Civil War" (Koestler, *Invisible Writing*, 68).

326 See Ball, *And Now My Soul Is Hardened*.
327 Ibid., 1.
328 Kondrashin, *Golod v SSSR*, vol. 1, bk. 2, doc. 473:60.
329 Graziosi, "'Lettres de Kharkov,'" doc. 4:24.
330 [Federal'noe arkhivnoe agentsvo], *Kollektsiia dokumentov*, doc. 173:1, doc. 177; Kornilov and Lavrova, *Besprizornost' na Urale*, doc. 81:317; Vaniukov, *Goldomor*, doc. 169:362.
331 Krivitsky, *In Stalin's Secret Service*, xviii.
332 Kornilov and Lavrova, *Besprizornost' na Urale*, 17. The overwhelming predominance of working-class waifs likely reflects the fact that the Urals, like the Ukraine, was very much an industrial as well as an agricultural region, as

Western Siberia was also becoming with the development of the country's third metallurgical base in the Kuzbass.
333 Wells, *Kapoot*, 104–5.
334 Volters, *Spetsialist v Sibiri*, 58–9.
335 Von Herwarth, *Against Two Evils*, 37.
336 Ibid., 37, 38.
337 [Federal'noe arkhivnoe agentsvo], *Kollektsiia dokumentov*, doc. 145:1.
338 Lievan, *British Documents*, 9, doc. 107:239. According to the 1926 census, it was 82 percent (Lorimer, *Population of the Soviet Union*, 67, table 26).
339 United Kingdom, FO 371/17251, no. 5797. The duchess, Katharine Ramsay (1874–1960), was a long-time Scottish Unionist MP whose interest in the Soviet Union arose from her humanitarian concern for the plight of the peasants and the workers (see her book *The Conscription of a People* [London: Philip Allan, 1931] and her pamphlet *Out of the Deep*) and her mercantile opposition to the dumping of Soviet output on the world market, especially timber, at "cut-throat prices" that "Soviet slave labour made possible" (Katharine, *Working Partnership*, 183, 185). She later became known as the "Red Duchess" on account of her support for the Republican side in the Spanish Civil War.
340 Viola, *Peasant Rebels under Stalin*, 120. For a description of the traditional way of life of the pre-industrial peasantry, see Shvetsova, *Zhizn' ot sokhi*. And for a realistic portrayal of the peasant's new way of life on the post-famine kolkhoz, see Abramov, *New Life*, which is akin to Alexander Solzhenitsyn's *One Day in the Life of Ivan Denisovich*.
341 Semenova, *Unichtozhennie kak klass*, 1:[2]. Indeed, two Russian authors of peasant recollections of the famine have concluded that collectivization changed the very psyche ("pyschotype") of the peasantry, for "[in the kolkhoz] it was no longer considered disgraceful to steal; industriousness was lost on account of the loss of incentives; drunkenness increased; the communal cohesion of everyday life disappeared; respect for oldsters and relatives declined; fear of a punitive government led to dissimulation, sanctimoniousness, and denouncement; and atheism generated immorality" (Lopatin and Lopatina, *Kollektivizatsiia i raskulachivanie*, 445).

Chapter Two

1 One of the first studies in English was by Dalrymple, "Soviet Famine of 1932–1934" (1964), wherein he states that "it [the famine] is scarcely known today" (250), although it was certainly known to expatriate survivors, of course.
2 For a comprehensive account of the elaborate deception of a variety of foreign visitors by Soviet officials about sundry deporable conditions in Stalinist Russia before the Second World War, much of it told in the voices of both the deceivers and the deceived, see Simkin, *Veliky obman*. In 1933, for example, three groups of 613 foreign workers and specialists were given free cruises in steamboats on the Volga River, and all of the towns that they visited had had a "face-lift" (à la "Potemkin villages") beforehand, and they were met by brass bands (ibid., 248).

It was impossible, however, to prevent every tourist from glimpsing starving peasants. For example, the wife of an American travel writer on a cut-rate guided train jaunt through southern European Russia in the summer of 1932 – on the eve of the famine's climax – was awakened one day at 4:00 a.m. by bedbugs:

> We have arrived at the station. My God! What a sight! I shall never forget it. Poverty, filth, disease and hunger everywhere. Women in rags and tatters are lying about in the dust and dirt half asleep with emaciated little babies sucking at their empty breasts. The people's clothes are actually tied on with bits of string and they look as if they had lived in them for years without taking them off. (Wells, *Kapoot*, 121, citing his wife's diary)

3 [Bullard], *Inside Stalin's Russia*, 203.
4 United Kingdom, FO 371/17251, no. 5797. Indeed, the very term "starvation" was eschewed and replaced by "provision difficulties." The memorable memorialist of the Gulag camps in Siberia's northeast, Varlam Shalamov, wrote that "alimentary dystrophy, the disease of the starving … was called by its real name only after the blockade of Leningrad [1941–44]. Before then dystrophy had various names … to denote what was just starvation" (Shalamov, *Kolyma Tales*, 1:104–5).

5 Lyons, *Assignment*, 443. Pilnyak, a realist writer who travelled widely both inside and outside the USSR, soon ran afoul of the regime (he declared himself a non-communist) but refused to leave his beloved country and strove vainly to compromise. In 1937 he was arrested, accused of Trotskyism and espionage, and summarily tried and shot.
6 Duranty, *Duranty Reports Russia*, 306. And the Russian word for a peasant – *muzhik* – has the same pejorative connotation of a bumpkin as it does in English.
7 See Engerman, *Modernization*, chap. 9, 194–243.
8 Burrell, *American Engineer*, 218.
9 Mitrany, *Marx against the Peasant*, 35, 207, 212. Russian serfdom, however, was characterized by a good deal of collective as well as individual action in the shape of the village commune (until 1906), so one might have expected Russian Marxists – theoretically speaking – to regard their country's peasants more benignly. But such does not seem to have been the case, possibly because Prime Minister Stolypin's "sturdy peasant proprietor" had been given free reign to develop after the uprisings of 1905.

Even after the quasi-abolition of serfdom in 1861 the term "peasant" was commonly pejorative, the popular attitude towards the class being derogatory. In the late 1850s, for example, a Russian general visited the writer and thinker Alexander Herzen, one of the founders of Russian socialism and agrarian populism, in self-imposed exile in London, and raised the "peasant question" (i.e., the question of whether to emancipate the peasants or not). The general asserted: "Our peasant is a fearful slacker, you know. He's a good chap, perhaps, but a drunkard and a slacker. Emancipate him at once, and he'll stop working, won't sow the fields and will simply die of hunger." Herzen retorted, "He won't really die of hunger, will he, because he will have sown wheat not for his master but for himself?" (Herzen, *My Past and Thoughts*, 530).
10 So-called because communism (Bolshevism, at least) was at war against enemies from both within (Whites mainly) and without (American, British, French, German, and Japanese forces and other foreign interventionists).
11 See Aleshkin and Vasil'ev, *Krest'ianskaia voina v Rossii*, here and there throughout.
12 Bondar and Matveev, *Istoricheskaia pamiat'*, 9.
13 Antipova et al., *Golod v SSSR*, doc. 94:292.

14 [Federal'noe arkhivnoe agentstvo], *Kollektsiia dokumentov*, doc. 81:5; Kondrashin, *Golod v SSSR*, 2, doc. 488:491.

15 Kopelev, *To Be Preserved Forever*, 259. The epithets "turkey" (*indiuk*) and "Hindu" (*Indus*) are puns on *indkhoz*, the Soviet acronym for *individual'noe khoziastvo* (individual peasant farmstead). Calling an "individualist" a "turkey" or a "Hindu" made it easier to deride him or her, of course.

Kopelev was apparently something of a model for the character of Lev Rubin in Alexander Solzhenitsyn's novel *The First Circle*, set in a *sharashka* (a scientific institute staffed by talented prisoners), where Rubin, a brilliant linguist and philologist, has been quite unjustly interned but nevertheless defends Stalin and the Soviet system.

16 Nechayev's pamphlet *The Revolutionary's Catechism* (1869) proclaimed the principle that all means are justified in furthering the cause of the revolution. He was the inspiration for Dostoyevsky's novel *The Possessed*.

17 Orlova, *Memoirs*, 207. The kolkhoz in question had a new manager every year and was frequently being subdivided or amalgamated, and the private plots of the kolkhozniks were continually being downsized or confiscated because their owners had not fulfilled their work quotas, while "half the kolkhozniks had not come back after the war, and those who had wouldn't have anything to do with the kolkhoz – they lived there but earned their money somewhere outside," and the "real work in the kolkhoz was done by the same women who'd been there since the start, in 1930" (Solzhenitsyn, *One Day in the Life*, 44, 45).

18 Born Vladimir Ilyich Ulyanov. "Lenin" was his nom de guerre as a revolutionary, referring to his exile in the basin of Eastern Siberia's Lena River.

19 This image was buttressed by the head of state, President Michael Kalinin (1875–1946), described by William Chamberlin as "a shrewd muzhik, with no influence on affairs of state, but with a certain decorative value for the regime because everything about him, his pale blue eyes, straw-colored beard, wrinkled face, clumsy manners, proclaimed his peasant origin" (Chamberlin, *Confessions*, 106). As such he was almost alone among the members of the leadership, and as such, too, perhaps it was telling that his figurehead position was powerless. He was, added Chamberlin, a "much simpler and less interesting figure" than the other Bolshevik leaders (ibid.).

20 [Steffens], *Autobiography*, 798. Steffens later told a friend that "I have seen the future, and it works." And he kept his faith in the Bolshevik promise, even

recognizing its atrocities but defending them as necessary for a better future. See Peter Hartshorn, *I Have Seen the Future*.
21 Hindus, *House without a Roof*, 220.
22 Lenin, *Polnoe sobranie sochinenii*, 38:9.
23 Lenin, "Comrade Workers, Forwards to the Last, Decisive Fight!," in *Collected Works*, 28:53–7. This exhortation was supposed to be put into effect by Lenin's "hanging order" in his telegram to Party officials in Penza Oblast, telling them to publicly hang by example at least one hundred landlords and kulaks who were rebelling against grain requisitions and to publicize their names, confiscate all of their grain, and execute the hostages, so that "people for hundreds of miles around will see, tremble, know, and scream out: let's choke and strangle these blood-sucking kulaks" (https://en.wikipedia.org/wiki/Lenin's_Hanging_Order; see also Pipes, *Unknown Lenin*, doc. 24:50–2).
24 Born Ioseb Besarionis Jughashvili in Georgia. "Stalin" was his revolutionary nickname, derived from "steel" (*stal*), which he made his official last name.
25 Talbot, *Khrushchev Remembers*, 109, 112, 113. The last remark was echoed in Khrushchev's memoirs: "Stalin regarded the collective farms and the household plots as places where you could shear the wool off the backs of the peasants as you would from sheep. His thinking was that after the fleece was removed, a new coat would grow" (Khrushchev, *Memoirs*, 2:318).
26 Kaganovich, "Ob itogakh," 2.
27 See, for example, Danilov, Manning, and Viola, *Tragediia sovetskoi derevni*, 3, docs. 114, 148, 152, 156, and 196 for 1932 and docs. 258–93 for 1933.
28 When this shibboleth was cited by a Soviet apologist who was trying to convince Panait Istrati of the necessity of violence against enemies of the Stalinist version of communism, the Romanian writer cracked, "All right, I can see the broken eggs; now where's this omelette of yours?" (Žižek, *Trouble in Paradise*, 30). Istrati was a knowledgeable critic of Stalin's Soviet Union as he was fluent in Russian, travelled widely in the country, and had contacts in high places; he lost faith before, not after, 1930 and the worst evils of collectivization (see Istrati, *Russia Unveiled*). Similarly, the Belgian Australian scholar Simon Leys (Pierre Ryckmans), known for his debunking of China's Cultural Revolution, referred to Mao as a leader who "broke eggs but never made an omelette" (*Times Literary Supplement*, 20 April 2018, 4).
29 Kondrashin, *Golod 1932–1933 godov*, 1st ed., 253.

30 Kurliandskii, *Stalin, vlast', religiia*, 88, citing the Russian State Archive of Social and Political History (hereafter RGASPI), f. 558, op. 11, d. 799, fols. 25, 30, 31, 34.

31 Ivnitskii, *Golod 1932–1933*, 192, citing RGASPI, f. 558, op. 1, d. 5,324, fol. 66; Ronina et al., "Oglianut'sia v razdum'e," 17. It is unclear whether or not Stalin meant that 25 to 30 million had starved *to death* or had been famished.

However, in August 1942 in Moscow Stalin told British prime minister Winston Churchill that 10 million had died during collectivization. He added, "It was fearful. Four years it lasted. It was absolutely necessary for Russia, if we were to avoid periodic famines, to plow the land with tractors. We must [had to] mechanise our agriculture ... It was all very bad and difficult – but necessary" (Churchill, *Second World War*, 4:447, 447–8). It would seem that Stalin was being candid and that his figure of 10 million deaths was very near the mark.

32 The first reference to the famine in the Russian scholarly literature occurred in Sharapov and Danilov, *Istoriia krest'ianstva SSSR*, 2:256, 265; an earlier version of this collective work had been cancelled in the autumn of 1964 immediately following Khrushchev's removal, which signalled the end of the short-lived "thaw" and the beginning of prolonged "stagnation" (*zastoi*) under Leonid Brezhnev and his like-minded successors (Danilov, *Istoriia krest'ianstva Rossii*, vol. 1, pt. 2, 229–348).

33 "Pismo T. P. Ryskulova k I. V. Stalinu, L. M. Kaganovichu, V. M. Molotovu," 9 March 1933, in Kvashonkin, Kosheleva, Rogovaya, and Khlevnyuk, *Sovetskoe rukovodstvo*, 204–25.

34 Kondrashin, *Golod 1932–1933 godov*, 1st ed., 252. Indeed, one theory postulates that Nadezhda's awareness prompted her to shoot herself in the early morning of 9 November 1932 after Stalin, during dinner, had cynically toasted the "destruction of the enemies of the state" and she had rebuked him by citing the starvation of the peasantry due to his policy of collectivization.

35 Kuznetsov and Terekhov, "Vazhnaia veka," 2; see also Kuznetsov and Terekhov, "Lessons of Defeat," 9–10.

36 At the end of 1927, when the Fifteenth Party Congress in December sealed the defeat of the oppositionists under Trotsky, Bukharin, and others, Josef ("Koba") Stalin's inner circle, or "team," included the tough Lazar Kaganovich, the most loyal member; the extremely hardworking and colourless Vyacheslav Molotov; the military veteran Klim Voroshilov; the educated

and cultured Valerian Kuibyshev; the Latvian proletarian Jan Rudzutak; Andrei Andreyev, another proletarian; Mikhail Kalinin, the peasant "elder statesman" of the group and the most popular Party figure after Stalin himself; the generous and sensitive Georgian Grigory ("Sergo") Ordzhonikidze; the Armenian Anastas Mikoyan, a trade specialist and a long-time survivor; and the personable Sergei Kirov, Stalin's close friend (murdered in 1934). All were members of the Politburo, but not all of them socialized with Stalin. What could be termed his "innermost circle" (with Kaganovich and Molotov) essentially constituted an executive triumvirate. The security specialist Lavrenty Beria, the son of a Georgian peasant, did not join Stalin's inner circle until after the famine (in 1932 Stalin rated him "a good organizer, an efficient capable functionary") (Davies et al., *Stalin-Kaganovich Correspondence*, doc. 58:182). See Fitzpatrick, *On Stalin's Team*.

37 For documentary particulars on "wreckers" at various levels of officialdom, see Mozokhin, *Politbiuro i "vrediteli."*

38 Stalin, *Works*, 13:256. This dogma was enshrined in the Soviet constitutions of 1918 and 1936.

39 Murin, *Pisatel' i vozhd*, 28–9, 68. An "Italian" (*Italian'ka* [Italian woman]) meant either working to rule or even striking – but why?

40 Resis, *Molotov Remembers*, 243, 243–4, 244. Molotov was the namesake of the "Molotov cocktail," the name given by Finnish soldiers to the homemade bottle grenades that they used against Russian tanks during the Winter War of 1939–40.

41 See Chuev, *Tak govoril Kaganovich*; and Kaganovich, *Pamiatnie zapiski*. Also very able (self-taught) and steely, Kaganovich allegedly originated the infamous rationalization of revolutionary violence in terms of having to break eggs in order to make an omelette (*Time Magazine*, 24 October 1932). He was sent to the Central Black Earth, the Ukraine, the North Caucasus, and Siberia to brutally enforce collectivization, kulakization, and the procurement of grain, and it was he who ordered the deportation to the North of all of the residents of three *stanitsas* (Cossack villages) in the North Caucasus, some forty-five thousand villagers altogether, as an example to others. In the 1930s, with the help of convict labour, he implemented "The General Plan for the Reconstruction of Moscow" (1930–9), which included the construction of the Moscow-Volga Canal and the Moscow Metro (the showcase subway system that bore his name until 1955, when he was expelled from the CPSU by

Khrushchev) as well the destruction of some four hundred historic landmarks and the introduction of the "Stalinist baroque" style, embodied in the seven "wedding cake" structures that dominated Moscow's skyline until the end of the century. Both Kaganovich and Molotov outlived Stalin by more than three decades, and although they were demoted for opposing Khrushchev, both of them, as well as Mikoyan, retired unscathed and died, unrepentant and peaceably, in their beds: Mikoyan at eighty-two in 1978, Molotov at ninety-six in 1986, Kaganovich at the age of ninety-seven (and demented) in 1991, without ever having been brought to account and without witnessing the demise of their beloved USSR.

42 Larina, *This I Cannot Forget*, 127.
43 Antipova et al., *Golod v SSSR*, doc. 126:385.
44 Von Herwarth, *Against Two Evils*, 39.
45 [Bullard], *Inside Stalin's Russia*, 116.
46 This possibility, however, did not prevent the Kremlin from finding and punishing culprits or scapegoats. In March 1933 seventy-five senior agricultural bureaucrats were arrested and tried on charges of "counter-revolutionary" activity and "sabotage" in the Ukraine, the North Caucasus, and Belorussia "with the aim," according to the OGPU, "of undermining the economic condition of the peasantry and creating a state of famine in the country by falsifying the figures on grain procurement and thereby leading the leadership to believe that grain was being hoarded." Thirty-five of the accused were shot, twenty-two were sentenced to ten years in prison, and eighteen were sentenced to eight years in prison ([Bullard], *Inside Stalin's Russia*, 228n17; Zelenin, "O nekotorykh 'belykh piatnakh'," 19n90, citing *Izvestiia*, 12 March 1933).
47 Antipova et al., *Golod v SSSR*, doc. 76:211, 216. Zhivanov's warning about Red Army soldiers being disaffected by the starvation of relatives (and friends) seems to have been unfounded, if we are to believe a German diplomat, who said that, although most of the recruits were the sons and daughters or brothers and sisters of starving peasants, they remained loyal to the regime because they enjoyed special rations, even though they were forbidden to take home-leave to rural areas, had their correspondence screened, and were ordered to write exhortatory letters to their families (Von Herwarth, *Against Two Evils*, 40).
48 Antipova et al., *Golod v SSSR*, doc. 126:385; [Federal Archival Agency], *Famine*

in the USSR, doc. 118:2; Kondrashin and Tiurina, "Govorit' o golode," doc. 26:126.

49 Smith and Smith, *I Was a Soviet Worker*, 196. Not every devout Bolshevik was as heartless as Yurov. It was rumoured in the capital's diplomatic community, for example, that Stalin's much younger and possibly bipolar second wife, Nadezhda Alliluyeva, fatally shot herself in 1932 as a result of her opposition to the violent campaign against the peasants ([Bullard], *Inside Stalin's Russia*, 203). The actual circumstances of her suicide are still not known, however.

50 Kopelev, *Education*, 250. During the famine's zenith in the winter of 1932–33 Kopelev was heatedly berated by his own peasant father not only for being blind to the catastrophe in the countryside but also for being responsible for its creation through his participation in rapacious grain requisitioning. The father's cri de coeur helped the son to realize that he had been misled by his blind faith in "scientific socialism," and he felt that there was no way to expiate his "sin," not even by prayer – all he could do was "not to forget, not to cover over, but to try to tell as much truth as I can as precisely as I can" (ibid., 267).

51 [Federal'noe arkhivnoe agentstvo], *Kollektsiia dokumentov*, doc. 59:141.

52 Vodopianova et al., *Mezhdu molotom i nakovalnei*, 1:73.

53 See Sholokhov, *Quiet Flows the Don* and *Virgin Soil Upturned*. To give Sholokhov his due, he was the first person in the Stalin period to mention the famine in the Soviet press when, in a collection of articles published in 1940 on the occasion of Stalin's sixtieth birthday, he wrote in his contribution that, in 1933 in the North Caucasus, enemies of the people, on the pretext of combatting sabotage in the kolkhozes, had deprived the kolkhozniks of grain, and that "all grain, including that given as an advance for workdays, was confiscated," "many communists ... were expelled from the Party and arrested," and "famine began in the kolkhoz" (Ivnitskii, *Golod 1932–1933*, 192, citing Pletnev, *Stalin*, 239). It was later the same year (9 September) that Stalin himself during a session of the Party's Central Committee acknowledged: "25–30 million of us, for example, starved, there was not enough grain, but we have come to live well today." But his speech was not published, and it was another half-century before the famine could be mentioned in print in the USSR (ibid., 192, citing RGASPI, f. 558, op. 1, d. 5,324, fol. 66). Sholokhov, incidentally, was awarded the 1965 Nobel Prize in Literature for *Quiet Flows the Don*, which some critics (notably Alexander Solzhenitsyn) contended was plagiarized, but the charge has not been proven.

54 Chukovskii, *Dni moei zhizni*, 311, 311–12, 312. This diary has been partially translated into English as [Chukovskii], *Kornei Chukovsky, Diary*.
55 Chukovskii, *Dni moei zhizni*, 337.
56 Gorky, "On the Russian Peasantry," 26. In a letter of 1934 to Stalin, whom he called the "Boss," Gorky expressed his "distrustful and even inimical attitude towards the peasant," "with all his individualistic notions of 'personal ownership'" (Barratt and Scherr, *Maksim Gorky*, letter 169:352).
57 Platonov, *Foundation Pit*, 153. Gorky's detestation of the peasantry may have stemmed at least in part from his horror at the bloody torching by peasants of a village store in Kazan Oblast in his youth (Barratt and Scherr, *Maksim Gorky*, 5).
58 Shentalinsky, *KGB's Literary Archive*, 261, citing *Pravda*, 15 November 1930, 2. Gorky wrote from Italy in 1926: "If the peasant and his grain were to disappear, the city-dweller would learn how to obtain grain in the laboratory. Creative labour is revolutionary; the labour of gathering is essentially conservative" (Barratt and Scherr, *Maksim Gorky*, letter 126:265–6).
59 For example, in the late spring of 1933 one P.I. Ivanov (possibly a pseudonym in order to avoid persecution) wrote to Gorky: "The Ukraine is becoming extinct from starvation. According to very rough estimates, no less than 1/3 of the population has already died off – 12–13 million human lives altogether." He added:

> Aleksey Maksimovich! If only you had seen all of this horror! If you had seen these wretched children, either with bloated faces or with shrivelled skin pulled away from their bones, really mummies with torment and hungry despair in their eyes ... They knock on our door every minute, begging for something to eat. If you had seen how they pick grain out of fresh dung, you would, like I, come to hate – no, not communism, not socialism – but today's leaders of communism. The number of orphans is in the millions, the number of abandoned [children] in the hundreds of thousands. Starvation has deadened maternal feeling and killed morality. Where, when, and under what regime has there been anything like this?

And the reason for the famine, Ivanov said, was the fact that "the village ha[d] given everything to the state, which has left it only the right to starve to death" (Kurliandskii, "Aleksey Maksimovich!," 218–19, 224, 224–5).

60 Leder, *My Life*, 312.
61 Klyuev, *Poems*, 60–1.
62 The Acmeists were members of a small group of Russian poets that was founded in the early years of the twentieth century and centred in St Petersburg. They rejected the vagueness and the affectations of the Symbolists. Their outstanding representatives were Anna Akhmatova and Osip Mandelstam, both of whom were repressed by Stalin.
63 [Mandelstam], *Osip Mandelstam*, 81.
64 Mandelstam, *Hope Abandoned*, 471.
65 For a complete translation of the poem, see Mandelstam, *Hope against Hope*, 13. Nadezhda managed to preserve many of her husband's poems by both memorizing and concealing them.
66 Medvedev, *Let History Judge*, 243–4, citing Pasternak's unpublished memoirs.
67 Pirozhkova, *At His Side*, 50–1.
68 Pasternak, *Doctor Zhivago*, 507.
69 Pirozhkova, *At His Side*, 18.
70 Freidin, *Isaac Babel's Selected Writings*, 322.
71 Only two of the stories have survived. Babel's downfall, incidentally, was due not to his writing but to his libido – a womanizer, he persisted in a longstanding relationship with the wife of the head of the secret police, Nikolai Yezhov. Babel's long-time mentor and protector, Maxim Gorky, was unable to save him, having died in 1936 under mysterious circumstances (possibly with the complicity of his "boss," Stalin, who had long indulged him).
72 For example, in 1931 Platonov examined collective and state farms in the Central Volga and the North Caucasus. One of the resultant entries in his notebooks reads: "North Caucasus Kray. State farm 'Svinovod' [Piggery] No. 22 ... 25% of the plan for construction has been fulfilled. There are no nails, iron, timber ... the milkmaids ran off from the herds, their superiors rounded them up and forced them to work – there are cases of suicide because of this ... the loss of livestock is 89–90%. Murrain [cattle plague] is down 1.5%" (Kornienko, "Istoriia teksta," 173).
73 The novel also foreshadows the fate of Moscow's Cathedral of Christ the Saviour, just upriver from the Kremlin, the holiest shrine of Russian Orthodoxy and the second largest church in Christendom (after St Peter's Basilica), which was demolished in 1931 to make room for the towering Palace of Soviets, whose foundation was not completed until 1939, leading Alfred Choler-

ton, of first the *News Chronicle* and then the *Daily Telegraph*, to quip that the definition of a reactionary was someone who could not distinguish the Palace of Soviets from a hole in the ground (Heckler, *Accidental Journalist*, 34). The site was made into an enormous swimming pool in the 1950s, which in turn gave way from 1995 to 2000, at enormous expense, to a rebuilt (and opulent) Cathedral of Christ the Saviour.

74 See Chandler, *Portable Platonov*.

75 See "Platonov, Andrei Platonovich," in the *Encyclopedia of Soviet Writers*, online at http://www.sovlit.net/bios/platonov.html.

76 Chamberlin, *Confessions*, 103–4, 104. At first, Chamberlin recalled, he strove for balance in his coverage, "partly because of the pressure of censorship, partly because of inability to tell of many cases of cruelty and injustice because of the certainty that this would bring down further reprisals on the victims, partly because, in fairness, I felt obliged to contradict some of the ignorant and extravagant hostile pictures of Soviet life which appeared abroad." He added that "the question of the influence of censorship on his reportage was not an easy question to answer, because the indirect forms of censorship were far more important than the blue-penciling of cables by the censor in the Commissariat for Foreign Affairs … Much more important … was the weapon of putting the recalcitrant correspondent on the blacklist of the Gay-Pay-Oo [OGPU], of expelling him from the country or refusing him permission to re-enter" (ibid., 102, 103).

77 Kondrashin, *Golod v SSSR*, 3, doc. 390:477.

78 Lyons, *Assignment*, 109. This vetting process, incidentally, rewarded the UPI man with "the discovery that journalists who sounded so cocksure in their published eulogies of the Bolshevik world were less certain and less eulogistic in their unpublished views" (ibid., 66). Born in Belorussia to a Jewish family but raised on New York City's East Side, Lyons (1898–1985) became an active young socialist in the 1910s and an enthusiastic supporter of the Bolsheviks in the 1920s. He left TASS to join United Press as its Moscow correspondent (1928–34). The experience completely disillusioned him, prompting him to famously label Stalin's Russia the "greatest show on earth" (ibid., 102) and making him a foe of the USSR and of communism for the rest of his life as well as a conservative commentator (he became an editor of *Reader's Digest* and the *National Review*) and a Cold War partisan.

79 Ibid., 542.

80 See Engerman, *Modernization*, 194–243.
81 Clyman, "Dares Warning of Death," 1, 3.
82 Clyman, "Russian Peasant," 1.
83 For the context of American correspondents in Moscow, see Bassow, *Moscow Correspondents*, esp. 66–75.
84 Ibid., 67; Lyons, *Assignment*, 545–7. According to the Belorussian-born American writer and journalist Maurice Hindus, who accompanied Barnes and Stoneman on their trip to the south, the *Herald-Tribune* correspondent Barnes avoided expulsion only after the renowned American newspaper editor and leader of the Progressive movement (and confidant of US presidents) William Allen White of the *Emporia* (Kansas) *Gazette* advised Commissar of Foreign Affairs Maxim Litvinov that such a move would jeopardize relations between the USSR and the United States (and at a time when the former was keen to gain American recognition, which came the next year) (Hindus, *House without a Roof*, 218). The cocksure (and conceited) Muggeridge of the *Guardian* called Barnes (1899–1940) "the most notable activist among the press corps ... an earnest [and] eager American reporter who kept us all on our toes" (Muggeridge, *Chronicles*, 234); in his diary, however, the same (albeit older) Muggeridge said that he had found Barnes to be "a quite exceptionally stupid man" (Bright-Holmes, *Like It Was*, 58). He became known as "Scoop" Barnes for having broken the famine story to American newspaper readers (Abbe, "Men of Cablese," 31). William Chamberlin felt that Barnes's "courageous, honest reporting in the face of the harassments and disabilities of censorship should have won him [rather than Duranty] a Pulitzer Prize" (Chamberlin, *Confessions*, 155).
85 Danilov, Manning, and Viola, *Tragediia sovetskoi derevni*, 3, doc. 267:644–5.
86 The affair caused a short-lived rupture in Anglo-Russian relations (the trial, incidentally, was covered for Reuters by Ian Fleming, the creator of James Bond). See Morrell, *Britain Confronts the Stalin Revolution*.
87 Muggeridge, *Chronicles*, 253, 256, 257, 260. Muggeridge (1903–1990), a member of the *Guardian*'s editorial staff, had become convinced by 1932 that capitalism had "irretrievably broken down ... [and] the Soviet regime seemed the only convincing alternative," and he "had a great longing to go to Russia, not just to look round, but to stay and bring up [his] family there." The newspaper's new editor, W.P. Crozier, "readily agreed to [his] going to Moscow to stand in for the *Guardian* correspondent there, William Henry

Chamberlin, who planned to go on extended leave." Muggeridge arrived in Moscow on 16 September, and already by 25 November he was "completely disillusioned," mainly by "the plan and [the fact that] all that doesn't conform, that's not mediocre, [is] crushed out of existence," although not by the tyranny and cruelty, which he considered "little things." He was repelled "more than anything" by "the atmosphere of repression, and want, and fear, and unhappiness (joylessness) everywhere; and of arrogance and corruption in the governing classes." He left the USSR in the spring of 1933 because Chamberlin had returned from leave to resume the *Guardian*'s Soviet coverage; besides, his money had nearly run out, and he believed that he would be expelled anyway after his famine articles appeared (Bright-Holmes, *Like It Was*, 13, 22, 48, 49, 73–4). Muggeridge called journalism in Moscow a "racket" (and by implication its practitioners "racketeers") (Muggeridge, "Russia Revealed"), and upon his return to England he published a satire of Western reporters in the Soviet capital, *Winter in Moscow* (1934). For an engaging but somewhat uncritical biography, see Hunter, *Malcolm Muggeridge*.

88 Jones (1905–1935) had obtained a first-class degree in French, German, and Russian at the University of Cambridge and had begun a doctorate in Russian history at the University of London under Bernard Pares, who came to regard him as his "best successor," and former prime minister (1916–22) Lloyd George hired him as a foreign affairs advisor (Pares, *Wandering Student*, 309–11). In 1935 Jones was killed in Inner Mongolia by bandits ("undoubtedly" at the behest of the Soviet secret police [Simkin, *Veliky obman*, 253]) while trying to enter the Soviet Union a fourth time. See Colley, *More Than a Grain of Truth*, and Gamache, *Gareth Jones*. His time in the USSR was dramatically fictionalized in the 2019 film *Mr Jones* (directed by Agnieszka Holland). In it, incidentally, Jones is identified with the Mr Jones in Orwell's *Animal Farm*, though he is merely the owner of the farm with that everyman name.

89 The efficacy of Jones's modus operandi was starkly illustrated by his interview of a peasant on the "Stalin Kolkhoz" in the Central Black Earth, first in the presence of the farm head, when the peasant told Jones "of the successes of the kolkhoz, of the enthusiasm of the country for the collective farm movement, and of the affection of the peasants for their young Bolshevist leader"; the next day, however, the same peasant, now alone, approached Jones and whispered, "It is terrible here in the kolkhoz. We cannot speak or

we will be sent away to Siberia as they sent the others [kulaks]. We are afraid. I had three cows. They took them away and now I only get a crust of bread. It is a thousand times worse now than before the Revolution; 1926 and 1927 were fine years, but now we dare not oppose the Communists or we shall be exiled. We have to keep quiet" (Jones, "Real Russia: The Peasant").

90 Colley, *More Than a Grain of Truth*, 225; [Jones], "Real Russia: The Outlook"; Jones, "Will There Be Soup"; Jones, "Famine Rules Russia"; Jones, "Balance-Sheet"; Jones, "Mr Jones Replies"; Jones, "Russia's Starvation"; Jones, "There Is No Bread"; Mowrer, "Russian Famine." For a complete listing of Jones's articles based upon his three visits to the USSR, see Gamache, *Gareth Jones*, 222–5.

Subsequently, Eugene Lyons, who described Jones as an "earnest and meticulous little man," was to allege that, after leaving the USSR, the Welshman had basically reported a summary of what he had been told by Moscow's foreign correspondents and journalists, although in order to protect them and to render his statements more authentic he had emphasized his covert trip to the south as his main source; Walter Duranty was to repeat this allegation. To his credit, however, Lyons did come more or less clean later, admitting that the capital's American correspondents had decided to disown Jones when pressed by their editors for famine news because to remain on amicable terms with the censors during the Metro-Vickers trial of British and Russian engineers "was for all of us a compelling professional necessity." "Throwing down Jones," he confessed, "was as unpleasant a chore to any of us in years of juggling facts to please dictatorial regimes – but throw him down we did, unanimously and in almost identical formulas of equivocation" (Lyons, *Assignment*, 575–6). Bassow, however, slants this affair somewhat differently, stating that the contingent of reporters was blackmailed by the Press Department, with Umansky declaring that unless they repudiated Jones's reportage they would not be accredited to cover the trial, so they agreed "in roundabout phrases that damned Jones a liar" and then celebrated the "filthy business" over vodka and *zakuski* (appetizers) with Umansky (Bassow, *Moscow Correspondents*, 68–9).

The breaking of the famine story was recounted quite differently, especially as regards timing, by Zara Witkin, the American engineer. He wrote that, after being refused permission in late August of 1933 to visit the Ukraine and the North Caucasus – "the first time that correspondents had been barred from a civilian area in peacetime" – the "fuming" American reporters (Barnes, Duranty, Lyons, Chamberlin, Stoneman, Louis Fischer of the *Nation*, Stanley Richardson of the Associated Press, and Linton Wells of the International News Service, plus ex-pat Maurice Hindus, who happened to be in Moscow after having been barred from his native village) assembled at the home of Barnes to decide what they had to do in order to "get the news." Lyons wanted to report on the famine but he had already been threatened with expulsion by the Soviet authorities at the beginning of the year for his story about the deportation of the thousands of residents of three Kuban stanitsas. Duranty stated that he would write nothing, saying, "What are a few million dead Russians in a situation like this? Quite unimportant. This is just an incident in the sweeping historical changes here. I think the entire matter is exaggerated." Barnes, Witkin continued, then proposed that they demand as a group to be allowed to see the famine conditions, but Duranty, Fischer, and Hindus demurred, whereupon Barnes left the room and telephoned a "sizzling dispatch about the famine" with an estimate of 1 million victims at the least. Upon the publication of this story on the front page of the New York *Herald-Tribune* the next day (Barnes, "Million Feared Dead," 7), every other American newspaper pressed their correspondents for confirmation, forcing their hands. The Soviet government had either to expel all of them or let Barnes stay, and it chose the latter course, for "the antagonism of the entire American press was too great a risk to run." It was upon this occasion, ended Witkin, that Duranty in his cablegram estimated 3 million deaths "of causes due to malnutrition" – his notorious euphemism for starvation ([Witkin], *American Engineer*, 207–10, 259).

Fischer (1896–1970), a Jewish American leftist who had been reporting from the Soviet Union since 1922, was described by Muggeridge as "a sallow, ponderous, inordinately earnest man, dear to Oumansky as one who had never once through the years veered from virtuously following the Party Line" (Muggeridge, *Chronicles*, 246). In the fall of 1932, Margaret Wettlin visited Fischer and found that he seemed to agree with Maurice Hindus's disenchantment with the Bolsheviks, yet, when pressed, this "serious" man with a "dark, brooding presence" did not elaborate but "just shook his head and said, 'Go home, little girl, go home'" (Wettlin, *Fifty Russian Winters*, 10, 11). Fischer denied the famine at the time but eventually had his epiphany – what he termed his "Kronstadt" (after the 1921 mutiny on that island naval base by the very sailors who in 1917, on behalf of the revolutionaries, had fired the signal from the battleship *Aurora* to storm the Winter Palace) – and admitted the existence of the famine, which "killed several million people" and stemmed from "an ingenious, twentieth-century form of wholesale serfdom" – that is, collectivization (Fischer, *Why I Became Pro-Soviet*, 22, 23; see also Crowl, *Angels in Stalin's Paradise*).

Fischer's Russian-born and pro-Marxist wife was even more culpable, never fully acknowledging either the 1917–21 or the 1928–34 famine. About the former she exulted: "Everybody was hungry, cold, and poor ... everybody suffered. But those who believed in the revolution suffered with exaltation. They were sacrificing themselves in order to rebuild the world." About the latter she enthused: "As in the first years after the revolution, people now starved and froze for the sake of a better future" and "those years were hard years, yet they were good years, full of exhilaration and renewed hopes in the possibilities of socialism" after that "ghost of capitalism, the NEP, that ugly detour from the road to socialism, was gone" (Fischer, *My Lives*, 10, 36, 36–7). After Stalin's bloody purges and his non-aggression pact with Nazi Germany, she finally apostatized.

91 Chamberlin (1897–1969) was the *Christian Science Monitor*'s man in Moscow, and sometimes he also reported to the *Manchester Guardian* as a "useful sideline" (Bright-Holmes, *Like It Was*, 13). Muggeridge described him: "He was a short, podgy, highly intelligent, droll man who neither drank nor smoked, his only form of self-indulgence being eating chocolate ... reckoning to consume his own weight annually." He and especially his Russian Jewish wife, Sonya, "had every intention of staying in the USSR for some time to come, and [he] very cleverly used his complaisant coverage in *The Guardian* to offset any sharp criticism of the régime he might essay in the *Monitor*. By playing off one against the other he managed to achieve the delicate balancing act of keeping on his feet in the USSR without becoming its committed stooge" (Muggeridge, *Chronicles*, 232, 233). Muggeridge allowed that Chamberlin "knows a lot about Russia" (Bright-Holmes, *Like It Was*, 16), and to Eugene Lyons he was the "best-informed and least sensational" of his American colleagues, being "always exact and scholarly and passionless" in his dispatches (Lyons, *Assignment*, 96, 147). James Abbe, who believed that no other American reporter knew the Soviet Union as well as Chamberlin, described his dispatches as factual and unadorned, although like every other corre-

spondent who wanted to remain in Moscow, he found it necessary "now and again to pull his punches," without, however, "wrangling with, or pandering to, the authorities" (Abbe, "Men of Cablese," 31). And William Strang, acting counsellor at the British Embassy, advised Whitehall that Chamberlin was "generally regarded as a well-informed and level-headed observer, who approaches this country with an unbiased mind" (Lievan, *British Documents*, 10, doc. 72:128). Like his fellow left-leaning journalists Lyons and Muggeridge, Chamberlin went to the Soviet Union "on a wave of pacifist-progressive sentiment, but soon soured on the régime," and two decades later he even became an "ardent supporter" of Joseph McCarthy (Muggeridge, *Chronicles*, 232, 241), the witch-hunting junior senator from one-time progressive Wisconsin who, in the early 1950s, sensationally investigated supposed communist subversion in the United States by means of scare tactics. Strang, incidentally, whom Reader Bullard rated "one of the best officials and most likeable men [he had] met" ([Bullard], *Inside Stalin's Russia*, 20), was to be the British negotiator – scorned by Molotov as a Foreign Office official "of the second class" – who was dispatched belatedly to Leningrad in August 1940 in an abortive attempt to make common cause with the USSR against Nazi Germany (Fitzpatrick, *On Stalin's Team*, 146).

92 And "there was no official censorship of mail correspondence" (Chamberlin, *Confessions*, 103).
93 Chamberlin, *Russia's Iron Age*, 97–8.
94 Chamberlin, *Confessions*, 155–6, 156–7. The concession, located near the town of Kropotkin in the Kuban, was managed by Dr Fritz Dittloff, a Prussian.
95 Chamberlin, *Russia's Iron Age*, 83–4.
96 Ibid., 86. Unorthodoxly, Sheboldayev had just a few years earlier advocated greater independence and more material rewards for kolkhozes. Born in Paris into an émigré physician's family that had returned to Russia in 1900, Sheboldayev had become involved in the revolutionary movement at the age of seventeen.
97 Ibid., 88. In fact, Western Siberia did suffer "a good deal of hardship and undernourishment."
98 A Yiddish writer, journalist, and playwright, Lang (1888–1970) was born in Lithuania, and in 1904 he had immigrated to the United States, where he became a labour union and socialist activist and the labour editor of the *Jewish Daily Forward*. His wife, Lucy Fox Robins Lang, was born in Kiev, and in the

United States she became an avowed and active anarchist. Presumably both were fluent in Yiddish, he in Lithuanian and Russian, and she in Ukrainian and Russian.

Lang's series of seven articles about Russia appeared initially in the *Jewish Daily Forward* and were reprinted two and a half years later in the conservative, Hearst-owned New York *Evening Journal* (15 May 1935, 1–2; 16 May 1935, 1–2; 17 May 1935, 1–2; 18 May 1935, 1–2; 20 May 1935, 1–2; 22 May 1935, 1–2; 23 May 1935, 1–2) as part of a campaign to discredit President Roosevelt's policy of cementing diplomatic relations with the USSR. They also reappeared in his wife's autobiography as a chapter entitled "Soviet Nightmare" (Lang, *Tomorrow Is Beautiful*, 257–69).

The articles were followed a week later by another series by Richard H. Sanger (1914–1976), the son of Roosevelt's assistant secretary of war. The younger Sanger and his wife went to the Soviet Union in 1933 to work as committed communists but left after eighteen months, thoroughly disillusioned. Upon their arrival at the beginning of July, he recounted, the famine had peaked in the Ukraine, the North Caucasus, the Central Volga, the Central Black Earth, and parts of Siberia, and the death rate from starvation remained high until September. He was convinced that in 1933 alone 4.5 million citizens starved to death and another 1 million perished from malnutrition-related diseases such as typhus. And, like Lang, he believed that the famine was solely human-made (Sanger, "Ex-Communist Bares Red Tyranny"). Years later Sanger became a foreign service officer in the US Department of State.

Lang's and Sanger's accounts were preceded from 18 to 27 February in Hearst's *Evening Journal* by yet another series on Soviet Russia by one Thomas Walker ... later found to be a hoax concocted by an American felon, Robert Green.

99 Walter Duranty (1884–1957) was the Moscow bureau chief of the *New York Times* from 1922 until 1934. By the end of the 1920s, according to colleague Eugene Lyons, he "reigned supreme" among the foreign reporters in the capital, and he was so much in demand that he was known as the "Unofficial American Ambassador" (Anonymous, *Experiences in Russia – 1931*, 85–6; Lyons, *Assignment*, 67). He gained an exclusive interview with Stalin in 1929, and in 1932 he won the Pulitzer Prize for a series of 1931 articles about the USSR. His reportage did more than anything else to influence American

opinion in favour of the Soviet state (Abbe, "Men of Cablese," 29). Lyons described him as "urbane, clever to a fault, a scintillating talker" and "curiously contemptuous of Russians," while the mercurial Muggeridge saw him as a "little sharp-witted energetic" Irishman from Liverpool (Muggeridge, *Chronicles*, 254). But it was Duranty's journalism that aroused controversy, particularly his coverage of the famine. He was accused of admitting the existence of starvation in private conversations but denying it in published dispatches (in a like vein Lyons recalled that his candid "spoken views of the Russian scene … would have shocked New York radicals who mistook him for a Soviet enthusiast" from his *Times* pieces [Lyons, *Assignment*, 67]). Duranty acknowledged to Muggeridge that "there was an appalling food shortage, if not a famine," and that it was the inevitable price of Bolshevik progress (adding, once more, "remember that you can't make omelettes without cracking eggs"). Muggeridge deemed him "a smart fellow, well dressed" but "despicable," and the two of them took a great dislike to each other (Bright-Holmes, *Like It Was*, 47). Yet, wrote the *Guardian*'s correspondent, "I always enjoyed his company; there was something vigorous, vivacious, preposterous, about his unscrupulousness which made his persistent lying somehow absorbing." He added that "it, of course, suited his material interests … to write everything the Soviet authorities wanted him to," so he "never had any trouble getting a visa, or a house, or interviews with whomever he wanted." His complicity was not only materially advantageous, Muggeridge believed, but also a result of an inferiority complex arising from being short, having lost part of a leg (in a train mishap), and lacking the aristocratic lineage and classical education that he claimed to have, so he admired the Stalin regime for its strength and ruthlessness ("I put my money on Stalin," he was wont to say) and the country for its vast size and large population. Also, by virtue of being the most talked-about man in Moscow among foreigners and the "great Russian expert in America," he gained repute (Muggeridge, *Chronicles*, 254–6).

A better opinion of Duranty was held by the news and fashion photographer James Abbe. He noted that Duranty read and spoke Russian, a "rare qualification" among his Moscow peers. He considered Duranty a "straight reporter," not an interpretive or investigative correspondent, as well as virtually a "one-city reporter," having seen little of the country or its people except Moscow, but he had "the knack of reading between the lines of

Soviet newspapers, and of whatever state documents [were] made public, getting more of the truth from them than 99 out of 100 Russians." Moreover, Abbe added, although "frequently criticized as being rabidly pro-Soviet, he had written many critical accounts of the breakdown and shortcomings of the [First] Five-Year Plan," although he did admit that, throughout his eleven years in Moscow, Duranty had never once jeopardized his standing with the Soviet authorities (Abbe, "Men of Cablese," 29).

Also, it was rumoured that Duranty was being blackmailed by the Soviet authorities (Muggeridge, *Chronicles*, 254, 255, 255–6), perhaps on sexual grounds (Conquest, *Reflections*, 1213). The British Embassy's William Strang reported: "Mr Duranty is a somewhat shady individual, who has been accused (though not on convincing evidence, as far as I can tell) of being in the pay of the Soviet Govt." (Carynnyk, Luciuk, and Kordan, *Foreign Office*, doc. 17:204). In a private conversation at the beginning of June 1931 with a member of the American Embassy in Berlin Duranty reportedly stated that, "in agreement with the New York Times and the Soviet authorities," his "official despatches always reflect[ed] the official opinion of the Soviet régime and not his own" (United States, Records of the Department of State, T1249, [2]). Another British Embassy staffer believed that Duranty hoped that his positive reportage would encourage American recognition of the USSR and earn him a position (such as press attaché) in the prospective American embassy (Taylor, *Stalin's Apologist*, 204).

Incidentally, the possibility of Western newspapers receiving "subsidies" from the Soviet government in return for "appropriate" reporting on the "success of the Five-Year Plan" is intimated by a letter from a Soviet diplomat in Paris to the Commissariat of the Interior in Moscow of 9 September 1933 about an article in *Le Matin* that was critical of the USSR: "With its campaign about the famine in the Ukraine, etc. the newspaper is clearly trying to blackmail a subsidy from us" (Kondrashin, *Khlebozagotovitel'naia politika*, 256, citing the Archive of the Foreign Policy of the Russian Federation [hereafter AVPRF], f. 05 [*sic*?], op. 13, p. 90, d. 14, fol. 72).

At any rate, seventy years after the famine a concerted (but unsuccessful) campaign was launched by the Ukrainian diaspora, notably in Canada and the United States, to have Duranty's Pulitzer Prize revoked, even though it was awarded for a series of eleven articles in the *New York Times* in 1931 and two in its magazine in 1932 that did *not* concern the famine (which had not yet climaxed or been publicized) and that in their own right are derivative but informative and not uncritical (one article is entitled "Stalin's Russia Is an Echo of Iron Ivan's"). After all, just because Duranty's famine denial was a "big lie" does not mean that his other reports are, ipso facto, mendacious. Perhaps, too, the objectors had an inflated opinion of the Pulitzer. Certainly, Duranty has become one of the bêtes noires of Ukrainian nationalists (see Crowl, *Angels*; Luciuk, *Not Worthy*; Taylor, *Stalin's Apologist*; and "Statement on Walter Duranty's [Pulitzer] Prize" online at https://www.pulitzer.org/news/statement-walter-duranty).

100 Lyons, *Assignment*, 572.
101 Chamberlin, *Confessions*, 155.
102 Duranty, *Duranty Reports Russia*, 279.
103 Ibid., 331. Whiting Williams wrote that, in the summer of 1933, Duranty "pooh-poohed all hunger rumors" but "now" (autumn) "confidentially admits five million" famine deaths (Williams, "Confidential Circular," n.p.). Whiting [Charles] Williams (1878–1975) was a multilingual charity organizer and management consultant from Ohio who famously went underground in the late 1910s and early 1920s in various countries in the Americas and Europe to investigate working conditions.
104 Anonymous, "Visitors Describe Famine," 6.
105 However, as the UPI's Eugene Lyons rightly cautioned listeners to, and readers of, the impressions of these various visitors and sojourners:

> Deeply rooted belief ... help[s] explain ... why two foreigners, equally honest and intelligent, having passed through the same routine of sight-seeing and interviews, emerge with diametrically opposite impressions of the Soviet land. What is to one a "gray, unsmiling population" is for the other the inspiring spectacle of a "grimly determined population." One speaks of "magnificent industrial discipline," the other of "factory serfs." One declaims about the tyranny of fashion having ended – "an uninhibited, unpretentious and truly democratic attitude towards clothes" ... The other dismisses this achievement of the revolution in some such phrase as "ragged, pathetically patched people." (Lyons, *Assignment*, 93)

106 Muggeridge, *Chronicles*, 243.

107 Lyons, *Assignment*, 573.
108 Hindus, *Green Worlds*, 327.
109 Ibid., 334, 335, 336. Similarly, near the end of his life Hindus wrote that, after the mid-1930s, "the threat of periodic famine, which for centuries had been ravaging the peasantry, has vanished from the Russian land. But at what a price!" (Hindus, *House without a Roof*, 222).
110 Hindus, *Green Worlds*, 342. Also, at the beginning of the famine's climax in the autumn of 1932 a fellow American, Margaret Wettlin, met Hindus at a Moscow hotel and he told her that his opinion had changed: "He was angry. He said he was through with this country. He said he couldn't forgive them [the Bolsheviks] for what they were doing to the peasants ... He said they were running away from the farms, driven away by hunger" (Wettlin, *Fifty Russian Winters*, 10).
111 Chukovsky, *Diary*, 313.
112 Smith, *D.S. Mirsky*, 233. At least Mirsky was correct on one of the two counts.
113 For a recent Russian study of the participants in, and the testimonials of, this empathetic Western curiosity, see Kulikova, *Novyi mir glazami starogo*; for the Soviet response to this interest, see David-Fox, *Showcasing the Great Experiment*.
114 Kaplan, *Lincoln Steffens*, 250; [Steffens], *Autobiography*, 799.
115 Muggeridge, *Chronicles*, 254.
116 Lievan, *British Documents*, 9, doc.134:293.
117 Rampersad, *Life of Langston Hughes*, 1:267.
118 Ibid., 265.
119 On this topic see Bullock, *Romancing the Revolution*. Actually, the interest of British leftists in Soviet Russia began in 1920 with the English Labour Delegation, led by H.G. Wells and Bertrand Russell, who, Pitirim Sorokin declared, "saw principally what the Communists [Bolsheviks] wanted to show them; they came in touch with few non-Communists, nor would they have been able to speak with many such had they so desired. They simply swallowed whatever bait the Soviet leaders offered them and went home impressed with the dictatorship of the proletariat, 'endless Communist enthusiasm,' and the devotion of the people to the Soviet Government" (Sorokin, *Leaves from a Rusian Diary*, 243). Wells, who was "placed under the constant guardianship of Gorky," was deceived (not only by Lenin in 1920 but also by Stalin in 1934); Russell was not, primarily because he was more empirical and bothered to roam urban and rural realities on his own.

120 Martin with Low, *Low's Russian Sketchbook*, 9.
121 Webb and Webb, *Soviet Communism*, 258, 259, 260, 261–3, 282–3, 282n2. This was a special limited edition printed by the authors for students in the classes of the Workers' Educational Association. The 2nd and 3rd editions of 1938 and 1941 omitted the question mark in the title of the 1st edition of 1935. Perhaps by then – even after the lethal purges – the Webbs were even more certain of a bright Soviet future?
122 Watt, *British Documents*, 11, doc. 186:262.
123 Chamberlin, *Russia's Iron Age*, 366–7.
124 Lyons, *Assignment*, 428–30. Shaw was a maverick about other causes, too, of course; for example, he endorsed eugenics and opposed vaccination.
125 Bright-Holmes, *Like It Was*, 22. Shaw was but one in a long list of foreign literary luminaries who revered Stalin (especially French writers – including Nobel laureates – like Henri Barbusse, André Gide, and Romain Rolland), although some of them were to recant. The Chilean poet Pablo Neruda, for example, referred to Stalin as "the angel of the Central Committee" and wrote a poetic tribute to him (and was awarded the Stalin Peace Prize in 1953).
126 Dalton, *Fateful Years*, 26, 28, 29.
127 Ibid., 28.
128 Koestler, *Invisible Writing*, 188. However, unlike many fellow leftists and many Soviets themselves, who found the new order exhilarating, Koestler – and many tourists – found it "terribly depressing":

> The drab streets, the unrelieved shabbiness and poverty, the grim pomposity of everything said and written, the all-pervading atmosphere of a reformatory school. The feeling of being cut off from the rest of the world. The boredom of newspapers which contained nothing critical or controversial, no crime, no sensation, no gossip, sex, scandal, human interest. The constant exhortations, the stereotyped uniformity of all and everything, the eternal portrait of Big Brother [Stalin] following you everywhere with his eyes. The overwhelming bleakness of an industrialized Neanderthal. (Ibid.)

129 Ibid., 19.
130 Muggeridge was to write a satirical fictional account of Western reporters in Moscow during the First Five-Year Plan (Muggeridge, *Winter in Moscow*). And see his "To Friends" for a scathing indictment of fellow travellers from

the West who denounced and protested injustices at home but overlooked them in Stalin's Russia.
131 Muggeridge, *Chronicles*, 243–5.
132 Cole, *The Life*, 190.
133 Foot, *Debts of Honour*, 139.
134 Katharine, *Working Partnership*, 185.
135 This reluctance helps to explain why the manuscript of George Orwell's *Animal Farm*, which Muggeridge rated "one of the few undoubted works of genius of our time," was rejected by fourteen publishers on the grounds that it was too hostile to the Soviet regime (one of the rejectors was T.S. Eliot at Faber and Faber) before finally being accepted and published in 1946 at the outset of the Cold War (Muggeridge, *Chronicles*, 272).
136 The Soviet Union invited 4,700 foreign workers to the country in 1930 and 10,000 in 1931 (Osokina, *Our Daily Bread*, 75).
137 Herman, *Coming Out of the Ice*, 14.
138 [Witkin], *American Engineer*, 30.
139 Ibid., 7.
140 Yet another, and even more pitiable, category of Western naïfs comprised hopeful ethnic immigrants returning to their historical homelands, such as the approximately six thousand North American Finns who immigrated to Soviet Karelia in the early 1930s. See Hokkanen and Hokkanen with Middleton, *Karelia*, and Sevander with Hertzel, *They Took My Father* (published in Russian as Sevander and Kherstel, *Oni zabrali u menia ottsa*).
141 Leningrad's British consul discovered in November 1933 that "Potyomkinization" meant window dressing quite literally in downtown Moscow, where, he observed: "Some of the [store] windows are 'dressed,' but a good deal of the stuff is dummy. I pass every day a confectioner's shop full of empty chocolate-boxes, and a provision shop which I thought well stocked until I saw that the butter was yellow paper and [the] Dutch cheeses painted wood" ([Bullard], *Inside Stalin's Russia*, 14). Governor Grigory Potyomkin, one of Empress Catherine II's lovers, allegedly had bogus, mobile "villages" erected along the banks of the Dniepr River in 1787 in order to impress Her Majesty during her six-month visit to war-torn South Russia, which had just been wrested from the Ottoman Turks and their Crimean Tatar vassals.
142 Herriot, *Eastward from Paris*, 213.
143 Ibid., 295n1.

144 Kupferman, *Au pays des Soviets*, 75, citing *Le Nouvelliste*, 14 September 1933.

145 Lang, *Tomorrow*, 263. To be fair to the Soviets, however, it should be noted that a similar sort of orchestration commonly accompanied, say, royal tours of the colonies and even ex-colonies of the British Empire (and still does), with roads being paved, buildings decorated, school children marshalled, and reportage genuflected, although the colonial subjects were not usually starving (with the exception of Bengal in 1943).

146 One possible exception was the sheltered and privileged daughter of a middle-level Soviet official, Tamara Petkevich, who in her memoir does not even mention the famine, which took place when she was a girl (between eight and fourteen years of age) in Leningrad. Following her father's arrest during the Great Terror, she, too, was exiled and became an actress in the Gulag, where she may well have learned of the famine from former kulaks. See Petkevich, *Memoir*.

147 But not because the editors of the mass dailies were unaware of the famine. In the late winter of 1932 the villager Ivan Litvinov, in the Central Black Earth Region, wrote in a letter (unpublished) to *Izvestia*:

> Every day throughout our district one sees entire strings of carts of starving Ukrainian peasants, both kolkhozniks and individual farmsteaders, and for a piece of bread they give all of their used stuff, such as shoes, clothes, and everything they have. When you ask them why they are starving, they answer: "We had a good crop but the Soviet authorities 'stocked' our grain and augmented their plans and tasks for us until we were left without a funt [pound] of grain." When you ask them who is to blame, they answer: "The Soviet authorities, who took the grain from us down to the last kernel, dooming us to starvation and destitution – worse than serfdom." (Kondrashin, *Golod v SSSR*, vol. 1, bk. 2, doc. 469:50)

And an anonymous Dynamo Moscow footballer wrote to the same paper at the beginning of July:

> Comrades, now the entire population of the USSR has come to realize the existence of the current catastrophic famine throughout the Ukraine and the Central Volga and of the relative famine throughout

the country, with the exception of the artificially supported and relatively satisfactory condition of Moscow, where the situation also worsens from day to day.

Masses of fugitives from the starving districts are filling the railroad stations, and masses are moving on foot to these stations, where there is still no leave to let them on the trains. One can meet groups of them at every step in the streets of Moscow. Together with this phenomenon, a mass of "little baggers" [*meshochniki*] come to our half-starving area to buy up something for their starving area. It is undoubtedly known to the authorities that potatoes from Moscow Obl[ast] are taken to Saratov Obl[ast], and that the same thing is repeated to a greater degree with flour. The refugees flee and carry with them news of the famine in the oblasts that makes one's hair stand on end. They tell us that their crop last year was good but that it was "taken" by the Bolsheviks. They tell us that the famine in Kamenets-Podolsk and other places has reached the point where they prefer to die from the fumes of the charcoal that they make in their izbas and from which entire families perish. (Kondrashin, *Golod v SSSR*, vol. 1, bk. 2, doc. 474:66)

148 Vilensky, *Till My Tale Is Told*, 173.
149 Elagin, *Ukroshchenie*, 46. For the horrific kulak trials of Agnes Pauls (Natasha Sawatsky) (1909–2013), the eldest daughter in a prosperous farming family in the Mennonite colony of Chortitza in South Russia who was kulakized, dispossessed, and deported to northern Siberia and who miraculously escaped and survived to live the last two-thirds of her life in Canada, see Pauls, *Refugee*.
150 Luogovskaya, *I Want to Live*, 59.
151 Kravchenko, *I Chose Freedom*, 111.
152 Zhober, *Kogda zhizn' tak deshego stoit*, 206.
153 Kondrashin and Tiurina, "Govorit' o golode," doc. 26:125.
154 Mandelstam, *Hope Abandoned*, 294–5. The author ends this paragraph with a footnote: "This produced extreme paranoia on the part of Stalin especially. Ilya Ehrenburg related to me a story of Khrushchov's [sic] about Koba attending a play in which the prominent Ukrainian actor Amvrosy Buchma took the part of a traitor and played it so well that the *vozhd* [leader] com-

155 After the collapse of the USSR an international consortium of researchers uncovered some two hundred diaries of the 1930s in official and private archives throughout the country (Garros, Korenevskaya, and Lahusen, *Intimacy and Terror*, xi).

156 Shaporina, *Dnevnik*, 1:86, 88, 90. Similarly, Solzhenitsyn wrote that "no Genghis Khan ever destroyed so many peasants as our glorious Organs, under the leadership of the Party" (Solzhenitsyn, *Gulag Archipelago*, vol. 3, bk. 6:363).

157 Prishvin, *Dnevniki*, 143.

158 Gorokhova, *Mountain of Crumbs*, 172–3.

159 Kaminskaya, *Final Judgement*, 20, 21–2.

160 Vilensky, *Till My Tale Is Told*, 124–5, 125, 126.

161 Wells, *Kapoot*, 111.

162 Ibid., 117.

163 Duranty, "Russians Hungry."

164 Mayakovsky, "*Vladimir Mayakovsky,*" 80. And for the benefit of any doubting capitalists he added much later (on the eve of his suicide) a famous couplet: "Eat your pineapple, chew your grouse: your last day dawns, you bourgeois louse" (ibid., 85).

165 Hellbeck, "Fashioning the Stalinist Soul," 364.

166 Ibid., 357.

167 Ibid., 355, 357. Earlier that winter Podlubny's mother, Yefrosinya, received a letter from her older sister in their native village in the Ukraine begging for help for her three children, who had been left to fend for themselves after their mother had been imprisoned for stealing state property (standing grain on a kolkhoz). The children wrote: "Aunt Frosya and brother Stopya! We are bloated from hunger, help us, if you can. Do not if you can't, we will have to die sooner or later anyway. But we want to live a little longer, our lives have been so short." Yefrosinya cried "bitter tears" but Stepan himself, "for some reason," merely smiled (ibid., 204–5, 205).

168 Clyman, "Russian Peasant Shot," 23.

169 Ciliga, *Russian Enigma*, 16.

170 Kondrashin, *Golod v SSSR*, 3, doc. 390:477.

(Note: the page begins mid-sentence: "mented that only someone who really was a traitor could act that well and ordered that the necessary measures be taken" (ibid., 324).)

Chapter Three

1 Kondrashin, *Golod 1932–1933*, 2nd ed., 105. And the Russian Orthodox Church's half-year of fasts largely coincided with the times of greatest peasant scarcity (Goldstein, *Kingdom of Rye*, 5–6).
2 Kondrashin, *Golod 1932–1933*, 2nd ed., 100, 105.
3 Jones, "Seizure of Land." Similarly, about the same time, Malcolm Muggeridge was unequivocal in asserting that the famine was "organized from within," "planned and deliberate," "not due to any natural catastrophe like failure of rain, or cyclone, or flooding," and "no external cause like bad weather or a blockade" (Muggeridge, *Chronicles*, 257; Muggeridge, *Winter in Moscow*, 138); Muggeridge, however, was much less well-travelled and less well-informed than Jones.
4 Jones described his simple method of investigative journalism in the preface to Heinz's published diary:

> With a knowledge of Russia and the Russian language, it was possible to get off the beaten path, to talk with grimy workers and rough peasants, as well as such leaders as Lenin's widow and Karl Radek. We visited vast engineering projects and factories, slept on the bug-infested floors of peasants' huts, shared black bread and cabbage soup with the villagers – in short, got into direct touch with the Russian people in their struggle for existence. (Anonymous, *Experiences in Russia – 1931*, Preface)

5 Perhaps, too, Jones's eagerness to publicize odious Bolshevik policies blinded him to natural factors.
6 Kondrashin, *Golod v SSSR*, 3:809n206. It should be noted, however, that a decade later, in a greatly revised second edition of his 2008 book, Kondrashin concluded that "the causes of the famine should be sought not in the 'will of God'" (i.e., the weather) but in the "hands of man" (i.e., policy), yet he also admitted that "the weather conditions of 1929 were more favourable [for the harvest] than in 1928," and that the year 1931 was "not at all favourable in terms of weather conditions," which were reflected in the lower yield and output of grain, with drought striking all of the Asiatic steppe, so that "on the whole it can be concluded that in 1931–33 the weather in the Volga Valley

was not at all favourable to agriculture." But I think he misses the point, which is that a reduction in the harvest by the weather means that there is less grain to be consumed and possibly not enough to feed everyone, unless a harvest failure in one part of the country is offset by a bumper harvest in the other – which seldom occurs. To him, perhaps, as to the Russian peasant, drought was so frequent, especially in the central and lower Volga Valley, as to be simply normal ("drought in the Volga Valley is a common occurrence") and therefore not a factor in the equation of causes (Kondrashin, *Golod 1932–1933*, 2nd ed., 117, 136, 168, 171).

7 Golubev and Dronin, *Geography of Droughts*, 16, fig. 1.
8 A French farmer and grain merchant who became minister of agriculture and visited the USSR in 1933, Victor Boret, felt that "Russian soil only nourishes the Russian people half as well as French soil nourishes the French" (Boret, *La paradis infernal*, 243).
9 For a cogent analysis of the less beneficial natural endowment of the USSR vis-à-vis North America in terms of size, topography, climate, and soil, see White, *Russia and America*, 44–55; for an informative treatment of two of the resultant "economic impacts" – frequent famines and infectious diseases – see ibid., 72–86.
10 A degree-month is one in which every day is warm enough (generally above 5°C, or 41°F) to allow plant growth.
11 Field, "Environmental Quality and Land Productivity," 9. Environmentally, the former Soviet Union/current Russian Federation is much more comparable to Canada, a "hard land," than to the United States, a "soft land" (in the sense of the amount of effort needed to extract the same benefits from their respective natural resources). But even in that case Canada is still favoured climatically on two counts: first, it is part of a smaller land mass than Russia and therefore less subject to temperature extremes and droughts (continentality), and second, it is much more open to the northward flow of subtropical air masses (warm and moist) in summer from the Caribbean Sea (as well as the relieving southward flow of Arctic air masses [cold and dry] in winter) because they are not impeded by North America's north-south trending mountain ranges (maritimity), whereas those from the Indian Ocean are barred from reaching Russia by the very high mountains and plateaus trending east-west along its southern boundary.
12 Gatrell, "'Bednaia' Rossiia," 218. If anything, the comparison worsened with

the dissolution of the USSR, when the country lost one-half of its population and one-quarter of its territory, including much of the former Soviet Union's most productive farmland: the Ukrainian steppe and wooded steppe, the Transcaucasian subtropics, the irrigated fields of Central Asia, the wheatbelt of northern Kazakhstan, and the dairylands of the former Baltic Republics of Estonia, Latvia, and Lithuania.

13 The higher yield of winter wheat is due to its longer and surer moisture supply from both autumn and spring rains as well as spring meltwater from winter snow cover; another advantage of winter wheat is the more even distribution of outlays over two seasons rather than one.

14 Climatologically, droughts are prolonged periods without rain and with low humidity and high temperatures that dry out the soil, so that plant roots do not receive enough moisture for growth. They are especially injurious when nighttime temperatures remain high (so that plants cannot "rest," i.e., maintain turgor) and when in spring there is only enough moisture in the soil to a depth of ten to twenty centimetres instead of a metre (so that in summer plant roots have no moisture and wither and die) (Buchinskii, *Zasukhi i sukhovei*, 5, 6).

15 Rudenko, *Zasukhi v SSSR*, 38, 45.

16 Ibid., 172, app. 3.

17 Buchinskii, *Zasukhi i sukhovei*, 43.

18 One centner (or "hundredweight") equals 220.5 pounds (100 kilograms, or 3 bushels of wheat), and since 1 hectare equals 2.47 acres and 1 bushel of wheat equals 60 pounds, then 1 centner per hectare equals 1⅚ bushels per acre.

19 Khrushchev, *Memoirs*, 2:313.

20 See Rolin, *Stalin's Meteorologist*.

21 Borisov, *Climates of the USSR*, 168; see also Rudenko, *Zasukhi v SSSR*, 17.

22 Cairns, *Soviet Famine*, 36. One of the earliest observers and recorders of sukhovei was the Russian naturalist Peter Simon Pallas, one of several talented German scientists who were invited by Peter the Great and Catherine the Great to come to Russia to live and work. Pallas experienced sukhovei at Tsaritsyn (Volgograd) in the summer of 1774: "in the fields there blew such a severe wind that it seemed to be coming from a stove, and so hard that it filled the air with dust rising from the steppe. Usually they arise about 2 o'clock in the afternoon and last until midnight, but they never blow after midnight" (quoted by Buchinskii, *Zasukhi i sukhovei*, 98).

23 Buchinskii, *Zasukhi i sukhovei*, 11, fig. 17.
24 Rudenko, *Zasukhi v SSSR*, 17.
25 Buchinskii, *Zasukhi i sukhovei*, 146, 161.
26 Joravsky, *Lysenko Affair*, 60; Roll-Hansen, *Lysenko Effect*, 65.
27 Cairns, "Agricultural Production," n.p. Cairns was seconded by Otto Schiller (United Kingdom, FO 371/17253, no. 6878).
28 Hindus, *Great Offensive*, 149.
29 Characteristically, Walter Duranty described it as a "partial drought" (Duranty, *Duranty Reports Russia*, 305).
30 Rudenko, *Zasukhi v SSSR*, 16.
31 Buchinsky, *Zasukhi i sukhovey*, 34; Rauner, "Synchronous Recurrence," 164; Rudenko, *Zasukhi v SSSR*, 168, app. 2.
32 Cairns, "Agricultural Production," n.p. Otto Schiller more or less agreed, attributing the harvest failure "to a considerable extent to unsatisfactory weather factors" (Schiller, "Agriculture," n.p.).
33 Rudenko, *Zasukhi v SSSR*, 164, app. 1.
34 Kondrashin, *Golod v SSSR*, vol. 1, bk. 2, doc. 560:199, 200.
35 Danilov, Manning, and Viola, *Tragediia sovetskoi derevni*, 3, doc. 76:203.
36 Jarman, *Soviet Union*, 4:350.
37 Cole, *The Life*, 119.
38 Cairns, "Agricultural Production," n.p.
39 Cairns, *Soviet Famine*, 83, 92.
40 Zelenin, "O nekotorykh 'belykh piatnakh,'" 8, 9.
41 Elmhirst, *Trip to Russia*, 58.
42 Cairns, *Soviet Famine*, 117.
43 Zelenin, "O nekotorykh 'belykh piatnakh,'" 8, citing the Central State Archive of the National Economy (TSGANKh), f. 1,562, op. 76, d. 160, fol. 22.
44 Duranty, *I Write*, 284.
45 Utley, *Lost Illusions*, 263.
46 Bednarek et al., *Holodomor*, doc. 125:351, doc. 181:476. The ambassador quoted Tsar Alexander II as having said that "a single rain in May can cover all the costs of the Turkish war [1877–78]."
47 Commission, *Report to Congress*, 456, 459.
48 Kondrashin, *Golod v SSSR*, 3, doc. 84:138, 139. In the Middle and Lower Volga, which were colder and drier than the Ukraine and the North Caucasus, the drought and sukhovei especially affected winter wheat, with the Middle

Volga losing almost one-third of its winter wheat acreage (Danilov, Manning, and Viola, *Tragediia sovetskoi derevni*, 3, doc. 348:781).
49 Kondrashin, *Golod v SSSR*, 3, doc. 330:412, doc. 377:460. The poet Isaac Babel wrote from Moscow at the end of the summer: "We are having a monstrous fall: every day it rains; it's midday and dark. It never stops pouring. This year's phenomenal bumper harvest is suffering quite a lot" (Babel, *Isaac Babel*, 240).
50 Carynnyk, Luciuk, and Kordan, *Foreign Office*, doc. 46:294, doc. 50:313; Watt, *British Documents*, 11, doc. 142:200; Williams, "Why Russia Is Hungry!," n.p.
51 Dronin and Bellinger, *Climate Dependence*, 130–5.
52 Buchinskii, *Zasukhi i sukovei*, 34.
53 Rudenko, *Zasukhi v SSSR*, 164, app. 1.
54 Watt, *British Documents*, 12, doc. 191:225, 226.
55 Bednarek et al., *Holodomor*, doc. 184:486; Commission, *Report to Congress*, 477, 480, 488, 489; Graziosi, "'Lettres de Kharkov,'" doc. 38:03; Watt, *British Documents*, 12, doc. 105:123, doc. 191:225, 226, doc. 201:237. In a telegram of 14 May 1934 Stalin and Molotov ordered the Ukrainian leadership, "in view of the threat of drought in some districts of the USSR," to replant the fall-sown winter grain that had perished with spring wheat and to sow more of the latter than had been sown of the former, as well as to plant the spring grain on land that had been designated for spring non-grain crops and on fallow, low-lying, and other vacant land (Kondrashin, *Golod v SSSR*, 3, doc. 248:329). Millet and corn ripened later than wheat; millet (like buckwheat) was a groat (grain) crop and wheat (like rye) was a bread crop, while corn (like oats) was a fodder crop.
56 Commission, *Report to Congress*, 489; Graziosi, "'Lettres de Kharkov,'" doc. 38:103.
57 Fischer, *Soviet Journey*, 172; Watt, *British Documents*, 12, doc. 164:189.
58 Bednarek et al., *Holodomor*, doc. 202:544.
59 Khripunov, *Dnevniki*, 369.

Chapter Four

1 David Engerman puts the proverb this way: "God makes a poor harvest, but human beings make a famine" (Engerman, *Modernization*, 194).
2 The first part of Collier's citation is actually Lord Byron's take ("He makes a

solitude, and calls it – peace!" [*The Bride of Abydos*, Canto II, sec. 20]) on Tacitus in *Agricola*, sec. 30 ("To plunder, to slaughter, to steal, these things they misname empire; and where they make a desert, they call it peace" – Caledonian chieftain Calgacus to the Britons at the Battle of the Grampians, referring to the Romans).

3 In at least one village in the northern Ukraine, however, some devout old men blamed the famine on godlessness. One of them told Gareth Jones in March 1933: "It is because the Communists have cursed God. They have tried to banish God from our midst, and the punishment has come in the form of death. When Holy Mother Russia believed in God, the fields became a mass of gold and the cattle and horses multiplied. But now the revenge has come for all the blasphemy and the evil which has been preached" (Jones, "There Is No Bread").

4 United States, Felix Cole to Secretary of State, 1.

5 Muggeridge, *Chronicles*, 257. Years later Eugene Lyons – now much more conservative – was equally unequivocal, if less vehement: "Russia has had many famines in its history, but the great famine of 1932–33 was in a class by itself. It was man-made, the direct and clearly foreseen result of a political decision" (Lyons, "My Six Years in Moscow," 271).

6 Golitsyn, *Memoirs*, 355.

7 On at least one occasion (1925) – *before* collectivization – Stalin spoke of "the dictatorship of the proletariat *and peasantry*" (Stalin, *Works*, 7:71, emphasis mine).

8 Schiller, "Agriculture," n.p.

9 [Muggeridge], "The Soviet and the Peasantry," 1:9.

10 Ganson, *Soviet Famine of 1946–47*, citing RGASPI, f. 397, op. 1, d. 21, fol. 5; [Khrushchev], *Khrushchev Remembers*, 107.

11 Khrushchev, *Memoirs*, 2:311–12.

12 Kaganovich, "Ukreplenie kolkhozov."

13 And, geographically, it meant the strategic dispersal of heavy industry to several bases in the country's interior, away from its borders with potential foreign enemies, who usually invaded from the west. In a letter of 12 July 1925 to Molotov, Stalin, then the Party's powerful general secretary following Lenin's death the year before, declared that the plan of the government's economic agencies to build factories in the borderlands (e.g., in St Petersburg and Rostov on Don) was "not expedient." He added:

In designing the construction program, I think that two considerations should be taken into account in addition to the principle of the factories' proximity to raw materials and fuel: the link with the countryside and the geographic-strategic footing of the new factories' location. Our basic interior is: the Urals, the Volga Region, the southern Black Earth Region (Tambov, Voronezh, Kursk, Oryol, etc.). These are exactly the areas (if you don't count the Urals) that are suffering from a lack of industry. Meanwhile, there are the areas that represent the most convenient rearguard for us in the event of military complications. Therefore, these are precisely the areas where industrial construction should be developed. (Lih, Naumov, and Khlevniuk, *Stalin's Letters to Molotov*, letter 1:85)

This policy was to underlie heavy industrialization under the First Five-Year Plan (1928–32), when the Donbass in the eastern Ukraine and Magnitogorsk in the southern Urals were favoured, as well as another, even remoter metallurgical base in the Kuzbass in the southeastern corner of Western Siberia. During the Second World War only the first of these three vital iron-and-steel complexes was overrun by the German invaders.

14 Schmemann, *Echoes*, 208.
15 For example, in August 1918 in Kaluga Oblast a Bolshevik squad under one Nazarov, the ruthless leader of a *kombed*, was massacred by peasants – save Nazarov himself, who was taken alive, disemboweled, and stuffed with grain (Schmemann, *Echoes*, 213).
16 Trotsky, *Revolution Betrayed*, 18.
17 Chamberlin, *Confessions*, 141. The peasants wanted their "own" land to use communally, as they always had, not necessarily to possess privately by virtue of legal title.
18 Dominique, *Secrets of Siberia*, 237.
19 Danilov, *Rural Russia*, 277. Grain dominated Russian agriculture; in 1926 it occupied five-sixths of the Soviet Union's sown area and provided more than one-quarter of the value of gross (and nearly one-third of net [marketed]) agricultural production (ibid.).
20 In 1927, in the RSFSR (with two-thirds of the USSR's peasant holdings), about 10 percent were "well-to-do," that is, kulaks, with up to 6 desyatinas (1 desyatina equals 2.7 acres or 1.09 hectares) of sown land, 2 horses and 2 cows,

buildings, and agricultural implements; about 40 percent were "middling" peasants (srednyaks) with up to 5 desyatinas of sown land, 1 cow, and 1 to 2 horses; and up to 50 percent were "poor labourers" (bednyaks) with 0 to 4 desyatinas of sown land, 0 to 1 cows, and 0 to 1 horses (Klimin, *Rossiiskoe krest'ianstvo v gody*, 1:217, 387).

21 Berelovich and Danilov, *Sovetskaia derevnia*, 2, doc. 276:657.
22 Danilov et al., *Kak lomali NEP*, 4:491; Kondrashin, *Golod v SSSR*, vol. 1, bk. 1, doc. 9:80.
23 Ivnitskii, *Golod 1932-1933*, 20–1; Werth, *Histoire*, 223.
24 Rogers, *There's Not a Bathing Suit*, 109, 109–10.
25 Osokina, *Our Daily Bread*, 29.
26 Grzhebin, "Kollektivizatsiia," 47.
27 One historian of the Stalin period has rated Scheffer "probably the finest foreign correspondent ever to work in the Soviet Union" (De Jonge, *Stalin*, 149).
28 Scheffer, *Seven Years*, 51.
29 Watt, *British Documents*, 9, doc. 50:122, doc. 57:130–1, doc. 62:137–8.
30 Ciliga, *Russian Enigma*, 30.
31 Ibid. A "confidential" memorandum to the British Embassy on the "corn [wheat] crisis" expressed surprise at the effectiveness of the peasant responses to the state's coercive measures:

> The peasants seem on the whole ... to be showing an unexampled power of adaptation and to have learnt to accommodate themselves to circumstances to a degree which, when one considers their low cultural level and the ingrained conservatism of peasants in general, was not to be expected. One ... sees it now in the question of the cultivation of corn, in which, as a result of the low corn prices, they have reduced the area under corn and have gone in for the better-paid "technical cultivation" (sugar beet, flax, hemp, seeds, etc.). (Watt, *British Documents*, 9, doc. 63:140)

32 Ibid., 9, doc. 62:136, 138.
33 Plakidin et al., "*I zabyt' po-prezhnomu nel'za*," 5.
34 Scheffer, *Seven Years*, 58. This analogy is probably derived from the Russian proverb "When you saw wood, dust [or sawdust] will fall" (Watt, *British Documents*, 9, doc. 72:167).

35 In 1928 tractors ploughed less than 1 percent of the sown area, and 10 percent of spring ploughing was still done with the light (shallow-cutting) wooden "scratch" plough (*sokha*), drawn by a single horse, with the rest done with the heavier (deeper-cutting) iron *plug*, drawn by a brace of horses or oxen; 75 percent of spring sowing and 45 percent of grain reaping was done by hand (Danilov, *Rural Russia*, 268–9, 269).
36 Ronina et al., "Oglianutsia v razdume," 14.
37 Kondrashin, *Khlebozagotovite'naia politika*, 33. This view was voiced by Grigory Petrovsky, the long-time chairman (1922–38) of the Soviet Executive Committee of the Ukraine, when he blamed the inability of the Soviet Union's peasants (more than four-fifths of its population) to feed all of its citizens (compared with less than one-half of France's doing just that) on their backwardness (Tauger, "Grain Crisis or Famine?," 170).
38 Osherowitch, *How People Live in Soviet Russia*, 137.
39 These policy options were subsequently lampooned in the following anecdote (Koestler, *Invisible Writing*, 72):

> Question: "What does it mean when there is food in the city but no food in the village?"
> Answer: "A Leftist, Trotskyite deviation."
> Question: "What does it mean when there is food in the village but no food in the city?"
> Answer: "A Rightist, Bukharinite deviation."
> Question: "What does it mean when there is no food in either the city or the village?"
> Answer: "The correct application of the general line."
> Question: "And what does it mean when there is food in both the village and the city?"
> Answer: "The horrors of capitalism."

40 Scheffer, *Seven Years*, 65.
41 Ciliga, *Russian Enigma*, 94.
42 Buchinskii, *Zasukhi i sukhovei*, 47; Joravsky, *Lysenko Affair*, 60; Rauner, "Synchronous Recurrence," 164; Roll-Hansen, *Lysenko Effect*, 65. For two winters in a row (1927–28 and 1928–29), owing to insufficient snow cover and excessive cold, the Ukraine suffered "a calamitous loss of winter wheat," the worst in nearly half a century, with as much as 90 percent of plantings killed in the

winter of 1927–28. This disaster prompted Lysenko's pseudo-scientific vernalization theory (Joravsky, *Lysenko Affair*, 60; Roll-Hansen, *Lysenko Effect*, 65).

43 The deputy commissar of finance found at the end of January 1928 that in the Urals "the peasants repeatedly pointed out that last year [1927], when the grain quality was poor, they received a higher price than this year, when the grain qualities are excellent," and that "the supply of scarce goods ... was significantly lower [by 40 percent] than last year," with the scarcest being tea, iron, textiles, metalware (especially nails), timber, and hides (Viola et al., *War against the Peasantry*, doc. 14:75–86.

44 Ibid., doc. 3:27–9.

45 Stalin, *Works*, 11:3, 4, 12.

46 Viola et al., *War against the Peasantry*, 17–18.

47 Resis, *Molotov Remembers*, 241, 242.

48 Ibid., 242.

49 In January 1928 the OGPU arrested (on charges of speculation) some three thousand private grain traders throughout the country, as well as 136 kulaks in Siberia and 80 in the Urals. The largest caches of grain that had been hidden by private traders (in anticipation of price rises) were uncovered in the Ukraine, however (Viola et al., *War against the Peasantry*, doc. 15:86–8). By 18 February in Siberia about 1,000 kulak peasants had been charged under Article 107 (the 1926 law on speculation) and about 700,000 puds (11,466 tonnes) of their grain had been confiscated as punishment "for plotting to withhold their surplus grain and for trying to frustrate grain procurement plans" (Danilov and Ivnitskii, *Dokumenty svidetel'stvuiut*, 100).

50 This aggressive approach was to become known as the "Siberian method" of grain procurement.

51 Shishkin, *Rossiia*, 176–7, 177, 180.

52 The Politburo was the political and economic executive, the inner circle of the government. From 1952 until 1966 it was was termed the Presidium.

53 Viola et al., *War against the Peasantry*, doc. 18:92.

54 The official Soviet version, in English, of this speech of 9 July 1928 on "Industrialization and the Grain Problem" has Stalin saying that the peasantry "not only pays the state the usual taxes, direct and indirect ... it also *overpays* in the relatively high prices for manufactured goods ... and it is more or less *underpaid* in the prices for agricultural produce" – all of which amounted to "something in the nature of a 'tribute,' of a supertax" (Stalin, *Works*, 11:167).

55 Viola et al., *War against the Peasantry*, doc. 19:98, 99, 101. The Bolsheviks also

wanted their country to regain its pre-war position as the primary supplier of grain to Western Europe, a position that had since been usurped by the United States, Canada, and Argentina. This goal would mean the export of at least 5 million tonnes annually (Kondrashin, *Khlebozagotovtel'naia politika*, 32).

56 For a detailed scholarly treatment of collectivization, see Davies, *Socialist Offensive*; Davies, *Soviet Collective Farm*; and Davies and Wheatcroft, *Years of Hunger*.

57 Curiously, Eugene Lyons subsequently contended (without attribution) that the decision to collectivize completely was postponed in "the hope of drawing in foreign capital," for "if enough goods could be produced to meet the food growers' demand for a fair return on their labor, the problem would be more than half solved," so "a decree invited the capitalists of the world to come in and develop Russia's resources practically on capitalist terms." He continued:

> Had the outside world, especially the United States before whose eyes the temptation was dangled most frankly, accepted the offer, there would perhaps have been no Five Year Plan, no liquidation of kulaks, no "Iron Age." The Great Depression might, indeed, have been less acute had world capital found a profitable outlet in the development of Russia's natural resources. But the bourgeois world still regarded Russia as an "economic vacuum," in the words of Herbert Hoover.

Lyons added that Hoover's election to the presidency in November 1928 created a "considerable flurry of optimism" in Moscow – despite his detestation of communists – for he was a mining engineer, and Moscow had a "fixation" on engineering (Lyons, *Assignment*, 323–4). Hoover's anti-communism was presumably sparked by his ARA experience with the Bolsheviks in 1921–22.

58 Stalin also needed a strong army as soon as possible to counter threats abroad – Japanese militarism and German Fascism, in particular. Its necessary strengthening was reflected in Voroshilov's revelation that, in 1931 alone, the Red Army reported four hundred deaths and two thousand woundings from accidents on the part of recruits in training (Kvashonkin et al., *Sovetskoe rukovodstvo*, doc. 102:184–5).

59 Shishkin, "Rossiia," 86–7, 88.

60 Ciliga justly noted that, after seizing power in 1917, the Bolsheviks found it much easier to liquidate and subdivide the thirty thousand gentry estates (which comprised one-half of Russia's farmland), as well as those of the church, than to liquidate 10 to 20 million of the country's 25 million peasant holdings in 1928 and merge them into a few hundred thousand kolkhozes and sovkhozes – in other words, it was easier for them to expropriate the property of a few hundred thousand nobles than that of a hundred thousand peasants. Moreover, the 1917 revolution was simpler, too, because it did not change the agricultural technology (and even allowed its slight regression), whereas the 1928 "great break" required technological modernization. And, finally, in expropriating all of the estates of the nobles the Bolsheviks excluded them from the rural economy, but in collectivizing the peasant holdings the Bolsheviks retained the peasants and adapted them to new ways (Ciliga, *Russian Enigma*, 105–6).
61 Klimin, *Rossiiskoe krest'ianstvo v gody*, 1:358, 388.
62 Lyons, *Assignment*, 323–4.
63 Hindus recalled his one-time neighbour, Adarya, "who bore and buried thirteen children in as many years," and the "red cock," the fire that consumed the wooden village once every decade on the average, creating "an endless procession of *pogoreltsi* [burned-downers] – peasants who had lost their homes through fire – who would make the rounds of villages begging for bread, for straw, for pieces of lumber with which to build new homes for themselves" (Hindus, *Red Bread*, 14, 15, 16), homes that were dark, smoky, dirty, unfloored izbas shared with livestock.
64 Superstitions such as the belief that milk, not water, had to be used to extinguish a fire ignited by lightning (Hindus, *Red Bread*, 16).
65 According to the prominent Russian historian of collectivization Nikolai Ivnitskii, himself of peasant descent, the Russian peasant, informed by centuries of experience, traditions, habits, and customs, was generally a conservative pragmatist, prejudiced against any innovation that might change his socio-economic position and way of life, unless by his own experience he had satisfied himself in practice that it was to his advantage (Ivnitskii, "Stalinskaia 'revoliutsiia sverkhu' i krest'ianstvo," 247).

Ivnitskii added that the muzhik supported the agrarian reforms of the Soviet authorities in 1917–18 (the liquidation of seigneurial landholding – his long-time dream – and the redistribution of land) but not the forcible measures of War Communism (grain requisitions, labour and cartage obligations, conscription into the Red Army), which were not in his best interests and turned him from a supporter of the Bolsheviks into an opponent. He did support the agrarian retreat of the NEP, but from the mid-1920s and especially the late 1920s his relationship with the Soviet authorities again became adversarial in the face of all-out collectivization, the application of force to those not wanting to enter the kolkhoz, and the annihilation of the kulaks. Ever practical and realistic, the muzhik simply saw no advantage to the kolkhoz (ibid., 247, 248).

66 Hindus was referring to "the ridges and the dead furrows which in Russia, in the absence of fences, have since days immemorial divided one strip of land from another ... [and] which stretch snake-like in every direction to the very horizon, and which, like a scourge, contaminate nearby fields with noxious weeds" (Hindus, *Red Bread*, 58).

67 "Mud! Mud! Mud! One could write a history of Russia in terms of mud," exclaimed the knowledgeable Hindus, who had been born and raised at the end of the nineteenth century in "a village where time [had] stopped" and who became a sympathetic but not completely uncritical witness to the collectivization project (Hindus, *Green Worlds*, 32).

68 Serge, *From Lenin to Stalin*, 80.

69 Lyons, *Assignment*, 99.

70 Hindus, *Red Bread*, 246.

71 Ibid., 254.

72 Dmitrienko and Shipilinoi, *Kak my zhili*, 42–3, 43.

73 This faltering was illustrated by a report of 13 November 1929 to the plenum of the Party's Central Committee by the Ukrainian Party's first secretary, Stanislav Kosior, who spoke thusly of the "negative side" of collectivization in the republic:

> In the Ukraine we have had, of course, dozens of excesses, we have had cases where sovkhozes were organized but the peasants lay down under the tractor and did not apply themselves to ploughing the land ... We have had some cases where whole villages turned themselves into collectives and then quickly collapsed, and we [the authorities] were driven away to the beat of a drum. We have had complete collectivization on the territory of dozens of villages, whereupon they all proved

to be hollow and artificial creations, and the population did not take part and knew nothing. There was even a case where one such collective challenged another to socialist competition and then within a few days they both collapsed. (Danilov and Ivnitskii, *Dokumenty svidetel'stvuiut*, 288–9)

74 Chamberlin, *Russia's Iron Age*, 77–8; see also Lyons, *Assignment*, 97.
75 Kondrashin, *Golod 1932–1933*, 2nd ed., 564.
76 "Preobrazhensky" means "transfigurer" as well as "transformer," as in the Transfiguration. It is one of a number of Russian surnames (and even place names) derived from major feasts of the Russian Orthodox Church, such as Rozhdestvensky (from Rozhdestvo, "The Nativity" [Christmas]), Voskresensky (from Voskresenie, "The Resurrection" [Easter Sunday]), Blagoveshchensky (from Blagoveshchenie, "The Annunciation"), and others.
77 Chamberlin, *Russia's Iron Age*, 79.
78 Resis, *Molotov Remembers*, 171.
79 Her assertion was presumably a reference to the communistic (and abortive) Conspiracy of Equals of Francis Baheuf, who was executed in 1797 by the Directorate.
80 Cairns, *Soviet Famine*, 58–9.
81 Danilov, Manning, and Viola, *Tragediia sovetskoi derevni*, 1, doc. 190:618. In February 1933, in a speech to the first national meeting of kolkhoz shock brigaders, Stalin said that, before 1928, every one hundred rural households comprised 4 to 5 kulak households, 8 to 10 "well-to-do" (zazhitochnik) households, 45 to 50 srednyak households, and about 35 bednyak households (Stalin, *Works*, 13:253).
82 Ibid., citing *Kollektivizatsiia sel'skogo khoziastva v Severnom raione (1927–1937 gg.): Sbornik dokumentov*, Vologda (1964), 174.
83 Shishkin, *Rossiia*, 185.
84 Kovalev, *Golosa*, 16.
85 Jones, "Reds Let Peasants Starve."
86 Sholokhov, *Virgin Soil Upturned*, 24.
87 As a one-time aristocrat noted, "in Siberia there had never been big landowners and ancient families – even the term *barin* (master) was unknown" (Golitsyn, *Memoirs*, 456).
88 Dominique, *Secrets of Siberia*, 236, 236–7.

89 Kotova, *Kollektivizatsiia*, doc. 137:591. As a result of this discrimination, reported the official, "counter-revolutionary" and "Socialist Revolutionary" (democratic socialist party) slogans – such as "the question of entry into the kolkhozes must be put to a national vote" and "kolkhozes without communists" – were heard in the kray (ibid.).
90 Fainsod, *Smolensk*, 258.
91 One indicator of their relative success is afforded by the difference in grain yields in the Lower Volga's Krasnoarmeisk District in 1929, a drought year, among kulak farms (14 puds per hectare), srednyak farms (12 puds), and bednyak and kolkhoz farms (9 puds) (Kondrashin, *Golod v SSSR*, vol. 1, bk. 1, doc. 65:147).
92 Platonov, "Among Animals and Plants," 117.
93 Kulakization was intended by the Bolsheviks to not only end the exploitation of human by human but to liquidate the kulaks as a "fifth column" in the struggle against capitalism and the expected conflict with the imperialist powers (Resis, *Molotov Remembers*, 254; Chuev, *Tak govoril Kaganovich*, 36, 45). Kaganovich even believed that "if we had not destroyed this fifth column we would not have beaten the Germans into the dust" (Chuev, *Tak govoril Kaganovich*, 36). This intention was part of the firm belief of the Stalinist leadership that the struggle against imperialism was a matter of the very survival of the Soviet Union (ibid., 59).
94 Lyons, *Assignment*, 97.
95 Williams, "*Why* Russia Is Hungry!," n.p.
96 Fischer, *My Lives*, 28.
97 In the Tsarist period Jews were confined to the Pale of Settlement in western Russia and were not allowed to own land, so their employment opportunities were restricted, particularly in agriculture.
98 Hindus, *Green Worlds*, 5.
99 Osokina, *Our Daily Bread*, 4.
100 Mochulsky, *Gulag Boss*, xxxv, 142.
101 Viola et al., *War against the Peasantry*, doc. 16:91. Eugene Lyons wrote: "the political legend then started and since raised to the dignity of official history is of a peasantry divided, with the government championing the poor peasants against their exploiting kulak neighbors," whereas "the simple fact is that the countryside, except for an inconsequential group of batraks, or landless peasants, was a solid phalanx in opposing the government" (Lyons, *Assignment*, 99).

102 Fischer, *My Lives*, 28.
103 Viola et al., *War against the Peasantry*, doc. 15:87.
104 Shaporina, *Dnevnik*, 87–8.
105 Danilov et al., *Kak lomali* NEP, 4:443, 490, 491; Kondrashin, *Golod v SSSR*, vol. 1, bk. 1, doc. 9:80.
106 Lyons, *Assignment*, 276. Alexander Solzhenitsyn noted the changing perception of the kulak, who in Tsarist Russia was commonly considered a "miserly, dishonest rural trader who grows rich not by his own labor but through someone else's, through usury and operating as a middleman." The Bolsheviks exploited this viewpoint, he continued, so that "after 1917 ... the name *kulak* began to be applied ... to all those who in any way hired workers, even if it was only when they were temporarily short of working hands in their own families," and "by 1930 *all strong peasants in general* were being so called – all peasants strong in management, strong in work, or even strong merely in convictions ... the *strength* of the peasantry," whereas they were really simply the "most industrious, enterprising, and level-headed peasants" (Solzhenitsyn, *Gulag Archipelago*, vol. 3, bk. 6:55, 352). It was at this time that the American mining engineer John Littlepage arrived and noted that the definition had become so arbitrary that one writer defined a kulak as a small-scale farmer who owned seven chickens instead of six – which, Littlepage added sardonically, was still better than the definition of a kulak as a rich peasant, as there were no such peasants in the entire country (Littlepage and Bess, *Search*, 77). John Scott (1912–1976), the American welder who worked at the new steel city of Magnitogorsk and glorified it in his book *Behind the Urals* (1942), recounted that in 1931 one of his fellow workers at the steel mill explained the basis for deciding who was to be "kulakized" (exposed and deprived):

> The poor peasants of the village get together in a meeting and decide: "So-and-so has six horses; we couldn't very well get along without those in the collective farm; besides he hired a man last year to help on the harvest." They notify the [O]GPU, and there you are. So-and-so gets five years. They confiscate his property and give it to the new collective farm. Sometimes they ship the whole family out. (Scott, *Behind the Urals*, 17–18)

Scott, incidentally, returned to the United States in 1942 with his Russian wife and got a job in the Office of Strategic Services (the precursor of the CIA),

where he was later identified as a Soviet agent under the code name of "Ivanov" by the NSA/FBI Verona project.
107 Solzhenitsyn, *Gulag Archipelago*, vol. 3, pt. 6:350, 355. For a detailed analysis of the various aspects of the "Great Break," especially its regional dimensions, see Sorokin, *1929*.
108 Viola et al., *War against the Peasantry*, 119.
109 Kondrashin, *Khlebozagotovitel'naia politika*, 33, 43, 44; Lih, Naumov, and Khlevniuk, *Stalin's Letters to Molotov*, letter 44:175.
110 Viola et al., *War against the Peasantry*, 319. One of the radical changes to the peasant's way of life was a different seasonal rhythm resulting from the stretching of the agricultural year over all of the twelve months, as the British Embassy reported: "The peasant of Tsarist Russia is generally accused of having spent the winter dozing near, or over, the big stove in his single-room dwelling; [but] as a member of a collective farm, he is coerced into tackling all sorts of tasks for which there was no time in the summer," including political activities and "preparatory campaigns" like tractor overhauling and seed preparation (Watt, *British Documents*, 12, doc. 237:287–8). Another change was a different daily rhythm, too. On one kolkhoz in the Zmiyov District of the Ukraine in 1933 it was found that a working day at ploughing time totalled twelve hours, but of these only four and a half were actually spent working; one was spent on subsidiary operations such as turning, harnessing and unharnessing, and lubricating; one and a half on smoking; three on dining; and two on driving from the village to the field and back ([Kaganovich], "Report").
111 Gritsenko, *Rossiiskaia i sovetskaia derevnia*, 237. So the kolkhozniks spent as much of their free time as possible on their personal plots, partly in order to supplement their own diet but mainly in order to produce surpluses for sale at the private village market (and the state responded by reducing the size of their plots and the amount of time they could devote to them).
112 Danilov et al., *Kak lomali NEP*, 4:254, 298, 328, 384, 493; Kondrashin, *Golod v SSSR*, vol. 1, bk. 1, doc. 4:74, doc. 5:74, doc. 6:75, doc. 7:77, doc. 9:82.
113 Danilov et al., *Kak lomali NEP*, 4:298, 384, 480, 490–4; Kondrashin, *Golod v SSSR*, vol. 1, bk. 1, doc. 4:73–4, doc. 7:77–8, doc. 9:78–83.
114 Danilov et al., *Kak lomali NEP*, 4:491; Kondrashin, *Golod v SSSR*, vol. 1, bk. 1, doc. 9:80.

115 Danilov et al., *Kak lomali NEP*, 4:493; Kondrashin, *Golod v SSSR*, vol. 1, bk.1, doc. 9:82.
116 Klimin, *Rossiiskoe krest'ianstvo v pervyi period*, 89. "Solovki" denoted the Solovetsky Islands, an archipelago in the White Sea in the north of European Russia. It epitomized isolation, insularity, and – literally – monastic privation, being the site of a monastery founded in 1429 and of an infamous prison established by the Bolsheviks in 1917 for some of the victims of their "Red Terror." It was Solzhenitsyn's "mother of the Gulag," that is, a prototype or testing ground for the methods and goals of the Cheka, the OGPU, and its successors. A Party loyalist who took part in collectivization and kulakization in the Lower Volga recalled in 1990 that "Solovki had become a synonym for old-style exile, and they [the peasants] feared these Solovetsky Islands more than the cruelest punishment" (Kotova, *Kollektivizatsiia*, 890). The archipelago is now a UNESCO World Heritage Site. See Robson, *Solovki*.
117 Viola et al., *War against the Peasantry*, 323.
118 Cherepnin, *Dnevnik lishentsa*, 119.
119 Bright-Holmes, *Like It Was*, 21. For another anecdote about "tempo," see Osherowitch, *How People Live in Soviet Russia*, 97–8.
120 Lyons, *Assignment*, 285.
121 Ivnitskii, "Stalinskaia 'revoliutsiia,'" 250, citing the Central State Archive of the Komi Republic (TSGAKR), f. 3, op. 1, d. 2,313, fols. 8, 46.
122 Kondrashin, *Golod 1932–1933*, 1st ed., 77–8.
123 Ibid., citing the former Kremlin Archive of the Politburo of the Central Committee of the CPSU (hereafter KAPCCCPSU), no fond, opis', delo, or folio cited.
124 Ibid., 253. The peasants were also rebelling against the closure and defilement of churches, the arrest and persecution of churchmen, and the closure of bazaars.
125 Ibid., citing KAPCCCPSU, no fond, opis', delo, or folio cited.
126 Golitsyn, *Memoirs*, 403. Another witness concurred: "During the collectivization of the local peasants a hitch arose: when it was explained that entry into the kolkhoz was not obligatory but must occur voluntarily, many peasants and even entire villages ... began to leave the kolkhozes." But in that case, he added, "it's true that detachments with machine guns would have been sent" (Cherepnin, *Dnevnik lishentsa*, 54). At one village in Belozersk Rayon astride

the uppermost Volga River, east of Leningrad, a kolkhoz (named for Lenin) of eighty-one households was established on 24 March 1930, and only a week later most of them applied to quit it, and by 26 April sixty-four households had left and re-subdivided the land into individual farmsteads, leaving seventeen households in the kolkhoz, none of which was "able-bodied" (Adon'eva, *Muzhskoi rod*, 109).

127 Kondrashin, *Khlebozagotovitel'naia politika*, 51.
128 Shvydkov, *Moi put'*, 15.
129 Schmemann, *Echoes*, 268.
130 Lyons, *Assignment*, 322.
131 [Jones], "Outlook for the Plan." Jones noted that the peasants went willingly to some industrial centres, "eager for travel and new experiences," but some places, such as the Donbass, "where living conditions are pitiable, where there are insufficient houses, and epidemics are rife, have an evil reputation in the villages." Indeed, there was an "exodus" from the Donets Basin such that train stations were jammed, transport disrupted, and coal output curtailed by those fleeing "the hunger and disease of that ill-famed district" (ibid.).
132 Zelenin, "O nekotorykh 'belykh piatnakh,'" 9, citing *Itogi vypolneniia pervogo piatiletnego plana razvitiia narodnogo khozaiastva Soyuza SSR* (Leningrad: Gosudarstvennoe izdatel'stvo "Standartizatsia I ratsionalizatsiia," 1933), 197.
133 Kondrashin, *Golod v SSSR*, vol. 1, bk. 1:20. In 1931 the rural-urban exodus totalled 4,100,300 persons – 2 million more than in 1930 (Kondrashin, *Khlebozagotovitel'naia politika*, 51). Incidentally, one historian has noted that collectivization provided "an almost limitless supply of nannies from the countryside" for the cities, where most Bolshevik functionaries employed nannies to mind their children, out of practical necessity for their outside-working wives (he added that, ironically, the leading Bolsheviks were wont to employ the most expensive nannies, whose opinions were generally reactionary) (Figes, *Whisperers*, 47, 48).
134 Danilov, Manning, and Viola, *Tragediia sovetskoi derevni*, 3, doc. 11:77; Kondrashin, *Khlebozagotovitel'naia politika*, 46. Thus, ironically, the peasants, in fleeing the villages, inadvertently helped to create a "grain famine" and, in flooding the cities, helped to create a "housing famine."
135 Kaganovich, "Ukreplenie kolkhozov," 2. As to sovkhozes, they were completely overshadowed by smaller-scale kolkhozes, the former numbering only

5,000 but the latter numbering more than 200,000 at the beginning of 1933 (ibid.).

136 Chamberlin, *Russia's Iron Age*, 66, 69. Peasant traditions died hard, however. At the beginning of 1935 one-quarter of peasant households (more than 13 million peasants) still operated as individual farmsteaders, according to GOSPLAN's commissar Valerian Kuibyshev (after whom the Volga bend city of Samara would be renamed, 1935–91) (Watt, *British Documents*, 12, doc. 238:289). Indeed, individual farmsteads boasted some advantages over kolkhozes and sovkhozes. As the NKVD (former OGPU) head of Chelyabinsk Rayon told his superiors in Moscow at the beginning of 1935, one of the chief causes of the slow pace of collectivization at that time was the "tolerant and anomalous policy with respect to the individual peasant farmsteader that actually places him in better conditions than the kolkhoznik." For example, more than 10 percent of farmsteads were exempted from taxation in 1934 as "poor and weak" farms; up to 60 percent of farmsteaders' income was derived from non-agricultural activities, including "earnings on the side in industry, hunting, fishing, etc." that escaped taxation, thanks to "poor accounting"; and farmsteaders seldom fulfilled the state obligations of building roads, repairing bridges, building and repairing schools, and felling and hauling firewood for schools – all of which had to be done by kolkhozniks. This situation, concluded the security officer, induced the individual farmsteader to believe that he could "sit out" the collectivization campaign and prompted the backward kolkhoznik to quit the kolkhoz for industry (Berelovich and Danilov, *Sovetskaia derevnia*, 4, doc. 3:41, 41–2, 42).

137 Kaganovich, "Ukreplenie kolkhozov," 2.

138 Vossler, *We'll Meet Again*, 57–8, 81, 91, 117, 129, 131, 136, 137, 138, 160, 164, 189, 222.

139 By the end of 1928 the price that the peasant received for his wheat was 40 percent below the London market price, but bread cost 30 percent more in Moscow than in London (Lievan, *British Documents*, 9, doc. 80:200). In 1931 Otto Schiller noted that "the fixing of the price paid by the State for grain, at a level which bears no relationship to general price levels in the country, constitutes an extremely heavy indirect taxation of agriculture." He added that "agricultural products, including grain, were traded on the market in provincial towns and villages at 6 to 10 times the state-controlled prices in city stores," leading him to conclude that "the principal burden of the enormous

State expenditure necessitated by the Five Year Plan rests on the shoulders of the peasant" (Schiller, "Agriculture," n.p.).

140 Between 1931 and 1934 the price of bread doubled (Watt, *British Documents*, 12, doc. 215:254).
141 For the collectivization experiences of seven individual peasant families in seven different villages in various regions of Russia (as part of their oral life histories recorded by interviewers in the early 1990s), see Kovalev, *Golosa krest'ian*.
142 For a comprehensive account of peasant resistance, see Viola, "Bab'i bunty."
143 Scott, *Behind the Urals*, 43.
144 For seventy-six such letters to Kalinin, see Kondrashin, *Golod v SSSR*, vol. 1, bk. 2, doc. 456:23–40.
145 The Party secretary of the Central Black Earth Region, for example, reported in mid-February of 1930 that, since the spring of 1929 (the second crackdown year of collectivization), deliberate slaughtering there, with women leading the campaign, had diminished cattle by one-half, sheep and goats by two-thirds, and pigs by seven-eighths (Ivnitskii, "Stalinskaia 'revoliutsiia sverkhu,'" 249, citing the State Archive of the National Economy [GANKh], f. 7,486, op. 1, d. 49, fol. 106).
146 Shaporina, *Dnevnik*, 1:89. By the summer of 1930, 200,000 to 250,000 peasant families had taken flight (Ivnitskii, "Stalinskaia 'revoliutsiia sverkhu,'" 249).
147 Danilov, Manning, and Viola, *Tragediia sovetskoi derevni*, 2, doc. 278:789.
148 Ivnitskii, *Golod 1932–1933*, 40; Ivnitskii, *Tragediia sovetskoi derevni*, 72–3.
149 Ibid., 55.
150 Osokina, *Our Daily Bread*, 53; see also ibid., 55, 56.
151 Cherepnin, *Dnevnik lishentsa*, 41.
152 For further details about this matter, see Viola, "Bab'i bunty."
153 The tactic of the *Italyanka* (work-to-rule) was explained to Andrew Cairns by a correspondent of the Polish Telegraph Agency: "Lenin said, 'The Russian soldiers won the war [of 1914–18] with their feet, by running away from it,' but I say the Russian peasants have won the collective farm battle with their bottoms, by sitting on them" (Cairns, *Soviet Famine*, 59). The correspondent obviously underestimated Stalin's resolve. Another version of this anecdote has Stalin complaining to Kalinin that his office was overrun with mice, whereupon Kalinin advised him to hang a sign on his office door saying "The Stalin Collective Farm," and then half of the mice would starve to death and

the other half would run away (Mel'nichenko, *Sovetskii anekdot*, no. 2215C, 474).

154 The Langs witnessed the deliberate destruction of grain at the end of the summer of 1933 in the Ukraine :

> We took a motor trip from Kiev into the country, and we came across a field in which the crops were burning. Here, as elsewhere, the grain had been left to perish, but sunshine had dried the stacks, and rebel peasants had set them on fire to prevent the government from harvesting the wheat. While soldiers fought the conflagrations, peasants looked on with a show of indifference. (Lang, "Soviet Nightmare," 262)

155 Bruski, "Bolshoi golod," 112.
156 Mikhailov, *Velikii dzhut*, 339.
157 [Kaganovich], "Report."
158 Vaniukov, *Golodomor*, doc. 63:161–2.
159 Kondrashin, *Khlebozagotovitel'naia politika*, 140–1.
160 [Kaganovich], "Report."
161 The "barbering" of ripening grain meant either squeezing the kernels out of the ears (spikes) or cutting off the ears whole.
162 Bruski, "Bol'shoi golod," 122–3, 123.
163 Kondrashin, *Golod v SSSR*, 2, doc. 385:507; Vaniukov, *Golodomor*, doc. 106:265.
164 Kondrashin, *Khlebozagotovitel'naia politika*, 113.
165 Kondrashin, *Golod 1932–1933*, 1st ed., 191.
166 Kondrashin, *Khlebozagotovitel'naia politika*, 113, citing RGASPI, f. 17, op. 2, d. 514, fols. 19–21.
167 Ivnitskii, *Golod 1932–1933*, 39–40; Ivnitskii, *Tragediia sovetskoi derevni*, 39–40. Elsewhere Ivnitskii gives a figure of 1,400 such acts in 1928 (Ivnitskii, *Golod 1932–1933*, 25). The grain belt refers to the grainlands of the natural zones of the wooded steppe and the grassy steppe of European Russia and Western Siberia.
168 Danilov, Manning, and Viola, *Tragediia sovetskoi derevni*, 1, doc. 181:608.
169 Shishkin, *Rossiia*, 192.
170 Ibid., 208. Boris Savinkov was a revolutionary terrorist who served with Yevno Azef in the leadership of the Socialist Revolutionary Party's combat branch, which succeeded in assassinating several ranking officials at the turn

of the century, when the assassination of Tsarist officials was *très au courant* among revolutionaries (Azef was subsequently exposed as a double agent for the Okhrana [or Okhranka], the Tsarist secret police).

171 Danilov, Manning, and Viola, *Tragediia sovetskoi derevni*, 2, doc. 278:788.
172 [Ivnitskii], "'Real Story'," 1–2.
173 Sevost'ianov et al., *"Sovershenno sekretno,"* vol. 10, pt. 2, doc. 327:535.
174 Shishkin, *Rossiia*, 180, citing Commissar of Military and Naval Affairs Kliment Voroshilov at a Party meeting of 10 April 1928.
175 Bednarek et al., *Holodomor*, doc. 88:256. For instance, in September of 1933 a soldier helping to investigate a Ukrainian village under suspicion of sabotage told Harry and Lucy Lang that one of two Red Army brothers from a neighbouring village who had heard of reports of famine at home obtained leave to visit his parents, whom he found dead from starvation, so he fetched his brother to see for himself, and "the two men became bandits, roving the countryside at night, getting their revenge" (Lang, "Soviet Nightmare," 261).
176 Tarkhova, *Krasnaia armiia*, 260, 260–1.
177 Jones, "Reds Let Peasants Starve."
178 Applebaum, *Gulag*, 291. Gulag survivor Varlam Shalamov wrote that the peasants made the best workers in the camps (Shalamov, *Kolyma Tales*, 1:454).
179 Kondrashin, *Khlebozagotovitel'naia politika*, 13–14, table 1, citing O.B. Mozokhin, *Pravo na respressii*, 2nd rev. ed. (Moscow: Kuchkovo pole, 2011), 353–480.
180 Lih, Naumov, and Khlevniuk, *Stalin's Letters to Molotov*, letter 63:211.
181 Watt, *British Documents*, 11, doc. 203:293. The essence of the tactic of terror was inadvertently expounded to the American reporter Ralph Barnes by a secret police official who, when asked by Barnes why innocent people were arrested in the Soviet Union, replied (after shaking with laughter for some time), "Of course we arrest innocent people ... otherwise, no one would be frightened. If people are only arrested for specific misdemeanours, all the others feel safe, and so are ripe for treason" (Muggeridge, *Chronicles*, 234–5). Muggeridge commented:

> By making justice subjective and arbitrary, every citizen can be plausibly arrested and charged at any time, with the result that they live in a permanent state of incipient guilt and fear, really feeling themselves to

be miserable offenders, not just in the eyes of God, but of their earthly rulers as well. Hence the so easily procured confessions [for the show trials], which do not need to be invented or extorted, but truly come from the heart. (Ibid., 235)

182 Bednarek et al., *Holodomor*, doc. 179:469.
183 "Dekulakization" is the customary translation of the Russian word *raskulachivanie*, which means "the classification of a peasant as a kulak," but it is confusing because in English the reverse is implied, as the prefix "de-" usually means "to undo," in this case "undoing a peasant's kulak status." This meaning would be appropriate if most of those being "undone" were genuine kulaks rather than peasants who had simply been classified as such for the purpose of persecution for having opposed collectivization, but it is more than likely that most of the "undoners" were actually srednyaks and bednyaks.
184 Danilov and Ivnitskii, *Dokumenty svidetel'stvuiut*, 342. In one instance two peasant houses that had been "decorated by craftsmen carpenters with carved lintels and window frames" were seized by the authorities as proof of kulakhood and their owners with their wives and children sent to Siberia (Golitsyn, *Memoirs*, 356).
185 Danilov, Manning, and Viola, *Tragediia sovetskoi derevni*, 2, doc. 254:699.
186 Torgov, *Perezhitoe*, 42.
187 Serge, *From Lenin to Stalin*, 77–8.
188 Krivitsky, *In Stalin's Secret Service*, xix.
189 Danilov and Ivnitskii, *Dokumenty svidetel'stuiut*, 465.
190 Krasilnikov, Salamatova, and Ushakova, *Korni ili shchepki*, 293–4. For a child survivor's "recollection of the manifold tragedy of a family of middle peasants in northern Russia in the 1930s," when "sturdy families of peasants who had worked without hired hands for endless hours were deprived of their good houses, cows, horses[,] mills – everything that we had gained with our own work" and "the children who were dekulakized by the Soviet came to know hunger and cold and all of the burdens of life and were essentially deprived of their childhood," see Berezina, *Raskulachivanie*.
191 Alexievich, *Second-Hand Time*, 129.
192 Solzhenitsyn, *Gulag Archipelago*, vol. 3, bk. 6:359.
193 Alexievich, *Second-Hand Time*, 267. In the 1990s an elderly peasant recalled

how easy it was to be denominated a kulak and dispossessed: "Two cows they had, and six children, and I guess they dressed neater than the rest, and for that they were repressed as kulaks" (Schmemann, *Echoes*, 268).

194 Krasilnikov, Salamatova, and Ushakova, *Korni ili shchepki*, 301, 350.
195 Ivnitskii, *Sud'ba raskulachennykh*, 290.
196 Pokrovskii, *Politbiuro i krest'ianstvo*, bk. 1, doc. 192:32.
197 Chamberlin, *Confessions*, 152.
198 For some of their stories, see Litvinenko and Riordan, *Memories of the Dispossessed*; see also Leshuk, *Days of Famine, Nights of Terror*; a collection of eighteen letters from exiled kulaks in 1930–35 in Milova, *Izgnanniki v svoei strane*, 434–68; and Alexopoulos, Hessler, and Tomoff, *Writing the Stalin Era*, 87–99.
199 Pokrovskii, *Politbiuro i krest'ianstvo*, bk. 1, doc. 16:36–7. Another survivor, a son, movingly recounted his exiled family's plight in the same part of Western Siberia:

> In the spring of 1931 about twenty thousand kulakized peasants deported from the grain-rich Altai and the Baraba Steppe were settled – or, more accurately, condemned to death or self-survival – on the conifered banks of the uninhabited Ket River [in the southeastern quarter of the Great Vasyugan Mire]. Arriving in the marshy taiga without a roof over their heads and amid an enormous swarm of midges, they found themselves in conditions of hard labour. They consumed broth with a pinch of flour, herbs, and the young shoots of bushes, and meanwhile they had to uproot trees, build little cabins ... A massive mortality ensued. Most families had many children, who suffered the most from the awful flour. The mothers, who were in no less agony, did not have the strength to save their children. Whole families died out. At the settlements of Gorodetsk, Palachka, Suiga, and Protochka after two years about two thousand [exiles] remained alive of the seven thousand and seven hundred sent there. In the settlement of Vostochka, where people from the Mountain Altai – unsuited to the climate of Narym [a settlement near the junction of the Ob and Ket Rivers] – had been brought, at least one-half died off.
>
> Of the eleven members of our family, seven were dead within six months. In the children's home, where I and the orphans were tended,

there were about two hundred youngsters, all of them the orphaned children of "kulaks." In each room of the children's home was hung the slogan: "Thank you, beloved Stalin, for our happy childhood." Is it not more than a little wondrous that those youngsters still left alive had to thank the great leader for having "gladdened them" by leaving them without fathers and mothers? (Ibid., doc. 27:43–4)

The experience of one of these families was also described by the son, who was "a direct witness to this terrible process of repression":

> My parents and our remaining relatives in the [village] commune offered to pay a rather large tax. In the town of Rubtsov they sold two horses and one sheep and paid the tax. Several days later our family was assessed a recurring and more severe tax. They sold nearly all of their remaining livestock and flour and paid the tax in honesty and without objection or indignation. The rural soviet [then] presented a third tax assessment, but it was impossible to pay it. They had only enough [means] to guarantee a minimum for survival. The family categorically refused to pay the third tax. The rural soviet called a meeting of all of the middle peasants who had refused to pay the tax and, for ignoring the demands of Soviet power, declared them enemies of the people – kulaks, subject to dekulakization with the confiscation of all of their property and deportation from the village. (Shvydkov, *Moi put'*, 28)

200 Kondrashin, *Golod 1932–1933*, 2nd ed., 132. For the horrific details of an official "top secret" report to Stalin on the deportation of kulaks to this island of Nazino on the Ob River, see Lopatin and Lopatina, *Kollektivizatsiia i raskulachivanie*, doc. 3:27–8.
201 See Davies et al., *Stalin-Kaganovich Correspondence*, doc. 8:70n6.
202 Ivnitskii, *Sud'ba raskulachenyykh*, 290.
203 Macqueen, "Survivors," 45.
204 Ivnitskii, *Sud'ba raskulachennykh*, 290, citing the State Archive of the Russian Federation (hereafter GARF), f. 9,479, op. 1, d. 24, fol. 4.
205 Ibid., 291.
206 Pokrovskii, *Politbiuro i krest'ianstvo*, bk. 2, doc. P-247:532.

207 Some of their children, however, neither forgot nor forgave. One of Svetlana Alexievich's witnesses to the experience of the Second World War by Soviet women at the front told her: "The children of the kulaks came back from exile. Their parents had been killed, and they served the German forces. They took their revenge" (Alexievich, *Unwomanly Face of War*, 321).
208 Leonhard, *Child of the Revolution*, 136.
209 Wells, *Kapoot*, 118, 119.
210 Lacassin, *Simenon*, 883, 903–4.
211 Vilensky, *Till My Tale Is Told*, 4. The "white gloves" allegory is sometimes rendered as "we [communists] don't wear kid gloves" (Grossman, *Life and Fate*, 286).
212 Kondrashin, *Golod 1932-1933*, 2nd ed., 131, table 2.
213 Berelovich and Danilov, *Sovetskaia derevnia*, vol. 3, bk. 1, doc. 268:771, doc. 269: 771–2; Ivnitskii, *Golod 1932–1933*, 61; Klimin, *Rossiiskoe krest'ianstvo v pervy period*, 224, 230; Klimin, *Rossiiskoe krest'ianstvo v zavershaiushchy period*, 634; Koenker and Bachman, *Revelations from the Russian Archives*, doc. 172:384–9; Pokrovskii, *Politbiuro i krest'ianstvo*, bk. 2, doc. P-146:309–10, doc. P-147:311, docs. P-148–62:312–27. By the spring of 1933, Gareth Jones estimated, 6 to 7 million kulaks had been exiled (Jones, "Seizure of Land"; Jones, "Balance-Sheet"); Victor Serge guessed "at least five million" (Serge, *From Lenin to Stalin*, 80).

The kulaks were not alone, moreover. For the context of their exile in terms of the "cleansing" of the borderlands of Koreans, Poles, and Finns in 1928–32 and the deportation of Gypsies (Roma), Poles, Germans, and Finns from the capital and the western frontier in 1933–36, followed by the banishment of Kurds and Armenians from the southern frontier in 1937–38, the removal of all Koreans from the eastern frontier in 1937, and finally the wholesale deportation from the frontline of more than half a dozen "nationalities" (ethnic groups) whose loyalties were deemed suspect during the Second World War (including Volga Germans, Crimean Tatars, Chechens, and Kalmyks), see Pobol' and Polian, *Stalinskie deportatsii 1928–1953*, 34–45, 45–75, 75–80, 80–97, and 273–614.
214 So-called presumably because of Gorky's early habit of wandering the country by riding freight cars as well as by walkabouting.
215 Littlepage and Bess, *In Search of Soviet Gold*, 72–3, 79.
216 For an especially gruesome account of the fate of some kulak exiles in Western Siberia, see Werth, *Cannibal Island*.

NOTES TO PAGES 176-9

217 Danilov, Manning, and Viola, *Tragediia sovetskoi derevni*, 3:14. The well-travelled, well-connected, and well-informed Otto Schiller, however, told his colleague, Andrew Cairns, that the death rate among kulak exiles was 50 percent (Cairns, *Soviet Famine*, 95).
218 Lyons, *Assignment*, 281–2, 284, 291–2.
219 Ibid., 283.
220 Solzhenitsyn, *Gulag Archipelago*, vol. 1, bk. 2:54, 57. For some voices of kulaks deported to Western Siberia, see Martynenko, *Kollektivizatsiia i raskulachivanie*.
221 Schiller, "Corn Growing."
222 Clyman, "Women Harvesters," 14. The muzhik added: "But we can't stop working because of that. There are people here who wouldn't work [in a kolkhoz]. Strangers now live in their houses; the fields don't stop bearing because the owners are dead" (ibid.) – in other words, some peasants chose to starve to death rather than to join a kolkhoz.
223 Grossman, *Everything Flows*, 86–7.
224 Lyons, *Assignment*, 491. He added that their "paralyzing indifference" produced "the greatest crop of weeds in recorded history," with weeds so thick that they broke the metal teeth of mechanical harvesters (ibid.).
225 Bruski, "Bol'shoi golod," 112.
226 Fischer, *Soviet Journey*, 171. The purblind Fischer was quick to add that "the peasants brought the calamity upon themselves" (ibid.), whereas the regime had provoked it.
227 Ibid., 170–1.
228 Duranty, *Duranty Reports Russia*, 305–6.
229 Bruski, "Bol'shoi golod," doc. 1:130.
230 Kaganovich, "Ukreplenie kolkhozov," 3.
231 Schiller, "Russia's Starving Peasants." Corpses lying by the roads and in the streets had become so commonplace as to be ignored by passersby.
232 Bruski, "Bol'shoi golod," 125.
233 Graziosi, "'Lettres de Kharkov,'" doc. 21:64.
234 Lyons, *Assignment*, 322.
235 Ronina et al., "Oglianutsia v razdume," 16.
236 [Federal Archival Agency], *Famine in the USSR*, doc. 39:82.
237 From 25.8 million to 20.6 million, according to an émigré economist and former cabinet minister under Kerensky's Provisional Government, Sergei Prokopovich (Serge [Kibalchich], *Memoirs of a Revolutionary*, 247).

238 Mandelstam, *Hope Abandoned*, 469.
239 [Federal Archival Agency], *Famine in the USSR*, doc. 38:81.
240 Ibid., doc. 40:83.
241 Ivnitskii, *Golod 1932–1933*, 246.
242 Indeed, Hans Blumenfeld, a German Jewish Communist pacifist, architect, and planner who worked in the USSR from 1930 until his expulsion from the Party in 1935 and from the country in 1937 (he eventually immigrated to Canada and obtained a university appointment) contended that "probably most deaths in 1933 were due to epidemics of typhus, typhoid fever, and dysentery" (Blumenfeld, *Life Begins at 65*, 153). Blumenfeld, however, was a life-long sympathizer of the Soviet experiment and tended to overlook or rationalize its misdeeds.
243 Lenin told the Seventh All-Russian Congress of Soviets at the end of 1919 that the country faced three main "scourges": war, starvation, and epidemics, particularly "lice, [the vector of] typhus, which is mowing down our soldiers" in the civil war, and he added that "either lice will triumph over socialism, or socialism will triumph over lice!" (Lenin, *Sochineniia*, 30:206).
244 Gantt, *Russian Medicine*, 152, 155, 156.
245 Volters, *Spetsialist v Sibiri*, 183.
246 Baroian, *Itogi*, 56, fig. 12.
247 Antipova, *Golod v SSSR*, doc. 79:230; Commission, *Report to Congress*, 468; Kondrashin, *Golod v SSSR*, 2, doc. 520:643; Vaniukov, *Golodomor*, doc. 64:165.
248 Commission, *Report to Congress*, 468; Kondrashin, *Golod v SSSR*, 2, doc. 520:643.
249 Bruski, "Bol'shoi golod," 118.
250 [Bullard], *Inside Stalin's Russia*, 159, 187.
251 Ibid., 188.
252 McVay and Luciuk, *Holy See*, doc. 13:17.
253 Wood, *Our Ally*, 176. Wood was eighty-four years of age when he dictated his memoir (ibid., 193).
254 Volters, *Spetsialist v Sibiri*, 183, 183–84, 184, 185, 186, 187.
255 Kondrashin, *Golod v SSSR*, 3, first supplement: 656. There raged another lethal disease termed "septic angina," which ran its course acutely: a high temperature, a rash, bleeding from the nose and throat, and necrotic angina. Its cause was alimentary toxicosis, which developed as a result of eating cereals (millet, wheat, rye) that had wintered under the snow. The disease was widespread during the famine years, notably in the Middle Volga (ibid.).

256 Bednarek et al., *Holodomor*, doc. 103:301; Kondrashin, *Golod v SSSR*, 2, doc. 315:422; 3, docs. 229–34:309–13; Vaniukov, *Golodomor*, doc. 94:243, doc. 101:258, doc. 149:335–8.
257 Kondrashin, *Khlebozagotovitel'naia politika*, 247.
258 Baroian, *Itogi*, 143, fig. 72.
259 Lievan, *British Documents*, 10, doc. 222:346. The city's drinking water was a problem throughout the Soviet period.
260 Kondrashin, *Golod v SSSR*, 3, first supplement: 656–7.
261 Baroian, *Itogi*, 77, fig. 24.
262 Commission, *Report to Congress*, 468; Watt, *British Documents*, 11, doc. 203:292.
263 Baroian, *Itogi*, 49, fig. 7.
264 At the beginning of the 1900s the Ministry of the Interior estimated that smallpox killed an average of forty-three thousand of the tsar's subjects yearly (and blinded many of the survivors) (ibid., 16).
265 Watt, *British Documents*, 11, doc. 141:198. The report added that "marmot hunters in Siberia have always had to run the risk of plague" (ibid.).
266 Gantt, *Russian Medicine*, 157.
267 Strøm, *Uncle Give Us Bread*, 34–5.
268 Carynnyk, Luciuk, and Kordan, *Foreign Office*, doc. 72:403.
269 *Brak* also means "marriage"!
270 Chamberlin, *Russia's Iron Age*, 91–2. As a kolkhoznik in Kolomna Rayon recalled: "In 1935 we were given a tractor – more grief. It ploughed so badly, so noisily" (Shcherbakov, *Na serdtse pali vse pechali*, 76). The main flaw in Soviet-made tractors was their faulty pistons (Elmhirst, *Trip to Russia*, 42). And the man in charge of the machine shop and yard at the German agricultural concession of "Drusag" in the North Caucasus told Andrew Cairns in 1932 that "the chief difficulty with Russian-made binders was that they would not bind" – they simply did not work (Cairns, *Soviet Famine*, 94).
271 Cairns, *Soviet Famine*, 89.
272 Hawker, *An Australian*, 6. Hawker spent June 1935 touring the wheatlands of the USSR, chiefly by airplane, travelling some three thousand miles (4,800 kilometres) (ibid., 5, 13).
273 Elmhirst, *Trip to Russia*, 51, 53, 59. *Verblyud* means "camel," a common draught animal in the North Caucasus at the time.
274 Clyman, "Peasants Live in Ground," 31.

275 Kondrashin, *Golod v sssr*, 3, doc. 125:184. Babbitt was bearing lining made of the soft alloy of the same name and used to lessen friction.
276 Bednarek et al., *Holodomor*, doc. 180:471.
277 Narkomzen sssr, *Sel'skoe khoziastvo sssr*, 217, table 67. See also Stalin, *Works*, 13:328. Otto Schiller was personally convinced that the ussr lost between one-half and two-thirds of its livestock in 1928–32 rather than the three-eighths officially reported (Cairns, *Soviet Famine*, 11). Schiller told Cairns that members of the staff of the Commissariat of Agriculture in Moscow had confided in him that the results of the February 1932 livestock census "were so catastrophical [sic] that they felt the figures must be wrong" (ibid). William Chamberlin estimated that between 1929 and 1934 the Soviet Union lost 42 percent of its livestock, including more than one-half of its horses and nearly one-half of its cattle (Chamberlin, *Russia's Iron Age*, 74).
278 Danilov and Ivnitskii, *Dokumenty svidetel'stvuiut*, 263–4.
279 Platonov, *The Return*, 148.
280 [Izmailov], *Dnevnik*, 1:295.
281 United Kingdom, fo 371/17253, no. 6878.
282 Kondrashin, *Khlebozagotovitel'naia politika*, 59; Vilensky, *Till My Tale Is Told*, 242. Another observer noted wryly: "Before entering the kolkhozes, the peasants slaughter their cattle. It seems just as well to gorge themselves with meat for once in their lives and secretly sell the leather, as to give their cattle to the state, with whose methods they are only too familiar" (Serge, *From Lenin to Stalin*, 75).
283 Kovalev, *Golosa krest'ian*, 15. For a piteous description of a peasant killing his favourite and pregnant mare to avoid having to give her to the kolkhoz, see the story "Kolyvushka," one of the two that have survived from Isaac Babel's *The Great Krinitsa* (Freidin, *Isaac Babel's Selected Writings*, 328–32).
284 Sholokhov, *Virgin Soil Upturned*, 157.
285 Kondrashin, *Golod 1932–1933*, 1st ed., 80.
286 Osherowitch, *How People Live in Soviet Russia*, 104.
287 Danilov and Ivnitskii, *Dokumenty svidetel'stvuiut*, 285.
288 This paucity was partly owing to the increase in the acreage of grain and industrial crops at the expense of natural meadows and pastures (Dronin and Belanger, *Climate Dependence*, 118).
289 Kondrashin, *Golod v sssr*, 3, doc. 186:252. The report also blamed deliberate misdiagnoses and the sabotage of prophylactic measures and quarantines by

veterinarians ("kulak wreckers") as well as insufficient feeding, inadequate sheltering, and unsatisfactory breeding (ibid., 252, 253, 253–4, 254). In 1935 an Australian observer cited poor feeding and poor breeding as the two main shortcomings of Soviet stock rearing (Hawker, *An Australian*, 55–6).

290 Kondrashin, *Golod v SSSR*, 3, doc. 177:238. In addition, the area's veterinarians were found to be lacking in both qualifications and medicines (ibid.).
291 Bednarek et al., *Holodomor*, doc. 103:301. His report added that the losses were worsened by grooms' sabotage (ibid.).
292 Cairns, "Agricultural Production," n.p.
293 [Federal Archival Agency], *Famine in the USSR*, doc. 18:45.
294 Bruski, "Bol'shoi golod," 111.
295 Danilov et al., *Kak lomali NEP*, 3, doc. 162:456.
296 Kondrashin, *Golod v SSSR*, 3, doc. 178:239.
297 United Kingdom, FO 371/17253, no. 4419.
298 Jones, "Seizure of Land," 5.
299 [Kaganovich], "Report."
300 Klimin, *Rossiiskoe krest'ianstvo v pervyi period*, 301, citing *Sotsialisticheskoe stroitel'stvo SSSR. Statisticheskii sbornik* (Moscow: GOSPLAN, 1935), 291.
301 [Federal Archival Agency], *Famine in the USSR*, doc. 18:45; Kondrashin, *Golod v SSSR*, vol. 1, bk. 2, doc. 600:228.
302 Jones, "Seizure of Land," 4.
303 Clyman, "Girl from New Toronto," 3.
304 Jarman, *Soviet Union*, 4:131.
305 Gheith and Jolluck, *Gulag Voices*, 35–6. The "Farsons" were made at the Kharkov Tractor Factory.
306 Kondrashin, *Golod v SSSR*, 2, doc. 81:169, 170.
307 Zaitsev et al., *Mologa*, 116.
308 [Jones], *"Tell Them We Are Starving,"* 94, 131.
309 [Kaganovich], "Report."
310 Bruski, "Bol'shoi golod," 111.
311 Kondrashin, *Golod v SSSR*, 2, doc. 132:215.
312 Gritsenko, *Rossiiskaia i sovetskaia derevnia*, 237.
313 Carynnyk, Luciuk, and Kordan, *Foreign Office*, doc. 72:402.
314 Cairns, "Agricultural Production," n.p.
315 [Kaganovich], "Report."
316 United Kingdom, FO 371/17253, no. 4419.

317 Carynnyk, Luciuk, and Jordan, *Foreign Office*, doc. 72:402.
318 Bednarek et al., *Holodomor*, doc. 94:280.
319 Strøm, *Uncle Give Us Bread*, 201.
320 Cairns, *Soviet Famine*, 85, 87; Kondrashin, *Golod v sssr*, 2, doc. 81:168–9, 169.
321 Cairns, *Soviet Famine*, 70; see also Cairns's remarks in Carynnyk, Luciuk, and Kordan, *Foreign Office*, doc. 8:99.
322 United Kingdom, FO 371/17253, no. 4419.
323 Wells, *Kapoot*, 114; Elmhirst, *Trip to Russia*, 24.
324 Duranty, *I Write As I Please*, 324.
325 Kvashonkin et al., *Sovetskoe rukovodstvo*, doc. 102:181, 181–2, 182, 183.
326 Cairns, *Soviet Famine*, 14, 15, 29.
327 Watt, *British Documents*, 12, doc. 128:154. Wild mustard (*Sinapis arvensis*) is an aggressive weed that can reduce the yield and the seed quality of spring cereals, sicken livestock with severe gastroenteritis, and host a variety of pests.
328 Even Maxim Gorky, the "great Soviet author," lent his voice in early 1933 to the "war upon weeds," which, he declared, "spoil, contaminate, devour a huge amount of hard-earned grain" (Gorki, "Maxim Gorki," 3). He added that he assumed that "the All-Union crusade upon weeds will be followed by a proclamation of a similar crusade against rats, mice and other rodents which destroy a huge amount of grain and food" (ibid.).
329 Graziosi, "'Lettres de Kharkov,'" doc. 38:103.
330 Hawker, *An Australian*, 13, 47.
331 Stefferud, *Plant Diseases*, 329, 332.
332 Cairns, *Soviet Famine*, 59.
333 Naumov, *Rzhavchina khlebnykh zlakov*, 3, 5.
334 The Italian Embassy in Moscow stated that the sugar beet plants had been "suffocated by parasitic plants [weeds] and pests [mainly *cecidomyia tritici*], so much so that the weight per hectare is one-third short" (Commission, *Report to Congress*, 437, 458).
335 Carynnyk, Luciuk, and Kordan, *Foreign Office*, doc. 8:99; Cairns, *Soviet Famine*, 80, 84; see also Cairns, *Soviet Famine*, 76, 77, 78, 80, 83, 84, 85, 88, 99.
336 Ibid., 99.
337 Watt, *British Documents*, 10, doc. 64:112.
338 [Menken], "Russian Impressions," 630. Menken found that "Verblyud" was "thick with problems": bad roads, a complex and cumbrous organization of

work, abundant weeds, mired tractors, and combines that operated successfully on dry, clean grain but were rendered useless by damp, weedy grain during the rainy harvest period (ibid.).

339 Clyman, "Peasants Live in Ground," 31. While touring "Verblyud" Clyman noticed that, beyond the farm buildings,

> the fields were dotted with dark black mounds. Thousands of barefooted peasants were now swarming out of them. When I came closer, I discovered that these lumps of earth were dugouts [zemlyankas]. There were rows and rows of them, built out of bits of wood and plastered over with cow dung and straw, [and] the doorways were so low that the people coming out of them were bent in [sic] double to crawl through.

She tried to enter one of them but "the stench of human body and cow dung was too great." These structures were the barracks for the seasonal workers – peasants – who, as unskilled workers (although they were in fact skilled workers because they "knew everything there was to know about the land"), were paid one ruble, ninety kopecks per day and fed in the third-class canteen, "where there was nothing but salted fish and boiled potatoes and corn mash to eat," plus a pound of black bread a day. The mechanics (one thousand of them) and workers, by contrast, lived in four-room flats and received "good pay and meat rations twice a week" in a first-class canteen (ibid.).

At the very same time the "Gigant" sovkhoz was also in a bad way, the French chargé d'affaires in Moscow reporting that the commissar of agriculture, Yakov Yakovlev, had found that: "On their own terms the farmers go to work at 9 o'clock in the morning, concern themselves primarily with preparing their lunch and return home after being content with clearing half a hectare. Barns are in a terrible state of filth and animals are dying for lack of forage" (McVay and Luciuk, *Holy See*, doc. 13:18).

340 At the same time, more and more "shoeless" specialists – those who had dirtied their hands (feet in this case) in the field with practical experience at the expense of academic learning and theoretical training (the preserve of the *zamknuty*, the "exclusive ones" or the "imprisoned ones") – came to the fore in response to Stalin's desire for quick results on the ground. A prime example was the geneticist Trofim Lysenko, whose machinations impaired agricultural innovation and contributed to the tragic death of Nikolai Vavilov.

341 Carynnyk, Luciuk, and Kordan, *Foreign Office*, doc. 72:403. Dittloff added that "the final death blow to the authority of the old school of manager, with technical training on a specific basis" had been dealt by the sensational Shakty trial of May 1928 (ibid.), when fifty-five non-communist managers and engineers working at the coal-mining centre of Shakty in the Donbass were accused of sabotaging production at the behest of French, German, and Polish capitalists (five of the accused were executed and thirty-eight were imprisoned). A purge of non-communist technicians throughout the country followed. The trial was a harbinger of the show trials a decade later.

342 Cairns, *Soviet Famine*, 59.

343 Graziosi, "'Lettres de Kharkov,'" doc. 38:103.

344 Elmhirst, *Trip to Russia*, 36–7.

345 Kondrashin, *Golod 1932–1933 godov*, 1st ed., 79.

346 This proverb was quoted by Kaganovich to illustrate the benefits of rotation ([Kaganovich], "Report").

347 Danilov, Manning, and Viola, *Tragediia sovetskoi derevni*, 3, doc. 162:456.

348 [Kaganovich], "Report."

349 Schiller, "Agriculture," n.p.

350 Kondrashin, *Golod v SSSR*, 3, doc. 249:330–40.

351 Davies et al., *Stalin-Kaganovich Correspondence*, doc. 18:94–5. Stalin, as was his wont, blamed others, in this case the transport sector's principal bureaucrats, for obstructionism (ibid.).

352 Carnnyk, Luciuk, and Kordan, *Foreign Office*, doc. 13:193.

353 Ibid., doc. 3:11.

354 Antipova et al., *Golod v SSSR*, doc. 14:85, doc. 15:86.

355 [Menken], "Russian Impressions," 584.

356 Zima, "Golod 1932–1933," 49.

357 Goichenko, *Skvoz raskulachivanie*, 242.

358 Ibid.

359 Ibid., 242–3.

360 [Izmailov], *Dnevnik*, 1:493.

361 United Kingdom, FO 371/17253, no. 6878. Schiller added that the looming crisis had been "somewhat obscured" and postponed by "the favourable harvest of 1930 due to climatic causes" (ibid.).

362 Danilov, Manning, and Viola, *Tragediia sovetskoi derevni*, 3, doc. 162:456–9; Kondrashin, *Golod v SSSR*, 2, doc. 12:53–6.

363 Ibid.

Chapter Five

1 Soviet statistics during the Stalin period (1928–53) differed in reliability between the unpublished and the published/broadcast/declared figures, the latter containing errors of both omission and commission (the various forms of statistical chicanery – the inflation or outright falsification of figures, forgery, and show work [*pokaza*] – were known colloquially as *tufta* [Mochulsky, *Gulag Boss*, 210], meaning "hogwash" or "crap"). During the 1920s and 1930s Soviet statisticians allegedly exhibited a high degree of honesty and professionalism, which was reflected in the published statistics – with the exception of those in the years 1928–31 and 1934–39, which were distorted by "the psychology of Constructivist [read 'creative'] planning," that is, political pressure by the authorities to cast the demographic and agricultural figures in a favourable light (Kondrashin, *Golod v SSSR*, 3:720–1; and Danilov, Manning, and Viola, *Tragediia sovetskoi derevni*, 3:866–7; see also Blium and Mespule, *Biurokraticheskaia anarkhiia*). The distortions of 1928–31 were explained by the British consul in Leningrad, Reader Bullard, in early 1932:

> There is no person in authority, from Stalin down, who would not sign a page of false statistics and think nothing of it. The few people who care for truth haven't the courage to stand up for it … and the Bolsheviks laugh at it, as they do at our conception of justice, as bourgeois. The Bolsheviks believe in what they call "proletarian truth," that is, any statement which for the moment advances the cause of the proletariat. ([Bullard], *Inside Stalin's Russia*, 90)

This attitude was expressed by Commissar of Trade Anastas Mikoyan in a speech to a Party plenum in November 1929, when he denounced "the bankruptcy of the bourgeois method of statistics" insofar as the old economists-cum-statisticians were "in favour of the policy of right deviation," and he declared "the necessity of reorganizing all of our statistics in a radical manner, involving the new – our – cadres, and, finally, seeing to it that Soviet statistics are a practical weapon in the hands of the proletarian dictatorship in the matter of socialist economic construction" (Danilov et al., *Kak lomali NEP*, 5:81). Otto Schiller was told confidentially by an official of the Commissariat of Agriculture that "all Russian statistics are compiled in three sets –

one for publication, one confidential set for the directors [of departments], and one very confidential set for the very high officials [commissars and Stalin's inner circle]" (Cairns, *Soviet Famine*, 38). This deception began at the very lowest level of officialdom (kolkhoz manager or even brigade leader) and continued up through the district and regional levels to the Kremlin itself in order to appear to meet the sacred targets of the Plan and not displease the higher bosses to whom they were answerable, for fear of incurring their wrath and (at a time of scarcity) being demoted or dismissed or (at a time of tyranny) jailed, exiled, or shot.

Because agricultural performance demonstrated the success or failure of the regime's pivotal and vaunted program of collectivization, it was particularly subject to statistical creativity. Victor Kondrashin has noted that Stalinist economic policy was oriented towards the solution of complex problems with the help of purely administrative (repressive) methods but without scientific evaluation; in agriculture this tendency resulted in an ignorance of the true extent of sowings, harvests, and procurements of grain, as well as their exaggeration, in order to satisfy the leadership's desire to increase commercial production as much as, and as fast as, possible (Kondrashin, *Khlebozagotovitel'naia politika*, 54, citing the Archive of the President of the Russian Federation [hereafter APRF], f. 3, op. 40, d. 81, fol. 133). "The authorities," Kondrashin has concluded, "simply forced Soviet statisticians to give the necessary figures on crops" (ibid.).

2 Narkomzem SSSR, *Sel'skoe khoziaistvo SSSR*, 208, table 29.
3 The 1928–31 average was a modest 7.7 centners per hectare; it was highest in the Central Black Earth (9.2) and the Ukraine (8.8) – both of them much higher than the drier and colder Lower and Middle Volga (5.9–6.1) (Ivnitskii, *Golod 1932–1933*, 68–9).
4 United Kingdom, FO 371/17253, no. 6878. And, according to Kaganovich, during the Second Five-Year Plan it was intended to open up to 4 million hectares of wheatland "in the non-chernozyom belt of the Union" and "no fewer than 5 million hec[tares] of virgin land" (Kondrashin, *Golod v SSSR*, 3, doc. 28:81).
5 Kondrashin, *Golod v SSSR*, 3, doc. 143:200–1.
6 Ibid., 3, doc. 235:315.
7 Ronina et al., "Oglianutsia v razdume," 17.
8 Cairns, "Agricultural Production."
9 Cairns, "Agricultural Production," citing GOSPLAN for the 1925–30 figures

and himself for the 1931–32 figures and the 1909–13 annual average; Tsentral'-noe upravlenie, *Narodnoe khoziaistvo SSSR ... 1932*, 121, table 5.1.
10 Carynnyk, Luciuk, and Kordan, *Foreign Office*, doc. 46:294.
11 Danilov, Manning, and Viola, *Tragediia sovetskoi derevni*, 3:854, table 6.
12 Kondrashin, *Golod v SSSR*, 3, doc. 249:330.
13 Ibid., doc. 51:103, 104. For a report from a state agricultural inspection body to the Central Committee about grain haulage and storage problems in 1931–33, see ibid., doc. 53:107–11.
14 Ivnitskii, *Golod 1932–1933*, 2.
15 Macqueen, "Survivors," 45.
16 Herman, *Coming Out of the Ice*, 39.
17 Veselovskii, *Problemy nashei zhizni*, 1:386.
18 Danilov, Manning, and Viola, *Tragediia sovetskoi derevni*, 1, doc. 38:147.
19 Lih, Naumov, and Khlevniuk, *Stalin's Letters to Molotov*, letter 42:169.
20 Ibid., letter 44:175.
21 Ibid., letter 57:201.
22 Ibid., letter 59:203, letter 60:205. One pud equals 16.38 kilograms or 36.113 pounds, so 1 centner equals 6.11 puds and 1 tonne equals 62.58 puds.
23 Mankov, "Iz dnevnika," 137.
24 Ivnitskii, *Golod 1932–1933*, 2.
25 Danilov, Manning, and Viola, *Tragediia sovetskoi derevni*, 2, doc. 226:615, 619.
26 Kondrashin, *Golod 1932–1933*, 2nd ed., 125.
27 Danilov, Manning, and Viola, *Tragediia sovetskoi derevni*, 2, doc. 226:615, 619.
28 Ivnitskii, *Golod 1932–1933 godov*, 247.
29 [Federal'noe arkhivnoe agentsvo], *Kollektsiia dokumentov*, doc. 18.
30 Lewin, "Taking Grain," 310; see also Werth, *Histoire*, 237. The Soviet norm, incidentally, for the minimum per capita consumption of grain by the peasants (for food, seed, and feed), based upon Tver Oblast in 1924, was 19 puds (686 pounds) – about 3 centners or one-third of a tonne – per year (Berelovich and Danilov, *Sovetskaia derevnia*, 2, doc. 164:231).
31 Ivnitskii, *Golod 1932–1933*, 67, 242.
32 Osokina, *Our Daily Bread*, 32–3.
33 Ibid., 35.
34 See Viola, *Best Sons of the Fatherland*. Much later, in 1955, Khrushchev would similarly mobilize the "Thirty Thousanders" to assist in the opening of the virgin and idle lands.
35 Sholokhov, *Virgin Soil Upturned*, 31, 33.

36 Golitsyn, *Memoirs*, 356.
37 Kondrashin, *Golod 1932–1933 godov*, 1st ed., 78.
38 Ibid., 49, citing APRF, f. 3, op. 40, d. 80, fols. 84–5.
39 Kondrashin, *Golod 1932–1933 godov*, 1st ed., 79.
40 Kravchenko, *I Chose Freedom*, 91, 92.
41 Kondrashin, *Golod v SSSR*, vol. 1, bk. 2, doc. 536:158–9.
42 Cairns, *Soviet Famine*, 60.
43 Danilov, Manning, and Viola, *Tragediia sovetskoi derevni*, 3, doc. 254:626, 627.
44 Kondrashin, *Golod 1932–1933*, 2nd ed., 179.
45 Kondrashin, *Khlebozagotovitel'naia politika*, 105.
46 Antipova et al., *Golod v SSSR*, doc. 65:187; Kondrashin and Tiurina, "Govorit' o golode," doc. 10:111, 112.
47 Kondrashin, *Golod 1932–1933*, 2nd ed., 229.
48 Antipova et al., *Golod v SSSR*, doc. 59:178; Kondrashin and Tiurina, "Govorit' o golode," doc. 6:107. The term *zapal* refers to the "withering" or "scorching" of grain during drought as the grain fails to ripen and dries out, the kernels becoming soft and puny; *tuman* normally means "fog" but seems to refer here to "haze," presumably *mgla*, with the dust particles in the air during sukhovei absorbing heat and increasing the air temperature.
49 Kondrashin, *Khlebozagotovitel'naia politika*, 130–1.
50 Ibid., 125.
51 Bondar and Matveev, *Istoricheskaia pamiat'*, 61; Grzhebin, "Kollektivizatsiia," 49.
52 Bondar and Matveev, *Istoricheskaia pamiat'*, 60; Danilov, Manning, and Viola, *Tragediia sovetskoi derevni*, 3:29; Grzhebin, "Kollektivizatsiia," 11.
53 Danilov, Manning, and Viola, *Tragediia sovetskoi derevni*, 3:29; Grzhebin, "Kollektivisatsiia," 50–1; Zelenin, "O nekotorikh 'belykh piatnakh'," 11.
54 Zelenin, "O nekotorikh 'belykh piatnakh'," 12, citing the Archive of Rostov Obkom of the KPSS (AROKPSS), f. 8, op. 1, d. 49, fol. 799 and d. 46, fols. 402–3.
55 Davies et al., *Stalin-Kaganovich Correpondence*, doc. 44:152, doc. 46:158.
56 Ibid., doc. 51:168n.
57 Kondrashin, *Khlebozagotovitel'naia politika*, 123, 124, citing APRF, f. 3, op. 40, d. 84, fols. 145–6, 148.
58 Medvedev, *Okruzhenie Stalina*, 118.
59 Antipova et al., *Golod v SSSR*, doc. 72:202; Kondrashin and Tiurina, "Govorit' o golode," doc. 16:118.

60 Kondrashin and Tiurina, "Govorit' o golode," docs. 17–18:119.
61 Kravchenko, *I Chose Freedom*, 111.
62 Kondrashin, *Khlebozagotovitel'naia politika*, 207, 207–8.
63 Ibid., 14, table 1, 230.
64 Danilov and Ivnitskii, *Dokumenty svidetel'stvuiut*, 270, citing *Materialy o rabote politotdelov MTS za 1933* (Moscow, 1934), 18, 40, 51, 69, 77, 87.
65 Kondrashin, *Golod v SSSR*, vol. 1, bk. 1, doc. 34:87–8.
66 Kondrashin, *Khlebozagotovitel'naia politika*, 64.
67 Kondrashin, *Golod 1932–1933 godov*, 1st ed., 81–2, 84–5.
68 Bruski, "Bol'shoi golod," 107–8.
69 Hindus, *Great Offensive*, 150, 151, 152. The peasants themselves, Hindus wrote, responded by sabotaging their field work, killing their livestock, and leaving for the large cities (ibid., 153, 154).
70 Antipova et al., *Golod v SSSR*, doc. 36:78.
71 Kondrashin, *Golod 1932–1933*, 2nd ed., 146.
72 [Bullard], *Inside Stalin's Russia*, 64.
73 Commission, *Report to Congress*, 457, 461.
74 Durant, *Tragedy of Russia*, 39.
75 Anonymous [Jack Heinz II], *Experiences in Russia – 1931*, 85. Victor Reuther, like his brother Walter a labour leader in the United States and for a while a worker in the USSR, was so circumspect as to be Durantyesque, writing that "the Soviet Union paid for all this [industrialization] by exporting its wheat and putting its people on a stringent diet" (Reuther, *Brothers Reuther*, 92).
76 Kondrashin, *Khlebozagotovitel'naia politika*, 147, table 10.
77 Stalin boasted that, by the end of the First Five-Year Plan, the state was procuring 1.2 billion to 1.4 billion puds (19,655,000 to 22,931,000 tonnes) of grain annually instead of the 500 million to 600 million puds (8,190,000 to 9,828,000 tonnes) before 1928 (Stalin, *Works*, 13:194).
78 Khlevniuk, Kvashonkin, Kosheleva, and Rogovaia, *Stalinskoe Politbiuro v 30-e gody*, doc. 130:146.
79 Antipova et al., *Golod v SSSR*, doc. 94:288.
80 Bednarek et al., *Holodomor*, doc. 202:544.
81 Barmine, *One Who Survived*, 246. Barmine also argued that the bumper harvest of 1933 and resultant better supply of food facilitated Stalin's later and bloody "counter-revolution" (in the form of Party purges and show trials) by winning support "in the politically unconscious masses of the population" – support further bolstered by the abolition of bread cards in early 1935 and

the granting of personal plots and a few livestock to collective farmers and the right to sell their own output on the open market (ibid., 253).

82 Kondrashin, *Khlebozagotovitel'naia politika*, 85. For the documentary basis of requisitioning and purchasing in 1933–34 that took into account the excesses and defects of procurement during the First Five-Year Plan in order to make procurement more effective, see Kondrashin and Mozokhin, *Posle "Velikogo pereloma."*

83 Ciliga, *Russian Enigma*, 517.

84 See, for example, Antipova et al., *Golod v SSSR*, docs. 22, 26–7, 38–40, 42, 46–7, 49, 55, 67, 86, 104, 108, 183–4; [Federal Archival Agency], *Famine in the USSR*, docs. 159, 190, 192, 194; [Federal'noe arkhivnoe agentstvo], *Kollektsiia dokumentov*, docs. 19, 23–24, 28, 30, 33, 39, 41, 47, 53, 58, 68, 74, 76, 98, 193; and Kondrashin, *Golod v SSSR*, 3, docs. 222, 250–384.

85 Antipova et al., *Golod v SSSR*, doc. 22:107–9.

86 Ibid., doc. 38:136–37.

87 Kondrashin, *Golod 1932–1933*, 2nd ed., 282, table 11; Kondrashin, *Khlebozagotovitel'naia politika*, 80, table 5; 186, table 11; 237, table 12.

88 Antipova et al., *Golod v SSSR*, doc. 42:141–2, [Federal'noe arkhivnoe agentstvo], *Kollektsiia dokumentov*, doc. 39.

89 [Federal Archival Agency], *Famine in the USSR*, doc. 159:1.

90 Kondrashin, *Khlebozagotovitel'naia politika*, 163–4.

91 Antipova et al., *Golod v SSSR*, doc. 126:385–6; [Federal Archival Agency], *Famine in the USSR*, doc. 118:2; Kondrashin and Tiurina, "Govorit' o golode," doc. 26:126.

92 Kondrashin, *Khlebozagotovitel'naia politika*, 165, citing the Central Archive of the Russian Federal Security Service (hereafter TSARFSB), f. 2, op. 11, d. 971, fols. 145–7.

93 Ibid., 167, 168, citing the Russian State Archive of the Economy (hereafter RGAE), f. 8,040, op. 8, d. 25, fols. 32–36.

94 Kondrashin, *Golod 1932–1933*, 2nd ed., 285.

95 Kondrashin, *Golod v SSSR*, vol. 2, 34:table 4; vol. 3, 20:table 1; vol. 3, 21:docs. 242, 325.

96 Ibid., 2:35.

97 Watt, *British Documents*, 11, doc. 203:292.

98 [Federal Archival Agency], *Famine in the USSR*, doc. 190; Kondrashin, *Khlebozagotovitel'naia politika*, 241–2, 242.

99 [Federal Archival Agency], *Famine in the USSR*, doc. 194.
100 On the "new NEP," see Davies, *Crisis and Progress*, 209–17; see also Jarman, *Soviet Union*, 4:573–7.
101 Such was the hunger at the famine's height, however, that a new threat appeared – the theft of produce, chickens, and even cows from the personal plots while their peasant tenants were absent, working in the fields (thieves who were caught were lynched). So now the starving peasants were stealing from each other instead of the kolkhozes, as in 1932.
102 For the original "model charter" of the kolkhoz of February to March 1930 and the revised charter of February 1935, see Danilov, Manning, and Viola, *Tragediia sovetskoi derevni*, 4:933, notes 111 and 112. Not surprisingly, under the 1935 charter the size of the personal plots of individual farmsteaders was to be "no higher" than that of kolkhozniks in the same district and even "10% less" than those of kolkhozniks in districts where there was not enough land for use as personal plots (ibid., doc. 157:417). For a typically lengthy but interesting discussion by Stalin with the delegates to a conference of superior kolkhozniks on the question of the allowable size of personal plots and the allowable number of personal livestock, see ibid., doc. 146:390–402.
103 Kondrashin, *Khlebozagotovitel'naia politika*, 217; Kondrashin, *Golod v SSSR*, 3:5, doc. 1:54–5. The measures did not prohibit decreases, so further relief was forthcoming when, owing to circumstances in some areas, the 1933 procurement plan was reduced by 787,690 tonnes to a level that was 1,777,225 tonnes lower than 1932's level and 7,811,258 tonnes lower than 1931's level (e.g., in the autumn Ukrainian Party secretary Khatayevich blamed "the extremely poor quality of sowing and the low sowing norms of autumn [winter] grain in 1932, the extreme infestation of fields by pests, the poor organization of harvesting, the acute shortage of workers, and the extreme strain on draught animals," while an OGPU report in the summer stated that in the North Caucasus cut and stooked grain had turned black and begun to spoil, uncut grain was shedding its kernels, milling was hampered by idle threshing machines, low output norms, the poor organization of work, and the lack of transport for the delivery of grain to depots [Kondrashin, *Khlebozagotovitel'naia politika*, 227, citing APRF, f. 3, op. 61, d. 794, fols. 96–108 and TSAFSB, f. 2, op. 11, d. 1,049, fols. 6–7; Kondrashin, *Golod v SSSR*, 3, doc. 30:82–3, doc. 109:169–70]).
104 A Polish diplomat reported that this concession generated a class of long-

distance bread traders who dealt solely in the buying and selling of bread. Carrying sacks and frequenting the railway stations, trains, and markets, they packed the third-class train cars, travelling to Kiev and even as far as Leningrad to buy bread rations and to Baku to buy corn flour (there were instances of single peasants travelling for two weeks and procuring up to ten puds of corn flour). The diplomat wrote:

> These new Soviet merchants have a portly physique and are acquainted with the conditions in faraway markets, prices, transporting conditions, [and] ways of paying bribes to the authorities – mainly the railway authorities for a proper treatment on the car, assistance with loading the grain, a place on the bench to sleep, and other privileges which are v[ery] important on a long journey.

The trade, he continued, was "extremely profitable," the traders usually reckoning that one-half of the grain would be kept for their own families and the other half sold at a profit of 100 percent, taking into account the cost of their travel and the cost of their load of grain (Bednarek et al., *Holodomor*, doc. 197:534–5).

105 Nikita Khrushchev recalled that Stalin even proposed the raising of rabbits and the growing of mushrooms at every workplace in order to help feed the workers, but the initial results were so mixed that people began to call the mushroom beds *grobnitsy* (tombs) instead of *gribnitsy* (mushroom cellars) (Khrushchev, *Memoirs*, 1:55). Actually, many urban families already had their own plots on unauthorized vacant land, where they grew vegetables, mostly potatoes, which were second only to bread as a Russian staple, and they also reared poultry and cattle in sheds near their plots or even in their flats (in 1932–33, at the peak of the famine, this "auxiliary economy" provided up to one-third of an industrial worker's milk and eggs and almost one-tenth of his or her vegetables, fruit, and fat [Osokina, *Our Daily Bread*, 110]). Willard Gorton, an American irrigation engineer who worked in Tashkent in the early 1930s, recounted an order issued by the superintendent of a dormitory: "It is also prohibited to have in the rooms chickens, dogs, suckling pigs, and other animals, including bears, as was noticed – I command all of these to be liquidated without leaving a trace!" (ibid.).

106 Davies et al., *Stalin-Kaganovich Correspondence*, doc. 25:116–17, 117, doc. 26:118, doc. 27:120, doc. 47:160–1; [Federal Archival Agency], *Famine in the*

USSR, doc. 195; Kondrashin, *Golod v SSSR*, 3, 5, doc. 5:59–64, doc. 227:306–7; Kondrashin, *Khlebozagotovitel'naia politika*, 86, 213, 220, 227, 230–1, 245.

107 Gritsenko, *Rossiiskaia i sovetskaia derevnia*, 194.
108 Watt, *British Documents*, 11, doc. 203:293, 294.
109 Bednarek et al., *Holodomor*, doc. 202:543.
110 Ciliga, *Russian Enigma*, 517.
111 Kondrashin, "Zerno v obmen na valiutu i stanki," 112.
112 Kondrashin, *Golod v SSSR*, vol. 1, bk. 1, doc. 228:385.
113 [Muggeridge], "The Soviet and the Peasantry," 2:13, 14. This "famine export" of grain was not new, having occurred only forty years earlier, when it likewise generated starvation. Then Tsar Alexander III's minister of finance (1887–92), Ivan Vyshnegradsky, declared, "we will be underfed, but we will export." In 1887–91 some 10 million tonnes of grain were exported in order to reduce the country's debt load and to secure credits for industrialization (Semenova, *Unichtozhennie kak klass*, 1:6) – a policy that helped to create the "king-sized famine" (*tsar golod*) of 1891–92 as well as substantial industrial advancement.
114 Ibid., 32.
115 Danilov et al., *Kak lomali NEP*, 5:79–81, 83; Kondrashin, *Golod v SSSR*, vol. 1, bk. 1, doc. 57:140.
116 Kondrashin, *Golod 1932–1933*, 2nd ed., 152–3; Kondrashin, *Khlebozagotovitel'naia politika*, 95, citing RGASPI, f. 17, op. 162, d. 10, fols. 41–2, 111.
117 Kondrashin, *Golod 1932–1933*, 2nd ed., 156.
118 Lih, Naumov, and Khlevniuk, *Stalin's Letters to Molotov*, letter 60:205. So determined was Stalin that he considered removing Mikoyan as commissar of trade because he was "not coping" with his job, that is, not doing what Stalin wanted (ibid.).
119 Osokina, *Our Daily Bread*, 44.
120 Ronina et al., "Oglianutsia v razdume," 16.
121 Kondrashin, *Golod v SSSR*, vol. 1, bk. 1, doc. 351:527–8.
122 Osokina, *Our Daily Bread*, 26.
123 The price that Soviet wheat fetched abroad would have been higher but for its inferior quality, so superior varieties were imported from Canada to improve domestic varieties (Kondrashin, *Khlebozagotovitel'naia politika*, 246).
124 Kondrashin, *Golod 1932–1933*, 2nd ed., 154–5; Kondrashin, *Khlebozagotovitel'naia politika*, 97.
125 Kondrashin and Tiurina, "Govorit' o golode," doc. 1:103.

126 Kondrashin, *Golod v SSSR*, 3, doc. 479:571.
127 Davies, Harrison, and Wheatcroft, *Economic Transformation*, 206.
128 Smith, *Soviet Foreign Trade*, 20.
129 Davies, Harrison, and Wheatcroft, *Economic Transformation*, 206–7.
130 Ibid., 208. And, according to Eugene Lyons, in the first half of 1931 the USSR exported 754,000 more tonnes of commodities than in the same period of 1930 but earned $63,730,000 less from them (Lyons, *Assignment*, 451).
131 Lyons, *Assignment*, 540.
132 Cairns, *Soviet Famine*, 40.
133 Williams, *Trading with the Bolsheviks*, here and there throughout.
134 Smith, *Soviet Foreign Trade*, 257.
135 Kondrashin, *Golod 1932–1933*, 2nd ed., 156.
136 Kondrashin, *Golod v SSSR*, vol. 1, bk. 1, doc. 225:381, doc. 226:381–2, doc. 227:382–3, doc. 228:383–6; Kondrashin, "Zerno v obmen na valiutu i stanki," 113.
137 Kondrashin, "Zerno v obmen na valiutu i stanki," 113. The Soviets also "categorically refused" to limit their grain acreage on the grounds that expansion was necessary to feed its increasing population, which was growing by 4 million per year (double Europe's rate, despite starvation) (Antipova et al., *Golod v SSSR*, doc. 71:161).
138 Davies et al., *Stalin-Kaganovich Correspondence*, doc. 6:65. In a September cypher to the other members of the inner circle Stalin and Molotov referred to the United States as "the current master of the financial world and our chief enemy," one that "is making and will make every effort to undermine our hard-currency position" (ibid., doc. 11:79).
139 Kondrashin, *Golod v SSSR*, vol. 1, bk. 1, doc. 227:383; Kondrashin, "Zerno v obmen na valiutu i stanki," 114. This first wheat conference, as well as the second in London in May, failed to reach an accord on export quotas, which were not agreed until the third conference in London in August 1933, and by then the Soviet Union was curtailing its grain exports.
140 Barmine, *One Who Survived*, 175. For Barmine's eyewitness account of this "desperate battle" by the Soviets to obtain credits and to meet payments on time for foreign machinery with "everything we could lay our hands on," see ibid., 174–7.
141 United States, Records of the Department of State, T1249, 1–2.
142 Kondrashin, *Golod v SSSR*, vol. 1, bk. 1, doc. 430:634; Kondrashin, "Zerno v obmen na valiutu i stanki," 113, citing RSASPI, f. 17, op. 162, d. 11, fol. 129.

143 Kondrashin, *Golod v SSSR*, vol. 1, bk. 1, doc. 240:392; Kondrashin, "Zerno v obmen na valiutu i stanki," 113.
144 Kondrashin, *Khlebozagotovitel'naia politika*, 100, table 7.
145 [Federal Archival Agency], *Famine in the USSR*, doc. 74:166.
146 Ibid., 96, 274, table 13; Kondrashin, *Golod 1932–1933*, 2nd ed., 443, table 22; Kondrashin, *Golod v SSSR*, 3:41, table 2.
147 Kondrashin, *Golod 1932–1933*, 2nd ed., 444, table 23; Kondrashin, *Golod v SSSR*, 3:41–2, table 3; Kondrashin, *Khlebozagotovitel'naia politika*, 275, table 14.
148 Kondrashin, "Zerno v obmen na valiutu i stanki," 113, citing Danilov, Manning, and Viola, *Tragediia sovetskoi derevni*, 3:53 and RSASPI, f. 17, op. 162, d. 9, fol. 102, d. 10, fol. 143, d.11, fol. 109.
149 Kondrashin, *Golod 1932–1933*, 2nd ed., 156; Kondrashin, *Khlebozagotovitel'naia politika*, 98, citing RGAE, f. 1,562, op. 329, d. 4, fol. 2.
150 The Russian historian Victor Kondrashin has been, if not the first, then the most vocal scholar to raise this matter (see especially Kondrashin, "Zerno v obmen na valiutu i stanki"). In his view "it can now be asserted with certainty that Stalin could not have begun collectivization with such haste and such force against the peasantry if the West had not bought Soviet grain" (Kondrashin, *Khlebozagotovitel'naia politika*, 33).
151 Kondrashin, "Zerno v obmen na valiutu i stanki," 112, citing *Sotsialisticheskoe stroitel'stvo SSSR. Statisticheskii sbornik* (Moscow: GOSPLAN, 1936), 687.
152 Ibid., 113.
153 Ibid., citing AVPRF, f. 54, op. 1, *papka* [file case] 1, d. 4, fol. 17.
154 Von Herwarth, *Against Two Evils*, 40–1.
155 Their reaction was expressed in a bitter ditty: "Rye and wheat have we exported, but on black pea and goosefoot are kolkhozniks supported" (Kondrashin, *Golod 1932–1933*, 2nd ed., 562). Black pea, or iron grass (*tsyganka*), is *Lathyrus niger*, a perennial legume. The relationship between exportation and starvation was noted by Maxim Gorky in a letter in the fall of 1930 with respect to the situation in Belorussia: "Ask Klara Zetkin [Clara Eissner, a German Marxist activist] how the [Soviet] Union's blue-collar and white-collar workers are starving and how this starvation is accompanied by the shipment abroad of everything we have of value" (Kondrashin, *Golod 1932–1933*, 2nd ed., 155).
156 Kondrashin, "Zerno v obmen na valiutu i stanki," 114.
157 Ibid.
158 An exception to this official discretion occurred in 1933 in Germany, where

an official propaganda campaign, with the participation of President Hindenburg and Chancellor Hitler, was begun against the Soviet Union's "famine export" of grain. The campaign included "an exhibit of letters from starving kolkhozniks in the German Volga Republic" and "a collection for the needs of the starving," but it was primarily concerned not with the plight of starving Germans in the USSR but, for example, with the anti-fascist campaign in the Soviet Union that had been prompted by the losses of German communists in the 1932 elections, "demonstrations" during a funeral in Moscow in June 1933 for Klara Tsetkin, and editorial caricatures of Hitler in the Soviet press. In the course of this growing diplomatic spat the special displeasure of the Kremlin was evoked by the publication in Germany of a report by Otto Schiller about his trip through the Ukraine and the famine there. Soviet diplomats asked how the German leadership would react if they, for instance, were to break diplomatic etiquette by going to "one of the forced labour camps" in Germany and then writing about it in the Soviet press. After an exchange of diplomatic notes and mutual concessions, the anti-fascist campaign in the Soviet Union was halted and the "famine exhibit" in Germany was closed. The conflict was settled, and economic relations between the two countries continued to develop (ibid., 114, citing AVPRF, f. 0,165 [sic?], op. 13, papka 154, d. 361, fols. 321, 322, 325; f. 05 [sic?], op. 13, papka 90, d. 14, fols. 89–78v. [sic]).

On a non-official level, in the summer of 1933 anti-Soviet groups in a number of Western European countries began to protest the famine in the Ukraine and the North Caucasus; for instance, French newspapers wrote that "the USSR [did] not have the right to export grain" because it was suffering a "famine," with "millions dying" (ibid., citing AVPRF, f. 05 [sic?], op. 13, papka 90, d. 14, fol. 70). And apparently some European periodicals were publicizing the "famine campaign" against the Soviet Union for commercial purposes, as a report by a Soviet diplomat to Moscow about the French newspaper *Le Matin* stated: "With its campaign about the famine in the Ukraine, etc., the newspaper is clearly trying to blackmail us for a subsidy" (ibid., citing AVPRF, f. 05 [sic?], op. 13, papka 90, d. 14, fol. 72). The implication is that the silence or perhaps even the support of some Western newspapers in their coverage of the USSR could be bought by the latter for the right price.

159 Kondrashin, *Khlebozagotovitel'naia politika*, 274–5. Indeed, with the benefit of hindsight it could be argued – perversely – that Western complicity was ben-

eficial because, by enabling Soviet industrialization and militarization, it created a future ally against the Axis in the Second World War, whose outcome would have been quite different without the Soviet Union's crucial participation as one of the Allies.

Chapter Six

The Kazakhs – officially termed "Kirghizes" until the mid-1920s – were the most populous but not the only nomadic (or semi-nomadic) people of the Asiatic Russian steppe (and semi-desert); other and smaller Sunni Muslim pastoralists, notably the actual (and nomadic) Kirghizes of mountainous Kirghizia below the Tien Shan, the nomadic Kalmyks of the left bank of the lower Volga River, and the semi-nomadic Karakalpaks of the lower reaches of the Amu Darya presumably suffered in the same manner and to the same degree as the Kazakhs.

1 The Kazakhs were "minoritized," too, by the involuntary resettlement in their republic of exiled kulaks and minority "nationalities" (ethnic groups), especially Ukrainians, Tatars, Germans, and others during the Stalin years, and by the voluntary settlement of Great Russians in the virgin lands of Kazakhstan's northern frontier under Khrushchev in the mid-1950s. For example, between the 1926 census and the suppressed 1937 census the number of Great Russians in the Kazakh SSR (officially demarcated in 1936) increased by 642,500 (although the 1937 census – as well as the published 1939 census – counted many Ukrainians, Belorussians, Jews, Mordvinians, and Bolgars as Great Russians) (Omarbekov, *Golodomor v Kazakhstane*, 8).

2 For background details, see Demko, *Russian Colonization*; Olcott, *Kazakhs*; and Pianciola, *Stalinismo di frontera*, which treats Russian colonization, Kazakh (and Kirghiz) depopulation, and governance during the 1905–36 period (for shorter English versions see Pianciola, "Collectivization Famine" and Pianciola, "Famine in the Steppe"). The most recent comprehensive and authoritative treatments of the Kazakh famine in English are Mikhailov, *Great Disaster*, based upon official documents and survivors' testimonies (although it is preoccupied with the pathological Party chief Filipp Goloshchyokin) and especially Cameron's excellent treatment, *The Hungry Steppe* (which is based upon state and Party documents and written and spoken recollections). See also Kindler, *Stalin's Nomads*.

3   The Basmachis (from Turkic *basmak*, "to attack" or "to raid") were a loose and motley group of anti-Russian and anti-Soviet rebels, rooted mainly in the villages.
4   Ryskozha, "Valery Mikhailov." In 1917–22 some 2 million people starved in Turkestan, of whom about 1 million (1,114,000 officially) died of hunger and disease, and one thousand children were rendered homeless (Mikhailov, *Great Disaster*, 81, 93).
5   Ryskozha, "Valery Mikhailov."
6   Tatimov and Tatimova, "Tragediia velikoi stepi," 55. The TOZ – Association for Communal Cultivation – was the simplest form of the kolkhoz, with all livestock remaining in private possession; it was most common in nomadic regions. The TOZ was abolished in 1938.
7   Pianciola, "Famine in the Steppe," 139–40, 140n11.
8   Danilov, Manning, and Viola, *Tragediia sovetskoi derevni*, 3, doc. 183:504; Nusinbaev and Zhienfaliev, *Golod v Kazakhskoi stepi*, doc. 7:152, 156.
9   Danilov, Manning, and Viola, *Tragediia sovetskoi derevni*, 3, doc. 183:507.
10 Littlepage and Bess, *In Search of Soviet Gold*, 108. At the same time the Kremlin even tried – albeit somewhat half-heartedly – to settle the Romany (Gypsies), the embodiment of itinerancy, onto "Gypsy kolkhozes" and into "Gypsy artels."
11 Occasionally *dzhut* is used figuratively, too, to connote a *golodomor* (killing by starving).
12 Omarbekov, *Golodomor v Kazakhstane*, 13. In the spring of 1919 the Kazakh delegates to the Seventh Congress of the Kirghiz Military-Revolutionary Committee had asked Lenin how it would be possible to undermine the economic power of the bais in the auls and he had replied: "Obviously, sooner or later you will have to pose the question of the re-distribution of livestock" ([Komissiia], 2).
13 "Special settlers" (exiled Russian and Ukrainian peasants) began to arrive in 1930, and most of them grew grain in the north or mined coal in the east at Karaganda.
14 Aldazhumanov et al., *Nasil'stvennaia kollektivizatsiia i golod v Kazakhstane*, doc. 67:188; see also Payne, "Seeing Like a Soviet State."
15 Ohayon, *La sédentarisation des Kazakhs*, 357–8; Pianciola, "Famine in the Steppe," 147. This repression followed hard on the heels of both a drought in 1927 and a "great *dzhut*" – a "silver frost" or "silver thaw" – in 1928, caused by

a deep freeze immediately after a spring thaw, leaving both pasture and foliage inaccessible to grazers and browsers under a hard layer of ice (Pianciola, "Famine in the Steppe," 147; Shayakhmetov, *Silent Steppe*, x). Also, an "appalling" smallpox epidemic in the winter of 1927–28 took many lives, especially in remote auls that had not been reached by vaccination campaigns; some Kazakhs were so terrified of the disease's effects (facial pockmarking, deafness, blindness) "that they never dared refer to the disease by name, and tried to appease it by calling it the 'holy illness' instead." Two months after this scourge there was an outbreak of measles, a virulent disease that proved fatal to some children still recovering from smallpox (Shayakhmetov, *Silent Steppe*, 109, 110–11, 111).

16 Cameron, "Kazakh Famine."
17 Cited by Cameron, *Hungry Steppe*, 105.
18 Ibid.
19 [Komissiia], "Prichiny goloda 30-kh godov," 4.
20 Ibid., 117.
21 Ibid., 6; Nusinbaev and Zhienfaliev, *Golod v Kazakhskoi stepi*, doc. 6:143n1; Omarbekov, *Golodomor v Kazakhstane*, 12.
22 Tatimov and Tatimova, "Tragediia velikoi stepi," 55.
23 Danilov, Manning, and Viola, *Tragediia sovetskoi derevni*, 3, doc. 172:483, doc. 183:503.
24 Shayakhmetov, *Silent Steppe*, 200.
25 Kvashonkin et al., *Sovetskoe rukovodstvo*, doc. 116:218.
26 [Komissiia], "Prichiny goloda 30-kh godov," 5.
27 Kondrashin, *Golod 1932–1933*, 2nd ed., 331, 333, 339.
28 Aldazhumanov et al., *Nasil'stvennaia kollektivizatsiia i golod*, doc. 67:185. Kazakhstan's grain yield – 27.5 puds per sown hectare in 1931 – was one of the lowest in the USSR (Kondrashin, *Golod 1932–1933*, 2nd ed., 342).
29 Shayakhmetov, *Silent Steppe*, 3. Shayakhmetov was a seven-year-old boy in 1929 when his father, a prosperous herdsman, was arrested as a kulak, dispossessed, and deported to a coal mine, where he died, leaving the family to wander Kazakhstan and survive on the charity of friends and relatives. See also Shayakhmetov, *Kazakh Teacher's Story*, the sequel to his moving memoir.
30 Omarbekov, *Golodomor v Kazakhstane*, 40.
31 Kondrashin, *Golod 1932–1933*, 2nd ed., 344.
32 Oleg Gubaidulin, "Velikii Dzhut," 2–3, citing Omarbekov. Western Kazakhstan

had to supply the North Caucasus and southern Kazakhstan had to supply the cotton centres of Uzbekistan (Samarkand, Tashkent, Namangan) with meat; in northern Kazakhstan special plants directly subordinate to Stalin were established (e.g., Moscow Meat, Leningrad Meat, All-Union Meat) (ibid., 1).

33 Kondrashin, *Golod v SSSR*, 3, doc. 180:242–3.
34 Nusinbaev and Zhienfaliev, *Golod v Kazakhskoi stepi*, doc. 9:187.
35 Kondrashin, *Golod v SSSR*, 3, doc. 180:241; Kondrashin, *Golod 1932–1933*, 2nd ed., 343, 358.
36 [Komissiia], "Prichiny goloda 30-kh godov," 5.
37 Omarbekov, *Golodomor v Kazakhstane*, 151.
38 Aldazhumanov et al., *Nasil'stvennaia kollektivizatsiia i golod*, doc. 67:185; Danilov, Manning, and Viola, *Tragediia sovetskoi derevni*, 3, doc. 183:504.
39 Aldazhumanov et al., *Nasil'stvennaia kollektivizatsiia i golod*, doc. 60:153–4.
40 Ibid., 154; Omarbekov, *Golodomor v Kazakhstane*, 50.
41 Mikhailov, *Great Disaster*, 355.
42 Kvashonkin et al., *Sovetskoe rukovodstvo*, doc. 116:205; Nusinbaev and Zhienfaliev, *Golod v Kazakhskoi stepi*, doc. 5:134, doc. 6:139, doc. 9:168; Shayakhmetov, *Silent Steppe*, 199, 225–6.
43 Kvashonkin et al., *Sovetskoe rukovodstvo*, doc. 116:211, 212, 214.
44 Tatimov and Tatimova, "Tragediia velikoi stepi," 57. Many Kazakhs developed scurvy when they refused to accept the new diet in the mines and factories of black bread and vegetables, animal products being scarce (Littlepage and Bess, *In Search of Soviet Gold*, 110).
45 Tatimov and Tatimova, "Tragediia velikoi stepi," 57.
46 Nusinbaev and Zhienfaliev, *Golod v Kazakhskoi stepi*, doc. 1:119, doc. 2:120.
47 Officially, 109,809 famine deaths (including, presumably, an unknown number of Kazakhs) were recorded for Kazakhstan in 1929 (Kondrashin, *Khlebozagotovitel'naia politika*, 45, citing TSARFSB, f. 2, op. 8, d. 744, fols. 103–5).
48 Shayakhmetov, *Silent Steppe*, 162, 163, 178, 184, 223.
49 Mikhailov, *Great Disaster*, 10–11.
50 Aldazhumanov et al., *Nasil'stvennaia kollektivizatsiia i golod*, doc. 60:154.
51 Zelenin, "O nekotorykh 'belykh piatnakh'," 6.
52 Kvashonkin et al., *Sovetskoe rukovodstvo*, doc. 116:206.
53 Mikhailov, *Great Disaster*, 16.
54 Cited by Cameron, *Hungry Steppe*, 156–7.

55 Shayakhmetov, *Silent Steppe*, 138. Food relief was given to 46,000 Kazakh families in November 1932 and to 105,000 families (330,000–350,000 Kazakhs) in March 1933, but at the end of that month there were still at least 100,000 Kazakh families who were starving and in need of relief (Omarbekov, *Golodomor v Kazakhstane*, 193).
56 Kvashonkin et al., *Sovetskoe rukovodstvo*, doc. 116:209.
57 Antipova et al., *Golod v SSSR*, doc. 157:452; Kondrashin, *Golod v SSSR*, 2, doc. 519:641; Vaniukov, *Golodomor*, doc. 155:343.
58 Omarbekov, *Golodomor v Kazakhstane*, 101. She added, "the local authorities assert that the destruction of the population is not from famine but from cholera, but in fact the population does not have it. The higher authorities do not report this but conceal it" (ibid.).
59 Ibid., 106.
60 Pianciola, "Famine in the Steppe," 170, citing GARF, f. 6,986, op. 1, d. 16, fols. 55–7. In 1929 alone 416 Kazakh families (1,845 Kazakhs) with 19,708 head of livestock fled to China (Pokrovskii, *Politbiuro i krest'ianstvo*, bk. 1, doc. 191:31). At first, at least, much of the Soviet-Chinese border was unguarded, and the Kazakhs knew secret routes (Shayakhmetov, *Silent Steppe*, 40–1).
61 [Komissiia], "Prichiny goloda 30-kh godov," 6. Another source, however, contends that by 1935 about 1 million Kazakhs had been repatriated (Ohayon, *La sédentarisation des Kazakhs*, 358).
62 Cited by Cameron, *Hungry Steppe*, 123.
63 Shayakhmetov, *Silent Steppe*, 39, 40.
64 Mikhailov, *Great Disaster*, 374–5; Nusinbaev and Zhienfaliev, *Golod v Kazakhskoi stepi*, doc. 9:168; see also Kvashonkin et al., *Sovetskoe rukovodstvo*, doc. 116:204, 205; and Mikhailov, *Velikii dzhut*, 343, 344. In addition, as of February 1933 some 300,000 Kazakhs had sought refuge elsewhere within Kazakhstan itself (Aldazhumanov et al., *Nasil'stvennaia kollektivizatsiia i golod*, doc. 75:207).
65 Mikhailov, *Great Disaster*, 375; Nusinbaev and Zhienfaliev, *Golod v Kazakhskoi stepi*, doc. 9:168. Nevertheless, owing to their nomadic tradition, it may still have been less daunting for them than for sedentary Eastern Slavic peasants to move.
66 Tatimov and Tatimova, "Tragediia velikoi stepi," 59.
67 Aldazhumanov et al., *Nasil'stvennaia kollektivizatsiia i golod*, doc. 75:207.
68 Kvashonkin et al., *Sovetskoe rukovodstvo*, doc. 116:206, 207.

69 Aldazhumanov et al., *Nasil'stvennaia kollektivizatsiia i golod*, doc. 75:208; Antipova et al., *Golod v SSSR*, docs. 171–2:488–90; Mikhailov, *Velikii dzhut*, 347; Pianciola, "Famine in the Steppe," 169; Vaniukov, *Golodomor*, doc. 173:374, 375.
70 Omarbekov, *Golodomor v Kazakhstane*, 99–100.
71 Pianciola, "Famine in the Steppe," 172, 173.
72 Solzhenitsyn, *Voices from the Gulag*, 78. Koumiss (*kumys*) is fermented mare's milk, a traditional Kazakh drink.
73 Ibid., 77. The meaning of "pap-man" is unclear, but the context implies "boss man" (*papa* means "papa," or "daddy," as well as "pope").
74 Aldazhumanov et al., *Nasil'stvennaia kollektivizatsiia i golod*, doc. 42:107–8; see also Mikhailov, *Great Disaster*, 306.
75 Kondrashin, *Golod v SSSR*, vol. 1, bk. 1, doc. 126:262.
76 Ibid., vol. 1, bk. 2, doc. 667:277–81; Vaniukov, *Golodomor*, doc. 30: 111–14.
77 Serge, *Memoirs of a Revolutionary*, 301, 302.
78 Goloshchyokin protested his innocence and his dismissal after seven and a half years of repression in a letter of 4 August 1933 to Stalin and Kaganovich in which he listed only some (thirty-three) of the accusations against him and decried the "unceremonious 'dressing-down' and frenzied defaming" to which he had been subjected (Kvashonkin et al., *Sovetskoe rukovodstvo*, doc. 136:245–9). He was an extremely believable scapegoat for the Kremlin's calamitous Kazakhstan campaign. In 1939 Beria ordered his arrest as a Trotskyite, and in 1941 he was shot without a trial (but "rehabilitated" in 1956 on the same day and the same month – 28 October – as his death).
79 Kvashonkin et al., *Sovetskoe rukovodstvo*, doc. 116:205, 207.
80 Alekseienko, "Demograficheskie posledstviia goloda," n.p.; Gubaidulin, "Velikii Dzhut," 3, citing Omarbekov. Cameron has estimated that 1.5 million of Kazakhstan's population of 6.5 million perished (Cameron, *Hungry Steppe*, 144, 175).
81 Mikhailov, *Great Disaster*, 355.
82 Omarbekov, *Golodomor v Kazakhstane*, 5.
83 Ibid., 5, 6–7.
84 Tatimov and Tatimova, "Tragediia velikoi stepi," 57.
85 Ibid., 59.
86 Ryskozha, "Valery Mikhailov."
87 Mikhailov, *Great Disaster*, 341–3.

Chapter Seven

1 According to the 1926 census, Ukrainians constituted 80 percent of the Ukraine's 29 million inhabitants, or 23.2 million, and 41 percent of the North Caucasus's 5.7 million inhabitants, or 2.3 million, for a total of 25.5 million (at the same time Great Russians formed 9 percent of the Ukraine's population, or 2.6 million [primarily urban], and 43 percent of the population of the North Caucasus, or 2.4 million [urban and rural]) (Lorimer, *Population of the Soviet Union*, table 25:63, table 65:162; Olesevych, *Statystychni tablytsi ukrainskoho naselennia*, table IIA:8, table IIC:22).
2 Lorimer, *Population of the Soviet Union*, 50; Olesevych, *Statystychni tablytsi ukrainskoho naselennia*, table IIA:16, table IIIC-A, I:105, table IIB.
3 This experienced peasantry and favourable environment explain why in 1914 and in 1940, when the Ukraine accounted for 25 to 30 percent of Tsarist and Soviet grain output, its grain yield per hectare exceeded the national average (and was double that of Kazakhstan) (Tsentral'noe statisticheskoe upravlenie, *Strana Sovetov za 50 let*, 134–5).
4 Khrushchev, *Memoirs*, 2:309, 313. Perhaps it was because of his esteem for the Ukraine that Khrushchev transferred the Crimea to it in 1954 (or perhaps it was simply because he considered the peninsula a natural geographical extension of the Ukraine, not of the RSFSR, especially after the return of the exiled Crimean Tatars at the end of the Second World War).
5 Alexievich, *Second-Hand Time*, 156. The same hyperbole is repeated by a different informant in Alexievich, *Unwomanly Face of War*, 321.
6 Ciliga, *Russian Enigma*, 101, 103.
7 Watt, *British Documents*, 11, doc. 49:62. It bears noting that potatoes, a major food crop, were much more prevalent in the northern periphery of the steppe zone, such as the Central Black Earth and the Upper Volga, and sunflowers, a minor food crop, much less so than in the Ukraine and the North Caucasus (and the Lower and Middle Volga), because potatoes were much less, and sunflowers much more, drought-resistant – meaning that the peasants to the north of the steppe were less likely to suffer in the event of either a harvest failure of grain or excessive grain procurements.
8 Kondrashin, *Golod 1932–1933*, 2nd ed., 367, 368; Kondrashin, *Khlebozagotovitel'naia politika*, 147, table 10. At the same time, on the average during the four-year period of 1930–33, the Ukraine was the principal producer of

Soviet grain at 29 percent, followed by the North Caucasus at 11 percent and the Central Black Earth at 10 percent, with the Lower Volga, the Middle Volga, and Western Siberia trailing at 7 percent each (Davies and Wheatcroft, *Years of Hunger*, 470, table 14a).

9 Kondrashin and Tiurina, "Govorit' o golode," 95.
10 Ibid., 95–6.
11 Kondrashin, *Golod v SSSR*, 3, doc. 415:502.
12 Bruski, "Bol'shoi golod," 105. This observation was corroborated in 1933 by the Italian ambassador, who wrote that the less bountiful farmlands north of the "famine frontier," that is, north of the steppe, represented "the territory on which the struggles for collectivization and for mandatory procurements [of grain] have not taken such violent forms as elsewhere: it is often the case that these areas were generally less fertile and the share of exactions imposed upon them have been lower and of the sort that at first enabled them to strike a certain balance between the harvest and individual needs" (Graziosi, "'Lettres de Kharkov,'" doc. 21:63).

Zhores Medvedev has pointed out that the peasants north of the steppe resisted collectivization less than those in the steppe because they were less productive and hence poorer (with fewer kulaks), and they perforce did more off-farm work – in other words, they had less to lose under collectivization and hence resisted less and suffered less (Medvedev, *Soviet Agriculture*, 86–7).

13 Schiller, "Agriculture," n.p. Similarly, Andrew Cairns observed that collectivization was "pushed harder" in the traditional grainlands of European Russia than elsewhere (Cairns, *Soviet Famine*, 4, 6). Such was the case from the outset: on 1 September 1928 the percentage of peasant holdings that had been collectivized in the Ukraine was 50 percent higher than the national average (3.3 percent and 2.1 percent, respectively), and on 1 October 1929 the ratio was the same (10.4 percent and 7.6 percent, respectively) (Ivnitskii, *Golod 1932–1933*, 12, 18–19).
14 It is worth noting in this regard that Ukrainians, whose population of 31 million in 1926 formed about one-fifth of the USSR's total, had played a disproportionately small role in the Bolshevik movement; a survey undertaken in 1922, for example, of 375,693 of 410,000 Party members and published in *Pravda* showed that less than 6 percent of them were Ukrainians (King, "Conditions in Russia," 35).

15 Grossman, *Forever Flowing*, 148–9, 149–50, 150.
16 Herriot, *Eastward from Paris*, 212.
17 Perhaps, too, Moscow was mindful that the Ukraine-North Caucasus-Lower Volga frontier had a history of violent rural dissent, for example, Stepan Razin's peasant rebellion of 1667–71, Yemelyan Pugachov's peasant rebellion of 1773–75, periodic Cossack revolts, and the Ukrainian uprisings of 1919.
18 The Ukraine's position was also notably strategic because it formed part of Russia's sensitive western frontier, the frontier that had been crossed by most of Russia's invaders.
19 Davies et al., *Stalin-Kaganovich Correspondence*, doc. 57:180.
20 In 1926 Ukrainians were more confined to their titular republic than any other SSR ethnic group except Armenians and Belorussians, constituting 80 percent of the Ukraine's population, with Great Russians, who were concentrated in the eastern Ukraine in Kharkov and the Donbass, constituting only 9 percent. This disproportion would change considerably by the end of the Soviet period, when Great Russians had more than doubled their share of the Ukraine's population.
21 At the height of the famine the Polish consulates in the Ukraine were flooded with visitors and letters pleading for protection against the abuses of the local authorities. One consul reported in early 1933:

> People are appealing to us who either have hitherto generally not wanted to hear about Poland or for a long time – mainly since 1924 – have not come to the consulate. Now they want to return to Poland, and all of them are trying to trace their actual or imaginary right to Polish citizenship and are complaining of unbearable poverty and starvation. In many cases the clients are grown men who weep when talking about their wives and children dying or swelling from starvation. (Bruski, "Bol'shoi golod," 116, 116–17, doc. 1:132)

The flood of supplicants became a trickle in the middle of March after mass arrests by the OGPU of recent visitors to the consulates; the OGPU also monitored letters to the consulates, with one consular official cracking that the OGPUists not only opened sealed letters but even unglued their stamps "in order to check whether or not there was anyone underneath them" (ibid., 117).

22 Lievan, *British Documents*, 9, doc. 77:196.
23 Stalin was referring to Symon Petlyura (1879–1926) and Józef Piłsudski (1867–1935), the former the recently deceased Ukrainian nationalist politician who had led the Ukraine's abortive struggle for independence after the October Revolution and the latter the de facto leader of the Second Polish Republic and father of modern Poland who wanted to enhance Poland's security through the decolonization of the peoples of the USSR and the establishment of a federation of independent states in the "intermarium," the broad peninsula between the Baltic and the Black Seas.
24 Davies et al., *Stalin-Kaganovich Correspondence*, doc. 57:180.
25 Ibid., 181. Andrei Sakharov, the talented scientist and respected human rights activist, accused Stalin of "Ukrainophobia," as well as anti-Semitism, but offered no evidence (Sakharov, *Progress*, 54). More reliably, perhaps, Nikita Khrushchev, in his famous "secret speech" of 25 February 1956 to a closed session of the Twentieth Congress of the CPSU about Stalin's abuses of Leninism and power, admitted that during and right after the Second World War Stalin had deported seven entire ethnic groups (including Volga Germans, Crimean Tatars, Kalmyks, and Chechens) for alleged collaboration with the German invaders, and he added, "The Ukrainians avoided meeting this fate only because there were too many of them and there was no place to which to deport them. Otherwise, he would have deported them also," presumably as punishment for disloyalty, some in the Ukraine having openly welcomed the enemy as liberators ([Khrushchev], *Anatomy of Terror*, 52). However, the premier may have been speaking jocularly; if not, Stalin was certainly powerful and ruthless enough to have relocated the Ukraine's nearly 24 million Ukrainians to Siberia, the Far East, or the Far North, which were certainly spacious enough to accommodate – if not sustain – them.
26 Watt, *British Documents*, 11, doc. 134:185–6.
27 Commission, *Report to Congress*, 424, 435. The consul was prescient with respect to "German consciousness." Alexander Solzhenitsyn contended that, after the outbreak of what the Russians term the "Second Great Patriotic War" in 1941, half of the population of the Don area was "eagerly waiting the Germans" – anyone but the Stalinists. He added that the union republics only wanted independence, the peasants only wanted freedom from the kolkhoz, and the workers only wanted freedom from feudal decrees, and if the Germans had not been "so hopelessly arrogant and stupid," had not pre-

served the kolkhoz for administrative convenience, and had not conceived the "obscene idea of turning Russia into a colony," the Stalin regime would not have survived (Solzhenitsyn, *Gulag Archipelago*, vol. 5, bk. 7:25, 26–7).

28 Commission, *Report to Congress*, 412, 413. Terence Martin has argued convincingly that "the grain requisitions terror triggered a nationalities terror" that was not, however, confined to the Ukraine (Martin, *Affirmative Action Empire*, 307). He has contended, too, that "collectivization was resisted more fiercely and more violently in the Soviet Union's non-[Great] Russian regions," thereby making Great Russians appear more loyal to the regime than other nationalities, and that as the USSR began in the early 1930s to adopt "a defensive foreign policy stance, the cross-border ethnic ties of the non-[Great] Russians became increasingly suspect" – meaning *all* non-Great Russians (ibid., 271).

29 Wells, *Kapoot*, 114.

30 Clyman, "Children Lived on Grass," 36. She added, "After this we understood why the village children always sprang up with stones to hurl at us as we passed. It was their revenge at something that could move faster than those spindly legs could carry them" (ibid.).

31 A Polish intelligence officer reported that he knew "from an absolutely trustworthy source" that in May–June some seven hundred corpses, on average, were collected nightly from the streets of Kiev (Bruski, "Bol'shoi golod," 121).

32 Goichenko, *Skvoz raskulachivanie i golodomor*, 207, 215, 216. Both of Goichenko's parents died in the famine.

33 Bruski, "Bol'shoi golod," 119.

34 Ibid., 120.

35 Mikhailov, *Great Disaster*, 346, citing *Kavkazskii kazak*, 1933, no. 3:6.

36 Vilensky, *Till My Tale Is Told*, 243–4.

37 Williams, "Confidential Circular," n.p.; Williams, "My Journey," n.p.

38 Sevost'ianov et al., "*Sovershenno sektretno*," vol. 10, pt. 3, doc. 460:426.

39 Bednarek et al., *Holodomor*, doc. 90:260–1.

40 Bruski, "Bol'shoi golod," doc. 3:139.

41 United Kingdom, FO 371/17253, no. 7753.

42 Kondrashin, *Golod v SSSR*, 3, doc. 182:244–6.

43 Bednarek et al., *Holodomor*, doc. 184:484.

44 Ibid., 483.

45 Ibid.

46 Ibid., 484. Walther was apparently citing Postyshev's speech of 19 November to a plenum of the Party's central committee.
47 Ibid., doc. 181:476, doc. 184:483.
48 Ibid., doc. 184:484.
49 Graziosi, "'Lettres de Kharkov,'" doc. 19:56.
50 Wells, *Kapoot*, 115. His sighting was matched by the two Americans from Atlanta motoring with Rhea Clyman, Alva Christensen and Mary De Give, who told Wells, "many times ... we saw the swollen bellied Russian children on all fours eating grass like so many sheep!" (ibid., 115, 116).
51 Kondrashin, *Golod v SSSR*, 2, doc. 353:469.
52 Danilov, Manning, and Viola, *Tragediia sovetskoi derevni*, 3, doc. 240:606; Kondrashin, *Golod v SSSR*, 2, doc. 203:296, 296–7.
53 Danilov, Manning, and Viola, *Tragediia sovetskoi derevni*, 3, doc. 240:608.
54 Ivnitskii, *Golod 1932–1933*, 35, 45; Ivnitskii, *Tragediia sovetskoi derevni*, 62.
55 Bruski, "Bol'shoi golod," 107.
56 The Cossacks usually fought on the side of the Whites because they had a tradition of service to tsardom and fewer grievances, having ample land, being exempt from taxation, and enjoying local autonomy under their elected atamans in return for their military services, so they were not as responsive as were the land-hungry peasants to the Bolshevik promise of "peace, land, and bread."
57 Chamberlin, *Russia's Iron Age*, 85.
58 Carynnyk, Luciuk, and Kordan, *Foreign Office*, doc. 72:401.
59 Chamberlin, *Russia's Iron Age*, 85.
60 Schiller, "Famine's Return to Russia."
61 Ibid., 85–6; Carynnyk, Luciuk, and Kordan, *Foreign Office*, doc. 72:401.
62 These wholesale deportations presaged those of seven ethnic groups a decade later during the Second World War (see Conquest, *Nation Killers*).
63 Schiller, "Famine's Return to Russia"; see also United Kingdom, FO 371/17251, no. 5797. For a list of some 6,250 famine victims of 1932–33 in five Cossack stanitsas, six Ukrainian khutors, and one Russian village in one district in the Kuban, giving their full name, date of death, and age at time of death, see Syncha (Forsova), *Uroki*.

Meanwhile, just across the border the Don Cossacks were being repressed too. When Rhea Clyman reached Rostov-on-Don (just over the Ukrainian border in Russia) at the end of August 1932 she found Red Army soldiers everywhere – "every inch of the Cossack region now has the imprint of a Red

Army heel," she wrote. Harvesting was being done under guard during the day, and the fields were patrolled at night. Later she learned that in November five thousand Don Cossack families had been deported to the north (Clyman, "Women Harvesters," 1, 14).

64 Carynnyk, Luciuk, and Kordan, *Foreign Office*, doc. 22:215.
65 United Kingdom, FO 371/17251, no. 1914.
66 Graziosi, "'Lettres de Kharkov,'" doc. 19:57.
67 Chamberlin, *Russia's Iron Age*, 83–4, 86; United Kingdom, FO 371/17253, no. 7753; Watt, *British Documents*, 11, doc. 203:293.
68 Kondrashin, *Golod v SSSR*, 2, doc. 265:384; Kondrashin and Tiurina, "Govorit' o golode," doc. 19:120.
69 Danilov, Manning, and Viola, *Tragediia sovetskoi derevni*, 3, doc. 258:634–5; [Federal Archival Agency], *Famine in the USSR 1929–1934*, doc. 38:81; Kondrashin, *Khlebozagotovitel'naia politika*, 149–50.
70 Kondrashin, *Khlebozagotovitel'naia politika*, 152, 153.
71 Danilov, Manning, and Viola, *Tragediia sovetskoi derevni*, 3, doc. 258:635.
72 Kondrashin, *Golod v SSSR*, 2, doc. 261:381.
73 [Federal Archival Agency], *Famine in the USSR 1929–1934*, doc. 40:83.
74 Kondrashin, *Golod v SSSR*, 3, doc. 203:271–2; Kondrashin, *Khlebozagotovitel'naia politika*, 243.
75 Kondrashin, *Golod v SSSR*, 3, doc. 203:272, 273.
76 Kondrashin, *Golod v SSSR*, 3, doc. 374:454; Kondrashin, *Khlebozagotovitel'naia politika*, 243.
77 Kondrashin, *Khlebozagotovitel'naia politika*, 243.
78 Kondrashin, *Golod v SSSR*, 3, doc. 374:454–5; see also Kondrashin, *Khlebozagotovitel'naia politika*, 244.
79 Bruski, "Bol'shoi golod," 123.
80 Ibid., doc. 3:141.
81 Ibid.
82 The Polish military attaché was kinder, estimating that the productivity of one peasant was equal to that of ten to twenty of the urban recruits (Bednarek et al., *Holodomor*, doc. 134:365).
83 Bruski, "Bol'shoi golod," doc. 3:144. These "undesirable elements" were not necessarily welcomed by the starving villagers, such as those of the hamlet of Popelnaya, who torched the belongings of several hundred of the unwanted newcomers (ibid., 124).
84 Ibid., doc. 3:145.

85 Some kolkhozes assigned a special detail of sexagenarian peasants to the fields, ostensibly to guard the crops but actually to "steal and hide dozens of centners of grain for themselves," while "so-called 'barbers' snipped whole sacks of spikes" that they baked on a griddle and ate whole (Bruski, "Bol'shoi golod," doc. 3:146, 147). The "personals" (individual farmsteaders) said, "it makes no difference whether or not the crop is gathered and marketed because we harvest for ourselves and hide as much as we can" (ibid., doc. 3:147).
86 Ibid., doc. 3:145–8.
87 Kondrashin, *Golod v SSSR*, 3, doc. 29:82.
88 Bruski, "Bol'shoi golod," 126.
89 Ibid., doc. 4:149. The bulletin added that the cost of this victory was the death of "at least 5,000,000 souls and the devastation of the Ukrainian village" (ibid.).

Epilogue

1 In the first half of the 1990s the Russian historian Victor Kondrashin did a survey of 617 witnesses to the famine in eighty villages of twenty-two rural rayons in the Volga Valley (Penza, Samara, Saratov, and Volgograd Oblasts) and the southern Urals (Orenburg Oblast). Their principal recollections included: "In nineteen thirty-three everyone ate goosefoot. Arms and legs swelled, and they died while walking," and "I did not fear frost and I did not fear the cold but I did fear the kolkhoz and starving to death there" (Kondrashin, "Golod v krest'ianskom mentalitete," 117).
2 Elagin, *Ukroshchenie iskusstv*, 46.
3 Burrell, *American Engineer*, 225.
4 Chukovskaia, *Zapiski*, 2:188–9. I am grateful to Constantin Ponomareff for this reference.
5 Vilensky, *Till My Tale Is Told*, xii.
6 Solzhenitsyn, *Gulag Archipelago*, vol. 3, bk. 6:368.
7 Czapski, *Inhuman Land*, 38. Miraculously, Czapski, a reserve officer, avoided the massacre of twenty-two thousand Polish officers by the Soviet secret police in the Katyn forest in the spring of 1940.
8 Mikhailov, *Great Disaster*, 377.
9 Khripunov, *Dnevniki*, 375.
10 The rationing of provisions began at the end of 1928 and ended in late 1935 (see here and there throughout Osokina, *Our Daily Bread*).

11 United Kingdom, Foreign Office, 4621/4621/38, no. 1.
12 Resis, *Molotov Remembers*, 148.
13 [Jones], "Outlook for the Plan."
14 Chamberlin, *Russia's Iron Age*, vii.
15 Poznansky, *Sotsial'nie kataklizmy v Sibiri*, 4.
16 The nomads provided chiefly meat, wool, and hides, mainly for the domestic market, while the peasants furnished chiefly grain for both the domestic and the foreign markets.
17 Grossman, *Love and Fate*, 707. In this epic novel of Russia's "Second Great Patriotic War" as experienced by the members of the Saposhnikov family, Grossman, a war correspondent for the Red Army's newspaper, often invokes the several atrocities of the Stalin period, including the famine.
18 Yet, despite Stalin's undeniable culpability, it was not accepted by all of his peasant victims, one of whom explained, "For us Stalin was God. We even cried when the radio announced his death," and God, of course, cannot be faulted (Lopatin and Lopatina, *Kollektivizatsiia i raskulachivanie*, doc. 127:392).
19 Veselovskii, *Problemy nashei zhizni*, 1:386.
20 Osherowitch, *How People Live in Soviet Russia*, 98.
21 See throughout Kondrashin, *Khlebozagotovitel'naia politika*.
22 The Bolshevik perception of the peasants was at least more realistic than that of the activists among the nineteenth-century intelligentsia like the Slavophiles, Populists, Tolstoyans, and Socialist Revolutionaries, who idealized Russian village life and saw the peasant as the embodiment of goodness and innocence – a view that was dispelled by Chekhov's dispassionate description in the nine sketches of "Peasants," perhaps his most popular and most translated short story, set in the village of Zhukovo, with its "dark, cramped and dirty" huts and "rough, dishonest, filthy, drunken" peasants living in "sheer, grinding poverty" (Hingley, *Oxford Chekhov*, 7:195–222).
23 Bright-Holmes, *Like It Was*, 41.
24 Barmine, *One Who Survived*, 175.
25 [Muggeridge], "The Soviet and the Peasantry," 3:9.
26 Serge, *From Lenin to Stalin*, 75.
27 Rayfield, *Stalin and His Hangmen*, 181, 186.
28 Bruski, "Bol'shoi golod," 127; see also doc. 2:135–6. The consul reached this conclusion on the basis of his observations during a trip from Kharkov to Moscow on 4–5 May (ibid., 127n86).

29 Lorimer, *Population of the Soviet Union*, 62.
30 Bednarek et al., *Holodomor*, doc. 181:474.
31 Gatalova, Kosheleva, and Rogovaia, TSK RKP(b) i natsional'nyi vopros. See, for instance, vol. 1, doc. 252:696–8, which attacks "counter-revolutionary elements – kulaks, former [White] officers, Petlyurists [nationalist partisans under Symon Petlyura in the early 1920s], supporters of the Kuban Rada [a Cossack-dominated popular assembly], and others" who had infiltrated the kolkhozes to sabotage grain procurement in the Ukraine, the North Caucasus, and the West Region. Academician Vladimir P. Kozlov, the head of Russia's Federal Archival Agency, has asserted in his foreword to a recent collection of archival documents about the famine that, in his country's central and regional archives, "not a single document has been discovered to support the concept of 'golodomor-genocide' in the Ukraine, and not even a hint of an ethnic motive has come to light in the documents ... which attest that the chief enemy of Soviet power at the time was an enemy on the basis of class, not ethnicity" (Antipova et al., *Golod v SSSR*, 7). For rebuttals of the holodomor thesis by Russian writers, see Chichirin, *Fenomen ukrainskogo "goloda"*; Chichirin, *Mif i pravda*; Kondrashin, *Golod 1932–1933*, 2nd ed.; and Shvetsov, *Novaia ideologiia*. Kondrashin, especially, demonstrates convincingly that ethnicity was not a factor in famine mortality (Kondrashin, *Golod 1932–1933*, 2nd ed., 401–22). The Russian-cum-American demographic historian Sergei Maksudov also asserts that the famine in the Ukraine was not genocidal (Maksudov, *Pobeda nad derevnei*, 10).
32 On 28 November 2006 the Ukraine's Supreme Assembly ruled that the "holodomor" of 1932–33 was an act of genocide against the Ukrainian people. The governments of several countries, including the Canadian Parliament and the United States Congress, have rashly declared likewise. On 2 April 2008 the State Duma of the Russian Federation memorialized the famine in a tribute to its victims, although a faction of the Communist Party tried vainly to block discussion of the resolution on the grounds that there were much more important matters to discuss that were worrying ordinary citizens. The majority of deputies, however, "grieved with the peoples of the former USSR on the 75th anniversary of the terrible tragedy – the famine of the 1930s that gripped much of the territory of the Soviet Union, whose peoples paid a huge price for industrialization." The resolution stresses that "many parts of the RSFSR (the Volga Valley, the Central Black Earth, the

North Caucasus, the Urals, the Crimea, part of Western Siberia), as well as Kazakhstan, the Ukraine, and Belorussia, suffered from the famine as the result of forcible collectivization" and that altogether about 7 million people starved to death in 1932–33. The resolution also stresses that "there is no historical evidence whatever that the famine was limited on the basis of ethnicity" and that "this tragedy bears no signs of genocide" and should not be a subject of political speculation (Anonymous, "Eto byla tragediia vsei strany"). On the same day in *Izvestiya* the Nobel Prize–winning writer Alexander Solzhenitsyn used the occasion to excoriate Ukrainian politicians for politicizing the famine as a Ukrainian holodomor, a "loopy fable," he wrote (Alexander Solzhenitsyn, "Swallowing Shameless Lies," *Guardian*, 3 April 2008).

33 Yet the 2019 film *Mr Jones* portrays an intrepid Gareth Jones uncovering a famine in the Ukraine only.
34 Kondrashin, *Golod 1932–1933*, 2nd ed., 8.
35 Or, as one of Stalin's biographers, Stephen Kotkin, has put it: "there was no 'Ukrainian' famine; the famine was Soviet" (Kotkin, *Stalin*, 129).
36 Solzhenitsyn, *Gulag Archipelago*, vol. 5, bk. 5:28, bk. 6:350, 351, 357.
37 Khripunov, *Dnevniki*, 369.
38 Kotkin, *Stalin*, 128.
39 Bednarek et al., *Holodomor*, doc. 184:486.
40 Ibid., doc. 202:543.
41 In a speech on 4 February 1931 to industry officials Stalin told his listeners to maintain their Bolshevik tempo because "to slacken the tempo would mean falling behind," and "those who fall behind get beaten." He elaborated:

> One feature of the history of old Russia was the continual beatings she suffered because of her backwardness. She was beaten by the Mongol khans. She was beaten by the Turkish beys. She was beaten by the Polish and Lithuanian gentry. She was beaten by the British and French industrialists. She was beaten by the Japanese barons. All beat her – because of her backwardness, because of her military backwardness, cultural backwardness, political backwardness, industrial backwardness, agricultural backwardness. They beat her because to do so was profitable and could be done with impunity.

"Such," Stalin added, "is the law of the exploiters – to beat the backward and the weak. It is the jungle law of capitalism." "That is why," he concluded, "we must no longer lag behind ... we are fifty or a hundred years behind the advanced countries. We must make good this distance in ten years. Either we do it, or we shall go under" (Stalin, *Works*, 13:40–1, 41). And to do it Stalin was willing to see the USSR "starve itself great," as American correspondents in Moscow were wont to say (Engerman, *Modernization*, 242).

42 Although apparently Stalin was capable of rationalizing a mistake, as an anonymous Soviet historian told Reader Bullard: "As Stalin said, if you don't make mistakes you'll never make anything" ([Bullard], *Inside Stalin's Russia*, 162).

43 Cited by Mikhailov, *Great Disaster*, 345. Incidentally, the fiancée of Bagritsky's son Vsevolod, who was killed in the Second World War, was Yelena Bonner, who would marry Andrei Sakharov, the dissident scientist, in 1972 (also incidentally, the pseudonym "Bagritsky" is derived from *bagrets*, meaning "crimson," presumably in honour of the association of communism with the colour red).

44 Kopelev, *No Jail for Thought*, 11, 11–12, 12, 13. The American edition is entitled *To Be Preserved Forever*. To his credit, later in life Kopelev realized and admitted his complicity.

45 Alexievich, *Second-Hand Time*, 254.

46 The origin of this aphorism supposedly dates to 1904, when Italian railway workers used this form of work stoppage instead of an actual strike, as it was more difficult for an employer to suppress such a "cold" strike.

47 Kondrashin, *Khlebozagotovitel'naia politika*, 297.

48 Quoted by Halberstadt, *Young Heroes*, 50.

49 Russia is not alone in this respect; Japan has not yet grappled with its fascist past, France has yet to fully confront the ignominy of Vichy France, Italy has yet to reckon fully with Mussolini's Ethiopian invasion and collaboration with Hitler, and Spain has yet to come fully to grips with Franco's Civil War and collaboration with Hitler. As a biographer of the historian "Prince" (Dmitry) Mirsky has written, Stalin's crimes amount "to an issue that their [Russians'] government has still not been able to confront, let alone attempt to exorcise or atone for by the institution of due process in identifying, investigating, and putting on trial the surviving perpetrators." He found that, for Russians who lived under Stalinism,

the attribution of all crimes to Stalin personally seems to be the most accessible way to fend off the idea of endemic national connivance and the guilt that is thereby entailed, and then perhaps to console themselves by resorting to the national myth that they were destined to suffer, purify themselves, and, Christ-like, save the world by taking upon themselves the worst ordeals it was capable of inflicting. (Smith, *D.S. Mirsky*, 228, 229)

50 Danilov, Manning, and Viola, *Tragediia sovetskoi derevni*, 3:33–4.
51 Kondrashin, *Golod v SSSR*, 3, doc. 478:568, table 3, 569, table 4. In the same two years in terms of ruble value the leading Soviet imports were machines and instruments, machine parts, and ferrous metals – in that order – and the leading exporter to the USSR was Germany, with up to one-half (and the United Kingdom a very distant second) (ibid., doc. 478:570, tables 6 and 7).
52 Ibid., doc. 478:568, table 3. Admittedly, it would have been difficult to increase timber exports insofar as much of the timber was cut by the unpaid kulak exiles created by compulsory collectivization.
53 Lyons, *Assignment*, 541–2.
54 Kuromiya, *Voices of the Dead*, 245.
55 Osokina, *Zoloto dlia industrializatsii*, 11.
56 Bondar and Matveev, *Istoricheskaia pamiat'*, 125, 126–7, 127; Osokina, "Legenda o meshke s khlebom," 90–1.
57 Ibid., 91.
58 Jones, "Russia's Starvation"; see also Jones, "Reds Let Peasants Starve."
59 Klimin, *Rossiiskoe krest'ianstvo v zavershaiushchy period*, 634.
60 Halberstadt, *Young Heroes*, 49.
61 Grossman, *Life and Fate*, 271.
62 Von Bremzen, *Mastering the Art*, 3, 147–9, 249–52.
63 Ibid., 4. The same stark contrast between the natural and the human likewise prevailed in Stalin's Soviet Union. And in the finale of his three-part cinematic cri de coeur for his native land, *The Cordillera of Dreams* (2019), Guzmán explores the protecting but isolating duality of the Andes – a situation that Russia, Tsarist and Soviet, has experienced along its mountainous southern and eastern but not its exposed western frontier.

BIBLIOGRAPHY

Primary Sources

Abbe, James E. *I Photograph Russia*. New York: Robert M. McBride and Co., 1934.
– "Men of Cablese." *New Outlook*, 162, no. 6 (1933): 27–32.
Adon'eva, S.B., ed. *Muzhskoi rod. Pervoe litso. Edinstvennoe chislo: Dnevniki D.I. Lukichova i D.P. Bespalova*. St Petersburg: Proppovsky Tsentr, 2013.
Aldazhumanov, K.S., M.K. Kairgaliev, V.P. Osipov, and Iu.I. Romanov, comps. *Nasil'stvennaia kollektivizatsiia i golod v Kazakhstane 1931–1933 gg: Sbornik dokumentov i materialov*. Almaty, KZ: Fond XXI veke, n.d.
Alexievich, Svetlana. *Last Witnesses: Unchildlike Stories*. Trans. Richard Pevear and Larissa Volokhonsky. New York: Penguin Books, 2019.
– *Second-Hand Time*. Trans. Bela Shayevich. London: Fitzcarraldo Editions, 2016.
– *The Unwomanly Face of War: An Oral History of Women in World War II*. Trans. Richard Pevear and Larissa Volokhonsky. New York: Random House, 2018.
Anonymous. A letter of 24 April 1933 from the Mennonite village of Woldenfuerst in the Kuban. https://www.garethjones.org/soviet_articles/holodomor_letters.htm.
Anonymous [Jack Heinz II]. *Experiences in Russia – 1931: A Diary*. Pittsburgh: Alton Press, 1932.
Anonymous. "Starving on the Volga." *New York Times*, 8 March 1892, 9.
– "Visitors Describe Famine in Ukraine." *New York Times*, 29 August 1933, 6.
Antipova, O.A. et al., comps. *Golod v SSSR 1930–1934 gg./Famine in the USSR, 1930–1934*. Moscow: Federal'noe arkhivnoe agentsvo, 2009.
Applebaum, Anne. *Red Famine: Stalin's War on Ukraine*. London: Allen Lane, 2017.
Ashmead-Bartlett, E. *Riddle of Russia*. London: Cassell, 1929.
Avdeenko, Aleksandr. "Otluchenie." *Znamia* no. 3 (March 1989): 5–73.
Barmine, Alexander. *One Who Survived: The Life Story of a Russian under the Soviets*. New York: G.P. Putnam's Sons, 1945.

Barnes, Ralph. "Million Feared Dead of Hunger in South Russia." *Herald-Tribune* (New York), 21 August 1933, 7.

Barratt, Andrew, and Barry P. Scherr, comps. and trans. *Maksim Gorky: Selected Letters*. Oxford: Clarendon Press, 1997.

Beal, Fred E. *Proletarian Journey: New England, Gastonia, Moscow*. New York: Hillman-Curl, 1937.

Bednarek, Jerzy, and Diana Bojko, eds. *Holodomor: The Great Famine in Ukraine, 1932–1933*. Trans. Dariusz Serówka. Warsaw-Kiev: Instytut Pamieci Narodowej, 2009. [Published in Polish as Bednarek, Jerzy, comp. and ed. *Hołodomor, 1932–1933: Wielki Głód na Ukrainie w dokumentach polskiej dyplomacji i wywiadu*. Warsaw: Polski Instytut Spraw Mi dzynarodowych, 2008.]

Berdinskikh, Viktor. *Rus' krest'ianskaia: Zrimyi mir russkoi derevni*. Moscow: Lomonosov, 2020.

Berelovich, A., and V. Danilov, eds. *Sovetskaia derevniia glazami VChK-OGPU-NKVD, 1918–1939: Dokumenty i materialy v 4 tomakh*. 4 vols. Moscow: ROSSPEN, 2000–12.

Berezina, Aleksandra. *Raskulachivanie*. Arkhangel'sk: Lotsiia, 2022.

Blumenfeld, Hans. *Life Begins at 65: The Not Entirely Candid Autobiography of a Drifter*. Montreal: Harvest House, 1987.

Bondar, N.I., and O.V. Matveev, comps. and eds. *Istoricheskaia pamiat' naseleniia Iuga Rossii o golode 1932–1933 gg: Materialy nauchno-prakticheskii konferentsii*. Krasnodar: Traditsiia and Plekhanovets, 2009.

Bratiushchenko, Iu.V. *Kogda arkhivy otkryvaiut sekrety*. St Petersburg: RDK-print, 2005.

Brezhnev, Leonid. *The Virgin Lands*. Trans. Robert Daglish. Moscow: Progress, 1978.

Bright-Holmes, John, ed. *Like It Was: The Diaries of Malcolm Muggeridge*. London: Collins, 1981.

Bruski, Yan Yatsek. "Bol'shoi golod na Ukraine v svete dokumentov polskoi diplomatii i razvedki." *Evropa* 21, no. 4 (2006): 97–152.

[Bullard, Reader]. *Inside Stalin's Russia: The Diaries of Reader Bullard, 1930–1934*. Ed. Julian and Margaret Bullard. Charlbury, UK: Day Books, 2000.

Bullard, Reader. *Camels Must Go: An Autobiography*. London: Faber and Faber, 1961.

Burrell, George A. *An American Engineer Looks at Russia*. Boston: Stratford, 1932.

BIBLIOGRAPHY

Cairns, Andrew. "Agricultural Production in Soviet Russia." United Kingdom, The National Archives, FO 371/17252, no. 345940.

Cairns, Andrew. *The Soviet Famine, 1932–33: An Eye-Witness Account of Conditions in the Spring and Summer of 1932*. Ed. Tony Kuz. Edmonton: Canadian Institute of Ukrainian Studies, 1989.

Carynnyk, Marco, Lubomyr Y. Luciuk, and Bohdan S. Kordan, eds. *The Foreign Office and the Famine: British Documents on Ukraine and the Great Famine of 1932–1933*. Kingston, ON/Vestal, NY: Limestone Press, 1988.

Cherepnin, N.P. *Dnevnik lishentsa: Kashin v 1930–1931 gg*. Moscow: Vishnevyi Pirog, 2011.

Christensen, Alva. "Girls Find Filth and Famine on Leaving Moscow." *Chicago Daily Tribune*, 18 January 1933, 8.

Chuev, Felix. *Tak govoril Kaganovich: Ispoved' stalinskogo apostola*. Moscow: Otechestvo, 1992. Reprinted in 2019.

Chukovskaia, Lidia. *Zapiski ob Anne Akhmatovoi*. Vol. 2. 5th rev. ed. Moscow: Soglasie, 1997.

Chukovskii, Kornei. *Dni moei zhizni*. Comp. E.Ts. Chukovskaia. Moscow: Boslen, 2009.

[Chukovskii, Kornei]. *Kornei Chukovsky, Diary, 1901–1969*. Trans. Michael Henry Heim, ed. Victor Erlich. New Haven, CT: Yale University Press, 2005.

Ciliga, Ante. *The Russian Enigma*. Trans. Fernand G. Fernier, Anne Cliff, Margaret Dewar, and Hugo Dewar. London: Ink Links, 1979.

Clyman, Rhea G. "Children Lived On Grass Only Food in Farm Area Grain Taken from Them." *Evening Telegram* (Toronto), 16 May 1933, 1, 36.

– "Dares Warning of Death to Discover Grim Secret of Russia's Famine-Land." *Evening Telegram* (Toronto), 10 May 1933, 1, 3.

– "Girl from New Toronto Begs Bread in Russia Father Lured by Job." *Evening Telegram* (Toronto), 15 May 1933, 1, 3.

– "Peasants Live in Ground Machines Rust in Fields on Russian State Farm." *Evening Telegram* (Toronto), 23 May 1933, 1, 31.

– "Russian Peasant Shot for 'Stealing' Own Cow to Give Children Food." *Evening Telegram* (Toronto), 30 May 1933, 1, 23.

– "Women Harvesters Toil under Threat of Rifles on Soviet 'Collective.'" *Evening Telegram* (Toronto), 22 May 1933, 1, 14.

– "Wrecks Litter Railroad Death Is a Commonplace in Georgian Mountains." *Evening Telegram* (Toronto), 31 May 1933, 1, 12.

Cockfield, Jamie H., ed. *Black Lebeda: The Russian Famine Diary of ARA Kazan District Supervisor J. Rives Childs, 1921–1923*. Macon, GA: Mercer University Press, 2006.

Commission on the Ukraine Famine. *Investigation of the Ukrainian Famine, 1932–1933: Oral History Project of the Commission on the Ukrainian Famine*. Ed. Leonid Hertz and James E. Mace. 3 vols. Washington, DC: United States Government Printing Office, 1990.

– *Investigation of the Ukrainian Famine, 1932–1933: Report to Congress*. Washington, DC: United States Government Printing Office, 1988.

Czapski, Józef. *Inhuman Land: Searching for the Truth in Soviet Russia, 1941–1942*. Trans. Antonia Lloyd-Jones. New York: New York Review Books, 2018.

Dalton, Hugh. *Fateful Years: Memoirs, 1931–1945*. London: Frederick Muller, 1957.

Danilov, Viktor, and Alexis Berelowitch. "Les documents sur la champagne soviétique 1918–1937." *Cahiers du monde russe* 35, no. 3 (1994): 633–82.

Danilov, V.P., N.A. Ivnitskii, eds. *Dokumenty svidetel'stvuiut: Iz istorii derevni nakanune i v khode kollektivizatsii 1927–1932 gg*. Moscow: Politizdat, 1989.

Danilov, V.P., O.V. Khlevniuk, and A.Iu. Vatlin, eds. *Kak lomali NEP: Stenogrammy plenumov TSK VKP(b) 1928–1929 gg*. 5 vols. Moscow: MFD, 2000.

Danilov, V., R. Manning, and L. Viola, eds. *Tragediia sovetskoi derevni. Kollektivizatsiia i raskulachivanie. Dokumenty i materialy v 5 tomakh 1927–1939*. 5 vols. Moscow: ROSSPEN, 1999–2004.

Davies, R.V., Oleg V. Khlevniuk, E.A. Rees, Liudmila P. Kosheleva, and Larisa A. Rogovaya, comps. and eds. *The Stalin-Kaganovich Correspondence, 1931–36*. Trans. Steven Shabad. New Haven, CT: Yale University Press, 2003.

Dmitrienko, N.M., and G.V. Shipilinoi, comps. *Kak my zhili: Vospominaniia i ustnie svidetel'stva tomskikh krest'ian*. Tomsk: Izdatel'stvo Tomskogo universiteta, 2014.

Dominique, Pierre. *Secrets of Siberia*. Trans. Warre B. Wells. London: Hutchinson, 1934.

Durant, Will. *Tragedy of Russia: Impressions from a Brief Visit*. New York: Simon and Schuster, 1933.

Duranty, Walter. "Russians Hungry, But Not Starving." *New York Times*, 31 March 1933.

Elagin, Iury. *Ukroshchenie iskustv*. New York: Izdatel'stvo imeni Chekhova, 1952.

Elmhirst, Leonard K. *Trip to Russia*. New York: New Republic, 1934.

[Federal Archival Agency of the Russian Federation]. *Famine in the USSR, 1929–1934 New Documentary Evidence / Golod v SSSR 1929–1934 gg. Novie Dokumenty.* Trans. Nikita B. Katz and Alexandra Dolgova. Moscow, 2009 (downloadable DVD).

[Federal'noe arkhivnoe agentstvo]. *Kollektsiia dokumentov GARF, RGAE, RGASPI, TSAFSB Rossii po teme "Golod v SSSR 1930-1934 gg."* http://www.rusarchives.ru/publication/hunger-ussr.

Fischer, Louis. *Soviet Journey.* Westport, CT: Greenwood Press, 1973. Reprint of the first edition of 1935.

Fischer, Louis, ed. *Thirteen Who Fled.* Trans. Gloria and Victor Fischer. New York: Harper Brothers, 1949.

Fischer, Markoosha. *My Lives in Russia.* 3rd ed. New York: Harper and Brothers, 1944.

Freidin, Gregory, ed. *Isaac Babel's Selected Writings.* Trans. Peter Constantine. New York: W.W. Norton, 2010.

Gaidukov, P.G., ed. *Aleksei Vasil'evich Oreshnikov: Dnevnik, 1915–1933.* Vol. 2. Moscow: Nauka, 2011.

Galygina, G.V. et al., comps. *Golod v Srednevolzhskom krae v 20-30-e gody XX veka: Golod v Samarskoi gubernii v 20-e gody XX veka: Sbornik dokumentov.* Vol. 1. Samara: RAKS-S, 2014.

Garros, Véronique, Natalia Korenevskaya, and Thomas Lahusen, eds. *Intimacy and Terror: Soviet Diaries of the 1930s.* Trans. Carol A. Flath. New York: New Press, 1995.

Gatalova, L.S., L.P. Kosheleva, and L.S. Rogovaia, comps. *TSK RKP(b) i natsional'nyi vopros.* 2 vols. Moscow: ROSSPEN, 2005-09.

Gerstein, Emma. *Moscow Memoirs: Memories of Anna Akhmatova, Osip Mandelstam, and Literary Russia under Stalin.* Trans. and ed. John Crowfoot. Woodstock, NY: Overlook Press, 1998.

Gheith, Jehanne M., and Katherine R. Jolluck, eds. *Gulag Voices: Oral Histories of Soviet Incarceration and Exile.* New York: Palgrave Macmillan, 2011.

Goichenko, D.D. *Skvoz raskulachivanie i golodomor: Svidetel'stvo ochevidtsa.* Ed. P.G. Protsenko. Moscow: Russkii put', 2006.

Golitsyn, Sergei. *Memoirs of a Survivor.* Trans. Nicholas Witter. London: Reportage Press, 2008.

Gorbachev, Mikhail. *Memoirs.* Trans. Georges Peronansky and Tatjana Varsavsky, ed. Martin McCauley. New York: Doubleday, 1996.

Gorki, M. "Maxim Gorki on the Fight against Weeds." *Moscow Daily News*, 18 February 1933, 3.
Gorky, Maxim, L. Auerbach, and S.G. Firin, eds. *Belomor: An Account of the Construction of the New Canal between the White Sea and the Baltic Sea*. Westport, CT: Hyperion Press, 1977.
Gorokhova, Elena. *Mountain of Crumbs: A Memoir*. New York: Simon and Schuster, 2009.
Graziosi, Andrea, *Lettere da Kharkov: La carestia in Ucraina e nel Caucaso del Nord nei rapport dei diplomatici italiani, 1932–33*. Turin: Einaudi, 1991.
Graziosi, Andrea, ed. "'Lettres de Kharkov': La famine en Ukraine et dans le Caucase du Nord à travers les rapports des diplomats italiens, 1932–1934." *Cahiers du monde russe et soviétique* 30, nos. 1–2 (1989): 5–106 [published in Italian as Andrea Graziosi, *Lettere da Kharkov: La carestia in Ucraina e nel Caucaso del Nord nei rapport dei diplomatici italiani, 1932–33*. Turin: Einaudi, 1991].
Griffin, Frederick. *Soviet Scene: A Newspaperman's Close-ups of New Russia*. Toronto: Macmillan, 1932.
– *Variety Show: Twenty Years of Watching the News Parade*. Toronto: Macmillan, 1936.
Gritsenko, N.F., comp. *Rossiiskaia i sovetskaia derevnia pervoi poloviny XX veka glazami krest'ian: Vzgliad iz emigratsii*. Moscow: Russkii put', 2009.
Hawker, C.A.S. *An Australian Looks at Russian Farms*. Adelaide: Advertiser Newspapers, 1936.
Hellbeck, Jochen. "Fashioning the Stalinist Soul: The Diary of Stepan Podlubnyi, 1931–1939." *Jahrbücher für Geschichte Osteuropas* 44, no. 3 (1996): 344–73.
– *Revolution on My Mind: Writing a Diary under Stalin*. Cambridge, MA: Harvard University Press, 2006.
– *Tagebuch aus Moskau, 1931–1939*. Munich: Deutscher Taschenbuch Verlag, 1996.
Herman, Victor. *Coming Out of the Ice: An Unexpected life*. New York: Harcourt Brace Jovanovich, 1979.
Herriot, Édouard. *Eastward from Paris*. Trans. Phyllis Megroz. London: Victor Gollancz, 1934.
Herzen, Alexander. *My Past and Thoughts: The Memoirs of Alexander Herzen*. Trans. Constance Garnett, rev. Humphrey Higgens, ed. Dwight Macdonald. Berkeley: University of California Press, 1999.
Iakhontov, S.D. *Vospominaniia, 1917–1942*. Ed. P.V. Akul'shin. Moscow-Riazan: AIRO-XXI and RGMU, 2017.

Ilyashov, Anatoli. "Victor Reuther on the Soviet Experience, 1933–35: An Interview." *International Review of Social History* 31, no. 3 (1986): 298–323.

Istrati, Panait. *Russia Unveiled*. Trans. R.J.S. Curtis. London: Allen and Unwin, 1931.

Ivanova, E.V., comp. *Vospominaniia Nikolaia i Mariny Chukovskikh*. Moscow: Knizhnyi Klub 36.6, 2015.

[Izmailov, Konstantin Fedorovich]. *Dnevnik Altaiskogo krest'ianina K.F. Izmailova*. Ed. Anna Baikalova. 2 vols. Moscow and Smolensk: Common Place, 2020.

Jarman, Robert, ed. *Soviet Union: Political Reports, 1917–1970*. Vols. 3–5. Cambridge, UK: Archive Editions, 2004.

Jones, Gareth. "Balance-Sheet of the Five-Year Plan." *Financial News* (London), 13 April 1933.

[Jones, Gareth]. "Famine Grips Russia, Millions Dying, Idle on Rise, Says Briton." *New York Evening Post*, 29 March 1933.

Jones, Gareth. "Famine Rules Russia: The 5-Year Plan Has Killed the Bread Supply." *Evening Standard* (London), 31 March 1933.

– "General Survey of Agricultural Conditions in the USSR." https://www.garethjones.org/soviet_articles/ussr_agriculture_1933.pdf.

– Jones, Gareth. A letter to his parents, 27 March 1933, in Gareth Vaughan Jones Papers, National Library of Wales, Aberystwyth.

– "Mr Jones Replies." *New York Times*, 13 May 1933, 12.

– "Outlook for the Plan: From the Farm to the Factory." *Times*, 15 October 1931.

– "My Russian Diary – I." *Star* (London), 22 October 1930.

[Jones, Gareth]. "Real Russia: Outlook for the Plan." *Times*, 15 October 1931.

Jones, Gareth. "Real Russia: The Peasant on the Farm." *Times*, 14 October 1931.

– "Reds Let Peasants Starve." *New York American*, 14 January 1935.

– "Russia's Starvation." *New York American*, 12 January 1935.

– "Seizure of Land and Slaughter of Livestock." *Western Mail* (Cardiff), 8 April 1933.

[Jones, Gareth]. *"Tell Them We Are Starving": The 1933 Soviet Diaries of Gareth Jones*. Ed. Lubomyr Y. Luciuk. Kingston, ON: Kashtan Press, 2015.

Jones, Gareth. "There Is No Bread." *New York Sunday American*, 13 January 1935.

– "Will There Be Soup? Russia Dreads the Coming Winter." *Western Mail* (Cardiff), 15 October 1932.

Kaganovich, L.M. "Ob itogakh Obedinënnogo TSK i TSKK VKP(b)." *Pravda*, 20 January 1933.

– *Pamiatnie zapiski rabochego, kommunista-bol'shevika, profsoiuznogo, partiinogo i sovetsko-gosudarstvennogo rabotnika*. Moscow: Bagrius, 1996.

[Kaganovich, L.M.]. "Report of L.M. Kaganovich at the First All-Union Congress of Collective Farm Shock Brigaders." *Moscow Daily News*, 20, 21, 22, 23, 24, 26, 28 February, 3 March 1933.

Kaganovich, L.M. "Ukreplenie kolkhozov i zadachi vesennogo seva." *Izvestiia*, 18 February 1933, 1–3 [available in English as "Report of L.M. Kaganovich at the First All-Union Congress of Collective Farm Shock Brigaders," *Moscow Daily News*, 20–24, 27–28 February, 3 March 1933].

Kalinin, M.N. *Izbrannie proizvedeniia v chetyrëkh tomakh*. Vol. 1. Moscow: Gospolizdat, 1960.

Kazmina-Berkbakka, Angelina. *Russkoe schast'e: Semeinaia khronika stalinskikh vremen*. St Petersburg: Aleteiia, 2012.

Khlevniuk, O.V., A.V. Kvashonkin, L.P. Kosheleva, and L.A. Rogovaia, comps. *Stalinskoe Politbiuro v 30-e gody: Sbornik dokumentov*. Moscow: AIRO-XX, 1995.

Khripunov, Ivan. *Dnevniki 1937–1941 godov*. Ed. S.I. Bykova. Moscow-Ekaterinburg: Kabinetny uchëny, 2021.

Khrushchev, Sergei, ed. *Memoirs of Nikita Khrushchev*. Trans. George Shriver. 2 vols. University Park: Pennsylvania State University Press, 2004–06.

[Khrushchev, N.S.]. *Anatomy of Terror: Khrushchev's Revelations about Stalin's Regime*. Washington, DC: Public Affairs Press, 1956.

– *Khrushchev Remembers*. Trans. and ed. Strobe Talbot. Boston: Little, Brown, 1970.

Klid, Bohdan, and Alexander J. Motyl, comps. and eds. *The Holodomor Reader: A Sourcebook on the Famine of 1932–1933 in Ukraine*. Edmonton and Toronto: Canadian Institute of Ukrainian Studies Press, 2012.

Koenker, Diane P., and Ronald D. Bachman, eds. *Revelations from the Russian Archives: Documents in English Translation*. Washington, DC: Library of Congress, 1997.

Koestler, Arthur. *The Invisible Writing: The Second Volume of an Autobiography, 1932–40*. London: Hutchinson, 1969.

Kondrashin, V.V., ed. *Golod v SSSR 1929–1934*. 3 vols. Moscow: Demokratiia, 2011–13.

Kondrashin, V.V., and O.B. Mozokhin, eds. *Posle "Velikogo pereloma": Khlebozagotovka i khlebozakupki v SSSR, 1933–1934*. Moscow: ROSSPEN, 2018.

Kondrashin, V.V., and E.A. Tiurina, eds. "'Govorit' o golode schitalos chut li ne kontrerevoliutsiei': Dokumenty rossiiskikh arkhivov o golode 1932–1933 gg. v SSSR." *Otechestvennie arkhivy* no. 2 (2009): 94–127.

Konstantin, Anatole. *A Red Boyhood: Growing Up under Stalin*. Columbia: University of Missouri Press, 2008.

Kornilov, G.E., and I.A. Lavrova, comps. *Besprizornost' na Urale v 1929–1941 gg.: Sbornik dokumentov i materialov*. Ekaterinburg: Izdatel'stvo AMB, 2009.

Kotova, I.V., comp. *Kollektivizatsiia na territorii Volgogradskoi oblasti. 1928–1932 gg. Dokumenty*. Volgograd: Kruton, 2011.

Kovalev, E.M., comp. *Golosa krest'ian: Sel'skaia Rossiia XX veka v krest'ianskikh memuarakh*. Moscow: Aspekt Press, 1996.

Kravchenko, Victor. *I Chose Freedom: The Personal and Political Life of a Soviet Official*. New York: Charles Scribner's Sons, 1946.

Kremlev [Brezkun], Sergei, ed. *Lavrentyi Beria: Spasennie dnevniki i lichnnie zapisi*. Moscow: Yauza-Press, 2016.

Krivitsky, W.G. *In Stalin's Secret Service*. New York: Enigma Books, 2000.

Kurliandskii, I.A. "'Aleksei Maksimovich! Esli by vy tol'ko videl ves etot uzhas!': A.M. Gorkii i golod 1932–1933 gg." In *Russkii istoricheskii sbornik*, ed. V.M. Lavrov et al., 207–40. Moscow: Kuchkogo pole, 2010.

Kvashonkin, A.V., L.P. Kosheleva, L.A. Rogovaya, and O.V. Khlevnyuk, comps. *Sovetskoe rukovodstvo. Perepiska. 1928–1941*. Moscow: ROSSPEN, 1999.

Lacassin, Francis, ed. *Simenon: Mes apprentissages. Reportages 1931–1946*. Paris: Omnibus, 2001.

Lang, Lucy Robins. "Soviet Nightmare." In *Tomorrow Is Beautiful*, 257–69. New York: Macmillan, 1948.

– *Tomorrow Is Beautiful*. New York: Macmillan, 1948.

Larina, Anna. *This I Cannot Forget: The Memoirs of Nikolai Bukharin's Widow*. Trans. Gary Kern. New York: W.W. Norton, 1993.

Leder, Mary M. *My Life in Stalinist Russia: An American Woman Looks Back*. Ed. Laurie Bernstein. Bloomington: Indiana University Press, 2001.

Lenin, V.I. "Comrade Workers, Forwards to the Last, Decisive Fight!" In *Collected Works*, 28:53–7. Moscow: Foreign Languages Publishing House, 1965.

– *Polnoe sobranie sochinenii*, 5th ed. Vol. 38. Moscow: Institut marksizma-leninizma pri TsK KPSS, 1958–66.

– *Sochineniia*. Vol. 30. 4th ed. Moscow: Gosudarstevennoe izdatel'stvo politicheskoi literatury, 1950.

Leonhard, Wolfgang. *Child of the Revolution.* Trans. C.M. Woodhouse. London: Ink Links, 1979.

Leshuk, Leonard, ed. *Days of Famine, Nights of Terror: Firsthand Accounts of Soviet Collectivization, 1928–1934,* 2nd rev. ed., trans. Raimund Rueger. Washington, DC: Europa University Press, 2000.

Lievan, Dominic, ed. *British Documents on Foreign Affairs: Reports and Papers from the Foreign Office Confidential Print. Series A: The Soviet Union, 1917–1939.* Vols. 9 and 10. Washington, DC: University Publications of America, 1986.

Lih, Lars T., Oleg V. Naumov, and Oleg V. Khlevniuk, eds. *Stalin's Letters to Molotov, 1925–1936.* Trans. Catherine A. Fitzpatrick. New Haven, CT: Yale University Press, 1995.

Littlepage, John D., and Demaree Bess. *In Search of Soviet Gold.* New York: Harcourt Brace, 1937.

Litvinenko, Olga, and James Riordan, comps. *Memories of the Dispossessed: Descendants of Kulak Families Tell Their Stories.* Trans. James Riordan. Nottingham, UK: Bramcote Press, 1998.

Lopatin, N.L., and L.N. Lopatina. *Kollektivizatsiia i raskulachivanie (ochevidtsi i dokumenty svidetel'stvuiut).* Kemerovo: Izdatel'stvo Aksiona, 2009.

Luciuk, Lubomyr, ed., *"Tell Them We Are Starving": The 1933 Soviet Diaries of Gareth Jones.* Kingston, ON: Kashtan Press, 2015.

Lugovskaya, Nina. *I Want to Live: The Diary of a Young Girl in Stalin's Russia.* Trans. Andrew Bromfield. New York: Houghton Mifflin, 2006.

Lyons, Eugene. "My Six Years in Moscow." In *As We See Russia* [by Members of the Overseas Press Club of America], 261–73. New York: E.P. Dutton, 1948.

Lyssyvets, Anastassia. *Raconte la vie heureuse …: Souvenirs d'une survivante de la Grande Famine en Ukraine.* Trans. Iryna Dmytrychyn. Paris: L'Harmattan, 2009.

Maillart, Ella. *Turkestan Solo.* London: G.P. Putnam's Sons, 1934.

Mandelstam, Nadezhda. *Hope Abandoned.* Trans. Max Hayward. New York: Atheneum, 1981.

– *Hope against Hope: A Memoir.* Trans. Max Hayward. New York: Atheneum, 1970.

Mankov, A.G. "Iz dnevnika 1933–1934 gg." *Zvezda* no. 5 (1994): 134–83.

Martynenko, Aleksei. *Kollektivizatsiia i raskulachivanie: Svidetel'sva ochevidtsev.* Moscow: Lavka Kirillitsa, 2018.

Masheev, V.N. *Narymskaia khronika 1930–1945: Tragediia spetspereselentsev. Dokumenty i vospominaniia.* Moscow: "Russkii put," 1997.

Matlin, M.G., comp. *Golod 1941–1945 gg. v ustnykh rasskazakh russkogo sel'skogo naseleniia Ul'ianovskogo Povolzh'ia.* Ul'ianovsk: FBGOU VO, 2017.

BIBLIOGRAPHY 447

– *Ustnie rasskazy o golode 1941–1945 gg. russkogo sel'skogo naseleniia Ul'ianovskogo Povolzh'ia*. Ul'ianovsk: FBGOU VO, 2018.

McVay, Athanasius D., and Lubomyr Y. Luciuk, eds. *The Holy See and the Holodomor: Documents from the Vatican Secret Archives on the Great Famine of 1932–1933 in Soviet Ukraine*. Kingston, ON: Kashtan Press, 2011.

[Menken, Jules]. "Russian Impressions." *Economist*, 8 October 1932, 629–30.

Milova, O.L., comp. *Izgnanniki s svoei strane: Pis'ma iz sovetskoi ssylki 1920–1930-kh godov*, 434–68. Moscow: Nauka, 2008.

Minskii muzhik [Dionisii Gorbatsevich]. *Chto ia videl v Sovetskoi Rossii? Iz moikh lichnykh nabliudeny*. Moscow: Common Place, 2018.

Mochulsky, Fyodor Vasilevich. *Gulag Boss: A Soviet Memoir*. Trans. and ed. Deborah Kaple. New York: Oxford University Press, 2011.

Mowrer, Edgar. "Russian Famine Now as Great as Starvation of 1921, Says Secretary to Lloyd George." *Chicago Daily News*, 29 March 1933, 2.

Mozokhin, O.B., ed. *Politbiuro i "vrediteli": Kampaniia po bor'be s vreditel'svom v sel'skom khoziaistve SSSR. Sbornik dokumentov*. Moscow: Kuchkovo pole, 2018.

Muggeridge, Malcolm. "Russia Revealed. IV. How the World Is Deceived: Art of Gulling Our Intelligentsia." *Morning Post* (London), 8 June 1933.

[Muggeridge, Malcolm]. "The Soviet and the Peasantry: An Observer's Notes. I, Famine in North Caucasus." *Guardian*, 25 March 1933, 13–14.

– "The Soviet and the Peasantry: An Observer's Notes. II, Hunger in the Ukraine." *Guardian*, 27 March 1933, 9–10.

– "The Soviet and the Peasantry: An Observer's Notes. III, Poor Harvest in Prospect." *Guardian*, 28 March 1933, 9–10.

Murin, Iurii, comp. *Pisatel' i vozhd: Perepiska M.A. Sholokhova s I.V. Stalinym*. Moscow: Rariotet, 1997.

Nadir, Moishe. "The Hungry Pain of Hunger." Trans. Philip Rahv. *New Masses* 7 (7 February 1933): 18.

Narkozem SSSR i Narkomsovkhoz. *Sel'skoe khoziaistvo SSSR: Ezhegodnik 1935*. Moscow: Gosudarstvennoe izdatel'stvo kolkhoznoi i sovkhoznoi literatury, 1936.

Negretov, P.I., comp. *V.G. Korolenkoi grazdanskoi voiny, 1917–1921: Biograficheskaia khronika*. Benson, VT: Chalidze Publications, 1985.

Nurtazina, Nazira. "Great Famine of 1931–1933 in Kazakhstan: A Contemporary's Reminiscences." *Acta Slavica Iaponica* no. 32 (2012): 105–29.

Nusinbaev, T., and N. Zhienfaliev, eds. *Golod v Kazakhskoi stepi (Pis'ma trevogi i boli)*. Almaty, KZ: Kazakh universitet, 1991.

Okunev, N.P. *V gody velikikh potriasenii: Dnevnik moskovskogo obyvatelia, 1914–1924*. Moscow: Kuchkovo pole, 2020.

Orlova, Raisa. *Memoirs*. Trans. Samuel Cioran. New York: Random House, 1983.

Osherowitch, Mendel. *How People Live in Soviet Russia: Impressions from a Journey*. Trans. Sharon Power, ed. Lubomyr Y. Luciuk. Kingston, ON: Kashtan Press, 2020.

Our Own Correspondent. "Great Soviet Drought." *Daily Telegraph*, 23 May 1934, 13.

Pauls, Helen Rose, ed. *Refugee*. Chilliwack, BC: Helen Rose Pauls, 2016.

Petkevich, Tamara. *Memoir of a Gulag Actress*. Trans. Yasha Klots and Ross Ufberg. DeKalb, IL: Northern Illinois University Press, 2010.

Pipes, Richard, ed. *Unknown Lenin: From the Secret Archive*. Trans. Catherine A. Fitzpatrick. New Haven, CT: Yale University Press, 1996.

Platonov, Andrei. *Zapisnie khnizhki: Materialy k biografii*. Ed. N.V. Kornienko. Moscow: Naselenie, 2000.

Pokrovskii, N.N., ed. *Politbiuro i krest'ianstvo: Vysyka, spetsposelenia, 1930–1940*. 2 bks. Moscow: ROSSPEN, 2005–06.

Poliakov, Iu.A. et al., eds. *Vsesoiuznaia perepis' naseleniia 1937 goda: Obshchie itogi. Sbornik dokumentov i materialov*. Moscow: ROSSPEN, 2007.

Reeves, Francis. *Russia Then and Now, 1892–1917: My Mission to Russia during the Famine of 1891–92*. London: G.P. Putnam's and Sons, 1917.

Resis, Albert, ed. *Molotov Remembers: Inside Kremlin Politics. Conversations with Felix Chuev*. Chicago: Ivan R. Dee, 1993. [The Russian edition of 1991 was republished in 2020 as Feliks Chuev. *140 besed s Molotovym: Vtoroi posle Stalina*.]

Robinson, Robert, with Jonathan Slevin. *Black on Red: My 44 Years Inside the Soviet Union*. Washington, DC: Acropolis Books, 1988.

Rogers, Will. *There's Not a Bathing Suit in Russia and Other Bare Facts*. New York: Albert and Charles Boni, 1927.

Sanger, R.H. "Ex-Communist Bares Red Tyranny." *New York Evening Journal*, 29 April 1935.

Scheffer, Paul. *Seven Years in Soviet Russia: With a Retrospect*. Trans. Arthur Livingston. London: Putnam, 1932.

Schiller, Otto. "Agriculture in the Soviet Union in the Year 1931." United Kingdom, The National Archives, FO 371/16335, no. 345940.

– "Corn Growing in Fields Where All the People Have Perished." *Daily Telegraph* (London), 30 August 1933.

– "Famine's Return to Russia." *Daily Telegraph* (London), 25 August 1933.

– "Russia's Starving Peasants." *Daily Telegraph* (London), 28 August 1933.
Scott, John. *Behind the Urals: An American Worker in Russia's City of Steel*. Ed. Stephen Kotkin. Bloomington: Indiana University Press, 1989.
Semenova, Elena, comp. and ed. *Unichtozhennie kak klass: K 90-letiu raskrest'ianivaniia Rossii*. 2 bks. Moscow: Traditsiia, 2020–22.
Serge, Victor. *From Lenin to Stalin*. Trans. Ralph Manheim. New York: Pathfinder Press, 1973.
– *Memoirs of a Revolutionary, 1901–1941*. Trans. Peter Sedgwick. London: Oxford University Press, 1963.
– *Russia Twenty Years After*. Trans. Max Shachtman. New York: Pioneer Publishers, 1937.
Sevost'ianov, G.N. et al., eds. *"Sovershenno sekretno": Lubianka-Stalinu o polozhenii v strane, 1932–1934 gg*. Vol. 10. Moscow: IRI RAN, 2017.
Seymour, June. *In the Moscow Manner*. London: Denis Archer, 1935.
Shaporina, L.V. *Dnevnik*. Ed. V.F. Petrova and V.N. Sazhin. 3rd ed., vol. 1. Moscow: Novoe Literaturnoe Obozrenie, 2017.
Shayakhmetov, Mukhamet. *A Kazakh Teacher's Story: Surviving the Silent Steppe*. Trans. Jan Butler. London: Stacey International, 2012.
– *The Silent Steppe: The Story of a Kazakh Nomad under Stalin*. Trans. Jan Butler. London: Stacey International, 2006.
Shcherbakov, ed. and comp. *Na serdtse pali vse pechali*. Moscow: Izdaltel'stvo Agey Tomesh, 2019.
Shishkin, V.A. *Rossiia v gody "velikogo pereloma" v vospriiatii inostrannogo diplomata, 1925–1931 gg*. St Petersburg: Dmitry Bulanin, 1999.
Shitts, I.I. *Dnevnik (mart 1928-avgust 1931)*. Paris: YMCA-Press, 1991. [Republished as *"I strakh, strakh bezumnyi ...": Dnevnik istorika, Mart 1928–Avgust 1931*. Moscow: Knizhny Klub Knigovek, 2022.]
Shvydkov, N.S. *Moi put': 1924–1985*. Moscow: Moskva, 2021.
Smith, Andrew, and Maria Smith. *I Was a Soviet Worker*. London: Robert Hale, 1937.
Smith, Homer. *Black Man in Red Russia*. Chicago: Johnson Publishing Co., 1964.
Solzhenitsyn, Alexander, ed., *Voices from the Gulag*. Trans. Kenneth Lantz. Evanston, IL: Northwestern University Press, 2010.
Sollohub, Edith. *The Russian Countess: Escaping Revolutionary Russia*. 2nd ed. Exeter, UK: Impress Books, 2017.
Sorokin, Pitirim. *Leaves from a Russian Diary*. New York: E.P. Dutton and Co., 1924.

– *Leaves – and Thirty Years After*. Boston: Beacon Press, 1950.

Stadling, Jonas, and Will Reason. *In the Land of Tolstoi: Experiences of Famine and Misrule in Russia*. New York: T. Whittaker, 1897.

Stalin, Joseph. *Selected Writings*. Westport, CT: Greenwood Press, 1970.

[Stalin, Joseph]. "Stalin's Speech at the Kolkhoz Congress." *Moscow Daily News*, 24 February 1933, 1.

Stalin, J.V. *Works*. Vols. 7, 11, 13. Moscow: Foreign Languages Publishing House, 1954–55.

Stalin, Joseph, and H.G. Wells. *Marxism vs. Liberalism: An Interview*. New York: New Century, 1945.

[Steffens, Lincoln]. *Autobiography*. New York: Harcourt Brace, 1931.

Storella, C.J., and A.K. Sokolov. *The Voice of the People: Letters from the Soviet Village, 1918–1932*. Trans. C.J. Storella. New Haven, CT: Yale University Press, 2013.

Strøm, Arne. *Uncle Give Us Bread*. London: George Allen and Unwin Ltd, 1936.

Talbot, Strobe, ed. and trans. *Khrushchev Remembers: The Last Testament*. Boston: Little, Brown and Co., 1974.

Tawdul, Adam J. "Famine in Russia Killed 10 Million." *New York American*, 18 August 1935.

Torgov, I.V. *Perezhitoe*. Moscow: Novyi Khronograf, 2014.

Tsentral'noe statisticheskoe upravlenie pri Sovete Ministrov SSSR. *Sel'skoe khoziastvo SSSR: Statisticheskii sbornik*. Moscow: Statistika, 1971.

Tsentral'noe statisticheskoe upravlenie pri Sovete Ministrov SSSR. *Strana Sovetov za 50 let: Sbornik statisticheskikh materialov*. Moscow: Statistika, 1967.

Tsentral'noe upravlenie narodnokhoziaistvennogo uchëta SSSR. *Narodnoe khoziaistvo SSSR: Statisticheskii spravochnik 1932*. Moscow-Leningrad: Gosudarstvennoe stosial'no-ekonomicheskoe izdatel'stvo, 1932.

Tsvetaeva, Marina. *Earthly Signs: Moscow Diaries, 1917–1922*. Trans. and ed. Jamey Gambrell. New York: New York Review Books, 2017.

United Kingdom. The National Archives, FO 371/17251, no. 5797, Duchess of Atholl to British Embassy, 2 August 1933, no. 6565, Golden to Shone, 31 August 1933; FO 371/17253, no. 4419, Strang to Simon, 6 June 1933, no. 6878, Coote to Simon, 12 September 1933, no. 7182, Strang to Simon, 30 September 1933, no. 7753, Strang to Simon, 27 October 1933; FO 4621/4621/38, no. 1, Strang to Simon, 1 August 1932.

United States. Foreign Affairs Committee. *Russia Relief*. London: Forgotten Books, 2018.

– National Archives and Records Administration. Records of the Department of

State. Central Decimal File 861.48/2450. Legation of the United States of America, Riga, Felix Cole to the Secretary of State, 4 October 1933.
– National Archives and Records Administration. Records of the Department of State, T1249, A.W. Kliefoth, "Memorandum," 4 June 1931.
Utley, Fred. *Lost Illusion*. Chicago: Henry Regnery, 1948.
Vaniukov, D., comp. *Golodomor*. Moscow: Knigovek, 2011.
Veselova, O.M. et al., comps. *Golod v Ukraïni, 1946–1947: Dokumenty i materiali*. Kyiv–New York: Vidavnitsvo M.P. Kots', 1996.
Veselovskii, V. S. *Problemy nashei zhizni: Vospominaniia*. Vol. 1. Moscow: Novyi Khronograf, 2018.
Vilensky, Simeon, ed. *Till My Tale Is Told: Women's Memoirs of the Gulag*. Trans. John Crowfoot, Marjorie Farquharson, Catriona Kelly, Sally Laird, and Cathy Porter. Bloomington: Indiana University Press, 1999.
Viola, Lynne, V.P. Danilov, N.A. Ivnitskii, and Denis Kozlov, eds. *The War against the Peasantry, 1927–1930: The Tragedy of the Soviet Countryside*. Trans. Steven Shabad. New Haven, CT: Yale University Press, 2005.
Vita-Finzi, Paolo. *Journal caucasien (1928–1931) suive de Carnet muscovite (1953)*. Paris: Editions L'Inventaire, 2000.
[Vladimirov, Ivan]. *Russia Accursed: Red Terror through the Eyes of an Artist*. Ed. Simon Hewitt. London: Ruzhnikov Publishing, 2020.
Vodopianova, E.K. et al., comps. *Mezhdu molotom i nakovalnei: Soiuz sovetskikh pisatelei SSSR. Dokumenty i kommentarii*. Vol. 1. Moscow: ROSSPEN, 2011.
Vodopianova, E.K., and V.V. Kondrashin, eds. "'…Nasha derevenia opustoshena do poslednego zernyshka': Iz dnevnikov literaturnogo kritika K.L. Zelinskogo i informatsionnykh svodok OGPU o golode v SSSR. 1933." *Otechestvennie arkhivy*, no. 1 (2009): 87–95.
Volters, Rudolf. *Spetsialist v Sibiri*, 2nd ed., trans. D. Khimel'nitskii. Novosibirsk: Izdatel'tsvo "Svin'in i synov'ia," 2010.
Von Herwarth, Johnnie. *Against Two Evils: Memoirs of a Diplomat-Soldier during the Third Reich*. London: Collins, 1981.
Vossler, Ronald J., ed. and trans. *We'll Meet Again: Germans in the Soviet Union Write Their Dakota Relatives, 1925–1937*. Fargo: North Dakota State Universities, 2000.
Watt, D. Cameron, ed. *British Documents on Foreign Affairs: Reports and Papers from Foreign Office Confidential Print. Series A: The Soviet Union, 1917–1939*. Vols. 11 and 12. Washington, DC: University Publications of America, 1986.

[Webb, Beatrice]. "Beatrice Webb's Typescript Diary, 4 January 1932–29 December 1934." LSE Digital Library. https://digital.library.lse.ac.uk/objects/lse:nut827hel.

Wells, Carveth. *Kapoot: The Narrative of a Journey from Leningrad to Mount Ararat in Search of Noah's Ark*. New York: Robert M. McBride, 1933.

Wells, H.G. *Russia in the Shadows*. Adelaide: University of Adelaide, 2016.

Wettlin, Margaret. *Fifty Russian Winters: An American Woman's Life in the Soviet Union*. New York: John Wiley and Sons, 1994.

Whitney, Thomas P., ed. *Khrushchev Speaks: Selected Speeches, Articles, and Press Conferences, 1949–1961*. Ann Arbor: University of Michigan Press, 1963.

Williams, Whiting. "Confidential Circular by Whiting Williams Dated October 20th 1933 Relating to His Summer Observations." https://www.garethjones.org/soviet_articles/williams_circular.htm.

– "My Journey through Famine-Stricken Russia." *Answers*, 24 February 1934.

– "*Why* Russia Is Hungry!" *Answers*, 4 March 1934.

[Witkin, Zara]. *American Engineer in Stalin's Russia: The Memoirs of Zara Witkin, 1932–1934*. Ed. Michael Gelb. Berkeley: University of California Press, 1991.

Wood, William A. *Our Ally as Told to Myriam Sieve*. New York: Charles Scribner's Sons, 1950.

Zaitsev, P.I., and A.A. Feniutin. *Mologa: do, vo vremia i posle zatopleniia, 1860–1950-e*. Rybinsk: Mediarost, 2019.

Zelenin, I.E. *Agrarnaia politika i sel'skoe khoziaistvo*. Moscow: RAN, 2001.

Zelënaia, Rina. *Dnevnik 1928–1938*. Ed. V. Nechaev. Moscow: Artist. Rezhissër. Teatr, 2021.

Zhober [Jobert], V., ed. *Kogda zhizn' tak deshego stoit …: Pis'ma O.A. Tolstoi-Voeikovoi, 1931–1933 gg*. St Petersburg: Nestor-Istoriia, 2012.

– *Russkaia sem'ia "Dans la tourmente déchaînée …": Pis'ma O.A. Tolstoi-Voeikovoi 1927–1930 gg.*, 2nd rev. ed. St Petersburg: Nestor-Istoriia, 2009.

Zima, V.F. "Golod 1932–1933 godov v pis'makh trudiashchikhsia Rossii." *Otechestvennaia istoriia* no. 2 (2006): 47–55.

Zlepko, D., ed. *Der ukrainische Hunger-Holocaust: Stalins verschwiegener Völkermord 1932/33 an 7 Millionen ukrainischen Bauern im Spiegel geheimgehaltener Akten des deutschen Auswärtigen Amtes*. Sonnenbühl, DE: Verlag Helmut Wild, 1988.

Secondary Sources

Abramov, Fyodor. *New Life: A Day on a Collective Farm*. New York: Grove Press, 1963.

Adamets, Serguei. "Famine in Nineteenth- and Twentieth-Century Russia: Mortality by Age, Cause, and Gender." In *Famine Demography: Perspectives from the Past and Present*, ed. Tim Dyson and Cormac Ó Gráda, 158–80. Oxford: Oxford University Press, 2002.

Alekseienko, A.N. "Demograficheskie posledstviia goloda v Kazakhstan nachala 30-kh godov (otsenka potër kazakhskogo etnosa)." *Demoskop Weekly* nos. 101–2, 17 February–2 March 2003.

Aleshkin, P.P., and Iu.A. Vasil'ev. *Krest'ianskaia voina v Rossii v usloviiakh povoennogo kommunizma i ee posledstvii (1918-1922 gg.)*. Moscow: Golos-Press, 2010.

– *Krest'ianskie vosstaniia v Rossii v 1918-1922 gg. Ot maknovshchiny do antonovshchiny*. Moscow: Veche, 2012.

Alexopoulos, Golfo, Julie Hessler, and Kiril Tomoff, eds. *Writing the Stalin Era: Sheila Fitzpatrick and Soviet Historiography*. New York: Palgrave Macmillan, 2011.

Anonymous. *American Correspondents and Journalists in Moscow 1917–1952: A Bibliography of their Books on the USSR*. Washington, DC: US Department of State, 1953.

– "Eto byla tragediia vsei strany: Gosudarstvennaia Duma priniala zaiavlenie 'Pamiati zhertv goloda 30-kh godov na territorii SSSR.'" *Parlamentskaia gazeta*, 3 April 2008.

– "Map of the Famine area of Soviet Russia in 1921." *Russian Information and Review* 1, no. 1 (1921): 3. https://commons.wikimedia.org/wiki/File:1921-Famine-map.jpg.

– "Map of Russia Showing the Districts Affected by the Famine." *Graphic*, 9 January 1892, 45. https://www.norkarussia.info/famine-1891-1892.html.

Applebaum, Anne. *Gulag: A History*. New York: Doubleday, 2003.

Babel, Nathalie, ed. *Isaac Babel: The Lonely Years, 1925–1939*. Trans. Andrew R. MacAndrew and Max Hayward. New York: Farrar and Straus, 1964.

Balan, Jars. "Rhea Clyman: A Forgotten Canadian Eyewitness to the Hunger of 1932." In *Women and the Holodomor Genocide: Victims, Survivors, Perpetrators*, ed. Victoria Malko, 91–117. Fresno: The Press at California State University, 2019.

Ball, Alan M. *And Now My Soul Is Hardened: Abandoned Children in Soviet Russia, 1918–1930*. Berkeley: University of California Press, 1996.

– *Russia's Last Capitalists: The Nepmen, 1921–1929*. Berkeley: University of California Press, 1990.

Baroian, O.V. *Itogi s infektsiiami v sssr i nekotorie aktual'nie voprosy sovremennoi epidemiologii*. Moscow: Izdatel'stvo Meditsina, 1968.

Bassow, Whitman. *The Moscow Correspondents: Reporting on Russia from the Revolution to Glasnost*. New York: William Morrow, 1988.

Blium, Alen, and Martina Mespule. *Biurokraticheskaia anarkhiia: Statistika i vlast' pri Staline*. Trans. V.M. Volodin. 2nd ed. [a translation of the French edition of 2003]. Moscow: ROSSPEN, 2008.

Boret, Victor. *La paradis infernal (URSS 1933)*. Paris: Librairie Aristide Quillet, 1933.

Borisenko, E.P., and V.M. Pasetskii. *Tysiacheletniaia letopis' neobychainykh iavlenii prirody*. Moscow: Mysl', 1988.

Borisov, A.A. *Climates of the USSR*. Trans. R.A. Ledward. Edinburgh: Oliver and Boyd, 1965.

Buchinskii, I. E. *Zasukhi i sukhovei*. Leningrad: Gidrometeoizdat, 1976.

Bullock, Ian. *Romancing the Revolution: The Myth of Soviet Democracy and the British Left*. Edmonton: Athabasca University Press, 2011.

Cameron, Sarah. *The Hungry Steppe: Famine, Violence, and the Making of Soviet Kazakhstan*. Ithaca, NY: Cornell University Press, 2018.

– "The Kazakh Famine of 1930–33 and the Politics of History in the Post-Soviet Space." *Kennan Institute Meeting Report* 29, no. 15 (2012): n.p.

Chamberlin, William Henry. *The Confessions of an Individualist*. New York: Macmillan, 1940.

– *Russia's Iron Age*. Boston: Little, Brown and Co., 1934.

Chandler, Robert, comp. *The Portable Platonov*. Trans. Robert and Elisabeth Chandler with Nadya Bourova et al. Moscow: GLAS, n.d.

Cherfas, Teresa. "Reporting Stalin's Famine: Jones and Muggeridge. A Case Study in Forgetting and Rediscovery." *Kritika: Explorations in Russian and Eurasian History* 14, no. 4 (2013): 775–804.

Chichirin, Ivan. *Fenomen ukrainiskogo "goloda" 1932–1933*. Moscow: Veche, 2022.

– *Mif i pravda o "Stalinskom golodomore": Ob ukrainskoi tragedii v 1932–1933 godakh*. Velikie Luki: Ivan Chicherin, 2009.

Churchill, Winston. *The Second World War*. Vol. 4. London: Cassell, 1948.

Cole, Margaret. *The Life of G.D.H. Cole*. London: Macmillan, 1971.

Colley, Margaret Siriol. *More Than a Grain of Truth: The Biography of Gareth Richard Vaughan Jones*. Newark, UK: N.L. and Margaret Colley, 2005.

Conquest, Robert. *Great Terror: Stalin's Purge of the Thirties*, rev. ed. New York: Macmillan, 1973.
– *Great Terror: A Reassessment*. New York: Oxford University Press, 1990.
– *Harvest of Sorrow: Soviet Collectivization and the Terror-Famine*. New York: Oxford University Press, 1986.
– *Nation Killers: The Soviet Deportation of Nationalities*, 2nd rev. ed. New York: Macmillan, 1970.
– *Reflections on a Ravaged Century*. New York: W.W. Norton, 2000.
Crowl, William. *Angels in Stalin's Paradise: Western Reporters in Soviet Russia, 1917 to 1937, a Case Study of Louis Fischer and Walter Duranty*. Lanham, MD: University Press of America, 1982.
Dalrymple, Dana G. "The Soviet Famine of 1932–1934." *Soviet Studies* 15, no. 3 (1964): 250–84.
Dando, William A. *The Geography of Famine*. New York: V.H. Winston and Sons and John Wiley and Sons, 1980.
– "Man-Made Famines: Some Geographical Insights from an Exploratory Study of a Millennium of Russian Famines." *Ecology of Food and Nutrition* 4 (1976): 219–34.
– "Soviet Famine." *Great Plains Rocky Mountain Geographical Journal* 5 (1973): 15–21.
Danilov, V.P. "Dinamika naseleniia SSSR za 1917–1929 gg. (Opyt arkheograficheskogo i istochnikovedcheskogo otbora dannykh dlia rekonstruktsii demograficheskogo protsessa)." *Arkheograficheskii ezhegodnik za 1968 god*, 242–53.
– *Istoriia krest'ianstva Rossii v XX veke: Izbrannie trudy*. Vol. 1, pt. 2. Moscow: ROSSPEN, 2011.
– *Rural Russia Under the New Regime*. Trans. Orlando Figes. Bloomington: Indiana University Press, 1988.
David-Fox, Michael. *Showcasing the Great Experiment: Cultural Diplomacy and Western Visitors to the Soviet Union, 1921–1941*. New York: Oxford University Press, 2012.
Davies, R.W. *Crisis and Progress in the Soviet Economy, 1931–1933*. Basingstoke, UK: Macmillan, 1996.
– *Socialist Offensive: The Collectivisation of Soviet Agriculture, 1929–1930*. Cambridge, MA: Harvard University Press, 1980.
– *The Soviet Collective Farm, 1929–1930*. Cambridge, MA: Harvard University Press, 1980.

Davies R.W., and Stephen G. Wheatcroft. *The Years of Hunger: Soviet Agriculture, 1931–1933*. Basingstoke, UK: Palgrave Macmillan, 2004.

Davies, R.W., Mark Harrison, and S.G. Wheatcroft, eds. *The Economic Transformation of the Soviet Union, 1913–1945*. Cambridge, UK: Cambridge University Press, 1994.

De Jonge, Alex. *Stalin, and the Shaping of the Soviet Union*. New York: Morrow, 1986.

Demko, George J. *The Russian Colonization of Kazakhstan, 1896–1916*. Bloomington: Indiana University Press, 1969.

Dikötter, Frank. *Mao's Great Famine: The History of China's Devastating Catastrophe, 1958–1962*. New York: Walker, 2010.

Dolot, Miron. *Execution by Hunger: The Hidden Holocaust*. New York: W.W. Norton, 1985.

Dronin, Nikolai M., and Edward G. Bellinger. *Climate Dependence and Food Problems in Russia, 1900–1990: The Interaction of Climate and Agricultural Policy and Their Effect on Food Problems*. Budapest: Central European Press, 2005.

Duranty, Walter. *Duranty Reports Russia*. New York: Viking, 1934.

– *I Write As I Please*. New York: Simon and Schuster, 1935.

Edmondson, Charles M. "Politics of Hunger: The Soviet Response to Famine." *Soviet Studies* 29, no. 4 (1977): 506–18.

Ellman, Michael. "1947 Soviet Famine and the Entitlement Approach to Famines." *Cambridge Journal of Economics* 24 (2000): 603–30.

– "Stalin and the Soviet Famine of 1932–33 Revisited." *Europe-Asia Studies* 59, no. 4 (2007): 663–93.

Engerman, David C. *Modernization from the Other Shore: American Intellectuals and the Romance of Russian Development*. Cambridge, MA: Harvard University Press, 2003.

Fainsod, Merle. *Smolensk under Soviet Rule*. Cambridge, MA: Harvard University Press, 1958.

Field, N.C. "Environmental Quality and Land Productivity: A Comparison of the Agricultural Land Base of the USSR and North America." *Canadian Geographer* 12, no. 1 (1968): 1–14.

Figes, Orlando. *Whisperers: Private Life in Stalin's Russia*. New York: Metropolitan Books, 2007.

Fischer, Louis. *Why I Became Pro-Soviet*. Delhi: Rajkamal Publications, n.d.

Fisher, H.H. *The Famine in Soviet Russia, 1919–1923: The Operations of the American Relief Administration*. New York: Macmillan, 1927.

Fitzpatrick, Sheila. *On Stalin's Team: The Years of Living Dangerously in Soviet Politics*. Princeton, NJ: Princeton University Press, 2015

– *Stalin's Peasants: Resistance and Survival in the Russian Village after Collectivization*. New York: Oxford University Press, 1994.

Foot, Michael. *Debts of Honour*. London: David Poynter, 1980.

Gamache, Ray. *Gareth Jones: Eyewitness to the Holodomor*. Cardiff, UK: Welsh Academic Press, 2013.

Ganson, Nicholas. *The Soviet Famine of 1946–47 in Global and Historical Perspective*. New York: Palgrave Macmillan, 2009.

Gantt, W. Horsley. *Russian Medicine*. New York: Paul B. Hoeber, 1937.

Gatrell, Peter. "'Bednaia' Rossiia: Rol' prirodnogo okruzheniia i deiiatel'nosti pravitel'stva v dolgovremennoi perspective ekonomicheskoi istorii Rossii." In *Ekonomicheskaia istoriia Rossii XIX-XX vv.: sovremenyi vzgliad*, ed. V.A. Vinogradov, 206–42. Moscow: ROSSPEN, 2000.

Golder, Frank Alfred, and Lincoln Hutchinson. *On the Trail of the Russian Famine*. Stanford, CA: Stanford University Press, 1927.

Goldman, Wendy Z., and Donald Filtzer, eds. *Hunger and War: Food Provisioning in the Soviet Union during World War II*. Bloomington: Indiana University Press, 2015.

Goldstein, Darra. *The Kingdom of Rye: A Brief History of Russian Food*. Oakland: University of California Press, 2022.

Golubev, Gennady, and Nikolai Dronin. *Geography of Droughts and Food Problems in Russia, 1900–2000*. Kassel, DE: Center for Environmental Systems Research, 2004.

Gorky, Maxim. "On the Russian Peasantry." *Journal of Peasant Studies* 4, no. 1 (1976): 11–27.

Graziosi, Andrea. "The Uses of Hunger: Stalin's Solution of the Peasant and National Questions in Soviet Ukraine, 1932 to 1933." In *Famines in European Economic History: The Last Great European Famines Reconsidered*, ed. Declan Curran, Lubomyr Luciuk, and Andrew G. Newby, 223–60. London and New York: Routledge, 2015.

– "Foreign Workers, 1920–40: Their Experience and Their Legacy." *International Labor and Working-Class History* no. 33 (Spring 1988): 38–59.

— *Stalinism, Collectivization and the Great Famine*. Cambridge, MA: Ukrainian Studies Fund, 2009.

Graziosi, Andrea, Lubomyr A. Hajda, and Halyna Hryn, eds. *After the Holodomor: The Enduring Impact of the Great Famine on Ukraine*. Cambridge, MA: Harvard University Press, 2014.

Grossman, Vasily. *Everything Flows*. Trans. Robert and Elizabeth Chandler with Anna Aslanyan. London: Harvill Secker, 2011.

— *Forever Flowing*. Trans. Thomas P. Whitney. London: Collins-Harvill, 1986.

— *Life and Fate*. Trans. Robert Chandler. London: Vintage Books, 2006.

Grzhebin, M.F., ed. "Kollektivizatsiia: Istoki, sushnost', posledstviia. Beseda za 'kruglom stolom.'" *Istoriia SSSR* 32, no. 3 (1989): 3–62.

Gubaidulin, Oleg. "Velikii Dzhut (Golodomor v Kazakhstane)." https://www.politforums.net/other/1232571431.html.

Halberstadt, Alex. *Young Heroes of the Soviet Union: A Memoir and a Reckoning*. London: Jonathan Cape, 2020.

Hale-Dorrell, Aaron T. *Corn Crusade: Khrushchev's Farming Revolution in the Post-Stalin Soviet Union*. New York: Oxford University Press, 2018.

Hartshorn, Peter. *I Have Seen the Future: A Life of Lincoln Steffens*. Berkeley: Counterpoint, 2011.

Heckler, Cheryl. *An Accidental Journalist: The Adventures of Edmund Stevens, 1934–1945*. Columbia: University of Missouri Press, 2007.

Hindus, Maurice. *The Great Offensive*. New York: Harrison Smith and Robert Haas, 1933.

— *Green Worlds: An Informal Chronicle*. New York: Doubleday, Doran, 1938.

— *House without a Roof: Russia after Forty-Three Years of Revolution*. Garden City, NY: Doubleday, 1961.

— *Red Bread: Collectivization in a Russian Village*. New York: Jonathan Cape and Harrison Smith, 1931.

Hingley, Ronald, trans. and ed. *The Oxford Chekhov*. Vol. 7. London: Oxford University Press, 1965.

Hokkanen, Lawrence, and Sylvia Hokkanen, with Anita Middleton. *Karelia: A Finnish-American Couple in Stalin's Russia*. St Cloud, MN: North Star Press, 1991.

Hryn, Halyna, ed. *Hunger by Design: The Great Ukrainian Famine and Its Soviet Context*. Cambridge, MA: Harvard Ukrainian Research Institute, 2008.

Hughes, Michael. *Inside the Enigma: British Officials in Russia, 1900–1939*. London: Hambeldon Press, 1997.

Hunczak, Taras, and Roman Serbyn, eds. *Famine in Ukraine 1932–1933: Genocide by Other Means*. New York: Shevchenko Scientific Society, 2007.

Hunter, Ian. *Malcolm Muggeridge: A Life*. Vancouver: Regent College Publishing, 2003.

Igort. *The Ukrainian and Russian Notebooks: Life and Death under Soviet Rule*. Trans. Jamie Richards. New York: Simon and Schuster, 2016.

Isajiw, Wsevolod W., ed. *Famine-Genocide in Ukraine, 1932–33: Western Archives, Testimonies, and New Research*. Toronto: Ukrainian Canadian Research and Documentation Centre, 2003.

Ivnitskii, N.A. *Golod 1932–1933 godov v SSSR: Ukraina•Kazakhstan•Severnyi Kavkaz•Povolzh'e•Tsentral'no-Chernozemnaia oblast'•Zapadnaia Sibir'•Ural*. Moscow: Sobranie, 2009.

– *Kollektivizatsiia i raskulachivanie (nachalo 30-kh godov)*. Moscow: Izdatel'stvo Magistr, 1996.

[Ivnitskii, N.A.]. "The 'Real Story' of Collectivization and Dekulakization." *WWICS News/Meeting Report*, 9 December 1997.

Ivnitskii, N.A. "Stalinskaia 'revoliutsiia sverkhu' i krest'ianstvo." In *Mentalitet i agrarnoe razvitie Rossii, XIX–XX vv*, ed. V.P. Danilov and L.V. Milov, 247–59. Moscow: ROSSPEN, 1996.

– *Sud'ba raskulachennykh v SSSR*. Moscow: Sobranie, 2004.

Joravsky, David. *The Lysenko Affair*. Chicago: University of Chicago Press, 1970.

Kahan, Arcadius. "Natural Calamities and Their Effect upon the Food Supply in Russia (An Introduction to a Catalogue)." *Jahrbücher für Geschichte Osteuropas* 16, no. 3 (1968): 353–77.

Kaminskaya, Dina. *Final Judgement: My Life as a Soviet Defence Lawyer*. Trans. Michael Glenny. London: Harvill Press, 1983.

Kaplan, Justin. *Lincoln Steffens: A Biography*. New York: Simon and Schuster, 1974.

Katharine, Duchess of Atholl. *Working Partnership: Being the Lives of John George, 8th Duke of Atholl ... and of his wife Katharine Marjory Ramsay*. London: Arthur Barker, 1958.

Keller, Bill. "Soviet Aide Admits Maps Were Faked for 50 Years." *New York Times*, 3 September 1988, sec. 1, 1–4.

Kern, Gary. *The Kravchenko Case: One Man's War on Stalin*. New York: Enigma Books, 2007.

Kessler, Gus. "The Passport System and State Control over Population Flows in the Soviet Union, 1932–1940." *Cahiers du monde russe* 12, nos. 2–4 (2001): 477–504.

Kindler, Robert. *Stalin's Nomads: Power and Famine in Kazakhstan*. Trans. Cynthia Klohr. Pittsburgh: Pittsburgh University Press, 2018.

King, William H. "Conditions in Russia." In United States, 68th Congress, 1st Session, *Senate Document No. 126*, 1–127. Washington, DC: Government Printing Office, 1924.

Klimin, I.I. *Rossiiskoe krest'ianstvo v gody novoi ekonomicheskoi politiki, 1921–1927*. Vol.1. St Petersburg: Izdatel'stvo Politekhnicheskogo universiteta, 2007.

– *Rossiiskoe krest'ianstvo nakanune "velikogo pereloma," 1928–1929 gg*. St Petersburg: VVM, 2010.

– *Rossiiskoe krest'ianstvo v pervyi period sploshnoi kollektivizatsii sel'skogo khoziaistva (1930–1932 gg.)*. St Petersburg: VVM, 2011.

– *Rossiiskoe krest'ianstvo v zavershaiushchii period sploshnoi kollektivizatsii sel'skogo khoziaistva (1933–1937 gg.)*. St Petersburg: VVM, 2012.

Klyuev, Nikolai. *Poems*. Trans. John Glad. Ann Arbor, MI: Ardis, 1977.

Koestler, Arthur. *Darkness at Noon*. Trans. Philip Boehm. New York: Scribner, 2019.

Komissiia Prezidiuma Verkhnogo Soveta Respubliki Kazakhstan. "Prichiny goloda 30-kh godov v Kazakhstane." [No longer online.]

Kondrashin, Viktor. *Golod 1932–1933 godov: Tragediia rossiiskoi derevni*. 1st ed. Moscow: ROSSPEN, 2008 [2nd ed. 2018].

– "Golod v krest'ianskom mentalitete." In *Mentalitet i agrarnoe razvitie Rossii (XIX–XX vv.)*, ed. V.P. Danilov and L.V. Milov, 115–23. Moscow: ROSSPEN, 1996.

– *Khlebozagotovitel'naia politika v gody pervoi piatiletki i ee rezul'taty, 1929–1933 gg*. Moscow: ROSSPEN, 2014.

– *Krest'ianstvo i gody Grazhdanskoi voiny*. Moscow-Berlin: DirectMedia, 2019.

– "Zerno v obmen na valiutu i stanki: Novie dokumenty rossiiskikh arkhivov ob uchastii zapadnoevropeiskikh stran v sovetskoi industrializatsii." *Klio* no. 3 [54] (2011): 112–15.

Kondrashin, V.V., ed. *Sovremennaia rossiisko-ukrainskaia istoriografiia goloda 1932–1933 v SSSR*. Moscow: ROSSPEN, 2011.

Kopelev, Lev. *To Be Preserved Forever*. Trans. and ed. Anthony Austin. Philadelphia: J.B. Lippincott, 1977. [Published in London by Secker and Warburg as *No Jail for Thought*.]

– *The Education of a True Believer*. Trans. Gary Kern. New York: Harper and Row, 1980.

Kornienko, N.V., ed. "Istoriia teksta i biografiia A. P. Platonova, 1926–1946." *Zdes' i teper'* 2, no. 1 (1993): 1–320.
Kotkin, Stephen. *Stalin: Waiting for Hitler, 1929–1941.* New York: Penguin Press, 2017.
Koval, Nikanor. *Krushilovka. Tridtsatogo goda. Povest'.* 2nd ed. Moscow: Russkii put', 2010.
Krasilnikov, Sergei, Marina Salamatova, and Svetlana Ushakova. *Korni ili shepki: Krest'ianskaia sem'ia na spetspolselenii v Zapadnoi Sibiri v 1930-kh-nachale 1950-kh gg.* Moscow: ROSSPEN, 2010.
Kulchytsky, Stanislav. *The Famine of 1932–1933 in Ukraine: An Anatomy of the Holodomor.* Edmonton: CIUS Press, 2018.
Kulikova, G.B. *Novyi mir glazami starogo. Sovetskaia Rossiia 1920-1930-kh godov glazami zapadnykh intellektualov: Ocherki dokumentirovannoi istorii.* Moscow: Institut rossiiskoi istorii RAN, 2013.
Kupferman, Fred. *Au pays des Soviets: Le voyage français en Union soviétique, 1917–1939.* Paris: Tallandier, 2007.
Kuriaev, Shamil. *Russkii khleb v zhernovakh ideologii.* St Petersburg: Aleteiia, 2019.
Kurliandskii, I.A. *Stalin, vlast', religiia.* Moscow: Kuchkovo pole, 2011.
Kurlyiw, Valentina. *Holodomor in Ukraine: The Genocidal Famine, 1932–1933. Learning Materials for Teachers and Students.* Edmonton: CIUS Press, 2019.
Kuromiya, Hiroaki. *Voices of the Dead: Stalin's Great Terror in the 1930s.* New Haven, CT: Yale University Press, 2007.
Kuznetsov, N., and R. Terekhov. "Lessons of Defeat of 'Splitters' at 1924 Congress." *Current Digest of the Soviet Press* 16, no. 21 (1964): 9–10.
– "Vazhnaia veka v zhizni Leninskoi partii." *Pravda,* 26 May 1964, 2.
Lewin, Moishe. "'Taking Grain': Soviet Policies of Agricultural Procurements before the War." In *Essays in Honour of E.H. Carr,* ed. C. Abramsky, 281–323. Hamden, CT: Archon Books, 1974.
Lewis, Robert A., Richard H. Rowland, and Ralph S. Clem. *Nationality and Population Change in Russia and the USSR: An Evaluation of Census Data, 1897–1970.* New York: Praeger, 1976.
Long, James W. "Volga Germans and the Famine of 1921." *Russian Review* 51 (1992): 510–25.
Lorimer, Frank. *The Population of the Soviet Union: History and Prospects.* Geneva: League of Nations, 1946.
Luciuk, Lubomyr, ed. *Not Worthy: Walter Duranty's Pulitzer Prize and the New York Times.* Kingston, ON: Kashtan Press, 2004.

Luciuk, Lubomyr Y., and Lisa Grekul, eds. *Reflections on the Great Famine of 1932–1933 in Soviet Ukraine*. Kingston, ON: Kashtan Press, 2008.

Lydolph, Paul E. *Climates of the Soviet Union*. Amsterdam: Elsevier, 1977.

Lyons, Eugene. *Assignment in Utopia*. London: George G. Harrap, 1937.

Macqueen, Angus. "Survivors." *Granta* 64 (Winter 1998): 37–54.

Madden, Cheryl, ed. *Holodomor: The Ukrainian Genocide 1932–1933*. [A special issue of *Canadian American Slavic Studies*, 37, no. 3 (2003).]

Maksudov, Sergei [Babyonyshev, Alexander]. *Pobeda nad derevnei: Demograficheskie poteri kollektivizatsii*. Moscow and Chelyabinsk: Sotsium, 2019.

Malysheva, M.P., and V.S. Poznanskii. "Golod na iuge Zapadnoi Sibiri v nachale 30-kh godov." *Gumanitarnie nauki v Sibiri* no. 1 (1995): 74–8.

[Mandelstam, Osip]. *Osip Mandelstam: 50 Poems*. Trans. Bernard Meares. New York: Persea Books, 2000.

Marples, David R. *Holodomor: Causes of the 1932–1933 Famine in Ukraine*. Saskatoon, SK: Heritage Press, 2011.

Martin, John H., and S.C. Salmon. "Rusts of Wheat, Oats, Barley, Rye." In *Plant Diseases: The Yearbook of Agriculture 1953*, ed. Alfred Stefferud, 329–43, 83rd Congress, 1st Session, House Document No. 122. Washington, DC: United States Department of Agriculture, 1953.

Martin, Kingsley, and drawings by David Low. *Low's Russian Sketchbook*. London: Victor Gollancz, 1932.

Martin, Terry. *The Affirmative Action Empire: Nations and Nationalism in the Soviet Union, 1923–1939*. Ithaca, NY: Cornell University Press, 2001.

Mayakovsky, Vladimir. *"Vladimir Mayakovsky" and Other Poems*. Trans. and ed. James Womack. Manchester, UK: Carcanet Press, 2016.

Medvedev, Roy. *Let History Judge: The Origins and Consequences of Stalinism*. Trans. and ed. George Shriver, rev. and enl. ed. New York: Columbia University Press, 1989.

– *Okruzhenie Stalina*, 2nd ed. Moscow: Molodaia Gvardiia, 2010.

Medvedev, Zhores. *Soviet Agriculture*. New York: W.W. Norton, 1987.

Mel'nichenko, M. *Sovetskii anekdot (Ukazatel' siuzhetov)*. Moscow: Novoe literaturnoe obozrenie, 2014.

Mikhailov, Valery. *The Great Disaster: Genocide of the Kazakhs*. Trans. Katharine Judelson. London: Stacey International, 2014.

– *Velikii dzhut: Dokumental'naia povest'*. Almaty, KZ: Mekter, 2008.

Milov, L.V. "Prirodno-klimaticheskii factor i osobennosti rossiiskogo istoricheskogo protsessa." *Voprosy istorii*, nos. 4–5 (1992): 37–56.
Mironin, Sigizmund. *'Golodomor' na Rusi*. Moscow: Algoritm, 2008.
Mironova, Natal'ia. *Velikaia epidemiia: Sypnoi tif v Rossii v pervye gody sovetskoi vlasti*. Moscow: Universitet Dmitriia Pozharskogo, 2020.
Mitrany, David. *Marx against the Peasant: A Study in Social Dogmatism*. New York: Collier Books, 1961.
Morgan, John. "Agriculture." In *Twelve Studies in Soviet Russia*, ed. Margaret I. Cole, 104–21. London: Victor Gollancz, 1933.
Morrell, Gordon W. *Britain Confronts the Stalin Revolution: Anglo-Soviet Relations and the Metro-Vickers Crisis*. Waterloo, ON: Wilfrid Laurier University Press, 1995.
Muggeridge, Malcolm. *Chronicles of Wasted Time*. Part 1: *The Green Stick*. London: Collins, 1972.
– "To Friends of the Soviet Union." *English Review* 56 (January 1934): 44–55.
– *Winter in Moscow*. London: Eyre and Spottiswoode, 1934.
Naumov, N.A., comp. *Rzhavchina khlebnykh zlakov v SSSR: Monografichreskaia svodka*. Moscow-Leningrad: Sel'skhozgiz, 1939.
Ohayon, Isabelle. *La sédentarisation des Kazakhs dans l'URSS de Staline: Collectivisation et changement social, 1928–1945*. Paris: Maisonneuve et Larose, 2006.
Olcott, Martha Brill. *The Kazakhs*, 2nd ed. Stanford: Hoover Institution Press, 1995.
Olesevych, Tymish. *Statystychni tablytsi ukrainskoho naselennia SSSR za perepysom 17 hrudnia 1926 roku*. Warsaw: Ukrainskyi naukovyi instytut, 1930.
Omarbekov, Talas. *Golodomor v Kazakhstane: Prichiny, masshtaby i itogi, 1930–1933 gg*. Almaty, KZ: ARYS, 2009.
Oreshkin, Dmitrii. *Dzhugafiliia i sovetskii statisticheskii epos*. Moscow: Mysl, 2019.
Osokina, Elena. *Alkhimiia sovetskoi industrializatsii: Vremia Torgsina*. Moscow: Novoe Literaturnoe Obozrenie, 2019.
– "Legenda o meshke s khlebom: Krizis snabzheniia v kontse 30-kh godov." *Rodina* 10 (1999): 87–91.
– *Our Daily Bread: Socialist Distribution and the Art of Survival in Stalin's Russia, 1927–1941*. Trans. Kate Transchel and Greta Bucher. Armonk, NY: M.E. Sharpe, 2001.
– "Torgsin, zoloto dlia industrializatsii." *Cahiers du monde russe* 47, no. 4 (2006), 715–47.

– "Victims of the Famine of 1933: How Many? An Analysis of Demographic Statistics of the Central State Archive of the National Economy of the USSR." *Russian Studies in History* 31, no. 2 (1992): 5–18.

– *Zoloto dlia industrializatsii: Torgsin*. Moscow: ROSSPEN, 2009.

Ovchinnikov, Aleksei. "Kiev otmechaet den' pamiati zhertv 1932–1933 godov." *Komsomol'skaia Pravda*, 22 November 2008.

Ozerov, Lev. *Portraits without Frames*. Trans. Maria Bloshteyn, Robert Chandler, Boris Dralyuk, and Irina Mashinski. New York: New York Review of Books, 2018.

Pannier, Bruce. "Kazakhstan: The Forgotten Famine." *Radio Free Europe/Radio Liberty*. http://www.rferl.org/a/1079304.html.

Pares, Sir Bernard. *Wandering Student: The Story of a Purpose*. Syracuse, NY: Syracuse University Press, 1948.

Pashuto, V.T. "Golodnie gody v Drevnei Rusi." In *Ezhegodnik po agrarnoi istorii Vostochnoi Evropy 1962 g.*, ed. V.K. Iatsunskii et al., 61–94. Minsk: Izdatel'stvo "Nauka i tekhnika," 1964.

Pasternak, Boris. *Doctor Zhivago*. Trans. Max Hayward and Manya Harari. New York: Pantheon, 1958.

Patenaude, Bertrand M. *The Big Show in Bololand: The American Relief Expedition to Soviet Russia in the Famine of 1921*. Stanford, CA: Stanford University Press, 2002.

Payne, Matthew J. "Seeing like a Soviet State: Settlement of Nomadic Kazakhs, 1928–1934." In *Writing the Stalin Era: Sheila Fitzpatrick and Soviet Historiography*, ed. Golfo Alexopoulos, Julie Hessler, and Kiril Tomoff, 59–86. New York: Palgrave Macmillan, 2011.

Pianciola, Niccolò. "Collectivization Famine in Kazakhstan, 1931–1933." In *Hunger by Design: The Great Ukrainian Famine and Its Soviet Context*, ed. Halyna Hryn, 103–16. Cambridge, MA: Harvard Ukrainian Research Institute, 2008.

– "Famine in the Steppe: The Collectivization of Agriculture and the Kazakh Herdsmen, 1928–1934." *Cahiers du monde russe* 45, nos. 1–2 (2004): 137–92.

– *Stalinismo di frontera: Colonizzazione Agricola, stermino dei nomadi e construzione statale in Asia central, 1905–1936*. Vincenza: Viella, 2009.

Pirozhkova, A.N. *At His Side: The Last Years of Isaac Babel*. Trans. Anne Frydman and Robert L. Busch. South Royalton, VT: Steerforth Press, 1996.

Plakidin, Vladimir I., Kseniia Fomicheva, and Anna Iukhneva. "*I zabyt' po-prezhnomu nel'za ...*" *Kniga pamiati repressii 30-kh g.g. protiv krest'ian v s. Maloe Igolkino*. Varezh: n.p., 2019.

Platonov, Andrei. "Among Animals and Plants." Trans. Robert and Elizabeth Chandler and Olga Meerson, *New Yorker*, 22 October 2007, 117–19, 122–8, 135, 137.
– *The Foundation Pit*. Trans. Robert and Elizabeth Chandler and Olga Meerson. New York: New York Review Books, 2009.
– *The Return and Other Stories*. Trans. Robert and Elizabeth Chandler and Angela Livingston. London: Harvill Press, 1999.
Pletnev, V.F., ed. *Stalin. K shestidesiatiletiiu so dnia rozhdeniia*. Moscow: Gosudarstvennoe izdatel'stvo khudozhestvennoi literatury, 1940.
Pobol', N.L., and P.M. Polian, comps. *Stalinskie deportatsii 1928–1953*. Moscow: Materik, 2005.
Poliakov, Iu.A., ed. *Naselenie Rossii v XX veke: Istoricheskie ocherki*. Vol. 1. Moscow: ROSSPEN, 2000.
Poliakov, V.A. *Golod v Povolzh'e, 1919–1925 gg: Proiskhozhdenie, osobennosti, posledstviia*. Volgograd: Volgogradskoe nauchnoe izdatel'stvo, 2007.
– *Pervyi sovetskii golod: Na meterialakh Povolzh'ia, 1919–1925 gg. Monografiia*. 2 vols. Volgograd: Izdatel'stvo Volgogradskogo gosudarstvennogo universiteta, 2019–21.
Poznanskii, V.S. *Sotsial'nie kataklizmy v Sibiri: Golod i epidemii v 20-30-e gody XX v.* Novosibirsk: Izdatel'stvo SO RAN, 2007.
Poznanskii, V.S., and M.P. Malysheva. "Golod na iuge Zapadnoi Sibiri v 1931–1932 gg." In *Vozvrashchenie pamiati: Istoriko-arkhivnyi almanakh*, 128–63. Novosibirsk: Izdatel'stvo SO RAN, 1997.
Pringle, Peter. *The Murder of Nikolai Vavilov: The Story of Stalin's Persecution of One of the Great Scientists of the Twentieth Century*. New York: Simon and Schuster, 2008.
Prishvin, M.M. *Dnevniki*. Ed. L.A. Riazanova and Ia.Z. Grishina. St Petersburg: Rostok, 2006.
Prokhorova, E.V., and E.D. Tverdiukova. *Prodovol'stvennyi rynok Petrograda-Leningrada perioda nepa*. St Petersburg: Gumanitarnaia Akademiia, 2019.
Prudnikova, E., and I. Chichirin. *Mifologiia "golodomora."* Moscow: OLMA, 2013.
[Pulitzer Prize Committee]. "Pulitzer Prizes: Statement on Walter Duranty's 1932 Prize," 21 November 2003. https://www.pulitzer.org/news/statement-walter-duranty.
Rakov, Aleksei. *"Derevniu opustoshaiut": Stalinskaia kollektivizatsiia i "raskulachivanie" na Urale v 1930-kh godakh*. Moscow: ROSSPEN, 2013.
Rampersad, Arnold. *The Life of Langston Hughes*, 2nd ed. New York: Oxford University Press, 2002.

Rauner, Iu.L. "Synchronous Recurrence of Droughts in the Grain-growing Regions of the Northern Hemisphere." *Soviet Geography: Review and Translation* 21, no. 3 (1980): 159–79.

Rayfield, Donald. *Stalin and His Hangmen*. New York: Random House, 2004.

Reuther, Victor G. *The Brothers Reuther and the Story of the UAW*. Boston: Houghton Mifflin, 1976.

Robbins, Richard G., Jr. *Famine in Russia, 1891–1892: The Imperial Government Responds to a Crisis*. New York: Columbia University Press, 1975.

Robson, Roy R. *Solovki: The Story of Russia Told through Its Most Remarkable Islands*. New Haven, CT: Yale University Press, 2004.

Rogalina, Nina. "Kollektivizatsiia v svete novykh dokumental'nykh publikastsii i sovremennoi istoriografii." In *XX vek i sel'skaia Rossiia: rossiiskie i iaponskie issledovateli'i v proekte "Istoriia rossiiskogo krest'ianstva v XX veke,"* ed. Hiroshi Okuda, 186–231. Tokyo: CIRJE, 2012.

Rolin, Olivier. *Stalin's Meteorologist: One Man's Untold Story of Love, Life and Death*. Trans. Ros Schwartz. London: Harvill Secker, 2017.

Roll-Hansen, Nils. *The Lysenko Effect: The Politics of Science*. Amherst, NY: Humanity Books, 2005.

Ronina, G., V.P. Danilov, M.A. Vyltsan, and N.A. Ivnitskii. "Oglianut'sia v razdum'e." *Sel'skaia nov'* no. 12 (1987): 14–17.

Rudenko, A.I., ed. *Zasukhi v SSSR: Ikh proiskhozhdenie, povtoriaemost' i vliianie na urozhai*. Leningrad: Gimiz, 1958.

Rudnytskyi, Omelian, Nataliia Levchuk, Oleh Wolowyna, and Pavlo Shevchuk. "Famine Losses in Ukraine in 1932 to 1933 within the Context of the Soviet Union." In *Famines in European Economic History: The Last Great European Famines Reconsidered*, ed. Declan Curran, Lubomyr Luciuk, and Andre G. Newby, 192–222. London and New York: Routledge, 2015.

Rudnytskyi, Omelian, Natalia Levchuk, Oleh Wolowyna, Pavlo Shevchuk, and All Kovbasiuk (Savchuk). "Demography of a Man-made Human Catastrophe: The Case of Massive Famine in Ukraine 1932–1933." *Canadian Studies in Population* 42, nos. 1–2 (2015): 53–80.

Ryskozha, Bolat. "Valery Mikhailov: Vo vremia goloda v Kazakhstane pogiblo 40 protsentov naseleniia." https://rus.azattyq.org/a/Valery_Mikhailov/1357347.html.

Sakharov, Andrei D. *Progress, Coexistence, and Intellectual Freedom*. Trans. New York Times. New York: W.W. Norton, 1968.

Scammell, Michael. *Koestler: The Indispensable Intellectual.* New York: Random House, 2009.

Schmemann, Serge. *Echoes of a Native Land: Two Centuries of a Russian Village.* New York: Vintage Books, 1997.

Sevander, Mayme, with Laurie Hertzel. *They Took My Father: Finnish Americans in Stalin's Russia.* Minneapolis: University of Minnesota Press, 2004.

Sen, Amartya. *Poverty and Famines: An Essay on Entitlement and Deprivation.* Oxford: Clarendon Press, 1981.

Sennikov, B.V. *Tambovskoe vosstanie 1918–1921 i raskrest'ianivanie Rossii 1929–1933 gg.* Moscow: Povest', 2004. [Reprint Ekaterinburg: AB CDE, 2020.]

Serbyn, Roman, and Bohdan Krawchenko, eds. *Famine in Ukraine, 1932–1933.* Edmonton: Canadian Institute of Ukrainian Studies, 1986.

Shalamov, Varlam. *Kolyma Tales.* Trans. John Glad. London: Penguin Books, 1994. [For a more recent translation of Shalamov's tales, see: *Kolyma Stories*, trans. Donald Rayfield (New York: New York Review Books, 2018), and *Sketches of the Criminal World: Further Kolyma Stories*, trans. Donald Rayfield (New York: New York Review Books, 2020).]

Sharapov, G.V., and V.P. Danilov. *Istoriia krest'ianstva SSSR: Istoriia sovetskogo krest'ianstva.* Vol. 2. Moscow: Nauka, 1986.

Shentalinsky, Vitaly. *The KGB's Literary Archive.* Trans. and ed. John Crowfoot. London: Harvill Press, 1995.

Sholokhov, Mikhail. *Quiet Flows the Don.* Trans. Robert Daglish, rev. and ed. Brian Murphy. London: J.M. Dent, 1996.

– *Virgin Soil Upturned.* Trans. Stephen Garry. London: Putnam, 1935.

Shvetsov, Iuryi. *Novaia ideologiia: Golodomor.* Moscow: Evropa, 2009.

Shvetsova, Liubov. *Zhizn' ot sokhi. Byt i traditsii russkikh krest'ian.* Moscow: Izdatel'stva AST, 2022.

Simkin, Lëv. *Velikyi obman. Chuzhestranitsy v strane bol'shevikov.* Moscow: Ekmos, 2022.

Sims, James Y., Jr. "Crop Failure of 1891: Soil Exhaustion, Technological Backwardness, and Russia's 'Agrarian Crisis.'" *Slavic Review* 41, no. 2 (1982): 236–50.

Smith, Douglas. *The Russian Job: The Forgotten Story of How America Saved the Soviet Union from Ruin.* New York: Farrar, Straus and Giroux, 2019.

Smith, G.S. *D.S. Mirsky: A Russian-English Life, 1890–1939.* New York: Oxford University Press, 2000.

Smith, Glen Alden. *Soviet Foreign Trade: Organization, Operations, and Policy, 1918–1971*. New York: Praeger, 1971.

Smith, R.E.F., and David Christian. *Bread and Salt: A Social and Economic History of Food and Drink in Russia*. Cambridge, UK: Cambridge University Press, 1984.

Solzhenitsyn, Aleksandr I. *Gulag Archipelago 1918–1956: An Experiment in Literary Investigation*. Trans. Thomas P. Whitney and Harry Willets. Vols. 1–3, 5–7. New York: Harper and Row, 1973–74.

– *One Day in the Life of Ivan Denisovich*. Trans. Max Hayward and Ronald Hingley. New York: Bantam Books, 1963.

Sorokin, A.K., ed. *1929: "Velikii perelom" i ego posledstviia. Materialy XII Mezhdurnarodnoi nauchnoi konferentsii. Ekaterinburg, 26–28 sentiabria 2019*. Moscow: ROSSPEN, 2020.

Sorokin, Pitirim A. *Man and Society in Calamity: The Effects of War, Revolution, Famine, Pestilence upon Human Mind, Behavior, Social Organization, and Cultural Life*. New York: E.P. Dutton and Co., 1942.

Stadnyuk, Ivan. *People Are Not Angels*. Trans. P.A. Spalding and I. Antonenko. London: Mono Press, 1963.

Stefferud, Alfred, ed. *Plant Diseases: The Yearbook of Agriculture 1953*, 83rd Congress, 1st Session, House Document No. 122. Washington, DC: United States Department of Agriculture, 1953.

Stepanov, M.G. *Otechestvennaia istoriografiia antikrest'ianskikh repressii v SSSR, 1929–1933 gg*. Abakan: Izdatel'stvo GOU VPO, 2010.

Syncha [Forsova], Svetlana. *Uroki nevydumannoi istorii. Golod 1932-1933 gg: Spiski zhertv goloda 1932-1933 godov po Korenovskomu rainou Krasnodararskogo kraia*. Krasnodar: Ekoinvest, 2009.

Tarkhova, Nonna. *Krasnaia armiia i stalinskaia kollektivizatsiia 1928–1933 gg*. Moscow: ROSSPEN, 2010.

Tatimov, Makash, and Miras Tatimova. "Tragediia velikoi stepi: O demograficheskoi katastrofe v Kazakahstane v tridtsatie gody." *Mysl'* no. 6 (2009): 55–60.

Tauger, Mark B. "Grain Crisis or Famine? The Ukrainian State Commission for Aid to Crop-Failure Victims and the Ukrainian Famine of 1928–29." In *Provincial Landscapes: Local Dimensions of Soviet Power, 1917–1953*, ed. Donald J. Raleigh, 146–70. Pittsburgh: University of Pittsburgh Press, 2001.

– "Modernisation in Soviet Agriculture." In *Modernisation in Russia since 1900*, ed. Markku Kangaspuro and Jeremy Smith, 84–103. Helsinki: Finnish Literature Society, 2006.

– "People's Commissariat of Agriculture." In *Decision-Making in the Stalinist Command Economy, 1932–37*, ed. E.A. Rees, 150–75. New York: St Martin's Press, 1997.
Taylor, S.J. *Stalin's Apologist: Walter Duranty – The New York Times's Man in Moscow*. New York: Oxford University Press, 1990.
Topolianskii, V.D., comp. *Vserossiiskii komitet pomoshchi golodaiushchim*. Moscow: MDF, 2014.
Tottle, Douglas. *Fraud, Famine and Fascism: The Ukrainian Genocide Myth from Hitler to Harvard*. Toronto: Progress Books, 1987.
Trotsky, Leon. *Revolution Betrayed*. Trans. Max Eastman. New York: Dover Publications, 2004.
Tsikhelashvili, N.Sh., and David Engerman. "Amerikanskaia pomosh' Rossii v 1921–1923 godakh: Konflikty i sotrudnichestvo." In *Amerikanskii ezhegodnik 1995*, 191–213. Moscow: Nauka, 1996.
Tzouliadis, Tim. *The Forsaken: An American Tragedy in Stalin's Russia*. London: Penguin, 2008.
Vallin, Jacques, France Meslé, Seguei Adamet, and Serhii Pyrozhkov. "A New Estimate of Ukrainian Population Losses during the Crises of the 1930s and 1940." *Population Studies* 56 (2009): 249–64.
Viola, Lynne. "Bab'i bunty and Peasant Women's Protests during Collectivization." *Russian Review* 45 (1986): 23–42.
– *The Best Sons of the Fatherland: Workers in the Vanguard of Soviet Collectivization*. New York: Oxford University Press, 1987.
– "Counternarratives of Soviet Life: Kulak Special Settlers in the First Person." In *Writing the Stalin Era: Sheila Fitzpatrick and Soviet Historiography*, ed. Golfo Alexopoulos, Julie Hessler, and Kiril Tomoff, 89–99. New York: Palgrave Macmillan, 2011.
– *Peasant Rebels under Stalin: Collectivization and the Culture of Peasant Resistance*. New York: Oxford University Press, 1996.
Volkov, Ivan Mefodievich. "Drought and Famine of 1946–47." *Russian Studies in History* 31, no. 2 (1992): 31–60.
Von Bremzen, Anya. *Mastering the Art: A Memoir of Food and Longing*. New York: Crown Publishers, 2013.
Walters, George J. *Wir Wollen Deutsche Bleiben: The Story of the Volga Germans*. Kansas City, MO: Halcyon Press, 1993.
Webb, Sidney, and Beatrice Webb. *Soviet Communism: A New Civilisation?* London: Longmans, Green and Co., 1935.

Weissman, Benjamin M. *Herbert Hoover and Famine Relief to Soviet Russia: 1921–1923*. Stanford, CA: Hoover Institution Press, 1974.

Werth, Nicholas. *Cannibal Island: Death in a Siberian Gulag*. Trans. Steven Rendall. Princeton, NJ: Princeton University Press, 2007.

– *Histoire de l'Union soviétique*. 6th rev. ed. Paris: Presses Universitaires de France, 2008.

Wheatcroft, S.G. "1891–92 Famine: Towards a More Detailed Analysis of Its Scale and Demographic Significance." In *Economy and Society in Russia and the Soviet Union, 1860–1930: Essays for Olga Crisp*, ed. Linda Edmondson and Peter Waldron, 44–64. London: St Martin's Press, 1992.

– "Eastern Europe (Russia and the USSR)." In *Famine in European History*, ed. Guido Alfani and Cormac Ó Gráda, 212–39. New York: Cambridge University Press, 2017.

White, Colin. *Russia and America: The Roots of Economic Convergence*. New York: Croom Helm, 1987.

Williams, Andrew J. *Trading with the Bolsheviks: The Politics of East-West Trade, 1920–39*. Manchester: Manchester University Press, 1992.

Zelenin, I.E. *Agrarnaia politika i sel'skoe khoziaistvo*. Moscow: RAN, 2001.

– "O nekotorikh 'belykh piatnakh' zvershaiushchego etapa sploshnoi kollektivizatsii." *Istoriia SSSR* 22, no. 2 (1989): 3–19.

Zima, V.F. *Golod 1921–1922 godov v Sovetskoi Rossii: Vlast' i tserkov'*. Moscow: Sobranie, 2015.

– *Golod v SSSR 1946–1947 godov: Proiskhozhdenie i posledstviia*. Moscow: RAN, 1996. [Republished in 2020.]

Žižek, Slavoj. *Trouble in Paradise: From the End of History to the End of Capitalism*. London: Allen Lane, 2014.

INDEX

Abbe, James, 332n211, 358n91, 360n99
Acmeists, 97, 352n62
Afghanistan, 250
Agricultural Training Farm and Experimental Station (Verblyud), 184–5, 196, 399n273, 402n338, 403n339. *See also* state farms (sovkhozes)
agriculture: challenges of, 125, 192–5, 312n59, 371n8, 402n327, 402n328, 402n334; diseases of, 195–6; impact of famine on, 59, 142; industry's dependence on, 53, 231–2; intensification of, 13, 15, 228, 311n56; management of, 196–8, 327n165, 403n340; mechanization of, 183–5, 189–91, 378n35, 381n60, 399n270; nomadism in, 76; policies of, 55–6, 124, 133–6, 281, 288, 370n3; production rates of, 137, 138, 154, 179, 202–6, 221–3; statistics for, 56, 405n1; transport of products of, 198–9. *See also* climate; collective farms (kolkhozes); collectivization; drought; fertilizers; food; grain; peasantry; Soviet Union; state farms (sovkhozes)
Akhmatova, Anna, 282, 352n62
Alexievich, Svetlana, 38, 171, 259, 290
alimentary dystrophy, 343n4
Alliluyeva, Nadezhda, 90, 347n34, 350n49
allotment gardens, 228
Altai Kray, 27, 40, 48–9, 54–5, 384n89; collective farms in, 72, 160, 199; famine in, 318n72; peasant uprising in, 87. *See also* Siberia
American Relief Administration, 10, 45, 326n151
Andreyev, Andrei, 272
"anecdotes," 18, 22, 23, 31, 53, 315n26
Anglo-Russian Trading Cooperative Society (ARCOS), 144
Animal Farm (Orwell), 366n135

anti-Semitism, 426n25
Antonov, Alexander, 87, 308n25
Argentina, 234–5
aristocracy, 6, 34, 87. *See also* "former persons"; Tsarist regime
Ashmead-Bartlett, Ellis, 24
Asiatic Russian steppe, 3, 12–14, 126, 128, 258, 370n6
Association for Communal Cultivation (TOZ), 418n6
atheism, 244–5
Australia, 198, 234–5

Babel, Isaac, 98–9, 352n71
Barmine, Alexander, 44, 223, 235, 285, 409n81
Barnes, Ralph, 103, 354n84, 355n90
"barracks socialism," 241
Basmachi Revolt, 240–1, 418n3
"bayization," 242. *See also* kulakization
Beal, Fred, 26, 30, 37, 317n54
bednyaks, 19, 140, 144, 376n20, 383n81, 393n183; arrest of, 272; and class, 155, 210–11; and collectivization, 150, 152, 314n13; persecution of, 171. *See also* kulaks; peasantry; srednyaks
Belgium, 236–7
Belomor Canal, 317n63, 340n323
Belorussia, 28, 76, 107–8, 153, 320n98; famine in, 76, 106, 224, 276, 349n46, 415n155, 432n32; population of, 417n2, 425n20; relocation from, 278
Bely, Andrei, 309n40
Benefit: A Poor Man's Chronicle (Platonov), 99
Beriozka, 35
Berlan, Pierre, 100
Berliner Tageblatt, 22, 140
Blok, Alexander, 10, 309n40

Blue Army of the peasants, 308n25
Blumenfeld, Hans, 398n242
Bolshevik regime, 6–8, 11, 307n24, 309n35, 317n61; agricultural policy of, 20, 55–6, 60, 134–6, 147, 281, 381n60; attitude towards peasantry of, 86–8, 150, 152, 212–13, 285; and Cossacks, 272–3; denomadization policy of, 241–2; dogmatism of, 289–92, 332n211, 405n1; economic policy of, 136–7, 142–3; finances of, 33–4; knowledge of the famine of, 93; peasant problem of, 137, 139–42; ruthlessness of, 169–70; support for, 51, 55; and the Ukraine, 262, 424n14. *See also* bureaucracy; Communist Party of the Soviet Union (CPSU); First Five Year Plan; New Economic Policy (NEP); Soviet Union
Bolshevism, 79, 135, 332n211, 344n10. *See also* communism; socialism
bread, 19–20, 35, 90, 314n18, 340n140; diet of, 39, 51; "famine," 62–3; fraud in, 268; search for, 28–9; traders of, 411n104. *See also* food; grain
breadlines, 19–22, 24, 25, 115, 319n85
Brezhnev, Leonid, 294, 311n56, 347n32
British Embassy, 17, 37, 54, 102–3, 328n185. *See also* Bullard, Reader; Cairns, Andrew
British Labour Party, 113, 115
Bryant, Louise, 109
bubonic plague, 179, 180, 182
Buchma, Amvrosy, 368n154
Budyonny, Semyon, 243
Bukharin, Nikolai, 92, 143, 149, 229, 347n36, 378n39
Bullard, Reader, 28–9, 45, 221, 331n202, 358n91
bureaucracy, 40, 169, 243, 323n120; abuses of, 249; access to food of, 42, 54; blame placed on, 404n351; denial of famine by, 81, 85, 92–4; dogmatism of, 135, 196, 219–20; exactions of, 141, 158, 210; failures of, 108, 116, 225; lies of, 119; scapegoating of, 91, 127, 144–5, 217, 349n46; statistical work of, 58, 405n1. *See also* Bolshevik regime; Soviet Union
"Burnt Ruins" (Klyuev), 96–7
Butyrka Prison, 99

"Caftan War," 86–7
Cairns, Andrew, 36–7, 39–42, 73–4, 287, 320n107, 323n120; on collectivization, 424n13; on Soviet agriculture, 127–8, 130, 188, 192–6, 198, 202

Calder, John, 43
Canada, 14, 15, 57, 234–5, 339n308, 432n32; agricultural productivity of, 198, 229, 230, 371n11, 379n55; imports from, 413n123; Ukrainian community of, 286–7, 360n99
cannibalism, 8, 10, 66, 68–71, 337n263; in Kazakhstan, 248–9; in North Caucasus, 271; in the Ukraine, 266
Capital: A Critique of Political Economy (Marx), 135
capitalism, 109, 113–16, 354n87, 433n41; in the countryside, 285; industrial, 86, 88, 135; industrial capitalism's complicity in the famine, 237–8; and world trade, 235–8, 414n138
censorship, 53, 95, 99; efficacy of, 115, 176, 353n76, 359n92; of foreign journalists, 85, 100–1, 103
Central Black Earth Region, 6, 53, 128, 154, 259, 286; livestock in, 188, 390n145; migration to, 258, 277; reporting from, 104; state procurement from, 210
Chamberlin, Sonya, 112–13, 358n91
Chamberlin, William, 17, 31, 55–6, 304n13, 314n7, 358n91; on censorship, 100; estimates of famine deaths by, 58; reporting of, 105–6, 287, 333n213, 353n76
charity, 60, 72, 73, 247, 291
Chechens, 270, 397n213, 426n25
Cheka, 6, 11, 300n6, 387n116. *See also* OGPU
Chekhov, Anton, 6, 431n22
chernozyom, 259, 261, 285, 286
Chevengur (Platonov), 5
children: abandonment of, 250–3, 341n325; deaths of, 75, 305n17; diseases of, 66; homeless, 80–3, 181, 418n4; mortality rates of, 44, 59; murder of, 69–71; orphaned, 10, 308n30, 310n48; starvation of, 264, 266–8
China, 42, 57, 110, 250, 421n60
cholera, 6, 10, 179, 180, 183, 421n58
Cholerton, Alfred, 103, 114
Christensen, Alva, 321n115, 428n50
Christian Science Monitor, 17, 105, 358n91
Chubar, Vlas, 217, 263
Chukovsky, Kornei, 95, 109
Ciliga, Ante, 4, 122, 141, 229, 259
Civil War (1918-1922), 6, 8, 20, 86–7, 307n24; cost of, 33, 137; lasting impact of, 262; Western intervention in, 207. *See also* White Army

INDEX

class war, 122, 125, 156, 274; and famine, 285, 290, 432n31
clergy, 86–7. See also Russian Orthodox Church
climate, 126–8, 130, 131, 200, 373n46; of the Central Black Earth region, 286; of the Ukraine, 259. See also agriculture; drought; Soviet Union
Clyman, Rhea, 38, 102, 122, 190, 321n115, 333n213; on children, 427n30; on collectivization, 185, 196, 264, 403n339
Cole, Margaret, 115, 129
collective farms (kolkhozes), 12, 19, 45, 146–7, 314n10; abandonment of, 27, 74, 79, 159–60, 179, 338n288, 387n126; failure of, 52, 67–8, 177, 355n89; famine on, 29, 40–1, 93–4, 122, 350n53; foreign tours of, 328n185; in literature, 95, 98; livestock on, 187, 189, 245, 268–9; management of, 196–7, 270, 411n102; mechanization of, 190; mortality rates on, 58–60; new policy for, 55–6, 224–8; production of, 203–4, 243–4; resistance to, 90, 130, 150–2, 165–6, 290, 432n31; size of, 161, 183, 196; state procurement from, 209–11, 213–14, 218–21; theft from, 166–7; triumph of, 292–3; work on, 178, 326n147, 386n110. See also collectivization; state farms (sovkhozes)
collectivization, 3, 19, 36, 45, 312n70, 316n40; as a cause of famine, 72, 90, 105, 132–4, 230, 237, 283, 288, 432n32; of Cossacks, 273–4; crisis of, 200–1, 290–1; data on, 405n1; and drought, 125; "excesses" of, 120, 213, 382n73; forced, 48, 55, 84, 260–1, 352n72; foreign reports of, 108, 110, 328n185; and grain production, 202, 206; impact on peasants of, 87, 179, 259, 342n341, 347n31, 347n34, 388n133; in literature, 95, 98–100; of livestock, 186–8, 244–6; pace of, 161, 381n60, 389n136; of pastoral nomads, 42, 240, 242–3, 250; policy of, 143–4, 146–7, 149–53, 157–8; resistance to, 106–7, 154, 159, 164–70, 264, 381n65, 424n12, 427n28; of Romany, 418n10; and supports and survival strategies during famine, 60–2; Western complicity in, 238–9, 415n150, 416n159; witnesses of, 117–18. See also collective farms (kolkhozes); state farms (sovkhozes)
colonialism, 240, 242

communism, 8, 11, 79, 307n24; atheism of, 375n3; construction of, 135, 289; disillusionment with, 114, 353n78; economic revolution of, 146; enemies of, 92; leaders of, 351n59; opposition to, 29; violence of, 57, 89. See also Bolshevism; socialism; War Communism
Communist Manifesto, The (Marx and Engels), 135
Communist Party of the Soviet Union (CPSU), 3, 11, 26; archives of, 300n6; knowledge of the famine of, 93, 118, 120–1; members of, 60; privileges of, 79. See also Bolshevik regime; bureaucracy
Cossacks, 87, 260, 425n17, 428n56; deportation of, 103, 105–6, 277; repression of, 216, 272–5, 428n63, 432n31. See also Kuban Valley
cotton, 26, 48, 149, 156, 419n32
counter-revolutionaries, 91, 92, 127, 269, 319n84, 432n31; among the bureaucracy, 349n46; among the peasantry, 216, 272, 276; support for, 93, 318n72
"Cow, The" (Platonov), 186
crime: caused by hunger, 44, 47, 62, 74, 83, 117, 251–2; on collective farms, 19; of peasant against peasant, 411n101; reporting on, 365n128
Crimea, 97, 122, 209, 233, 328n185, 423n4, 432n32. See also Tatars

dacha, 74, 338n294
Dalton, Hugh, 113
De Give, Mary, 321n115, 428n50
dekulakization, 168, 170–1, 289, 393n183. See also kulakization
denomadization, 242, 244, 248, 250. See also sedentarization
deportation: of Cossacks, 103, 273–5; of ethnic groups, 396n213, 428n62; of farmsteaders, 225; of kulaks, 153, 155, 157, 170, 174, 176; of pastoralists, 242; resistance of, 188; of Ukrainians, 258. See also migration
Derzhinsky, Felix, 6
Dittloff, Fritz, 192, 196, 273, 333n213, 359n94, 404n341
Doctor Zhivago (Pasternak), 98
Donbass, 207, 230, 262, 388n131, 404n341
drought, 6, 8, 9, 12, 124–9, 132, 372n14; as a

cause of famine, 370n6; "pendulum principle" of, 14–15, 312n70. *See also* agriculture; climate
Drusag (German-Russian Seed Joint-Stock Company), 105, 192, 196, 323n120, 333n213, 359n94
Durant, Will, 42, 221
Duranty, Walter, 10, 86, 102, 333n213, 354n84; reporting by, 106–7, 120–1, 355n90, 360n99, 363n103
dysentery, 10, 179, 181, 398n242

Eikhe, Robert, 251
Eisenstein, Sergei, 86
epidemic diseases, 6, 10, 12, 27, 179–82, 299n2, 310n44; in Kazakhstan, 246–8, 418n15; of livestock, 188. *See also* malnutrition; various diseases
ethnicity, 82, 176, 262, 270, 366n140, 426n25; and deportation, 398n213, 417n1, 426n25; and famine, 154–5, 258, 285, 287, 432n31, 432n32; of the Ukraine, 321n115, 331n202, 425n20. *See also* genocide
ethnocide, 254, 255
European Russian steppe, 3, 12–14, 258–60; agricultural zone of, 287; crops in, 194; drought on, 125, 126, 128; famine in, 37; fodder production of, 300n4. *See also* North Caucasus Region; Ukraine, the
Everything Flows (Grossman), 177

Fabians, 113, 321n115
famines, general, 3, 143–4, 299n2; causes of, 87, 125–6, 134, 178, 230, 304n13, 375n5; definition of, 24; denial of, 85; end of, 15; mortality rates of, 56–60, 71, 332n208
farmsteaders, 389n136; grain concealment by, 272; migration of, 275; plot-sizes of, 411n102; relief for, 225–7; repression of, 216, 273; state procurement from, 209, 213; Ukrainian, 259; war on, 285. *See also* kulaks
fascism, 53, 115, 380n58. *See also* Germany
fertilizers, 15, 152, 178, 197
First All-Union Conference of Stakhanovites, 56, 330n197
First All-Union Congress of Collective Farm Shock Brigaders, 45, 91, 177
First Circle, The (Solzhenitsyn), 345n15
First Five Year Plan, 17, 19, 34, 120, 314n7,

332n211; cost of, 389n139; foreign reporting on, 360n99; grain harvest of, 204; industrial policy of, 283, 375n13; introduction of, 146; results of, 160, 221, 223, 409n77; shortfalls of, 237. *See also* Bolshevik regime; collectivization; industrialization
First International Wheat Conference, 235, 414n139
First World War, 8, 33, 137, 240, 250, 282
Fischer, Louis, 177, 221, 355n90
food: assistance of, 224–7; export of, 72; prices of, 23, 26, 55; search for, 21, 24, 28–33, 43, 47–51, 73–6; seizure of, 40, 87; "surrogates" for, 37, 62–8, 251, 335n243, 335n244. *See also* bread; breadlines; grain; livestock; potatoes; rationing
"food squads," 6
Foot, Michael, 115
Ford Motor Company, 115, 319n84, 332n208
"former persons," 4, 21, 35, 315n19
Foundation Pit, The (Platonov), 99
Fourteen Little Red Huts (Platonov), 99–100
France, 100, 234–7, 261, 292, 327n173, 378n37, 434n49

Gantt, Horsley W., 45, 57, 179
gender, 59, 81, 165, 333n216, 333n217
"General Idea," 135, 378n39
General Line, The (Eisenstein), 86
genocide, 4, 246, 254, 300n6, 432n31. *See also* golodomor; holodomor
gentry, 60, 84, 137; estates of, 140–1, 146, 381n60, 381n65. *See also* aristocracy; Tsarist regime
Georgia, 29, 263, 321n115
Germany, 207, 236–7, 239, 323n120, 358n91, 380n58; collaboration with, 426n25; complicity in the famine of, 238, 292; imports by, 291; Soviet invasion by, 426n27; trade with USSR of, 234, 235, 415n158, 435n51
Gigant sovkoz, 185, 196, 403n339. *See also* state farms (sovkhozes)
Godunov, Boris, 11, 305n15
Goichenko, Dmitry, 264–5
gold, 33–5, 72, 231, 235
golodomor, 288, 418n11, 432n31
Goloshchyokin, Filipp Isayevich, 241–3, 250, 254, 422n78
"Goloshchyokin's genocide," 246, 254

INDEX
475

Gorbachev, Mikhail, 293
Gorbatsevich, Dionisy, 55
Gorky, Maxim, 27–8, 96, 109, 134, 317n63, 351n56–351n59, 396n214; and agriculture, 402n328, 415n155; death of, 352n71; Writers' Brigade of, 340n323
grain: and class war, 156; cultivation of, 12–15, 300n4, 311n53, 312n63, 372n13, 376n19; diseases of, 195–6, 408n48; export of, 26, 28, 34, 72, 142, 206–8, 230–8, 291, 338n285, 379n55, 413n113; growing conditions of, 126–30, 132, 192–5, 370n6; harvest of, 131, 154, 279–80; hoarding of, 9, 272, 430n85; loan of, 224–7; loss of, 198, 402n327, 402n328; price of, 8, 139–40, 379n43, 389n139; private traders of, 154, 379n49; production of, 197, 202–4, 259–60, 406n3, 419n28; sabotage of, 165–7, 391n154; seizure of, 20, 27, 38, 40, 80, 133, 307n24, 318n72, 346n23, 367n147; state procurement of, 144–5, 149, 208–21, 263, 284, 312n72, 411n103; theft of, 61–2, 122–3, 249, 368n167; transport of, 198–9. *See also* agriculture
Grankina, Nadezhda, 120
Great Depression, 34, 78, 228, 231–3, 238, 292, 380n57
Great Krinitsa, The (Babel), 99
Great Leap Forward, 110
"Great Plan for the Transformation of Nature" (1948), 311n57
Great Russians, 260–2, 283, 286–7, 306n20, 316n34, 316n46; children of, 82; in Kazakhstan, 255, 417n1, 418n13; loyalty to Stalin of, 427n28; in the Ukraine, 423n1, 425n20
Great Terror, 109–10, 114, 282–3, 291, 315n32, 328n175. *See also* purges
Griffin, Frederick, 77, 339n308
Grossman, Vasily, 177, 261, 335n244, 431n17
Gulag camps, 12, 88, 319n84, 328n175, 387n116; accounts of, 343n4; death in, 106; peasants in, 169, 392n178

Hawker, Charles, 55–6, 399n272
Hearst, William Randolph, 300n6
Heinz, John, 124, 370n4
Herman, Sam, 115
Herman, Victor, 32, 115, 207, 319n84
Herriot, Édouard, 116–17, 261
Herzen, Alexander, 344n9

Hindus, Maurice, 107–8, 112, 354n84, 355n90, 364n109, 381n67; disillusionment of, 364n110
Holocaust, 283
holodomor, 4, 38, 288, 300n6, 432n31, 432n32
Hoover, Herbert, 380n57
housing, 25, 43; condition of, 277–8, 284; shortage of, 49, 51, 160, 388n134
Hughes, Langston, 110–11
hunger strikes, 23, 30
Hurdy-Gurdy, The (Platonov), 99

ideology, 94, 120, 122, 169, 363n105. *See also* Bolshevik regime; communism; "General Idea"; socialism
imperialism, 240
industrialization, 4, 17, 135, 142, 146; financing of, 33–4, 72, 120, 139, 206–7, 221, 237–9, 413n113; impact of famine on, 51–2; and the peasantry, 149, 387n131; policy of, 223, 233, 283, 375n13; price of, 432n32; resistance of, 264; Western complicity in, 238–9, 416n159
industrial strikes, 45, 52, 137, 317n54, 326n146
industry, 17, 38, 45, 76, 283; and agriculture, 139; focus of, 184; impact of famine on, 51, 53; labour for, 160, 387n131; modernization of, 230; policies for, 135–7; provisioning of, 144–5, 155
influenza, 6, 179
Ingushes, 270
intellectuals, 79, 169, 262
Intourist, 39, 73, 120, 174, 185, 339n308. *See also* tourists
Iran, 250
Isayev, Uraz, 246, 248
Istoriia krest'ianstva SSSR (Sharapov and Danilov), 347n32
Istrati, Panait, 346n28
Italy, 27, 115, 230, 235–7, 434n49
Italyanka, 165, 291, 390n153
Izmailov, Konstantin, 40, 48–9, 54–5, 186

Japan, 207, 239, 380n58
Jewish Daily Forward, 18, 106, 359n98
Jewish populace, 39, 316n34, 384n97
Jones, Gareth, 46, 50–1, 323n120, 326n155, 355n88; famine reporting by, 104–5, 124–5, 287, 355n89, 355n90; journalism of, 370n4
journalists: censorship of, 85, 300n6, 355n90;

foreign, 100–4, 114, 354n87, 365n130; methods of, 370n4; silences of, 176, 287

Kaganovich, Lazar, 29, 61, 89, 335n230, 347n36, 348n41; denial of famine by, 92; enforcement of procurement by, 215–17; tyranny of, 283, 291
Kalinin, Mikhail, 5, 10, 116, 136, 261, 345n19, 347n36; letters to, 158, 164, 240, 247, 249
Kalmyks, 4, 396n213, 417n1, 426n25
"Kazakhicide," 254
Kazakhs, 42, 48–9, 241, 287, 417n1; ethnocide of, 254–7; loss of livestock of, 246; migration of, 250–4, 421n61, 421n64, 421n65; sedentarization of, 243–5, 420n44; starvation of, 246–9, 254, 258, 420n47, 421n55
Kazakhstan, 6, 12–15, 58, 81, 300n4, 419n28; collectivization of, 243–6; devastation of, 285; disease in, 181–2, 418n15; drought in, 125, 128, 129; economy of, 242, 419n32; famine in, 29, 37, 42–3, 240–1, 247–55, 420n47, 421n55, 422n80; migration to, 258; settlement in, 417n1; state procurement from, 209
Kharkov (Kharkiv), the Ukraine, 30, 321n115; factories in, 51–2; famine in, 38–9; migration to, 337n281; orphaned children in, 268, 341n325
Kharkov Tractor Factory, 32, 199, 401n305
Khatayevich, Mendel, 198–201, 215, 411n103
Khrushchev, Nikita S., 3, 10, 12–15, 27, 89; agricultural reforms of, 135, 293, 312n70; "secret speech" of, 426n25; on the Ukraine, 259, 423n4
Kibalchich, Victor (Victor Serge), 4, 253, 299n2
Kiev (Kyiv), 5, 30, 69, 306n20; famine in, 92, 94, 264–5, 427n31; mobilization of the population of, 279
Kirgizians, 42, 48–9, 254. See also Kazakhs
Klyuev, Nikolai, 96–7
Koestler, Arthur, 30, 32, 74, 75–6, 319n85; disillusionment of, 365n128; on the famine, 113–14
kolkhozes. See collective farms (kolkhozes)
kolkhozniks. See peasantry
Komsomol, 88, 117, 169
Kopelev, Lev, 87–8, 94, 289–90, 345n15, 350n50, 434n44

Korolenko, Vladimir, 8–10
Kosior, Stanislav, 93–4, 185, 188, 214, 217, 263
Kravchenko, Victor, 117, 212, 321n111
Krivitsky, Walter, 81
Kuban Valley, 97, 192, 196, 258; destruction of, 272–5, 277; epidemic in, 106, 182; repressions of, 216; Western reporters in, 103, 194
Kulagin, Peter, 93
kulakization, 157, 159, 171, 175–6, 384n93, 385n106; and deportation, 394n199; in Kazakhstan, 242, 249–50; in the Ukraine, 261; witness to, 117, 289. See also dekulakization
kulaks, 11, 19, 21, 333n222, 334n222, 376n20; arrest of, 272; assistance of, 60; classification as, 383n81, 393n183, 393n184, 393n193; and collectivization, 148, 151–6; commercial production of, 141; deportation of, 171–4, 394n199, 396n213, 397n217, 417n1, 435n52; elimination of, 157, 170, 174–6, 269, 290, 384n93; as enemies of Marxism, 87–9, 91, 143–4, 211, 285, 346n23; livestock of, 188; persecution of, 108, 117, 119, 122, 217, 355n89, 368n149, 385n106; resistance of, 159, 396n207, 424n112; state procurement from, 210; Ukrainians as, 261. See also bednyaks; peasantry; srednyaks

Lang, Harry, 106, 359n98
Lang, Lucy, 35, 116, 341n325, 359n98
League of Nations, 239, 300n6
Leder, Mary, 78
Le Matin, 107, 360n99, 415n158
Lenin, Vladimir Ilyich (Ulyanov), 10, 88–9, 109–10, 307n24, 345n18; economic policy of, 138, 142; mausoleum of, 18, 21
Leningrad: famine in, 22, 25–6, 31, 44, 49, 308n30; peasants in, 78, 337n281; provisioning of, 245; reporting from, 106; siege of, 333n217, 343n4
Le Petit Parisien, 50, 327n173
lishentsy. See "former persons"
literature, 95–100
Littlepage, John, 22, 175–6, 242, 315n32, 385n106
Little Russians. See Ukrainians
Litvinov, Ivan, 367n147
Litvinov, Maxim, 354n84
livestock, 13, 290, 300n4; breeding of, 237;

care for, 400n289, 401n290; fodder for, 68; herders of, 42; in Kazakhstan, 241–5, 248; loss of, 185–9, 197, 268–9, 352n72, 394n199, 400n277; seizure of, 6, 19, 40, 170, 252, 418n12; slaughter of, 27, 164, 171, 390n145, 400n282; supply of, 227; support of in famine, 61, 64; theft of, 62, 251
Lucchini, Pierre, 325n128
Lugansk, 5, 189
Lugovskaya, Nina, 328n175
Lunacharsky, Anatoly, 8–9, 95
Lyons, Eugene, 17, 21, 58, 332n211, 353n78; on the cause of famine, 375n5; on censorship, 101, 107, 356n90; on other reporters, 314n7, 358n91, 360n99; reporting by, 103, 113; on visitors to the USSR, 363n105
Lysenko, Trofim, 13, 313n72, 327n165, 378n42, 403n340

Machine and Tractor Stations (MTS), 12, 13, 191, 201, 210; payment of, 228; repression of, 218
Magnitogorsk, 315n33, 375n13, 385n106
Maillart, Ella, 325n133
malaria, 106, 179, 180, 182, 274
malnutrition, 16–17; death by, 26, 107, 179–82, 359n98; diseases of, 10, 12, 67, 179–80, 299n2, 343n4; of livestock, 188, 245; of peasants, 40, 66, 83; and work, 131. *See also* epidemic diseases; starvation
Manchester Guardian, 45, 103, 300n6, 354n87, 358n91
Mandelstam, Nadezhda, 118, 179, 352n65
Mandelstam, Osip, 97–8, 352n62
Man'kov, Arkady, 49–50
Marino Sanatorium, 81
Marxism, 86–7, 135
Mayakovsky, Vladimir, 121
McCarthy, Joseph, 358n91
mental illness, 66, 71, 177. *See also* cannibalism
Metropolitan Vickers, 103, 354n86, 355n90
mgla, 127, 408n48
migration, 73–4, 76–80; of children, 82–3; to cities, 160, 290; and disease, 182; of Kazakhs, 250–4; prevention of, 275, 337n281; of Ukrainians, 258. *See also* deportation; "passportization"; peasantry
Mikoyan, Anastas, 15, 31, 319n80, 348n41

militarization, 136, 206, 208, 233, 239, 416n159. *See also* Red Army
Minsk, Belorussia, 35, 106
Mirsky, Dmitry S., 109
Molotov, Vyascheslav, 29, 307n24, 347n36, 348n40, 348n41; denial of famine by, 92; enforcement of procurement by, 216–17; grain requisitioning by, 144; tyranny of, 283, 291
Mongolia, 250, 355n88
Morozov, Pavlik, 167
Moscow: famine in, 9–10, 20–5, 29–31, 43–4, 50–1, 367n147; peasants in, 75, 78, 337n281; provisioning of, 245
Muggeridge, Malcolm, 45–6, 326n151, 326n155, 354n87; on the cause of the famine, 134, 370n3; famine reporting by, 103; on foreign visitors to the USSR, 114–15; on other reporters, 354n84, 356n90, 358n91, 360n99, 365n130
Muslims, 240–1, 244, 417n1

Narkomtorg, 23
nationalism, 262, 263, 286. *See also* Ukrainian nationalists
nationalization, 135, 137, 146
"neo-NEP," 224, 227, 229, 409n81
Nepmen, 91, 138, 143–4, 175
Neruda, Pablo, 365n125
Nevadovskaya, Tatyana, 255
New Economic Policy (NEP), 19, 33, 138–9, 300n6, 307n24; end of, 142–3; harvest of, 206, 210; and peasants, 147, 241; and private traders, 91; support for, 381n65. *See also* Bolshevik regime
New York *Evening Journal*, 359n98
New York Times, 10, 106–7, 120–1, 360n99
NKVD, 241, 293, 328n175, 389n136. *See also* OGPU
nomadism, 42, 48, 76, 242, 250. *See also* denomadization; Kazakhs
nomads, 72, 133, 240–4, 284–6, 431n16. *See also* Kazakhs
North Caucasus Region, 6, 423n1, 423n8, 425n17; cannibalism in, 70–1; collectivization in, 157, 352n72; devastation of, 194, 270–1, 274–5; drought in, 125, 128, 132, 154; exports from, 231, 233; famine in, 37, 46–7, 258, 259–60, 350n53; migration from, 79,

276–7; mortality rates in, 58, 59, 333n213; orphaned children in, 81; reporting from, 105–6; resettlement of, 277; in the Second World War, 323n120; state procurement from, 209–10, 215–16, 272
Novosibirsk, Siberia, 41–2, 145, 181, 320n107

OGPU, 16, 36, 300n6, 313n2; policing of peasants by, 61–2, 269, 276–7; political force of, 146; press censorship by, 103, 353n76; prisons of, 387n116; provisioning of, 79, 80, 165; reporting on the famine by, 93; suppression of the peasantry by, 159, 169, 379n49, 425n21; tactics of, 392n181
oil, 234, 235, 291–2, 313n72
Old and New (Eisenstein), 86
Omsk, Siberia, 41–2, 144, 252
One Day in the Life of Ivan Denisovich (Solzhenitsyn), 88
On the Russian Peasantry (Gorky), 96
Orenburg, 14, 120, 126, 253, 430n1
Orlova, Raisa, 88
Orwell, George, 366n135
Osherowitch, Mendel, 18, 39
Ovey, Esmond, 25, 46, 85, 259

"passportization," 79, 83, 277, 337n281
Pasternak, Boris, 8, 98
Pauls, Agnes, 368n149
peasant commune, 60, 73, 137, 146, 344n9
peasant rebellion, 20, 425n17. *See also* political unrest
peasantry: apathy of, 177–8, 390n153, 397n224; attitudes toward, 85–6, 108, 344n9, 347n34, 351n56, 431n22; blamed for famine, 72, 94, 111–12, 121–2, 378n37, 387n134; classes of, 16, 19; on collective farms, 146–51, 161–4; defeat of, 83–4, 95, 171, 269–70, 281, 430n89; as enemies of Marxism, 86–91, 96, 143–4; and famine, 5, 7–9, 21, 22, 36–7, 39–40, 307n24; foreign reporting about, 104–5, 292; health of, 179–83; livelihoods of, 124, 138–41, 407n30; livestock of, 187–8; and mechanization, 190–1; migration of, 42–3, 51, 73–80, 179, 337n281, 390n146; mobility of, 275–9, 388n131, 388n133; mortality rates of, 58, 60, 305n17, 332n208; and the Orthodox Church, 387n124; political unrest of, 11, 20, 27, 35–6, 52, 145, 159, 318n72, 325n128; production of, 141–2, 377n31, 431n16; purge of, 293; resistance of, 130, 137, 159–60, 164–9, 290–1, 376n15, 381n65, 384n101; starvation of, 45–7, 131, 133, 397n231; state exactions from, 210–13, 220–1, 389n139; support strategies of, 60–2; terrorization of, 271–2; in the Ukraine, 264; war on, 154–5, 157–8, 223, 259, 284–6, 300n6; workload of, 192–3, 386n110, 386n111. *See also* bednyaks; class war; collective farms (kolkhozes); collectivization; dekulakization; kulaks; srednyaks; state farms (sovkhozes)
People's Commissariats, 300n6. *See also* bureaucracy
Petkevich, Tamara, 367n146
Petlyura, Symon, 263, 269, 426n23, 432n31
Petrograd. *See* Leningrad
Pilnyak, Boris, 85–6, 88, 344n5
Piłsudski, Józef, 263, 426n23
"Pitchfork Movement," 87
Platonov (Klimentov), Andrei, 5, 59, 96, 99–100, 186, 352n72
Podlubny, Stepan, 121, 369n167
Poland, 73, 195, 235–7, 425n21; threat of, 218, 262–3, 276, 426n23
Politburo, 145, 157, 166, 210, 347n36, 379n52; food distribution by, 224, 227; procurements by, 215, 231; trade policy of, 235–7
political unrest, 11, 23; in Kazakhstan, 243; lack of, 83; of the proletariat, 28; suppression of, 72–3; of workers, 52. *See also* peasant rebellion; peasantry
"politotdels," 218–19
Possessed, The (Dostoyevsky), 345n16
Postyshev, Pavel, 215–16, 263, 428n46
potatoes, 22, 26, 32, 48, 423n7; diet of, 39, 51
Potyomkin villages, 366n141
Preobrazhensky, Yevgeny, 149, 383n76
press, 100, 354n87; international, 415n158; Soviet, 117, 360n99, 367n147. *See also* journalists
Prishvin, Mikhail, 119
private property, 88, 135, 234, 261; collectivization of, 60, 62, 147, 151, 154, 157, 245; destruction of, 19, 278; seizure of, 122, 163, 170–1, 177, 381n60, 385n106, 394n199
private traders, 154, 175. *See also* Nepmen
Privin, Yevgeny Natanovich, 17

INDEX

proletariat, 86, 88, 122; creation of, 242; dictatorship of, 135, 364n119, 375n7, 405n1; rural, 146; victory of, 154–5. *See also* workers
propaganda, 115, 176, 183, 364n119
prostitution, 43
Pugachov, Yemelyan, 425n17
Pulitzer Prize, 354n84, 360n99
purges, 17, 23, 110, 114; of agricultural officials, 127, 216; of Kazakhs, 241; of old Bolsheviks, 44, 114, 136, 215, 251, 276, 319n85; of peasants, 293; support for, 409n81; of technicians, 404n341; threat of, 158; of Ukrainian nationalists, 30, 263; victims of, 127n165, 330n200; of writers, 99, 344n5. *See also* Great Terror; show trials

Quiet Flows the Don (Sholokhov), 95, 350n53
Quisling, Vidkund, 262

racism, 110, 244
rail network, 24, 48, 102, 233; bread traders on, 411n104; children on, 250, 268; exiles on, 29, 171, 179, 268, 277, 368n147; failure of, 127, 198–9, 279–80; journalists on, 104, 287; search for food on, 75–80, 82, 275. *See also* migration; "passportization"
Ramsay, Katharine, Duchess of Atholl, 85, 115, 342n339
rationing, 16, 21–3, 25, 32, 430n10; in cities, 160; and economic reform, 137; end of, 55; for exiles, 172; for foreigners, 44, 112–13; and fraud, 315n33; and mortality, 59, 283; for workers, 51
Razin, Stepan, 425n17
Red Army, 6, 36, 53; grain reserve of, 131, 208; help with the harvest of, 228; political force of, 146; provisioning of, 72, 79, 91, 137, 144, 165, 245, 349n47; settlement of soldiers of, 277; strength of, 93, 380n58; suppression of the peasantry by, 159, 169, 428n63
Red Cavalry (Babel), 98–9
Red Cross, 10, 72
"Red Terror," 6, 135, 282, 387n116
Reed, John, 109
Repair-Technical Stations (RTS), 13
Richardson, Stanley, 333n213, 357n90
Robins, Raymond, 89
Robinson, Robert, 332n208
Romania, 73, 195, 235, 262

Romany, 418n10
Rosen, Joseph, 45, 326n151
Rostov-on-Don, 103, 126, 216, 237, 428n63
RSFSR, 11, 14, 261, 300n4, 432n32; drought in, 132; livestock supply of, 186; peasant population of, 167, 376n20. *See also* Great Russians
Rudenko, Mykola, 45, 326n148
Russell, Bertrand, 364n119
Russia (non-Soviet), 5–6, 8–11, 305n15. *See also* Great Russians; RSFSR; Russian Federation; Tsarist regime
Russian army, 8
Russian Federation, 332n205, 371n11, 432n32
Russian Orthodox Church, 60, 140–1, 352n73, 370n1, 381n60
Russification, 240, 263, 281
Ryskulov, Turar, 246, 248–50, 254

Sakharov, Andrei, 426n25, 434n43
Sanger, Richard H., 359n98
Scheffer, Paul, 22, 23, 25, 140–1, 377n27
Schiller, Otto, 39–40, 42, 48, 323n120; on agriculture, 135, 197, 200, 206, 261, 270, 389n139, 400n277; on mortality rates, 55, 59, 186, 229, 333n213, 397n217; on the peasantry, 92–3, 132, 176, 178, 223, 273–4; reporting by, 287, 288–9, 415n158
scorbutus (scurvy), 179–82, 420n44
Scott, John, 164, 385n106
Second Five Year Plan, 52, 204, 406n3
Second World War, 12, 282, 300n6, 323n120, 375n13, 426n27; deportation of populations during, 396n213, 428n62; Soviet carnage of, 291, 293, 396n207
sedentarization, 42, 240, 242–3, 246
serfdom, 11, 86, 344n9; collectivization as, 149, 170, 212, 226, 229, 355n90
Serge, Victor. *See* Kibalchich, Victor (Victor Serge)
settler colonialism, 240, 242, 244, 417n1
Shaginyan, Marietta, 94
Shakty trial, 404n341
Shalamov, Varlam, 343n4, 392n178
Shaporina, Lyubov, 25–6, 118, 154, 164
Shaw, George Bernard, 99, 112–13, 365n124
Shayakhmetov, Mukhamet, 244, 247, 250, 419n29
Sheboldayev, Boris, 106, 215, 273, 359n96

Shitts, Ivan, 299n2, 315n19
Sholokhov, Mikhail, 91, 95, 151, 187, 211, 350n53
show trials, 103, 354n86, 355n90, 392n181. *See also* Great Terror; purges
Siberia, 6, 13, 53; disease in, 181, 182; drought in, 125, 128, 129; exile to, 171, 394n199; famine in, 29, 39–41, 46, 54, 194; migration to, 10, 251, 252; oil production in, 312n72; opposition to collectivization in, 164, 168; orphaned children in, 81; peasant revolt in, 87; state procurement from, 144–5, 209, 423n8. *See also* Altai Kray
Simenon, George, 174
smallpox, 163, 179, 181–3, 399n264, 418n15
Smith, Homer, 43, 77
socialism, 94, 113, 115, 138, 143, 229; belief in, 350n50, 351n59, 356n90; building of, 26, 28, 81, 150, 284, 289; and the defeat of the peasantry, 284; and food, 283; foreign help for, 196; propaganda for, 23, 80, 94, 219; victory of, 246, 398n243; violence of, 57. *See also* "barracks socialism"; Bolshevism; class war; communism; "state capitalism"
"socialist realism," 28
Socialist Revolutionaries (SRS), 153, 168, 276, 431n22
Sollohub, Edith, 307n24, 308n30
Solovetsky Islands, 127, 157, 387n116
Solzhenitsyn, Alexander, 8, 283, 332n208, 345n15, 350n53, 432n32; on collectivization, 61, 73, 79, 154, 171, 178, 288; on the German occupation, 426n27; Gulag of, 88, 125, 387n116. See also *First Circle, The* (Solzhenitsyn); *One Day in the Life of Ivan Denisovich* (Solzhenitsyn)
Sorokin, Pitirim, 6–8, 10, 309n35, 364n119
Soviet Central Asia, 10, 30, 37, 48, 241
Soviet Gold Trust, 175
Soviet Union, 33–4, 62, 240, 255, 299n1; agricultural environment of, 13–15, 125–6, 131–2, 195, 287, 371n12; agricultural production of, 141–2, 179, 202–6, 221–3, 259–60, 423n8; deportation of ethnicities by, 396n213, 428n62; disillusionment with, 176, 354n87, 359n98; exports of, 231–9, 291, 413n123, 414n130; famine in, 5–12, 16–17, 134, 282–3, 285, 287–8, 300n6, 304n13, 432n32; food culture of, 293; health care in, 180–2; immigration to, 78, 340n313, 366n136, 366n140; imports of, 292, 312n72, 435n51; isolation of, 136, 229–30, 380n57; migration within, 79, 179; military strength of, 380n58; official statistics of, 56–7, 330n200, 331n202, 349n46, 405n1; population of, 274, 414n137, 424n14; procurements by, 208–9, 215, 246; republics of, 262–3; response to famine of, 71–2, 85, 249, 337n280, 338n285, 421n55; security of, 83, 207, 221, 384n93, 415n158, 427n28, 433n41; state press of, 101; state violence in, 23, 29, 284, 348n41; tax exactions of, 210; visitors to, 44, 109–16, 129. *See also* Bolshevik regime; bureaucracy; Khrushchev, Nikita S.; Stalin, Joseph
sovkhozes. *See* state farms (sovkhozes)
Spain, 115, 434n49
"special settlements," 171–3, 277
srednyaks, 19, 140–1, 144, 376n20, 383n81, 393n183; arrest of, 272; and collectivization, 151; livestock of, 188; persecution of, 170–1. *See also* bednyaks; kulaks; peasantry
Stalin, Joseph, 3, 12–13, 311n57, 346n24, 426n25, 434n49; agricultural policy of, 19, 126–7, 169, 223–4, 281; apologists for, 108, 109, 114, 117; attitude towards peasantry of, 89–90, 139, 346n25; economic policy of, 143, 146, 156–7, 229–30; grain requisitioning by, 144–5; hatred of, 332n211; hypocrisy of, 56; knowledge of the famine of, 89–91, 94, 347n31, 350n53; purges of, 217–18, 293, 315n32, 330n200; responsibility for famine of, 72, 134, 291, 300n6, 431n18, 434n42; support for, 28, 51, 119, 212, 365n125, 409n81; trade policy of, 231; tyranny of, 282–3, 287, 294; and violence, 57, 98, 170
Stalinism, 3–4, 221, 292, 307n24, 434n49
Stalin Peace Prize, 365n125
stanitsas, 103, 216, 273–4. *See also* Cossacks
starvation, 3, 12, 16, 46–8, 299n2, 304n13; cause of, 133, 237, 276; in the cities, 284, 308n30; denial of, 111, 113, 116, 291, 360n99; and disease, 181, 183; foreign reporting on, 58; ideological justification for, 120–2, 355n90, 368n167, 413n113; impact of, 21, 24, 67, 292, 333n214, 359n98; of Kazakhs, 246–54; of kulak exiles, 172–3; official response to, 26, 45, 343n4; of peasants, 22, 27–9, 37, 40–1, 54; planned, 168, 288–9, 300n6; and

political unrest, 52–3; of Russian villages, 273–4; of workers, 26, 30, 42, 415n155. *See also* cannibalism
"Stary Krim" (Mandelstam), 97
"state capitalism," 138. *See also* socialism
State Commission for the Electrification of Russia (GOELRO), 137
state farms (sovkhozes), 13, 146, 184–5, 314n10, 388n135, 403n339; livestock on, 245, 269; management of, 197, 217–18, 270; mechanization of, 189–90; new policy for, 224, 227; size of, 196; state procurement from, 209, 213, 218. *See also* Agricultural Training Farm and Experimental Station (Verblyud); collective farms (kolkhozes); Gigant sovkoz
State Hermitage Museum, 10, 34
Steffens, Lincoln, 88, 109, 110, 345n20
"steppe golodomor," 254
Stoneman, William, 103, 354n84, 356n90
St Petersburg. *See* Leningrad
Strang, William, 358n91, 360n99
Strøm, Arne, 43, 183, 325n137
Strong, Anna Louise, 110, 176
suicide, 29, 32, 66, 78, 173, 219, 352n72
sukhovei, 127–8, 130, 192, 372n22, 373n48, 408n48
Symbolist poets, 309n40, 352n62

"Tambov Brotherhood," 87
Tashkent, Uzbekistan, 26, 47, 104, 419n32
Tatars, 64, 119, 254, 396n213, 417n1, 423n4, 426n25
Terekhov, Roman, 90–1
terrorism, 159, 164, 168–70, 392n181; famine as, 291; of grain requisitions, 427n28; against peasants, 271–2; state, 23, 29. *See also* purges
timber, 172–3, 207, 234, 238, 291–2, 342n339, 435n52; scarcity of, 352n72, 379n43; targets for, 218
"Time of Troubles," 8, 305n15, 310n47
Tolstaya-Voyeikova, Olga, 35, 49, 118
Tolstoy, Leo, 6
Tomsk, Siberia, 29, 145, 172
Torgov, Igor, 170
Torgsin (All-Union Association for Trade with Foreigners on the Territory of the USSR), 33–5, 44, 45, 47, 325n138; food sales of, 320n89; foreign customers of, 320n97; state profits from, 291–2
tourists, 4, 34, 44, 85, 107, 343n2. *See also* Intourist
TOZ, 418n6
Trans-Siberian Railway, 82
Tretyakov Gallery, 34
Trotsky, Leon, 92, 138, 142–3, 227, 229, 347n36
Trotskyism, 99, 344n5
Tsarist regime, 6, 11, 114, 305n15, 316n46, 391n170; Cossack support for, 272, 428n56; grain exports of, 413n113; grain harvest of, 204, 206; imperialism of, 240; kulaks under, 152. *See also* aristocracy; "former persons"; gentry; serfdom
tuberculosis, 26, 100, 181, 182
Tulaikov, Nikolai, 12
Turkestan, 10, 240, 250, 285, 325n128, 418n4
Turkey, 33, 250
TurkSib Railway, 327n166
Twenty-Five Thousanders, 211–12, 243, 289
typhoid, 10, 179–83, 309n41, 398n242
typhus, 10, 26, 27, 94, 179–82, 309n41; as leading cause of death, 398n242; scourge of, 398n243

Uigurs, 254
Ukraine, the, 4, 262–3, 306n20, 425n18; cannibalism in, 69–70; climate of, 127–8, 132, 378n42; collectivization of, 157, 179, 382n73, 424n13; devastation of, 264–8, 285, 286, 430n89; epidemic disease in, 180–2; exports from, 231, 233; famine in, 6, 9, 21, 37–9, 46, 47, 93–4, 258–60, 300n6; genocide in, 432n31, 432n32; harvest in, 154, 177, 192–6, 203–4, 423n3, 423n8; industrial workers in, 51–2; livestock of, 188–9; and migration, 76, 79, 275, 276–7; mortality rates in, 58, 59, 331n202, 332n208, 332n210, 333n213, 333n214; observations of, 98–9, 104–7, 116–17; orphaned children in, 83; peasant revolt in, 159, 425n17; populations of, 261, 423n1, 425n20; relief for, 224–5; resettlement of, 277–80; state procurement from, 144, 209–10, 214–15, 217, 219–20, 379n49, 411n103; wheat production of, 14, 15, 90, 129, 131, 185, 300n4, 374n55. *See also holodomor*
Ukrainian nationalists, 6, 30, 262–3, 300n6, 306n20, 360n99; in North America, 286–8

Ukrainians, 3–4, 316n46; children of, 82; collaboration with Nazi Germany of, 426n25; collectivization of, 260–1; famine deaths of, 331n202; in Kazakhstan, 254, 255, 417n1, 418n13; loss of, 258–9; in the Soviet Union, 424n14, 425n20
Umansky, Konstantin, 101–2, 356n90
Union for the Struggle for Discipline, 212
United Kingdom, 207, 234–7, 291, 435n51; complicity in the famine of, 238, 239, 292. *See also* British Embassy
United States: agricultural productivity of, 125, 371n11; as enemy of the USSR, 414n138; recognition of the USSR by, 207, 239, 360n99, 380n57; trade with USSR of, 234–8, 292; Ukrainian community of, 286–7, 432n32
UPI, 103, 113, 332n211, 353n78
Urals, 6, 13; disease in, 182; drought in, 125, 128, 129; grain requisitioning in, 144; industry in, 207, 230; orphaned children in, 81
urbanization, 233
USSR. *See* Soviet Union
Utley, Freda, 28, 55, 131, 318n66
Uzbekistan, 26, 419n32
Uzbeks, 254

Vavilov, Nikolai, 48, 327n165, 403n340
venereal disease, 183
Verblyud. *See* Agricultural Training Farm and Experimental Station (Verblyud)
Virgin and Idle Lands Program (VILP), 13–15, 126, 255, 300n4, 311n56, 312n63
Virgin Soil Upturned (Sholokhov), 95
"Volga famine" (1921-22), 6–11, 306n19, 308n30
Volga German Republic, 60, 64, 323n120, 426n25
Volga Valley Region, 6, 13, 127; agriculture in, 200–1, 222–3, 384n91, 423n8; during the Civil War, 87; collectivization of, 157; drought in, 125, 128, 129, 132, 306n19, 307n23, 370n6, 373n48; exports from, 233; famine in, 37, 46; livestock in, 189; and migration, 79, 251, 253; mortality rates in, 59–60, 333n213; orphaned children in, 81; state procurement from, 209–10, 215–16

Volovich, Hava, 266–7
Volters, Rudolf, 41–2, 47, 82, 180–1, 324n126
Voroshilov, Kliment, 194, 347n36, 380n58
Vyvyan, John, 16

Waldhauer, Oskar, 10
Wangenheim, Alexei, 126–7
War Communism, 75, 86, 136–7, 344n10, 381n65
Webb, Beatrice and Sidney, 111–12, 321n115, 365n121
Wells, Carveth, 78, 264, 271
Wells, H.G., 57, 308n30, 326n144, 364n119
Western Siberia. *See* Siberia
Wettlin, Margaret, 44, 356n90, 364n110
White, William Allen, 354n84
White Army, 86–7, 106, 109, 207, 261; Cossacks in, 272–3, 428n56
White Russians, 316n46. *See also* Belorussia
Williams, Whiting (Charles), 131, 152, 268, 333n214, 363n103
Witkin, Zara, 43–4, 115–16, 325n134, 332n211, 355n90
Wood, William, 181, 398n253
workers: allotment gardens for, 228, 412n105; attitudes towards peasants of, 87, 122, 225; conscription of, 137; and famine, 25–6, 30, 38, 40–1, 47–8, 50–1; income of, 268; migration of, 74–5; mobilization for the harvest of, 278–80, 429n82; orphaned children of, 82, 341n332; political unrest of, 11, 51–3, 319n76; provisioning of, 91, 165; rationing for, 21–3, 324n126; "shock," 61, 326n147; support for state of, 169, 211–12. *See also* Twenty-Five Thousanders
World War I. *See* First World War
World War II. *See* Second World War

Yagoda, Genrikh, 215, 276
Yakovlev, Yakov, 220, 403n339
Yezhov, Nikolai 241, 352n71
Yushchenko, Viktor, 333n214

Zakheim, Judel, 175
Zatmilova, Galina, 117
zazhitochniks, 19, 27, 150, 170–1, 383n81
Zelënaia, Rina, 76
zemlyankas, 68, 78, 253, 340n311, 403n339

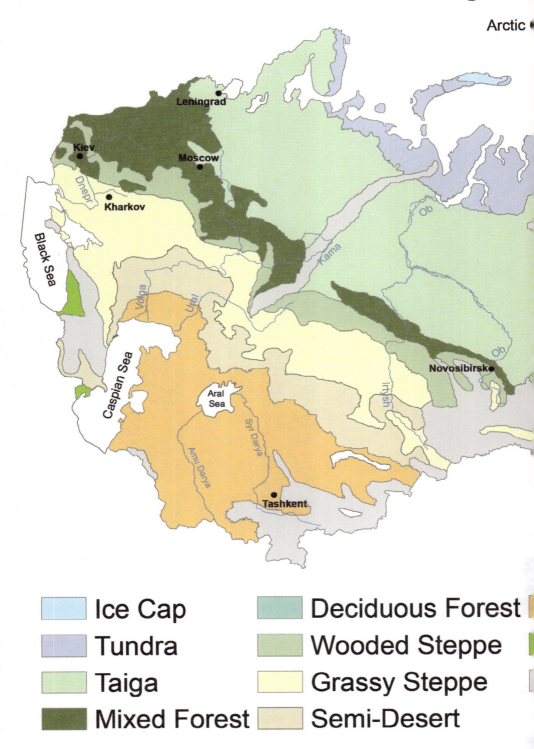